CW01103064

THE CTS NEW
SUNDAY MISSAL
2013

PEOPLE'S EDITION

WITH THE NEW TRANSLATION OF THE MASS

Sundays Year C

From First Sunday of Advent 2012
to Christ the King 2013

Texts approved for use
in England and Wales, Scotland, and Ireland.

CATHOLIC TRUTH SOCIETY

Catholic Truth Society
40-46 Harleyford Road, London, SE11 5AY
First Published 2012

ISBN

The CTS New Sunday Missal 2013 (RM13): 978 1 86082 813 3

Cover design, compilation and typographical design and layout
© 2012 Catholic Truth Society

Concordat cum originali: Paul Moynihan

Imprimatur: ✠ Peter Smith, Archbishop of Southwark, 15 August 2012.

Acknowledgements:

The CTS is grateful for the help of the Association for Latin in the Liturgy in the preparation of this volume.

Extracts from scripture (excepting Psalm texts) from the Jerusalem Bible © 1966 Darton Longman and Todd and Doubleday & Company Inc.

The English translation of the Gospel Readings for the Palm Sunday Procession from the Catholic Edition of the Revised Standard Version of the Bible © 1965, 1966 by the Division of Christian Education of the National Council of the Churches of Christ in the United States of America. Used by permission. All rights reserved.

Psalm texts from the Grail Psalms © 1963 The Grail (England).

New English Translation 2010, granted recognitio by the Congregation for Divine Worship and the Discipline of the Sacraments, for the dioceses of the Bishops' Conferences of England and Wales (Prot. N. 915/06/L, 28 March 2010), and Scotland, (Prot. N. 1021/07/L, 23 June 2010), and Ireland (Prot. N. 516/05/L, 18 June 2010).

The English translation and chants of The Roman Missal © 2010, International Commission on English in the Liturgy Corporation. All rights reserved.

Latin text of Missale Romanum, Libreria Editrice Vaticana omnia sibi vindicat iura. Sine eiusdem licentia scripto data nemini liceat hunc Missale denuo imprimere aut in aliam linguam vertere © 2003, Libreria Editrice Vaticana.

Papal Magisterium used for introductions to feasts and seasons © Libreria Editrice Vaticana, Vatican City State

Rite of Eucharistic Exposition and Benediction taken from *Holy Communion and Worship of the Eucharist Outside Mass* (The Roman Ritual) Vol. 1, Approved by the Bishops' Conference of England and Wales, Ireland and Scotland and confirmed by decree of the Sacred Congregation for the Sacraments and Divine Worship 29th May 1976.

Rosary Meditations and material for Preparation for Mass and Thanksgiving after Mass taken from *Eucharistic Adoration* D667 first published CTS, 2004.

TABLE OF CONTENTS

Preparation for Mass		5
The Order of Mass		9
Thanksgiving After Mass		152
2 December	First Sunday of Advent	161
8 December	Immaculate Conception	164
9 December	Second Sunday of Advent	170
16 December	Third Sunday of Advent	174
23 December	Fourth Sunday of Advent	178
25 December	The Nativity of the Lord	182
30 December	The Holy Family	200
1 January	Solemnity of Mary, the Holy Mother of God	205
6 January	Epiphany of the Lord	210
13 January	Baptism of the Lord	218
20 January	Second Sunday in Ordinary Time	224
27 January	Third Sunday in Ordinary Time	228
3 February	Fourth Sunday in Ordinary Time	233
10 February	Fifth Sunday in Ordinary Time	238
13 February	Ash Wednesday	242
17 February	First Sunday of Lent	250
24 February	Second Sunday of Lent	255
1 March	Saint David (Wales)	260
3 March	Third Sunday of Lent	263
10 March	Fourth Sunday of Lent	268
17 March	Fifth Sunday of Lent	273
17 March	Saint Patrick	274
19 March	Saint Joseph	279
24 March	Palm Sunday	284
	The Sacred Paschal Triduum	304
28 March	Thursday of the Lord's Supper	305
29 March	Good Friday	315
30 March	Easter Vigil	343
31 March	Mass during the day	386
7 April	Second Sunday of Easter	391
8 April	Annunciation of the Lord	396
14 April	Third Sunday of Easter	401
21 April	Fourth Sunday of Easter	406
23 April	Saint George (England)	409
28 April	Fifth Sunday of Easter	413

TABLE OF CONTENTS

5 May	Sixth Sunday of Easter	417
12 May	Seventh Sunday of Easter (Scotland)	422
12 May	Ascension (England, Wales & Ireland)	426
19 May	Pentecost	434
26 May	The Most Holy Trinity	453
2 June	The Most Holy Body and Blood of Christ	458
7 June	The Most Sacred Heart of Jesus	464
9 June	Tenth Sunday in Ordinary Time	469
16 June	Eleventh Sunday in Ordinary Time	473
23 June	Twelfth Sunday in Ordinary Time	477
24 June	Nativity of Saint John the Baptist	481
29 June	Saints Peter and Paul (Ireland & Scotland)	490
30 June	Saints Peter and Paul (England & Wales)	490
30 June	Thirteeth Sunday in Ordinary Time (Ireland & Scotland)	499
7 July	Fourteenth Sunday in Ordinary Time	502
14 July	Fifteenth Sunday in Ordinary Time	506
21 July	Sixteenth Sunday in Ordinary Time	511
28 July	Seventeenth Sunday in Ordinary Time	515
4 August	Eighteenth Sunday in Ordinary Time	520
11 August	Nineteenth Sunday in Ordinary Time	525
15 August	Assumption of the Blessed Virgin Mary	530
18 August	Twentieth Sunday in Ordinary Time	538
25 August	Twenty-First Sunday in Ordinary Time	542
1 September	Twenty-Second Sunday in Ordinary Time	545
8 September	Twenty-Third Sunday in Ordinary Time	549
15 September	Twenty-Fourth Sunday in Ordinary Time	554
22 September	Twenty-Fifth Sunday in Ordinary Time	559
29 September	Twenty-Sixth Sunday in Ordinary Time	563
6 October	Twenty-Seventh Sunday in Ordinary Time	567
13 October	Twenty-Eight Sunday in Ordinary Time	571
20 October	Twenty-Ninth Sunday in Ordinary Time	574
27 October	Thirtieth Sunday in Ordinary Time	578
1 November	All Saints	582
2 November	Commemoration of all the Faithful Departed	587
3 November	Thirty-First Sunday in Ordinary Time	594
10 November	Thirty-Second Sunday in Ordinary Time	598
17 November	Thirty-Third Sunday in Ordinary Time	602
24 November	Our Lord Jesus Christ, King of the Universe	606
30 November	Saint Andrew (Scotland)	610
Rite of Eucharistic Exposition and Benediction		615

PREPARATION FOR MASS

Prayer of Saint Ambrose

I draw near, loving Lord Jesus Christ,
to the table of your most
  delightful banquet
in fear and trembling,
a sinner, presuming not
  upon my own merits,
but trusting rather in your
  goodness and mercy.
I have a heart and body
  defiled by my many offences,
a mind and tongue
over which I have kept no good watch.
Therefore, O loving God,
  O awesome Majesty,
I turn in my misery, caught in snares,
to you the fountain of mercy,
hastening to you for healing,
flying to you for protection;
and while I do not look forward
  to having you as Judge,
I long to have you as Saviour.
To you, O Lord, I display my wounds,
to you I uncover my shame.
I am aware of my many and great sins,
for which I fear,
but I hope in your mercies,
which are without number.
Look upon me, then,
  with eyes of mercy,
Lord Jesus Christ, eternal King,
God and Man, crucified for mankind.
Listen to me,
  as I place my hope in you,
have pity on me, full of miseries
  and sins,
you, who will never cease
to let the fountain of compassion flow.
Hail, O Saving Victim,

Oratio S. Ambrosii

Ad mensam dulcissimi convivii tui,
  pie Domine Iesu Christe,
ego peccator de propriis meis
  meritis nihil præsumens,
sed de tua confidens misericordia
  et bonitate,
accedere vereor et contremisco.
Nam cor et corpus habeo multis
  criminibus maculatum,
mentem et linguam non
  caute custoditam.

Ergo, o pia Deitas,
  o tremenda maiestas,
ego miser,
  inter angustias deprehensus,
ad te fontem misericordiæ recurro,
ad te festino sanandus,
sub tuam protectionem fugio;
et, quem Iudicem sustinere nequeo,
Salvatorem habere suspiro.
Tibi, Domine, plagas meas ostendo,
tibi verecundiam meam detego.
Scio peccata mea multa
  et magna, pro quibus timeo:
spero in misericordias tuas,
  quarum non est numerus.
Respice ergo in me oculis
  misericordiæ tuæ,
Domine Iesu Christe, Rex æterne,
  Deus et homo,
crucifixus propter hominem.
Exaudi me sperantem in te:
miserere mei pleni miseriis
  et peccatis,
tu qui fontem miserationis
numquam manare cessabis.
Salve, salutaris victima,

offered for me and
    for the whole human race
on the wood of the Cross.
Hail, O noble and precious Blood,
flowing from the wounds
of Jesus Christ, my crucified Lord,
and washing away the sins
    of all the world.
Remember, Lord, your creature,
whom you redeemed by your Blood.
I am repentant of my sins,
I desire to put right what I have done.
Take from me, therefore, most
    merciful Father,
all my iniquities and sins,
so that, purified in mind and body,
I may worthily taste the Holy of Holies.
And grant that this sacred foretaste
of your Body and Blood
which I, though unworthy,
    intend to receive,
may be the remission of my sins,
the perfect cleansing of my faults,
the banishment of shameful thoughts,
and the rebirth of right sentiments;
and may it encourage
a wholesome and
    effective performance
of deeds pleasing to you
and be a most firm defence
    of body and soul
against the snares of my enemies.
Amen.

Prayer of Saint Thomas Aquinas

Almighty eternal God,
behold, I come to the Sacrament
of your Only Begotten Son,
our Lord Jesus Christ,
as one sick to the physician of life,
as one unclean to

pro me et omni humano genere
    in patibulo Crucis oblata.

Salve, nobilis et pretiose Sanguis,
de vulneribus crucifixi Domini mei
    Iesu Christi profluens,
et peccata totius mundi abluens.

Recordare, Domine, creaturæ tuæ,
quam tuo Sanguine redemisti.
Pænitet me peccasse,
cupio emendare quod feci.
Aufer ergo a me, clementissime Pater,
omnes iniquitates et peccata mea,
ut, purificatus mente et corpore,
digne degustare merear
    Sancta sanctorum.
Et concede, ut hæc sancta
    prælibatio Corporis
    et Sanguinis tui,
quam ego indignus
    sumere intendo,
sit peccatorum meorum remissio,
sit delictorum perfecta purgatio,
sit turpium cogitationum effugatio
ac bonorum sensuum regeneratio,
operumque tibi placentium
    salubris efficacia,
animæ quoque et corporis
contra inimicorum meorum
    insidias firmissima tuitio.
Amen.

Oratio S. Thomæ Aquinatis

Omnipotens sempiterne Deus,
ecce accedo ad sacramentum
    Unigeniti Filii tui,
Domini nostri Iesu Christi,
accedo tamquam infirmus
    ad medicum vitæ

the fountain of mercy,
as one blind to the light
   of eternal brightness,
as one poor and needy to
   the Lord of heaven and earth.
I ask, therefore, for the abundance
   of your immense generosity,
that you may graciously cure
   my sickness,
wash away my defilement,
give light to my blindness,
enrich my poverty,
clothe my nakedness,
so that I may receive
   the bread of Angels,
the King of kings and Lord of lords,
with such reverence and humility,
such contrition and devotion,
such purity and faith,
such purpose and intention
as are conducive to the salvation of
   my soul.
Grant, I pray, that I may receive
not only the Sacrament
   of the Lord's Body and Blood,
but also the reality and power
   of that Sacrament.
O most gentle God,
grant that I may so receive
the Body of your Only Begotten
   Son our Lord Jesus Christ,
which he took from
   the Virgin Mary,
that I may be made worthy
   to be incorporated into his
   Mystical Body
and to be counted among
   its members.
O most loving Father,
grant that I may at last gaze for ever
upon the unveiled face
	immundus ad
	   fontem misericordiæ,
	cæcus ad lumen claritatis æternæ,
	pauper et egenus ad
	   Dominum cæli et terræ.
	Rogo ergo immensæ largitatis
	   tuæ abundantiam,
	quatenus meam curare
	   digneris infirmitatem,
	lavare fœditatem,
	   illuminare cæcitatem,
	ditare paupertatem,
	   vestire nuditatem,
	ut panem Angelorum,
	   Regem regum
	   et Dominum dominantium,
	tanta suscipiam reverentia
	   et humilitate,
	tanta contritione et devotione,
	   tanta puritate et fide,
	tali proposito et intentione,
	sicut expedit saluti animæ meæ.
	Da mihi, quæso,
	   dominici Corporis et Sanguinis
	non solum suscipere sacramentum,
	sed etiam rem
	   et virtutem sacramenti.
	O mitissime Deus,
	da mihi Corpus Unigeniti Filii tui,
	Domini nostri Iesu Christi,
	quod traxit de Virgine Maria,
	   sic suscipere,
	ut corpori suo mystico
	merear incorporari
	et inter eius membra connumerari.
	
	O amantissime Pater,
	   concede mihi dilectum
	   Filium tuum,

of your beloved Son,
whom I, a wayfarer,
propose to receive now veiled
  under these species:
Who lives and reigns with you
  for ever and ever.
Amen.
	quem nunc velatum
	  in via suscipere propono,
	revelata tandem facie
	  perpetuo contemplari:
	Qui tecum vivit et regnat
	in sæcula sæculorum.
	Amen.

PRAYER BEFORE MASS

O God, to whom every heart is open, every desire known and from whom no secrets are hidden; purify the thoughts of our hearts by the inspiration of your Holy Spirit, that we may perfectly love you, and worthily praise your holy name. Amen.

Before Holy Communion

Prayer for Help

O God, help me to make a good Communion. Mary, my dearest mother, pray to Jesus for me. My dear Angel Guardian, lead me to the Altar of God.

Act of Faith

O God, because you have said it, I believe that I shall receive the Sacred Body of Jesus Christ to eat, and his Precious Blood to drink. My God, I believe this with all my heart.

Act of Humility

My God, I confess that I am a poor sinner; I am not worthy to receive the Body and Blood of Jesus, on account of my sins. Lord, I am not worthy to receive you under my roof; but only say the word, and my soul will be healed.

Act of Sorrow

My God, I detest all the sins of my life. I am sorry for them, because they have offended you, my God, you who are so good. I resolve never to commit sin any more. My good God, pity me, have mercy on me, forgive me.

Act of Adoration

O Jesus, great God, present on the Altar, I bow down before you.
I adore you.

Act of Love and Desire

Jesus, I love you. I desire with all my heart to receive you. Jesus, come into my poor soul, and give me your Flesh to eat and your Blood to drink.

Give me your whole Self, Body, Blood, Soul and Divinity, that I may live for ever with you.

THE ORDER OF MASS

ORDO MISSÆ CUM POPULO

THE INTRODUCTORY RITES

Before Mass begins, the people gather in a spirit of recollection, preparing for their participation in the Mass.

All stand during the entrance procession.

SIGN OF THE CROSS

After the Entrance Chant, the Priest and the faithful sign themselves with the Sign of the Cross:

Priest: In nómine Patris, et Fílii, et Spíritus Sancti.

A-men.

Response: Amen.

GREETING

The Priest greets the people, with one of the following:

1. **Pr.** Grátia Dómini nostri Iesu Christi,
   et cáritas Dei,
   et communicátio Sancti Spíritus
   sit cum ómnibus vobis.

Et cum spí-ri-tu tu-o.

   R. Et cum spíritu tuo.

2. **Pr.** Grátia vobis et pax a Deo Patre nostro
   et Dómino Iesu Christo.
   R. Et cum spíritu tuo.

3. **Pr.** Dóminus vobíscum.
   R. Et cum spíritu tuo.

The Priest, or a Deacon, or another minister, may very briefly introduce the faithful to the Mass of the day.

# THE ORDER OF MASS WITH A CONGREGATION

THE INTRODUCTORY RITES

Before Mass begins, the people gather in a spirit of recollection, preparing for their participation in the Mass.

All stand during the entrance procession.

SIGN OF THE CROSS

After the Entrance Chant, the Priest and the faithful sign themselves with the Sign of the Cross:

Priest: In the name of the Father, and of the Son, and of the Holy Spirit.

A-men.

Response: Amen.

GREETING

The Priest greets the people, with one of the following:

1. **Pr.** The grace of our Lord Jesus Christ,
    and the love of God,
    and the communion of the Holy Spirit
    be with you all.

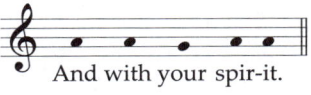

    And with your spir-it.

    R. And with your spirit.

2. **Pr.** Grace to you and peace from God our Father
    and the Lord Jesus Christ.
    R. And with your spirit.

3. **Pr.** The Lord be with you.
    R. And with your spirit.

The Priest, or a Deacon, or another minister, may very briefly introduce the faithful to the Mass of the day.

PENITENTIAL ACT*

There are three forms of the Penitential Act which may be chosen from as appropriate. Each Penitential Act begins with the invitation to the faithful by the Priest:

Pr. Fratres, agnoscámus peccáta nostra,
   ut apti simus ad sacra mystéria celebránda.

A brief pause for silence follows.
Then one of the following forms is used:

**1. Confíteor Deo omnipoténti et vobis, fratres,
quia peccávi nimis
cogitatióne, verbo, ópere et omissióne:**

(and, striking their breast, they say:)

**mea culpa, mea culpa, mea máxima culpa.
Ideo precor beátam Mariám semper Vírginem,
omnes Angelos et Sanctos,
et vos, fratres, oráre pro me
ad Dóminum Deum nostrum.**

2. Pr. Miserére nostri, Dómine.

Qui- a peccá- vi- mus ti- bi.

R. Quia peccávimus tibi.

Pr. Osténde nobis, Dómine, misericórdiam tuam.

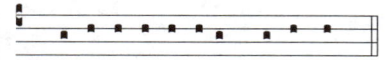

Et sa- lu- tá- re tu- um da no- bis.

R. Et salutáre tuum da nobis.

---

* From time to time on Sundays, especially in Easter Time, instead of the customary Penitential Act, the blessing and sprinkling of water may take place (as in pp.16-21) as a reminder of Baptism.

PENITENTIAL ACT*

There are three forms of the Penitential Act which may be chosen from as appropriate. Each Penitential Act begins with the invitation to the faithful by the Priest:

Pr. Brethren (brothers and sisters),
  let us acknowledge our sins,
  and so prepare ourselves to celebrate the sacred mysteries.

A brief pause for silence follows.

Then one of the following forms is used:

**1. I confess to almighty God
and to you, my brothers and sisters,
that I have greatly sinned,
in my thoughts and in my words,
in what I have done and in what I have failed to do,**

(and, striking their breast, they say:)

**through my fault, through my fault,
through my most grievous fault;
therefore I ask blessed Mary ever-Virgin,
all the Angels and Saints,
and you, my brothers and sisters,
to pray for me to the Lord our God.**

---

2. Pr. Have mercy on us, O Lord.

♪ For we have sinned a-gainst you.

  R. For we have sinned against you.

  Pr. Show us, O Lord, your mercy.

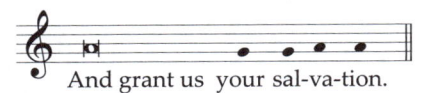

♪ And grant us your sal-va-tion.

  R. And grant us your salvation.

---

* From time to time on Sundays, especially in Easter Time, instead of the customary Penitential Act, the blessing and sprinkling of water may take place (as in pp.16-21) as a reminder of Baptism.

Invocations naming the gracious works of the Lord may be made, as in the example below:

3. Pr. Qui missus es sanáre contrítos corde:
   Kýrie, eléison.

Ký- ri- e, e- lé- i- son.

R. Kýrie, eléison.

Pr. Qui peccatóres vocáre venísti:
   Christe, eléison.

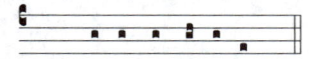

Chri- ste, e- lé- i- son.

R. Christe, eléison.

Pr. Qui ad déxteram Patris sedes, ad interpellándum pro nobis:
   Kýrie, eléison.

Ký- ri- e, e- lé- i- son.

R. Kýrie, eléison.

The absolution by the Priest follows:

Pr. Misereátur nostri omnípotens Deus
   et, dimíssis peccátis nostris,
   perdúcat nos ad vitam ætérnam.

A-men.

R. Amen.

The Kýrie, eléison (Lord, have mercy) invocations follow, unless they have just occurred.

Pr. Kýrie, eléison.

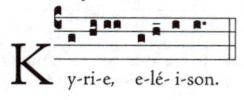

Ky-ri-e, e-lé- i-son.

THE INTRODUCTORY RITES

Invocations naming the gracious works of the Lord may be made, as in the example below:

3. Pr. You were sent to heal the contrite of heart:
Lord, have mercy. Or: Kýrie, eléison.

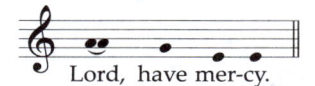

Lord, have mer-cy. Or: repeat music/words from Latin, p.14.

R. Lord, have mercy.

Pr. You came to call sinners:
Christ, have mercy. Or: Christe, eléison.

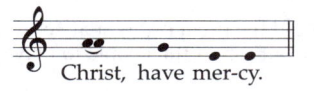

Christ, have mer-cy. Or: repeat music/words from Latin, p.14.

R. Christ, have mercy.

Pr. You are seated at the right hand of the Father to intercede for us:
Lord, have mercy. Or: Kýrie, eléison.

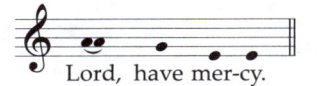

Lord, have mer-cy. Or: repeat music/words from Latin, p.14.

R. Lord, have mercy.

The absolution by the Priest follows:

Pr. May almighty God have mercy on us,
forgive us our sins,
and bring us to everlasting life.

A-men.

R. Amen.

The Kýrie, eléison (Lord, have mercy) invocations follow, unless they have just occurred.

Pr. Lord, have mercy.

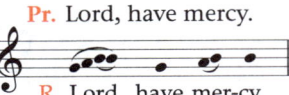

R. Lord, have mer-cy.

Pr. Christe, eléison.

R. Chris-te, e-lé-i-son.

Pr. Kýrie eléison.

R. Ky-ri-e, e-lé-i-son. **Vel:** R. Ky-ri-e, e-lé-i-son.

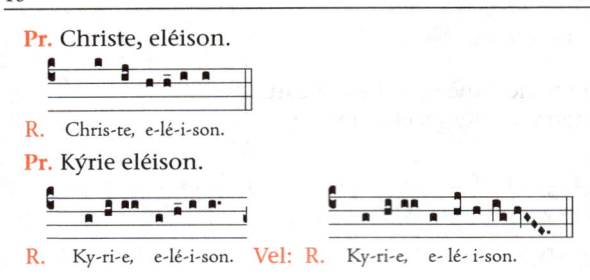

RITE FOR THE BLESSING AND SPRINKLING OF WATER

If this rite is celebrated during Mass, it takes the place of the usual Penitential Act at the beginning of Mass. After the greeting, the Priest calls upon the people to pray in these or similar words:

Dominum Deum nostrum, fratres carissimi,
suppliciter deprecemur,
ut hanc creaturam aquæ benedicere dignetur,
super nos aspergendam in nostri memoriam baptismi.
Ipse autem nos adiuvare dignetur,
ut fideles Spiritui, quem accepimus, maneamus.

And after a brief pause for silence, he continues with hands joined:

Omnipotens sempiterne Deus, qui voluisti ut per aquam,
fontem vitæ ac purificationis principium,
etiam animæ mundarentur
æternæque vitæ munus exciperent,
dignare, quæsumus, hanc aquam ✠ benedicere,
qua volumus hac die tua, Domine, communiri.
Fontem vivum in nobis tuæ gratiæ renovari
et ab omni malo spiritus et corporis
per ipsam nos defendi concedas,
ut mundis tibi cordibus propinquare
tuamque digne salutem valeamus accipere.
Per Christum Dominum nostrum.
R. Amen.

Pr. Christ, have mercy.

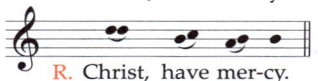

R. Christ, have mer-cy.

Pr. Lord, have mercy.

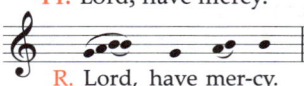

R. Lord, have mer-cy.

RITE FOR THE BLESSING AND SPRINKLING OF WATER

If this rite is celebrated during Mass, it takes the place of the usual Penitential Act at the beginning of Mass. After the greeting, the Priest calls upon the people to pray in these or similar words:

Dear brethren (brothers and sisters),
let us humbly beseech the Lord our God
to bless this water he has created,
which will be sprinkled on us
as a memorial of our Baptism.
May he help us by his grace
to remain faithful to the Spirit we have received.

And after a brief pause for silence, he continues with hands joined:

Almighty ever-living God,
who willed that through water,
the fountain of life and the source of purification,
even souls should be cleansed
and receive the gift of eternal life;
be pleased, we pray, to ✠ bless this water,
by which we seek protection on this your day, O Lord.
Renew the living spring of your grace within us
and grant that by this water we may be defended
from all ills of spirit and body,
and so approach you with hearts made clean
and worthily receive your salvation.
Through Christ our Lord.
R. Amen.

Or:

Domine Deus omnipotens,
qui es totius vitæ corporis et animæ fons et origo,
hanc aquam, te quæsumus, ✠ benedicas,
qua fidenter utimur
ad nostrorum implorandam veniam peccatorum
et adversus omnes morbos inimicique insidias
tuæ defensionem gratiæ consequendam.
Præsta, Domine, ut, misericordia tua interveniente,
aquæ vivæ semper nobis saliant in salutem,
ut mundo tibi corde appropinquare possimus,
et omnia corporis animæque pericula devitemus.
Per Christum Dominum nostrum.
R. Amen.

Or, during Easter Time:

Domine Deus omnipotens,
precibus populi tui adesto propitius;
et nobis, mirabile nostræ creationis opus,
sed et redemptionis nostræ mirabilius, memorantibus,
hanc aquam ✠ benedicere tu dignare.
Ipsam enim tu fecisti,
ut et arva fecunditate donaret,
et levamen corporibus nostris munditiamque præberet.
Aquam etiam tuæ ministram misericordiæ condidisti;
nam per ipsam solvisti tui populi servitutem,
illiusque sitim in deserto sedasti;
per ipsam novum foedus nuntiaverunt prophetæ,
quod eras cum hominibus initurus;
per ipsam denique, quam Christus in Iordane sacravit,
corruptam naturæ nostræ substantiam
in regenerationis lavacro renovasti.
Sit igitur hæc aqua nobis suscepti baptismatis memoria,
et cum fratribus nostris, qui sunt in Paschate baptizati,
gaudia nos tribuas sociare.
Per Christum Dominum nostrum.
R. Amen.

THE INTRODUCTORY RITES

Or:

Almighty Lord and God,
who are the source and origin of all life,
whether of body or soul,
we ask you to ✠ bless this water,
which we use in confidence
to implore forgiveness for our sins
and to obtain the protection of your grace
against all illness and every snare of the enemy.
Grant, O Lord, in your mercy,
that living waters may always spring up for our salvation,
and so may we approach you with a pure heart
and avoid all danger to body and soul.
Through Christ our Lord.
R. Amen.

Or, during Easter Time:

Lord our God,
in your mercy be present to your people's prayers,
and, for us who recall the wondrous work of our creation
and the still greater work of our redemption,
graciously ✠ bless this water.
For you created water to make the fields fruitful
and to refresh and cleanse our bodies.
You also made water the instrument of your mercy:
for through water you freed your people from slavery
and quenched their thirst in the desert;
through water the Prophets proclaimed the new covenant
you were to enter upon with the human race;
and last of all,
through water, which Christ made holy in the Jordan,
you have renewed our corrupted nature
in the bath of regeneration.
Therefore, may this water be for us
a memorial of the Baptism we have received,
and grant that we may share
in the gladness of our brothers and sisters
who at Easter have received their Baptism.
Through Christ our Lord.
R. Amen.

Where the circumstances of the place or the custom of the people suggest that the mixing of salt be preserved in the blessing of water, the Priest may bless salt, saying:

Supplices te rogamus, omnipotens Deus,
ut hanc creaturam salis
benedicere ✠ tua pietate digneris,
qui per Eliseum prophetam in aquam mitti eam iussisti,
ut sanaretur sterilitas aquæ.
Præsta, Domine, quæsumus,
ut, ubicumque hæc salis et aquæ commixtio
fuerit aspersa,
omni impugnatione inimici depulsa,
præsentia Sancti tui Spiritus nos iugiter custodiat.
Per Christum Dominum nostrum.
R. Amen.

Then he pours the salt into the water, without saying anything.
Afterward, taking the aspergillum, the Priest sprinkles himself and the ministers, then the clergy and people, moving through the church, if appropriate.
Meanwhile, one of the following chants, or another appropriate chant is sung.

Outside Easter Time

Antiphon Ps 50:9
Asperges me, Domine, hyssopo et mundabor:
lavabis me, et super nivem dealbabor.

During Easter Time

Antiphon Cf. Ez 47:1-2,9
Vidi aquam egredientem de templo,
a latere dextro, alleluia;
et omnes, ad quos pervenit aqua ista, salvi facti sunt,
et dicent: alleluia, alleluia.

When he returns to his chair and the singing is over, the Priest stands facing the people and, with hands joined, says:

Deus omnipotens nos a peccatis purificet,
et per huius Eucharistiæ celebrationem dignos nos reddat,
qui mensæ regni sui participes efficiamur.
R. Amen.

Then, when it is prescribed, the hymn Gloria in excelsis (Glory to God in the highest) is sung or said.

THE INTRODUCTORY RITES

Where the circumstances of the place or the custom of the people suggest that the mixing of salt be preserved in the blessing of water, the Priest may bless salt, saying:

We humbly ask you, almighty God:
be pleased in your faithful love to bless ✠ this salt
you have created,
for it was you who commanded the prophet Elisha
to cast salt into water,
that impure water might be purified.
Grant, O Lord, we pray,
that, wherever this mixture of salt and water is sprinkled,
every attack of the enemy may be repulsed
and your Holy Spirit may be present
to keep us safe at all times.
Through Christ our Lord.

R. Amen.

Then he pours the salt into the water, without saying anything.
Afterward, taking the aspergillum, the Priest sprinkles himself and the ministers, then the clergy and people, moving through the church, if appropriate.
Meanwhile, one of the following chants, or another appropriate chant is sung.

Outside Easter Time

Antiphon   Ps 50:9

Sprinkle me with hyssop, O Lord, and I shall be cleansed;
wash me and I shall be whiter than snow.

During Easter Time

Antiphon   Cf. Ez 47:1-2,9

I saw water flowing from the Temple,
from its right-hand side, alleluia:
and all to whom this water came
were saved and shall say: alleluia, alleluia.

When he returns to his chair and the singing is over, the Priest stands facing the people and, with hands joined, says:

May almighty God cleanse us of our sins,
and through the celebration of this Eucharist
make us worthy to share at the table of his Kingdom.

R. Amen.

Then, when it is prescribed, the hymn Gloria in excelsis (Glory to God in the highest) is sung or said.

THE GLORIA

On Sundays (outside Advent and Lent), Solemnities and Feast Days, this hymn is either sung or said:

Glória in excélsis Deo. Et in terra pax homínibus bonæ voluntátis. Laudámus te. Benedícimus te. Adorámus te. Glorificámus te. Grátias ágimus tibi propter magnam glóriam tuam. Dómine Deus, Rex cæléstis, Deus Pater omnípotens. Dómine Fili unigénite, Iesu Christe. Dómine Deus, Agnus Dei, Fílius Patris, Qui tollis peccáta mundi, miserére nobis. Qui tollis peccáta mundi, súscipe deprecatiónem nostram. Qui sedes ad déxteram Patris, miseré-

THE GLORIA

On Sundays (outside Advent and Lent), Solemnities and Feast Days, this hymn is either sung or said:

Glo-ry to God in the high-est,

and on earth peace to peo-ple of good will.

We praise you, we bless you, we a-dore you, we glo-ri-fy you,

we give you thanks for your great glo-ry,

Lord God, heav-en-ly King, O God, al-might-y Fa-ther.

Lord Je-sus Christ, On-ly Be-got-ten Son,

Lord God, Lamb of God, Son of the Fa-ther,

you take a-way the sins of the world, have mer-cy on us;

you take a-way the sins of the world, re-ceive our prayer;

you are seat-ed at the right hand of the Fa-ther, have mer-cy on us.

...re nobis. Quóni-am tu solus Sanctus. Tu solus Dó-mi-nus Tu so-lus Al-tíssimus, Ie-su Christe. Cum Sancto Spí-ri-tu, in gló-ri-a De-i Pa-tris. A- men.

Glória in excélsis Deo
et in terra pax homínibus bonæ voluntátis.

Laudámus te,
benedícimus te,
adorámus te,
glorificámus te,
grátias ágimus tibi propter magnam glóriam tuam,
Dómine Deus, Rex cæléstis,
Deus Pater omnípotens.

Dómine Fili Unigénite, Iesu Christe,
Dómine Deus, Agnus Dei, Fílius Patris,
qui tollis peccáta mundi, miserére nobis;
qui tollis peccáta mundi, súscipe deprecatiónem nostram.
Qui sedes ad déxteram Patris, miserére nobis.

Quóniam tu solus Sanctus, tu solus Dóminus, tu solus Altíssimus,
Iesu Christe, cum Sancto Spíritu: in glória Dei Patris.
Amen.

When this hymn is concluded, the Priest, says: **Pr.** Orémus.
And all pray in silence. Then the Priest says the Collect prayer, which ends:
R. Amen.

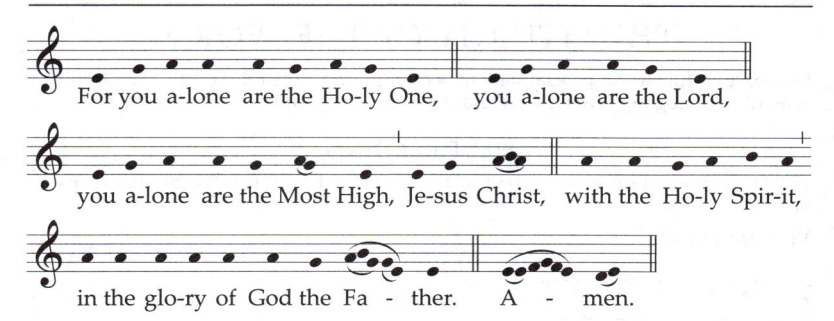

THE INTRODUCTORY RITES

For you alone are the Holy One, you alone are the Lord, you alone are the Most High, Jesus Christ, with the Holy Spirit, in the glory of God the Father. Amen.

Glory to God in the highest,
and on earth peace to people of good will.

We praise you,
we bless you,
we adore you,
we glorify you,
we give you thanks for your great glory,
Lord God, heavenly King,
O God, almighty Father.

Lord Jesus Christ, Only Begotten Son,
Lord God, Lamb of God, Son of the Father,
you take away the sins of the world, have mercy on us;
you take away the sins of the world, receive our prayer;
you are seated at the right hand of the Father,
have mercy on us.

For you alone are the Holy One,
you alone are the Lord,
you alone are the Most High,
Jesus Christ,
with the Holy Spirit,
in the glory of God the Father.
Amen.

When this hymn is concluded, the Priest, says: **Pr.** Let us pray.
And all pray in silence. Then the Priest says the Collect prayer, which ends:
R. Amen.

THE LITURGY OF THE WORD

By hearing the word proclaimed in worship, the faithful again enter into the unending dialogue between God and the covenant people.

FIRST READING

The reader goes to the ambo and proclaims the First Reading, while all sit and listen. The reader ends:

Verbum Dómini.

De- o grá- ti- as

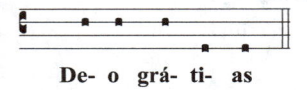

R. Deo grátias.

It is appropriate to have a brief time of quiet between readings as those present take the word of God to heart.

PSALM

The psalmist or cantor sings or says the Psalm, with the people making the response.

SECOND READING

On Sundays and certain other days there is a second reading. The reader ends:

Verbum Dómini.

De- o grá- ti- as

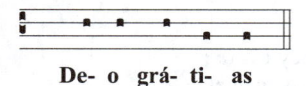

R. Deo grátias.

GOSPEL

The assembly stands for the Gospel Acclamation. Except during Lent the Acclamation is:

R. Allelúia!

During Lent the following forms may be used or another similar phrase:

R. Laus tibi, Christe, Rex ætérnæ glóriæ! Or:
R. Laus et honor tibi, Dómine Iesu! Or:
R. Glória et laus tibi, Christe! Or:
R. Glória tibi, Christe, Verbo Dei!

THE LITURGY OF THE WORD

By hearing the word proclaimed in worship, the faithful again enter into the unending dialogue between God and the covenant people.

FIRST READING

The reader goes to the ambo and proclaims the First Reading, while all sit and listen. The reader ends:

The word of the Lord.

Thanks be to God.

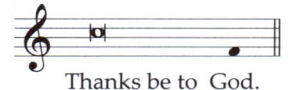

R. Thanks be to God.

It is appropriate to have a brief time of quiet between readings as those present take the word of God to heart.

PSALM

The psalmist or cantor sings or says the Psalm, with the people making the response.

SECOND READING

On Sundays and certain other days there is a second reading. The reader ends:

The word of the Lord.

Thanks be to God.

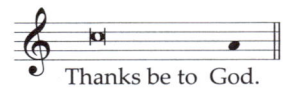

R. Thanks be to God.

GOSPEL

The assembly stands for the Gospel Acclamation. Except during Lent the Acclamation is:

R. Alleluia!

During Lent the following forms may be used or another similar phrase:

R. Praise to you, O Christ, king of eternal glory! Or:

R. Praise and honour to you, Lord Jesus! Or:

R. Glory and praise to you, O Christ! Or:

R. Glory to you, O Christ, you are the Word of God!

At the ambo the Deacon, or the Priest says:
Pr. Dóminus vobíscum.

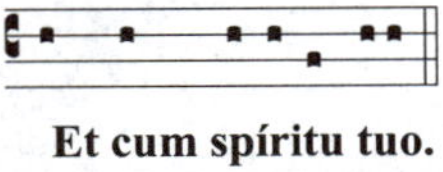

Et cum spíritu tuo.

R. Et cum spíritu tuo.
Pr. Léctio sancti Evangélii secúndum **N.**

He makes the Sign of the Cross on the book and, together with the people, on his forehead, lips, and breast.

Glória tibi Dómine.

R. Glória tibi, Dómine.

At the end of the Gospel:
Pr. Verbum Dómini.

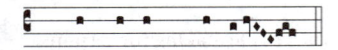

Laus ti-bi, Christe.

R. Laus tibi, Christe.

THE HOMILY

Then follows the Homily, which is preached by a Priest or Deacon on all Sundays and Holydays of Obligation. After a brief silence all stand.

THE CREED

On Sundays and Solemnities, the Profession of Faith will follow. Especially during Lent and Easter Time, the Apostles' Creed may be used.

THE NICENO-CONSTANTINOPOLITAN CREED

Credo in unum De- um, Patrem omni-poténtem factó-rem cæli et terræ, vi-sibili-um óm-nium et invi-si-bí- lium. Et in unum Dó-

THE LITURGY OF THE WORD

At the ambo the Deacon, or the Priest says:
Pr. The Lord be with you.

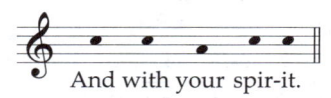

And with your spir-it.

R. And with your spirit.
Pr. A reading from the holy Gospel according to **N.**

He makes the Sign of the Cross on the book and, together with the people, on his forehead, lips, and breast.

Glory to you, O Lord.

R. Glory to you, O Lord.

At the end of the Gospel:
Pr. The Gospel of the Lord.

Praise to you, Lord Je-sus Christ.

R. Praise to you, Lord Jesus Christ.

THE HOMILY

Then follows the Homily, which is preached by a Priest or Deacon on all Sundays and Holydays of Obligation. After a brief silence all stand.

THE CREED

On Sundays and Solemnities, the Profession of Faith will follow. Especially during Lent and Easter Time, the Apostles' Creed may be used.

THE NICENO-CONSTANTINOPOLITAN CREED

I be-lieve in one God, the Fa-ther al-might-y, mak-er of heav-en and earth, of all things vis-i-ble and in-vis-i-ble.

...minum Iesum Christum, Fílium Dei unigénitum. Et ex Patre natum ante ómnia sǽcula. Deum de Deo, lumen de lumine, Deum verum de Deo vero. Génitum, non factum, consubstantiálem Patri: per quem ómnia facta sunt. Qui propter nos homines et propter nostram salútem descéndit de cælis. Et in-

At the words that follow, up to and including et homo factus est, *all bow.*

carnátus est de Spíritu Sancto ex María Vírgine, et homo factus est. Crucifíxus étiam pro nobis sub Póntio Piláto, passus et sepúltus est. Et resurréxit tértia die, secúndum Scriptúras, Et ascéndit in cælum, sedet ad déxteram Patris. Et íterum

THE LITURGY OF THE WORD

I believe in one Lord Jesus Christ, the Only Begotten Son of God, born of the Father before all ages. God from God, Light from Light, true God from true God, begotten, not made, consubstantial with the Father; through him all things were made. For us men and for our salvation he came down from

At the words that follow, up to and including and became man, *all bow.*

heaven, and by the Holy Spirit was incarnate of the Virgin Mary, and became man.

For our sake he was crucified under Pontius Pilate, he suffered death and was buried, and rose again on the third day in accordance with the Scriptures. He ascended into heaven

ventúrus est cum glória, iudicáre vivos et mórtuos, cuius regni non erit finis. Et in Spíritum Sanctum, Dóminum et vivificántem: qui ex Patre Filióque procédit. Qui cum Patre et Fílio simul adorátur et conglorificátur: qui locútus est per prophétas. Et unam, sanctam, cathólicam et apostólicam Ecclésiam. Confíteor unum baptísma in remissiónem peccatórum. Et exspécto resurrectiónem mortuórum. Et vitam ventúri sǽculi. Amen

and is seated at the right hand of the Fa-ther. He will come a-gain in glo-ry to judge the living and the dead and his kingdom will have no end.

I be-lieve in the Ho-ly Spir-it, the Lord, the giv-er of life, who pro-ceeds from the Father and the Son, who with the Fa-ther and the Son is adored and glo-ri-fied, who has spoken through the proph-ets. I be-lieve in one, ho-ly, ca-tho-lic and a-pos-tol-ic Church. I con-fess one Bap-tism for the for-give-ness of sins and I look for-ward to the res-ur-rec-tion of the dead and the life of the world to come. A - men.

Credo in unum Deum,
Patrem omnipoténtem,
factórem cæli et terræ,
visibílium ómnium et invisibílium.

Et in unum Dóminum Iesum Christum,
Fílium Dei Unigénitum,
et ex Patre natum ante ómnia sǽcula.
Deum de Deo, lumen de lúmine,
    Deum verum de Deo vero,
génitum, non factum, consubstantiálem Patri:
per quem ómnia facta sunt.
Qui propter nos hómines et propter nostram salútem
descéndit de cælis.

(all bow)

Et incarnátus est de Spíritu Sancto
ex María Vírgine, et homo factus est.

Crucifíxus étiam pro nobis sub Póntio Piláto;
passus et sepúltus est,
et resurréxit tértia die, secúndum Scriptúras,
et ascéndit in cælum, sedet ad déxteram Patris.

Et íterum ventúrus est cum glória,
    iudicáre vivos et mórtuos,
cuius regni non erit finis.

Et in Spíritum Sanctum, Dóminum et vivificántem:
qui ex Patre Filióque procédit.
Qui cum Patre et Fílio simul adorátur et conglorificátur:
qui locútus est per prophétas.

Et unam, sanctam, cathólicam et apostólicam Ecclésiam.
Confíteor unum baptísma in remissiónem peccatórum.
Et exspécto resurrectiónem mortuórum,
et vitam ventúri sǽculi. Amen.

THE LITURGY OF THE WORD

I believe in one God,
the Father almighty,
maker of heaven and earth,
of all things visible and invisible.

I believe in one Lord Jesus Christ,
the Only Begotten Son of God,
born of the Father before all ages.
God from God, Light from Light,
true God from true God,
begotten, not made, consubstantial with the Father;
through him all things were made.
For us men and for our salvation
he came down from heaven,

(all bow)

and by the Holy Spirit was incarnate of the Virgin Mary,
and became man.

For our sake he was crucified under Pontius Pilate,
he suffered death and was buried,
and rose again on the third day
in accordance with the Scriptures.
He ascended into heaven
and is seated at the right hand of the Father.
He will come again in glory
to judge the living and the dead
and his kingdom will have no end.

I believe in the Holy Spirit, the Lord, the giver of life,
who proceeds from the Father and the Son,
who with the Father and the Son is adored and glorified,
who has spoken through the prophets.

I believe in one, holy, catholic and apostolic Church.
I confess one Baptism for the forgiveness of sins
and I look forward to the resurrection of the dead
and the life of the world to come. Amen.

THE APOSTLES' CREED

Credo in Deum, Patrem omnipoténtem,
Creatórem cæli et terræ,
et in Iesum Christum, Fílium eius únicum,
Dóminum nostrum,

at the words that follow up to and including Maria Virgine, all bow.

qui concéptus est de Spíritu Sancto,
natus ex María Vírgine,
passus sub Póntio Piláto,
crucifíxus, mórtuus, et sepúltus,
descéndit ad ínferos,
tértia die resurréxit a mórtuis,
ascéndit ad cælos,
sedet ad déxteram Dei Patris omnipoténtis,
inde ventúrus est iudicáre vivos et mórtuos.

Credo in Spíritum Sanctum,
sanctam Ecclésiam cathólicam,
Sanctórum communiónem,
remissiónem peccatórum,
carnis resurrectiónem,
vitam ætérnam. Amen.

THE PRAYER OF THE FAITHFUL (BIDDING PRAYERS)

Intentions will normally be for the Church; for the world; for those in particular need; and for the local community. After each there is time for silent prayer, followed by the next intention, or concluded with a sung phrase such as Christe audi nos, or Christe exaudi nos, or by a responsory such as:

R. **Præsta, ætérne omnípotens Deus.** Or:
R. **Te rogámus audi nos.** Or:
R. **Kýrie, eléison.**

The Priest concludes the Prayer with a collect.

THE APOSTLES' CREED

**I believe in God,
the Father almighty
Creator of heaven and earth,
and in Jesus Christ, his only Son, our Lord,**

at the words that follow up to and including the Virgin Mary, all bow.

**who was conceived by the Holy Spirit,
born of the Virgin Mary,
suffered under Pontius Pilate,
was crucified, died and was buried;
he descended into hell;
on the third day he rose again from the dead;
he ascended into heaven,
and is seated at the right hand of God
    the Father almighty;
from there he will come to judge the living and the dead.**

**I believe in the Holy Spirit,
the holy catholic Church,
the communion of saints,
the forgiveness of sins,
the resurrection of the body,
and life everlasting. Amen.**

THE PRAYER OF THE FAITHFUL (BIDDING PRAYERS)

Intentions will normally be for the Church; for the world; for those in particular need; and for the local community. After each there is time for silent prayer, followed by the next intention, or concluded with a sung phrase such as Christ, hear us, or Christ graciously hear us, or by a responsory such as:

Let us pray to the Lord.
- **R. Grant this, almighty God.** Or:
- **R. Lord, have mercy.** Or:
- **R. Kýrie, eléison.**

The Priest concludes the Prayer with a collect.

THE LITURGY OF THE EUCHARIST

For Catholics, the Eucharist is the source and summit of the whole Christian life.

After the Liturgy of the Word, the people sit and the Offertory Chant begins. The faithful express their participation by making an offering, bringing forward bread and wine for the celebration of the Eucharist and perhaps other gifts to relieve the needs of the Church and of the poor.

PREPARATORY PRAYERS

Standing at the altar, the Priest takes the paten with the bread and holds it slightly raised above the altar with both hands, saying:

Pr. Benedíctus es, Dómine, Deus univérsi,
 quia de tua largitáte accépimus panem,
 quem tibi offérimus,
 fructum terræ et óperis mánuum hóminum:
 ex quo nobis fiet panis vitæ.
R. Benedíctus Deus in sǽcula.

The Priest then takes the chalice and holds it slightly raised above the altar with both hands, saying:

Pr. Benedíctus es, Dómine, Deus univérsi,
 quia de tua largitáte accépimus vinum,
 quod tibi offérimus,
 fructum vitis et óperis mánuum hóminum,
 ex quo nobis fiet potus spiritális.
R. Benedíctus Deus in sǽcula.

The Priest completes additional personal preparatory rites, and the people rise as he says:

Pr. Oráte, fratres:
 ut meum ac vestrum sacrifícium
 acceptábile fiat apud Deum Patrem omnipoténtem.

**R. Suscípiat Dóminus sacrifícium de mánibus tuis
 ad laudem et glóriam nóminis sui,
 ad utilitátem quoque nostram
 totiúsque Ecclésiæ suæ sanctæ.**

PRAYER OVER THE OFFERINGS

The Priest says the Prayer over the Offerings, at the end of which the people acclaim:
R. Amen.

THE LITURGY OF THE EUCHARIST

For Catholics, the Eucharist is the source and summit of the whole Christian life.

After the Liturgy of the Word, the people sit and the Offertory Chant begins. The faithful express their participation by making an offering, bringing forward bread and wine for the celebration of the Eucharist and perhaps other gifts to relieve the needs of the Church and of the poor.

PREPARATORY PRAYERS

Standing at the altar, the Priest takes the paten with the bread and holds it slightly raised above the altar with both hands, saying:

Pr. Blessed are you, Lord God of all creation,
for through your goodness we have received
the bread we offer you:
fruit of the earth and work of human hands,
it will become for us the bread of life.

R. Blessed be God for ever.

The Priest then takes the chalice and holds it slightly raised above the altar with both hands, saying:

Pr. Blessed are you, Lord God of all creation,
for through your goodness we have received
the wine we offer you:
fruit of the vine and work of human hands,
it will become our spiritual drink.

R. Blessed be God for ever.

The Priest completes additional personal preparatory rites, and the people rise as he says:

Pr. Pray, brethren (brothers and sisters),
that my sacrifice and yours
may be acceptable to God,
the almighty Father.

**R. May the Lord accept the sacrifice at your hands
for the praise and glory of his name,
for our good
and the good of all his holy Church.**

PRAYER OVER THE OFFERINGS

The Priest says the Prayer over the Offerings, at the end of which the people acclaim:

R. Amen.

THE EUCHARISTIC PRAYER

Extending his hands, the Priest says:
Pr. Dóminus vobíscum.

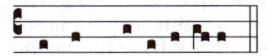

Et cum spí-ri-tu tu-o.

R. **Et cum spíritu tuo.**

Pr. Sursum corda.

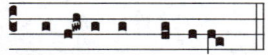

Habémus ad Dóminum.

R. **Habémus ad Dóminum.**

Pr. Grátias agámus Dómino Deo nostro.

Dignum et iustum est.

R. **Dignum et iustum est.**

The Priest continues with the Preface appropriate to the Season or Feast at the end of which all sing or say:

Sanc-tus, * Sanc-tus, Sanc-tus Dó-mi-nus De-us Sá-ba-oth. Ple-ni sunt cæ-li et ter-ra gló-ri-a tu-a. Ho-sán-na in ex-cél-sis. Be-ne-díc-tus qui ve-nit in nómine Dómini. Ho-sán-na in excél-sis.

THE EUCHARISTIC PRAYER

Extending his hands, the Priest says:

Pr. The Lord be with you.

R. And with your spir-it.

R. And with your spirit.

Pr. Lift up your hearts.

R. We lift them up to the Lord.

R. We lift them up to the Lord.

Pr. Let us give thanks to the Lord our God.

R. It is right and just.

R. It is right and just.

The Priest continues with the Preface appropriate to the Season or Feast at the end of which all sing or say:

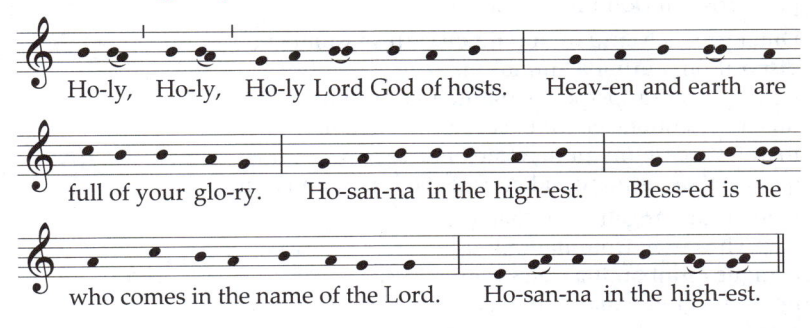

Ho-ly, Ho-ly, Ho-ly Lord God of hosts. Heav-en and earth are full of your glo-ry. Ho-san-na in the high-est. Bless-ed is he who comes in the name of the Lord. Ho-san-na in the high-est.

Sanctus, Sanctus, Sanctus Dóminus Deus Sábaoth.
Pleni sunt cæli et terra glória tua.
Hosánna in excélsis.
Benedíctus qui venit in nómine Dómini.
Hosánna in excélsis.

After the Sanctus the congregation kneels for the remainder of the Eucharistic Prayer. (Texts for the four principal Eucharistic Prayers follow: Eucharistic Prayer I at p.80, II at p.92, III at p.100, IV at p.110.)

PREFACES

ADVENT

PRÆFATIO I DE ADVENTU

De duobus adventibus Christi

In Missis de tempore a prima dominica Adventus usque ad diem 16 decembris

Vere dignum et iustum est, æquum et salutare,
nos tibi semper et ubique gratias agere:
Domine, sancte Pater, omnipotens æterne Deus:
per Christum Dominum nostrum.

Qui, primo adventu in humilitate carnis assumptæ,
dispositionis antiquæ munus implevit,
nobisque salutis perpetuæ tramitem reseravit:
ut, cum secundo venerit in suæ gloria maiestatis,
manifesto demum munere capiamus,
quod vigilantes nunc audemus exspectare promissum.

Et ideo cum Angelis et Archangelis,
cum Thronis et Dominationibus,
cumque omni militia cælestis exercitus,
hymnum gloriæ tuæ canimus,
sine fine dicentes:

Sanctus, Sanctus, Sanctus Dominus Deus Sabaoth. . .

**Holy, Holy, Holy Lord God of hosts.
Heaven and earth are full of your glory.
Hosanna in the highest.
Blessed is he who comes in the name of the Lord.
Hosanna in the highest.**

After the Sanctus the congregation kneels for the remainder of the Eucharistic Prayer. (Texts for the four principal Eucharistic Prayers follow: Eucharistic Prayer I at p.81, II at p.93, III at p.101, IV at p.111.)

PREFACES

ADVENT

PREFACE I OF ADVENT

The two comings of Christ

From the First Sunday of Advent until 16 December

It is truly right and just, our duty and our salvation,
always and everywhere to give you thanks,
Lord, holy Father, almighty and eternal God,
through Christ our Lord.

For he assumed at his first coming
the lowliness of human flesh,
and so fulfilled the design you formed long ago,
and opened for us the way to eternal salvation,
that, when he comes again in glory and majesty
and all is at last made manifest,
we who watch for that day
may inherit the great promise
in which now we dare to hope.

And so, with Angels and Archangels,
with Thrones and Dominions,
and with all the hosts and Powers of heaven,
we sing the hymn of your glory,
as without end we acclaim:

Holy, Holy, Holy Lord God of hosts. . .

PRÆFATIO II DE ADVENTU

De duplici exspectatione Christi
17 decembris-24 decembris

Vere dignum et iustum est, æquum et salutare,
nos tibi semper et ubique gratias agere:
Domine, sancte Pater, omnipotens æterne Deus:
per Christum Dominum nostrum.

Quem prædixerunt cunctorum præconia prophetarum,
Virgo Mater ineffabili dilectione sustinuit,
Ioannes cecinit affuturum et adesse monstravit.
Qui suæ nativitatis mysterium
tribuit nos prævenire gaudentes,
ut et in oratione pervigiles
et in suis inveniat laudibus exsultantes.

Et ideo cum Angelis et Archangelis,
cum Thronis et Dominationibus,
cumque omni militia cælestis exercitus,
hymnum gloriæ tuæ canimus,
sine fine dicentes:
Sanctus, Sanctus, Sanctus Dominus Deus Sabaoth. . .

CHRISTMAS

PRÆFATIO I DE NATIVITATE DOMINI

De Christo luce

Vere dignum et iustum est, æquum et salutare,
nos tibi semper et ubique gratias agere:
Domine, sancte Pater, omnipotens æterne Deus:

Quia per incarnati Verbi mysterium
nova mentis nostræ oculis lux tuæ claritatis infulsit:
ut, dum visibiliter Deum cognoscimus,
per hunc in invisibilium amorem rapiamur.

Et ideo cum Angelis et Archangelis,
cum Thronis et Dominationibus,
cumque omni militia cælestis exercitus,
hymnum gloriæ tuæ canimus, sine fine dicentes:
Sanctus, Sanctus, Sanctus Dominus Deus Sabaoth. . .

PREFACE II OF ADVENT

The twofold expectation of Christ
17 December-24 December

It is truly right and just, our duty and our salvation,
always and everywhere to give you thanks,
Lord, holy Father, almighty and eternal God,
through Christ our Lord.

For all the oracles of the prophets foretold him,
the Virgin Mother longed for him
with love beyond all telling,
John the Baptist sang of his coming
and proclaimed his presence when he came.

It is by his gift that already we rejoice
at the mystery of his Nativity,
so that he may find us watchful in prayer
and exultant in his praise.

And so, with Angels and Archangels,
with Thrones and Dominions,
and with all the hosts and Powers of heaven,
we sing the hymn of your glory,
as without end we acclaim:

Holy, Holy, Holy Lord God of hosts...

CHRISTMAS

PREFACE I OF THE NATIVITY OF THE LORD

Christ the Light

It is truly right and just, our duty and our salvation,
always and everywhere to give you thanks,
Lord, holy Father, almighty and eternal God.

For in the mystery of the Word made flesh
a new light of your glory has shone upon the eyes of our mind,
so that, as we recognise in him God made visible,
we may be caught up through him in love of things invisible.

And so, with Angels and Archangels,
with Thrones and Dominions,
and with all the hosts and Powers of heaven,
we sing the hymn of your glory,
as without end we acclaim:

Holy, Holy, Holy Lord God of hosts...

PRÆFATIO II DE NATIVITATE DOMINI

De restauratione universa in Incarnatione

Vere dignum et iustum est, æquum et salutare,
nos tibi semper et ubique gratias agere:
Domine, sancte Pater, omnipotens æterne Deus:
per Christum Dominum nostrum.

Qui, in huius venerandi festivitate mysterii,
invisibilis in suis, visibilis in nostris apparuit,
et ante tempora genitus esse cœpit in tempore;
ut, in se erigens cuncta deiecta,
in integrum restitueret universa,
et hominem perditum ad cælestia regna revocaret.

Unde et nos, cum omnibus Angelis te laudamus,
iucunda celebratione clamantes:

Sanctus, Sanctus, Sanctus Dominus Deus Sabaoth. . .

PRÆFATIO III DE NATIVITATE DOMINI

De commercio in Incarnatione Verbi

Vere dignum et iustum est, æquum et salutare,
nos tibi semper et ubique gratias agere:
Domine, sancte Pater, omnipotens æterne Deus:
per Christum Dominum nostrum.

Per quem hodie commercium nostræ reparationis effulsit,
quia, dum nostra fragilitas a tuo Verbo suscipitur,
humana mortalitas non solum
in perpetuum transit honorem,
sed nos quoque, mirando consortio, reddit æternos.

Et ideo, choris angelicis sociati,
te laudamus in gaudio confitentes:

Sanctus, Sanctus, Sanctus Dominus Deus Sabaoth. . .

PREFACE II OF THE NATIVITY OF THE LORD

The restoration of all things in the Incarnation

It is truly right and just, our duty and our salvation,
always and everywhere to give you thanks,
Lord, holy Father, almighty and eternal God,
through Christ our Lord.

For on the feast of this awe-filled mystery,
though invisible in his own divine nature,
he has appeared visibly in ours;
and begotten before all ages,
he has begun to exist in time;
so that, raising up in himself all that was cast down,
he might restore unity to all creation
and call straying humanity back to the heavenly Kingdom.

And so, with all the Angels, we praise you,
as in joyful celebration we acclaim:

Holy, Holy, Holy Lord God of hosts. . .

PREFACE III OF THE NATIVITY OF THE LORD

The exchange in the Incarnation of the Word

It is truly right and just, our duty and our salvation,
always and everywhere to give you thanks,
Lord, holy Father, almighty and eternal God,
through Christ our Lord.

For through him the holy exchange that restores our life
has shone forth today in splendour:
when our frailty is assumed by your Word
not only does human mortality receive unending honour
but by this wondrous union we, too, are made eternal.

And so, in company with the choirs of Angels,
we praise you, and with joy we proclaim:

Holy, Holy, Holy Lord God of hosts. . .

PRÆFATIO DE EPIPHANIA DOMINI
De Christo lumine gentium

Vere dignum et iustum est, æquum et salutare,
nos tibi semper et ubique gratias agere:
Domine, sancte Pater, omnipotens æterne Deus:

Quia ipsum in Christo salutis nostræ mysterium
hodie ad lumen gentium revelasti,
et, cum in substantia nostræ mortalitatis apparuit,
nova nos immortalitatis eius gloria reparasti.

Et ideo cum Angelis et Archangelis,
cum Thronis et Dominationibus,
cumque omni militia cælestis exercitus,
hymnum gloriæ tuæ canimus,
sine fine dicentes:

Sanctus, Sanctus, Sanctus Dominus Deus Sabaoth. . .

LENT
PRÆFATIO I DE QUADRAGESIMA
De spiritali significatione Quadregesimæ

Vere dignum et iustum est, æquum et salutare,
nos tibi semper et ubique gratias agere:
Domine, sancte Pater, omnipotens æterne Deus:
per Christum Dominum nostrum.

Quia fidelibus tuis dignanter concedis
quotannis paschalia sacramenta
in gaudio purificatis mentibus exspectare:
ut, pietatis officia et opera caritatis propensius exsequentes,
frequentatione mysteriorum, quibus renati sunt,
ad gratiæ filiorum plenitudinem perducantur.

Et ideo cum Angelis et Archangelis,
cum Thronis et Dominationibus,
cumque omni militia cælestis exercitus,
hymnum gloriæ tuæ canimus,
sine fine dicentes:

Sanctus, Sanctus, Sanctus Dominus Deus Sabaoth. . .

PREFACE OF THE EPIPHANY OF THE LORD
Christ the light of the nations

It is truly right and just, our duty and our salvation,
always and everywhere to give you thanks,
Lord, holy Father, almighty and eternal God.

For today you have revealed the mystery
of our salvation in Christ
as a light for the nations,
and, when he appeared in our mortal nature,
you made us new by the glory of his immortal nature.

And so, with Angels and Archangels,
with Thrones and Dominions,
and with all the hosts and Powers of heaven,
we sing the hymn of your glory,
as without end we acclaim:

Holy, Holy, Holy Lord God of hosts. . .

LENT
PREFACE I OF LENT
The spiritual meaning of Lent

It is truly right and just, our duty and our salvation,
always and everywhere to give you thanks,
Lord, holy Father, almighty and eternal God,
through Christ our Lord.

For by your gracious gift each year
your faithful await the sacred paschal feasts
with the joy of minds made pure,
so that, more eagerly intent on prayer
and on the works of charity,
and participating in the mysteries
by which they have been reborn,
they may be led to the fullness of grace
that you bestow on your sons and daughters.

And so, with Angels and Archangels,
with Thrones and Dominions,
and with all the hosts and Powers of heaven,
we sing the hymn of your glory,
as without end we acclaim:

Holy, Holy, Holy Lord God of hosts. . .

PRÆFATIO II DE QUADRAGESIMA

De spiritali pænitentia

Vere dignum et iustum est, æquum et salutare,
nos tibi semper et ubique gratias agere:
Domine, sancte Pater, omnipotens æterne Deus:

Qui filiis tuis ad reparandam mentium puritatem,
tempus præcipuum salubriter statuisti,
quo, mente ab inordinatis affectibus expedita,
sic incumberent transituris
ut rebus potius perpetuis inhærerent.

Et ideo, cum Sanctis et Angelis universis,
te collaudamus, sine fine dicentes:
Sanctus, Sanctus, Sanctus Dominus Deus Sabaoth...

PRÆFATIO III DE QUADRAGESIMA

De fructibus abstinentiæ

Vere dignum et iustum est, æquum et salutare,
nos tibi semper et ubique gratias agere:
Domine, sancte Pater, omnipotens æterne Deus:

Qui nos per abstinentiam tibi gratias referre voluisti,
ut ipsa et nos peccatores ab insolentia mitigaret,
et, egentium proficiens alimento,
imitatores tuæ benignitatis efficeret.

Et ideo, cum innumeris Angelis,
una te magnificamus laudis voce dicentes:

Sanctus, Sanctus, Sanctus Dominus Deus Sabaoth...

PRÆFATIO IV DE QUADRAGESIMA

De fructibus ieiunii

Vere dignum et iustum est, æquum et salutare,
nos tibi semper et ubique gratias agere:
Domine, sancte Pater, omnipotens æterne Deus:

Qui corporali ieiunio vitia comprimis, mentem elevas,
virtutem largiris et præmia:
per Christum Dominum nostrum.

PREFACE II OF LENT

Spiritual penance

It is truly right and just, our duty and our salvation,
always and everywhere to give you thanks,
Lord, holy Father, almighty and eternal God.

For you have given your children a sacred time
for the renewing and purifying of their hearts,
that, freed from disordered affections,
they may so deal with the things of this passing world
as to hold rather to the things that eternally endure.

And so, with all the Angels and Saints,
we praise you, as without end we acclaim:

Holy, Holy, Holy Lord God of hosts. . .

PREFACE III OF LENT

The fruits of abstinence

It is truly right and just, our duty and our salvation,
always and everywhere to give you thanks,
Lord, holy Father, almighty and eternal God.

For you will that our self-denial should give you thanks,
humble our sinful pride,
contribute to the feeding of the poor,
and so help us imitate you in your kindness.

And so we glorify you with countless Angels,
as with one voice of praise we acclaim:

Holy, Holy, Holy Lord God of hosts. . .

PREFACE IV OF LENT

The fruits of fasting

It is truly right and just, our duty and our salvation,
always and everywhere to give you thanks,
Lord, holy Father, almighty and eternal God.

For through bodily fasting you restrain our faults,
raise up our minds,
and bestow both virtue and its rewards,
through Christ our Lord.

Per quem maiestatem tuam laudant Angeli,
adorant Dominationes, tremunt Potestates.
Cæli cælorumque Virtutes, ac beata Seraphim,
socia exsultatione concelebrant.

Cum quibus et nostras voces ut admitti iubeas, deprecamur,
supplici confessione dicentes:

Sanctus, Sanctus, Sanctus Dominus Deus Sabaoth...

PRÆFATIO I DE PASSIONE DOMINI

De virtute Crucis

Vere dignum et iustum est, æquum et salutare,
nos tibi semper et ubique gratias agere:
Domine, sancte Pater, omnipotens æterne Deus:

Quia per Filii tui salutiferam passionem
sensum confitendæ tuæ maiestatis totus mundus accepit,
dum ineffabili crucis potentia
iudicium mundi et potestas emicat Crucifixi.

Unde et nos, Domine, cum Angelis et Sanctis universis,
tibi confitemur, in exsultatione dicentes:

Sanctus, Sanctus, Sanctus Dominus Deus Sabaoth...

EASTER

PRÆFATIO PASCHALIS I

De mysterio paschali

Vere dignum et iustum est, æquum et salutare:
Te quidem, Domine, omni tempore confiteri,
sed in hac potissimum nocte (die) gloriosius prædicare,
(sed in hoc potissimum gloriosius prædicare,)
cum Pascha nostrum immolatus est Christus.

Ipse enim verus est Agnus
qui abstulit peccata mundi.
Qui mortem nostram moriendo destruxit,
et vitam resurgendo reparavit.

Quapropter, profusis paschalibus gaudiis,
totus in orbe terrarum mundus exsultat.

Through him the Angels praise your majesty,
Dominions adore and Powers tremble before you.
Heaven and the Virtues of heaven and the blessed Seraphim
worship together with exultation.
May our voices, we pray, join with theirs
in humble praise, as we acclaim:

Holy, Holy, Holy Lord God of hosts. . .

PREFACE I OF THE PASSION OF THE LORD

The power of the Cross

It is truly right and just, our duty and our salvation,
always and everywhere to give you thanks,
Lord, holy Father, almighty and eternal God.

For through the saving Passion of your Son
the whole world has received a heart
to confess the infinite power of your majesty,
since by the wondrous power of the Cross
your judgement on the world is now revealed
and the authority of Christ crucified.

And so, Lord, with all the Angels and Saints,
we, too, give you thanks, as in exultation we acclaim:

Holy, Holy, Holy Lord God of hosts. . .

EASTER

PREFACE I OF EASTER

The Paschal Mystery

It is truly right and just, our duty and our salvation,
at all times to acclaim you, O Lord,
but (on this night / on this day / in this time) above all
to laud you yet more gloriously,
when Christ our Passover has been sacrificed.

For he is the true Lamb
who has taken away the sins of the world;
by dying he has destroyed our death,
and by rising, restored our life.

Therefore, overcome with paschal joy,
every land, every people exults in your praise

Sed et supernæ virtutes atque angelicæ potestates
hymnum gloriæ tuæ concinunt, sine fine dicentes:

Sanctus, Sanctus, Sanctus Dominus Deus Sabaoth. . .

PRÆFATIO PASCHALIS II

De vita nova in Christo

Vere dignum et iustum est, æquum et salutare:
Te quidem, Domine, omni tempore confiteri,
sed in hoc potissimum gloriosius prædicare,
cum Pascha nostrum immolatus est Christus.

Per quem in æternam vitam filii lucis oriuntur,
et regni cælestis atria fidelibus reserantur.
Quia mors nostra est eius morte redempta,
et in eius resurrectione vita omnium resurrexit.

Quapropter, profusis paschalibus gaudiis,
totus in orbe terrarum mundus exsultat.
Sed et supernæ virtutes atque angelicæ potestates
hymnum gloriæ tuæ concinunt, sine fine dicentes:

Sanctus, Sanctus, Sanctus Dominus Deus Sabaoth. . .

PRÆFATIO PASCHALIS III

De Christo vivente et semper interpellante pro nobis

Vere dignum et iustum est, æquum et salutare:
Te quidem, Domine, omni tempore confiteri,
sed in hoc potissimum gloriosius prædicare,
cum Pascha nostrum immolatus est Christus.

Qui se pro nobis offerre non desinit,
nosque apud te perenni advocatione defendit;
qui immolatus iam non moritur,
sed semper vivit occisus.

Quapropter, profusis paschalibus gaudiis,
totus in orbe terrarum mundus exsultat.
Sed et supernæ virtutes atque angelicæ potestates
hymnum gloriæ tuæ concinunt, sine fine dicentes:

Sanctus, Sanctus, Sanctus Dominus Deus Sabaoth. . .

and even the heavenly Powers, with the angelic hosts,
sing together the unending hymn of your glory,
as they acclaim:

Holy, Holy, Holy Lord God of hosts. . .

PREFACE II OF EASTER

New life in Christ

It is truly right and just, our duty and our salvation,
at all times to acclaim you, O Lord,
but in this time above all to laud you yet more gloriously,
when Christ our Passover has been sacrificed.

Through him the children of light rise to eternal life
and the halls of the heavenly Kingdom
are thrown open to the faithful;
for his Death is our ransom from death,
and in his rising the life of all has risen.

Therefore, overcome with paschal joy,
every land, every people exults in your praise
and even the heavenly Powers, with the angelic hosts,
sing together the unending hymn of your glory,
as they acclaim:

Holy, Holy, Holy Lord God of hosts. . .

PREFACE III OF EASTER

Christ living and always interceding for us

It is truly right and just, our duty and our salvation,
at all times to acclaim you, O Lord,
but in this time above all to laud you yet more gloriously,
when Christ our Passover has been sacrificed.

He never ceases to offer himself for us
but defends us and ever pleads our cause before you:
he is the sacrificial Victim who dies no more,
the Lamb, once slain, who lives for ever.

Therefore, overcome with paschal joy,
every land, every people exults in your praise
and even the heavenly Powers, with the angelic hosts,
sing together the unending hymn of your glory,
as they acclaim:

Holy, Holy, Holy Lord God of hosts. . .

PRÆFATIO PASCHALIS IV

De restauratione universi per mysterium paschale

Vere dignum et iustum est, æquum et salutare:
Te quidem, Domine, omni tempore confiteri,
sed in hoc potissimum gloriosius prædicare,
cum Pascha nostrum immolatus est Christus.

Quia, vetustate destructa, renovantur universa deiecta,
et vitæ nobis in Christo reparatur integritas.

Quapropter, profusis paschalibus gaudiis,
totus in orbe terrarum mundus exsultat.
Sed et supernæ virtutes atque angelicæ potestates
hymnum gloriæ tuæ concinunt, sine fine dicentes:

Sanctus, Sanctus, Sanctus Dominus Deus Sabaoth...

PRÆFATIO PASCHALIS V

De Christo sacerdote et victima

Vere dignum et iustum est, æquum et salutare:
Te quidem, Domine, omni tempore confiteri,
sed in hoc potissimum gloriosius prædicare,
cum Pascha nostrum immolatus est Christus.

Qui, oblatione corporis sui,
antiqua sacrificia in crucis veritate perfecit,
et, seipsum tibi pro nostra salute commendans,
idem sacerdos, altare et agnus exhibuit.

Quapropter, profusis paschalibus gaudiis,
totus in orbe terrarum mundus exsultat.
Sed et supernæ virtutes atque angelicæ potestates
hymnum gloriæ tuæ concinunt, sine fine dicentes:

Sanctus, Sanctus, Sanctus Dominus Deus Sabaoth...

PREFACE IV OF EASTER

The restoration of the universe through the Paschal Mystery

It is truly right and just, our duty and our salvation,
at all times to acclaim you, O Lord,
but in this time above all to laud you yet more gloriously,
when Christ our Passover has been sacrificed.

For, with the old order destroyed,
a universe cast down is renewed,
and integrity of life is restored to us in Christ.

Therefore, overcome with paschal joy,
every land, every people exults in your praise
and even the heavenly Powers, with the angelic hosts,
sing together the unending hymn of your glory,
as they acclaim:

Holy, Holy, Holy Lord God of hosts...

PREFACE V OF EASTER

Christ, Priest and Victim

It is truly right and just, our duty and our salvation,
at all times to acclaim you, O Lord,
but in this time above all to laud you yet more gloriously,
when Christ our Passover has been sacrificed.

By the oblation of his Body,
he brought the sacrifices of old to fulfilment
in the reality of the Cross
and, by commending himself to you for our salvation,
showed himself the Priest, the Altar, and the Lamb of sacrifice.

Therefore, overcome with paschal joy,
every land, every people exults in your praise
and even the heavenly Powers, with the angelic hosts,
sing together the unending hymn of your glory,
as they acclaim:

Holy, Holy, Holy Lord God of hosts...

PRÆFATIO I DE ASCENSIONE DOMINI

De mysterio Ascensionis

Vere dignum et iustum est, æquum et salutare,
nos tibi semper et ubique gratias agere:
Domine, sancte Pater, omnipotens æterne Deus:

Quia Dominus Iesus, Rex gloriæ,
peccati triumphator et mortis,
mirantibus Angelis, ascendit (hodie) summa cælorum,
Mediator Dei et hominum,
Iudex mundi Dominusque virtutum;
non ut a nostra humilitate discederet,
sed ut illuc confideremus, sua membra, nos subsequi
quo ipse, caput nostrum principiumque, præcessit.

Quapropter, profusis paschalibus gaudiis,
totus in orbe terrarum mundus exsultat.
Sed et supernæ virtutes atque angelicæ potestates
hymnum gloriæ tuæ concinunt, sine fine dicentes:
Sanctus, Sanctus, Sanctus Dominus Deus Sabaoth...

PRÆFATIO II DE ASCENSIONE DOMINI

De mysterio Ascensionis

Vere dignum et iustum est, æquum et salutare,
nos tibi semper et ubique gratias agere:
Domine, sancte Pater, omnipotens æterne Deus:
per Christum Dominum nostrum.

Qui post resurrectionem suam
omnibus discipulis suis manifestus apparuit,
et ipsis cernentibus est elevatus in cælum,
ut nos divinitatis suæ tribueret esse participes.

Quapropter, profusis paschalibus gaudiis,
totus in orbe terrarum mundus exsultat.
Sed et supernæ virtutes atque angelicæ potestates
hymnum gloriæ tuæ concinunt, sine fine dicentes:

Sanctus, Sanctus, Sanctus Dominus Deus Sabaoth...

PREFACE I OF THE ASCENSION OF THE LORD

The mystery of the Ascension

It is truly right and just, our duty and our salvation,
always and everywhere to give you thanks,
Lord, holy Father, almighty and eternal God.

For the Lord Jesus, the King of glory,
conqueror of sin and death,
ascended (today) to the highest heavens,
as the Angels gazed in wonder.

Mediator between God and man,
judge of the world and Lord of hosts,
he ascended, not to distance himself from our lowly state
but that we, his members, might be confident of following
where he, our Head and Founder, has gone before.

Therefore, overcome with paschal joy,
every land, every people exults in your praise
and even the heavenly Powers, with the angelic hosts,
sing together the unending hymn of your glory,
as they acclaim:

Holy, Holy, Holy Lord God of hosts...

PREFACE II OF THE ASCENSION OF THE LORD

The mystery of the Ascension

It is truly right and just, our duty and our salvation,
always and everywhere to give you thanks,
Lord, holy Father, almighty and eternal God,
through Christ our Lord.

For after his Resurrection
he plainly appeared to all his disciples
and was taken up to heaven in their sight,
that he might make us sharers in his divinity.

Therefore, overcome with paschal joy,
every land, every people exults in your praise
and even the heavenly Powers, with the angelic hosts,
sing together the unending hymn of your glory,
as they acclaim:

Holy, Holy, Holy Lord God of hosts...

PRÆFATIO I DE DOMINICIS « PER ANNUM »
De mysterio paschali et de populo Dei

Vere dignum et iustum est, æquum et salutare,
nos tibi semper et ubique gratias agere:
Domine, sancte Pater, omnipotens æterne Deus:
per Christum Dominum nostrum.

Cuius hoc mirificum fuit opus per paschale mysterium,
ut de peccato et mortis iugo ad hanc gloriam vocaremur,
qua nunc genus electum, regale sacerdotium,
gens sancta et acquisitionis populus diceremur,
et tuas annuntiaremus ubique virtutes,
qui nos de tenebris ad tuum admirabile lumen vocasti.

Et ideo cum Angelis et Archangelis,
cum Thronis et Dominationibus,
cumque omni militia cælestis exercitus,
hymnum gloriæ tuæ canimus,
sine fine dicentes:

Sanctus, Sanctus, Sanctus Dominus Deus Sabaoth. . .

PRÆFATIO II DE DOMINICIS « PER ANNUM »
De mysterio salutis

Vere dignum et iustum est, æquum et salutare,
nos tibi semper et ubique gratias agere:
Domine, sancte Pater, omnipotens æterne Deus:
per Christum Dominum nostrum.

Qui, humanis miseratus erroribus,
de Virgine nasci dignatus est.
Qui, crucem passus, a perpetua morte nos liberavit
et, a mortuis resurgens, vitam nobis donavit æternam.

Et ideo cum Angelis et Archangelis,
cum Thronis et Dominationibus,
cumque omni militia cælestis exercitus,
hymnum gloriæ tuæ canimus,
sine fine dicentes:

Sanctus, Sanctus, Sanctus Dominus Deus Sabaoth. . .

PREFACE I OF THE SUNDAYS IN ORDINARY TIME

The Paschal Mystery and the People of God

It is truly right and just, our duty and our salvation,
always and everywhere to give you thanks,
Lord, holy Father, almighty and eternal God,
through Christ our Lord.

For through his Paschal Mystery,
he accomplished the marvellous deed,
by which he has freed us from the yoke of sin and death,
summoning us to the glory of being now called
a chosen race, a royal priesthood,
a holy nation, a people for your own possession,
to proclaim everywhere your mighty works,
for you have called us out of darkness
into your own wonderful light.

And so, with Angels and Archangels,
with Thrones and Dominions,
and with all the hosts and Powers of heaven,
we sing the hymn of your glory,
as without end we acclaim:

Holy, Holy, Holy Lord God of hosts. . .

PREFACE II OF THE SUNDAYS IN ORDINARY TIME

The mystery of salvation

It is truly right and just, our duty and our salvation,
always and everywhere to give you thanks,
Lord, holy Father, almighty and eternal God,
through Christ our Lord.

For out of compassion for the waywardness that is ours,
he humbled himself and was born of the Virgin;
by the passion of the Cross he freed us from unending death,
and by rising from the dead he gave us life eternal.

And so, with Angels and Archangels,
with Thrones and Dominions,
and with all the hosts and Powers of heaven,
we sing the hymn of your glory,
as without end we acclaim:

Holy, Holy, Holy Lord God of hosts. . .

PRÆFATIO III DE DOMINICIS « PER ANNUM »
De salvatione hominis per hominem

Vere dignum et iustum est, æquum et salutare,
nos tibi semper et ubique gratias agere:
Domine, sancte Pater, omnipotens æterne Deus:

Ad cuius immensam gloriam pertinere cognoscimus
ut mortalibus tua deitate succurreres;
sed et nobis provideres de ipsa
mortalitate nostra remedium,
et perditos quosque unde perierant, inde salvares,
per Christum Dominum nostrum.

Per quem maiestatem tuam adorat exercitus Angelorum,
ante conspectum tuum in æternitate lætantium.

Cum quibus et nostras voces ut admitti iubeas, deprecamur,
socia exsultatione dicentes:

Sanctus, Sanctus, Sanctus Dominus Deus Sabaoth. . .

PRÆFATIO IV DE DOMINICIS « PER ANNUM »
De historia salutis

Vere dignum et iustum est, æquum et salutare,
nos tibi semper et ubique gratias agere:
Domine, sancte Pater, omnipotens æterne Deus:
per Christum Dominum nostrum.

Ipse enim nascendo vetustatem hominum renovavit,
patiendo delevit nostra peccata,
æternæ vitæ aditum præstitit a mortuis resurgendo,
ad te Patrem ascendendo cælestes ianuas reseravit.

Et ideo, cum Angelorum atque Sanctorum turba,
hymnum laudis tibi canimus, sine fine dicentes:
Sanctus, Sanctus, Sanctus Dominus Deus Sabaoth. . .

PREFACE III OF THE SUNDAYS IN ORDINARY TIME

The salvation of man by a man

It is truly right and just, our duty and our salvation,
always and everywhere to give you thanks,
Lord, holy Father, almighty and eternal God.

For we know it belongs to your boundless glory,
that you came to the aid of mortal beings with your divinity
and even fashioned for us a remedy out of mortality itself,
that the cause of our downfall
might become the means of our salvation,
through Christ our Lord.

Through him the host of Angels adores your majesty
and rejoices in your presence for ever.
May our voices, we pray, join with theirs
in one chorus of exultant praise, as we acclaim:

Holy, Holy, Holy Lord God of hosts...

PREFACE IV OF THE SUNDAYS IN ORDINARY TIME

The history of salvation

It is truly right and just, our duty and our salvation,
always and everywhere to give you thanks,
Lord, holy Father, almighty and eternal God,
through Christ our Lord.

For by his birth he brought renewal
to humanity's fallen state,
and by his suffering cancelled out our sins;
by his rising from the dead
he has opened the way to eternal life,
and by ascending to you, O Father,
he has unlocked the gates of heaven.

And so, with the company of Angels and Saints,
we sing the hymn of your praise,
as without end we acclaim:

Holy, Holy, Holy Lord God of hosts...

PRÆFATIO V DE DOMINICIS « PER ANNUM »

De creatione

Vere dignum et iustum est, æquum et salutare,
nos tibi semper et ubique gratias agere:
Domine, sancte Pater, omnipotens æterne Deus:

Qui omnia mundi elementa fecisti,
et vices disposuisti temporum variari;
hominem vero formasti ad imaginem tuam,
et rerum ei subiecisti universa miracula,
ut vicario munere dominaretur omnibus quæ creasti,
et in operum tuorum magnalibus iugiter te laudaret,
per Christum Dominum nostrum.

Unde et nos cum omnibus Angelis te laudamus,
iucunda celebratione clamantes:

Sanctus, Sanctus, Sanctus Dominus Deus Sabaoth...

PRÆFATIO VI DE DOMINICIS « PER ANNUM »

De pignore æterni Paschatis

Vere dignum et iustum est, æquum et salutare,
nos tibi semper et ubique gratias agere:
Domine, sancte Pater, omnipotens æterne Deus:

In quo vivimus, movemur et sumus,
atque in hoc corpore constituti
non solum pietatis tuæ cotidianos experimur effectus,
sed æternitatis etiam pignora iam tenemus.
Primitias enim Spiritus habentes,
per quem suscitasti Iesum a mortuis,
paschale mysterium speramus nobis esse perpetuum.

Unde et nos cum omnibus Angelis te laudamus,
iucunda celebratione clamantes:

Sanctus, Sanctus, Sanctus Dominus Deus Sabaoth...

PREFACE V OF THE SUNDAYS IN ORDINARY TIME

Creation

It is truly right and just, our duty and our salvation,
always and everywhere to give you thanks,
Lord, holy Father, almighty and eternal God.

For you laid the foundations of the world
and have arranged the changing of times and seasons;
you formed man in your own image
and set humanity over the whole world in all its wonder,
to rule in your name over all you have made
and for ever praise you in your mighty works,
through Christ our Lord.

And so, with all the Angels, we praise you,
as in joyful celebration we acclaim:

Holy, Holy, Holy Lord God of hosts. . .

PREFACE VI OF THE SUNDAYS IN ORDINARY TIME

The pledge of the eternal Passover

It is truly right and just, our duty and our salvation,
always and everywhere to give you thanks,
Lord, holy Father, almighty and eternal God.

For in you we live and move and have our being,
and while in this body
we not only experience the daily effects of your care,
but even now possess the pledge of life eternal.

For, having received the first fruits of the Spirit,
through whom you raised up Jesus from the dead,
we hope for an everlasting share in the Paschal Mystery.

And so, with all the Angels, we praise you,
as in joyful celebration we acclaim:

Holy, Holy, Holy Lord God of hosts. . .

PRÆFATIO VII DE DOMINICIS « PER ANNUM »

De salute per obœdientiam Christi

Vere dignum et iustum est, æquum et salutare,
nos tibi semper et ubique gratias agere:
Domine, sancte Pater, omnipotens æterne Deus:

Quia sic mundum misericorditer dilexisti,
ut ipsum nobis mitteres Redemptorem,
quem absque peccato
in nostra voluisti similitudine conversari,
ut amares in nobis quod diligebas in Filio,
cuius obœdientia sumus ad tua dona reparati,
quæ per inobœdientiam amiseramus peccando.

Unde et nos, Domine, cum Angelis et Sanctis universis
tibi confitemur, in exsultatione dicentes:

Sanctus, Sanctus, Sanctus Dominus Deus Sabaoth. . .

PRÆFATIO VIII DE DOMINICIS « PER ANNUM »

De Ecclesia adunata ex unitate Trinitatis

Vere dignum et iustum est, æquum et salutare,
nos tibi semper et ubique gratias agere:
Domine, sancte Pater, omnipotens æterne Deus:

Quia filios, quos longe peccati crimen abstulerat,
per sanguinem Filii tui Spiritusque virtute,
in unum ad te denuo congregare voluisti:
ut plebs, de unitate Trinitatis adunata,
in tuæ laudem sapientiæ multiformis
Christi corpus templumque Spiritus nosceretur Ecclesia.

Et ideo, choris angelicis sociati,
te laudamus in gaudio confitentes:

Sanctus, Sanctus, Sanctus Dominus Deus Sabaoth. . .

PREFACE VII OF THE SUNDAYS IN ORDINARY TIME

Salvation through the obedience of Christ

It is truly right and just, our duty and our salvation,
always and everywhere to give you thanks,
Lord, holy Father, almighty and eternal God.

For you so loved the world
that in your mercy you sent us the Redeemer,
to live like us in all things but sin,
so that you might love in us what you loved in your Son,
by whose obedience we have been restored to those gifts of yours
that, by sinning, we had lost in disobedience.

And so, Lord, with all the Angels and Saints,
we, too, give you thanks, as in exultation we acclaim:

Holy, Holy, Holy Lord God of hosts. . .

PREFACE VIII OF THE SUNDAYS IN ORDINARY TIME

The Church united by the unity of the Trinity

It is truly right and just, our duty and our salvation,
always and everywhere to give you thanks,
Lord, holy Father, almighty and eternal God.

For, when your children were scattered afar by sin,
through the Blood of your Son and the power of the Spirit,
you gathered them again to yourself,
that a people, formed as one by the unity of the Trinity,
made the body of Christ and the temple of the Holy Spirit,
might, to the praise of your manifold wisdom,
be manifest as the Church.

And so, in company with the choirs of Angels,
we praise you, and with joy we proclaim:

Holy, Holy, Holy Lord God of hosts. . .

PRÆFATIO I DE SS.MA EUCHARISTIA

De sacrificio et de sacramento Christi

Vere dignum et iustum est, æquum et salutare,
nos tibi semper et ubique gratias agere:
Domine, sancte Pater, omnipotens æterne Deus:
per Christum Dominum nostrum.

Qui, verus æternusque Sacerdos,
formam sacrificii perennis instituens,
hostiam tibi se primus obtulit salutarem,
et nos, in sui memoriam, præcepit offerre.
Cuius carnem pro nobis immolatam
dum sumimus, roboramur,
et fusum pro nobis sanguinem dum potamus, abluimur.

Et ideo cum Angelis et Archangelis,
cum Thronis et Dominationibus,
cumque omni militia cælestis exercitus,
hymnum gloriæ tuæ canimus,
sine fine dicentes:

Sanctus, Sanctus, Sanctus Dominus Deus Sabaoth...

PRÆFATIO II DE SS.MA EUCHARISTIA

De fructibus Sanctissimæ Eucharistiæ

Vere dignum et iustum est, æquum et salutare,
nos tibi semper et ubique gratias agere:
Domine, sancte Pater, omnipotens æterne Deus:
per Christum Dominum nostrum.

Qui cum Apostolis suis in novissima cena convescens,
salutiferam crucis memoriam prosecuturus in sæcula,
Agnum sine macula se tibi obtulit,
perfectæ laudis munus acceptum.

Quo venerabili mysterio fideles tuos alendo sanctificas,
ut humanum genus, quod continet unus orbis,
una fides illuminet, caritas una coniungat.

Ad mensam igitur accedimus tam mirabilis sacramenti,
ut, gratiæ tuæ suavitate perfusi,
ad cælestis formæ imaginem transeamus.

PREFACE I OF THE MOST HOLY EUCHARIST

The Sacrifice and the Sacrament of Christ

It is truly right and just, our duty and our salvation,
always and everywhere to give you thanks,
Lord, holy Father, almighty and eternal God,
through Christ our Lord.

For he is the true and eternal Priest,
who instituted the pattern of an everlasting sacrifice,
and was the first to offer himself as the saving Victim,
commanding us to make this offering as his memorial.
As we eat his flesh that was sacrificed for us,
we are made strong,
and, as we drink his Blood that was poured out for us,
we are washed clean.

And so, with Angels and Archangels,
with Thrones and Dominions,
and with all the hosts and Powers of heaven,
we sing the hymn of your glory,
as without end we acclaim:

Holy, Holy, Holy Lord God of hosts. . .

PREFACE II OF THE MOST HOLY EUCHARIST

The fruits of the Most Holy Eucharist

It is truly right and just, our duty and our salvation,
always and everywhere to give you thanks,
Lord, holy Father, almighty and eternal God,
through Christ our Lord.

For at the Last Supper with his Apostles,
establishing for the ages to come the saving memorial of the Cross,
he offered himself to you as the unblemished Lamb,
the acceptable gift of perfect praise.

Nourishing your faithful by this sacred mystery,
you make them holy, so that the human race,
bounded by one world,
may be enlightened by one faith
and united by one bond of charity.

And so, we approach the table of this wondrous Sacrament,
so that, bathed in the sweetness of your grace,
we may pass over to the heavenly realities here foreshadowed.

Propter quod cælestia tibi atque terrestria
canticum novum concinunt adorando,
et nos cum omni exercitu Angelorum proclamamus,
sine fine dicentes:

Sanctus, Sanctus, Sanctus Dominus Deus Sabaoth. . .

PRÆFATIO I DE APOSTOLIS

De Apostolis pastoribus populi Dei

Vere dignum et iustum est, æquum et salutare,
nos tibi semper et ubique gratias agere:
Domine, sancte Pater, omnipotens æterne Deus:

Qui gregem tuum, Pastor æterne, non deseris,
sed per beatos Apostolos continua protectione custodis,
ut iisdem rectoribus gubernetur,
quos Filii tui vicarios eidem contulisti præesse pastores.

Et ideo cum Angelis et Archangelis,
cum Thronis et Dominationibus,
cumque omni militia cælestis exercitus,
hymnum gloriæ tuæ canimus,
sine fine dicentes:

Sanctus, Sanctus, Sanctus Dominus Deus Sabaoth. . .

PRÆFATIO II DE APOSTOLIS

De apostolico fundamento et testimonio

Vere dignum et iustum est, æquum et salutare,
nos tibi semper et ubique gratias agere:
Domine, sancte Pater, omnipotens æterne Deus:
per Christum Dominum nostrum.

Quoniam Ecclesiam tuam
in apostolicis tribuisti consistere fundamentis,
ut signum sanctitatis tuæ in terris maneret ipsa perpetuum,
et cælestia præberet cunctis hominibus documenta.

Quapropter nunc et usque in sæculum
cum omni militia Angelorum
devota tibi mente concinimus,
clamantes atque dicentes:

Sanctus, Sanctus, Sanctus Dominus Deus Sabaoth. . .

Therefore, all creatures of heaven and earth
sing a new song in adoration,
and we, with all the host of Angels,
cry out, and without end we acclaim:

Holy, Holy, Holy Lord God of hosts...

PREFACE I OF APOSTLES

The Apostles, shepherds of God's people

It is truly right and just, our duty and our salvation,
always and everywhere to give you thanks,
Lord, holy Father, almighty and eternal God.

For you, eternal Shepherd, do not desert your flock,
but through the blessed Apostles
watch over it and protect it always,
so that it may be governed
by those you have appointed shepherds
to lead it in the name of your Son.

And so, with Angels and Archangels,
with Thrones and Dominions,
and with all the hosts and Powers of heaven,
we sing the hymn of your glory,
as without end we acclaim:

Holy, Holy, Holy Lord God of hosts...

PREFACE II OF APOSTLES

The apostolic foundation and witness

It is truly right and just, our duty and our salvation,
always and everywhere to give you thanks,
Lord, holy Father, almighty and eternal God,
through Christ our Lord.

For you have built your Church
to stand firm on apostolic foundations,
to be a lasting sign of your holiness on earth
and offer all humanity your heavenly teaching.

Therefore, now and for ages unending,
with all the host of Angels,
we sing to you with all our hearts,
crying out as we acclaim:

Holy, Holy, Holy Lord God of hosts...

PRÆFATIO I DE SANCTIS MARTYRIBUS
De signo et exemplo martyrii

Vere dignum et iustum est, æquum et salutare,
nos tibi semper et ubique gratias agere:
Domine, sancte Pater, omnipotens æterne Deus:

Quoniam beati martyris N. pro confessione nominis tui,
ad imitationem Christi,
sanguis effusus tua mirabilia manifestat,
quibus perficis in fragilitate virtutem,
et vires infirmas ad testimonium roboras,
per Christum Dominum nostrum.

Et ideo, cum cælorum Virtutibus,
in terris te iugiter celebramus,
maiestati tuæ sine fine clamantes:

Sanctus, Sanctus, Sanctus Dominus Deus Sabaoth...

PRÆFATIO II DE SANCTIS MARTYRIBUS
De mirabilibus Dei in martyrum victoria

Vere dignum et iustum est, æquum et salutare,
nos tibi semper et ubique gratias agere:
Domine, sancte Pater, omnipotens æterne Deus:

Quoniam tu magnificaris in tuorum laude Sanctorum,
et quidquid ad eorum pertinet passionem,
tuæ sunt opera miranda potentiæ:
qui huius fidei tribuis clementer ardorem,
qui suggeris perseverantiæ firmitatem,
qui largiris in agone victoriam,
per Christum Dominum nostrum.

Propter quod cælestia tibi atque terrestria
canticum novum concinunt adorando,
et nos cum omni exercitu Angelorum
proclamamus, sine fine dicentes:
Sanctus, Sanctus, Sanctus Dominus Deus Sabaoth...

PREFACE I OF HOLY MARTYRS
The sign and example of martyrdom

It is truly right and just, our duty and our salvation,
always and everywhere to give you thanks,
Lord, holy Father, almighty and eternal God.

For the blood of your blessed Martyr N.,
poured out like Christ's to glorify your name,
shows forth your marvellous works,
by which in our weakness you perfect your power
and on the feeble bestow strength to bear you witness,
through Christ our Lord.

And so, with the Powers of heaven,
we worship you constantly on earth,
and before your majesty
without end we acclaim:

Holy, Holy, Holy Lord God of hosts. . .

PREFACE II OF HOLY MARTYRS

The wonders of God in the victory of the Martyrs

It is truly right and just, our duty and our salvation,
always and everywhere to give you thanks,
Lord, holy Father, almighty and eternal God.

For you are glorified when your Saints are praised;
their very sufferings are but wonders of your might:
in your mercy you give ardour to their faith,
to their endurance you grant firm resolve,
and in their struggle the victory is yours,
through Christ our Lord.

Therefore, all creatures of heaven and earth
sing a new song in adoration,
and we, with all the host of Angels,
cry out, and without end we acclaim:

Holy, Holy, Holy Lord God of hosts. . .

PRÆFATIO I DE DEFUNCTIS

De spe resurrectionis in Christo

Vere dignum et iustum est, æquum et salutare,
nos tibi semper et ubique gratias agere:
Domine, sancte Pater, omnipotens æterne Deus:
per Christum Dominum nostrum.

In quo nobis spes beatæ resurrectionis effulsit,
ut, quos contristat certa moriendi condicio,
eosdem consoletur futuræ immortalitatis promissio.
Tuis enim fidelibus, Domine, vita mutatur, non tollitur,
et, dissoluta terrestris huius incolatus domo,
æterna in cælis habitatio comparatur.

Et ideo cum Angelis et Archangelis,
cum Thronis et Dominationibus,
cumque omni militia cælestis exercitus,
hymnum gloriæ tuæ canimus,
sine fine dicentes:

Sanctus, Sanctus, Sanctus Dominus Deus Sabaoth. . .

PRÆFATIO II DE DEFUNCTIS

Christus mortuus est pro vita nostra

Vere dignum et iustum est, æquum et salutare,
nos tibi semper et ubique gratias agere:
Domine, sancte Pater, omnipotens æterne Deus:
per Christum Dominum nostrum.

Ipse enim mortem unus accepit,
ne omnes nos moreremur;
immo unus mori dignatus est,
ut omnes tibi perpetuo viveremus.

Et ideo, choris angelicis sociati,
te laudamus in gaudio confitentes:

Sanctus, Sanctus, Sanctus Dominus Deus Sabaoth. . .

PREFACE I FOR THE DEAD

The hope of resurrection in Christ

It is truly right and just, our duty and our salvation,
always and everywhere to give you thanks,
Lord, holy Father, almighty and eternal God,
through Christ our Lord.

In him the hope of blessed resurrection has dawned,
that those saddened by the certainty of dying
might be consoled by the promise of immortality to come.
Indeed for your faithful, Lord,
life is changed not ended,
and, when this earthly dwelling turns to dust,
an eternal dwelling is made ready for them in heaven.

And so, with Angels and Archangels,
with Thrones and Dominions,
and with all the hosts and Powers of heaven,
we sing the hymn of your glory,
as without end we acclaim:

Holy, Holy, Holy Lord God of hosts. . .

PREFACE II FOR THE DEAD

Christ died so that we might live

It is truly right and just, our duty and our salvation,
always and everywhere to give you thanks,
Lord, holy Father, almighty and eternal God,
through Christ our Lord.

For as one alone he accepted death,
so that we might all escape from dying;
as one man he chose to die,
so that in your sight we all might live for ever.

And so, in company with the choirs of Angels,
we praise you, and with joy we proclaim:

Holy, Holy, Holy Lord God of hosts. . .

PRÆFATIO III DE DEFUNCTIS

Christus, salus et vita

Vere dignum et iustum est, æquum et salutare,
nos tibi semper et ubique gratias agere:
Domine, sancte Pater, omnipotens æterne Deus:
per Christum Dominum nostrum:

Qui est salus mundi, vita hominum, resurrectio mortuorum.

Per quem maiestatem tuam adorat exercitus Angelorum,
ante conspectum tuum in æternitate lætantium.
Cum quibus et nostras voces ut admitti iubeas, deprecamur,
socia exsultatione dicentes:

Sanctus, Sanctus, Sanctus Dominus Deus Sabaoth. . .

PRÆFATIO IV DE DEFUNCTIS

De vita terrena ad gloriam cælestem

Vere dignum et iustum est, æquum et salutare,
nos tibi semper et ubique gratias agere:
Domine, sancte Pater, omnipotens æterne Deus:

Cuius imperio nascimur, cuius arbitrio regimur,
cuius præcepto in terra, de qua sumpti sumus,
peccati lege absolvimur.
Et, qui per mortem Filii tui redempti sumus,
ad ipsius resurrectionis gloriam
tuo nutu excitamur.

Et ideo, cum Angelorum atque Sanctorum turba,
hymnum laudis tibi canimus, sine fine dicentes:

Sanctus, Sanctus, Sanctus Dominus Deus Sabaoth. . .

PREFACE III FOR THE DEAD

Christ, the salvation and the life

It is truly right and just, our duty and our salvation,
always and everywhere to give you thanks,
Lord, holy Father, almighty and eternal God,
through Christ our Lord.

For he is the salvation of the world,
the life of the human race,
the resurrection of the dead.

Through him the host of Angels adores your majesty
and rejoices in your presence for ever.
May our voices, we pray, join with theirs
in one chorus of exultant praise, as we acclaim:

Holy, Holy, Holy Lord God of hosts. . .

PREFACE IV FOR THE DEAD

From earthly life to heavenly glory

It is truly right and just, our duty and our salvation,
always and everywhere to give you thanks,
Lord, holy Father, almighty and eternal God.

For it is at your summons that we come to birth,
by your will that we are governed,
and at your command that we return,
on account of sin,
to that earth from which we came.

And when you give the sign,
we who have been redeemed by the Death of your Son,
shall be raised up to the glory of his Resurrection.

And so, with the company of Angels and Saints,
we sing the hymn of your praise,
as without end we acclaim:

Holy, Holy, Holy Lord God of hosts. . .

PRÆFATIO V DE DEFUNCTIS

De resurrectione nostra per victoriam Christi

Vere dignum et iustum est, æquum et salutare,
nos tibi semper et ubique gratias agere:
Domine, sancte Pater, omnipotens æterne Deus:

Quia, etsi nostri est meriti quod perimus,
tuæ tamen est pietatis et gratiæ
quod, pro peccato morte consumpti,
per Christi victoriam redempti,
cum ipso revocamur ad vitam.

Et ideo, cum cælorum Virtutibus,
in terris te iugiter celebramus,
maiestati tuæ sine fine clamantes:

Sanctus, Sanctus, Sanctus Dominus Deus Sabaoth. . .

PREFACE V FOR THE DEAD

Our resurrection through the victory of Christ

It is truly right and just, our duty and our salvation,
always and everywhere to give you thanks,
Lord, holy Father, almighty and eternal God.

For even though by our own fault we perish,
yet by your compassion and your grace,
when seized by death according to our sins,
we are redeemed through Christ's great victory,
and with him called back into life.

And so, with the Powers of heaven,
we worship you constantly on earth,
and before your majesty
without end we acclaim:

Holy, Holy, Holy Lord God of hosts. . .

EUCHARISTIC PRAYER I
(THE ROMAN CANON)

Pr. Te ígitur, clementíssime Pater,
per Iesum Christum, Fílium tuum,
Dóminum nostrum,
súpplices rogámus ac pétimus,
uti accépta hábeas
et benedícas ✠ hæc dona, hæc múnera,
hæc sancta sacrifícia illibáta,
in primis, quæ tibi offérimus
pro Ecclésia tua sancta cathólica:
quam pacificáre, custodíre, adunáre
et régere dignéris toto orbe terrárum:
una cum fámulo tuo Papa nostro **N.**
et Antístite nostro **N.***
et ómnibus orthodóxis atque cathólicæ
et apostólicæ fídei cultóribus.

Commemoration of the Living.
Meménto, Dómine,
famulórum famularúmque tuárum **N.** et **N.**
et ómnium circumstántium,
quorum tibi fides cógnita est et nota devótio,
pro quibus tibi offérimus:
vel qui tibi ófferunt hoc sacrifícium laudis,
pro se suísque ómnibus:
pro redemptióne animarúm suárum,
pro spe salútis et incolumitátis suæ:
tibíque reddunt vota sua
ætérno Deo, vivo et vero.

Within the Action
Communicántes,
et memóriam venerántes,
in primis gloriósæ semper Vírginis Maríæ,
Genetrícis Dei et Dómini nostri Iesu Christi:
† sed et beáti Ioseph, eiúsdem Vírginis Sponsi,
et beatórum Apostolórum ac Mártyrum tuórum,
Petri et Pauli, Andréæ,
(Iacóbi, Ioánnis,
Thomæ, Iacóbi, Philíppi,

---

*Mention may be made here of the Coadjutor Bishop or Auxiliary Bishops.

EUCHARISTIC PRAYER I
(THE ROMAN CANON)

Pr. To you, therefore, most merciful Father,
we make humble prayer and petition
through Jesus Christ, your Son, our Lord:
that you accept
and bless ✠ these gifts, these offerings,
these holy and unblemished sacrifices,
which we offer you firstly
for your holy catholic Church.
Be pleased to grant her peace,
to guard, unite and govern her
throughout the whole world,
together with your servant **N.** our Pope
and **N.** our Bishop,*
and all those who, holding to the truth,
hand on the catholic and apostolic faith.

Commemoration of the Living.

Remember, Lord, your servants **N.** and **N.**
and all gathered here,
whose faith and devotion are known to you.
For them, we offer you this sacrifice of praise
or they offer it for themselves
and all who are dear to them:
for the redemption of their souls,
in hope of health and well-being,
and paying their homage to you,
the eternal God, living and true.

Within the Action

In communion with those whose memory we venerate,
especially the glorious ever-Virgin Mary,
Mother of our God and Lord, Jesus Christ,
† and blessed Joseph, her Spouse,
your blessed Apostles and Martyrs,
Peter and Paul, Andrew,
(James, John,
Thomas, James, Philip,

---

*Mention may be made here of the Coadjutor Bishop or Auxiliary Bishops.

Bartholomǽi, Matthǽi,
Simónis et Thaddǽi:
Lini, Cleti, Cleméntis, Xysti,
Cornélii, Cypriáni,
Lauréntii, Chrysógoni,
Ioánnis et Pauli,
Cosmæ et Damiáni)
et ómnium Sanctórum tuórum;
quorum méritis precibúsque concédas,
ut in ómnibus protectiónis tuæ muniámur auxílio.
(Per Christum Dóminum nostrum. Amen.)

PROPER FORMS OF THE COMMUNICANTES

On the Nativity of the Lord and throughout the Octave

Communicántes,
et (noctem sacratíssimam) diem sacratíssimum celebrántes,
(qua) quo beátæ Maríæ intemeráta virgínitas
huic mundo édidit Salvatórem:
sed et memóriam venerántes,
in primis eiúsdem gloriósæ semper Vírginis Maríæ,
Genetrícis eiúsdem Dei et Dómini nostri Iesu Christi: †

On the Epiphany of the Lord

Communicántes,
et diem sacratíssimum celebrántes,
quo Unigénitus tuus, in tua tecum glória coætérnus,
in veritáte carnis nostræ visibíliter corporális appáruit:
sed et memóriam venerántes,
in primis gloriósæ semper Vírginis Maríæ,
Genetrícis eiúsdem Dei et Dómini nostri Iesu Christi: †

From the Mass of the Easter Vigil until the Second Sunday of Easter

Communicántes,
et (noctem sacratíssimam) diem sacratíssimum celebrántes
Resurrectiónis Dómini nostri Iesu Christi secúndum carnem:
sed et memóriam venerántes,
in primis gloriósæ semper Vírginis Maríæ,
Genetrícis eiúsdem Dei et Dómini nostri Iesu Christi: †

Bartholomew, Matthew,
Simon and Jude;
Linus, Cletus, Clement, Sixtus,
Cornelius, Cyprian,
Lawrence, Chrysogonus,
John and Paul,
Cosmas and Damian)
and all your Saints;
we ask that through their merits and prayers,
in all things we may be defended
by your protecting help.
(Through Christ our Lord. Amen.)

PROPER FORMS OF THE COMMUNICANTES

On the Nativity of the Lord and throughout the Octave

>Celebrating the most sacred night (day)
on which blessed Mary the immaculate Virgin
brought forth the Saviour for this world,
and in communion with those whose memory we venerate,
especially the glorious ever-Virgin Mary,
Mother of our God and Lord, Jesus Christ, †

On the Epiphany of the Lord

>Celebrating the most sacred day
on which your Only Begotten Son,
eternal with you in your glory,
appeared in a human body, truly sharing our flesh,
and in communion with those whose memory we venerate,
especially the glorious ever-Virgin Mary,
Mother of our God and Lord, Jesus Christ, †

From the Mass of the Easter Vigil until the Second Sunday of Easter

>Celebrating the most sacred night (day)
of the Resurrection of our Lord Jesus Christ in the flesh,
and in communion with those whose memory we venerate,
especially the glorious ever-Virgin Mary,
Mother of our God and Lord, Jesus Christ, †

On the Ascension of the Lord

>Communicántes,
et diem sacratíssimum celebrántes,
quo Dóminus noster, Unigénitus Fílius tuus,
unítam sibi fragilitátis nostræ substántiam
in glóriæ tuæ déxtera collocávit:
sed et memóriam venerántes,
in primis gloriósæ semper Vírginis Maríæ,
Genetrícis eiúsdem Dei et Dómini nostri Iesu Christi: †

On Pentecost Sunday

>Communicántes,
et diem sacratíssimum Pentecóstes celebrántes,
quo Spíritus Sanctus
Apóstolis in ígneis linguis appáruit:
sed et memóriam venerántes,
in primis gloriósæ semper Vírginis Maríæ,
Genetrícis Dei et Dómini nostri Iesu Christi: †

Hanc ígitur oblatiónem servitútis nostræ,
sed et cunctæ famíliæ tuæ,
quǽsumus, Dómine, ut placátus accípias:
diésque nostros in tua pace dispónas,
atque ab ætérna damnatióne nos éripi
et in electórum tuórum iúbeas grege numerári.
(Per Christum Dóminum nostrum. Amen.)

From the Mass of the Easter Vigil until the Second Sunday of Easter

>Hanc ígitur oblatiónem servitútis nostræ,
sed et cunctæ famíliæ tuæ,
quam tibi offérimus
pro his quoque, quos regeneráre dignátus es ex aqua et Spíritu Sancto,
tríbuens eis remissiónem ómnium peccatórum,
quǽsumus, Dómine, ut placátus accípias:
diésque nostros in tua pace dispónas,
atque ab ætérna damnatióne nos éripi
et in electórum tuórum iúbeas grege numerári.
(Per Christum Dóminum nostrum. Amen.)

On the Ascension of the Lord

>Celebrating the most sacred day
>on which your Only Begotten Son, our Lord,
>placed at the right hand of your glory
>our weak human nature,
>which he had united to himself,
>and in communion with those whose memory we venerate,
>especially the glorious ever-Virgin Mary,
>Mother of our God and Lord, Jesus Christ, †

On Pentecost Sunday

>Celebrating the most sacred day of Pentecost,
>on which the Holy Spirit
>appeared to the Apostles in tongues of fire,
>and in communion with those whose memory we venerate,
>especially the glorious ever-Virgin Mary,
>Mother of our God and Lord, Jesus Christ, †

Therefore, Lord, we pray:
graciously accept this oblation of our service,
that of your whole family;
order our days in your peace,
and command that we be delivered from eternal damnation
and counted among the flock of those you have chosen.
(Through Christ Our Lord. Amen.)

From the Mass of the Easter Vigil until the Second Sunday of Easter

>Therefore, Lord, we pray:
>graciously accept this oblation of our service,
>that of your whole family,
>which we make to you
>also for those to whom you have been pleased to give
>the new birth of water and the Holy Spirit,
>granting them forgiveness of all their sins;
>order our days in your peace,
>and command that we be delivered from eternal damnation
>and counted among the flock of those you have chosen.
>(Through Christ our Lord. Amen.)

Quam oblatiónem tu, Deus, in ómnibus, quæsumus,
benedíctam, adscríptam, ratam,
rationábilem, acceptabilémque fácere dignéris:
ut nobis Corpus et Sanguis fiat dilectíssimi Fílii tui,
Dómini nostri Iesu Christi.

Qui, prídie quam paterétur,
accépit panem in sanctas ac venerábiles manus suas,
et elevátis óculis in cælum
ad te Deum Patrem suum omnipoténtem,
tibi grátias agens benedíxit,
fregit,
dedítque discípulis suis, dicens:

Accípite et manducáte ex hoc omnes:
hoc est enim Corpus meum,
quod pro vobis tradétur.

Símili modo, postquam cenátum est,
accípiens et hunc præclárum cálicem
in sanctas ac venerábiles manus suas,
item tibi grátias agens benedíxit,
dedítque discípulis suis dicens:

Accípite et bíbite ex eo omnes:
hic est enim calix Sánguinis mei
novi et ætérni testaménti,
qui pro vobis et pro multis effundétur
in remissiónem peccatórum.
Hoc fácite in meam commemoratiónem.

EUCHARISTIC PRAYER I

Be pleased, O God, we pray,
to bless, acknowledge,
and approve this offering in every respect;
make it spiritual and acceptable,
so that it may become for us
the Body and Blood of your most beloved Son,
our Lord Jesus Christ.

On the day before he was to suffer,
he took bread in his holy and venerable hands,
and with eyes raised to heaven
to you, O God, his almighty Father,
giving you thanks, he said the blessing,
broke the bread
and gave it to his disciples, saying:

TAKE THIS, ALL OF YOU, AND EAT OF IT,
FOR THIS IS MY BODY,
WHICH WILL BE GIVEN UP FOR YOU.

In a similar way, when supper was ended,
he took this precious chalice
in his holy and venerable hands,
and once more giving you thanks, he said the blessing
and gave the chalice to his disciples, saying:

TAKE THIS, ALL OF YOU, AND DRINK FROM IT,
FOR THIS IS THE CHALICE OF MY BLOOD,
THE BLOOD OF THE NEW AND ETERNAL COVENANT,
WHICH WILL BE POURED OUT FOR YOU AND FOR MANY
FOR THE FORGIVENESS OF SINS.
DO THIS IN MEMORY OF ME.

Pr. Mystérium fídei.

The people continue, acclaiming one of the following:

Mortem tu-am annunti-ámus, Dómi-ne, et tu-am resurrecti-ó-nem confi-témur, do-nec vé-ni-as.

**1. Mortem tuam annuntiámus, Dómine,
et tuam resurrectiónem confitémur, donec vénias.**

Quoti-escúmque manducámus panem hunc et cálicem bíbimus, mortem tu-am annunti-ámus, Dómine, donec vé- ni-as.

**2. Quotiescúmque manducámus panem hunc
et cálicem bíbimus,
mortem tuam annuntiámus, Dómine, donec vénias.**

Salvátor mundi, salva nos, qui per crucem et resurrecti-ónem tu-am li-be-rá- sti nos.

**3. Salvátor mundi, salva nos,
qui per crucem et resurrectiónem tuam liberásti nos.**

EUCHARISTIC PRAYER I

Pr. The mystery of faith.

The people continue, acclaiming one of the following:

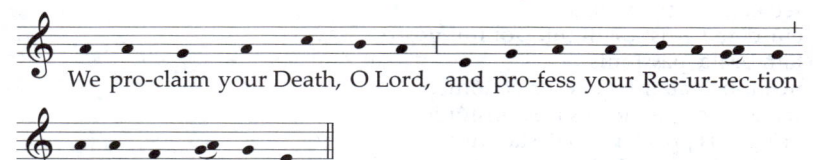

We proclaim your Death, O Lord, and profess your Resurrection until you come again.

**1. We proclaim your Death, O Lord,
and profess your Resurrection
until you come again.**

When we eat this Bread and drink this Cup, we proclaim your Death, O Lord, until you come again.

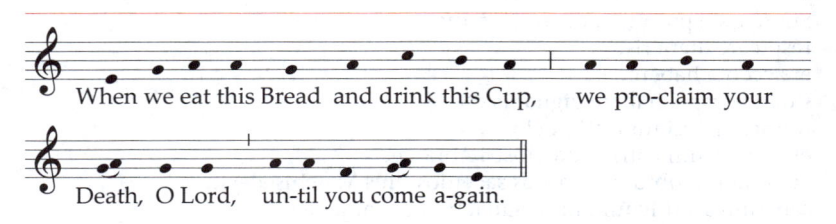

**2. When we eat this Bread and drink this Cup,
we proclaim your Death, O Lord,
until you come again.**

Save us, Saviour of the world, for by your Cross and Resurrection you have set us free.

**3. Save us, Saviour of the world,
for by your Cross and Resurrection
you have set us free.**

Only in Ireland: **4. My Lord and my God.**

Pr. Unde et mémores, Dómine,
nos servi tui,
sed et plebs tua sancta,
eiúsdem Christi, Fílii tui, Dómini nostri,
tam beátæ passiónis,
necnon et ab ínferis resurrectiónis,
sed et in cælos gloriósæ ascensiónis:
offérimus præcláræ maiestáti tuæ
de tuis donis ac datis
hóstiam puram,
hóstiam sanctam,
hóstiam immaculátam,
Panem sanctum vitæ ætérnæ
et Cálicem salútis perpétuæ.

Supra quæ propítio ac seréno vultu
respícere dignéris:
et accépta habére,
sícuti accépta habére dignátus es
múnera púeri tui iusti Abel,
et sacrifícium Patriárchæ nostri Abrahæ,
et quod tibi óbtulit summus sacérdos tuus Melchísedech,
sanctum sacrifícium, immaculátam hóstiam.

Súpplices te rogámus, omnípotens Deus:
iube hæc perférri per manus sancti Angeli tui
in sublíme altáre tuum,
in conspéctu divínæ maiestátis tuæ;
ut, quotquot ex hac altáris participatióne
sacrosánctum Fílii tui Corpus et Sánguinem sumpsérimus,
omni benedictióne cælésti et grátia repleámur
(Per Christum Dóminum nostrum. Amen.)

Commemoration of the Dead.

Meménto étiam, Dómine, famulórum famularúmque tuárum **N.** et **N.**,
qui nos præcessérunt cum signo fídei,
et dórmiunt in somno pacis.
Ipsis, Dómine, et ómnibus in Christo quiescéntibus,
locum refrigérii, lucis et pacis,
ut indúlgeas, deprecámur.
(Per Christum Dóminum nostrum. Amen.)

Nobis quoque peccatóribus fámulis tuis,
de multitúdine miseratiónum tuárum sperántibus,

EUCHARISTIC PRAYER I

Pr. Therefore, O Lord,
as we celebrate the memorial of the blessed Passion,
the Resurrection from the dead,
and the glorious Ascension into heaven
of Christ, your Son, our Lord,
we, your servants and your holy people,
offer to your glorious majesty
from the gifts that you have given us,
this pure victim,
this holy victim,
this spotless victim,
the holy Bread of eternal life
and the Chalice of everlasting salvation.

Be pleased to look upon these offerings
with a serene and kindly countenance,
and to accept them,
as once you were pleased to accept
the gifts of your servant Abel the just,
the sacrifice of Abraham, our father in faith,
and the offering of your high priest Melchizedek,
a holy sacrifice, a spotless victim.

In humble prayer we ask you, almighty God:
command that these gifts be borne
by the hands of your holy Angel
to your altar on high
in the sight of your divine majesty,
so that all of us, who through this participation at the altar
receive the most holy Body and Blood of your Son,
may be filled with every grace and heavenly blessing.
(Through Christ our Lord. Amen.)

Commemoration of the Dead.

Remember also, Lord, your servants **N.** and **N.**,
who have gone before us with the sign of faith
and rest in the sleep of peace.
Grant them, O Lord, we pray,
and all who sleep in Christ,
a place of refreshment, light and peace.
(Through Christ our Lord. Amen.)

To us, also, your servants, who, though sinners,
hope in your abundant mercies,

partem áliquam et societátem donáre dignéris
cum tuis sanctis Apóstolis et Martýribus:
cum Ioánne, Stéphano,
Matthía, Bárnaba,
(Ignátio, Alexándro,
Marcellíno, Petro,
Felicitáte, Perpétua,
Agatha, Lúcia,
Agnéte, Cæcília, Anastásia)
et ómnibus Sanctis tuis:
intra quorum nos consórtium,
non æstimátor mériti,
sed véniæ, quǽsumus, largítor admítte.
Per Christum Dóminum nostrum.

Per quem hæc ómnia, Dómine,
semper bona creas, sanctíficas, vivíficas, benedícis,
et præstas nobis.

Pr. Per ipsum, et cum ipso, et in ipso,
est tibi Deo Patri omnipoténti,
in unitáte Spíritus Sancti,
omnis honor et glória
per ómnia sǽcula sæculórum.

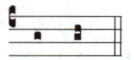

A-men.
R. **Amen.**

Then follows the Communion Rite, p.120.

EUCHARISTIC PRAYER II

Pr. Dóminus vóbiscum.
R. **Et cum spíritu tuo.**
Pr. Sursum corda.
R. **Habémus ad Dóminum.**
Pr. Grátias agámus Dómino Deo nostro.
R. **Dignum et iustum est.**
Pr. Vere dignum et iustum est, æquum et salutáre, nos tibi, sancte Pater,

graciously grant some share
and fellowship with your holy Apostles and Martyrs:
with John the Baptist, Stephen,
Matthias, Barnabas,
(Ignatius, Alexander,
Marcellinus, Peter,
Felicity, Perpetua,
Agatha, Lucy,
Agnes, Cecilia, Anastasia)
and all your Saints;
admit us, we beseech you,
into their company,
not weighing our merits,
but granting us your pardon,
through Christ our Lord.

Through whom
you continue to make all these good things, O Lord;
you sanctify them, fill them with life,
bless them, and bestow them upon us.

Pr. Through him, and with him, and in him,
O God, almighty Father,
in the unity of the Holy Spirit,
all glory and honour is yours,
for ever and ever.

A-men.

R. Amen.

Then follows the Communion Rite, p.121.

EUCHARISTIC PRAYER II

Pr. The Lord be with you.
R. And with your spirit.
Pr. Lift up your hearts.
R. We lift them up to the Lord.
Pr. Let us give thanks to the Lord our God.
R. It is right and just.
Pr. It is truly right and just, our duty and our salvation,

semper et ubíque grátias ágere
per Fílium dilectiónis tuæ Iesum Christum,
Verbum tuum per quod cuncta fecísti:
quem misísti nobis Salvatórem et Redemptórem,
incarnátum de Spíritu Sancto et ex Vírgine natum.

Qui voluntátem tuam adímplens
et pópulum tibi sanctum acquírens
exténdit manus cum paterétur,
ut mortem sólveret et resurrectiónem manifestáret.

Et ídeo cum Angelis et ómnibus Sanctis
glóriam tuam prædicámus, una voce dicéntes:

The people sing or say aloud the Sanctus.

Sanctus, * Sanc-tus, Sanc-tus Dó-mi-nus De-us Sá-ba-oth. Ple-ni sunt cæ-li et ter-ra gló-ri-a tu-a. Ho-sán-na in ex-cél-sis. Be-ne-díc-tus qui ve-nit in nómine Dómini. Ho-sán-na in excél-sis.

Sanctus, Sanctus, Sanctus Dóminus Deus Sábaoth.
Pleni sunt cæli et terra glória tua.
Hosánna in excélsis.
Benedíctus qui venit in nómine Dómini.
Hosánna in excélsis.

Pr. Vere Sanctus es, Dómine, fons omnis sanctitátis.
Hæc ergo dona, quǽsumus,
Spíritus tui rore sanctífica,
ut nobis Corpus et ✠ Sanguis fiant
Dómini nostri Iesu Christi.

EUCHARISTIC PRAYER II

always and everywhere to give you thanks, Father most holy,
through your beloved Son, Jesus Christ,
your Word through whom you made all things,
whom you sent as our Saviour and Redeemer,
incarnate by the Holy Spirit and born of the Virgin.

Fulfilling your will and gaining for you a holy people,
he stretched out his hands as he endured his Passion,
so as to break the bonds of death and manifest the resurrection.

And so, with the Angels and all the Saints
we declare your glory,
as with one voice we acclaim:

The people sing or say aloud the Sanctus.

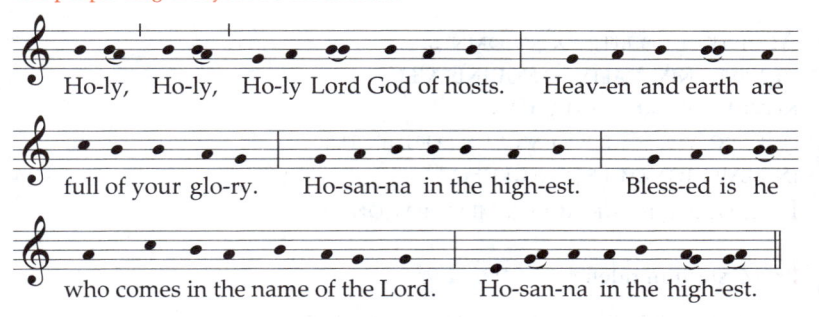

Ho-ly, Ho-ly, Ho-ly Lord God of hosts. Heav-en and earth are full of your glo-ry. Ho-san-na in the high-est. Bless-ed is he who comes in the name of the Lord. Ho-san-na in the high-est.

Holy, Holy, Holy Lord God of hosts.
Heaven and earth are full of your glory.
Hosanna in the highest.
Blessed is he who comes in the name of the Lord.
Hosanna in the highest.

Pr. You are indeed Holy, O Lord,
the fount of all holiness.
Make holy, therefore, these gifts, we pray,
by sending down your Spirit upon them like the dewfall,
so that they may become for us
the Body and ✠ Blood of our Lord Jesus Christ.

Qui cum Passióni voluntárie traderétur,
accépit panem et grátias agens fregit,
dedítque discípulis suis, dicens:

Accípite et manducáte ex hoc omnes:
hoc est enim Corpus meum,
quod pro vobis tradétur.

Símili modo, postquam cenátum est,
accípiens et cálicem,
íterum grátias agens dedit discípulis suis, dicens:

Accípite et bíbite ex eo omnes:
hic est enim calix Sánguinis mei
novi et ætérni testaménti,
qui pro vobis et pro multis effundétur
in remissiónem peccatórum.
Hoc fácite in meam commemoratiónem.

Pr. Mystérium fídei.

The people continue, acclaiming one of the following:

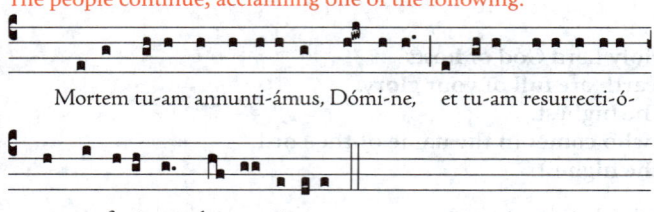

Mortem tu-am annunti-ámus, Dómi-ne, et tu-am resurrecti-ó-nem confi-témur, do-nec vé-ni-as.

**1. Mortem tuam annuntiámus, Dómine,
et tuam resurrectiónem confitémur, donec vénias.**

EUCHARISTIC PRAYER II

At the time he was betrayed
and entered willingly into his Passion,
he took bread and, giving thanks, broke it,
and gave it to his disciples, saying:

TAKE THIS, ALL OF YOU, AND EAT OF IT,
FOR THIS IS MY BODY,
WHICH WILL BE GIVEN UP FOR YOU.

In a similar way, when supper was ended,
he took the chalice
and, once more giving thanks,
he gave it to his disciples, saying:

TAKE THIS, ALL OF YOU, AND DRINK FROM IT,
FOR THIS IS THE CHALICE OF MY BLOOD,
THE BLOOD OF THE NEW AND ETERNAL COVENANT,
WHICH WILL BE POURED OUT FOR YOU AND FOR MANY
FOR THE FORGIVENESS OF SINS.

DO THIS IN MEMORY OF ME.

Pr. The mystery of faith.

The people continue, acclaiming one of the following:

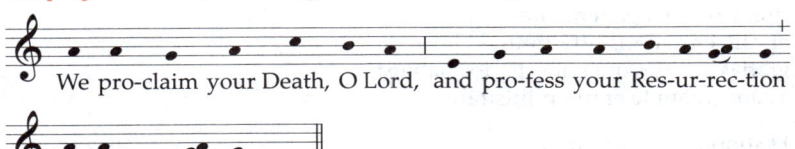

We pro-claim your Death, O Lord, and pro-fess your Res-ur-rec-tion un-til you come a-gain.

**1. We proclaim your Death, O Lord,
and profess your Resurrection
until you come again.**

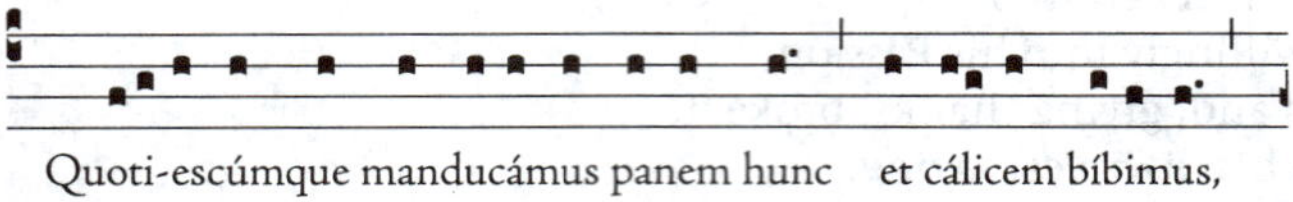

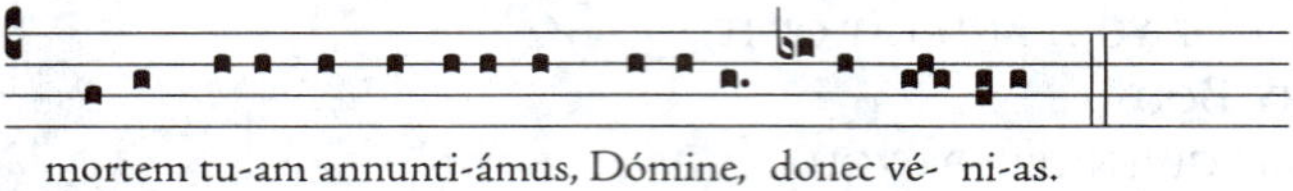

Quoti-escúmque manducámus panem hunc et cálicem bíbimus, mortem tu-am annunti-ámus, Dómine, donec vé- ni-as.

**2. Quotiescúmque manducámus panem hunc
et cálicem bíbimus,
mortem tuam annuntiámus, Dómine, donec vénias.**

Salvátor mundi, salva nos, qui per crucem et resurrecti-ónem tu-am li-be-rá- sti nos.

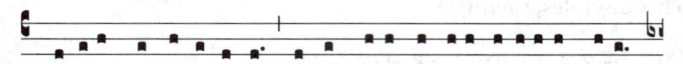

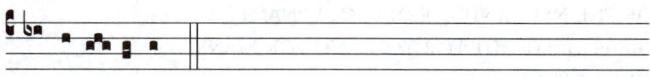

**3. Salvátor mundi, salva nos,
qui per crucem et resurrectiónem tuam liberásti nos.**

Pr. Mémores ígitur mortis et resurrectiónis eius,
tibi, Dómine, panem vitæ
et cálicem salútis offérimus,
grátias agéntes quia nos dignos habuísti
astáre coram te et tibi ministráre.

Et súpplices deprecámur
ut Córporis et Sánguinis Christi partícipes
a Spíritu Sancto congregémur in unum.

Recordáre, Dómine, Ecclésiæ tuæ toto orbe diffúsæ,
ut eam in caritáte perfícias
una cum Papa nostro **N.** et Epíscopo nostro **N.***
et univérso clero.

---

* Mention may be made here of the Coadjutor Bishop or Auxiliary Bishops.

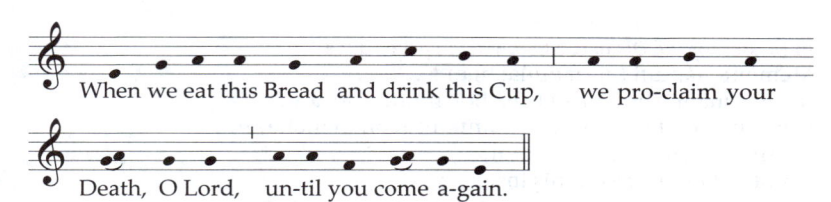

EUCHARISTIC PRAYER II

♪ *When we eat this Bread and drink this Cup, we pro-claim your Death, O Lord, un-til you come a-gain.*

2. **When we eat this Bread and drink this Cup,
we proclaim your Death, O Lord,
until you come again.**

♪ *Save us, Sav-iour of the world, for by your Cross and Res-ur-rec-tion you have set us free.*

3. **Save us, Saviour of the world,
for by your Cross and Resurrection
you have set us free.**

Only in Ireland: **4.** **My Lord and my God.**

Pr. Therefore, as we celebrate
the memorial of his Death and Resurrection,
we offer you, Lord,
the Bread of life and the Chalice of salvation,
giving thanks that you have held us worthy
to be in your presence and minister to you.

Humbly we pray
that, partaking of the Body and Blood of Christ,
we may be gathered into one by the Holy Spirit.

Remember, Lord, your Church,
spread throughout the world,
and bring her to the fullness of charity,
together with **N.** our Pope and **N.** our Bishop*
and all the clergy.

---

*Mention may be made here of the Coadjutor Bishop or Auxiliary Bishops.

In Masses for the Dead, the following may be added:
Meménto fámuli tui (fámulæ tuæ) N.,
quem (quam) (hódie) ad te ex hoc mundo vocásti.
Concéde, ut, qui (quæ) complantátus (complantáta) fuit
    similitúdini mortis Fílii tui,
simul fiat et resurrectiónis ipsíus.

Meménto étiam fratrum nostrórum,
qui in spe resurrectiónis dormiérunt,
omniúmque in tua miseratióne defunctórum,
et eos in lumen vultus tui admítte.
Omnium nostrum, quǽsumus, miserére,
ut cum beáta Dei Genetríce Vírgine María,
beátis Apostólis et ómnibus Sanctis,
qui tibi a sǽculo placuérunt,
ætérnæ vitæ mereámur esse consórtes,
et te laudémus et glorificémus
per Fílium tuum Iesum Christum.

Per ipsum, et cum ipso, et in ipso,
est tibi Deo Patri omnipoténti,
in unitáte Spíritus Sancti,
omnis honor et glória
per ómnia sǽcula sæculórum.

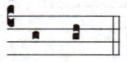

A-men.
R. Amen.

Then follows the Communion Rite, p.120.

EUCHARISTIC PRAYER III

Pr. Vere Sanctus es, Dómine,
et mérito te laudat omnis a te cóndita creatúra,
quia per Fílium tuum,
Dóminum nostrum Iesum Christum,
Spíritus Sancti operánte virtúte,
vivíficas et sanctíficas univérsa,
et pópulum tibi congregáre non désinis,

In Masses for the Dead, the following may be added:
Remember your servant **N.**,
whom you have called **(**today**)**
from this world to yourself.
Grant that he **(**she**)** who was united with your Son in a death like his,
may also be one with him in his Resurrection.

Remember also our brothers and sisters
who have fallen asleep in the hope of the resurrection,
and all who have died in your mercy:
welcome them into the light of your face.
Have mercy on us all, we pray,
that with the Blessed Virgin Mary, Mother of God,
with the blessed Apostles,
and all the Saints who have pleased you throughout the ages,
we may merit to be coheirs to eternal life,
and may praise and glorify you
through your Son, Jesus Christ.

Through him, and with him, and in him,
O God, almighty Father,
in the unity of the Holy Spirit,
all glory and honour is yours,
for ever and ever.

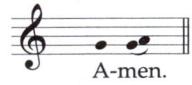

A-men.

R. Amen.

Then follows the Communion Rite, p.121.

EUCHARISTIC PRAYER III

Pr. You are indeed Holy, O Lord,
and all you have created
rightly gives you praise,
for through your Son our Lord Jesus Christ,
by the power and working of the Holy Spirit,
you give life to all things and make them holy,
and you never cease to gather a people to yourself,

ut a solis ortu usque ad occásum
oblátio munda offerátur nómini tuo.

Súpplices ergo te, Dómine, deprecámur,
ut hæc múnera, quæ tibi sacránda detúlimus,
eódem Spíritu sanctificáre dignéris,
ut Corpus et ✠ Sanguis fiant
Fílii tui Dómini nostri Iesu Christi,
cuius mandáto hæc mystéria celebrámus.

Ipse enim in qua nocte tradebátur
accépit panem
et tibi grátias agens benedíxit,
fregit, dedítque discípulis suis, dicens:

Accípite et manducáte ex hoc omnes:
hoc est enim Corpus meum,
quod pro vobis tradétur.

Símili modo, postquam cenátum est,
accípiens cálicem,
et tibi grátias agens benedíxit,
dedítque discípulis suis, dicens:

Accípite et bíbite ex eo omnes:
hic est enim calix Sánguinis mei
novi et ætérni testaménti,
qui pro vobis et pro multis effundétur
in remissiónem peccatórum.
Hoc fácite in meam commemoratiónem.

EUCHARISTIC PRAYER III

so that from the rising of the sun to its setting
a pure sacrifice may be offered to your name.

Therefore, O Lord, we humbly implore you:
by the same Spirit graciously make holy
these gifts we have brought to you for consecration,
that they may become the Body and ✠ Blood
of your Son our Lord Jesus Christ,
at whose command we celebrate these mysteries.

For on the night he was betrayed
he himself took bread,
and, giving you thanks, he said the blessing,
broke the bread and gave it to his disciples, saying:

Take this, all of you, and eat of it,
for this is my Body,
which will be given up for you.

In a similar way, when supper was ended,
he took the chalice,
and, giving you thanks, he said the blessing,
and gave the chalice to his disciples, saying:

Take this, all of you, and drink from it,
for this is the chalice of my Blood,
the Blood of the new and eternal covenant,
which will be poured out for you and for many
for the forgiveness of sins.
Do this in memory of me.

Pr. Mystérium fídei.

The people continue, acclaiming one of the following:

Mortem tu-am annunti-ámus, Dómi-ne, et tu-am resurrecti-ó-nem confi-témur, do-nec vé-ni-as.

1. **Mortem tuam annuntiámus, Dómine,
et tuam resurrectiónem confitémur, donec vénias.**

Quoti-escúmque manducámus panem hunc et cálicem bíbimus, mortem tu-am annunti-ámus, Dómine, donec vé- ni-as.

2. **Quotiescúmque manducámus panem hunc
et cálicem bíbimus,
mortem tuam annuntiámus, Dómine, donec vénias.**

Salvátor mundi, salva nos, qui per crucem et resurrecti-ónem tu-am li-be-rá- sti nos.

3. **Salvátor mundi, salva nos,
qui per crucem et resurrectiónem tuam liberásti nos.**

EUCHARISTIC PRAYER III

Pr. The mystery of faith.

The people continue, acclaiming one of the following:

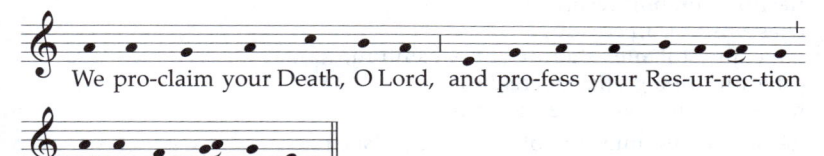

We proclaim your Death, O Lord, and profess your Resurrection until you come again.

**1. We proclaim your Death, O Lord,
and profess your Resurrection
until you come again.**

When we eat this Bread and drink this Cup, we proclaim your Death, O Lord, until you come again.

**2. When we eat this Bread and drink this Cup,
we proclaim your Death, O Lord,
until you come again.**

Save us, Saviour of the world, for by your Cross and Resurrection you have set us free.

**3. Save us, Saviour of the world,
for by your Cross and Resurrection
you have set us free.**

Only in Ireland: **4. My Lord and my God.**

Pr. Mémores ígitur, Dómine,
eiúsdem Fílii tui salutíferæ passiónis
necnon mirábilis resurrectiónis
et ascensiónis in cælum,
sed et præstolántes álterum eius advéntum,
offérimus tibi, grátias referéntes,
hoc sacrifícium vivum et sanctum.

Réspice, quǽsumus, in oblatiónem Ecclésiæ tuæ
et, agnóscens Hóstiam,
cuius volúisti immolatióne placári,
concéde, ut qui Córpore et Sánguine Fílii tui refícimur,
Spíritu eius Sancto repléti,
unum corpus et unus spíritus inveniámur in Christo.

Ipse nos tibi perfíciat munus ætérnum,
ut cum eléctis tuis hereditátem cónsequi valeámus,
in primis cum beatíssima Vírgine, Dei Genetríce, María,
cum beátis Apóstolis tuis et gloriósis Martýribus
(cum Sancto **N.**: the saint of the day or Patron Saint)
et ómnibus Sanctis,
quorum intercessióne
perpétuo apud te confídimus adiuvári.

Hæc Hóstia nostræ reconciliatiónis profíciat,
quǽsumus, Dómine,
ad totíus mundi pacem atque salútem.
Ecclésiam tuam, peregrinántem in terra,
in fide et caritáte firmáre dignéris
cum fámulo tuo Papa nostro **N.** et Epíscopo nostro **N.***,
cum episcopáli órdine et univérso clero
et omni pópulo acquisitiónis tuæ.

Votis huius famíliæ, quam tibi astáre voluísti,
adésto propítius.
Omnes fílios tuos ubíque dispérsos
tibi, clemens Pater, miserátus coniúnge.

---

*Mention may be made here of the Coadjutor Bishop or Auxiliary Bishops.

EUCHARISTIC PRAYER III

Pr. Therefore, O Lord, as we celebrate the memorial
of the saving Passion of your Son,
his wondrous Resurrection
and Ascension into heaven,
and as we look forward to his second coming,
we offer you in thanksgiving
this holy and living sacrifice.

Look, we pray, upon the oblation of your Church
and, recognising the sacrificial Victim by whose death
you willed to reconcile us to yourself,
grant that we, who are nourished
by the Body and Blood of your Son
and filled with his Holy Spirit,
may become one body, one spirit in Christ.

May he make of us
an eternal offering to you,
so that we may obtain an inheritance with your elect,
especially with the most Blessed Virgin Mary, Mother of God,
with your blessed Apostles and glorious Martyrs
(with Saint **N.**: the Saint of the day or Patron Saint)
and with all the Saints,
on whose constant intercession in your presence
we rely for unfailing help.

May this Sacrifice of our reconciliation,
we pray, O Lord,
advance the peace and salvation of all the world.
Be pleased to confirm in faith and charity
your pilgrim Church on earth,
with your servant **N.** our Pope and **N.** our Bishop*,
the Order of Bishops, all the clergy,
and the entire people you have gained for your own.

Listen graciously to the prayers of this family,
whom you have summoned before you:
in your compassion, O merciful Father,
gather to yourself all your children
scattered throughout the world.

---

*Mention may be made here of the Coadjutor Bishop or Auxiliary Bishops.

† Fratres nostros defúnctos
et omnes qui, tibi placéntes, ex hoc sǽculo transiérunt,
in regnum tuum benígnus admítte,
ubi fore sperámus,
ut simul glória tua perénniter satiémur,
per Christum Dóminum nostrum,
per quem mundo bona cuncta largíris. †

Per ipsum, et cum ipso, et in ipso,
est tibi Deo Patri omnipoténti,
in unitáte Spíritus Sancti,
omnis honor et glória
per ómnia sǽcula sæculórum.

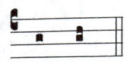

A-men.
R. Amen.

Then follows the Communion Rite, p.120.

When this Eucharistic Prayer is used in Masses for the Dead, the following may be said:
† Meménto fámuli tui (fámulæ tuæ) **N.**,
quem (quam) (hódie) ad te ex hoc mundo vocásti.
Concéde, ut, qui (quæ) complantátus (complantáta)
    fuit símilitúdini mortis Fílii tui,
simul fiat et resurrectiónis ipsíus,
quando mórtuos suscitábit in carne de terra
et corpus humilitátis nostræ
configurábit córpori claritátis suæ.
Sed et fratres nostros defúnctos,
et omnes qui, tibi placéntes, ex hoc sǽculo transiérunt,
in regnum tuum benígnus admítte,
ubi fore sperámus,
ut simul glória tua perénniter satiémur,
quando omnem lácrimam abstérges ab óculis nostris,
quia te, sícuti es, Deum nostrum vidéntes,
tibi símiles érimus cuncta per sǽcula,
et te sine fine laudábimus,
per Christum Dóminum nostrum,
per quem mundo bona cuncta largíris. †

† To our departed brothers and sisters
and to all who were pleasing to you
at their passing from this life,
give kind admittance to your kingdom.
There we hope to enjoy for ever the fullness of your glory
through Christ our Lord,
through whom you bestow on the world all that is good. †

Through him, and with him, and in him,
O God, almighty Father,
in the unity of the Holy Spirit,
all glory and honour is yours,
for ever and ever.

A-men.

R. Amen.
Then follows the Communion Rite, p.121.

When this Eucharistic Prayer is used in Masses for the Dead, the following may be said:
† Remember your servant **N.**
whom you have called (today)
from this world to yourself.
Grant that he (she) who was united with your Son in a death like his,
may also be one with him in his Resurrection,
when from the earth
he will raise up in the flesh those who have died,
and transform our lowly body
after the pattern of his own glorious body.
To our departed brothers and sisters, too,
and to all who were pleasing to you
at their passing from this life,
give kind admittance to your kingdom.
There we hope to enjoy for ever the fullness of your glory,
when you will wipe away every tear from our eyes.
For seeing you, our God, as you are,
we shall be like you for all the ages
and praise you without end,
through Christ our Lord,
through whom you bestow on the world all that is good. †

EUCHARISTIC PRAYER IV

Pr. Dóminus vóbiscum.
R. Et cum spíritu tuo.
Pr. Sursum corda.
R. Habémus ad Dóminum.
Pr. Grátias agámus Dómino Deo nostro.
R. Dignum et iustum est.

Pr. Vere dignum est tibi grátias ágere,
vere iustum est te glorificáre, Pater sancte,
quia unus es Deus vivus et verus,
qui es ante sǽcula et pérmanes in ætérnum,
inaccessíbilem lucem inhábitans;
sed et qui unus bonus atque fons vitæ cuncta fecísti,
ut creatúras tuas benedictiónibus adimpléres
multásque lætificáres tui lúminis claritáte.

Et ídeo coram te innúmeræ astant turbæ Angelórum,
qui die ac nocte sérviunt tibi
et, vultus tui glóriam contemplántes,
te incessánter gloríficant.

Cum quibus et nos et, per nostram vocem,
omnis quæ sub cælo est creatúra
nomen tuum in exsultatióne confitémur, canéntes:

The people sing or say aloud the Sanctus.

Sanctus, * Sanc-tus, Sanc-tus Dó-mi-nus De-us Sá-ba-oth. Pleni sunt cæ-li et ter-ra gló-ri-a tu-a. Ho-sán-na in ex-cél-sis. Be-ne-díc-tus qui ve-nit in nómine Dómini. Ho-sán-na in excél-sis.

EUCHARISTIC PRAYER IV

Pr. The Lord be with you.
R. And with your spirit.
Pr. Lift up your hearts.
R. We lift them up to the Lord.
Pr. Let us give thanks to the Lord our God.
R. It is right and just.

Pr. It is truly right to give you thanks,
truly just to give you glory, Father most holy,
for you are the one God living and true,
existing before all ages and abiding for all eternity,
dwelling in unapproachable light;
yet you, who alone are good, the source of life,
have made all that is,
so that you might fill your creatures with blessings
and bring joy to many of them by the glory of your light.

And so, in your presence are countless hosts of Angels,
who serve you day and night
and, gazing upon the glory of your face,
glorify you without ceasing.

With them we, too, confess your name in exultation,
giving voice to every creature under heaven,
as we acclaim:

The people sing or say aloud the Sanctus.

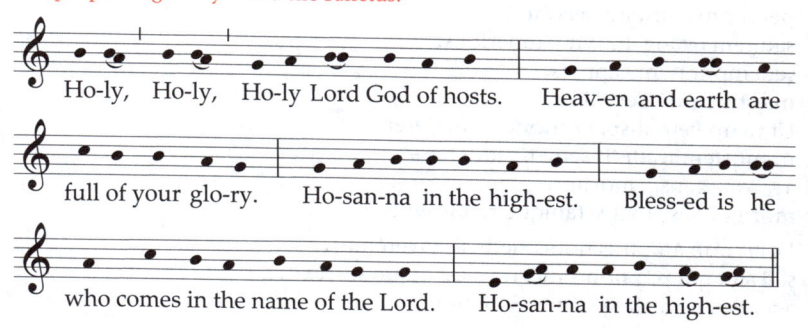

Ho-ly, Ho-ly, Ho-ly Lord God of hosts. Heav-en and earth are full of your glo-ry. Ho-san-na in the high-est. Bless-ed is he who comes in the name of the Lord. Ho-san-na in the high-est.

Sanctus, Sanctus, Sanctus Dóminus Deus Sábaoth.
Pleni sunt cæli et terra glória tua.
Hosánna in excélsis.
Benedíctus qui venit in nómine Dómini.
Hosánna in excélsis.

Pr. Confitémur tibi, Pater sancte,
quia magnus es et ómnia ópera tua
in sapiéntia et caritáte fecísti.
Hóminem ad tuam imáginem condidísti,
eíque commisísti mundi curam univérsi,
ut, tibi soli Creatóri sérviens,
creatúris ómnibus imperáret.
Et cum amicítiam tuam, non obœ́diens, amisísset,
non eum dereliquísti in mortis império.
Omnibus enim misericórditer subvenísti,
ut te quæréntes invenírent.
Sed et fœdera plúries homínibus obtulísti
eósque per prophétas erudísti in exspectatióne salútis.

Et sic, Pater sancte, mundum dilexísti,
ut, compléta plenitúdine témporum,
Unigénitum tuum nobis mítteres Salvatórem.
Qui, incarnátus de Spíritu Sancto
et natus ex María Vírgine,
in nostra condiciónis forma est conversátus
per ómnia absque peccáto;
salútem evangelizávit paupéribus,
redemptiónem captívis,
mæstis corde lætítiam.
Ut tuam vero dispensatiónem impléret,
in mortem trádidit semetípsum
ac, resúrgens a mórtuis,
mortem destrúxit vitámque renovávit.

Et, ut non ámplius nobismetípsis viverémus,
sed sibi qui pro nobis mórtuus est atque surréxit,
a te, Pater, misit Spíritum Sanctum
primítias credéntibus,

EUCHARISTIC PRAYER IV

Holy, Holy, Holy Lord God of hosts.
Heaven and earth are full of your glory.
Hosanna in the highest.
Blessed is he who comes in the name of the Lord.
Hosanna in the highest.

Pr. We give you praise, Father most holy,
for you are great
and you have fashioned all your works
in wisdom and in love.
You formed man in your own image
and entrusted the whole world to his care,
so that in serving you alone, the Creator,
he might have dominion over all creatures.
And when through disobedience he had lost your friendship,
you did not abandon him to the domain of death.
For you came in mercy to the aid of all,
so that those who seek might find you.
Time and again you offered them covenants
and through the prophets
taught them to look forward to salvation.

And you so loved the world, Father most holy,
that in the fullness of time
you sent your Only Begotten Son to be our Saviour.
Made incarnate by the Holy Spirit
and born of the Virgin Mary,
he shared our human nature
in all things but sin.
To the poor he proclaimed the good news of salvation,
to prisoners, freedom,
and to the sorrowful of heart, joy.
To accomplish your plan,
he gave himself up to death,
and, rising from the dead,
he destroyed death and restored life.

And that we might live no longer for ourselves
but for him who died and rose again for us,
he sent the Holy Spirit from you, Father,

qui, opus suum in mundo perfíciens,
omnem sanctificatiónem compléret.

Quǽsumus ígitur, Dómine,
ut idem Spíritus Sanctus
hæc múnera sanctificáre dignétur,
ut Corpus et ✠ Sanguis fiant
Dómini nostri Iesu Christi
ad hoc magnum mystérium celebrándum,
quod ipse nobis relíquit in fœdus ætérnum.

Ipse enim, cum hora venísset
ut glorificarétur a te, Pater sancte,
ac dilexísset suos qui erant in mundo,
in finem diléxit eos:
et cenántibus illis
accépit panem, benedíxit ac fregit,
dedítque discípulis suis, dicens:

Accípite et manducáte ex hoc omnes:
hoc est enim Corpus meum,
quod pro vobis tradétur.

Símili modo
accípiens cálicem, ex genímine vitis replétum,
grátias egit, dedítque discípulis suis, dicens:

Accípite et bíbite ex eo omnes:
hic est enim calix Sánguinis mei
novi et ætérni testaménti,
qui pro vobis et pro multis effundétur
in remissiónem peccatórum.
Hoc fácite in meam commemoratiónem.

Pr. Mystérium fídei.

The people continue, acclaiming one of the following:

EUCHARISTIC PRAYER IV

as the first fruits for those who believe,
so that, bringing to perfection his work in the world,
he might sanctify creation to the full.

Therefore, O Lord, we pray:
may this same Holy Spirit
graciously sanctify these offerings,
that they may become
the Body and ✠ Blood of our Lord Jesus Christ
for the celebration of this great mystery,
which he himself left us
as an eternal covenant.

For when the hour had come
for him to be glorified by you, Father most holy,
having loved his own who were in the world,
he loved them to the end:
and while they were at supper,
he took bread, blessed and broke it,
and gave it to his disciples, saying:

TAKE THIS, ALL OF YOU, AND EAT OF IT,
FOR THIS IS MY BODY,
WHICH WILL BE GIVEN UP FOR YOU.

In a similar way,
taking the chalice filled with the fruit of the vine,
he gave thanks,
and gave the chalice to his disciples, saying:

TAKE THIS, ALL OF YOU, AND DRINK FROM IT,
FOR THIS IS THE CHALICE OF MY BLOOD,
THE BLOOD OF THE NEW AND ETERNAL COVENANT,
WHICH WILL BE POURED OUT FOR YOU AND FOR MANY
FOR THE FORGIVENESS OF SINS.
DO THIS IN MEMORY OF ME.

Pr. The mystery of faith.

The people continue, acclaiming one of the following:

Mortem tu-am annunti-ámus, Dómi-ne, et tu-am resurrecti-ó-

nem confi-témur, do-nec vé-ni-as.

**1. Mortem tuam annuntiámus, Dómine,
et tuam resurrectiónem confitémur, donec vénias.**

Quoti-escúmque manducámus panem hunc et cálicem bíbimus,

mortem tu-am annunti-ámus, Dómine, donec vé- ni-as.

**2. Quotiescúmque manducámus panem hunc
et cálicem bíbimus,
mortem tuam annuntiámus, Dómine, donec vénias.**

Salvátor mundi, salva nos, qui per crucem et resurrecti-ónem tu-am

li-be-rá- sti nos.

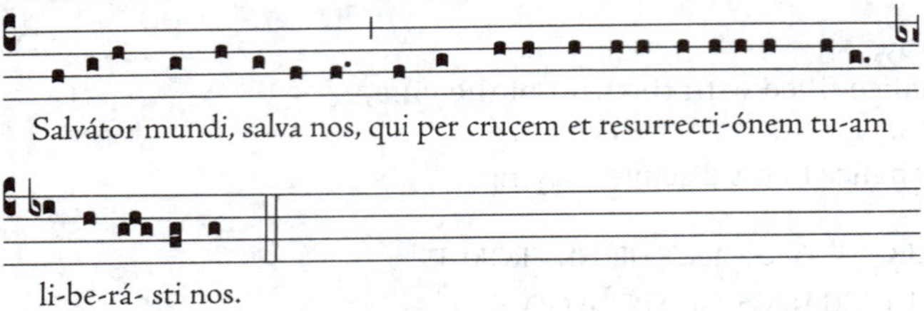

**3. Salvátor mundi, salva nos,
qui per crucem et resurrectiónem tuam liberásti nos.**

Pr. Unde et nos, Dómine, redemptiónis nostræ memoriále nunc celebrántes,
mortem Christi
eiúsque descénsum ad ínferos recólimus,
eius resurrectiónem
et ascensiónem ad tuam déxteram profitémur,

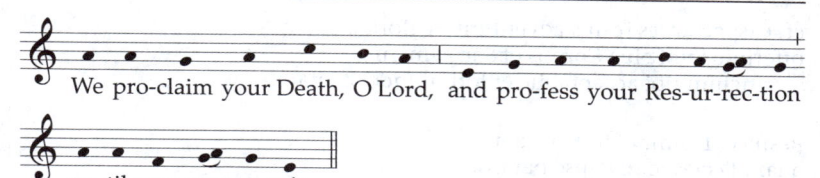

EUCHARISTIC PRAYER IV

We proclaim your Death, O Lord, and profess your Resurrection until you come again.

**1. We proclaim your Death, O Lord,
and profess your Resurrection
until you come again.**

When we eat this Bread and drink this Cup, we proclaim your Death, O Lord, until you come again.

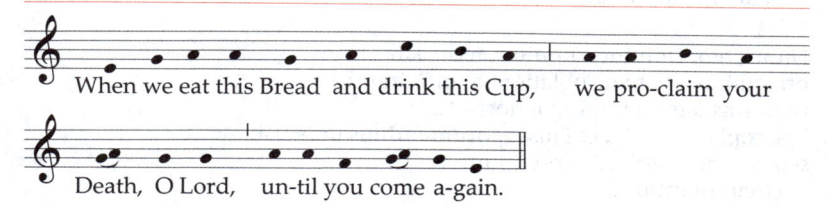

**2. When we eat this Bread and drink this Cup,
we proclaim your Death, O Lord,
until you come again.**

Save us, Saviour of the world, for by your Cross and Resurrection you have set us free.

**3. Save us, Saviour of the world,
for by your Cross and Resurrection
you have set us free.**

Only in Ireland: **4. My Lord and my God.**

Pr. Therefore, O Lord,
as we now celebrate the memorial of our redemption,
we remember Christ's Death
and his descent to the realm of the dead,
we proclaim his Resurrection
and his Ascension to your right hand,

et, exspectántes ipsíus advéntum in glória,
offérimus tibi eius Corpus et Sánguinem,
sacrifícium tibi acceptábile et toti mundo salutáre.

Réspice, Dómine, in Hóstiam,
quam Ecclésiæ tuæ ipse parásti,
et concéde benígnus ómnibus
qui ex hoc uno pane participábunt et cálice,
ut, in unum corpus a Sancto Spíritu congregáti,
in Christo hóstia viva perficiántur,
ad laudem glóriæ tuæ.

Nunc ergo, Dómine, ómnium recordáre,
pro quibus tibi hanc oblatiónem offérimus:
in primis fámuli tui, Papæ nostri **N.**,
Epíscopi nostri **N.***, et Episcopórum órdinis univérsi,
sed et totíus cleri, et offeréntium,
et circumstántium,
et cuncti pópuli tui,
et ómnium, qui te quærunt corde sincéro.

Meménto étiam illórum,
qui obiérunt in pace Christi tui,
et ómnium defunctórum,
quorum fidem tu solus cognovísti.

Nobis ómnibus, fíliis tuis, clemens Pater, concéde,
ut cæléstem hereditátem cónsequi valeámus
cum beáta Vírgine, Dei Genetríce, María,
cum Apóstolis et Sanctis tuis
in regno tuo, ubi cum univérsa creatúra,
a corruptióne peccáti et mortis liberáta,
te glorificémus per Christum Dóminum nostrum,
per quem mundo bona cuncta largíris.

Per ipsum, et cum ipso, et in ipso,
est tibi Deo Patri omnipoténti,
in unitáte Spíritus Sancti,
omnis honor et glória
per ómnia sǽcula sæculórum.

---
* Mention may be made here of the Coadjutor Bishop or Auxiliary Bishops.

and, as we await his coming in glory,
we offer you his Body and Blood,
the sacrifice acceptable to you
which brings salvation to the whole world.

Look, O Lord, upon the Sacrifice
which you yourself have provided for your Church,
and grant in your loving kindness
to all who partake of this one Bread and one Chalice
that, gathered into one body by the Holy Spirit,
they may truly become a living sacrifice in Christ
to the praise of your glory.

Therefore, Lord, remember now
all for whom we offer this sacrifice:
especially your servant **N.** our Pope,
N. our Bishop,* and the whole Order of Bishops,
all the clergy,
those who take part in this offering,
those gathered here before you,
your entire people,
and all who seek you with a sincere heart.

Remember also
those who have died in the peace of your Christ
and all the dead,
whose faith you alone have known.

To all of us, your children,
grant, O merciful Father,
that we may enter into a heavenly inheritance
with the Blessed Virgin Mary, Mother of God,
and with your Apostles and Saints in your kingdom.
There, with the whole of creation,
freed from the corruption of sin and death,
may we glorify you through Christ our Lord,
through whom you bestow on the world all that is good.

Through him, and with him, and in him,
O God, almighty Father,
in the unity of the Holy Spirit,
all glory and honour is yours,
for ever and ever.

---

*Mention may be made here of the Coadjutor Bishop or Auxiliary Bishops.

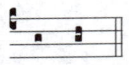

A-men.

R. Amen.

Then follows the Communion Rite.

THE COMMUNION RITE

The eating and drinking together of the Lord's Body and Blood in a Paschal meal is the culmination of the Eucharist

THE LORD'S PRAYER

After the chalice and paten have been set down, the congregation stands and the Priest says:

Pr. Præcéptis salutáribus móniti,
et divína institutióne formáti,
audémus dícere:

Together with the people, he continues:

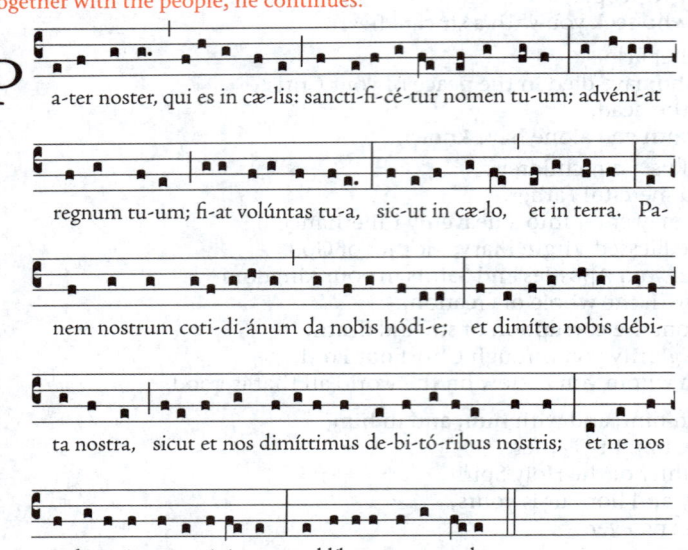

Pater noster, qui es in cælis: sancti-fi-cé-tur nomen tu-um; advéni-at regnum tu-um; fi-at volúntas tu-a, sic-ut in cæ-lo, et in terra. Panem nostrum coti-di-ánum da nobis hódi-e; et dimítte nobis débita nostra, sicut et nos dimíttimus de-bi-tó-ribus nostris; et ne nos indúcas in tenta-ti-ó-nem; sed líbera nos a ma-lo.

THE COMMUNION RITE

R. **Amen.**

Then follows the Communion Rite.

THE COMMUNION RITE

The eating and drinking together of the Lord's Body and Blood in a Paschal meal is the culmination of the Eucharist

THE LORD'S PRAYER

After the chalice and paten have been set down, the congregation stands and the Priest says:

Pr. At the Saviour's command
and formed by divine teaching,
we dare to say:

Together with the people, he continues:

Our Father, who art in heaven, hallowed be thy name; thy kingdom come, thy will be done on earth as it is in heaven. Give us this day our daily bread, and forgive us our trespasses, as we forgive those who trespass against us; and lead us not into temptation, but deliver us from evil.

R. Pater noster, qui es in cælis:
sanctificétur nomen tuum;
advéniat regnum tuum;
fiat volúntas tua, sicut in cælo, et in terra.
Panem nostrum cotidiánum da nobis hódie;
et dimítte nobis debíta nostra,
sicut et nos dimíttimus debitóribus nostris;
et ne nos indúcas in tentatiónem;
sed líbera nos a malo.

Pr. Líbera nos, quǽsumus, Dómine, ab ómnibus malis,
da propítius pacem in diébus nostris,
ut, ope misericórdiæ tuæ adiúti,
et a peccáto simus semper líberi
et ab omni perturbatióne secúri:
exspectántes beátam spem
et advéntum Salvatóris nostri Iesu Christi.

Qui-a tu-um est regnum, et po-téstas,

et gló- ri- a in saecu-la.

R. Quia tuum est regnum,
et potéstas, et glória
in sǽcula.

THE PEACE

Pr. Dómine Iesu Christe, qui dixísti Apostólis tuis:
Pacem relínquo vobis, pacem meam do vobis:
ne respícias peccáta nostra,
sed fidem Ecclésiæ tuæ;
eámque secúndum voluntátem tuam
pacificáre et coadunáre dignéris.
Qui vivis et regnas in sǽcula sæculórum.

R. Amen.

THE COMMUNION RITE

**R. Our Father, who art in heaven,
hallowed be thy name;
thy kingdom come,
thy will be done
on earth as it is in heaven.
Give us this day our daily bread,
and forgive us our trespasses,
as we forgive those who trespass against us;
and lead us not into temptation,
but deliver us from evil.**

Pr. Deliver us, Lord, we pray, from every evil,
graciously grant peace in our days,
that, by the help of your mercy,
we may be always free from sin
and safe from all distress,
as we await the blessed hope
and the coming of our Saviour, Jesus Christ.

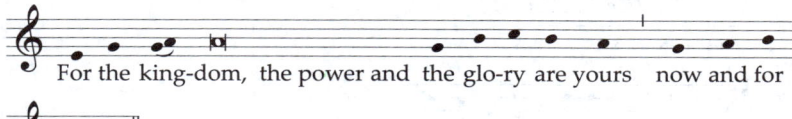

For the king-dom, the power and the glo-ry are yours now and for ev-er.

**R. For the kingdom,
the power and the glory are yours
now and for ever.**

THE PEACE

Pr. Lord Jesus Christ,
who said to your Apostles:
Peace I leave you, my peace I give you;
look not on our sins,
but on the faith of your Church,
and graciously grant her peace and unity
in accordance with your will.
Who live and reign for ever and ever.
R. Amen.

Pr. Pax Dómini sit semper vobíscum.

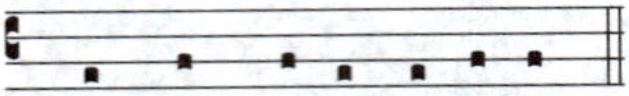

Et cum spí-ri- tu tu- o.
R. Et cum spíritu tuo.

Then, if appropriate, the Deacon, or the Priest, adds:
Pr. Offérte vobis pacem.
And all offer one another the customary sign of peace.

BREAKING OF THE BREAD

Then the Priest takes the host, breaks it over the paten, and places a small piece in the chalice. Meanwhile the following is sung or said:

Agnus De-i, * qui tol-lis pec-cá-ta mundi:

mi-se-ré-re no-bis.

Ag-nus De-i, * qui tol-lis pec-cá-ta mundi:

mi-se-ré-re no-bis.

Ag-nus De-i, * qui tol-lis pec-cá-ta mun-di:

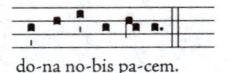

do-na no-bis pa-cem.

THE COMMUNION RITE

Pr. The peace of the Lord be with you always.

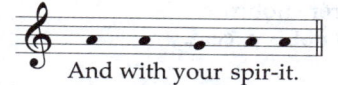

And with your spir-it.

R. And with your spirit.

Then, if appropriate, the Deacon, or the Priest, adds:
Pr. Let us offer each other the sign of peace.
And all offer one another the customary sign of peace.

BREAKING OF THE BREAD

Then the Priest takes the host, breaks it over the paten, and places a small piece in the chalice. Meanwhile the following is sung or said:

Lamb of God,* you take a-way the sins of the world,

have mer-cy on us.

Lamb of God,* you take a-way the sins of the world,

have mer-cy on us.

Lamb of God,* you take a-way the sins of the world,

grant us peace.

The invocation may even be repeated several times if the fraction is prolonged. Only the final time, however, is grant us peace said.

Agnus Dei, qui tollis peccáta mundi: miserére nobis.
Agnus Dei, qui tollis peccáta mundi: miserére nobis.
Agnus Dei, qui tollis peccáta mundi: dona nobis pacem.

Then the Priest, with hands joined, says quietly:

Domine Iesu Christe, Fili Dei vivi,
qui ex voluntate Patris,
cooperante Spiritu Sancto,
per mortem tuam mundum vivificasti:
libera me per hoc sacrosanctum Corpus et Sanguinem tuum
ab omnibus iniquitatibus meis et universis malis:
et fac me tuis semper inhærere mandatis,
et a te numquam separari permittas.

Or:

Perceptio Corporis et Sanguinis tui, Domine Iesu Christe,
non mihi proveniat in iudicium et condemnationem:
sed pro tua pietate prosit mihi
ad tutamentum mentis et corporis,
et ad medelam percipiendam.

INVITATION TO COMMUNION

All kneel. The Priest genuflects, takes the host and, holding it slightly raised above the paten or above the chalice says aloud:

Pr. Ecce Agnus Dei, ecce qui tollit peccáta mundi.
Beáti qui ad cenam Agni vocáti sunt.
**R. Dómine, non sum dignus, ut intres sub tectum meum,
sed tantum dic verbo, et sanábitur ánima mea.**

While the Priest is receiving the Body of Christ, the Communion Chant begins.

COMMUNION PROCESSION

After the priest has reverently consumed the Body and Blood of Christ he takes the paten or ciborium and approaches the communicants.
The Priest raises the host slightly and shows it to each of the communicants, saying:
Pr. Corpus Christi.
R. Amen.

Lamb of God, you take away the sins of the world, have mercy on us.
Lamb of God, you take away the sins of the world, have mercy on us.
Lamb of God, you take away the sins of the world, grant us peace.

Then the Priest, with hands joined, says quietly:
Lord Jesus Christ, Son of the living God,
who, by the will of the Father
and the work of the Holy Spirit,
through your Death gave life to the world,
free me by this, your most holy Body and Blood,
from all my sins and from every evil;
keep me always faithful to your commandments,
and never let me be parted from you.

Or:
May the receiving of your Body and Blood,
Lord Jesus Christ,
not bring me to judgement and condemnation,
but through your loving mercy
be for me protection in mind and body
and a healing remedy.

INVITATION TO COMMUNION

All kneel. The Priest genuflects, takes the host and, holding it slightly raised above the paten or above the chalice says aloud:
Pr. Behold the Lamb of God,
    behold him who takes away the sins of the world.
    Blessed are those called to the supper of the Lamb.

R. Lord, I am not worthy
    that you should enter under my roof,
    but only say the word
    and my soul shall be healed.

While the Priest is receiving the Body of Christ, the Communion Chant begins.

COMMUNION PROCESSION

After the priest has reverently consumed the Body and Blood of Christ he takes the paten or ciborium and approaches the communicants.
The Priest raises the host slightly and shows it to each of the communicants, saying:
Pr. The Body of Christ.
R. Amen.

When Communion is ministered from the chalice:
Pr. Sanguis Christi.
R. Amen.
After the distribution of Communion, if appropriate, a sacred silence may be observed for a while, or a psalm or other canticle of praise or a hymn may be sung.

PRAYER AFTER COMMUNION

Then, the Priest says:
Pr. Orémus.
All stand and pray in silence for a while, unless silence has just been observed. Then the Priest says the Prayer after Communion, at the end of which the people acclaim:
R. Amen.

THE CONCLUDING RITES

The Mass closes, sending the people forth to put what they have celebrated into effect in their daily lives.

Any brief announcements follow here. Then the dismissal takes place.

Pr. Dóminus vóbiscum.

Et cum spí-ri-tu tu-o.

R. Et cum spíritu tuo.

The Priest blesses the people, saying:

Pr. Benedícat vos omnípotens Deus,
Pater, et Fílius, ✠ et Spíritus Sanctus.

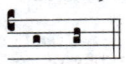

A-men.
R. Amen.

When Communion is ministered from the chalice:
Pr. The Blood of Christ.
R. Amen.

After the distribution of Communion, if appropriate, a sacred silence may be observed for a while, or a psalm or other canticle of praise or a hymn may be sung.

PRAYER AFTER COMMUNION

Then, the Priest says:
Pr. Let us pray.

All stand and pray in silence for a while, unless silence has just been observed. Then the Priest says the Prayer after Communion, at the end of which the people acclaim:
R. Amen.

THE CONCLUDING RITES

The Mass closes, sending the people forth to put what they have celebrated into effect in their daily lives.

Any brief announcements follow here. Then the dismissal takes place.

Pr. The Lord be with you.

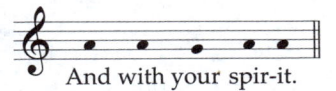

And with your spir-it.

R. And with your spirit.

The Priest blesses the people, saying:

Pr. May almighty God bless you,
the Father, and the Son, ✠ and the Holy Spirit.

A-men.

R. Amen.

Then the Deacon, or the Priest himself says the Dismissal:

Pr. Ite, missa est.

> Or:

Pr. Ite, ad Evangélium Dómini annuntiándum.

> Or:

Pr. Ite in pace, glorificándo vita vestra Dóminum.

De- o grá- ti-as.

R. Deo grátias.

> Or:

Pr. Ite in pace.

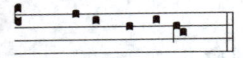

De- o grá- ti- as.

R. Deo grátias.

Then the Priest venerates the altar as at the beginning. After making a profound bow with the ministers, he withdraws.

THE CONCLUDING RITES

Then the Deacon, or the Priest himself says the Dismissal:
Pr. Go forth, the Mass is ended.
  Or:
Pr. Go and announce the Gospel of the Lord.
  Or:
Pr. Go in peace, glorifying the Lord by your life.

R. Thanks be to God.

R. Thanks be to God.
  Or:
Pr. Go in peace.

R. Thanks be to God.

R. Thanks be to God.

Then the Priest venerates the altar as at the beginning. After making a profound bow with the ministers, he withdraws.

SOLEMN BLESSINGS

The following blessings may be used, at the discretion of the Priest, at the end of the celebration of Mass, or of a Liturgy of the Word, or of the Office, or of the Sacraments.
The Deacon or, in his absence, the Priest himself, says the invitation: *Inclinate vos ad benedictionem*. Then the Priest, with hands extended over the people, says the blessing, with all responding: Amen.

I. For Celebrations in the Different Liturgical Times

1. In Adventu

Omnipotens et misericors Deus, cuius Unigeniti adventum
et præteritum creditis, et futurum exspectatis,
eiusdem adventus vos illustratione sanctificet
et sua benedictione locupletet.
R. Amen.

In præsentis vitæ stadio reddat vos in fide stabiles,
spe gaudentes, et in caritate efficaces.
R. Amen.

Ut, qui de adventu Redemptoris nostri
secundum carnem devota mente lætamini,
in secundo, cum in maiestate sua venerit,
præmiis æternæ vitæ ditemini.
R. Amen.

Et benedictio Dei omnipotentis,
Patris, et Filii, ✠ et Spiritus Sancti,
descendat super vos et maneat semper.
R. Amen.

2. In Nativitate Domini

Deus infinitæ bonitatis,
qui incarnatione Filii sui mundi tenebras effugavit,
et eius gloriosa nativitate
hanc noctem (diem) sacratissimam irradiavit,
effuget a vobis tenebras vitiorum,
et irradiet corda vestra luce virtutum.
R. Amen.

Quique eius salutiferæ nativitatis gaudium magnum
pastoribus ab Angelo voluit nuntiari,
ipse mentes vestras suo gaudio impleat,
et vos Evangelii sui nuntios efficiat.
R. Amen.

SOLEMN BLESSINGS

The following blessings may be used, at the discretion of the Priest, at the end of the celebration of Mass, or of a Liturgy of the Word, or of the Office, or of the Sacraments.

The Deacon or, in his absence, the Priest himself, says the invitation: Bow down for the blessing. Then the Priest, with hands extended over the people, says the blessing, with all responding: Amen.

I. For Celebrations in the Different Liturgical Times

1. Advent

May the almighty and merciful God,
by whose grace you have placed your faith
in the First Coming of his Only Begotten Son
and yearn for his coming again,
sanctify you by the radiance of Christ's Advent
and enrich you with his blessing.
R. Amen.

As you run the race of this present life,
may he make you firm in faith,
joyful in hope and active in charity.
R. Amen.

So that, rejoicing now with devotion
at the Redeemer's coming in the flesh,
you may be endowed with the rich reward of eternal life
when he comes again in majesty.
R. Amen.

And may the blessing of almighty God,
the Father, and the Son, ✠ and the Holy Spirit,
come down on you and remain with you for ever.
R. Amen.

2. The Nativity of the Lord

May the God of infinite goodness,
who by the Incarnation of his Son has driven darkness from the world
and by that glorious Birth has illumined this most holy night (day),
drive far from you the darkness of vice
and illumine your hearts with the light of virtue.
R. Amen.

May God, who willed that the great joy
of his Son's saving Birth
be announced to shepherds by the Angel,
fill your minds with the gladness he gives
and make you heralds of his Gospel.
R. Amen.

Et, qui per eius incarnationem terrena cælestibus sociavit,
dono vos suæ pacis et bonæ repleat voluntatis,
et vos faciat Ecclesiæ consortes esse cælestis.
R. Amen.

Et benedictio Dei omnipotentis,
Patris, et Filii, ✠ et Spiritus Sancti,
descendat super vos et maneat semper.
R. Amen.

3. Initio anni

Deus, fons et origo totius benedictionis,
gratiam vobis concedat,
benedictionis suæ largitatem infundat,
atque per totum annum vos salvos et incolumes protegat.
R. Amen.

Custodiat fidei vobis integritatem,
tribuat spei longanimitatem,
perseverantem usque ad finem
cum sancta patientia caritatem.
R. Amen.

Dies et actus vestros in sua pace disponat,
preces hic et ubique exaudiat,
et ad vitam æternam feliciter vos perducat.
R. Amen.

Et benedictio Dei omnipotentis,
Patris, et Filii, ✠ et Spiritus Sancti,
descendat super vos et maneat semper.
R. Amen.

4. In Epiphania Domini

Deus, qui vos de tenebris vocavit in admirabile lumen suum,
suam vobis benedictionem benignus infundat,
et corda vestra fide, spe et caritate stabiliat.
R. Amen.

Et quia Christum sequimini confidenter,
qui hodie mundo apparuit lux relucens in tenebris,
faciat et vos lucem esse fratribus vestris.
R. Amen.

SOLEMN BLESSINGS

And may God, who by the Incarnation
brought together the earthly and heavenly realm,
fill you with the gift of his peace and favour
and make you sharers with the Church in heaven.
R. Amen.

And may the blessing of almighty God,
the Father, and the Son, ✠ and the Holy Spirit,
come down on you and remain with you for ever.
R. Amen.

3. The Beginning of the Year

May God, the source and origin of all blessing,
grant you grace,
pour out his blessing in abundance,
and keep you safe from harm throughout the year.
R. Amen.

May he give you integrity in the faith,
endurance in hope,
and perseverance in charity
with holy patience to the end.
R. Amen.

May he order your days and your deeds in his peace,
grant your prayers in this and in every place,
and lead you happily to eternal life.
R. Amen.

And may the blessing of almighty God,
the Father, and the Son, ✠ and the Holy Spirit,
come down on you and remain with you for ever.
R. Amen.

4. The Epiphany of the Lord

May God, who has called you
out of darkness into his wonderful light,
pour out in kindness his blessing upon you
and make your hearts firm
in faith, hope and charity.
R. Amen.

And since in all confidence you follow Christ,
who today appeared in the world
as a light shining in darkness,
may God make you, too,
a light for your brothers and sisters.
R. Amen.

Quatenus, peregrinatione peracta,
perveniatis ad eum, quem magi stella prævia quæsierunt,
et gaudio magno, lucem de luce,
Christum Dominum invenerunt.
R. Amen.

Et benedictio Dei omnipotentis,
Patris, et Filii, ✠ et Spiritus Sancti,
descendat super vos et maneat semper.
R. Amen.

5. De Passione Domini

Deus, Pater misericordiarum, qui Unigeniti sui passione
tribuit vobis caritatis exemplum,
præstet ut, per servitium Dei et hominum,
percipiatis suæ benedictionis ineffabile donum.
R. Amen.

Ut ab eo sempiternæ vitæ munus obtineatis,
per cuius temporalem mortem, æternam vos evadere creditis.
R. Amen.

Quatenus, cuius humilitatis sequimini documenta,
eius resurrectionis possideatis consortia.
R. Amen.

Et benedictio Dei omnipotentis,
Patris, et Filii, ✠ et Spiritus Sancti,
descendat super vos et maneat semper.
R. Amen.

6. Tempore paschali

Deus, qui per resurrectionem Unigeniti sui
dignatus est vobis bonum redemptionis
adoptionisque conferre,
sua benedictione vos tribuat congaudere.
R. Amen.

And so when your pilgrimage is ended,
may you come to him
whom the Magi sought as they followed the star
and whom they found with great joy, the Light from Light,
who is Christ the Lord.
R. Amen.

And may the blessing of almighty God,
the Father, and the Son, ✠ and the Holy Spirit,
come down on you and remain with you for ever.
R. Amen.

5. The Passion of the Lord

May God, the Father of mercies,
who has given you an example of love
in the Passion of his Only Begotten Son,
grant that, by serving God and your neighbour,
you may lay hold of the wondrous gift of his blessing.
R. Amen.

So that you may receive the reward of everlasting life from him,
through whose earthly Death
you believe that you escape eternal death.
R. Amen.

And by following the example of his self-abasement,
may you possess a share in his Resurrection.
R. Amen.

And may the blessing of almighty God,
the Father, and the Son, ✠ and the Holy Spirit,
come down on you and remain with you for ever.
R. Amen.

6. Easter Time

May God, who by the Resurrection of his Only Begotten Son
was pleased to confer on you
the gift of redemption and of adoption,
give you gladness by his blessing.
R. Amen.

Et quo redimente percepistis donum perpetuæ libertatis,
eo largiente hereditatis æternæ consortes effici valeatis.
R. Amen.

Et cui resurrexisti in baptismate iam credendo,
adiungi mereamini in patria cælesti nunc recte vivendo.
R. Amen.

Et benedictio Dei omnipotentis,
Patris, et Filii, ✠ et Spiritus Sancti,
descendat super vos et maneat semper.
R. Amen.

7. In Ascensione Domini

Benedicat vos omnipotens Deus,
cuius Unigenitus hodierna die cælorum alta penetravit,
et vobis, ubi est ipse, ascendendi aditum reservavit.
R. Amen.

Concedat ut, sicut Christus post resurrectionem suam
visus est discipulis manifestus,
ita vobis in iudicium veniens
appareat pro æternitate placatus.
R. Amen.

Et qui eum consedere Patri in sua creditis maiestate,
ipsum usque in finem sæculi vobiscum permanere
secundum eius promissionem læti valeatis experire.
R. Amen.

Et benedictio Dei omnipotentis,
Patris, et Filii, ✠ et Spiritus Sancti,
descendat super vos et maneat semper.
R. Amen.

8. De Spiritu Sancto

Deus, Pater luminum, qui discipulorum mentes
Spiritus Paracliti infusione dignatus est illustrare,
sua vos faciat benedictione gaudere,
et perpetuo donis eiusdem Spiritus abundare.
R. Amen.

May he, by whose redeeming work
you have received the gift of everlasting freedom,
make you heirs to an eternal inheritance.
R. Amen.

And may you, who have already risen with Christ
in Baptism through faith,
by living in a right manner on this earth,
be united with him in the homeland of heaven.
R. Amen.

And may the blessing of almighty God,
the Father, and the Son, ✠ and the Holy Spirit,
come down on you and remain with you for ever.
R. Amen.

7. The Ascension of the Lord

May almighty God bless you,
for on this very day his Only Begotten Son
pierced the heights of heaven
and unlocked for you the way
to ascend to where he is.
R. Amen.

May he grant that,
as Christ after his Resurrection
was seen plainly by his disciples,
so when he comes as Judge
he may show himself merciful to you for all eternity.
R. Amen.

And may you, who believe he is seated
with the Father in his majesty,
know with joy the fulfilment of his promise
to stay with you until the end of time.
R. Amen.

And may the blessing of almighty God,
the Father, and the Son, ✠ and the Holy Spirit,
come down on you and remain with you for ever.
R. Amen.

8. The Holy Spirit

May God, the Father of lights,
who was pleased to enlighten the disciples' minds
by the outpouring of the Spirit, the Paraclete,
grant you gladness by his blessing
and make you always abound with the gifts of the same Spirit.
R. Amen.

Ignis ille, qui super discipulos mirandus apparuit,
corda vestra ab omni malo potenter expurget,
et sui luminis infusione perlustret.
R. Amen.

Quique dignatus est in unius fidei confessione
diversitatem adunare linguarum,
in eadem fide perseverare vos faciat,
et per illam a spe ad speciem pervenire concedat.
R. Amen.

Et benedictio Dei omnipotentis,
Patris, et Filii, ✠ et Spiritus Sancti,
descendat super vos et maneat semper.
R. Amen.

9. Per annum, I

Benedicat vobis Dominus, et custodiat vos.
R. Amen.

Illuminet faciem suam super vos, et misereatur vestri.
R. Amen.

Convertat vultum suum ad vos, et donet vobis suam pacem.
R. Amen.

Et benedictio Dei omnipotentis,
Patris, et Filii, ✠ et Spiritus Sancti,
descendat super vos et maneat semper.
R. Amen.

10. Per annum, II

Pax Dei, quæ exsuperat omnem sensum,
custodiat corda vestra et intellegentias vestras
in scientia et caritate Dei,
et Filii sui, Domini nostri Iesu Christi.
R. Amen.

Et benedictio Dei omnipotentis,
Patris, et Filii, ✠ et Spiritus Sancti,
descendat super vos et maneat semper.
R. Amen.

11. Per annum, III

Omnipotens Deus sua vos clementia benedicat,
et sensum in vobis sapientiæ salutaris infundat.
R. Amen.

May the wondrous flame that appeared above the disciples,
powerfully cleanse your hearts from every evil
and pervade them with its purifying light.
R. Amen.

And may God, who has been pleased to unite many tongues
in the profession of one faith,
give you perseverance in that same faith
and, by believing, may you journey from hope to clear vision.
R. Amen.

And may the blessing of almighty God,
the Father, and the Son, ✠ and the Holy Spirit,
come down on you and remain with you for ever.
R. Amen.

9. Ordinary Time I

May the Lord bless you and keep you.
R. Amen.

May he let his face shine upon you
and show you his mercy.
R. Amen.

May he turn his countenance towards you
and give you his peace.
R. Amen.

And may the blessing of almighty God,
the Father, and the Son, ✠ and the Holy Spirit,
come down on you and remain with you for ever.
R. Amen.

10. Ordinary Time II

May the peace of God,
which surpasses all understanding,
keep your hearts and minds
in the knowledge and love of God,
and of his Son, our Lord Jesus Christ.
R. Amen.

And may the blessing of almighty God,
the Father, and the Son, ✠ and the Holy Spirit,
come down on you and remain with you for ever.
R. Amen.

11. Ordinary Time III

May almighty God bless you in his kindness
and pour out saving wisdom upon you.
R. Amen.

Fidei documentis vos semper enutriat,
et in sanctis operibus, ut perseveretis, efficiat.
R. Amen.

Gressus vestros ad se convertat,
et viam vobis pacis et caritatis ostendat.
R. Amen.

Et benedictio Dei omnipotentis,
Patris, et Filii, ✠ et Spiritus Sancti,
descendat super vos et maneat semper.
R. Amen.

12. Per annum, IV

Deus totius consolationis dies vestros in sua pace disponat,
et suæ vobis benedictionis dona concedat.
R. Amen.

Ab omni semper perturbatione vos liberet,
et corda vestra in suo amore confirmet.
R. Amen.

Quatenus donis spei, fidei et caritatis divites,
et præsentem vitam transigatis in opere efficaces,
et possitis ad æternam pervenire felices.
R. Amen.

Et benedictio Dei omnipotentis,
Patris, et Filii, ✠ et Spiritus Sancti,
descendat super vos et maneat semper.
R. Amen.

13. Per annum, V

Omnipotens Deus universa a vobis adversa semper excludat,
et suæ super vos benedictionis dona propitiatus infundat.
R. Amen.

Corda vestra efficiat divinis intenta eloquiis,
ut repleri possint gaudiis sempiternis.
R. Amen.

Quatenus, quæ bona et recta intellegentes,
viam mandatorum Dei inveniamini semper currentes,
et civium supernorum efficiamini coheredes.
R. Amen.

Et benedictio Dei omnipotentis,
Patris, et Filii, ✠ et Spiritus Sancti,
descendat super vos et maneat semper.
R. Amen.

May he nourish you always with the teachings of the faith
and make you persevere in holy deeds.
R. Amen.

May he turn your steps towards himself
and show you the path of charity and peace.
R. Amen.

And may the blessing of almighty God,
the Father, and the Son, ✠ and the Holy Spirit,
come down on you and remain with you for ever.
R. Amen.

12. Ordinary Time IV

May the God of all consolation order your days in his peace
and grant you the gifts of his blessing.
R. Amen.

May he free you always from every distress
and confirm your hearts in his love.
R. Amen.

So that on this life's journey
you may be effective in good works,
rich in the gifts of hope, faith and charity,
and may come happily to eternal life.
R. Amen.

And may the blessing of almighty God,
the Father, and the Son, ✠ and the Holy Spirit,
come down on you and remain with you for ever.
R. Amen.

13. Ordinary Time V

May almighty God always keep every adversity far from you
and in his kindness pour out upon you the gifts of his blessing.
R. Amen.

May God keep your hearts attentive to his words,
that they may be filled with everlasting gladness.
R. Amen.

And so, may you always understand what is good and right,
and be found ever hastening along
in the path of God's commands,
made coheirs with the citizens of heaven.
R. Amen.

And may the blessing of almighty God,
the Father, and the Son, ✠ and the Holy Spirit,
come down on you and remain with you for ever.
R. Amen.

14. Per annum, VI

Benedicat vos Deus omni benedictione cælesti,
sanctosque vos et puros
in conspectu suo semper efficiat;
divitias gloriæ suæ in vos abundanter effundat,
verbis veritatis instruat, Evangelio salutis erudiat,
et caritate fraterna semper locupletet.
Per Christum Dominum nostrum.
R. Amen.

Et benedictio Dei omnipotentis,
Patris, et Filii, ✠ et Spiritus Sancti,
descendat super vos et maneat semper.
R. Amen.

II. For Celebrations of the Saints

15. De beata Maria Virgine

Deus, qui per beatæ Mariæ Virginis partum
genus humanum sua voluit benignitate redimere,
sua vos dignetur benedictione ditare.
R. Amen.

Eiusque semper et ubique patrocinia sentiatis,
per quam auctorem vitæ suscipere meruistis.
R. Amen.

Et qui hodierna die devotis mentibus convenistis,
spiritalium gaudiorum cælestiumque præmiorum
vobiscum munera reportetis.
R. Amen.

Et benedictio Dei omnipotentis,
Patris, et Filii, ✠ et Spiritus Sancti,
descendat super vos et maneat semper.
R. Amen.

16. De sanctis Petro et Paulo

Benedicat vos omnipotens Deus,
qui in beati Petri confessione vos saluberrima stabilivit,
et per eam in Ecclesiæ soliditate fidei fundavit.
R. Amen.

Et quos beati Pauli instruxit indefessa prædicatione,
suo semper exemplo doceat Christo fratres lucrifacere.
R. Amen.

14. Ordinary Time VI

May God bless you with every heavenly blessing,
make you always holy and pure in his sight,
pour out in abundance upon you the riches of his glory,
and teach you with the words of truth;
may he instruct you in the Gospel of salvation,
and ever endow you with fraternal charity.
Through Christ our Lord.
R. Amen.

And may the blessing of almighty God,
the Father, and the Son, ✠ and the Holy Spirit,
come down on you and remain with you for ever.
R. Amen.

II. For Celebrations of the Saints

15. The Blessed Virgin Mary

May God, who through the childbearing of the Blessed Virgin Mary
willed in his great kindness to redeem the human race,
be pleased to enrich you with his blessing.
R. Amen.

May you know always and everywhere
the protection of her,
through whom you have been found worthy to receive
the author of life.
R. Amen.

May you, who have devoutly gathered on this day,
carry away with you the gifts of spiritual joys and heavenly rewards.
R. Amen.

And may the blessing of almighty God,
the Father, and the Son, ✠ and the Holy Spirit,
come down on you and remain with you for ever.
R. Amen.

16. Saints Peter and Paul, Apostles

May almighty God bless you,
for he has made you steadfast in Saint Peter's saving confession
and through it has set you on the solid rock of the Church's faith.
R. Amen.

And having instructed you
by the tireless preaching of Saint Paul,
may God teach you constantly by his example
to win brothers and sisters for Christ.
R. Amen.

Ut Petrus clave, Paulus verbo,
ope intercessionis uterque
in illam patriam nos certent inducere,
ad quam meruerunt illi, alter cruce, alter gladio,
feliciter pervenire.
R. Amen.

Et benedictio Dei omnipotentis,
Patris, et Filii, ✠ et Spiritus Sancti,
descendat super vos et maneat semper.
R. Amen.

17. De Apostolis
Deus, qui vos in apostolicis tribuit consistere fundamentis,
benedicere vobis dignetur
beatorum Apostolorum N. et N. (beati Apostoli N.)
meritis intercedentibus gloriosis.
R. Amen.

Et apostolicis præsidiis vos pro cunctis faciat testes veritatis,
qui vos eorum munerari documentis voluit et exemplis.
R. Amen.

Ut eorum intercessione
ad æternæ patriæ hereditatem pervenire possitis,
per quorum doctrinam fidei firmitatem possidetis.
R. Amen.

Et benedictio Dei omnipotentis,
Patris, et Filii, ✠ et Spiritus Sancti,
descendat super vos et maneat semper.
R. Amen.

18. De omnibus Sanctis
Deus, gloria et exsultatio Sanctorum,
benedicat vos benedictione perpetua,
qui vobis tribuit eximiis suffragiis roborari.
R. Amen.

Eorum intercessione a præsentibus malis liberati,
et exemplis sanctæ conversationis instructi,
in servitio Dei fratrumque inveniamini semper intenti.
R. Amen.

So that by the keys of St Peter and the words of St Paul,
and by the support of their intercession,
God may bring us happily to that homeland
that Peter attained on a cross
and Paul by the blade of a sword.
R. Amen.

And may the blessing of almighty God,
the Father, and the Son, ✠ and the Holy Spirit,
come down on you and remain with you for ever.
R. Amen.

17. The Apostles

May God, who has granted you
to stand firm on apostolic foundations,
graciously bless you through the glorious merits
of the holy Apostles N. and N. (the holy Apostle N.).
R. Amen.

And may he, who endowed you
with the teaching and example of the Apostles,
make you, under their protection,
witnesses to the truth before all.
R. Amen.

So that through the intercession of the Apostles,
you may inherit the eternal homeland,
for by their teaching you possess firmness of faith.
R. Amen.

And may the blessing of almighty God,
the Father, and the Son, ✠ and the Holy Spirit,
come down on you and remain with you for ever.
R. Amen.

18. All Saints

May God, the glory and joy of the Saints,
who has caused you to be strengthened
by means of their outstanding prayers,
bless you with unending blessings.
R. Amen.

Freed through their intercession from present ills
and formed by the example of their holy way of life,
may you be ever devoted
to serving God and your neighbour.
R. Amen.

Quatenus cum iis omnibus
valeatis illius patriæ vos gaudia possidere,
in qua filios suos supernis coniungi civibus
in pace perpetua sancta lætatur Ecclesia.
R. Amen.

Et benedictio Dei omnipotentis,
Patris, et Filii, ✠ et Spiritus Sancti,
descendat super vos et maneat semper.
R. Amen.

III. Other Blessings

19. In dedicatione ecclesiæ

Deus, Dominus cæli et terræ,
qui vos hodie ad huius domus dedicationem adunavit,
ipse vos cælesti benedictione faciat abundare.
R. Amen.

Concedatque vobis fieri templum suum
et habitaculum Spiritus Sancti,
qui omnes filios dispersos voluit in Filio suo congregari.
R. Amen.

Quatenus feliciter emundati,
habitatorem Deum in vobismetipsis possitis habere,
et æternæ beatitudinis hereditatem
cum omnibus Sanctis possidere.
R. Amen.

Et benedictio Dei omnipotentis,
Patris, et Filii, ✠ et Spiritus Sancti,
descendat super vos et maneat semper.
R. Amen.

20. In celebrationibus pro defunctis

Benedicat vos Deus totius consolationis,
qui hominem ineffabili bonitate creavit,
et in resurrectione Unigeniti sui
spem credentibus resurgendi concessit.
R. Amen.

Nobis, qui vivimus, veniam tribuat pro peccatis,
et omnibus defunctis locum concedat lucis et pacis.
R. Amen.

So that, together with all,
you may possess the joys of the homeland,
where Holy Church rejoices
that her children are admitted in perpetual peace
to the company of the citizens of heaven.
R. Amen.

And may the blessing of almighty God,
the Father, and the Son, ✠ and the Holy Spirit,
come down on you and remain with you for ever.
R. Amen.

III. Other Blessings

19. For the Dedication of a Church

May God, the Lord of heaven and earth,
who has gathered you today for the dedication of this church,
make you abound in heavenly blessings.
R. Amen.

And may he, who has willed that all his scattered children
should be gathered together in his Son,
grant that you may become his temple
and the dwelling place of the Holy Spirit.
R. Amen.

And so, when you are thoroughly cleansed,
may God dwell within you
and grant you to possess with all the Saints
the inheritance of eternal happiness.
R. Amen.

And may the blessing of almighty God,
the Father, and the Son, ✠ and the Holy Spirit,
come down on you and remain with you for ever.
R. Amen.

20. In Celebrations for the Dead

May the God of all consolation bless you,
for in his unfathomable goodness he created the human race,
and in the Resurrection of his Only Begotten Son
he has given believers the hope of rising again.
R. Amen.

To us who are alive, may God grant pardon for our sins,
and to all the dead, a place of light and peace.
R. Amen.

Ut omnes cum Christo sine fine feliciter vivamus,
quem resurrexisse a mortuis veraciter credimus.
R. Amen.

Et benedictio Dei omnipotentis,
Patris, et Filii, ✠ et Spiritus Sancti,
descendat super vos et maneat semper.
R. Amen.

SOLEMN BLESSINGS

So may we all live happily for ever with Christ,
whom we believe truly rose from the dead.
R. Amen.

And may the blessing of almighty God,
the Father, and the Son, ✠ and the Holy Spirit,
come down on you and remain with you for ever.
R. Amen.

THANKSGIVING AFTER MASS

Prayer of Saint Thomas Aquinas

I give you thanks,
Lord, holy Father,
   almighty and eternal God,
who have been pleased
   to nourish me,
a sinner and your
   unworthy servant,
with the precious Body and Blood
of your Son, our Lord Jesus Christ:
this through no merits of mine,
but due solely to
   the graciousness of your mercy.

And I pray that this
   Holy Communion
may not be for me an offence
   to be punished,
but a saving plea for forgiveness.
May it be for me the armour of faith,
and the shield of good will.
May it cancel my faults,
destroy concupiscence
   and carnal passion,
increase charity and patience,
   humility and obedience
and all the virtues,
may it be a firm defence against
   the snares of all my enemies,
both visible and invisible,
the complete calming of
   my impulses,
both of the flesh and of the spirit,
a firm adherence to you,
   the one true God,
and the joyful completion of my
   life's course.

Oratio S. Thomas Aquinatis

Gratias tibi ago, Domine,
sancte Pater,
   omnipotens æterne Deus,
qui me peccatorem,
   indignum famulum tuum,
nullis meis meritis, sed sola
   dignatione misericordiæ tuæ
satiare dignatus es pretioso Corpore
   et Sanguine Filii tui,
Domini nostri Iesu Christi.

Et precor,
   ut hæc sancta communio
non sit mihi reatus ad pœnam,
sed intercessio salutaris ad veniam.
Sit mihi armatura fidei,
   et scutum bonæ voluntatis.
Sit vitiorum meorum evacuatio,
concupiscentiæ
   et libidinis exterminatio,
caritatis et patientiæ,
   humilitatis et obœdientiæ,
omniumque virtutum
   augmentatio:
contra insidias
   inimicorum omnium
tam visibilium quam invisibilium,
   firma defensio:
motuum meorum, tam carnalium
   quam spiritalium,
perfecta quietatio:
in te uno ac vero Deo
   firma adhæsio,
atque finis mei felix consummatio.

And I beseech you to lead me,
   a sinner,
to that banquet beyond all telling,
where with your Son and the
   Holy Spirit
you are the true light of
   your Saints,
fullness of satisfied desire,
   eternal gladness,
consummate delight and
   perfect happiness.
Through Christ our Lord.
Amen.

Prayer to the Most Holy Redeemer

Soul of Christ, sanctify me.
Body of Christ, save me.
Blood of Christ, embolden me.
Water from the side of Christ,
   wash me.

Passion of Christ, strengthen me.
O good Jesus, hear me.
Within your wounds hide me.
Never permit me to be parted
   from you.

From the evil Enemy defend me.
At the hour of my death call me
and bid me come to you,
that with your Saints
   I may praise you
for age upon age.
Amen.

Prayer of Self-Offering

Receive, Lord, my entire freedom.
Accept the whole of my memory,
my intellect and my will.

Et precor te,
   ut ad illud ineffabile convivium
me peccatorem perducere digneris,
ubi tu, cum Filio tuo et
   Spiritu Sancto,
Sanctis tuis es lux vera,
   satietas plena,
gaudium sempiternum,
iucunditas consummata et
   felicitas perfecta.
Per Christum Dominum nostrum.
Amen.

Aspirationes ad Ss.mum Redemptorem

Anima Christi, sanctifica me.
Corpus Christi, salva me.
Sanguis Christi, inebria me.
Aqua lateris Christi, lava me.

Passio Christi, conforta me.
O bone Iesu, exaudi me.
Intra tua vulnera absconde me.
Ne permittas me separari a te.

Ab hoste maligno defende me.
In hora mortis meæ voca me.
Et iube me venire ad te,
ut cum Sanctis tuis laudem te
in sæcula sæculorum.

Amen.

Oblatio sui

Suscipe, Domine,
   universam meam libertatem.
Accipe memoriam, intellectum
   atque voluntatem omnem.

Whatever I have or possess,
it was you who gave it to me;
I restore it to you in full,
and I surrender it completely
to the guidance of your will.
Give me only love of you
together with your grace,
and I am rich enough
and ask for nothing more.
Amen.

Prayer to Our Lord Jesus Christ Crucified

Behold, O good and loving Jesus,
that I cast myself on my knees
 before you
and, with the greatest fervour
 of spirit,
I pray and beseech you to instill
 into my heart
ardent sentiments of faith,
 hope and charity,
with true repentance for my sins
and a most firm purpose
 of amendment.
With deep affection and sorrow
I ponder intimately
and contemplate in my mind
 your five wounds,
having before my eyes what
 the prophet David
had already put in your mouth
 about yourself, O good Jesus:
They have pierced my hands and
 my feet;
they have numbered all my bones
 (Ps 21:17-18).

Quidquid habeo vel possideo,
 mihi largitus es:
id tibi totum restituo,
ac tuæ prorsus voluntati
 trado gubernandum.
Amorem tui solum cum gratia tua
 mihi dones,
et dives sum satis, nec aliud
 quidquam ultra posco.
Amen.

Oratio ad Dominum nostrum Iesum Christum Crucifixum

En ego, o bone et dulcissime Iesu,
ante conspectum tuum genibus
 me provolvo,
ac maximo animi ardore te oro
 atque obtestor,
ut meum in cor vividos fidei,
 spei et caritatis sensus,
atque veram peccatorum
 meorum pœnitentiam,
eaque emendandi firmissimam
 voluntatem velis imprimere;

dum magno animi affectu et dolore
tua quinque vulnera mecum
 ipse considero
ac mente contemplor,
illud præ oculis habens,
quod iam in ore ponebat tuo David
 propheta de te, o bone Iesu:

Foderunt manus meas
 et pedes meos:
dinumeraverunt omnia ossa mea
 (Ps 21:17-18).

THANKSGIVING AFTER MASS

The Universal Prayer Attributed to Pope Clement XI

I believe, O Lord,
    but may I believe more firmly;
I hope,
    but may I hope more securely;
I love,
    but may I love more ardently;
I sorrow,
    but may I sorrow more deeply.

I adore you as my first beginning;
I long for you as my last end;
I praise you as my
    constant benefactor;
I invoke you as my
    gracious protector.

By your wisdom direct me,
by your righteousness restrain me,
by your indulgence console me,
by your power protect me.

I offer you, Lord, my thoughts to
    be directed to you,
my words, to be about you,
my deeds, to respect your will,
my trials, to be endured for you.

I will whatever you will,
I will it because you will it,
I will it in the way you will it,
I will it for as long as you will it.

Lord, enlighten my understanding,
    I pray:
arouse my will,
cleanse my heart,
sanctify my soul.

Oratio universalis sub nomine Clementis Pp. XI vulgata

Credo, Domine,
    sed credam firmius;
spero, sed sperem securius;
amo, sed amem ardentius;
doleo, sed doleam vehementius.

Adoro te ut primum principium;
desidero ut finem ultimum;
laudo ut benefactorem perpetuum;
invoco ut defensorem propitium.

Tua me sapientia dirige,
iustitia contine,
clementia solare,
potentia protege.

Offero tibi, Domine, cogitanda,
    ut sint ad te;
dicenda, ut sint de te;
facienda, ut sint secundum te;
ferenda, ut sint propter te.

Volo quidquid vis,
volo quia vis,
volo quomodo vis,
volo quamdiu vis.

Oro, Domine:
    intellectum illumines,
voluntatem inflammes,
cor emundes,
animam sanctifices.

May I weep for past sins, repel future temptations, correct evil inclinations, nurture appropriate virtues.	Defleam præteritas iniquitates, repellam futuras tentationes, corrigam vitiosas propensiones, excolam idoneas virtutes.
Give me, good God, love for you, hatred for myself, zeal for my neighbour, contempt for the world.	Tribue mihi, bone Deus, amorem tui, odium mei, zelum proximi, contemptum mundi.
May I strive to obey superiors, to help those dependent on me, to have care for my friends, forgiveness for my enemies.	Studeam superioribus obœdire, inferioribus subvenire, amicis consulere, inimicis parcere.
May I conquer sensuality by austerity, avarice by generosity, anger by gentleness, lukewarmness by fervour.	Vincam voluptatem austeritate, avaritiam largitate, iracundiam lenitate, tepiditatem fervore.
Render me prudent in planning, steadfast in dangers, patient in adversity, humble in prosperity.	Redde me prudentem in consiliis, constantem in periculis, patientem in adversis, humilem in prosperis.
Make me, O Lord, attentive at prayer, moderate at meals, diligent in work, steadfast in intent.	Fac, Domine, ut sim in oratione attentus, in epulis sobrius, in munere sedulus, in proposito firmus.
May I be careful to maintain interior innocence, outward modesty, exemplary behaviour, a regular life.	Curem habere innocentiam interiorem, modestiam exteriorem, conversationem exemplarem, vitam regularem.
May I be always watchful in subduing nature, in nourishing grace, in observing your law, in winning salvation.	Assidue invigilem naturæ domandæ, gratiæ fovendæ, legi servandæ, saluti promerendæ.

THANKSGIVING AFTER MASS

May I learn from you
how precarious are earthly things,
how great divine things,
how fleeting is time,
how lasting things eternal.

Grant that I may prepare for death,
fear judgement,
flee hell,
gain paradise.
Through Christ our Lord.
Amen.

Prayers to the Blessed Virgin Mary

O Mary, Virgin and
   Mother most holy,
behold, I have received your
   most dear Son,
whom you conceived in
   your immaculate womb,
brought forth, nursed and
   embraced most tenderly.
Behold him at whose sight
you used to rejoice and be filled
   with all delight;
him whom, humbly and lovingly,
once again I present
and offer him to you
to be clasped in your arms,
to be loved by your heart,
and to be offered up to
   the Most Holy Trinity
as the supreme worship of adoration,
for your own honour and glory
and for my needs and for those of
   the whole world.
I ask you therefore,
   most loving Mother:

Discam a te quam tenue quod
   terrenum,
quam grande quod divinum,
quam breve quod temporaneum,
quam durabile quod æternum.

Da, ut mortem præveniam,
iudicium pertimeam,
infernum effugiam,
paradisum obtineam.
Per Christum Dominum nostrum.
Amen.

Orationes ad B. Mariam Virginem

O Maria, Virgo
   et Mater sanctissima,
ecce suscepi dilectissimum
   Filium tuum,
quem immaculato utero
   tuo concepisti,
genuisti, lactasti atque suavissimis
   amplexibus strinxisti.
Ecce, cuius aspectu lætabaris
   et omnibus deliciis replebaris,
illum ipsum tibi humiliter
   et amanter repræsento et offero,

tuis bracchiis constringendum,
   tuo corde amandum,

sanctissimæque Trinitati in
   supremum latriæ cultum,
pro tui ipsius honore et gloria
et pro meis totiusque mundi
   necessitatibus, offerendum.
Rogo ergo te, piissima Mater,

entreat for me the forgiveness
of all my sins
and, in abundant measure, the grace
of serving him in the future more faithfully,
and at the last, final grace,
so that with you I may praise him
for all the ages of ages.
Amen.

Hail, Mary, full of grace, the Lord is with thee;
blessed art thou amongst women,
and blessed is the fruit of thy womb, Jesus.
Holy Mary, Mother of God,
pray for us sinners
now and at the hour of our death.
Amen.

impetra mihi veniam omnium peccatorum meorum,
uberemque gratiam ipsi deinceps fidelius serviendi,
ac denique gratiam finalem,
ut eum tecum laudare possim
per omnia sæcula sæculorum.

Amen.

Ave Maria, gratia plena, Dominus tecum;
benedicta tu in mulieribus,
et benedictus fructus ventris tui, Iesus.
Sancta Maria, Mater Dei,
ora pro nobis peccatoribus
nunc et in hora mortis nostræ.
Amen.

AFTER HOLY COMMUNION

Act of Faith

O Jesus, I believe that I have received your Flesh to eat and your Blood to drink, because you have said it, and your word is true. All that I have and all that I am are your gift and now you have given me yourself.

Act of Adoration

O Jesus, my God, my Creator, I adore you, because from your hands I came and with you I am to be happy for ever.

Act of Humility

O Jesus, I am not worthy to receive you, and yet you have come to me that my poor heart may learn of you to be meek and humble.

Act of Love

Jesus, I love you; I love you with all my heart. You know that I love you, and wish to love you daily more and more.

Act of Thanksgiving

My good Jesus, I thank you with all my heart. How good, how kind you are to me. Blessed be Jesus in the most holy Sacrament of the Altar.

Act of Offering

O Jesus, receive my poor offering.
Jesus, you have given yourself to me,
and now let me give myself to you:
I give you my body, that I may be chaste and pure.
I give you my soul, that I may be free from sin.
I give you my heart, that I may always love you.
I give you my every breath that I shall breathe,
and especially my last.
I give you myself in life and in death,
that I may be yours for ever and ever.

For Yourself

O Jesus, wash away my sins with your Precious Blood.

O Jesus, the struggle against temptation is not yet finished. My Jesus, when temptation comes near me, make me strong against it. In the moment of temptation may I always say: "My Jesus, mercy! Mary, help!"

O Jesus, may I lead a good life; may I die a happy death. May I receive you before I die. May I say when I am dying: "Jesus, Mary and Joseph, I give you my heart and my soul".

Listen now for a moment to Jesus Christ; perhaps he has something to say to you. Answer Jesus in your heart, and tell him all your troubles. Then say:

For Perseverance

Jesus, I am going away for a time, but, I trust, not without you. You are with me by your grace. I resolve never to leave you by mortal sin. Although I am so weak I have such hope in you. Give me grace to persevere. Amen.

IF I CAN'T GET TO MASS

Spiritual Communion

Spiritual Communion is the heartfelt desire to receive Our Lord, even when we are unable because of the distance or for some other reason. This desire to receive him through spiritual Communion is an act of love which prolongs our thanksgiving even when we are not in the Eucharistic presence of Our Lord. The wish to live constantly in his presence can be fuelled by acts of love and desire to be united with him and is a means of drawing more deeply from the life of the Holy Spirit dwelling within our souls in the state of grace. 'The effects of a sacrament can be received by desire. Although in such a case the sacrament is not received physically . . . nevertheless the actual reception of the sacrament itself brings with it fuller effect than receiving it through desire alone' (St Thomas Aquinas). The writings of the saints reveal many formulae for making a spiritual Communion:

Acts of Spiritual Communion

My Jesus, I believe that You are truly present in the Most Holy Sacrament. I love You above all things, and I desire to receive You into my soul. Since I cannot at this moment receive You sacramentally, come at least spiritually into my heart. I embrace You as being already there and unite myself wholly to You. Never permit me to be separated from You. Amen.

(St Alphonsus Liguori)

I wish, my Lord, to receive You with the purity, humility and devotion with which your Most Holy Mother received You, with the spirit and fervour of the saints. Come, Lord Jesus.

Give me, good Lord, a longing to be with You ... give me warmth, delight and quickness in thinking upon You. And give me Your grace to long for Your holy sacraments, and specially to rejoice in the presence of Your very blessed Body, Sweet Saviour Christ, in the Holy Sacrament of the altar.

(St Thomas More)

FIRST SUNDAY OF ADVENT

In Advent, the liturgy frequently repeats and assures us, as if to overcome our natural diffidence, that God "comes": he comes to be with us in every situation of ours, he comes to dwell among us, to live with us and within us; he comes to fill the gaps that divide and separate us; he comes to reconcile us with him and with one another. He comes into human history to knock at the door of every man and every woman of good will, to bring to individuals, families and peoples the gifts of brotherhood, harmony and peace. This is why Advent is par excellence the season of hope in which believers in Christ are invited to remain in watchful and active waiting, nourished by prayer and by the effective commitment to love.

(Pope Benedict XVI)

Entrance Antiphon   Cf. Ps 24:1-3

To you, I lift up my soul,
O my God.
In you, I have trusted;
   let me not be put to shame.
Nor let my enemies exult over me;
and let none who hope in you
   be put to shame.

Ant. ad introitum

Ad te levavi animam meam,
Deus meus, in te confido,
   non erubescam.
Neque irrideant me inimici mei,
etenim universi qui te exspectant
   non confundentur.

The Gloria in excelsis (Glory to God in the highest) is not said.

Collect

Grant your faithful, we pray,
   almighty God,
the resolve to run forth to meet
   your Christ
with righteous deeds at his coming,
so that, gathered at his right hand,
they may be worthy to possess
   the heavenly Kingdom.
Through our Lord Jesus Christ,
   your Son,
who lives and reigns with you
   in the unity of the Holy Spirit,
one God, for ever and ever.

Collecta

Da, quæsumus, omnipotens Deus,
hanc tuis fidelibus voluntatem,
ut, Christo tuo venienti iustis
   operibus occurrentes,
eius dexteræ sociati, regnum
   mereantur possidere cæleste.
Per Dominum nostrum Iesum
   Christum Filium tuum,
qui tecum vivit et regnat
   in unitate Spiritus Sancti,
Deus, per omnia sæcula sæculorum.

FIRST READING

A reading from the prophet Jeremiah   33:14-16
I will make a virtuous Branch grow for David.

See, the days are coming – it is the Lord who speaks – when I am going to fulfil the promise I made to the House of Israel and the House of Judah:

'In those days and at that time,
I will make a virtuous Branch grow for David,
who shall practise honesty and integrity in the land.
In those days Judah shall be saved
and Israel shall dwell in confidence.
And this is the name the city will be called:
The Lord-our-integrity.'

The word of the Lord.

Responsional Psalm   Ps 24:4-5,8-9,10,14. R. v.1

R. **To you, O Lord, I lift up my soul.**

Lord, make me know your ways.
Lord, teach me your paths.
Make me walk in your truth, and teach me:
for you are God my saviour. R.

The Lord is good and upright.
He shows the path to those who stray,
he guides the humble in the right path;
he teaches his way to the poor. R.

His ways are faithfulness and love
for those who keep his covenant and will.
The Lord's friendship is for those who revere him;
to them he reveals his covenant. R.

SECOND READING

A reading from the first letter of St Paul to the Thessalonians   3:12-4:2
May the Lord confirm your hearts in holiness when Christ comes.

May the Lord be generous in increasing your love and make you love one another and the whole human race as much as we love you. And may he so confirm your hearts in holiness that you may be blameless in the sight of our God and Father when our Lord Jesus Christ comes with all his saints.

Finally, brothers, we urge you and appeal to you in the Lord Jesus to make more and more progress in the kind of life that you are meant to live: the life that God wants, as you learnt from us, and as you are already living it. You have not forgotten the instructions we gave you on the authority of the Lord Jesus.

The word of the Lord.

Gospel Acclamation

Ps 84:8

R. **Alleluia, alleluia!**
Let us see, O Lord, your mercy
and give us your saving help.
R. **Alleluia!**

GOSPEL

A reading from the holy Gospel according to Luke 21:25-28,34-36
Your liberation is near at hand.

Jesus said to his disciples: 'There will be signs in the sun and moon and stars; on earth nations in agony, bewildered by the clamour of the ocean and its waves; men dying of fear as they await what menaces the world, for the powers of heaven will be shaken. And then they will see the Son of Man coming in a cloud with power and great glory. When these things begin to take place, stand erect, hold your heads high, because your liberation is near at hand.

'Watch yourselves, or your hearts will be coarsened with debauchery and drunkenness and the cares of life, and that day will be sprung on you suddenly, like a trap. For it will come down on every living man on the face of the earth. Stay awake, praying at all times for the strength to survive all that is going to happen, and to stand with confidence before the Son of Man.'

The Gospel of the Lord.

The Creed is said.

Prayer over the Offerings	Super oblata

Accept, we pray, O Lord,
    these offerings we make,
gathered from among
    your gifts to us,
and may what you grant us
	Suscipe, quæsumus,
	    Domine, munera,
	quæ de tuis offerimus
	    collata beneficiis,
	et, quod nostræ devotioni concedis

to celebrate devoutly here below,
gain for us the prize
   of eternal redemption.
Through Christ our Lord.

Preface I of Advent, pp.42-43.

Communion Antiphon   Ps 84:13
The Lord will bestow his bounty,
and our earth shall yield its increase.

Prayer after Communion
May these mysteries, O Lord,
in which we have participated,
profit us, we pray,
for even now, as we walk amid
   passing things,
you teach us by them to love
   the things of heaven
and hold fast to what endures.
Through Christ our Lord.

effici temporali,
tuæ nobis fiat præmium
   redemptionis æternæ.
Per Christum Dominum nostrum.

Ant. ad communionem
Dominus dabit benignitatem,
et terra nostra dabit fructum suum.

Post communionem
Prosint nobis, quæsumus, Domine,
   frequentata mysteria,
quibus nos,
   inter prætereuntia ambulantes,
iam nunc instituis amare cælestia
   et inhærere mansuris.
Per Christum Dominum nostrum.

A formula of Solemn Blessing, pp.132-133, may be used.

8 December

THE IMMACULATE CONCEPTION OF THE BLESSED VIRGIN MARY

On the path of Advent shines the star of Mary Immaculate, "a sign of certain hope and comfort" (Lumen Gentium, n. 68). To reach Jesus, the true light, the sun that dispels all the darkness of history, we need light near us, human people who reflect Christ's light and thus illuminate the path to take. And what person is more luminous than Mary? Who can be a better star of hope for us than she, the dawn that announced the day of salvation? For this reason, the liturgy has us celebrate today, as Christmas approaches, the Solemn Feast of the Immaculate Conception of Mary: the mystery of God's grace that enfolded her from the first instant of her existence as the creature destined to be Mother of the Redeemer, preserving her from the stain of original sin. Looking at her, we recognise the loftiness and beauty of God's plan for everyone: to become holy and immaculate in love, in the image of our Creator.

(Pope Benedict XVI)

Solemnity

Entrance Antiphon   Is 61:10

I REJOICE heartily in the Lord,
in my God is the joy of my soul;
for he has clothed me with a robe
    of salvation,
and wrapped me in a mantle
    of justice,
like a bride adorned with her jewels.

Ant. ad introitum

GAUDENS gaudebo in Domino,
et exsultabit anima mea
    in Deo meo;
quia induit me vestimentis salutis,
et indumento iustitiæ
    circumdedit me,
quasi sponsam ornatam
    monilibus suis.

The Gloria in excelsis (Glory to God in the highest) is said.

Collect

O God, who by the Immaculate
    Conception of the Blessed Virgin
prepared a worthy dwelling
    for your Son,
grant, we pray,
that, as you preserved her
    from every stain
by virtue of the Death of your Son,
    which you foresaw,
so, through her intercession,
we, too, may be cleansed
    and admitted to your presence.
Through our Lord Jesus Christ,
    your Son,
who lives and reigns with you
    in the unity of the Holy Spirit,
one God, for ever and ever.

Collecta

Deus, qui per immaculatam
    Virginis Conceptionem
dignum Filio tuo
    habitaculum præparasti,
quæsumus, ut, qui ex morte
    eiusdem Filii tui prævisa,
eam ab omni labe præservasti,
nos quoque mundos,
    eius intercessione,
ad te pervenire concedas.
Per Dominum nostrum Iesum
    Christum Filium tuum,
qui tecum vivit et regnat
    in unitate Spiritus Sancti,
Deus, per omnia sæcula sæculorum.

FIRST READING

A reading from the book of Genesis   3:9-15,20

I will make you enemies of each other; your offspring and her offspring.

After Adam had eaten of the tree, the Lord God called to him, 'Where are you?' he asked. 'I heard the sound of you in the garden,' he replied. 'I was afraid because I was naked, so I hid.' 'Who told you that you were naked?' he asked. 'Have you been eating of the tree I forbade you to eat?' The man replied, 'It was the woman you put with me; she gave me the fruit, and I

ate it.' Then the Lord God asked the woman, 'What is this you have done?'
The woman replied, 'The serpent tempted me and I ate.'

Then the Lord God said to the serpent, 'Because you have done this,
'Be accursed beyond all cattle,
all wild beasts.
You shall crawl on your belly and eat dust
every day of your life.
I will make you enemies of each other:
you and the woman,
your offspring and her offspring.
It will crush your head
and you will strike its heel.'

The man named his wife 'Eve' because she was the mother of all those who live.

The word of the Lord.

Responsional Psalm

Ps 97:1-4. R. v.1

R. **Sing a new song to the Lord
for he has worked wonders.**

Sing a new song to the Lord
for he has worked wonders.
His right hand and his holy arm
have brought salvation. R.

The Lord has made known his salvation;
has shown his justice to the nations.
He has remembered his truth and love
for the house of Israel. R.

All the ends of the earth have seen
the salvation of our God.
Shout to the Lord all the earth,
ring out your joy. R.

SECOND READING

A reading from the letter of St Paul to the Ephesians

1:3-6,11-12

Before the world was made, God chose us in Christ.

Blessed be God the Father of our Lord Jesus Christ,
who has blessed us with all the spiritual blessings of heaven in Christ.

Before the world was made, he chose us, chose us in Christ,
to be holy and spotless, and to live through love in his presence,
determining that we should become his adopted sons,
    through Jesus Christ
for his own kind purposes,
to make us praise the glory of his grace,
his free gift to us in the Beloved.
And it is in him that we were claimed as God's own,
chosen from the beginning,
under the predetermined plan of the one who guides all things
as he decides by his own will;
chosen to be,
for his greater glory,
the people who would put their hopes in Christ before he came.

The word of the Lord.

Gospel Acclamation   Cf. Lk 1:28

R. **Alleluia, alleluia!**
Hail, Mary, full of grace; the Lord is with thee!
Blessed art thou among women.
R. **Alleluia!**

GOSPEL

A reading from the holy Gospel according to Luke   1:26-38

Rejoice, so highly favoured! The Lord is with you.

The angel Gabriel was sent by God to a town in Galilee called Nazareth, to a virgin betrothed to a man named Joseph, of the house of David; and the virgin's name was Mary. He went in and said to her, 'Rejoice, so highly favoured! The Lord is with you.' She was deeply disturbed by these words and asked herself what this greeting could mean, but the angel said to her, 'Mary, do not be afraid; you have won God's favour. Listen! You are to conceive and bear a son, and you must name him Jesus. He will be great and will be called Son of the Most High. The Lord God will give him the throne of his ancestor David; he will rule over the House of Jacob for ever and his reign will have no end.' Mary said to the angel, 'But how can this come about, since I am a virgin?' 'The Holy Spirit will come upon you' the angel answered, 'and the power of the Most High will cover you with its shadow. And so the child will be holy and will be called Son of God. Know this too: your kinswoman Elizabeth has, in her old age, herself conceived a son, and she whom people called barren is now in her sixth month, for nothing is impossible to God.' 'I am the handmaid of the Lord,' said Mary, 'let what you have said be done to me.' And the angel left her.

The Gospel of the Lord.

The Creed is said.

Prayer over the Offerings

Graciously accept the saving sacrifice which we offer you, O Lord,
on the Solemnity of the
  Immaculate Conception
of the Blessed Virgin Mary,
and grant that, as we profess her,
on account of your prevenient grace,
to be untouched by any stain of sin,
so, through her intercession,
we may be delivered from all
  our faults.
Through Christ our Lord.

Preface: The Mystery of Mary and the Church.

It is truly right and just,
  our duty and our salvation,
always and everywhere
  to give you thanks,
Lord, holy Father,
  almighty and eternal God.

For you preserved the most Blessed
  Virgin Mary
from all stain of original sin,
so that in her, endowed with
  the rich fullness of your grace,
you might prepare a worthy
  Mother for your Son
and signify the beginning
  of the Church,
his beautiful Bride without spot
  or wrinkle.

Super oblata

Salutarem hostiam,
quam in sollemnitate
  immaculatæ Conceptionis
beatæ Virginis Mariæ tibi,
  Domine, offerimus,
suscipe dignanter, et præsta,
ut, sicut illam tua gratia præveniente
ab omni labe
  profitemur immunem,
ita, eius intercessione, a culpis
  omnibus liberemur.
Per Christum Dominum nostrum.

Præfatio: De mysterio Mariæ et Ecclesiæ.

Vere dignum et iustum est,
  æquum et salutare,
nos tibi semper et ubique
  gratias agere:
Domine, sancte Pater,
  omnipotens æterne Deus:

Qui beatissimam Virginem Mariam
ab omni originalis culpæ
  labe præservasti,
ut in ea,
  gratiæ tuæ plenitudine ditata,
dignam Filio tuo
  Genetricem præparares
et Sponsæ eius Ecclesiæ,
sine ruga vel macula formosæ,
  signares exordium.

She, the most pure Virgin,
    was to bring forth a Son,
the innocent Lamb who would
    wipe away our offences;
you placed her above all others
to be for your people an advocate
    of grace
and a model of holiness.
And so, in company with the choirs
    of Angels,
we praise you, and with joy
    we proclaim:

Holy, Holy, Holy Lord God of hosts...

Communion Antiphon

Glorious things are spoken of you,
    O Mary,
for from you arose the sun of justice,
Christ our God.

Prayer after Communion

May the Sacrament we have received,
O Lord our God,
heal in us the wounds of that fault
from which in a singular way
you preserved Blessed Mary in her
    Immaculate Conception.
Through Christ our Lord.

Filium enim erat purissima
    Virgo datura,
qui crimina nostra Agnus
    innocens aboleret;
et ipsam præ omnibus tuo
    populo disponebas
advocatam gratiæ
    et sanctitatis exemplar.
Et ideo, choris angelicis sociati,
te laudamus in gaudio confitentes:

Sanctus, Sanctus, Sanctus. . .

Ant. ad communionem

Gloriosa dicta sunt de te, Maria,
quia ex te ortus est sol iustitiæ,
Christus Deus noster.

Post communionem

Sacramenta quæ sumpsimus,
Domine Deus noster,
illius in nobis culpæ
    vulnera reparent,
a qua immaculatam beatæ
    Mariæ Conceptionem
singulariter præservasti.
Per Christum Dominum nostrum.

A formula of Solemn Blessing, pp.132-133, may be used.

9 December

SECOND SUNDAY OF ADVENT

On this Sunday the Liturgy presents to us the Gospel passage in which St Luke prepares the scene on which Jesus is about to enter and begin his public ministry. The Evangelist focuses the spotlight on to John the Baptist, who was the Precursor of the Messiah, and with great precision outlines the space-time coordinates of his preaching. The Evangelist evidently wanted to warn those who read or hear about it that the Gospel is not a legend but the account of a true story, that Jesus of Nazareth is a historical figure who fits into that precise context. After this ample historical introduction, the subject becomes "the word of God", presented as a power that comes down from Heaven and settles upon John the Baptist.

(Pope Benedict XVI)

Entrance Antiphon Cf. Is 30:19,30

O PEOPLE of Sion, behold,
the Lord will come to save
the nations,
and the Lord will make the glory
of his voice heard
in the joy of your heart.

Ant. ad introitum

POPULUS Sion, ecce Dominus
veniet ad salvandas gentes;
et auditam faciet Dominus gloriam
vocis suæ
in lætitia cordis vestri.

The Gloria in excelsis (Glory to God in the highest) is not said.

Collect

Almighty and merciful God,
may no earthly undertaking
hinder those
who set out in haste to meet
your Son,
but may our learning
of heavenly wisdom
gain us admittance to his company.
Who lives and reigns with you
in the unity of the Holy Spirit,
one God, for ever and ever.

Collecta

Omnipotens et misericors Deus,
in tui occursum Filii festinantes
nulla opera terreni actus impediant,
sed sapientiæ cælestis eruditio nos
faciat eius esse consortes.
Qui tecum vivit et regnat
in unitate Spiritus Sancti,
Deus, per omnia sæcula sæculorum.

FIRST READING

A reading from the prophet Baruch 5:1-9

God means to show your splendour to every nation.

Jerusalem, take off your dress of sorrow and distress,
put on the beauty of the glory of God for ever,
wrap the cloak of the integrity of God around you,
put the diadem of the glory of the Eternal on your head:
since God means to show your splendour to every nation under heaven,
since the name God gives you for ever will be,
'Peace through integrity, and honour through devotedness.'
Arise, Jerusalem, stand on the heights
and turn your eyes to the east:
see your sons reassembled from west and east
at the command of the Holy One, jubilant that God has remembered them.
Though they left you on foot,
with enemies for an escort,
now God brings them back to you
like royal princes carried back in glory.
For God has decreed the flattening
of each high mountain, of the everlasting hills,
the filling of the valleys to make the ground level
so that Israel can walk in safety under the glory of God.
And the forests and every fragrant tree will provide shade
for Israel at the command of God;
for God will guide Israel in joy by the light of his glory
with his mercy and integrity for escort.

The word of the Lord.

Responsional Psalm

Ps 125. R. v.3

**R. What marvels the Lord worked for us!
Indeed we were glad.**

When the Lord delivered Zion from bondage
it seemed like a dream.
Then was our mouth filled with laughter,
on our lips there were songs. R.

The heathens themselves said: 'What marvels
the Lord worked for them!'
What marvels the Lord worked for us!
Indeed we were glad. R.

Deliver us, O Lord, from our bondage
as streams in dry land.
Those who are sowing in tears
will sing when they reap. R.

They go out, they go out, full of tears
carrying seed for the sowing:
they come back, they come back, full of song,
carrying their sheaves. R.

R. **What marvels the Lord worked for us!**
Indeed we were glad.

SECOND READING

A reading from the letter of St Paul to the Philippians 1:4-6,8-11
Be pure and blameless for the day of Christ.

Every time I pray for all of you, I pray with joy, remembering how you have helped to spread the Good News from the day you first heard it right up to the present. I am quite certain that the One who began this good work in you will see that it is finished when the Day of Christ Jesus comes. God knows how much I miss you all, loving you as Christ Jesus loves you. My prayer is that your love for each other may increase more and more and never stop improving your knowledge and deepening your perception so that you can always recognise what is best. This will help you to become pure and blameless, and prepare you for the Day of Christ, when you will reach the perfect goodness which Jesus Christ produces in us for the glory and praise of God.

The word of the Lord.

Gospel Acclamation Lk 3:4,6

R. **Alleluia, alleluia!**

Prepare a way for the Lord,
make his paths straight,
and all mankind shall see the salvation of God.

R. **Alleluia!**

GOSPEL

A reading from the holy Gospel according to Luke 3:1-6
All mankind shall see the salvation of God.

In the fifteenth year of Tiberius Caesar's reign, when Pontius Pilate was governor of Judaea, Herod tetrarch of Galilee, his brother Philip tetrarch of the lands of Ituraea and Trachonitis, Lysanias tetrarch of Abilene, during the pontificate of Annas and Caiaphas, the word of God came to John son of Zechariah, in the wilderness. He went through the whole Jordan district proclaiming a baptism of repentance for the forgiveness of sins, as it is written in the book of sayings of the prophet Isaiah:

> A voice cries in the wilderness:
> Prepare a way for the Lord,
> make his paths straight.
> Every valley will be filled in,
> every mountain and hill be laid low,
> winding ways will be straightened
> and rough roads made smooth.
> And all mankind shall see the salvation of God.

The Gospel of the Lord.

The Creed is said.

Prayer over the Offerings

Be pleased, O Lord, with our
　humble prayers and offerings,
and, since we have no merits
　to plead our cause,
come, we pray, to our rescue
with the protection of your mercy.
Through Christ our Lord.

Preface I of Advent, pp.42-43.

Communion Antiphon Ba 5:5;4:36

Jerusalem, arise and stand upon
　the heights,
and behold the joy which comes
　to you from God.

Super oblata

Placare, Domine, quæsumus,
nostræ precibus humilitatis
　et hostiis,
et, ubi nulla suppetunt
　suffragia meritorum,
tuæ nobis indulgentiæ
　succurre præsidiis.
Per Christum Dominum nostrum.

Ant. ad communionem

Ierusalem, surge et sta in excelso,
et vide iucunditatem,
　quæ veniet tibi a Deo tuo.

Prayer after Communion

Replenished by the food
   of spiritual nourishment,
we humbly beseech you, O Lord,
that, through our partaking
   in this mystery,
you may teach us to judge wisely
   the things of earth
and hold firm to the things
   of heaven.
Through Christ our Lord.

Post communionem

Repleti cibo spiritalis alimoniæ,
supplices te, Domine, deprecamur,
ut, huius participatione mysterii,
doceas nos terrena
   sapienter perpendere,
et cælestibus inhærere.
Per Christum Dominum nostrum.

A formula of Solemn Blessing, pp.132-133, may be used.

16 December

THIRD SUNDAY OF ADVENT

The first Reading of Mass is an invitation to joy. The Prophet Zephaniah at the end of the seventh century B.C. spoke to the city of Jerusalem and its people with these words: "Sing aloud, O daughter of Zion; shout, O Israel! Rejoice and exult with all your heart, O daughter of Jerusalem...! [T]he Lord your God is in your midst" As in the times of the Prophet Zephaniah, it is particularly to those being tested and to "life's wounded and orphans of joy" that God's Word is being addressed in a special way. To transform the world, God chose a humble young girl from a village in Galilee, Mary of Nazareth, and challenged her with this greeting: "Hail, full of grace, the Lord is with you". In these words lies the secret of an authentic Christmas. God repeats them to the Church, to each one of us: Rejoice, the Lord is close!

(Pope Benedict XVI)

Entrance Antiphon   Ph 4:4-5

REJOICE in the Lord always;
again I say, rejoice.
Indeed, the Lord is near.

Ant. ad introitum

GAUDETE in Domino semper:
iterum dico, gaudete.
Dominus enim prope est.

The Gloria in excelsis (Glory to God in the highest) is not said.

16 DECEMBER

Collect

O God, who see how your people faithfully await the feast
   of the Lord's Nativity,
enable us, we pray,
to attain the joys of so great
   a salvation
and to celebrate them always with solemn worship
   and glad rejoicing.
Through our Lord Jesus Christ,
   your Son,
who lives and reigns with you
   in the unity of the Holy Spirit,
one God, for ever and ever.

Collecta

Deus, qui conspicis populum tuum nativitatis dominicæ festivitatem
   fideliter exspectare,
præsta, quæsumus,
ut valeamus ad tantæ salutis
   gaudia pervenire,
et ea votis sollemnibus alacri
   semper lætitia celebrare.
Per Dominum nostrum Iesum
   Christum Filium tuum,
qui tecum vivit et regnat
   in unitate Spiritus Sancti,
Deus, per omnia sæcula sæculorum.

FIRST READING

A reading from the prophet Zephaniah   3:14-18

The Lord will dance with shouts of joy for you as on a day of festival.

Shout for joy, daughter of Zion,
Israel, shout aloud!
Rejoice, exult with all your heart,
daughter of Jerusalem!
The Lord has repealed your sentence;
he has driven your enemies away.
The Lord, the king of Israel, is in your midst;
you have no more evil to fear.
When that day comes, word will come to Jerusalem:
Zion, have no fear,
do not let your hands fall limp.
The Lord your God is in your midst,
a victorious warrior.
He will exult with joy over you,
he will renew you by his love;
he will dance with shouts of joy for you
as on a day of festival.

   The word of the Lord.

Responsorial Psalm
Is 12:2-6. R. v.6

R. **Sing and shout for joy**
for great in your midst is the Holy One of Israel.

Truly, God is my salvation,
I trust, I shall not fear.
For the Lord is my strength, my song,
he became my saviour.
With joy you will draw water
from the wells of salvation. R.

Give thanks to the Lord, give praise to his name!
Make his mighty deeds known to the peoples!
Declare the greatness of his name. R.

Sing a psalm to the Lord
for he has done glorious deeds,
make them known to all the earth!
People of Zion, sing and shout for joy
for great in your midst is the Holy One of Israel. R.

SECOND READING

A reading from the letter of St Paul to the Philippians 4:4-7
The Lord is very near.

I want you to be happy, always happy in the Lord; I repeat, what I want is your happiness. Let your tolerance be evident to everyone: the Lord is very near. There is no need to worry; but if there is anything you need, pray for it, asking God for it with prayer and thanksgiving, and that peace of God, which is so much greater than we can understand, will guard your hearts and your thoughts, in Christ Jesus.

The word of the Lord.

Gospel Acclamation
Is 61:1 (Lk 4:18)

R. **Alleluia, alleluia!**
The spirit of the Lord has been given to me.
He has sent me to bring good news to the poor.
R. **Alleluia!**

GOSPEL

A reading from the holy Gospel according to Luke 3:10-18

What must we do?

When all the people asked John, 'What must we do?' he answered, 'If anyone has two tunics he must share with the man who has none, and the one with something to eat must do the same.' There were tax collectors too who came for baptism, and these said to him, 'Master what must we do?' He said to them, 'Exact no more than your rate.' Some soldiers asked him in their turn, 'What about us? What must we do?' He said to them, 'No intimidation! No extortion! Be content with your pay!'

A feeling of expectancy had grown among the people, who were beginning to think that John might be the Christ, so John declared before them all, 'I baptise you with water, but someone is coming, someone who is more powerful than I am, and I am not fit to undo the strap of his sandals; he will baptise you with the Holy Spirit and fire. His winnowing-fan is in his hand to clear his threshing-floor and to gather the wheat into his barn; but the chaff he will burn in a fire that will never go out.' As well as this, there were many other things he said to exhort the people and to announce the Good News to them.

The Gospel of the Lord.

The Creed is said.

Prayer over the Offerings

May the sacrifice of our worship,
    Lord, we pray,
be offered to you unceasingly,
to complete what was begun
    in sacred mystery
and powerfully accomplish
    for us your saving work.
Through Christ our Lord.

Preface I of Advent, pp.42-43.

Super oblata

Devotionis nostræ tibi,
    Domine, quæsumus,
hostia iugiter immoletur,
quæ et sacri peragat
    instituta mysterii
et salutare tuum nobis
    potenter operetur.
Per Christum Dominum nostrum.

Communion Antiphon   Cf. Is 35:4

Say to the faint of heart:
    Be strong and do not fear.
Behold, our God will come,
    and he will save us.

Ant. ad communionem

Dicite: Pusillanimes, confortamini
    et nolite timere:
ecce Deus noster veniet
    et salvabit nos.

Prayer after Communion	Post communionem
We implore your mercy, Lord, that this divine sustenance may cleanse us of our faults and prepare us for the coming feasts. Through Christ our Lord.	Tuam, Domine, clementiam imploramus, ut hæc divina subsidia, a vitiis expiatos, ad festa ventura nos præparent. Per Christum Dominum nostrum

A formula of Solemn Blessing, pp.132-133, may be used.

23 December

FOURTH SUNDAY OF ADVENT

With the Fourth Sunday of Advent, the Lord's Birth is at hand. With the words of the Prophet Micah, the Liturgy invites us to look at Bethlehem, the little town in Judea that witnessed the great event. Unfortunately, in our day, it does not represent an attained and stable peace, but rather a peace sought with effort and hope. Yet God is never resigned to this state of affairs, so that this year too, in Bethlehem and throughout the world, the mystery of Christmas will be renewed in the Church. Today, as in the times of Jesus, Christmas is not a fairy-tale for children but God's response to the drama of humanity in search of true peace.

(Pope Benedict XVI)

Entrance Antiphon Cf. Is 45:8	Ant. ad introitum
DROP down dew from above, you heavens, and let the clouds rain down the Just One; let the earth be opened and bring forth a Saviour.	RORATE, cæli, desuper, et nubes pluant iustum; aperiatur terra et germinet Salvatorem.

The Gloria in excelsis (Glory to God in the highest) is not said.

23 DECEMBER

Collect

Pour forth, we beseech you, O Lord,
your grace into our hearts,
that we, to whom the Incarnation
   of Christ your Son
was made known by
   the message of an Angel,
may by his Passion and Cross
be brought to the glory
   of his Resurrection.
Who lives and reigns with you
   in the unity of the Holy Spirit,
one God, for ever and ever.

Collecta

Gratiam tuam,
   quæsumus, Domine,
mentibus nostris infunde,
   ut qui, Angelo nuntiante,
Christi Filii tui
   incarnationem cognovimus,
per passionem eius et crucem
ad resurrectionis
   gloriam perducamur.
Qui vivis et regnas cum Deo Patre
   in unitate Spiritus Sancti,
Deus, per omnia sæcula sæculorum.

FIRST READING

A reading from the prophet Micah 5:1-4

Out of you will be born the one who is to rule over Israel.

The Lord says this:

   You, Bethlehem Ephrathah,
   the least of the clans of Judah,
   out of you will be born for me
   the one who is to rule over Israel;
   his origin goes back to the distant past,
   to the days of old.
   The Lord is therefore going to abandon them
   till the time when she who is to give birth gives birth.
   Then the remnant of his brothers will come back
   to the sons of Israel.
   He will stand and feed his flock
   with the power of the Lord,
   with the majesty of the name of his God.
   They will live secure, for from then on he will extend his power
   to the ends of the land.
   He himself will be peace.

The word of the Lord.

Responsorial Psalm

Ps 79:2-3,15-16,18-19. R. v.4

R. **God of hosts, bring us back;
let your face shine on us and we shall be saved.**
O shepherd of Israel, hear us,
shine forth from your cherubim throne.
O Lord, rouse up your might,
O Lord, come to our help. R.

God of hosts, turn again, we implore,
look down from heaven and see.
Visit this vine and protect it,
the vine your right hand has planted. R.

May your hand be on the man you have chosen,
the man you have given your strength.
And we shall never forsake you again:
give us life that we may call upon your name. R.

SECOND READING

A reading from the letter to the Hebrews

10:5-10

Here I am! I am coming to obey your will.

This is what Christ said, on coming into the world:

> You who wanted no sacrifice or oblation,
> prepared a body for me.
> You took no pleasure in holocausts or sacrifices for sin;
> then I said,
> just as I was commanded in the scroll of the book,
> 'God, here I am! I am coming to obey your will.'

Notice that he says first: You did not want what the Law lays down as the things to be offered, that is: the sacrifices, the oblations, the holocausts and the sacrifices for sin, and you took no pleasure in them; and then he says: Here I am! I am coming to obey your will. He is abolishing the first sort to replace it with the second. And this will was for us to be made holy by the offering of his body made once and for all by Jesus Christ.

The word of the Lord.

Gospel Acclamation

Lk 1:38

R. **Alleluia, alleluia!**
I am the handmaid of the Lord:
let what you have said be done to me.
R. **Alleluia!**

GOSPEL

A reading from the holy Gospel according to Luke   1:39-45

Why should I be honoured with a visit from the mother of my Lord?

Mary set out and went as quickly as she could to a town in the hill country of Judah. She went into Zechariah's house and greeted Elizabeth. Now as soon as Elizabeth heard Mary's greeting, the child leapt in her womb and Elizabeth was filled with the Holy Spirit. She gave a loud cry and said, 'Of all women you are the most blessed, and blessed is the fruit of your womb. Why should I be honoured with a visit from the mother of my Lord? For the moment your greeting reached my ears, the child in my womb leapt for joy. Yes, blessed is she who believed that the promise made her by the Lord would be fulfilled.'

The Gospel of the Lord.

The Creed is said.

Prayer over the Offerings | Super oblata

May the Holy Spirit, O Lord,
sanctify these gifts laid upon
    your altar,
just as he filled with his power the
    womb of the Blessed Virgin Mary.
Through Christ our Lord.

Altari tuo, Domine,
    superposita munera
Spiritus ille sanctificet,
qui beatæ Mariæ viscera
    sua virtute replevit.
Per Christum Dominum nostrum.

Preface II of Advent, pp.44-45.

Communion Antiphon   Is 7:14 | Ant. ad communionem

Behold, a Virgin shall conceive
    and bear a son;
and his name will be called
    Emmanuel.

Ecce Virgo concipiet,
    et pariet filium;
et vocabitur nomen eius
    Emmanuel.

Prayer after Communion | Post communionem

Having received this pledge
    of eternal redemption,
we pray, almighty God,
that, as the feast day of our
    salvation draws ever nearer,
so we may press forward
    all the more eagerly

Sumpto pignore
    redemptionis æternæ,
quæsumus, omnipotens Deus,
ut quanto magis dies salutiferæ
    festivitatis accedit,
tanto devotius proficiamus

to the worthy celebration of the mystery of your Son's Nativity. Who lives and reigns for ever and ever.	ad Filii tui digne nativitatis mysterium celebrandum. Qui vivit et regnat in sæcula sæculorum.

A formula of Solemn Blessing, pp.132-133 may be used.

25 December

THE NATIVITY OF THE LORD

The Gospel from Matthew proposes to us precisely the account of Jesus's birth. However, the Evangelist introduces it with a summary of his genealogy, which he sets at the beginning as a prologue. Here the full evidence of Mary's role in salvation history stands out: Mary's being is totally relative to Christ and in particular to his Incarnation. "Jacob the father of Joseph the husband of Mary, of whom Jesus was born, who is called Christ". The lack of continuity in the layout of the genealogy immediately meets the eye; we do not read "begot" but instead: "Mary, of whom Jesus was born who is called Christ". Precisely in this we perceive the beauty of the plan of God who, respecting the human being, makes him fertile from within, causing the most beautiful fruit of his creative and redeeming work to develop in the humble Virgin of Nazareth. Then the Evangelist brings on stage the figure of Joseph, his inner drama, his robust faith and his exemplary rectitude. Behind Joseph's thoughts and deliberations is his love for God and his firm determination to obey him. But how is it possible not to feel that Joseph's distress, hence his prayers and his decision, were motivated at the same time by esteem and love for his betrothed? God's beauty and that of Mary are inseparable in Joseph's heart; he knows that there can be no contradiction between them; he seeks the answer in God and finds it in the light of the Word and of the Holy Spirit: "The Virgin shall be with child and give birth to a son, and they shall call him Emmanuel (which means, God with us)".

(Pope Benedict XVI)

Solemnity

At the Vigil Mass

24 December

This Mass is used on the evening of 24 December, either before or after First Vespers (Evening Prayer I) of the Nativity.

Entrance Antiphon   Cf. Ex 16:6-7 | Ant. ad introitum

TODAY you will know that the Lord will come,
and he will save us,
and in the morning you will see his glory.

HODIE scietis, quia veniet Dominus, et salvabit nos,
et mane videbitis gloriam eius.

The Gloria in excelsis (Glory to God in the highest) is said.

Collect | Collecta

O God, who gladden us year by year
as we wait in hope for our redemption,
grant that, just as we joyfully welcome
your Only Begotten Son
   as our Redeemer,
we may also merit to face
   him confidently
when he comes again as our Judge.
Who lives and reigns with you
   in the unity of the Holy Spirit,
one God, for ever and ever.

Deus, qui nos redemptionis nostræ
annua exspectatione lætificas,
præsta, ut Unigenitum tuum,
quem læti suscipimus Redemptorem,
venientem quoque Iudicem securi
   videre mereamur,
Dominum nostrum,
   Iesum Christum.
Qui tecum vivit et regnat
   in unitate Spiritus Sancti,
Deus, per omnia sæcula sæculorum.

FIRST READING

A reading from the prophet Isaiah   62:1-5

The Lord takes delight in you.

About Zion I will not be silent,
about Jerusalem I will not grow weary,
until her integrity shines out like the dawn
and her salvation flames like a torch.
The nations then will see your integrity,
all the kings your glory,
and you will be called by a new name,
one which the mouth of the Lord will confer.
You are to be a crown of splendour in the hand of the Lord,
a princely diadem in the hand of your God;
no longer are you to be named 'Forsaken'

nor your land 'Abandoned',
but you shall be called 'My Delight'
and your land 'The Wedded';
for the Lord takes delight in you
and your land will have its wedding.
Like a young man marrying a virgin,
so will the one who built you wed you,
and as the bridegroom rejoices in his bride,
so will your God rejoice in you.

The word of the Lord.

Responsorial Psalm
Ps 88:4-5,16-17,27,29. R. Cf. v.2

R. **I will sing for ever of your love, O Lord.**

'I have made a covenant with my chosen one;
I have sworn to David my servant:
I will establish your dynasty for ever
and set up your throne through all ages.' R.

Happy the people who acclaim such a king,
who walk, O Lord, in the light of your face,
who find their joy every day in your name,
who make your justice the source of their bliss. R.

'He will say to me: "You are my father,
my God, the rock who saves me."
I will keep my love for him always;
for him my covenant shall endure.' R.

SECOND READING

A reading from the Acts of the Apostles
13:16-17,22-25

Paul's witness to Christ, the son of David.

When Paul reached Antioch in Pisidia, he stood up in the synagogue, held up a hand for silence and began to speak:

'Men of Israel, and fearers of God, listen! The God of our nation Israel chose our ancestors, and made our people great when they were living as foreigners in Egypt; then by divine power he led them out.

'Then he made David their king, of whom he approved in these words, "I have selected David son of Jesse, a man after my own heart, who will carry out my whole purpose." To keep his promise, God has raised up for Israel one of David's descendants, Jesus, as Saviour, whose coming was heralded by John when he proclaimed a baptism of repentance for the whole people of Israel. Before John ended his career he said, "I am not the one you imagine me to be; that one is coming after me and I am not fit to undo his sandal."'

The word of the Lord.

Gospel Acclamation

R. **Alleluia, alleluia!**
Tomorrow there will be an end to the sin of the world
and the saviour of the world will be our king.
R. **Alleluia!**

GOSPEL

A reading from the holy Gospel according to Matthew 1:1-25

The ancestry of Jesus Christ, the son of David.

A genealogy of Jesus Christ, the son of David, son of Abraham:
Abraham was the father of Isaac,
Isaac the father of Jacob,
Jacob the father of Judah and his brothers,
Judah the father of Perez and Zerah, Tamar being their mother,
Perez the father of Hezron,
Hezron the father of Ram,
Ram the father of Amminadab,
Amminadab the father of Nahshon,
Nahshon the father of Salmon,
Salmon was the father of Boaz, Rahab being his mother,
Boaz the father of Obed, Ruth being his mother,
Obed was the father of Jesse;
and Jesse was the father of King David.
David was the father of Solomon, whose mother had been Uriah's wife,
Solomon was the father of Rehoboam,
Rehoboam the father of Abijah,
Abijah the father of Asa,
Asa was the father of Jehoshaphat,
Jehoshaphat the father of Joram,
Joram the father of Azariah,
Azariah was the father of Jotham,
Jotham the father of Ahaz,
Ahaz the father of Hezekiah,
Hezekiah was the father of Manasseh,
Manasseh the father of Amon,

Amon the father of Josiah;
and Josiah was the father of Jechoniah and his brothers.
Then the deportation to Babylon took place.

After the deportation to Babylon:
Jechoniah was the father of Shealtiel,
Shealtiel the father of Zerubbabel,
Zerubbabel was the father of Abiud,
Abiud the father of Eliakim,
Eliakim the father of Azor,
Azor was the father of Zadok,
Zadok the father of Achim,
Achim the father of Eliud,
Eliud was the father of Eleazar,
Eleazar the father of Matthan,
Matthan the father of Jacob,
and Jacob was the father of Joseph the husband of Mary; of her was born Jesus who is called Christ.

The sum of generations is therefore: fourteen from Abraham to David; fourteen from David to the Babylonian deportation; and fourteen from the Babylonian deportation to Christ.

[This is how Jesus Christ came to be born. His mother Mary was betrothed to Joseph; but before they came to live together she was found to be with child through the Holy Spirit. Her husband Joseph, being a man of honour and wanting to spare her publicity, decided to divorce her informally. He had made up his mind to do this when the angel of the Lord appeared to him in a dream and said, 'Joseph son of David, do not be afraid to take Mary home as your wife, because she has conceived what is in her by the Holy Spirit. She will give birth to a son and you must name him Jesus, because he is the one who is to save his people from their sins.' Now all this took place to fulfil the words spoken by the Lord through the prophet:

The Virgin will conceive and give birth to a son
and they will call him Emmanuel,

a name which means 'God-is-with-us'. When Joseph woke up he did what the angel of the Lord had told him to do: he took his wife to his home and, though he had not had intercourse with her, she gave birth to a son; and he named him Jesus.

The Gospel of the Lord.]

Shorter Form, verses 18-25. Read between [ ]
The Creed is said.
All kneel at the words and by the Holy Spirit was incarnate.

Prayer over the Offerings

As we look forward, O Lord,
to the coming festivities,
may we serve you
    all the more eagerly
for knowing that in them
you make manifest the beginnings
    of our redemption.
Through Christ our Lord.

Super oblata

Tanto nos, Domine, quæsumus,
promptiore servitio hæc præcurrere
    concede sollemnia,
quanto in his constare principium
nostræ redemptionis ostendis.
Per Christum Dominum nostrum.

Preface I, II or III of the Nativity of the Lord, pp.44-47

Communion Antiphon   Cf. Is 40:5

The glory of the Lord
    will be revealed,
and all flesh will see the salvation
    of our God.

Ant. ad communionem

Revelabitur gloria Domini,
et videbit omnis caro salutare
    Dei nostri.

Prayer after Communion

Grant, O Lord, we pray,
that we may draw new vigour
from celebrating the Nativity
    of your Only Begotten Son,
by whose heavenly mystery
    we receive both food and drink.
Who lives and reigns
    for ever and ever.

Post communionem

Da nobis, quæsumus, Domine,
Unigeniti Filii tui recensita
    nativitate vegetari,
cuius cælesti mysterio pascimur
    et potamur.
Qui vivit et regnat
    in sæcula sæculorum.

A formula of Solemn Blessing, pp.132-135, may be used.

At the Mass during the Night

25 December

God's sign is simplicity. God's sign is the baby. God's sign is that he makes himself small for us. This is how he reigns. He does not come with power and outward splendour. He comes as a baby – defenceless and in need of our help. He does not want to overwhelm us with his strength. He takes away our fear of his greatness. He asks for our love: so he makes himself a child. He wants nothing other from us than our love, through which we spontaneously learn to enter into his feelings, his thoughts and his will – we learn to live with him and to practise with him that humility of renunciation that belongs to the very essence of love. God made himself small so that we could understand him, welcome him, and love him.

(Pope Benedict XVI)

THE NATIVITY OF THE LORD

On the Nativity of the Lord all Priests may celebrate or concelebrate three Masses, provided the Masses are celebrated at their proper times.

Entrance Antiphon — Ps 2:7

THE Lord said to me:
You are my Son.
It is I who have begotten you this day.

Or:

Let us all rejoice in the Lord,
　for our Saviour has been born
　　in the world.
Today true peace has come down
　to us from heaven.

Ant. ad introitum

DOMINUS dixit ad me:
Filius meus es tu,
ego hodie genui te.

Vel:

Gaudeamus omnes in Domino,
quia Salvator noster natus
　est in mundo.
Hodie nobis de cælo pax
　vera descendit.

The Gloria in excelsis (Glory to God in the highest) is said.

Collect

O God, who have made
　this most sacred night
radiant with the splendour
　of the true light,
grant, we pray, that we,
　who have known the mysteries
　of his light on earth,
may also delight in his gladness
　in heaven.
Who lives and reigns with you
　in the unity of the Holy Spirit,
one God, for ever and ever.

Collecta

Deus, qui hanc sacratissimam
　noctem
veri luminis fecisti
　illustratione clarescere,
da, quæsumus, ut, cuius in terra
　mysteria lucis agnovimus,
eius quoque gaudiis perfruamur
　in cælo.
Qui tecum vivit et regnat
　in unitate Spiritus Sancti,
Deus, per omnia sæcula sæculorum.

FIRST READING

A reading from the prophet Isaiah　　　　9:1-7
A Son is given to us.

The people that walked in darkness
has seen a great light;
on those who live in a land of deep shadow
a light has shone.
You have made their gladness greater,
you have made their joy increase;
they rejoice in your presence

as men rejoice at harvest time,
as men are happy when they are dividing the spoils.
For the yoke that was weighing on him,
the bar across his shoulders,
the rod of his oppressor,
these you break as on the day of Midian.
For all the footgear of battle,
every cloak rolled in blood,
is burnt,
and consumed by fire.
For there is a child born for us,
a son given to us
and dominion is laid on his shoulders;
and this is the name they give him:
Wonder-Counsellor, Mighty-God,
Eternal-Father, Prince-of-Peace.
Wide is his dominion
in a peace that has no end,
for the throne of David
and for his royal power,
which he establishes and makes secure
in justice and integrity.
From this time onwards and for ever,
the jealous love of the Lord of hosts will do this.

The word of the Lord.

Responsional Psalm

Ps 95:1-3,11-13. R. Lk 2:11

R. **Today a saviour has been born to us;
he is Christ the Lord.**

O sing a new song to the Lord,
sing to the Lord all the earth.
O sing to the Lord, bless his name. R.

Proclaim his help day by day,
tell among the nations his glory
and his wonders among all the peoples. R.

Let the heavens rejoice and earth be glad,
let the sea and all within it thunder praise,

let the land and all it bears rejoice,
all the trees of the wood shout for joy
at the presence of the Lord for he comes,
he comes to rule the earth. R.

With justice he will rule the world,
he will judge the peoples with his truth. R.

R. **Today a saviour has been born to us;
he is Christ the Lord.**

SECOND READING

A reading from the letter of St Paul to Titus 2:11-14

God's grace has been revealed to the whole human race.

God's grace has been revealed, and it has made salvation possible for the whole human race and taught us that what we have to do is to give up everything that does not lead to God, and all our worldly ambitions; we must be self-restrained and live good and religious lives here in this present world, while we are waiting in hope for the blessing which will come with the Appearing of the glory of our great God and saviour Christ Jesus. He sacrificed himself for us in order to set us free from all wickedness and to purify a people so that it could be his very own and would have no ambition except to do good.

The word of the Lord.

Gospel Acclamation Lk 2:10-11

R. **Alleluia, alleluia!**
I bring you news of great joy:
today a saviour has been born to us, Christ the Lord.
R. **Alleluia!**

GOSPEL

A reading from the holy Gospel according to Luke 2:1-14

Today a saviour has been born to you.

Caesar Augustus issued a decree for a census of the whole world to be taken. This census – the first – took place while Quirinius was governor of Syria, and everyone went to his own town to be registered. So Joseph set out from the town of Nazareth in Galilee and travelled up to Judaea, to the town of David called Bethlehem, since he was of David's House and line, in order to be registered together with Mary, his betrothed, who was with child. While they were there the time came for her to have her child, and she gave birth to a son, her first-born. She wrapped him in swaddling clothes, and laid him in a manger because there was no room for them at the inn. In the countryside close by there were shepherds who lived in the fields and took it in turns to watch their flocks during the night. The angel of the Lord appeared to them and the glory of the Lord shone round them. They were terrified, but the angel said, 'Do not be afraid. Listen, I bring you news of great joy, a joy to be shared by the whole people. Today in the town of David a saviour has been born to you; he is Christ the Lord. And here is a sign for you: you will find a baby wrapped in swaddling clothes and lying in a manger.' And suddenly with the angel there was a great throng of the heavenly host, praising God and singing:

> 'Glory to God in the highest heaven,
> and peace to men who enjoy his favour'.

The Gospel of the Lord.

The Creed is said. All kneel at the words and by the Holy Spirit was incarnate.

Prayer over the Offerings	Super oblata
May the oblation of this day's feast be pleasing to you, O Lord, we pray, that through this most holy exchange we may be found in the likeness of Christ, in whom our nature is united to you. Who lives and reigns for ever and ever.	Grata tibi sit, Domine, quæsumus, hodiernæ festivitatis oblatio, ut, per hæc sacrosancta commercia, in illius inveniamur forma, in quo tecum est nostra substantia. Qui vivit et regnat in sæcula sæculorum.

Preface I, II or III of the Nativity of the Lord, pp.44-47.

Communion Antiphon Jn 1:14	Ant. ad communionem
The Word became flesh, and we have seen his glory.	Verbum caro factum est, et vidimus gloriam eius.

Prayer after Communion	Post communionem
Grant us, we pray, O Lord our God, that we, who are gladdened by participation in the feast of our Redeemer's Nativity,	Da nobis, quæsumus, Domine Deus noster, ut, qui nativitatem Redemptoris nostri frequentare gaudemus,

may through an honourable way
   of life become worthy of union
   with him.
Who lives and reigns
   for ever and ever.

dignis conversationibus
ad eius mereamur
   pervenire consortium.
Per Christum Dominum nostrum.

A formula of Solemn Blessing, pp.132-135, may be used.

At the Mass at Dawn

The shepherds, the simple souls, were the first to come to Jesus in the manger and to encounter the Redeemer of the world. The wise men from the East, representing those with social standing and fame, arrived much later. The shepherds lived nearby. They only needed to "come over", as we do when we go to visit our neighbours. The wise men, however, lived far away. They had to undertake a long and arduous journey in order to arrive in Bethlehem. And they needed guidance and direction. Today too there are simple and lowly souls who live very close to the Lord. They are, so to speak, his neighbours and they can easily go to see him. But most of us in the world today live far from Jesus Christ, the incarnate God who came to dwell amongst us. In all kinds of ways, God has to prod us and reach out to us again and again, so that we can manage to escape from the muddle of our thoughts and activities and discover the way that leads to him. But a path exists for all of us. The Lord provides everyone with tailor-made signals.

(Pope Benedict XVI)

Entrance Antiphon Cf. Is 9:1,5; Lk 1:33

TODAY a light will shine upon us,
   for the Lord is born for us;
and he will be called Wondrous God,
Prince of peace, Father of future ages:
and his reign will be without end.

Ant. ad introitum

LUX fulgebit hodie super nos,
   quia natus est nobis Dominus;
et vocabitur admirabilis, Deus,
   Princeps pacis,
Pater futuri sæculi:
   cuius regni non erit finis.

The Gloria in excelsis (Glory to God in the highest) is said.

Collect

Grant, we pray, almighty God,
that, as we are bathed in the new
   radiance of your incarnate Word,
the light of faith, which illumines
   our minds,

Collecta

Da, quæsumus, omnipotens Deus,
ut dum nova incarnati Verbi
   tui luce perfundimur,
hoc in nostro resplendeat opere,
quod per fidem fulget in mente.

may also shine through in our deeds.
Through our Lord Jesus Christ,
  your Son,
who lives and reigns with you
  in the unity of the Holy Spirit,
one God, for ever and ever.

Per Dominum nostrum Iesum
  Christum Filium tuum,
qui tecum vivit et regnat
  in unitate Spiritus Sancti,
Deus, per omnia sæcula sæculorum.

FIRST READING

A reading from the prophet Isaiah 62:11-12

Look, your saviour comes.

This the Lord proclaims
to the ends of the earth:

> Say to the daughter of Zion, 'Look,
> your saviour comes,
> the prize of his victory with him,
> his trophies before him.'
> They shall be called 'The Holy People',
> 'The Lord's Redeemed'.
> And you shall be called 'The-sought-after',
> 'City-not-forsaken'.

The word of the Lord.

Responsorial Psalm Ps 96:1,6,11-12

R. **This day new light will shine upon the earth:
the Lord is born for us.**

The Lord is king, let earth rejoice,
the many coastlands be glad.
The skies proclaim his justice;
all peoples see his glory. R.

Light shines forth for the just
and joy for the upright of heart.
Rejoice, you just, in the Lord;
give glory to his holy name. R.

SECOND READING

A reading from the letter of St Paul to Titus   3:4-7

It was for no reason except his own compassion that he saved us.

When the kindness and love of God our saviour for mankind were revealed, it was not because he was concerned with any righteous actions we might have done ourselves; it was for no reason except his own compassion that he saved us, by means of the cleansing water of rebirth and by renewing us with the Holy Spirit which he has so generously poured over us through Jesus Christ our saviour. He did this so that we should be justified by his grace, to become heirs looking forward to inheriting eternal life.

The word of the Lord.

Gospel Acclamation   Lk 2:14

R. **Alleluia, alleluia!**
Glory to God in the highest heaven,
and peace to men who enjoy his favour.

R. **Alleluia!**

GOSPEL

A reading from the holy Gospel according to Luke   2:15-20

The shepherds found Mary and Joseph and the baby.

Now when the angels had gone from them into heaven, the shepherds said to one another, 'Let us go to Bethlehem and see this thing that has happened which the Lord has made known to us.' So they hurried away and found Mary and Joseph, and the baby lying in the manger. When they saw the child they repeated what they had been told about him, and everyone who heard it was astonished at what the shepherds had to say. As for Mary, she treasured all these things and pondered them in her heart. And the shepherds went back glorifying and praising God for all they had heard and seen; it was exactly as they had been told.

The Gospel of the Lord.

The Creed is said. All kneel at the words *and by the Holy Spirit was incarnate*.

Prayer over the Offerings | Super oblata

May our offerings be worthy,
   we pray, O Lord,
of the mysteries of the Nativity
   this day,
	Munera nostra, quæsumus, Domine,
	nativitatis hodiernæ mysteriis
	   apta proveniant,

that, just as Christ was born a man
and also shone forth as God,
so these earthly gifts may confer
on us what is divine.
Through Christ our Lord.

ut sicut homo genitus idem
præfulsit et Deus,
sic nobis hæc terrena substantia
conferat quod divinum est.
Per Christum Dominum nostrum.

Preface I, II or III of the Nativity of the Lord, pp.44-47.

Communion Antiphon Cf. Zc 9:9
Rejoice, O Daughter Sion; lift up
praise, Daughter Jerusalem:
Behold, your King will come,
the Holy One and Saviour
of the world.

Ant. ad communionem
Exsulta, filia Sion, lauda,
filia Ierusalem:
ecce Rex tuus veniet sanctus
et salvator mundi.

Prayer after Communion
Grant us, Lord, as we honour
with joyful devotion
the Nativity of your Son,
that we may come to know
with fullness of faith
the hidden depths of this mystery
and to love them
ever more and more.
Through Christ our Lord.

Post communionem
Da nobis, Domine,
Filii tui nativitatem
læta devotione colentibus,
huius arcana mysterii
et plena fide cognoscere,
et pleniore caritatis ardore diligere.
Per Christum Dominum nostrum.

A formula of Solemn Blessing, pp.132-135 may be used.

At the Mass during the Day

Saint John, in his Gospel, went to the heart of the matter: "He came to his own home, and his own people received him not". This refers first and foremost to Bethlehem: the Son of David comes to his own city, but has to be born in a stable, because there is no room for him at the inn. Then it refers to Israel: the one who is sent comes among his own, but they do not want him. And truly, it refers to all mankind: he through whom the world was made, the primordial Creator-Word, enters into the world, but he is not listened to, he is not received. These words refer ultimately to us, to each individual and to society as a whole. Do we have time for our neighbour who is in need of a word from us, from me, or in need of my affection? Do we have time and space for God? Can he enter into our lives? Does he find room in us, or have we occupied all the available space in our thoughts, our actions, our lives for ourselves?

(Pope Benedict XVI)

Entrance Antiphon   Cf. Is 9:5

A CHILD is born for us,
  and a son is given to us;
his sceptre of power rests
  upon his shoulder,
and his name will be called
  Messenger of great counsel.

Ant. ad introitum

PUER natus est nobis,
  et filius datus est nobis,
cuius imperium super
  humerum eius,
et vocabitur nomen eius magni
  consilii Angelus.

The Gloria in excelsis (Glory to God in the highest) is said.

Collect

O God, who wonderfully created
  the dignity of human nature
and still more wonderfully
  restored it,
grant, we pray,
that we may share in the divinity
  of Christ,
who humbled himself to share
  in our humanity.
Who lives and reigns with you
  in the unity of the Holy Spirit,
one God, for ever and ever.

Collecta

Deus, qui humanæ
  substantiæ dignitatem
et mirabiliter condidisti,
  et mirabilius reformasti,
da, quæsumus, nobis eius
  divinitatis esse consortes,
qui humanitatis nostræ fieri
  dignatus est particeps.
Qui tecum vivit et regnat
  in unitate Spiritus Sancti,
Deus, per omnia sæcula sæculorum.

FIRST READING

A reading from the prophet Isaiah   52:7-10

All the ends of the earth shall see the salvation of our God.

How beautiful on the mountains,
are the feet of one who brings good news,
who heralds peace, brings happiness,
proclaims salvation,
and tells Zion,
'Your God is king!'
Listen! Your watchmen raise their voices,
they shout for joy together,
for they see the Lord face to face,
as he returns to Zion.
Break into shouts of joy together,
you ruins of Jerusalem;
for the Lord is consoling his people,

redeeming Jerusalem.
The Lord bares his holy arm
in the sight of all the nations,
and all the ends of the earth shall see
the salvation of our God.

The word of the Lord.

Responsorial Psalm

Ps 97:1-6. R. v.3

R. **All the ends of the earth have seen the salvation of our God.**

Sing a new song to the Lord
for he has worked wonders.
His right hand and his holy arm
have brought salvation. R.

The Lord has made known his salvation;
has shown his justice to the nations.
He has remembered his truth and love
for the house of Israel. R.

All the ends of the earth have seen
the salvation of our God.
Shout to the Lord all the earth,
ring out your joy. R.

Sing psalms to the Lord with the harp,
with the sound of music.
With trumpets and the sound of the horn
acclaim the King, the Lord. R.

SECOND READING

A reading from the letter to the Hebrews

1:1-6

God has spoken to us through his Son.

At various times in the past and in various different ways, God spoke to our ancestors through the prophets; but in our own time, the last days, he has spoken to us through his Son, the Son that he has appointed to inherit everything and through whom he made everything there is. He is the radiant light of God's glory and the perfect copy of his nature, sustaining the universe by his powerful command; and now that he has destroyed the defilement of sin, he has gone to take his place in heaven at the right hand of divine Majesty. So he is now as far above the angels as the title which he has inherited is higher than their own name.

God has never said to any angel: You are my Son, today I have become your father; or: I will be a father to him and he a son to me. Again, when he brings the First-born into the world, he says: Let all the angels of God worship him.

The word of the Lord.

Gospel Acclamation.

R. **Alleluia, alleluia!**
A hallowed day has dawned upon us.
Come, you nations, worship the Lord,
for today a great light has shone down upon the earth.

R. **Alleluia!**

GOSPEL

A reading from the holy Gospel according to John 1:1-18
The Word was made flesh, and lived among us.

[In the beginning was the Word:
the Word was with God
and the Word was God.
He was with God in the beginning.
Through him all things came to be,
not one thing had its being but through him.
All that came to be had life in him
and that life was the light of men,
a light that shines in the dark,
a light that darkness could not overpower.]

A man came, sent by God.
His name was John.
He came as a witness,
as a witness to speak for the light,
so that everyone might believe through him.
He was not the light,
only a witness to speak for the light.

[The Word was the true light
that enlightens all men;
and he was coming into the world.
He was in the world
that had its being through him,

and the world did not know him.
He came to his own domain
and his own people did not accept him.
But to all who did accept him
he gave power to become children of God,
to all who believe in the name of him
who was born not out of human stock
or urge of the flesh
or will of man
but of God himself.
The Word was made flesh,
he lived among us,
and we saw his glory,
the glory that is his as the only Son of the Father,
full of grace and truth.]

John appears as his witness. He proclaims:
'This is the one of whom I said:
He who comes after me
ranks before me
because he existed before me.'

Indeed, from his fullness we have, all of us, received –
yes, grace in return for grace,
since, though the Law was given through Moses,
grace and truth have come through Jesus Christ.
No one has ever seen God,
it is the only Son, who is nearest to the Father's heart,
who has made him known.

[The Gospel of the Lord.]

Shorter Form, verses 1-5, 9-14. Read between [ ]

The Creed is said. All kneel at the words and by the Holy Spirit was incarnate.

Prayer over the Offerings

Make acceptable, O Lord,
   our oblation on this solemn day,
when you manifested
   the reconciliation
that makes us wholly pleasing
   in your sight

Super oblata

Oblatio tibi sit, Domine,
   hodiernæ sollemnitatis accepta,
qua et nostræ reconciliationis
   processit perfecta placatio,

and inaugurated for us the fullness of divine worship.
Through Christ our Lord.

et divini cultus nobis est indita plenitudo.
Per Christum Dominum nostrum.

Preface I, II or III of the Nativity of the Lord, pp.44-47.

Communion Antiphon Cf. Ps 97:3

All the ends of the earth have seen the salvation of our God.

Ant. ad communionem

Viderunt omnes fines terræ salutare Dei nostri.

Prayer after Communion

Grant, O merciful God,
that, just as the Saviour of the world, born this day,
is the author of divine generation for us,
so he may be the giver even of immortality.
Who lives and reigns
for ever and ever.

Post communionem

Præsta, misericors Deus,
ut natus hodie Salvator mundi,
sicut divinæ nobis generationis est auctor,
ita et immortalitatis sit ipse largitor.
Qui vivit et regnat
in sæcula sæculorum.

A formula of Solemn Blessing, pp.132-135, may be used.

30 December

THE HOLY FAMILY OF JESUS, MARY AND JOSEPH

If we aspire to a deeper understanding of Jesus's life and mission, we must draw close to the mystery of the Holy Family of Nazareth to observe and listen. Today's liturgy offers us a providential opportunity to do so. For every believer, and especially for Christian families, the humble dwelling place in Nazareth is an authentic school of the Gospel. Here we admire, put into practice, the divine plan to make the family an intimate community of life and love; here we learn that every Christian family is called to be a small "domestic church" that must shine with the Gospel virtues. Recollection and prayer, mutual understanding and respect, personal discipline and community asceticism and a spirit of sacrifice, work and solidarity are typical features that make the family of Nazareth a model for every home.

(Blessed Pope John Paul II)

Feast

Entrance Antiphon   Lk 2:16

THE shepherds went in haste,
and found Mary and Joseph
and the Infant lying in a manger.

Ant. ad introitum

VENERUNT pastores festinantes,
et invenerunt Mariam
et Ioseph et Infantem positum
in præsepio.

The Gloria in excelsis (Glory to God in the highest) is said.

Collect

O God, who were pleased to give us
the shining example
of the Holy Family,
graciously grant that we may
imitate them
in practising the virtues of family life
and in the bonds of charity,
and so, in the joy of your house,
delight one day in eternal rewards.
Through our Lord Jesus Christ,
your Son,
who lives and reigns with you
in the unity of the Holy Spirit,
one God, for ever and ever.

Collecta

Deus, qui præclara nobis
sanctæ Familiæ
dignatus es exempla præbere,
concede propitius,
ut, domesticis virtutibus caritatisque
vinculis illam sectantes,
in lætitia domus tuæ præmiis
fruamur æternis.
Per Dominum nostrum Iesum
Christum Filium tuum,
qui tecum vivit et regnat
in unitate Spiritus Sancti,
Deus, per omnia sæcula sæculorum.

The readings for Year C are included in full below. The readings for Year A may also be used on this feast: Si 3:3-7,14-17; Ps 127:1-5; Col 3:12-21; Col 3:15,16.

FIRST READING

A reading from the first book of Samuel   1:20-22,24-28

Samuel is made over to the Lord for the whole of his life.

Hannah conceived and gave birth to a son, and called him Samuel 'since' she said 'I asked the Lord for him.'

When a year had gone by, the husband Elkanah went up again with all his family to offer the annual sacrifice to the Lord and to fulfil his vow. Hannah, however, did not go up, having said to her husband, 'Not before the child is weaned. Then I will bring him and present him before the Lord and he shall stay there for ever.'

When she had weaned him, she took him up with her together with a three-year old bull, an ephah of flour and a skin of wine, and she brought him to the temple of the Lord at Shiloh; and the child was with them. They slaughtered the bull and the child's mother came to Eli. She said, 'If you please, my lord. As you live, my lord, I am the woman who stood here beside you, praying to the Lord. This is the child I prayed for, and the Lord granted me what I asked him. Now I make him over to the Lord for the whole of his life. He is made over to the Lord.'

There she left him, for the Lord.

The word of the Lord.

Responsorial Psalm   Ps 83:2-3,5-6,9-10. R. v.5

R. **They are happy who dwell in your house, O Lord.**

How lovely is your dwelling place,
Lord, God of hosts.
My soul is longing and yearning,
is yearning for the courts of the Lord.
My heart and my soul ring out their joy
to God, the living God. R.

They are happy, who dwell in your house,
for ever singing your praise.
They are happy, whose strength is in you;
they walk with ever growing strength. R.

O Lord, God of hosts, hear my prayer,
give ear, O God of Jacob.
Turn your eyes, O God, our shield,
look on the face of your anointed. R.

SECOND READING

A reading from the first letter of St John   3:1-2,21-24

We are called God's children, and that is what we are.

Think of the love that the Father has lavished on us,
by letting us be called God's children;
and that is what we are.
Because the world refused to acknowledge him,
therefore it does not acknowledge us.

My dear people, we are already the children of God
but what we are to be in the future has not yet been revealed,
all we know is, that when it is revealed
we shall be like him
because we shall see him as he really is.

My dear people,
if we cannot be condemned by our own conscience,
we need not be afraid in God's presence,
and whatever we ask him,
we shall receive,
because we keep his commandments
and live the kind of life that he wants.
His commandments are these:
that we believe in the name of his Son Jesus Christ
and that we love one another
as he told us to.
Whoever keeps his commandments
lives in God and God lives in him.
We know that he lives in us
by the Spirit that he has given us.

The word of the Lord.

Gospel Acclamation

Cf. Ac 16:14

R. **Alleluia, alleluia!**
Open our heart, O Lord,
to accept the words of your Son.
R. **Alleluia!**

GOSPEL

A reading from the holy Gospel according to Luke

2:41-52

Jesus is found by his parents sitting among the doctors.

Every year the parents of Jesus used to go to Jerusalem for the feast of the Passover. When he was twelve years old, they went up for the feast as usual. When they were on their way home after the feast, the boy Jesus stayed behind in Jerusalem without his parents knowing it. They assumed he was with the caravan, and it was only after a day's journey that they went to look for him among their relations and acquaintances. When they failed to find him they went back to Jerusalem looking for him everywhere.

Three days later, they found him in the Temple, sitting among the doctors, listening to them, and asking them questions; and all those who heard him were astounded at his intelligence and his replies. They were overcome when they saw him, and his mother said to him, 'My child, why have you done this to us? See how worried your father and I have been, looking for you.' 'Why were you looking for me?' he replied. 'Did you not know that I must be busy with my Father's affairs?' But they did not understand what he meant.

He then went down with them and came to Nazareth and lived under their authority. His mother stored up all these things in her heart. And Jesus increased in wisdom, in stature, and in favour with God and men.

The Gospel of the Lord.

The Creed is said.

Prayer over the Offerings

We offer you, Lord,
   the sacrifice of conciliation,
humbly asking that,
through the intercession of the Virgin
   Mother of God and Saint Joseph,
you may establish our families firmly
   in your grace and your peace.
Through Christ our Lord.

Super oblata

Hostiam tibi placationis offerimus,
   Domine,
suppliciter deprecantes,
ut, Deiparæ Virginis beatique
   Ioseph interveniente suffragio,
familias nostras in tua gratia
   firmiter et pace constituas.
Per Christum Dominum nostrum.

Preface I, II or III of the Nativity of the Lord, pp.44-47.

Communion Antiphon   Ba 3:38

Our God has appeared on the earth,
   and lived among us.

Ant. ad communionem

Deus noster in terris visus est,
et cum hominibus conversatus est.

Prayer after Communion

Bring those you refresh
   with this heavenly Sacrament,
most merciful Father,
to imitate constantly the example
   of the Holy Family,
so that, after the trials of this world,
we may share their company for ever.
Through Christ our Lord.

Post communionem

Quos cælestibus reficis sacramentis,
fac, clementissime Pater,
sanctæ Familiæ exempla
   iugiter imitari,
ut, post ærumnas sæculi,
eius consortium
   consequamur æternum.
Per Christum Dominum nostrum.

1 January

SOLEMNITY OF MARY, THE HOLY MOTHER OF GOD

The Octave of Christmas ends on the first day of the new year, which is dedicated to the Blessed Virgin, venerated as the Mother of God. The Gospel reminds us that she "kept all these things, pondering them in her heart" (Lk 2:19). So she did in Bethlehem, on Golgotha at the foot of the cross, and on the day of Pentecost, when the Holy Spirit descended in the Upper Room. And so she does today too. The Mother of God and of human beings keeps in her heart all of humanity's problems, great and difficult, and meditates upon them. The Alma Redemptoris Mater walks with us and guides us with motherly tenderness towards the future. Thus she helps humanity cross all the "thresholds" of the years, the centuries, the millenniums, by sustaining their hope in the One who is the Lord of history.

(Blessed Pope John Paul II)

Entrance Antiphon

HAIL, Holy Mother,
 who gave birth to the King
who rules heaven and earth for ever.

Or: Cf. Is 9:1,5; Lk 1:33

Today a light will shine upon us,
 for the Lord is born for us;
and he will be called Wondrous God,
Prince of peace, Father of future ages:
and his reign will be without end.

Ant. ad introitum

SALVE, sancta Parens,
 enixa puerpera Regem,
qui cælum terramque regit
 in sæcula sæculorum.

Vel:

Lux fulgebit hodie super nos,
quia natus est nobis Dominus;
et vocabitur admirabilis, Deus,
 Princeps pacis,
Pater futuri sæculi:
 cuius regni non erit finis.

The Gloria in excelsis (Glory to God in the highest) is said.

Collect

O God, who through the fruitful
   virginity of Blessed Mary
bestowed on the human race
the grace of eternal salvation,
grant, we pray,
that we may experience
   the intercession of her,
through whom we were
   found worthy
to receive the author of life,
our Lord Jesus Christ, your Son.
Who lives and reigns with you
   in the unity of the Holy Spirit,
one God, for ever and ever.

Collecta

Deus, qui salutis æternæ,
beatæ Mariæ virginitate fecunda,
humano generi præmia præstitisti,
   tribue, quæsumus,
ut ipsam pro nobis
   intercedere sentiamus,
per quam meruimus
   auctorem vitæ suscipere,
Dominum nostrum Iesum
   Christum, Filium tuum.
Qui tecum vivit et regnat
   in unitate Spiritus Sancti,
Deus, per omnia sæcula sæculorum.

FIRST READING

A reading from the book of Numbers 6:22-27

They are to call down my name on the sons of Israel, and I will bless them.

The Lord spoke to Moses and said, 'Say this to Aaron and his sons: "This is how you are to bless the sons of Israel. You shall say to them:

   May the Lord bless you and keep you.
   May the Lord let his face shine on you and be gracious to you.
   May the Lord uncover his face to you and bring you peace."

This is how they are to call down my name on the sons of Israel, and I will bless them.'

   The word of the Lord.

Responsorial Psalm   Ps 66:2-3,5,6,8. R. v.2
R. O God, be gracious and bless us.

God, be gracious and bless us
and let your face shed its light upon us.
So will your ways be known upon earth
and all nations learn your saving help. R.

Let the nations be glad and exult
for you rule the world with justice.
With fairness you rule the peoples,
you guide the nations on earth. R.

Let the peoples praise you, O God;
let all the peoples praise you.
May God still give us his blessing
till the ends of the earth revere him. R.

SECOND READING

A reading from the letter of St Paul to the Galatians 4:4-7

God sent his Son, born of a woman.

When the appointed time came, God sent his Son, born of a woman, born a subject of the Law, to redeem the subjects of the Law and to enable us to be adopted as sons. The proof that you are sons is that God has sent the Spirit of his Son into our hearts: the Spirit that cries, 'Abba, Father', and it is this that makes you a son, you are not a slave any more; and if God has made you son, then he has made you heir.

The word of the Lord.

Gospel Acclamation Heb 1:1-2

R. **Alleluia, alleluia!**

At various times in the past
and in various different ways,
God spoke to our ancestors through the prophets;
but in our own time, the last days,
he has spoken to us through his Son.

R. **Alleluia!**

GOSPEL

A reading from the holy Gospel according to Luke 2:16-21

They found Mary and Joseph and the baby ... When the eighth day came, they gave him the name Jesus.

The shepherds hurried away to Bethlehem and found Mary and Joseph, and the baby lying in the manger. When they saw the child they repeated what they had been told about him, and everyone who heard it was astonished at what the shepherds had to say. As for Mary, she treasured all these things and pondered them in her heart. And the shepherds went back glorifying and praising God for all they had heard and seen; it was exactly as they had been told.

When the eighth day came and the child was to be circumcised, they gave him the name Jesus, the name the angel had given him before his conception.

The Gospel of the Lord.

The Creed is said.

Prayer over the Offerings

O God, who in your kindness begin
    all good things
and bring them to fulfilment,
grant to us, who find joy
    in the Solemnity of the holy
    Mother of God,
that, just as we glory in the
    beginnings of your grace,
so one day we may rejoice
    in its completion.
Through Christ our Lord.

Super oblata

Deus, qui bona cuncta inchoas
    benignus et perficis,
da nobis, de sollemnitate sanctæ
    Dei Genetricis lætantibus,
sicut de initiis tuæ gratiæ gloriamur,
ita de perfectione gaudere.
Per Christum Dominum nostrum.

Preface: The Motherhood of the Blessed Virgin Mary.

It is truly right and just,
    our duty and our salvation,
always and everywhere to give
    you thanks,
Lord, holy Father,
    almighty and eternal God,
and to praise, bless,
    and glorify your name
on the Solemnity of the Motherhood
of the Blessed ever-Virgin Mary.

For by the overshadowing
    of the Holy Spirit
she conceived your
    Only Begotten Son,
and without losing the glory
    of virginity,
brought forth into the world
    the eternal Light,
Jesus Christ our Lord.

Præfatio: De Maternitate beatæ Mariæ Virginis.

Vere dignum et iustum est,
    æquum et salutare,
nos tibi semper
    et ubique gratias agere:
Domine, sancte Pater,
    omnipotens æterne Deus:

Et te in Maternitate
beatæ Mariæ semper Virginis
    collaudare,
benedicere et prædicare.

Quæ et Unigenitum tuum Sancti
    Spiritus obumbratione concepit,
et, virginitatis gloria permanente,
lumen æternum mundo effudit,
Iesum Christum Dominum nostrum.

Through him the Angels praise
   your majesty,
Dominions adore and Powers
   tremble before you.
Heaven and the Virtues of heaven
   and the blessed Seraphim
worship together with exultation.
May our voices, we pray,
   join with theirs
in humble praise, as we acclaim:

Holy, Holy, Holy Lord God of hosts...

Communion Antiphon   Heb 13:8

Jesus Christ is the same yesterday,
   today, and for ever.

Prayer after Communion

We have received this heavenly
   Sacrament with joy, O Lord:
grant, we pray,
that it may lead us to eternal life,
for we rejoice to proclaim
   the blessed ever-Virgin Mary
Mother of your Son
   and Mother of the Church.
Through Christ our Lord.

Per quem maiestatem
   laudant Angeli,
adorant Dominationes,
   tremunt Potestates.
Cæli cælorumque Virtutes,
   ac beata Seraphim,
socia exsultatione concelebrant.
Cum quibus et nostras voces ut
   admitti iubeas, deprecamur,
supplici confessione dicentes:

Sanctus, Sanctus, Sanctus...

Ant. ad communionem

Iesus Christus heri et hodie,
   ipse et in sæcula.

Post communionem

Sumpsimus, Domine,
   læti sacramenta cælestia:
præsta, quæsumus,
ut ad vitam nobis
   proficiant sempiternam,
qui beatam semper Virginem Mariam
Filii tui Genetricem
   et Ecclesiæ Matrem
profiteri gloriamur.
Per Christum Dominum nostrum.

A formula of Solemn Blessing, pp.132-135, may be used.

6 January

THE EPIPHANY OF THE LORD

Men and women of every generation need on their pilgrim journey to be directed: what star can we therefore follow? After coming to rest "over the place where the child was", the purpose of the star that guided the Magi ended, but its spiritual light is always present in the Word of the Gospel, which is still able today to guide every person to Jesus. This same Word, which is none other than the reflection of Christ, true man and true God, is authoritatively echoed by the Church for every well-disposed heart. The Church too, therefore, carries out the mission of the star for humanity. But something of the sort could be said of each Christian, called to illuminate the path of the brethren by word and example of life.

(Pope Benedict XVI)

Solemnity

At the Vigil Mass

This Mass is used on the evening of the day before the Solemnity, either before or after First Vespers (Evening Prayer I) of the Epiphany.

Entrance Antiphon Cf. Ba 5:5	Ant. ad introitum

ARISE, Jerusalem,
    and look to the East
and see your children gathered from
    the rising to the setting of the sun.
	SURGE, Ierusalem,
	    et circumspice ad orientem
	et vide congregatos filios tuos
	a solis ortu usque ad occasum.

The Gloria in excelsis (Glory to God in the highest) is said.

Collect	Collecta

May the splendour of your majesty,
    O Lord, we pray,
shed its light upon our hearts,
that we may pass through
    the shadows of this world
and reach the brightness
    of our eternal home.
	Corda nostra, quæsumus, Domine,
	tuæ maiestatis splendor illustret,
	quo per mundi huius tenebras
	    transire valeamus,
	et perveniamus ad patriam

Through our Lord Jesus Christ, your Son, who lives and reigns with you in the unity of the Holy Spirit, one God, for ever and ever. claritatis æternæ.	Per Dominum nostrum Iesum Christum Filium tuum, qui tecum vivit et regnat in unitate Spiritus Sancti, Deus, per omnia sæcula sæculorum.

FIRST READING

A reading from the prophet Isaiah 60:1-6

Above you the glory of the Lord appears.

Arise, shine out Jerusalem, for your light has come,
the glory of the Lord is rising on you,
though night still covers the earth
and darkness the peoples.

Above you the Lord now rises
and above you his glory appears.
The nations come to your light
and kings to your dawning brightness.

Lift up your eyes and look around:
all are assembling and coming towards you,
your sons from far away
and daughters being tenderly carried.

At this sight you will glow radiant,
your heart throbbing and full;
since the riches of the sea will flow to you;
the wealth of the nations come to you;

camels in throngs will cover you,
and dromedaries of Midian and Ephah;
everyone in Sheba will come,
bringing gold and incense
and singing the praise of the Lord.

The word of the Lord.

Responsial Psalm Ps 71:1-2,7-8,10-13. R. Cf. v.11

R. **All nations shall fall prostrate before you, O Lord.**

O God, give your judgement to the king,
to a king's son your justice,
that he may judge your people in justice
and your poor in right judgement. R.

In his days justice shall flourish
and peace till the moon fails.
He shall rule from sea to sea,
from the Great River to earth's bounds. R.

The Kings of Tarshish and the sea coasts
shall pay him tribute.
The kings of Sheba and Seba
shall bring him gifts.
Before him all kings shall fall prostrate,
all nations shall serve him. R.

For he shall save the poor when they cry
and the needy who are helpless.
He will have pity on the weak
and save the lives of the poor. R.

SECOND READING

A reading from the letter of St Paul to the Ephesians 3:2-3,5-6

It has now been revealed that pagans share the same inheritance.

You have probably heard how I have been entrusted by God with the grace he meant for you, and that it was by a revelation that I was given the knowledge of the mystery. This mystery that has now been revealed through the Spirit to his holy apostles and prophets was unknown to any men in past generations; it means that pagans now share the same inheritance, that they are parts of the same body, and that the same promise has been made to them, in Christ Jesus, through the gospel.

The word of the Lord.

Gospel Acclamation Mt 2:2

R. **Alleluia, alleluia!**
We saw his star as it rose
and have come to do the Lord homage.
R. **Alleluia!**

GOSPEL

A reading from the holy Gospel according to Matthew 2:1-12

We saw his star and have come to do the king homage.

After Jesus had been born at Bethlehem in Judaea during the reign of King Herod, some wise men came to Jerusalem from the east. 'Where is the infant king of the Jews?' they asked. 'We saw his star as it rose and have come to do him homage.' When King Herod heard this he was perturbed, and so was the whole of Jerusalem. He called together all the chief priests and the scribes of the people, and enquired of them where the Christ was to be born. 'At Bethlehem in Judaea,' they told him 'for this is what the prophet wrote:

And you, Bethlehem, in the land of Judah
you are by no means least among the leaders of Judah,
for out of you will come a leader
who will shepherd my people Israel.'

Then Herod summoned the wise men to see him privately. He asked them the exact date on which the star had appeared, and sent them on to Bethlehem. 'Go and find out all about the child,' he said 'and when you have found him, let me know, so that I too may go and do him homage.' Having listened to what the king had to say, they set out. And there in front of them was the star they had seen rising; it went forward and halted over the place where the child was. The sight of the star filled them with delight, and going into the house they saw the child with his mother Mary, and falling to their knees they did him homage. Then, opening their treasures, they offered him gifts of gold and frankincense and myrrh. But they were warned in a dream not to go back to Herod, and returned to their own country by a different way.

The Gospel of the Lord.

The Creed is said.

Prayer over the Offerings | Super oblata

Accept we pray, O Lord, our offerings, in honour of the appearing
of your Only Begotten Son
and the first fruits of the nations,
that to you praise may be rendered
and eternal salvation be ours.
Through Christ our Lord.

Suscipe, quæsumus, Domine, munera nostra
pro apparitione Unigeniti Filii tui
et primitiis gentium dicata,
ut et tibi celebretur laudatio
et nobis fiat æterna salvatio.
Per Christum Dominum nostrum.

Preface of the Epiphany of the Lord, pp.48-49.

Communion Antiphon Cf. Rv 21:23

The brightness of God illumined
　the holy city Jerusalem,
and the nations will walk by its light.

Ant. ad communionem

Claritas Dei illuminavit civitatem
　sanctam Ierusalem
et ambulabant gentes in lumine eius.

Prayer after Communion

Renewed by sacred nourishment,
we implore your mercy, O Lord,
that the star of your justice
may shine always bright in our minds
and that our true treasure may ever
　consist in our confession of you.
Through Christ our Lord.

Post communionem

Sacra alimonia renovati,
tuam, Domine,
　misericordiam deprecamur,
ut semper in mentibus nostris
　tuæ appareat stella iustitiæ
et noster in tua sit
　confessione thesaurus.
Per Christum Dominum nostrum.

A formula of Solemn Blessing, pp.134-137, may be used.

At the Mass during the Day

Entrance Antiphon Cf.Ml 3:1;1Ch 29:12

BEHOLD, the Lord,
　the Mighty One, has come;
and kingship is in his grasp,
　and power and dominion.

Ant. ad introitum

ECCE advenit
　Dominator Dominus;
et regnum in manu eius
　et potestas et imperium.

The Gloria in excelsis (Glory to God in the highest) is said.

Collect

O God, who on this day
revealed your Only Begotten Son
　to the nations
by the guidance of a star,
grant in your mercy
that we, who know you already
　by faith,
may be brought to behold
　the beauty of your sublime glory.
Through our Lord Jesus Christ,
　your Son,
who lives and reigns with you
　in the unity of the Holy Spirit,
one God, for ever and ever.

Collecta

Deus, qui hodierna die
　Unigenitum tuum
gentibus stella duce revelasti,
concede propitius, ut qui iam
　te ex fide cognovimus,
usque ad contemplandam speciem
　tuæ celsitudinis perducamur.
Per Dominum nostrum Iesum
　Christum Filium tuum,
qui tecum vivit et regnat
　in unitate Spiritus Sancti,
Deus, per omnia sæcula sæculorum.

FIRST READING

A reading from the prophet Isaiah   60:1-6

Above you the glory of the Lord appears.

Arise, shine out Jerusalem, for your light has come,
the glory of the Lord is rising on you,
though night still covers the earth
and darkness the peoples.
Above you the Lord now rises
and above you his glory appears.
The nations come to your light
and kings to your dawning brightness.

Lift up your eyes and look around:
all are assembling and coming towards you,
your sons from far away
and daughters being tenderly carried.

At this sight you will glow radiant,
your heart throbbing and full;
since the riches of the sea will flow to you;
the wealth of the nations come to you;

camels in throngs will cover you,
and dromedaries of Midian and Ephah;
everyone in Sheba will come,
bringing gold and incense
and singing the praise of the Lord.

The word of the Lord.

Responsorial Psalm   Ps 71:1-2,7-8,10-13. R. Cf. v.11

R. **All nations shall fall prostrate before you, O Lord.**

O God, give your judgement to the king,
to a king's son your justice,
that he may judge your people in justice
and your poor in right judgement. R.

In his days justice shall flourish
and peace till the moon fails.
He shall rule from sea to sea,
from the Great River to earth's bounds. R.

The Kings of Tarshish and the sea coasts
shall pay him tribute.
The kings of Sheba and Seba
shall bring him gifts.
Before him all kings shall fall prostrate,
all nations shall serve him. R.

For he shall save the poor when they cry
and the needy who are helpless.
He will have pity on the weak
and save the lives of the poor. R.

R. **All nations shall fall prostrate before you, O Lord.**

SECOND READING

A reading from the letter of St Paul to the Ephesians   3:2-3,5-6
It has now been revealed that pagans share the same inheritance.

You have probably heard how I have been entrusted by God with the grace he meant for you, and that it was by a revelation that I was given the knowledge of the mystery. This mystery that has now been revealed through the Spirit to his holy apostles and prophets was unknown to any men in past generations; it means that pagans now share the same inheritance, that they are parts of the same body, and that the same promise has been made to them, in Christ Jesus, through the gospel.

The word of the Lord.

Gospel Acclamation   Mt 2:2

R. **Alleluia, alleluia!**
We saw his star as it rose
and have come to do the Lord homage.
R. **Alleluia!**

GOSPEL

A reading from the holy Gospel according to Matthew   2:1-12
We saw his star and have come to do the king homage.

After Jesus had been born at Bethlehem in Judaea during the reign of King Herod, some wise men came to Jerusalem from the east. 'Where is the infant king of the Jews?' they asked. 'We saw his star as it rose and have come to do him homage.' When King Herod heard this he was perturbed, and so was the whole of Jerusalem. He called together all the chief priests and the scribes of the people, and enquired of them where the Christ was to be born. 'At Bethlehem in Judaea,' they told him 'for this is what the prophet wrote:

> And you, Bethlehem, in the land of Judah
> you are by no means least among the leaders of Judah,
> for out of you will come a leader
> who will shepherd my people Israel.'

Then Herod summoned the wise men to see him privately. He asked them the exact date on which the star had appeared, and sent them on to Bethlehem. 'Go and find out all about the child,' he said 'and when you have found him, let me know, so that I too may go and do him homage.' Having listened to what the king had to say, they set out. And there in front of them was the star they had seen rising; it went forward and halted over the place where the child was. The sight of the star filled them with delight, and going into the house they saw the child with his mother Mary, and falling to their knees they did him homage. Then, opening their treasures, they offered him gifts of gold and frankincense and myrrh. But they were warned in a dream not to go back to Herod, and returned to their own country by a different way.

The Gospel of the Lord.

The Creed is said.

Prayer over the Offerings

Look with favour, Lord, we pray,
on these gifts of your Church,
in which are offered now not gold
   or frankincense or myrrh,
but he who by them is proclaimed,
sacrificed and received, Jesus Christ.
Who lives and reigns
   for ever and ever.

Super oblata

Ecclesiæ tuæ, quæsumus, Domine,
   dona propitius intuere,
quibus non iam aurum,
   thus et myrrha profertur,
sed quod eisdem muneribus
declaratur, immolatur et sumitur,
   Iesus Christus.
Qui vivit et regnat
   in sæcula sæculorum.

Preface of the Epiphany of the Lord, pp.48-49.

Communion Antiphon Cf. Mt 2:2

We have seen his star in the East,
and have come with gifts to adore
the Lord.

Ant. ad communionem

Vidimus stellam eius in Oriente,
et venimus cum muneribus
adorare Dominum.

Prayer after Communion

Go before us with heavenly light,
O Lord,
always and everywhere,
that we may perceive with clear sight
and revere with true affection
the mystery in which you have
willed us to participate.
Through Christ our Lord.

Post communionem

Cælesti lumine, quæsumus,
Domine,
semper et ubique nos præveni,
ut mysterium, cuius nos participes
esse voluisti,
et puro cernamus intuitu,
et digno percipiamus affectu.
Per Christum Dominum nostrum.

A formula of Solemn Blessing, pp. 134-137, may be used.

13 January

THE BAPTISM OF THE LORD

Feast

Entrance Antiphon Cf. Mt 3:16-17

AFTER the Lord was baptised,
the heavens were opened,
and the Spirit descended upon him
like a dove,
and the voice of the
Father thundered:
This is my beloved Son,
with whom I am well pleased.

Ant. ad introitum

BAPTIZATO Domino,
aperti sunt cæli,
et sicut columba super eum
Spiritus mansit,
et vox Patris intonuit:
Hic est Filius meus dilectus,
in quo mihi bene complacui.

The Gloria in excelsis (Glory to God in the highest) is said.

Collect

Almighty ever-living God,
who, when Christ had been
  baptised in the River Jordan
and as the Holy Spirit descended
  upon him,
solemnly declared him your
  beloved Son,
grant that your children
  by adoption,
reborn of water and the Holy Spirit,
may always be well pleasing to you.
Through our Lord Jesus Christ,
  your Son,
who lives and reigns with you in
  the unity of the Holy Spirit,
one God, for ever and ever.

Or:

O God, whose Only Begotten Son
has appeared in our very flesh,
grant, we pray, that we may be
  inwardly transformed
through him whom we recognise
  as outwardly like ourselves.
Who lives and reigns with you in
  the unity of the Holy Spirit,
one God, for ever and ever.

Collecta

Omnipotens sempiterne Deus,
qui Christum, in Iordane
  flumine baptizatum,
Spiritu Sancto super eum
  descendente,
dilectum Filium tuum
  sollemniter declarasti,
concede filiis adoptionis tuæ,
ex aqua et Spiritu Sancto renatis,
ut in beneplacito tuo
  iugiter perseverent.
Per Dominum nostrum
  Iesum Christum Filium tuum,
qui tecum vivit et regnat
  in unitate Spiritus Sancti,
Deus, per omnia sæcula sæculorum.

Vel:

Deus, cuius Unigenitus in
  substantia nostræ carnis apparuit,
præsta, quæsumus,
ut per eum, quem similem nobis
  foris agnovimus,
intus reformari mereamur.
Qui tecum vivit et regnat
  in unitate Spiritus Sancti,
Deus, per omnia sæcula sæculorum.

The readings for Year C are included in full below. The readings for Year A may also be used on this feast: Is 42:1-4,6-7; Ps 28:1-4,9-10; Ac 10:34-38; Cf. Mk 9:7.

FIRST READING

A reading from the prophet Isaiah   40:1-5.9-11
The glory of the Lord shall be revealed and all mankind shall see it.

'Console my people, console them'
says your God.
'Speak to the heart of Jerusalem
and call to her
that her time of service is ended,
that her sin is atoned for,

that she has received from the hand of the Lord
double punishment for all her crimes.'

A voice cries, 'prepare in the wilderness
a way for the Lord.
Make a straight highway for our God
across the desert.
Let every valley be filled in,
every mountain and hill be laid low,
let every cliff become a plain,
and the ridges a valley;
then the glory of the Lord shall be revealed
and all mankind shall see it;
for the mouth of the Lord has spoken.'

Go up on a high mountain,
joyful messenger to Zion.
Shout with a loud voice,
joyful messenger to Jerusalem.
Shout without fear,
say to the towns of Judah,
'Here is your God.'

Here is the Lord coming with power,
his arm subduing all things to him.
The prize of his victory is with him,
his trophies all go before him.
He is like a shepherd feeding his flock,
gathering lambs in his arms,
holding them against his breast
and leading to their rest the mother ewes.

The word of the Lord.

Responsorial Psalm

Ps 103:1-2,3-4,24-25,27-30. R. v.1

R. Bless the Lord, my soul!
Lord God, how great you are.

Lord God, how great you are,
clothed in majesty and glory,
wrapped in light as in a robe!
You stretch out the heavens like a tent. R.

Above the rains you build your dwelling.
You make the clouds your chariot,
you walk on the wings of the wind,
you make the winds your messengers
and flashing fire your servants. R.

How many are your works, O Lord!
In wisdom you have made them all.
The earth is full of your riches.
There is the sea, vast and wide,
with its moving swarms past counting
living things great and small. R.

All of these look to you
to give them their food in due season.
You give it, they gather it up:
you open your hand, they have their fill. R.

You take back your spirit, they die,
returning to the dust from which they came.
You send forth your spirit, they are created;
and you renew the face of the earth. R.

SECOND READING

A reading from the letter of St Paul to Titus 2:11-14, 3:4-7

He saved us by the cleansing water of rebirth and by renewing us with the Holy Spirit.

God's grace has been revealed, and it has made salvation possible for the whole human race and taught us that what we have to do is to give up everything that does not lead to God, and all our worldly ambitions; we must be self-restrained and live good and religious lives here in this present world, while we are waiting in hope for the blessing which will come with the Appearing of the glory of our great God and saviour Christ Jesus. He sacrificed himself for us in order to set us free from all wickedness and to purify a people so that it could be his very own and would have no ambition except to do good.

When the kindness and love of God our saviour for mankind were revealed, it was not because he was concerned with any righteous actions we might have done ourselves; it was for no reason except his own compassion that he saved us, by means of the cleansing water of rebirth and by renewing us with the Holy Spirit which he has so generously poured over us through Jesus Christ our saviour. He did this so that we should be justified by his grace, to become heirs looking forward to inheriting eternal life.

The word of the Lord.

Gospel Acclamation

Cf. Lk 3:13

R. **Alleluia, alleluia!**
Someone is coming, said John, someone greater than I.
He will baptise you with the Holy Spirit and with fire.
R. **Alleluia!**

GOSPEL

A reading from the holy Gospel according to Luke 3:15-16,21-22
While Jesus after his own baptism was at prayer, heaven opened.

A feeling of expectancy had grown among the people, who were beginning to think that John might be the Christ, so John declared before them all, 'I baptise you with water, but someone is coming, someone who is more powerful than I am and I am not fit to undo the strap of his sandals; he will baptise you with the Holy Spirit and fire.'

Now when all the people had been baptised and while Jesus after his own baptism was at prayer, heaven opened and the Holy Spirit descended on him in bodily shape, like a dove. And a voice came from heaven, 'You are my Son, the Beloved; my favour rests on you.'

The Gospel of the Lord.
The Creed is said.

Prayer over the Offerings

Accept, O Lord, the offerings
we have brought to honour the
  revealing of your beloved Son,
so that the oblation of your faithful
may be transformed into the
  sacrifice of him
who willed in his compassion
to wash away the sins of the world.
Who lives and reigns
  for ever and ever.

Super oblata

Suscipe munera, Domine,
in dilecti Filii tui revelatione delata,
ut fidelium tuorum oblatio
  in eius sacrificium transeat,
qui mundi voluit peccata
  miseratus abluere.
Qui vivit et regnat
  in sæcula sæculorum.

13 JANUARY

Preface: The Baptism of the lord.

It is truly right and just, our duty and our salvation,
always and everywhere
to give you thanks,
Lord, holy Father,
almighty and eternal God.

For in the waters of the Jordan
you revealed with signs
and wonders a new Baptism,
so that through the voice
that came down from heaven
we might come to believe in your
Word dwelling among us,
and by the Spirit's descending
in the likeness of a dove
we might know that Christ
your Servant
has been anointed with the oil
of gladness
and sent to bring the good news
to the poor.

And so, with the Powers of heaven,
we worship you constantly on earth,
and before your majesty
without end we acclaim:
Holy, Holy, Holy Lord God of hosts...

Communion Antiphon Jn 1:32,34

Behold the One of whom
John said:
I have seen and testified that this is
the Son of God.

Præfatio: de Baptismate domini.

Vere dignum et iustum est,
æquum et salutare,
nos tibi semper et ubique
gratias agere:
Domine, sancte Pater,
omnipotens æterne deus:

Qui miris signasti mysteriis novum
in Iordane lavacrum,
ut, per vocem de cælo delapsam,
habitare Verbum tuum inter
homines crederetur;

et, per Spiritum in columbæ
specie descendentem,
Christus Servus tuus oleo
perungi lætitiæ
ac mitti ad evangelizandum
pauperibus nosceretur.

Et ideo cum cælorum virtutibus
in terris te iugiter celebramus,
maiestati tuæ sine fine clamantes:

Sanctus, Sanctus, Sanctus. . .

Ant. ad communionem

Ecce de quo dicebat Ioannes:
Ego vidi et testimonium perhibui,
quia hic est Filius Dei.

Prayer after Communion

Nourished with these sacred gifts,
we humbly entreat your mercy,
    O Lord,
that, faithfully listening to your
    Only Begotten Son,
we may be your children
    in name and in truth.
Through Christ our Lord.

Post communionem

Sacro munere satiati,
clementiam tuam, Domine,
    suppliciter exoramus,
ut, Unigenitum tuum
    fideliter audientes,
filii tui vere nominemur et simus.
Per Christum Dominum nostrum.

20 January

SECOND SUNDAY IN ORDINARY TIME

Entrance Antiphon — Ps 65:4

ALL the earth shall bow down
before you, O God,
and shall sing to you,
shall sing to your name,
    O Most High!

Ant. ad introitum

OMNIS terra adoret te, Deus,
et psallat tibi;
psalmum dicat nomini tuo,
    Altissime.

Collect

Almighty ever-living God,
who govern all things,
both in heaven and on earth,
mercifully hear the pleading
    of your people
and bestow your peace on
    our times.
Through our Lord Jesus Christ,
    your Son,
who lives and reigns with you
    in the unity of the Holy Spirit,
one God, for ever and ever.

Collecta

Omnipotens sempiterne Deus,
qui cælestia simul
    et terrena moderaris,
supplicationes populi tui
    clementer exaudi,
et pacem tuam nostris
    concede temporibus.
Per Dominum nostrum Iesum
    Christum Filium tuum,
qui tecum vivit et regnat
    in unitate Spiritus Sancti,
Deus, per omnia sæcula sæculorum.

FIRST READING

A reading from the prophet Isaiah

62:1-5

The bridegroom rejoices in his bride.

About Zion I will not be silent,
about Jerusalem I will not grow weary,
until her integrity shines out like the dawn
and her salvation flames like a torch.
The nations then will see your integrity,
all the kings your glory,
and you will be called by a new name,
one which the mouth of the Lord will confer.
You are to be a crown of splendour in the hand of the Lord,
a princely diadem in the hand of your God;
no longer are you to be named 'Forsaken',
nor your land 'Abandoned',
but you shall be called 'My Delight'
and your land 'The Wedded';
for the Lord takes delight in you
and your land will have its wedding.
Like a young man marrying a virgin,
so will the one who built you wed you,
and as the bridegroom rejoices in his bride,
so will your God rejoice in you.

The word of the Lord.

Responsional Psalm

Ps 95:1-3,7-10. R. v.3

R. **Proclaim the wonders of the Lord**
among all the peoples.

O sing a new song to the Lord,
sing to the Lord all the earth.
O sing to the Lord, bless his name. R.

Proclaim his help day by day,
tell among the nations his glory
and his wonders among all the peoples. R.

Give the Lord, you families of peoples,
give the Lord glory and power,
give the Lord the glory of his name. R.

Worship the Lord in his temple.
O earth, tremble before him.
Proclaim to the nations: 'God is king.'
He will judge the peoples in fairness. R.

R. **Proclaim the wonders of the Lord among all the peoples.**

SECOND READING

A reading from the first letter of St Paul to the Corinthians   12:4-11

One and the same Spirit, who distributes gifts to different people just as he chooses.

There is a variety of gifts but always the same Spirit; there are all sorts of service to be done, but always to the same Lord; working in all sorts of different ways in different people, it is the same God who is working in all of them. The particular way in which the Spirit is given to each person is for a good purpose. One may have the gift of preaching with wisdom given him by the Spirit; another may have the gift of preaching instruction given him by the same Spirit; and another the gift of faith given by the same Spirit; another again the gift of healing, through this one Spirit; one, the power of miracles; another, prophecy; another the gift of recognising spirits, another the gift of tongues and another the ability to interpret them. All these are the work of one and the same Spirit, who distributes different gifts to different people just as he chooses.

The word of the Lord.

Gospel Acclamation   Cf. Jn 6:63,68

R. **Alleluia, alleluia!**
Your words are spirit, Lord,
and they are life:
you have the message of eternal life.
R. **Alleluia!**

Or: Cf. 2 Th 2:14

R. **Alleluia, alleluia!**
Through the Good News God called us
to share the glory of our Lord Jesus Christ.
R. **Alleluia!**

GOSPEL

A reading from the holy Gospel according to John 2:1-11

This was the first of the signs given by Jesus: it was given at Cana in Galilee.

There was a wedding at Cana in Galilee. The mother of Jesus was there, and Jesus and his disciples had also been invited. When they ran out of wine, since the wine provided for the wedding was all finished, the mother of Jesus said to him, 'They have no wine.' Jesus said, 'Woman why turn to me? My hour has not come yet.' His mother said to the servants, 'Do whatever he tells you.' There were six stone water jars standing there, meant for the ablutions that are customary among the Jews; each could hold twenty or thirty gallons. Jesus said to the servants, 'Fill the jars with water,' and they filled them to the brim. 'Draw some out now' he told them 'and take it to the steward.' They did this; the steward tasted the water, and it had turned into wine. Having no idea where it came from – only the servants who had drawn the water knew – the steward called the bridegroom and said, 'People generally serve the best wine first, and keep the cheaper sort till the guests have plenty to drink; but you have kept the best wine till now.'

This was the first of the signs given by Jesus: it was given at Cana in Galilee. He let his glory be seen, and his disciples believed in him.

The Gospel of the Lord.

Prayer over the Offerings

Grant us, O Lord, we pray,
that we may participate worthily
   in these mysteries,
for whenever the memorial
   of this sacrifice is celebrated
the work of our redemption
   is accomplished.
Through Christ our Lord.

Super oblata

Concede nobis,
   quæsumus, Domine,
hæc digne frequentare mysteria,
quia, quoties huius hostiæ
   commemoratio celebratur,
opus nostræ redemptionis exercetur.
Per Christum Dominum nostrum.

Preface of Sundays in Ordinary Time I-VIII, pp.60-67.

Communion Antiphon Cf. Ps 22:5

You have prepared a table before me,
and how precious is the chalice
   that quenches my thirst.

Ant. ad communionem

Parasti in conspectu meo mensam,
et calix meus inebrians quam
   præclarus est!

Or: 1 Jn 4:16

We have come to know
   and to believe
in the love that God has for us.

Prayer after Communion

Pour on us, O Lord,
   the Spirit of your love,
and in your kindness
make those you have nourished
by this one heavenly Bread
one in mind and heart.
Through Christ our Lord.

Vel:

Nos cognovimus
   et credidimus caritati,
quam Deus habet in nobis.

Post communionem

Spiritum nobis, Domine,
   tuæ caritatis infunde,
ut, quos uno cælesti pane satiasti,
una facias pietate concordes.
Per Christum Dominum nostrum.

---

27 January

THIRD SUNDAY IN ORDINARY TIME

Entrance Antiphon   Cf. Ps 95:1,6

O SING a new song to the Lord;
   sing to the Lord, all the earth.
In his presence are majesty
   and splendour,
strength and honour
   in his holy place.

Collect

Almighty ever-living God,
direct our actions according
   to your good pleasure,
that in the name of your beloved Son
we may abound in good works.
Through our Lord Jesus Christ,
   your Son,
who lives and reigns with you
   in the unity of the Holy Spirit,
one God, for ever and ever.

Ant. ad introitum

CANTATE Domino
   canticum novum,
cantate Domino, omnis terra.
Confessio et pulchritudo
   in conspectu eius,
sanctitas et magnificentia
   in sanctificatione eius.

Collecta

Omnipotens sempiterne Deus,
dirige actus nostros
   in beneplacito tuo,
ut in nomine dilecti Filii tui
mereamur bonis operibus abundare.
Per Dominum nostrum Iesum
   Christum Filium tuum,
qui tecum vivit et regnat
   in unitate Spiritus Sancti,
Deus, per omnia sæcula sæculorum.

FIRST READING

A reading from the book of Nehemiah 8:2-6,8-10

Ezra read from the law of God and the people understood what was read.

Ezra the priest brought the Law before the assembly, consisting of men, women, and children old enough to understand. This was the first day of the seventh month. On the square before the Water Gate, in the presence of the men and women, and children old enough to understand, he read from the book from early morning till noon; all the people listened attentively to the Book of the Law.

Ezra the scribe stood on a wooden dais erected for the purpose. In full view of all the people – since he stood higher than all the people – Ezra opened the book; and when he opened it all the people stood up. Then Ezra blessed the Lord, the great God, and all the people raised their hands and answered, 'Amen! Amen!'; then they bowed down and, face to the ground, prostrated themselves before the Lord. And Ezra read from the Law of God, translating and giving the sense, so that the people understood what was read.

Then Nehemiah – His Excellency – and Ezra, priest and scribe (and the Levites who were instructing the people) said to all the people, 'This day is sacred to the Lord your God. Do not be mournful, do not weep.' For the people were all in tears as they listened to the words of the Law.

He then said, 'Go, eat the fat, drink the sweet wine, and send a portion to the man who has nothing prepared ready. For this day is sacred to our Lord. Do not be sad: the joy of the Lord is your stronghold.'

The word of the Lord.

Responsional Psalm

Ps 18:8-10,15. R. Jn 6:63

R. **Your words are spirit, Lord,
and they are life.**

The law of the Lord is perfect,
it revives the soul.
The rule of the Lord is to be trusted,
it gives wisdom to the simple. R.

The precepts of the Lord are right,
they gladden the heart.
The command of the Lord is clear,
it gives light to the eyes. R.

The fear of the Lord is holy,
abiding for ever.
The decrees of the Lord are truth
and all of them just. R.

May the spoken words of my mouth,
the thoughts of my heart,
win favour in your sight, O Lord,
my rescuer, my rock! R.

R. **Your words are spirit, Lord,
and they are life.**

SECOND READING

A reading from the first letter of St Paul to the Corinthians 12:12-30

You together are Christ's body; but each of you is a different part of it.

[Just as a human body, though it is made up of many parts is a single unit because all these parts, though many, make one body, so it is with Christ. In the one Spirit we were all baptised, Jews as well as Greeks, slaves as well as citizens, and one Spirit was given to us all to drink.

Nor is the body to be identified with any one of its many parts.] If the foot were to say, 'I am not a hand and so I do not belong to the body,' would that mean that it stopped being part of the body? If the ear were to say, 'I am not an eye, and so I do not belong to the body,' would that mean that it is not a part of the body? If your whole body was just one eye, how would you hear anything? If it was just one ear, how would you smell anything?

Instead of that, God put all the separate parts into the body on purpose. If all the parts were the same, how could it be a body? As it is, the parts are many but the body is one. The eye cannot say to the hand, 'I do not need you,' nor can the head say to the feet, 'I do not need you.'

What is more, it is precisely the parts of the body that seem to be the weakest which are the indispensable ones; and it is the least honourable parts of the body that we clothe with the greatest care. So our more improper parts get decorated in a way that our more proper parts do not need. God has arranged the body so that more dignity is given to the parts which are without it, and so that there may not be disagreements inside the body, but that each part may be equally concerned for all the others. If one part is hurt, all parts are hurt with it. If one part is given special honour, all parts enjoy it.

[Now you together are Christ's body; but each of you is a different part of it.] In the Church, God has given the first place to apostles, the second to prophets, the third to teachers; after them, miracles, and after them the gift of healing; helpers, good leaders, those with many languages. Are all of them apostles, or all of them prophets, or all of them teachers? Do they all have the gift of miracles, or all have the gift of healing? Do all speak strange languages, and all interpret them?

[The word of the Lord.]

Shorter Form, verses 12-14,17. Read between [ ]

Gospel Acclamation

Lk 4:18

R. **Alleluia, alleluia!**
The Lord has sent me to bring the good news to the poor,
to proclaim liberty to captives.
R. **Alleluia!**

GOSPEL

A reading from the holy Gospel according to Luke

1:1-4,4:14-21

The text is being fulfilled today.

Seeing that many others have undertaken to draw up accounts of the events that have taken place among us, exactly as these were handed down to us by those who from the outset were eyewitnesses and ministers of the word, I in my turn, after carefully going over the whole story from the beginning, have decided to write an ordered account for you, Theophilus, so that your Excellency may learn how well founded the teaching is that you have received.

Jesus, with the power of the Spirit in him, returned to Galilee; and his reputation spread throughout the countryside. He taught in their synagogues and everyone praised him.

He came to Nazara, where he had been brought up, and went into the synagogue on the sabbath day as he usually did. He stood up to read, and they handed him the scroll of the prophet Isaiah. Unrolling the scroll he found the place where it is written:

> The spirit of the Lord has been given to me, for he has anointed me.
> He has sent me to bring the good news to the poor,
> to proclaim liberty to captives
> and to the blind new sight,
> to set the downtrodden free,
> to proclaim the Lord's year of favour.

He then rolled up the scroll, gave it back to the assistant and sat down. And all eyes in the synagogue were fixed on him. Then he began to speak to them, 'This text is being fulfilled today even as you listen.'

The Gospel of the Lord.

Prayer over the Offerings

Accept our offerings, O Lord,
   we pray,
and in sanctifying them
grant that they may profit us
   for salvation.
Through Christ our Lord.

Super oblata

Munera nostra, Domine,
   suscipe placatus,
quæ sanctificando
   nobis, quæsumus,
salutaria fore concede.
Per Christum Dominum nostrum.

Preface of Sundays in Ordinary Time I-VIII, pp.60-67.

Communion Antiphon Cf. Ps 33:6

Look toward the Lord
   and be radiant;
let your faces not be abashed.

Ant. ad communionem

Accedite ad Dominum
   et illuminamini,
et facies vestræ non confundentur.

Or: Jn 8:12

I am the light of the world,
   says the Lord;
whoever follows me will not walk
   in darkness,
but will have the light of life.

Prayer after Communion

Grant, we pray, almighty God,
that, receiving the grace
by which you bring us to new life,
we may always glory in your gift.
Through Christ our Lord.

Vel:

Ego sum lux mundi, dicit Dominus:
qui sequitur me non ambulat
   in tenebris,
sed habebit lumen vitæ.

Post communionem

Præsta nobis, quæsumus,
   omnipotens Deus,
ut, vivificationis tuæ
   gratiam consequentes,
in tuo semper munere gloriemur.
Per Christum Dominum nostrum.

---

3 February

FOURTH SUNDAY IN ORDINARY TIME

Entrance Antiphon   Ps 105:47

SAVE us, O Lord our God!
And gather us from the nations,
to give thanks to your holy name,
and make it our glory to praise you.

Collect

Grant us, Lord our God,
that we may honour you
   with all our mind,
and love everyone in truth of heart.
Through our Lord Jesus Christ,
   your Son,
who lives and reigns with you
   in the unity of the Holy Spirit,
one God, for ever and ever.

Ant. ad introitum

SALVOS nos fac,
Domine Deus noster,
et congrega nos de nationibus,
ut confiteamur nomini sancto tuo,
et gloriemur in laude tua.

Collecta

Concede nobis,
   Domine Deus noster,
ut te tota mente veneremur,
et omnes homines rationabili
   diligamus affectu.
Per Dominum nostrum Iesum
   Christum Filium tuum,
qui tecum vivit et regnat
   in unitate Spiritus Sancti,
Deus, per omnia sæcula sæculorum.

FIRST READING

A reading from the prophet Jeremiah   1:4-5,17-19

I have appointed you as prophet to the nations.

In the days of Josiah, the word of the Lord was addressed to me, saying,

'Before I formed you in the womb I knew you;
before you came to birth I consecrated you;
I have appointed you as prophet to the nations.
So now brace yourself for action.
Stand up and tell them
all I command you.
Do not be dismayed at their presence,
or in their presence I will make you dismayed.
I, for my part, today will make you
into a fortified city,
a pillar of iron,
and a wall of bronze
to confront all this land:
the kings of Judah, its princes,
its priests and the country people.
They will fight against you
but shall not overcome you,
for I am with you to deliver you –
it is the Lord who speaks.'

The word of the Lord.

Responsorial Psalm   Ps 70:1-6,15,17. R. v.15

R. **My lips will tell of your help.**

In you, O Lord, I take refuge;
let me never be put to shame.
In your justice rescue me, free me:
pay heed to me and save me. R.

Be a rock where I can take refuge,
a mighty stronghold to save me;
for you are my rock, my stronghold.
Free me from the hand of the wicked. R.

It is you, O Lord, who are my hope,
my trust, O Lord, since my youth.
On you I have leaned from my birth,
from my mother's womb you have been my help. R.

My lips will tell of your justice
and day by day of your help.
O God, you have taught me from my youth
and I proclaim your wonders still. R.

SECOND READING

A reading from the first letter of St Paul to the Corinthians 12:31-13:13

There are three things that last: faith, hope and love; and the greatest of these is love.

Be ambitious for the higher gifts. And I am going to show you a way that is better than any of them.

If I have all the eloquence of men or of angels, but speak without love, I am simply a gong booming or a cymbal clashing. If I have the gift of prophecy, understanding all the mysteries there are, and knowing everything, and if I have faith in all its fulness, to move mountains, but without love, then I am nothing at all. If I give away all that I possess, piece by piece, and if I even let them take my body to burn it, but am without love, it will do me no good whatever.

[Love is always patient and kind; it is never jealous; love is never boastful or conceited; it is never rude or selfish; it does not take offence, and is not resentful. Love takes no pleasure in other people's sins but delights in the truth; it is always ready to excuse, to trust, to hope, and to endure whatever comes.

Love does not come to an end. But if there are gifts of prophecy, the time will come when they must fail; or the gift of languages, it will not continue for ever; and knowledge – for this, too, the time will come when it must fail. For our knowledge is imperfect and our prophesying is imperfect; but once perfection comes, all imperfect things will disappear. When I was a child, I used to talk like a child, and think like a child, and argue like a child, but now I am a man, all childish ways are put behind me. Now we are seeing a dim reflection in a mirror; but then we shall be seeing face to face. The knowledge that I have now is imperfect; but then I shall know as fully as I am known.

In short, there are three things that last: faith, hope and love; and the greatest of these is love.

The word of the Lord.]

Shorter Form, verses 4-13. Read between [ ]

Gospel Acclamation
Jn 14:5

R. **Alleluia, alleluia!**
I am the Way, the Truth and the Life, says the Lord;
no one can come to the Father except through me.
R. **Alleluia!**

Or:
Lk 4:18

R. **Alleluia, alleluia!**
The Lord sent me to bring the good news to the poor,
to proclaim liberty to captives.
R. **Alleluia!**

GOSPEL

A reading from the holy Gospel according to Luke
4:21-30

Like Elijah and Elisha, Jesus is not sent to the Jews only.

Jesus began to speak in the synagogue, 'This text is being fulfilled today even as you listen.' And he won the approval of all, and they were astonished by the gracious words that came from his lips.

They said, 'This is Joseph's son, surely?' But he replied, 'No doubt you will quote me the saying, "Physician, heal yourself" and tell me, "We have heard all that happened in Capernaum, do the same here in your own countryside."' And he went on, 'I tell you solemnly, no prophet is ever accepted in his own country.

'There were many widows in Israel, I can assure you, in Elijah's day, when heaven remained shut for three years and six months and a great famine raged throughout the land, but Elijah was not sent to any one of these: he was sent to a widow at Zarephath, a Sidonian town. And in the prophet Elisha's time there were many lepers in Israel, but none of these was cured, except the Syrian, Naaman.'

When they heard this everyone in the synagogue was enraged. They sprang to their feet and hustled him out of the town; and they took him up to the brow of the hill their town was built on, intending to throw him down the cliff, but he slipped through the crowd and walked away.

The Gospel of the Lord.

Prayer over the Offerings

O Lord, we bring to your altar
these offerings of our service:
be pleased to receive them, we pray,
and transform them
into the Sacrament
   of our redemption.
Through Christ our Lord.

Super oblata

Altaribus tuis, Domine,
munera nostræ
   servitutis inferimus,
quæ, placatus assumens,
sacramentum nostræ
   redemptionis efficias.
Per Christum Dominum nostrum.

Preface of Sundays in Ordinary Time I-VIII, pp.60-67.

Communion Antiphon Cf. Ps 30:17-18

Let your face shine on your servant.
Save me in your merciful love.
O Lord, let me never be put to shame,
   for I call on you.

Ant. ad communionem

Illumina faciem tuam super
   servum tuum,
et salvum me fac in tua misericordia.
Domine, non confundar,
   quoniam invocavi te.

Or: Mt 5:3-4

Blessed are the poor in spirit,
for theirs is the Kingdom of Heaven.
Blessed are the meek,
   for they shall possess the land.

Vel:

Beati pauperes spiritu,
quoniam ipsorum
   est regnum cælorum.
Beati mites,
   quoniam ipsi possidebunt terram.

Prayer after Communion

Nourished by these redeeming gifts,
we pray, O Lord,
that through this help
   to eternal salvation
true faith may ever increase.
Through Christ our Lord.

Post communionem

Redemptionis nostræ munere
   vegetati, quæsumus, Domine,
ut hoc perpetuæ salutis auxilio
fides semper vera proficiat.
Per Christum Dominum nostrum.

10 February

FIFTH SUNDAY IN ORDINARY TIME

Entrance Antiphon   Ps 94:6-7

O COME, let us worship God
and bow low before the God
who made us,
for he is the Lord our God.

Ant. ad introitum

VENITE, adoremus Deum,
et procidamus ante Dominum,
qui fecit nos;
quia ipse est Dominus Deus noster.

Collect

Keep your family safe, O Lord,
  with unfailing care,
that, relying solely on the hope
  of heavenly grace,
they may be defended always
  by your protection.
Through our Lord Jesus Christ,
  your Son,
who lives and reigns with you
  in the unity of the Holy Spirit,
one God, for ever and ever.

Collecta

Familiam tuam,
  quæsumus, Domine,
continua pietate custodi,
ut, quæ in sola spe gratiæ
  cælestis innititur,
tua semper protectione muniatur.
Per Dominum nostrum Iesum
  Christum Filium tuum,
qui tecum vivit et regnat
  in unitate Spiritus Sancti,
Deus, per omnia sæcula sæculorum.

FIRST READING

A reading from the prophet Isaiah   6:1-8

Here I am, send me.

In the year of King Uzziah's death I saw the Lord seated on a high throne; his train filled the sanctuary; above him stood seraphs, each one with six wings.

  And they cried out one to another in this way,
  'Holy, holy, holy is the Lord of hosts.
  His glory fills the whole earth.'

The foundations of the threshold shook with the voice of the one who cried out, and the Temple was filled with smoke. I said:

  'What a wretched state I am in! I am lost,
  for I am a man of unclean lips
  and I live among a people of unclean lips,
  and my eyes have looked at the King, the Lord of hosts.'

Then one of the seraphs flew to me, holding in his hand a live coal which he had taken from the altar with a pair of tongs. With this he touched my mouth and said:

'See now, this has touched your lips,
your sin is taken away,
your iniquity is purged.'

Then I heard the voice of the Lord saying:

'Whom shall I send? Who will be our messenger?'

I answered, 'Here I am, send me.'

The word of the Lord.

Responsorial Psalm

Ps 137:1-5,7-8. R. v.1

R. **Before the angels I will bless you, O Lord.**

I thank you, Lord, with all my heart,
you have heard the words of my mouth.
Before the angels I will bless you.
I will adore before your holy temple. R.

I thank you for your faithfulness and love
which excel all we ever knew of you.
On the day I called, you answered;
you increased the strength of my soul. R.

All earth's kings shall thank you
when they hear the words of your mouth.
They shall sing of the Lord's ways:
'How great is the glory of the Lord!' R.

You stretch out your right hand and save me.
Your hand will do all things for me.
Your love, O Lord, is eternal,
discard not the work of your hand. R.

SECOND READING

A reading from the first letter of St Paul to the Corinthians 15:1-11
I preach what they preach, and this is what you all believed.

Brothers, I want to remind you of the gospel I preached to you, the gospel that you received and in which you are firmly established; because the gospel will save you only if you keep believing exactly what I preached to you – believing anything else will not lead to anything.

Well then, [in the first place, I taught you what I had been taught myself, namely that Christ died for our sins, in accordance with the scriptures; that he was buried; and that he was raised to life on the third day, in accordance with the scriptures; that he appeared first to Cephas and secondly to the Twelve. Next he appeared to more than five hundred of the brothers at the same time, most of whom are still alive, though some have died; then he appeared to James, and then to all the apostles; and last of all he appeared to me too; it was as though I was born when no one expected it.]

I am the least of the apostles; in fact, since I persecuted the Church of God, I hardly deserve the name apostle; but by God's grace that is what I am, and the grace that he gave me has not been fruitless. On the contrary, I, or rather the grace of God that is with me, have worked harder than any of the others; [but what matters is that I preach what they preach, and this is what you all believed.

The word of the Lord.]

Shorter Form, verses 3-8,11. Read between [ ]

Gospel Acclamation
Jn 15:15

R. **Alleluia, alleluia!**
I call you friends, says the Lord,
because I have made known to you
everything I have learnt from my Father.
R. **Alleluia!**
Or:
Mt 4:19

R. **Alleluia, alleluia!**
Follow me, says the Lord,
and I will make you fishers of men.
R. **Alleluia!**

GOSPEL

A reading from the holy Gospel according to Luke 5:1-11

They left everything and followed him.

Jesus was standing one day by the lake of Gennesaret, with the crowd pressing round him listening to the word of God, when he caught sight of two boats close to the bank. The fishermen had gone out of them and were washing their nets. He got into one of the boats – it was Simon's – and asked him to put out a little from the shore. Then he sat down and taught the crowds from the boat.

When he had finished speaking he said to Simon, 'Put out into deep water and pay out your nets for a catch.' 'Master,' Simon replied 'we worked hard all night long and caught nothing, but if you say so, I will pay out the nets.' And when they had done this they netted such a huge number of fish that their nets began to tear, so they signalled to their companions in the other boats to come and help them; when these came, they filled the two boats to sinking point.

When Simon Peter saw this he fell at the knees of Jesus saying 'Leave me, Lord; I am a sinful man.' For he and all his companions were completely overcome by the catch they had made; so also were James and John, sons of Zebedee, who were Simon's partners. But Jesus said to Simon, 'Do not be afraid; from now on it is men you will catch.' Then, bringing their boats back to land, they left everything and followed him.

The Gospel of the Lord.

Prayer over the Offerings | Super oblata

O Lord our God,
who once established these
   created things
to sustain us in our frailty,
grant, we pray,
that they may become for us now
the Sacrament of eternal life.
Through Christ our Lord.

Domine Deus noster,
   qui has potius creaturas
ad fragilitatis nostræ
   subsidium condidisti,
tribue, quæsumus,
ut etiam æternitatis nobis
   fiant sacramentum.
Per Christum Dominum nostrum.

Preface of Sundays in Ordinary Time I-VIII, pp.60-67.

Communion Antiphon Cf. Ps106:8-9 | Ant. ad communionem

Let them thank the Lord
   for his mercy,
his wonders for the children of men
for he satisfies the thirsty soul,
and the hungry he fills
   with good things.

Confiteantur Domino
   misericordiæ eius,
et mirabilia eius filiis hominum,
quia satiavit animam inanem,
et animam esurientem
   satiavit bonis.

Or: Mt 5:5-6 | Vel:

Blessed are those who mourn,
   for they shall be consoled.
Blessed are those who hunger
   and thirst for righteousness,
for they shall have their fill.

Beati qui lugent,
   quoniam ipsi consolabuntur.
Beati qui esuriunt
   et sitiunt iustitiam,
quoniam ipsi saturabuntur.

Prayer after Communion

O God, who have willed
   that we be partakers
in the one Bread and the one Chalice,
grant us, we pray, so to live that,
   made one in Christ,
we may joyfully bear fruit
for the salvation of the world.
Through Christ our Lord.

Post communionem

Deus, qui nos de uno pane
   et de uno calice
participes esse voluisti,
da nobis, quæsumus, ita vivere, ut,
   unum in Christo effecti,
fructum afferamus pro mundi
   salute gaudentes.
Per Christum Dominum nostrum.

13 February

ASH WEDNESDAY

In the course of today's Mass, ashes are blessed and distributed. These are made from the olive branches or branches of other trees that were blessed the previous year.

Entrance Antiphon Ws 11:24,25,27

YOU are merciful to all, O Lord,
   and despise nothing that you
   have made.
You overlook people's sins,
   to bring them to repentance,
and you spare them,
   for you are the Lord our God.

Ant. ad introitum

MISERERIS omnium, Domine,
   et nihil odisti eorum
   quæ fecisti,
dissimulans peccata hominum
   propter pænitentiam
et parcens illis,
   quia tu es Dominus Deus noster.

The Penitential Act is omitted, and the Distribution of Ashes takes its place.

Collect

Grant, O Lord, that we may begin
   with holy fasting
this campaign of Christian service,
so that, as we take up battle
   against spiritual evils,
we may be armed with weapons
   of self-restraint.
Through our Lord Jesus Christ,
   your Son,
who lives and reigns with you
   in the unity of the Holy Spirit,
one God, for ever and ever.

Collecta

Concede nobis, Domine,
præsidia militiæ christianæ sanctis
   inchoare ieiuniis,
ut, contra spiritales
   nequitias pugnaturi,
continentiæ muniamur auxiliis.
Per Dominum nostrum
   Iesum Christum Filium tuum,
qui tecum vivit et regnat
   in unitate Spiritus Sancti,
Deus, per omnia sæcula sæculorum.

FIRST READING

A reading from the prophet Joel 2:12-18

Let your hearts be broken, not your garments torn.

'Now, now – it is the Lord who speaks –
come back to me with all your heart,
fasting, weeping, mourning.'
Let your hearts be broken not your garments torn,
turn to the Lord your God again,
for he is all tenderness and compassion,
slow to anger, rich in graciousness,
and ready to relent.
Who knows if he will not turn again, will not relent,
will not leave a blessing as he passes,
oblation and libation
for the Lord your God?
Sound the trumpet in Zion!
Order a fast,
proclaim a solemn assembly,
call the people together,
summon the community,
assemble the elders,
gather the children,
even the infants at the breast.
Let the bridegroom leave his bedroom
and the bride her alcove.
Between vestibule and altar let the priests,
the ministers of the Lord, lament.
Let them say,
'Spare your people, Lord!
Do not make your heritage a thing of shame,
a byword for the nations.
Why should it be said among the nations,
"Where is their God?"'
Then the Lord, jealous on behalf of his land,
took pity on his people.

    The word of the Lord.

Responsorial Psalm

Ps 50:3-6,12-14,17. R. v.3

R. **Have mercy on us, O Lord, for we have sinned.**

Have mercy on me, God, in your kindness.
In your compassion blot out my offence.
O wash me more and more from my guilt
and cleanse me from my sin. R.

My offences truly I know them;
my sin is always before me.
Against you, you alone, have I sinned:
what is evil in your sight I have done. R.

A pure heart create for me, O God,
put a steadfast spirit within me.
Do not cast me away from your presence,
nor deprive me of your holy spirit. R.

Give me again the joy of your help;
with a spirit of fervour sustain me.
O Lord, open my lips
and my mouth shall declare your praise. R.

SECOND READING

A reading from the second letter of St Paul to the Corinthians 5:20-6:2

Be reconciled to God ... now is the favourable time.

We are ambassadors for Christ; it is as though God were appealing through us, and the appeal that we make in Christ's name is: be reconciled to God. For our sake God made the sinless one into sin, so that in him we might become the goodness of God. As his fellow workers, we beg you once again not to neglect the grace of God that you have received. For he says: At the favourable time, I have listened to you, on the day of salvation I came to your help. Well, now is the favourable time; this is the day of salvation.

The word of the Lord.

Gospel Acclamation

Ps 50:12,14

R. **Praise to you, O Christ, king of eternal glory!**
A pure heart create for me, O God,
and give me again the joy of your help.
R. **Praise to you, O Christ, king of eternal glory!**

13 FEBRUARY

Or:

R. **Praise to you, O Christ, king of eternal glory!**
Harden not your hearts today,
but listen to the voice of the Lord.
R. **Praise to you, O Christ, king of eternal glory!**

Cf. Ps 94:8

GOSPEL

A reading from holy Gospel according to Matthew

6:1-6,16-18

Your Father, who sees all that is done in secret, will reward you.

Jesus said to his disciples:

'Be careful not to parade your good deeds before men to attract their notice; by doing this you will lose all reward from your Father in heaven. So when you give alms, do not have it trumpeted before you; this is what the hypocrites do in the synagogues and in the streets to win men's admiration. I tell you solemnly, they have had their reward. But when you give alms, your left hand must not know what your right is doing; your almsgiving must be secret, and your Father who sees all that is done in secret will reward you.

'And when you pray, do not imitate the hypocrites: they love to say their prayers standing up in the synagogues and at the street corners for people to see them. I tell you solemnly, they have had their reward. But when you pray go to your private room and, when you have shut your door, pray to your Father who is in that secret place, and your Father who sees all that is done in secret will reward you.

'When you fast do not put on a gloomy look as the hypocrites do: they pull long faces to let men know they are fasting. I tell you solemnly, they have had their reward. But when you fast, put oil on your head and wash your face, so that no one will know you are fasting except your Father who sees all that is done in secret; and your Father who sees all that is done in secret will reward you.'

The Gospel of the Lord.

Blessing and Distribution of Ashes

After the Homily, the Priest, standing with hands joined, says:

Dear brethren (brothers and sisters),
 let us humbly ask God our Father
that he be pleased to bless
 with the abundance of his grace
these ashes, which we will put
 on our heads in penitence.

Deum Patrem, fratres carissimi,
 suppliciter deprecemur,
ut hos cineres, quos pænitentiæ causa
capitibus nostris imponimus,
ubertate gratiæ suæ
 benedicere dignetur.

After a brief prayer in silence, and, with hands extended, he continues:

O God, who are moved
 by acts of humility
and respond with forgiveness
 to works of penance,
lend your merciful ear to our prayers
and in your kindness pour out
 the grace of your ✠ blessing
on your servants who are marked
 with these ashes,
that, as they follow
 the Lenten observances,
they may be worthy to come
 with minds made pure
to celebrate the Paschal Mystery
 of your Son.
Who lives and reigns
 for ever and ever.

R. Amen.

Or:

O God, who desire not
 the death of sinners,
but their conversion,
mercifully hear our prayers
and in your kindness be pleased
 to bless ✠ these ashes,
which we intend to receive
 upon our heads,
that we, who acknowledge
 we are but ashes
and shall return to dust,

Deus, qui humiliatione flecteris
 et satisfactione placaris,
aurem tuæ pietatis precibus
 nostris inclina,
et super famulos tuos,
horum cinerum aspersione contactos,
gratiam tuæ benedictionis ✠
 effunde propitius,
ut, quadragesimalem
 observantiam prosequentes,
ad Filii tui paschale
 mysterium celebrandum
purificatis mentibus
 pervenire mereantur.
Per Christum Dominum nostrum.

R. Amen.

Vel:

Deus, qui non mortem
 sed conversionem
desideras peccatorum,
preces nostras clementer exaudi,
et hos cineres,
quos capitibus nostris
 imponi decernimus,
benedicere ✠ pro tua pietate dignare,
ut qui nos cinerem esse
et in pulverem
 reversuros cognoscimus,

13 FEBRUARY

may, through a steadfast
   observance of Lent,
gain pardon for sins
   and newness of life
after the likeness of your Risen Son.
Who lives and reigns
   for ever and ever.

R. Amen.

quadragesimalis exercitationis studio,
peccatorum veniam
et novitatem vitæ,
ad imaginem Filii tui resurgentis,
   consequi valeamus.
Qui vivit et regnat
   in sæcula sæculorum.

R. Amen.

He sprinkles the ashes with holy water, without saying anything.

Then the Priest places ashes on the head of all those present who come to him, and says to each one:

Repent, and believe in the Gospel.

Or:

Remember that you are dust,
   and to dust you shall return.

Pænitemini, et credite Evangelio.

Vel:

Memento, homo, quia pulvis es,
   et in pulverem reverteris.

Meanwhile, the following are sung:

Antiphon 1

Let us change our garments
   to sackcloth and ashes,
let us fast and weep before the Lord,
that our God, rich in mercy,
   might forgive us our sins.

Antiphona 1

Immutemur habitu,
   in cinere et cilicio,
ieiunemus,
   et ploremus ante Dominum,
quia multum misericors est
dimittere peccata nostra
   Deus noster.

Antiphon 2   Cf. Jl 2:17; Est 4:17

Let the priests,
   the ministers of the Lord,
stand between the porch and
   the altar and weep and cry out:
Spare, O Lord, spare your people;
do not close the mouths of those
   who sing your praise, O Lord.

Antiphona 2

Inter vestibulum et altare
plorabunt sacerdotes
   ministri Domini,
et dicent: Parce, Domine,
   parce populo tuo,
et ne claudas ora canentium te,
   Domine.

Antiphon 3   Ps 50:3

Blot out my transgressions, O Lord.

Antiphona 3

Dele, Domine, iniquitatem meam.

This may be repeated after each verse of Psalm 50

| (Have mercy on me, O God). | Miserere mei, Deus. |

Responsory Cf. Ba 3:2; Ps 78:9	Responsorium
R. Let us correct our faults which we have committed in ignorance, let us not be taken unawares by the day of our death, looking in vain for leisure to repent. * Hear us, O Lord, and show us your mercy, for we have sinned against you. V. Help us, O God our Saviour; for the sake of your name, O Lord, set us free. * Hear us, O Lord. . .	R. Emendemus in melius, quæ ignoranter peccavimus, ne subito præoccupati die mortis quæramus spatium pænitentiæ, et invenire non possumus. *Attende, Domine, et miserere, quia peccavimus tibi. V. Adiuva nos, Deus salutaris noster, et propter honorem nominis tui, Domine, libera nos. *Attende, Domine. . .

Another appropriate chant may also be sung.

After the distribution of ashes, the Priest washes his hands and proceeds to the Universal Prayer, and continues the Mass in the usual way.

The Creed is not said.

The Liturgy of the Eucharist

Prayer over the Offerings	Super oblata

As we solemnly offer
the annual sacrifice for
   the beginning of Lent,
we entreat you, O Lord,
that, through works of penance
   and charity,
we may turn away from
   harmful pleasures
and, cleansed from our sins,
   may become worthy
to celebrate devoutly the Passion
   of your Son.
Who lives and reigns
   for ever and ever.
	Sacrificium quadragesimalis initii
	   sollemniter immolamus,
	te, Domine, deprecantes,
	ut per pænitentiæ
	   caritatisque labores
	a noxiis voluptatibus temperemus,
	et, a peccatis mundati,
	ad celebrandam Filii tui passionem
	mereamur esse devoti.
	Qui vivit et regnat
	   in sæcula sæculorum.

Preface III or IV of Lent, pp.50-53.

Communion Antiphon Cf. Ps 1:2-3

He who ponders the law
   of the Lord day and night
will yield fruit in due season.

Prayer after Communion

May the Sacrament we have
   received sustain us, O Lord,
that our Lenten fast may
   be pleasing to you
and be for us a healing remedy.
Through Christ our Lord.

Ant. ad communionem

Qui meditabitur in lege
   Domini die ac nocte,
dabit fructum suum in tempore suo.

Post communionem

Percepta nobis, Domine,
præbeant sacramenta subsidium,
ut tibi grata sint nostra ieiunia,
et nobis proficiant ad medelam.
Per Christum Dominum nostrum.

For the dismissal, the Priest stands facing the people and, extending his hands over them, says this prayer:

Prayer over the People

Pour out a spirit of compunction,
   O God,
on those who bow before
   your majesty,
and by your mercy may they
   merit the rewards you promise
to those who do penance.
Through Christ our Lord.

Oratio super populum

Super inclinantes se tuæ maiestati,
   Deus,
spiritum compunctionis
   propitius effunde,
et præmia pænitentibus repromissa
misericorditer consequi mereantur.
Per Christum Dominum nostrum.

The blessing and distribution of ashes may also take place outside Mass. In this case, the rite is preceded by a Liturgy of the Word, with the Entrance Antiphon, the Collect, and the readings with their chants as at Mass. Then there follow the Homily and the blessing and distribution of ashes. The rite is concluded with the Universal Prayer, the Blessing, and the Dismissal of the Faithful.

17 February

FIRST SUNDAY OF LENT

St Luke recounts that after receiving Baptism from John, "Jesus, full of the Holy Spirit, returned from the Jordan, and was led by the Spirit for forty days in the wilderness, tempted by the devil" (Lk 4:1). There is a clear insistence on the fact that the temptations were not just an incident on the way, but rather the consequence of Jesus's decision to carry out the mission entrusted to him by the Father: to live, to the very end, his reality as the beloved Son who trusts totally in him. Christ came into the world to set us free from sin and from the ambiguous fascination of planning our life while leaving God out. He did not do so with loud proclamations but rather by fighting the tempter himself, until the Cross. This example applies to everyone: the world is improved by starting with oneself, changing, with God's grace, everything in one's life that is not going well.

(Pope Benedict XVI)

Entrance Antiphon Cf. Ps 90:15-16

WHEN he calls on me,
  I will answer him;
I will deliver him and give him glory,
I will grant him length of days.

Ant. ad introitum

INVOCABIT me,
  et ego exaudiam eum;
eripiam eum, et glorificabo eum,
longitudine dierum adimplebo eum.

The Gloria in excelsis (Glory to God in the highest) is not said.

Collect

Grant, almighty God,
through the yearly observances
  of holy Lent,
that we may grow in understanding
of the riches hidden in Christ
and by worthy conduct pursue
  their effects.
Through our Lord Jesus Christ,
  your Son,
who lives and reigns with you
  in the unity of the Holy Spirit,
one God, for ever and ever.

Collecta

Concede nobis, omnipotens Deus,
ut, per annua quadragesimalis
  exercitia sacramenti,
et ad intellegendum Christi
  proficiamus arcanum,
et effectus eius digna
  conversatione sectemur.
Per Dominum nostrum Iesum
  Christum Filium tuum,
qui tecum vivit et regnat
  in unitate Spiritus Sancti,
Deus, per omnia sæcula sæculorum.

FIRST READING

A reading from the book of Deuteronomy
The creed of the chosen people.
26:4-10

Moses said to the people: 'The priest shall take the pannier from your hand and lay it before the altar of the Lord your God. Then, in the sight of the Lord your God, you must make this pronouncement:

"My father was a wandering Aramaean. He went down into Egypt to find refuge there, few in numbers; but there he became a nation, great, mighty, and strong. The Egyptians ill-treated us, they gave us no peace and inflicted harsh slavery on us. But we called on the Lord, the God of our fathers. The Lord heard our voice and saw our misery, our toil and our oppression; and the Lord brought us out of Egypt with mighty hand and outstretched arm, with great terror, and with signs and wonders. He brought us here and gave us this land, a land where milk and honey flow. Here then I bring the first-fruits of the produce of the soil that you, Lord, have given me." You must then lay them before the Lord your God, and bow down in the sight of the Lord your God.'

The word of the Lord.

Responsorial Psalm

Ps 90:1-2,10-15. R. v.15

R. **Be with me, O Lord, in my distress.**

He who dwells in the shelter of the Most High
and abides in the shade of the Almighty
says to the Lord: 'My refuge
my stronghold, my God in whom I trust!' R.

Upon you no evil shall fall,
no plague approach where you dwell.
For you has he commanded his angels,
to keep you in all your ways. R.

They shall bear you upon their hands
lest you strike your foot against a stone.
On the lion and the viper you will tread
and trample the young lion and the dragon. R.

His love he set on me, so I will rescue him;
protect him for he knows my name.
When he calls I shall answer: 'I am with you.'
I will save him in distress and give him glory. R.

SECOND READING

A reading from the letter of St Paul to the Romans 10:8-13

The creed of the Christian.

Scripture says: The word, that is the faith we proclaim, is very near to you, it is on your lips and in your heart. If your lips confess that Jesus is Lord and if you believe in your heart that God raised him from the dead, then you will be saved. By believing from the heart you are made righteous; by confessing with your lips you are saved. When scripture says: those who believe in him will have no cause for shame, it makes no distinction between Jew and Greek: all belong to the same Lord who is rich enough, however many ask his help, for everyone who calls on the name of the Lord will be saved.

The word of the Lord.

Gospel Acclamation Mt 4:4

R. **Praise to you, O Christ, king of eternal glory!**
Man does not live on bread alone,
but on every word that comes from the mouth of God.
R. **Praise to you, O Christ, king of eternal glory!**

GOSPEL

A reading from the holy Gospel according to Luke 4:1-13

Jesus was led by the Spirit through the wilderness and was tempted there.

Filled with the Holy Spirit, Jesus left the Jordan and was led by the Spirit through the wilderness being tempted there by the devil for forty days. During that time he ate nothing and at the end he was hungry. Then the devil said to him, 'If you are the Son of God, tell this stone to turn into a loaf.' But Jesus replied 'Scripture says: Man does not live on bread alone.'

Then leading him to a height, the devil showed him in a moment of time all the kingdoms of the world and said to him, 'I will give you all this power and the glory of these kingdoms, for it has been committed to me and I give it to anyone I choose. Worship me, then, and it shall all be yours.' But Jesus answered him, 'Scripture says:

You must worship the Lord your God,
and serve him alone.'

Then he led him to Jerusalem and made him stand on the parapet of the Temple. 'If you are the Son of God,' he said to him 'throw yourself down from here, for scripture says:

He will put his angels in charge of you
to guard you,
and again:
They will hold you up on their hands
in case you hurt your foot against a stone.'
But Jesus answered him, 'It has been said:
You must not put the Lord your God to the test.'
Having exhausted all these ways of tempting him, the devil left him, to return at the appointed time.

The Gospel of the Lord.

The Creed is said.

Prayer over the Offerings

Give us the right dispositions,
O Lord, we pray,
to make these offerings,
for with them we celebrate
the beginning
of this venerable and sacred time.
Through Christ our Lord.

Preface: The Temptation of the Lord.

It is truly right and just,
our duty and our salvation,
always and everywhere
to give you thanks,
Lord, holy Father,
almighty and eternal God,
through Christ our Lord.

By abstaining forty long days
from earthly food,
he consecrated through his fast
the pattern of our Lenten observance
and, by overturning all the snares
of the ancient serpent,
taught us to cast out the leaven
of malice,
so that, celebrating worthily
the Paschal Mystery,

Super oblata

Fac nos, quæsumus, Domine,
his muneribus offerendis
convenienter aptari,
quibus ipsius venerabilis
sacramenti celebramus
exordium.
Per Christum Dominum nostrum.

Praefatio: De tentatione Domini.

Vere dignum et iustum est,
aequum et salutare,
nos tibi semper et ubique
gratias agere:
Domine, sancte Pater, omnipotens
aeterne Deus:
per Christum Dominum nostrum:

Qui quadraginta diebus,
terrenis abstinens alimentis,
formam huius observantiae
ieiunio dedicavit,
et, omnes evertens antiqui
serpentis insidias,
fermentum malitiae nos
docuit superare,
ut, paschale mysterium dignis
mentibus celebrantes,

we might pass over at last
  to the eternal paschal feast.

And so, with the company
  of Angels and Saints,
we sing the hymn of your praise,
as without end we acclaim:

Holy, Holy, Holy Lord God of hosts...

Communion Antiphon — Mt 4:4
One does not live by bread alone,
but by every word that comes forth
  from the mouth of God.

Or: — Cf. Ps 90:4
The Lord will conceal you
  with his pinions,
and under his wings you will trust.

Prayer after Communion
Renewed now with heavenly bread,
by which faith is nourished,
  hope increased,
and charity strengthened,
we pray, O Lord,
that we may learn to hunger
  for Christ,
the true and living Bread,
and strive to live by every word
which proceeds from your mouth.
Through Christ our Lord.

Prayer over the People
May bountiful blessing,
  O Lord, we pray,
come down upon your people,
that hope may grow in tribulation,
virtue be strengthened
  in temptation,
and eternal redemption be assured.
Through Christ our Lord.

---

ad pascha demum
  perpetuum transeamus.

Et ideo, cum Angelorum
  atque Sanctorum turba,
hymnum laudis tibi canimus,
  sine fine dicentes:

Sanctus, Sanctus, Sanctus. . .

Ant. ad communionem
Non in solo pane vivit homo,
sed in omni verbo quod procedit
  de ore Dei.

Vel:
Scapulis suis obumbrabit
  tibi Dominus,
et sub pennis eius sperabis.

Post communionem
Cælesti pane refecti,
quo fides alitur, spes provehitur
  et caritas roboratur,

quæsumus, Domine,
ut ipsum, qui est panis vivus
  et verus, esurire discamus,
et in omni verbo,
  quod procedit de ore tuo,
vivere valeamus.
Per Christum Dominum nostrum.

Oratio super populum
Super populum tuum,
  Domine, quæsumus,
benedictio copiosa descendat,
ut spes in tribulatione succrescat,
virtus in tentatione firmetur,
æterna redemptio tribuatur.
Per Christum Dominum nostrum.

24 February

SECOND SUNDAY OF LENT

Another detail proper to St Luke's narrative deserves emphasis: the mention of the topic of Jesus' conversation with Moses and Elijah, who appeared beside him when he was transfigured. As the Evangelist tells us, they "talked with him ... and spoke of his departure" (in Greek, éxodos), "which he was to accomplish at Jerusalem" (9:31). Therefore, Jesus listens to the Law and the Prophets who spoke to him about his death and Resurrection. In his intimate dialogue with the Father, he did not depart from history, he did not flee the mission for which he came into the world, although he knew that to attain glory he would have to pass through the Cross. On the contrary, Christ enters more deeply into this mission, adhering with all his being to the Father's will; he shows us that true prayer consists precisely in uniting our will with that of God. For a Christian, therefore, to pray is not to evade reality and the responsibilities it brings, but rather, fully to assume them, trusting in the faithful and inexhaustible love of the Lord.

(Pope Benedict XVI)

Entrance Antiphon   Cf. Ps 26:8-9

OF you my heart has spoken:
    Seek his face.
It is your face, O Lord, that I seek;
    hide not your face from me.

Or: Cf. Ps 24:6,2,22

Remember your compassion,
    O Lord,
and your merciful love,
    for they are from of old.
Let not our enemies exult over us.
Redeem us, O God of Israel,
    from all our distress.

Ant. ad introitum

TIBI dixit cor meum quæsivi
    vultum tuum,
vultum tuum, Domine, requiram.
Ne avertas faciem tuam a me.

Vel:

Reminiscere miserationum tuarum,
    Domine,
et misericordiæ tuæ,
    quæ a sæculo sunt.
Ne umquam dominentur nobis
    inimici nostri;
libera nos, Deus Israel, ex omnibus
    angustiis nostris.

The Gloria in excelsis (Glory to God in the highest) is not said.

Collect

O God, who have commanded us
to listen to your beloved Son,
be pleased, we pray,
to nourish us inwardly by your word,
that, with spiritual sight made pure,
we may rejoice to behold your glory.
Through our Lord Jesus Christ,
   your Son,
who lives and reigns with you
   in the unity of the Holy Spirit,
one God, for ever and ever.

Collecta

Deus, qui nobis dilectum Filium
   tuum audire præcepisti,
verbo tuo interius
   nos pascere digneris,
ut, spiritali purificato intuitu,
gloriæ tuæ lætemur aspectu.
Per Dominum nostrum Iesum
   Christum Filium tuum,
qui tecum vivit et regnat
   in unitate Spiritus Sancti,
Deus, per omnia sæcula sæculorum.

FIRST READING

A reading from the book of Genesis   15:5-12,17-18

God enters into a Covenant with Abraham, the man of faith.

Taking Abram outside the Lord said, 'Look up to heaven and count the stars if you can. Such will be your descendants' he told him. Abram put his faith in the Lord, who counted this as making him justified.

'I am the Lord' he said to him 'who brought you out of Ur of the Chaldaeans to make you heir to this land.' 'My Lord, the Lord' Abram replied 'how am I to know that I shall inherit it?' He said to him, 'Get me a three-year-old heifer, a three-year-old goat, a three-year-old ram, a turtledove and a young pigeon.' He brought him all these, cut them in half and put half on one side and half facing it on the other; but the birds he did not cut in half. Birds of prey came down on the carcasses but Abram drove them off.

Now as the sun was setting Abram fell into a deep sleep, and terror seized him. When the sun had set and darkness had fallen, there appeared a smoking furnace and a firebrand that went between the halves. That day the Lord made a Covenant with Abram in these terms:

'To your descendants I give this land,
from the wadi of Egypt to the Great River.'

The word of the Lord.

Responsorial Psalm   Ps 26:1,7-9,13-14. R. v.1

R. **The Lord is my light and my help.**

The Lord is my light and my help;
whom shall I fear?

The Lord is the stronghold of my life;
before whom shall I shrink? R.

O Lord, hear my voice when I call;
have mercy and answer.
Of you my heart has spoken:
'Seek his face.' R.

It is your face, O Lord, that I seek;
hide not your face.
Dismiss not your servant in anger;
you have been my help. R.

I am sure I shall see the Lord's goodness
in the land of the living.
Hope in him, hold firm and take heart.
Hope in the Lord! R.

SECOND READING

A reading from the letter of St Paul to the Philippians 3:17-4:1

Christ will transfigure our bodies into copies of his glorious body.

My brothers, be united in following my rule of life. Take as your models everybody who is already doing this and study them as you used to study us. I have told you often, and I repeat it today with tears, there are many who are behaving as the enemies of the cross of Christ. They are destined to be lost. They make foods into their god and they are proudest of something they ought to think shameful; the things they think important are earthly things. [For us, our homeland is in heaven, and from heaven comes the saviour we are waiting for, the Lord Jesus Christ, and he will transfigure these wretched bodies of ours into copies of his glorious body. He will do that by the same power with which he can subdue the whole universe.

So then, my brothers and dear friends, do not give way but remain faithful in the Lord. I miss you very much, dear friends; you are my joy and my crown.

The word of the Lord.]

Shorter Form, 3:20-4:1. Read between [ ]

Gospel Acclamation

Mt 17:5

R. **Glory and praise to you, O Christ!**
From the bright cloud the Father's voice was heard:
'This is my Son, the Beloved. Listen to him.'
R. **Glory and praise to you, O Christ!**

GOSPEL

A reading from the holy Gospel according to Luke 9:28-36

As Jesus prayed, the aspect of his face was changed.

Jesus took with him Peter and John and James and went up the mountain to pray. As he prayed, the aspect of his face was changed and his clothing became brilliant as lightning. Suddenly there were two men there talking to him; they were Moses and Elijah appearing in glory, and they were speaking of his passing which he was to accomplish in Jerusalem. Peter and his companions were heavy with sleep, but they kept awake and saw his glory and the two men standing with him. As these were leaving him, Peter said to Jesus, 'Master, it is wonderful for us to be here; so let us make three tents, one for you, one for Moses and one for Elijah.' – He did not know what he was saying. As he spoke, a cloud came and covered them with shadow; and when they went into the cloud the disciples were afraid. And a voice came from the cloud saying, 'This is my Son, the Chosen One. Listen to him.' And after the voice had spoken, Jesus was found alone. The disciples kept silence and, at that time, told no one what they had seen.

The Gospel of the Lord.

The Creed is said.

Prayer over the Offerings

May this sacrifice, O Lord, we pray,
cleanse us of our faults
and sanctify your faithful
   in body and mind
for the celebration
   of the paschal festivities.
Through Christ our Lord.

Preface: The Transfiguration of the Lord.

It is truly right and just,
   our duty and our salvation,
always and everywhere
   to give you thanks,
Lord, holy Father,
   almighty and eternal God,
through Christ our Lord.

For after he had told the disciples
   of his coming Death,

Super oblata

Hæc hostia, Domine, quæsumus,
   emundet nostra delicta,
et ad celebranda festa paschalia
fidelium tuorum corpora
   mentesque sanctificet.
Per Christum Dominum nostrum.

Praefatio: De transfiguratione Domini.

Vere dignum et iustum est,
   aequum et salutare,
nos tibi semper et ubique
   gratias agere:
Domine, sancte Pater,
   omnipotens aeterne Deus:
per Christum Dominum nostrum:

Qui, propria morte
   praenuntiata discipulis,

on the holy mountain
> he manifested to them his glory,
to show, even by the testimony
> of the law and the prophets,
that the Passion leads to the glory
> of the Resurrection.

And so, with the Powers of heaven,
we worship you constantly on earth,
and before your majesty
without end we acclaim:
Holy, Holy, Holy Lord God of hosts...

Communion Antiphon Mt 17:5
This is my beloved Son,
> with whom I am well pleased;
listen to him.

Prayer after Communion
As we receive these glorious mysteries,
we make thanksgiving to you,
> O Lord,
for allowing us while still on earth
to be partakers even now
> of the things of heaven.
Through Christ our Lord.

Prayer over the People
Bless your faithful, we pray, O Lord,
with a blessing that endures for ever,
and keep them faithful
to the Gospel of your
> Only Begotten Son,
so that they may always desire
> and at last attain
that glory whose beauty he showed
> in his own Body,
to the amazement of his Apostles.
Through Christ our Lord.

---

in monte sancto suam eis
> aperuit claritatem,
ut per passionem, etiam lege
> prophetisque testantibus,
ad gloriam resurrectionis
> perveniri constaret.

Et ideo, cum caelorum Virtutibus,
in terris te iugiter celebramus,
maiestati tuae sine fine clamantes:
Sanctus, Sanctus, Sanctus. . .

Ant. ad communionem
Hic est Filius meus dilectus,
in quo mihi bene complacui;
ipsum audite.

Post communionem
Percipientes, Domine,
> gloriosa mysteria,
gratias tibi referre satagimus,
quod, in terra positos,
iam cælestium præstas
> esse participes.
Per Christum Dominum nostrum.

Oratio super populum
Benedic, Domine, fideles tuos
> benedictione perpetua,
et fac eos Unigeniti tui Evangelio
> sic adhærere,
ut ad illam gloriam, cuius in se
> speciem Apostolis ostendit,
et suspirare iugiter et feliciter
> valeant pervenire.
Per Christum Dominum nostrum.

In Wales

1 March

SAINT DAVID, BISHOP, PATRON OF WALES

Saint David was one of the great saints of the sixth century, that golden age of saints and missionaries in these isles, and he was thus a founder of the Christian culture which lies at the root of modern Europe. David's preaching was simple yet profound: his dying words to his monks were, "Be joyful, keep the faith, and do the little things". It is the little things that reveal our love for the one who loved us first (Cf. 1 Jn 4:19) and that bind people into a community of faith, love and service. May Saint David's message, in all its simplicity and richness, continue to resound today, drawing the hearts of people to renewed love for Christ and his Church.

(Pope Benedict XVI)

Solemnity

Entrance Antiphon
Is 52:7

How beautiful upon the mountains are the feet of him
who brings glad tidings of peace,
bearing good news, announcing salvation!

The Gloria in excelsis (Glory to God in the highest) is said.

Collect
O God, who graciously bestowed on your Bishop Saint David of Wales
the virtue of wisdom and the gift of eloquence
and made him an example of prayer and pastoral zeal,
grant that, through his intercession
your Church may ever prosper and render you joyful praise.
Through our Lord Jesus Christ, your Son,
who lives and reigns with you in the unity of the Holy Spirit,
one God, for ever and ever.

Alternative readings may be chosen from the Common of Pastors, or from the Common of Holy Men and Women.

FIRST READING

A reading from the letter of St Paul to the Philippians   3:8-14

I am racing for the finish, for the prize to which God calls us upward to receive in Christ Jesus.

I believe nothing can happen that will outweigh the supreme advantage of knowing Christ Jesus my Lord. For him I have accepted the loss of everything, and I look on everything as so much rubbish if only I can have Christ and be given a place in him. I am no longer trying for perfection by my own efforts, the perfection that comes from the Law, but I want only the perfection that comes through faith in Christ, and is from God and based on faith. All I want is to know Christ and the power of his resurrection and to share his sufferings by reproducing the pattern of his death. That is the way I can hope to take my place in the resurrection of the dead. Not that I have become perfect yet. I have not yet won, but I am still running, trying to capture the prize for which Christ Jesus captured me. I can assure you my brothers, I am far from thinking that I have already won. All I can say is that I forget the past and I strain ahead for what is still to come; I am racing for the finish, for the prize to which God calls us upwards to receive in Christ Jesus.

The word of the Lord.

Responsorial Psalm

Ps 1:14,6. R. Ps 39:5

R. **Happy the man who has placed his trust in the Lord.**

Happy indeed is the man
who follows not the counsel of the wicked;
nor lingers in the way of sinners
nor sits in the company of scorners,
but whose delight is the law of the Lord
and who ponders his law day and night. R.

He is like a tree that is planted
beside the flowing waters,
that yields its fruit in due season
and whose leaves shall never fade;
and all that he does shall prosper. R.

Not so are the wicked, not so!
For they like winnowed chaff
shall be driven away by the wind.
For the Lord guards the way of the just
but the way of the wicked leads to doom. R.

A second reading is chosen from the options given on p.260.

Gospel Acclamation
Mt 23:9-10

R. **Glory to you, O Christ, you are the Word of God.**
If you make my word your home
you will indeed be my disciples,
and you will learn the truth, says the Lord.
R. **Glory to you, O Christ, you are the Word of God.**

GOSPEL

A reading from the holy Gospel according to Matthew 5:13-19
You are the light of the world.

Jesus said to his disciples: 'You are the salt of the earth. But if salt becomes tasteless, what can make it salty again? It is good for nothing, and can only be thrown out to be trampled underfoot by men.

'You are the light of the world. A city built on a hill-top can not be hidden. No one lights a lamp to put it under a tub; they put it on the lamp-stand where it shines for everyone in the house. In the same way your light must shine in the sight of men, so that, seeing your good works, they may give the praise to your Father in heaven.'

The Gospel of the Lord.

The Creed is said.

Prayer over the Offerings

Look with favour, O Lord, we pray,
on the offerings we set upon this sacred altar
on the feast day of the Bishop Saint David,
that, bestowing on us your pardon,
our oblations may give honour to your name.
Through Christ our Lord.

Communion Antiphon
Cf. 1 Co 1:23-24

We proclaim Christ crucified,
Christ, the power of God, and the wisdom of God.

Prayer after Communion

We pray, almighty God,
that we, who are fortified by the power of this Sacrament,
may learn through the example of your Bishop Saint David
to seek you always above all things
and to bear in this world the likeness of the New Man.
Who lives and reigns for ever and ever.

3 March

THIRD SUNDAY OF LENT

In today's Gospel passage, Jesus is questioned on certain distressing events. In the face of the easy conclusion of considering evil as an effect of divine punishment, Jesus restores the true image of God who is good and cannot desire evil. Jesus asks us to interpret these events differently, putting them in the perspective of conversion: misfortunes, sorrowful events must not awaken curiosity in us or the quest for presumed sins; instead they must be opportunities for reflection, in order to overcome the illusion of being able to live without God, and to reinforce, with the Lord's help, the commitment to change our way of life.

(Pope Benedict XVI)

Entrance Antiphon Cf. Ps 24:15-16

MY eyes are always on the Lord,
   for he rescues my feet
from the snare.
Turn to me and have mercy on me,
   for I am alone and poor.

Or: Cf. Ezk 36:23-26

When I prove my holiness
   among you,
I will gather you from all
   the foreign lands;
and I will pour clean water upon you
and cleanse you from
   all your impurities,
and I will give you a new spirit,
   says the Lord.

Ant. ad introitum

OCULI mei semper
   ad Dominum,
quia ipse evellet de laqueo
   pedes meos.
Respice in me et miserere mei,
quoniam unicus et pauper sum ego.

Vel:

Cum sanctificatus fuero in vobis,
congregabo vos de universis terris;
et effundam super vos
   aquam mundam,
et mundabimini ab omnibus
   inquinamentis vestris,
et dabo vobis spiritum novum,
   dicit Dominus.

The Gloria in excelsis (Glory to God in the highest) is not said.

Collect

O God, author of every mercy
 and of all goodness,
who in fasting, prayer and almsgiving
have shown us a remedy for sin,
look graciously on this confession
 of our lowliness,
that we, who are bowed down
 by our conscience,
may always be lifted up
 by your mercy.
Through our Lord Jesus Christ,
 your Son,
who lives and reigns with you
 in the unity of the Holy Spirit,
one God, for ever and ever.

Collecta

Deus, omnium misericordiarum
 et totius bonitatis auctor,
qui peccatorum remedia in ieiuniis,
orationibus et eleemosynis
 demonstrasti,
hanc humilitatis nostræ
 confessionem propitius intuere,
ut, qui inclinamur
 conscientia nostra,
tua semper misericordia sublevemur.
Per Dominum nostrum Iesum
 Christum Filium tuum,
qui tecum vivit et regnat
 in unitate Spiritus Sancti,
Deus, per omnia sæcula sæculorum.

FIRST READING

A reading from the book of Exodus   3:1-8,13-15

I Am has sent me to you.

Moses was looking after the flock of Jethro, his father-in-law, priest of Midian. He led his flock to the far side of the wilderness and came to Horeb, the mountain of God. There the angel of the Lord appeared to him in the shape of a flame of fire, coming from the middle of a bush. Moses looked; there was the bush blazing but it was not being burnt up. 'I must go and look at this strange sight,' Moses said 'and see why the bush is not burnt.' Now the Lord saw him go forward to look, and God called to him from the middle of the bush. 'Moses, Moses!' he said. 'Here I am' he answered. 'Come no nearer' he said. 'Take off your shoes, for the place on which you stand is holy ground. I am the God of your father,' he said 'the God of Abraham, the God of Isaac and the God of Jacob.' At this Moses covered his face, afraid to look at God.

And the Lord said, 'I have seen the miserable state of my people in Egypt. I have heard their appeal to be free of their slave-drivers. Yes, I am well aware of their sufferings. I mean to deliver them out of the hands of the Egyptians and bring them up out of that land to a land rich and broad, a land where milk and honey flow.'

Then Moses said to God, 'I am to go, then, to the sons of Israel and say to them, "The God of your fathers has sent me to you". But if they ask me what his name is, what am I to tell them?' And God said to Moses, 'I Am who I Am. This' he added 'is what you must say to the sons of Israel: "The Lord, the God of your fathers, the God of Abraham, the God of Isaac, and the God of Jacob, has sent me to you." This is my name for all time; by this name I shall be invoked for all generations to come.'

The word of the Lord

Responsorial Psalm

Ps 102:1-4,6-8,11. R. v.8

R. **The Lord is compassion and love.**

My soul, give thanks to the Lord,
all my being, bless his holy name.
My soul give thanks to the Lord
and never forget all his blessings. R.

It is he who forgives all your guilt,
who heals every one of your ills,
who redeems your life from the grave,
who crowns you with love and compassion. R.

The Lord does deeds of justice,
gives judgement for all who are oppressed.
He made known his ways to Moses
and his deeds to Israel's sons. R.

The Lord is compassion and love,
slow to anger and rich in mercy.
For as the heavens are high above the earth
so strong is his love for those who fear him. R.

SECOND READING

A reading from the first letter of St Paul to the Corinthians   10:1-6,10-12

The life of the people under Moses in the desert was written down to be a lesson for us.

I want to remind you, brothers, how our fathers were all guided by a cloud above them and how they all passed through the sea. They were all baptised into Moses in this cloud and in this sea; all ate the same spiritual food and all drank the same spiritual drink since they all drank from the spiritual rock that followed them as they went, and that rock was Christ. In spite of this, most of them failed to please God and their corpses littered the desert.

These things all happened as warnings for us, not to have the wicked lusts for forbidden things that they had. You must never complain: some of them did, and they were killed by the Destroyer.

All this happened to them as a warning, and it was written down to be a lesson for us who are living at the end of the age. The man who thinks he is safe must be careful that he does not fall.

The word of the Lord.

Gospel Acclamation
Mt 4:17

R. **Glory to you, O Christ, you are the Word of God!**
Repent, says the Lord,
for the kingdom of heaven is close at hand.
R. **Glory to you, O Christ, you are the Word of God!**

GOSPEL

A reading from the holy Gospel according to Luke 13:1-9

Unless you repent you will all perish as they did.

Some people arrived and told Jesus about the Galileans whose blood Pilate had mingled with that of their sacrifices. At this he said to them, 'Do you suppose these Galileans who suffered like that were greater sinners than any other Galileans? They were not, I tell you. No; but unless you repent you will all perish as they did. Or those eighteen on whom the tower at Siloam fell and killed them? Do you suppose that they were more guilty than all the other people living in Jerusalem? They were not, I tell you. No; but unless you repent you will all perish as they did.'

He told this parable: 'A man had a fig tree planted in his vineyard, and he came looking for fruit on it but found none. He said to the man who looked after the vineyard, "Look here, for three years now I have been coming to look for fruit on this fig tree and finding none. Cut it down: why should it be taking up the ground?" "Sir," the man replied "leave it one more year and give me time to dig round it and manure it: it may bear fruit next year; if not, then you can cut it down."'

The Gospel of the Lord.

The Creed is said.

Prayer over the Offerings

Be pleased, O Lord,
   with these sacrificial offerings,
and grant that we who beseech
   pardon for our own sins,
may take care to forgive
   our neighbour.
Through Christ our Lord.

Preface I or II of Lent, pp.48-51.

Communion Antiphon Cf. Ps 83:4-5

The sparrow finds a home,
and the swallow a nest for her young:
by your altars, O Lord of hosts,
   my King and my God.
Blessed are they who dwell
   in your house,
for ever singing your praise.

Prayer after Communion

As we receive the pledge
of things yet hidden in heaven
and are nourished while still on earth
with the Bread that comes
   from on high,
we humbly entreat you, O Lord,
that what is being brought about
   in us in mystery
may come to true completion.
Through Christ our Lord.

Prayer over the People

Direct, O Lord, we pray,
   the hearts of your faithful,
and in your kindness grant
   your servants this grace:
that, abiding in the love of you
   and their neighbour,
they may fulfil the whole
   of your commands.
Through Christ our Lord.

Super oblata

His sacrificiis, Domine,
   concede placatus,
ut, qui propriis oramus
   absolvi delictis,
fraterna dimittere studeamus.
Per Christum Dominum nostrum.

Ant. ad communionem

Passer invenit sibi domum,
et turtur nidum,
   ubi reponat pullos suos:
altaria tua, Domine virtutum,
   Rex meus, et Deus meus!
Beati qui habitant in domo tua,
in sæculum sæculi laudabunt te.

Post communionem

Sumentes pignus cælestis arcani,
et in terra positi iam superno
   pane satiati,
te, Domine, supplices deprecamur,
ut, quod in nobis mysterio geritur,
   opere impleatur.
Per Christum Dominum nostrum.

Oratio super populum

Rege, Domine, quæsumus,
   tuorum corda fidelium,
et servis tuis hanc gratiam
   largire propitius,
ut in tui et proximi
   dilectione manentes
plenitudinem mandatorum
   tuorum adimpleant.
Per Christum Dominum nostrum.

10 March

FOURTH SUNDAY OF LENT

On this Fourth Sunday of Lent, the Gospel of the father and the two sons better known as the Parable of the "Prodigal Son" (Lk 15:11-32) is proclaimed. This passage of St Luke constitutes one of the peaks of spirituality and literature of all time. After Jesus has told us of the merciful Father, things are no longer as they were before. We now know God; he is our Father who out of love created us to be free and endowed us with a conscience, who suffers when we get lost and rejoices when we return. The two sons represent two immature ways of relating to God: rebellion and childish obedience. Both these forms are surmounted through the experience of mercy. Only by experiencing forgiveness, by recognizing one is loved with a freely given love, a love greater than our wretchedness but also than our own merit, do we at last enter into a truly filial and free relationship with God.

(Pope Benedict XVI)

Entrance Antiphon Cf. Is 66:10-11

REJOICE, Jerusalem,
and all who love her.
Be joyful, all who were in mourning;
exult and be satisfied at her
    consoling breast.

Ant. ad introitum

LÆTARE, Ierusalem,
et conventum facite,
    omnes qui diligitis eam;
gaudete cum lætitia,
    qui in tristitia fuistis,
ut exsultetis, et satiemini ab
    uberibus consolationis vestræ.

The Gloria in excelsis (Glory to God in the highest) is not said.

Collect

O God, who through your Word
reconcile the human race
    to yourself in a wonderful way,
grant, we pray,
that with prompt devotion
    and eager faith
the Christian people may hasten
toward the solemn celebrations
    to come.

Collecta

Deus, qui per Verbum tuum
humani generis reconciliationem
    mirabiliter operaris,
præsta, quæsumus,
    ut populus christianus
prompta devotione et alacri fide
ad ventura sollemnia
    valeat festinare.

Through our Lord Jesus Christ, your Son, who lives and reigns with you in the unity of the Holy Spirit, one God, for ever and ever.	Per Dominum nostrum Iesum Christum Filium tuum, qui tecum vivit et regnat in unitate Spiritus Sancti, Deus, per omnia sæcula sæculorum.

FIRST READING

A reading from the book of Joshua   5:9-12

The People of God keep the Passover on their entry into the promised land.

The Lord said to Joshua, 'Today I have taken the shame of Egypt away from you.'

The Israelites pitched their camp at Gilgal and kept the Passover there on the fourteenth day of the month, at evening in the plain of Jericho. On the morrow of the Passover they tasted the produce of that country, unleavened bread and roasted ears of corn, that same day. From that time, from their first eating of the produce of that country, the manna stopped falling. And having manna no longer, the Israelites fed from that year onwards on what the land of Canaan yielded.

The word of the Lord.

Responsorial Psalm   Ps 33:2-7. R. v.9

R. **Taste and see that the Lord is good.**

I will bless the Lord at all times,
his praise always on my lips;
in the Lord my soul shall make its boast.
The humble shall hear and be glad. R.

Glorify the Lord with me.
Together let us praise his name.
I sought the Lord and he answered me;
from all my terrors he set me free. R.

Look towards him and be radiant;
let your faces not be abashed.
This poor man called; the Lord heard him
and rescued him from all his distress. R.

SECOND READING

A reading from the second letter of St Paul to the Corinthians 5:17-21

God reconciled us to himself through Christ.

For anyone who is in Christ, there is a new creation; the old creation has gone, and now the new one is here. It is all God's work. It was God who reconciled us to himself through Christ and gave us the work of handing on this reconciliation. In other words, God in Christ was reconciling the world to himself, not holding men's faults against them, and he has entrusted to us the news that they are reconciled. So we are ambassadors for Christ; it is as though God were appealing through us, and the appeal that we make in Christ's name is: be reconciled to God. For our sake God made the sinless one into sin, so that in him we might become the goodness of God.

The word of the Lord.

Gospel Acclamation Lk 15:18

R. **Praise and honour to you, Lord Jesus!**
I will leave this place and go to my father and say:
'Father, I have sinned against heaven and against you.'
R. **Praise and honour to you, Lord Jesus!**

GOSPEL

A reading from the holy Gospel according to Luke 15:1-3,11-32

Your brother here was dead and has come to life.

The tax collectors and the sinners were all seeking the company of Jesus to hear what he had to say, and the Pharisees and the scribes complained. 'This man' they said 'welcomes sinners and eats with them.' So he spoke this parable to them:

'A man had two sons. The younger said to his father, "Father, let me have the share of the estate that would come to me." So the father divided the property between them. A few days later, the younger son got together everything he had and left for a distant country where he squandered his money on a life of debauchery.

'When he had spent it all, that country experienced a severe famine, and now he began to feel the pinch, so he hired himself out to one of the local inhabitants who put him on his farm to feed the pigs. And he would willingly have filled his belly with the husks the pigs were eating but no one offered him anything. Then he came to his senses and said,

"How many of my father's paid servants have more food than they want, and here am I dying of hunger! I will leave this place and go to my father and say: Father, I have sinned against heaven and against you; I no longer deserve to be called your son; treat me as one of your paid servants." So he left the place and went back to his father.

'While he was still a long way off, his father saw him and was moved with pity. He ran to the boy, clasped him in his arms and kissed him tenderly. Then his son said, "Father, I have sinned against heaven and against you. I no longer deserve to be called your son." But the father said to his servants, "Quick! Bring out the best robe and put it on him; put a ring on his finger and sandals on his feet. Bring the calf we have been fattening, and kill it; we are going to have a feast, a celebration, because this son of mine was dead and has come back to life; he was lost and is found." And they began to celebrate.

'Now the elder son was out in the fields, and on his way back, as he drew near the house, he could hear music and dancing. Calling one of the servants he asked what it was all about. "Your brother has come" replied the servant "and your father has killed the calf we had fattened because he has got him back safe and sound." He was angry then and refused to go in, and his father came out to plead with him; but he answered his father, "Look, all these years I have slaved for you and never once disobeyed your orders, yet you never offered me so much as a kid for me to celebrate with my friends. But, for this son of yours, when he comes back after swallowing up your property – he and his women – you kill the calf we had been fattening."

'The father said, "My son, you are with me always and all I have is yours. But it is only right we should celebrate and rejoice, because your brother here was dead and has come to life; he was lost and is found."'

The Gospel of the Lord.

The Creed is said.

Prayer over the Offerings

We place before you
   with joy these offerings,
which bring eternal remedy, O Lord,
praying that we may both faithfully revere them
and present them to you, as is fitting,
for the salvation of all the world.
Through Christ our Lord.

Super oblata

Remedii sempiterni munera, Domine,
lætantes offerimus,
   suppliciter exorantes,
ut eadem nos et fideliter venerari,
et pro salute mundi congruenter exhibere perficias.
Per Christum Dominum nostrum.

Preface I or II of Lent, pp.48-51.

Communion Antiphon   Lk 15:32

You must rejoice, my son,
for your brother was dead
   and has come to life;
he was lost and is found.

Prayer after Communion

O God, who enlighten everyone
   who comes into this world,
illuminate our hearts, we pray,
with the splendour of your grace,
that we may always ponder
what is worthy and pleasing
   to your majesty
and love you in all sincerity.
Through Christ our Lord.

Prayer over the People

Look upon those who call to you,
   O Lord,
and sustain the weak;
give life by your unfailing light
to those who walk in the shadow
   of death,
and bring those rescued
   by your mercy from every evil
to reach the highest good.
Through Christ our Lord.

Ant. ad communionem

Oportet te, fili, gaudere,
quia frater tuus mortuus fuerat,
   et revixit;
perierat, et inventus est.

Post communionem

Deus, qui illuminas
   omnem hominem
venientem in hunc mundum,
illumina, quæsumus, corda nostra
   gratiæ tuæ splendore,
ut digna ac placita maiestati tuæ
   cogitare semper,
et te sincere diligere valeamus.
Per Christum Dominum nostrum.

Oratio super populum

Tuere, Domine, supplices tuos,
   sustenta fragiles,
et inter tenebras
   mortalium ambulantes
tua semper luce vivifica,
atque a malis omnibus
   clementer ereptos,
ad summa bona pervenire concede.
Per Christum Dominum nostrum.

FIFTH SUNDAY OF LENT

We have reached the Fifth Sunday of Lent in which the liturgy this year presents to us the Gospel episode of Jesus who saves an adulterous woman condemned to death. St John the Evangelist highlights one detail: while his accusers are insistently interrogating him, Jesus bends down and starts writing with his finger on the ground. St Augustine notes that this gesture portrays Christ as the divine legislator: in fact, God wrote the law with his finger on tablets of stone. Thus Jesus is the Legislator, he is Justice in person. And what is his sentence? "Let him who is without sin among you be the first to throw a stone at her." These words are full of the disarming power of truth that pulls down the wall of hypocrisy and opens consciences to a greater justice, that of love, in which consists the fulfilment of every precept.

(Pope Benedict XVI)

Entrance Antiphon   Cf. Ps 42:1-2

GIVE me justice, O God,
   and plead my cause against
a nation that is faithless.
From the deceitful and cunning
   rescue me,
for you, O God, are my strength.

Ant. ad introitum

IUDICA me, Deus,
   et discerne causam meam
de gente non sancta;
ab homine iniquo et doloso eripe me,
quia tu es Deus meus
   et fortitudo mea.

The Gloria in excelsis (Glory to God in the highest) is not said.

Collect

By your help, we beseech you,
   Lord our God,
may we walk eagerly
   in that same charity
with which, out of love for the world,
your Son handed himself
   over to death.
Through our Lord Jesus Christ,
   your Son,
who lives and reigns with you
   in the unity of the Holy Spirit,
one God, for ever and ever.

Collecta

Quæsumus, Domine Deus noster,
   ut in illa caritate
qua Filius tuus diligens mundum
   morti se tradidit,
inveniamur ipsi, te opitulante,
   alacriter ambulantes.
Per Dominum nostrum Iesum
   Christum Filium tuum,
qui tecum vivit et regnat
   in unitate Spiritus Sancti,
Deus, per omnia sæcula sæculorum.

In Ireland

17 March

SAINT PATRICK, BISHOP, PATRON OF IRELAND

St Patrick (385-461) was born into a Christian Romano-British family. His first encounter with Ireland was as a slave after he was captured by raiders at the age of sixteen. After escaping, he probably studied in Gaul and was ordained a priest. Around 432 he returned to Ireland as a missionary bishop and succeeded in consolidating the faith in large parts of the country.

Entrance Antiphon
Gn 12:1-2

Go from your country and your kindred and your father's house to the land that I will show you.
I will make of you a great nation, and I will bless you,
and make your name great, so that you will be a blessing.

The Gloria in excelsis (Glory to God in the highest) is said.

Collect

Lord, through the work of Saint Patrick in Ireland
we have come to acknowledge the mystery of the one true God
and give thanks for our salvation in Christ;
grant by his prayers
that we who celebrate this festival
may keep alive the fire of faith he kindled.
Through our Lord Jesus Christ, your Son,
who lives and reigns with you in the unity of the Holy Spirit,
one God, for ever and ever.

FIRST READING

A reading from the prophet Isaiah
43:16-21

See, I am doing a new deed, and I will give my chosen people drink.

Thus says the Lord,
who made a way through the sea,
a path in the great waters;
who put chariots and horse in the field

and a powerful army,
which lay there never to rise again,
snuffed out, put out like a wick:

> No need to recall the past,
> no need to think about what was done before.
> See, I am doing a new deed,
> even now it comes to light; can you not see it?
> Yes, I am making a road in the wilderness,
> paths in the wilds.
>
> The wild beasts will honour me,
> jackals and ostriches,
> because I am putting water in the wilderness
> (rivers in the wild)
> to give my chosen people drink.
> The people I have formed for myself
> will sing my praises.

The word of the Lord.

Responsional Psalm

Ps 125. R. v.3

R. **What marvels the Lord worked for us!**
Indeed we were glad.

When the Lord delivered Zion from bondage,
it seemed like a dream.
Then was our mouth filled with laughter,
on our lips there were songs. R.

The heathens themselves said: 'What marvels
the Lord worked for them!'
What marvels the Lord worked for us!
Indeed we were glad. R.

Deliver us, O Lord, from our bondage
as streams in dry land.
Those who are sowing in tears
will sing when they reap. R.

They go out, they go out, full of tears,
carrying seed for the sowing:
they come back, they come back, full of song,
carrying their sheaves. R.

SECOND READING

A reading from the letter of St Paul to the Philippians 3:8-14

Reproducing the pattern of his death, I have accepted the loss of everything for Christ.

I believe nothing can happen that will outweigh the supreme advantage of knowing Christ Jesus my Lord. For him I have accepted the loss of everything, and I look on everything as so much rubbish if only I can have Christ and be given a place in him. I am no longer trying for perfection by my own efforts, the perfection that comes from the Law, but I want only the perfection that comes through faith in Christ, and is from God and based on faith. All I want is to know Christ and the power of his resurrection and to share his sufferings by reproducing the pattern of his death. That is the way I can hope to take my place in the resurrection of the dead. Not that I have become perfect yet: I have not yet won, but I am still running, trying to capture the prize for which Christ Jesus captured me. I can assure you my brothers, I am far from thinking that I have already won. All I can say is that I forget the past and I strain ahead for what is still to come; I am racing for the finish, for the prize to which God calls us upwards to receive in Christ Jesus.

The word of the Lord.

Gospel Acclamation   Cf. Am 5:14

R. **Praise to you, O Christ, king of eternal glory!**
Seek good and not evil so that you may live,
and that the Lord God of hosts may really be with you.
R. **Praise to you, O Christ, king of eternal glory!**

Or: Jl 2:12-13

R. **Praise to you, O Christ, king of eternal glory!**
Now, now – it is the Lord who speaks –
come back to me with all your heart,
for I am all tenderness and compassion.
R. **Praise to you, O Christ, king of eternal glory!**

GOSPEL

A reading from the holy Gospel according to John 8:1-11

If there is one of you who has not sinned, let him be the first to throw a stone at her.

Jesus went to the Mount of Olives. At daybreak he appeared in the Temple again; and as all the people came to him, he sat down and began to teach them.

The scribes and Pharisees brought a woman along who had been caught committing adultery; and making her stand there in full view of everybody, they said to Jesus, 'Master, this woman was caught in the very act of committing adultery, and Moses has ordered us in the Law to condemn women like this to death by stoning. What have you to say?' They asked him this as a test, looking for something to use against him. But Jesus bent down and started writing on the ground with his finger. As they persisted with their question, he looked up and said, 'If there is one of you who has not sinned, let him be the first to throw a stone at her.' Then he bent down and wrote on the ground again. When they heard this they went away one by one, beginning with the eldest, until Jesus was left alone with the woman, who remained standing there. He looked up and said, 'Woman, where are they? Has no one condemned you?' 'No one, sir,' she replied. 'Neither do I condemn you,' said Jesus 'go away, and don't sin any more.'

The Gospel of the Lord.

The Creed is said.

Prayer over the Offerings

Hear us, almighty God,
and, having instilled in your servants
the teachings of the Christian faith,
graciously purify them
by the working of this sacrifice.
Through Christ our Lord.

Preface I or II of Lent, pp.48-51.

Communion Antiphon Jn 8:10-11

Has no one condemned you, woman?
No one, Lord.
Neither shall I condemn you.
From now on, sin no more.

Prayer after Communion

We pray, almighty God,
that we may always be counted
    among the members of Christ,
in whose Body and Blood
    we have communion.
Who lives and reigns
    for ever and ever.

Super oblata

Exaudi nos, omnipotens Deus,
et famulos tuos, quos fidei
    christianæ eruditionibus imbuisti,
huius sacrificii tribuas
    operatione mundari.
Per Christum Dominum nostrum.

Ant. ad communionem

Nemo te condemnavit, mulier?
    Nemo, Domine.
Nec ego te condemnabo:
    iam amplius noli peccare.

Post communionem

Quæsumus, omnipotens Deus,
ut inter eius membra
    semper numeremur,
cuius Corpori communicamus
    et Sanguini.
Qui vivit et regnat
    in sæcula sæculorum.

Prayer over the People

Bless, O Lord, your people,
who long for the gift of your mercy,
and grant that what,
   at your prompting, they desire
they may receive by your
   generous gift.
Through Christ our Lord.

Oratio super populum

Benedic, Domine, plebem tuam,
quæ munus tuæ
   miserationis exspectat,
et concede, ut, quod,
   te inspirante, desiderat,
te largiente percipiat.
Per Christum Dominum nostrum.

In Ireland

SAINT PATRICK, BISHOP, PATRON OF IRELAND

Prayer over the Offerings

Lord, accept this pure sacrifice
which, through the labours of Saint Patrick,
your grateful people make
to the glory of your name.
Through Christ our Lord.

Preface

It is truly right and just, our duty and our salvation,
always and everywhere to give you thanks,
Lord, holy Father, almighty and eternal God,
and to proclaim your greatness with due praise
as we honour Saint Patrick.

For you drew him through daily prayer
in captivity and hardship
to know you as a loving Father.

You chose him out of all the world
to return to the land of his captors,
that they might acknowledge Jesus Christ, their Redeemer.

In the power of your Spirit you directed his paths
to win the sons and daughters of the Irish
to the service of the Triune God.

And so, with the Angels and Archangels,
and with the great multitude of the Saints,
we sing the hymn of your praise, as without end we acclaim:

Holy, Holy, Holy Lord God of hosts ...

Communion Antiphon
Cf. Mt 8:11

Many will come from east and west
and sit down with Abraham, Isaac and Jacob
at the feast in the Kingdom of Heaven, says the Lord.

Prayer after Communion

Strengthen us, O Lord, by this sacrament
so that we may profess the faith taught by Saint Patrick
and to proclaim it in our way of living.
Through Christ our Lord.

Solemn Blessing

May God the Father, who called us together
to celebrate this feast of Saint Patrick,
bless you, protect you and keep you faithful.
R. Amen.

May Christ the Lord, the High King of Heaven,
be near you at all times and shield you from evil.
R. Amen.

May the Holy Spirit, who is the source of all holiness,
make you rich in the love of God's people.
R. Amen.

And may the blessing of almighty God,
the Father, and the Son, ✠ and the Holy Spirit,
come down on you and remain with you for ever.
R. Amen.

---

19 March

SAINT JOSEPH, SPOUSE OF THE BLESSED VIRGIN MARY

The figure of this great Saint, even though remaining somewhat hidden, is of fundamental importance in the history of salvation. Above all, as part of the tribe of Judah, he united Jesus to the Davidic lineage so that, fulfilling the promises regarding the Messiah, the Son of the Virgin Mary may truly be called the "son of David". The Gospel of Matthew highlights in a special way the Messianic prophecies which reached fulfilment through the role that

Joseph played: the birth of Jesus in Bethlehem; his journey through Egypt, where the Holy Family took refuge; the nickname, the "Nazarene". In all of this he showed himself, like his spouse Mary, an authentic heir of Abraham's faith: faith in God who guides the events of history according to his mysterious salvific plan. His greatness, like Mary's, stands out even more because his mission was carried out in the humility and hiddenness of the house of Nazareth. Moreover, God himself, in the person of his Incarnate Son, chose this way and style of life – humility and hiddenness – in his earthly existence. From the example of Saint Joseph we all receive a strong invitation to carry out with fidelity, simplicity and modesty the task that Providence has entrusted to us.

(Pope Benedict XVI)

Solemnity

Entrance Antiphon — Cf. Lk 12:42

BEHOLD, a faithful and prudent steward,
whom the Lord set over
   his household.

Ant. ad introitum

ECCE fidelis servus et prudens, quem constituit Dominus super familiam suam.

The Gloria in excelsis (Glory to God in the highest) is said.

Collect

Grant, we pray, almighty God,
that by Saint Joseph's intercession
your Church may constantly
   watch over
the unfolding of the mysteries
   of human salvation,
whose beginnings you entrusted
   to his faithful care.
Through our Lord Jesus Christ,
   your Son,
who lives and reigns with you
   in the unity of the Holy Spirit,
one God, for ever and ever.

Collecta

Præsta, quæsumus,
   omnipotens Deus,
ut humanæ salutis mysteria,
cuius primordia beati Ioseph fideli
   custodiæ commisisti,
Ecclesia tua, ipso intercedente,
   iugiter servet implenda.
Per Dominum nostrum Iesum
   Christum Filium tuum,
qui tecum vivit et regnat
   in unitate Spiritus Sancti,
Deus, per omnia sæcula sæculorum.

FIRST READING

A reading from the second book of Samuel   7:4-5,12-14,16

The Lord will give him the throne of his ancestor David.

The word of the Lord came to Nathan:

   'Go and tell my servant David, "Thus the Lord speaks: When your days are ended and you are laid to rest with your ancestors, I will preserve the offspring of your body after you and make his sovereignty secure. (It is he who shall build a house for my name and I will make his royal throne secure for ever.) I will be a father to him and he a son to me. Your House and your sovereignty will always stand secure before me and your throne be established for ever."'

The word of the Lord.

Responsional Psalm

Ps 88:2-5,27,29. R. v.37

R. **His dynasty shall last for ever.**

I will sing for ever of your love, O Lord;
through all ages my mouth will proclaim your truth.
Of this I am sure, that your love lasts for ever,
that your truth is firmly established as the heavens. R.

'I have made a covenant with my chosen one;
I have sworn to David my servant:
I will establish your dynasty for ever
and set up your throne through all ages.' R.

He will say to me: 'You are my father,
my God, the rock who saves me.'
I will keep my love for him always;
for him my covenant shall endure. R.

SECOND READING

A reading from the letter of St Paul to the Romans 4:13,16-18,22

Though it seemed Abraham's hope could not be fulfilled, he hoped and he believed.

The promise of inheriting the world was not made to Abraham and his descendants on account of any law but on account of the righteousness which consists in faith. That is why what fulfils the promise depends on faith, so that it may be a free gift and be available to all of Abraham's descendants, not only those who belong to the Law but also to those who belong to the faith of Abraham who is the father of all of us. As scripture says: I have made you the ancestor of many nations – Abraham is our father in the eyes of God, in whom he put his faith, and who brings the dead to life and calls into being what does not exist.

Though it seemed Abraham's hope could not be fulfilled, he hoped and he believed, and through doing so he did become the father of many nations exactly as he had been promised: Your descendants will be as many as the stars. This is the faith that was 'considered as justifying him'.

The word of the Lord.

Gospel Acclamation
Ps 83:5

R. **Glory and praise to you, O Christ.**
They are happy who dwell in your house, O Lord,
for ever singing your praise.
R. **Glory and praise to you, O Christ.**

GOSPEL

A reading from the holy Gospel according to Matthew 1:16,18-21,24

Joseph did what the angel of the Lord had told him to do.

Jacob was the father of Joseph the husband of Mary; of her was born Jesus who is called Christ.

This is how Jesus Christ came to be born. His mother Mary was betrothed to Joseph; but before they came to live together she was found to be with child through the Holy Spirit. Her husband Joseph, being a man of honour and wanting to spare her publicity, decided to divorce her informally. He had made up his mind to do this when the angel of the Lord appeared to him in a dream and said, 'Joseph son of David, do not be afraid to take Mary home as your wife, because she has conceived what is in her by the Holy Spirit. She will give birth to a son and you must name him Jesus, because he is the one who is to save his people from their sins.' When Joseph woke up he did what the angel of the Lord had told him to do.

The Gospel of the Lord

ALTERNATIVE GOSPEL

A reading from the holy Gospel according to Luke 2:41-51

See how worried your father and I have been, looking for you.

Every year the parents of Jesus used to go to Jerusalem for the feast of the Passover. When he was twelve years old, they went up for the feast as usual. When they were on their way home after the feast, the boy Jesus stayed behind in Jerusalem without his parents knowing it. They assumed he was with the caravan, and it was only after a day's journey that they went to look for him among their relations and acquaintances. When they failed to find him they went back to Jerusalem looking for him everywhere.

Three days later, they found him in the Temple, sitting among the doctors, listening to them, and asking them questions; and all those who heard him were astounded at his intelligence and his replies. They were overcome when they saw him and his mother said to him, 'My child, why have you done this to us? See how worried your father and I have been, looking for you.' 'Why were you looking for me?' he replied. 'Did you not know that I must be busy with my Father's affairs?' But they did not understand what he meant.

He then went down with them and came to Nazareth and lived under their authority.

The Gospel of the Lord.

The Creed is said.

Prayer over the Offerings

We pray, O Lord,
that, just as Saint Joseph
    served with loving care
your Only Begotten Son,
    born of the Virgin Mary,
so we may be worthy to minister
with a pure heart at your altar.
Through Christ our Lord.

Preface: The mission of Saint Joseph.

It is truly right and just,
    our duty and our salvation,
always and everywhere
    to give you thanks,
Lord, holy Father,
    almighty and eternal God,
and on the Solemnity of Saint Joseph
to give you fitting praise,
to glorify you and bless you.

For this just man was given by you
as spouse to the Virgin Mother of God
and set as a wise and faithful servant
in charge of your household
to watch like a father over your
    Only Begotten Son,
who was conceived by the
    overshadowing of the Holy Spirit,
our Lord Jesus Christ.

Through him the Angels praise
    your majesty,

Super oblata

Quæsumus, Domine, ut,
    sicut beatus Ioseph
Unigenito tuo,
    nato de Maria Virgine,
pia devotione deserviit,
ita et nos mundo corde
tuis altaribus mereamur ministrare.
Per Christum Dominum nostrum.

Præfatio: De missione sancti Ioseph.

Vere dignum et iustum est,
    æquum et salutare,
nos tibi semper et ubique
    gratias agere:
Domine, sancte Pater,
    omnipotens æterne Deus:
Et te in sollemnitate beati Ioseph
debitis magnificare præconiis,
    benedicere et prædicare.

Qui et vir iustus, a te Deiparæ
    Virgini Sponsus est datus,
et fidelis servus ac prudens,
super Familiam tuam est constitutus,
ut Unigenitum tuum,
Sancti Spiritus obumbratione
    conceptum,
paterna vice custodiret,
Iesum Christum Dominum nostrum.

Per quem maiestatem tuam
    laudant Angeli,

Dominions adore and Powers tremble before you.
Heaven and the Virtues of heaven and the blessed Seraphim
worship together with exultation.

May our voices, we pray, join with theirs
in humble praise, as we acclaim:

Holy, Holy, Holy Lord God of hosts...

Communion Antiphon Mt 25:21

Well done, good and faithful servant. Come, share your master's joy.

Prayer after Communion

Defend with unfailing protection, O Lord, we pray,
the family you have nourished with food from this altar,
as they rejoice at the Solemnity of Saint Joseph,
and graciously keep safe your gifts among them.
Through Christ our Lord.

---

adorant Dominationes, tremunt Potestates.
Cæli cælorumque Virtutes, ac beata Seraphim,
socia exsultatione concelebrant.

Cum quibus et nostras voces ut admitti iubeas, deprecamur,
supplici confessione dicentes:

Sanctus, Sanctus, Sanctus...

Ant. ad communionem

Euge, serve bone et fidelis: intra in gaudium Domini tui.

Post communionem

Familiam tuam, quæsumus, Domine,
quam de beati Ioseph sollemnitate lætantem
ex huius altaris alimonia satiasti,
perpetua protectione defende,
et tua in ea propitiatus dona custodi.
Per Christum Dominum nostru.

---

24 March

PALM SUNDAY OF THE PASSION OF THE LORD

It is a moving experience each year on Palm Sunday as we go up the mountain with Jesus, towards the Temple, accompanying him on his ascent. But what are we really doing when we join this procession as part of the throng which went up with Jesus to Jerusalem and hailed him as King of Israel? Does it have anything to do with the reality of our life and our world? To answer this, we must first be clear about what Jesus himself wished to do and actually did. He was journeying towards the Temple in the Holy City, towards that place which for Israel ensured in a particular way God's closeness to his people. The ultimate goal of his pilgrimage was the heights of God himself; to those heights he wanted to lift every human being. Our procession today is meant, then, to be an image of something deeper, to reflect the fact that, together with Jesus, we are setting out on pilgrimage along the high road that leads to the living God.

(Pope Benedict XVI)

On this day the Church recalls the entrance of Christ the Lord into Jerusalem to accomplish his Paschal Mystery. Accordingly, the memorial of this entrance of the Lord takes place at all Masses, by means of the Procession or the Solemn Entrance before the principal Mass or the Simple Entrance before other Masses. The Solemn Entrance, but not the Procession, may be repeated before other Masses that are usually celebrated with a large gathering of people.

It is desirable that, where neither the Procession nor the Solemn Entrance can take place, there be a sacred celebration of the Word of God on the messianic entrance and on the Passion of the Lord, either on Saturday evening or on Sunday at a convenient time.

The Commemoration of the Lord's Entrance into Jerusalem

First Form: The Procession

At an appropriate hour, a gathering takes place at a smaller church or other suitable place other than inside the church to which the procession will go. The faithful hold branches in their hands.

Wearing the red sacred vestments as for Mass, the Priest and the Deacon, accompanied by other ministers, approach the place where the people are gathered. Instead of the chasuble, the Priest may wear a cope, which he leaves aside when the procession is over, and puts on a chasuble.

Meanwhile, the following antiphon or another appropriate chant is sung.

Ant. Mt 21:9	Ant.
Hosanna to the Son of David; blessed is he who comes in the name of the Lord, the King of Israel. Hosanna in the highest.	Hosanna filio David: benedictus qui venit in nomine Domini. Rex Israel: Hosanna in excelsis.

After this, the Priest and people sign themselves, while the Priest says: In the name of the Father, and of the Son, and of the Holy Spirit. Then he greets the people in the usual way. A brief address is given, in which the faithful are invited to participate actively and consciously in the celebration of this day, in these or similar words:

Dear brethren (brothers and sisters),
since the beginning of Lent until now
we have prepared our hearts
    by penance and charitable works.
Today we gather together to herald
    with the whole Church
the beginning of the celebration
of our Lord's Paschal Mystery,
that is to say, of his Passion
    and Resurrection.
For it was to accomplish this mystery
that he entered his own city
    of Jerusalem.
Therefore, with all faith
    and devotion,
let us commemorate
the Lord's entry into the city
    for our salvation,
following in his footsteps,
so that, being made by his grace
    partakers of the Cross,
we may have a share also in his
    Resurrection and in his life.

Fratres carissimi,
postquam iam ab initio
    Quadragesimæ corda nostra
pænitentia et operibus
    caritatis præparavimus,
hodierna die congregamur,
ut cum tota Ecclesia præludamus
paschale Domini nostri mysterium,
eius nempe passionem
    atque resurrectionem,
ad quod implendum
ipse ingressus est civitatem
    suam Ierusalem.
Quare cum omni fide et devotione
    memoriam agentes
huius salutiferi ingressus,
    sequamur Dominum,
ut, per gratiam consortes
    effecti crucis,
partem habeamus resurrectionis
    et vitæ.

After the address, the Priest says one of the following prayers with hands extended.

Let us pray.
Almighty ever-living God,
sanctify ✠ these branches
    with your blessing,
that we, who follow Christ the King
    in exultation,
may reach the eternal Jerusalem
    through him.
Who lives and reigns
    for ever and ever.
R. Amen.

Or:

Increase the faith of those who
    place their hope in you, O God,

Oremus.
Omnipotens sempiterne Deus,
hos palmites tua
    benedictione ✠ sanctifica,
ut nos, qui Christum Regem
    exsultando prosequimur,
per ipsum valeamus ad æternam
    Ierusalem pervenire.
Qui vivit et regnat
    in sæcula sæculorum.
R. Amen.

Vel:

Auge fidem in te sperantium, Deus,
et supplicum preces

and graciously hear the prayers
  of those who call on you,
that we, who today hold high
  these branches
to hail Christ in his triumph,
may bear fruit for you by good
  works accomplished in him.
Who lives and reigns
  for ever and ever.
R. Amen.

clementer exaudi,
ut, qui hodie Christo triumphanti
  palmites exhibemus,
in ipso fructus tibi bonorum
  operum afferamus.
Qui vivit et regnat
  in sæcula sæculorum.
R. Amen.

He sprinkles the branches with holy water without saying anything.

Then a Deacon or, if there is no Deacon, a Priest, proclaims in the usual way the Gospel concerning the Lord's entrance according to one of the four Gospels. If appropriate, incense may be used.

GOSPEL

A reading from the holy Gospel according to Luke   19:28-40

Blessings on him who comes in the name of the Lord.

Jesus went on ahead, going up to Jerusalem.
When he drew near to Bethphage and Bethany,
at the mount that is called Olivet,
he sent two disciples,
saying, 'Go into the village opposite,
where on entering you will find a colt tied,
on which no one has ever yet sat;
untie it and bring it here.
If any one asks you,
"Why are you untying it?"
you shall say this,
"The Lord has need of it."'
So those who were sent
went away and found it as he had told them.
And as they were untying the colt,
its owners said to them,
'Why are you untying the colt?'
And they said,
'The Lord has need of it.'
And they brought it to Jesus,
and throwing their garments on the colt
they set Jesus upon it.

And as he rode along,
they spread their garments on the road.
As he was drawing near,
at the descent of the Mount of Olives,
the whole multitude of the disciples
began to rejoice and praise God with a loud voice
for all the mighty works that they had seen,
saying,
'Blessed is the King who comes in the name of the Lord!
Peace in heaven and glory in the highest!'
And some of the Pharisees in the multitude said to him,
'Teacher, rebuke your disciples.'
He answered,
'I tell you, if these were silent,
the very stones would cry out.'

The Gospel of the Lord.

After the Gospel, a brief homily may be given. Then, to begin the Procession, an invitation may be given by a Priest or a Deacon or a lay minister, in these or similar words:

Dear brethren (brothers and sisters), like the crowds who acclaimed Jesus in Jerusalem, let us go forth in peace.	Imitemur, fratres carissimi, turbas acclamantes Iesum, et procedamus in pace.
Or:	*Vel:*
Let us go forth in peace.	Procedamus in pace.
In this latter case, all respond:	
In the name of Christ. Amen.	In nomine Christi. Amen.

The Procession to the church where Mass will be celebrated then sets off in the usual way. If incense is used, the thurifer goes first, carrying a thurible with burning incense, then an acolyte or another minister, carrying a cross decorated with palm branches according to local custom, between two ministers with lighted candles. Then follow the Deacon carrying the Book of the Gospels, the Priest with the ministers, and, after them, all the faithful carrying branches.

As the Procession moves forward, the following or other suitable chants in honour of Christ the King are sung by the choir and people.

24 MARCH

Antiphon 1

The children of the Hebrews,
   carrying olive branches,
went to meet the Lord,
   crying out and saying:
Hosanna in the highest.

Antiphona 1

Pueri Hebræorum,
   portantes ramos olivarum,
obviaverunt Domino,
   clamantes et dicentes:
Hosanna in excelsis.

If appropriate, this antiphon is repeated between the strophes of the following Psalm.

PSALM 23

The Lord's is the earth
   and its fullness,*
the world, and those who dwell in it.
It is he who set it on the seas;*
on the rivers he made it firm. Ant.

Who shall climb the mountain
   of the Lord?*
The clean of hands and pure of heart,
whose soul is not set on vain things,†
who has not sworn
   deceitful words.* Ant.

Blessings from the Lord
   shall he receive,*
and right reward from the God
   who saves him.
Such are the people who seek him,*
who seek the face of the God
   of Jacob. Ant.

O gates, lift high your heads,†
grow higher, ancient doors.*
Let him enter, the king of glory!
Who is this king of glory?*
The Lord, the mighty, the valiant;
the Lord, the valiant in war. Ant.

O gates, lift high your heads;†
grow higher, ancient doors.*
Let him enter, the king of glory!
Who is this king of glory?*
He, the Lord of hosts,
he is the king of glory. Ant.

Domini est terra et plenitudo eius,*
   orbis terrarum et qui habitant in eo.
Quia ipse super maria fundavit eum*
et super flumina firmavit eum. Ant.

Quis ascendet in montem Domini,*
   aut quis stabit in loco sancto eius?
Innocens manibus et mundo corde,†
qui non levavit ad vana
   animam suam,*
nec iuravit in dolum. Ant.

Hic accipiet benedictionem
   a Domino*
et iustificationem a Deo salutari suo.
Hæc est generatio
   quærentium eum,*
quærentium faciem Dei Iacob. Ant.

Attollite, portæ, capita vestra,†
et elevamini, portæ æternales,*
et introibit rex gloriæ.
Quis est iste rex gloriæ?*
Dominus fortis et potens,
Dominus potens in prœlio. Ant.

Attollite, portæ, capita vestra, †
et elevamini, portæ æternales,*
et introibit rex gloriæ.
Quis est iste rex gloriæ?*
Dominus virtutum ipse est
   rex gloriæ. Ant.

Antiphon 2

The children of the Hebrews spread
  their garments on the road,
crying out and saying:
  Hosanna to the Son of David;
blessed is he who comes
  in the name of the Lord.

Antiphona 2

Pueri Hebræorum vestimenta
  prosternebant in via,
et clamabant dicentes:
  Hosanna filio David;
benedictus, qui venit
  in nomine Domini.

If appropriate, this antiphon is repeated between the strophes of the following Psalm.

PSALM 46

All peoples, clap your hands.*
Cry to God with shouts of joy!
For the Lord, the Most high,
  is awesome,*
the great king over all the earth. Ant.
He humbles peoples under us*
and nations under our feet.
Our heritage he chose for us,*
the pride of Jacob whom he loves.
God goes up with shouts of joy.*
The Lord goes up
  with trumpet blast. Ant.
Sing praise for God; sing praise!*
Sing praise to our king; sing praise!
God is king of all earth.*
Sing praise with all your skill. Ant.
God reigns over the nations.*
God sits upon his holy throne.
The princes of the peoples
  are assembled
with the people of the God
  of Abraham. †
The rulers of the earth belong
  to God,*
who is greatly exalted. Ant.

Omnes gentes, plaudite manibus,*
iubilate Deo in voce exsultationis,
quoniam Dominus Altissimus,
  terribilis,*
rex magnus super omnem terram. Ant.
Subiecit populos nobis,*
et gentes sub pedibus nostris.
Elegit nobis hereditatem nostram,*
gloriam Iacob, quem dilexit.
Ascendit Deus in iubilo,*
et Dominus in voce tubæ. Ant.
Psallite Deo, psallite;*
psallite regi nostro, psallite.
Quoniam rex omnis terræ Deus,*
psallite sapienter. Ant.
Regnavit Deus super gentes,*
Deus sedet super sedem
  sanctam suam.
Principes populorum congregati sunt
cum populo Dei Abraham,†
quoniam Dei sunt scuta terræ:*
vehementer elevatus est. Ant.

Hymn to Christ the King

Chorus:

Glory and honour and praise be to
  you, Christ, King and Redeemer,
to whom young children cried out
  loving Hosannas with joy.
All repeat: Glory and honour. . .

Hymnus ad Christum Regem

Gloria, laus et honor tibi sit,
  rex Christe redemptor,
cui puerile decus prompsit
  Hosanna pium.
Omnes repetunt: Gloria, laus. . .

Chorus:
Israel's King are you, King David's
   magnificent offspring;
you are the ruler who come blest
   in the name of the Lord.
All repeat: Glory and honour. . .

Chorus:
Heavenly hosts on high unite
   in singing your praises;
men and women on earth
   and all creation join in.
All repeat: Glory and honour. . .

Chorus:
Bearing branches of palm, Hebrews
   came crowding to greet you;
see how with prayers and hymns
   we come to pay you our vows.
All repeat: Glory and honour. . .

Chorus:
They offered gifts of praise to you,
   so near to your Passion;
see how we sing this song now
   to you reigning on high.
All repeat: Glory and honour. . .

Chorus:
Those you were pleased to accept;
   now accept our gifts of devotion,
good and merciful King,
   lover of all that is good.
All repeat: Glory and honour. . .

Israel es tu rex, Davidis
   et inclita proles,
nomine qui in Domini,
   rex benedicte, venis.
Omnes repetunt: Gloria, laus. . .

Cœtus in excelsis te laudat
   cælicus omnis,
et mortalis homo,
   et cuncta creata simul.
Omnes repetunt: Gloria, laus. . .

Plebs Hebræa tibi cum palmis
   obvia venit;
cum prece, voto,
   hymnis adsumus ecce tibi.
Omnes repetunt: Gloria, laus. . .

Hi tibi passuro solvebant
   munia laudis;
nos tibi regnanti
   pangimus ecce melos.
Omnes repetunt: Gloria, laus. . .

Hi placuere tibi,
   placeat devotio nostra:
rex bone, rex clemens,
   cui bona cuncta placent.
Omnes repetunt: Gloria, laus. . .

As the procession enters the church, there is sung the following responsory or another chant, which should speak of the Lord's entrance.

R. As the Lord entered the holy city,
the children of the Hebrews
proclaimed the resurrection of life.
*Waving their branches of palm,
   they cried:
Hosanna in the Highest.

R. Ingrediente Domino
   in sanctam civitatem,
Hebræorum pueri, resurrectionem
   vitæ pronuntiantes,
*Cum ramis palmarum:
Hosanna, clamabant, in excelsis.

V. When the people heard that Jesus was coming to Jerusalem, they went out to meet him.	V. Cum audisset populus, quod Iesus veniret Hierosolymam, exierunt obviam ei.
*Waving their branches. . .	*Cum ramis. . .

When the Priest arrives at the altar, he venerates it and, if appropriate, incenses it. Then he goes to the chair, where he puts aside the cope, if he has worn one, and puts on the chasuble. Omitting the other Introductory Rites of the Mass and, if appropriate, the Kyrie (Lord, have mercy), he says the Collect of the Mass, and then continues the Mass in the usual way.

Second Form: The Solemn Entrance

When a procession outside the church cannot take place, the entrance of the Lord is celebrated inside the church by means of a Solemn Entrance before the principal Mass.

Holding branches in their hands, the faithful gather either outside, in front of the church door, or inside the church itself. The Priest and ministers and a representative group of the faithful go to a suitable place in the church outside the sanctuary, where at least the greater part of the faithful can see the rite.

While the Priest approaches the appointed place, the antiphon Hosanna or another appropriate chant is sung. Then the blessing of branches and the proclamation of the Gospel of the Lord's entrance into Jerusalem take place. After the Gospel, the Priest processes solemnly with the ministers and the representative group of the faithful through the church to the sanctuary, while the responsory As the Lord entered or another appropriate chant is sung.

Arriving at the altar, the Priest venerates it. He then goes to the chair and, omitting the Introductory Rites of the Mass and, if appropriate, the Kyrie (Lord, have mercy), he says the Collect of the Mass, and then continues the Mass in the usual way.

Third Form: The Simple Entrance

At all other Masses of this Sunday at which the Solemn Entrance is not held, the memorial of the Lord's entrance into Jerusalem takes place by means of a Simple Entrance.

While the Priest proceeds to the altar, the Entrance Antiphon with its Psalm or another chant on the same theme is sung. Arriving at the altar, the Priest venerates it and goes to the chair. After the Sign of the Cross, he greets the people and continues the Mass in the usual way.

At other Masses, in which singing at the entrance cannot take place, the Priest, as soon as he has arrived at the altar and venerated it, greets the people, reads the Entrance Antiphon, and continues the Mass in the usual way.

24 MARCH

Entrance Antiphon Cf. Jn 12:1,12-13; Ps 23:9-10

SIX days before the Passover,
when the Lord came into
  the city of Jerusalem,
the children ran to meet him;
in their hands they carried
  palm branches
and with a loud voice cried out:

*Hosanna in the highest!
Blessed are you, who have come
  in your abundant mercy!

O gates, lift high your heads;
grow higher, ancient doors.
Let him enter, the king of glory!
Who is this king of glory?
He, the Lord of hosts,
  he is the king of glory.

*Hosanna in the highest!
Blessed are you, who have come
  in your abundant mercy!

Ant. ad introitum

ANTE sex dies sollemnis Paschæ,
  quando venit Dominus
in civitatem Ierusalem,
occurrerunt ei pueri:
et in manibus portabant
  ramos palmarum
et clamabant voce magna, dicentes:

*Hosanna in excelsis:
Benedictus, qui venisti
  in multitudine misericordiæ tuæ.
Attollite, portæ, capita vestra,
et elevamini, portæ æternales,
et introibit rex gloriæ.
Quis est iste rex gloriæ?
Dominus virtutum ipse est
  rex gloriæ.

*Hosanna in excelsis:
Benedictus, qui venisti
  in multitudine misericordiæ tuæ.

At the Mass

After the Procession or Solemn Entrance the Priest begins the Mass with the Collect.

Collect

Almighty ever-living God,
who as an example of humility
  for the human race to follow
caused our Saviour to take flesh
  and submit to the Cross,
graciously grant that we may heed
  his lesson of patient suffering
and so merit a share
  in his Resurrection.
Who lives and reigns with you
  in the unity of the Holy Spirit,
one God, for ever and ever.

Collecta

Omnipotens sempiterne Deus,
qui humano generi, ad imitandum
  humilitatis exemplum,
Salvatorem nostrum carnem sumere,
et crucem subire fecisti,
concede propitius,
ut et patientiæ ipsius
  habere documenta
et resurrectionis consortia mereamur.
Qui tecum vivit et regnat
  in unitate Spiritus Sancti,
Deus, per omnia sæcula sæculorum.

FIRST READING

A reading from the prophet Isaiah 50:4-7

I did not cover my face against insult - I know I shall not be shamed.

The Lord has given me
a disciple's tongue.
So that I may know how to reply to the wearied
he provides me with speech.
Each morning he wakes me to hear,
to listen like a disciple.
The Lord has opened my ear.
For my part, I made no resistance,
neither did I turn away.
I offered my back to those who struck me,
my cheeks to those who tore at my beard;
I did not cover my face
against insult and spittle.
The Lord comes to my help,
so that I am untouched by the insults.
So, too, I set my face like flint,
I know I shall not be shamed.

   The word of the Lord.

Responsional Psalm Ps 21:8-9,17-20,23-24. R. v.2

R. My God, my God, why have you forsaken me?

All who see me deride me.
They curl their lips, they toss their heads.
'He trusted in the Lord, let him save him;
let him release him if this is his friend.' R.

Many dogs have surrounded me,
a band of the wicked beset me.
They tear holes in my hands and my feet.
I can count every one of my bones. R.

They divide my clothing among them.
They cast lots for my robe.
O Lord, do not leave me alone,
my strength, make haste to help me! R.

I will tell of your name to my brethren
and praise you where they are assembled.
'You who fear the Lord give him praise;
all sons of Jacob, give him glory.
Revere him, Israel's sons.' R.

SECOND READING

A reading from the letter of St Paul to the Philippians 2:6-11

He humbled himself, but God raised him high.

His state was divine,
yet Christ Jesus did not cling
to his equality with God
but emptied himself
to assume the condition of a slave,
and became as men are;
and being as all men are,
he was humbler yet,
even to accepting death,
death on a cross.
But God raised him high
and gave him the name
which is above all other names
so that all beings
in the heavens, on earth and in the underworld,
should bend the knee at the name of Jesus
and that every tongue should acclaim
Jesus Christ as Lord,
to the glory of God the Father.

The word of the Lord.

Gospel Acclamation Ph 2:8-9

R. **Praise to you, O Christ, king of eternal glory.**
Christ was humbler yet,
even to accepting death, death on a cross.
But God raised him high
and gave him the name which is above all names.
R. **Praise to you, O Christ, king of eternal glory.**

The narrative of the Lord's Passion is read without candles and without incense, with no greeting or signing of the book. It is read by a Deacon or, if there is no Deacon, by a Priest. It may also be read by readers, with the part of Christ, if possible, reserved to a Priest.

Deacons, but not others, ask for the blessing of the Priest before singing the Passion, as at other times before the Gospel.

GOSPEL

The passion of our Lord Jesus Christ according to Luke 22:14-23:56

The symbols in the following passion narrative represent:

N Narrator J Jesus O Other single speaker

C Crowd, or more than one speaker

N When the hour came Jesus took his place at table, and the apostles with him. And he said to them,

J I have longed to eat this Passover with you before I suffer; because, I tell you, I shall not eat it again until it is fulfilled in the kingdom of God.

N Then, taking a cup, he gave thanks and said,

J Take this and share it among you, because from now on, I tell you, I shall not drink wine until the kingdom of God comes.

N Then he took some bread, and when he had given thanks, broke it and gave it to them, saying,

J This is my body which will be given for you; do this as a memorial of me.

N He did the same with the cup after supper, and said,

J This cup is the new covenant in my blood which will be poured out for you.

And yet, here with me on the table is the hand of the man who betrays me. The Son of Man does indeed go to his fate even as it has been decreed, but alas for that man by whom he is betrayed!

N And they began to ask one another which of them it could be who was to do this thing.

A dispute arose also between them about which should be reckoned the greatest, but he said to them,

J Among pagans it is the kings who lord it over them, and those who have authority over them are given the title Benefactor. This must not happen with you. No; the greatest among you must behave as if he were the youngest, the leader as if he were the one who serves. For who is the greater: the one at table or the one who serves? The one at table, surely? Yet here I am among you as one who serves!

You are the men who have stood by me faithfully in my trials; and now I confer a kingdom on you, just as my Father conferred one on me: you will eat and drink at my table in my kingdom, and you will sit on thrones to judge the twelve tribes of Israel.

Simon, Simon! Satan, you must know, has got his wish to sift you all like wheat; but I have prayed for you, Simon, that your faith may not fail, and once you have recovered, you in your turn must strengthen your brothers.

N He answered,
O Lord, I would be ready to go to prison with you, and to death.
N Jesus replied,
J I tell you, Peter, by the time the cock crows today you will have denied three times that you know me.
N He said to them,
J When I sent you out without purse or haversack or sandals, were you short of anything?
N They answered,
C No.
N He said to them,
J But now if you have a purse, take it: if you have a haversack, do the same; if you have no sword, sell your cloak and buy one, because I tell you these words of scripture have to be fulfilled in me: He let himself be taken for a criminal. Yes, what scripture says about me is even now reaching its fulfilment.
N They said,
C Lord, there are two swords here now.
N He said to them,
J That is enough!
N He then left the upper room to make his way as usual to the Mount of Olives, with the disciples following. When they reached the place he said to them,
J Pray not to be put to the test.
N Then he withdrew from them, about a stone's throw away, and knelt down and prayed, saying,
J Father, if you are willing, take this cup away from me. Nevertheless, let your will be done, not mine.
N Then an angel appeared to him coming from heaven to give him strength. In his anguish he prayed even more earnestly and his sweat fell to the ground like great drops of blood.

    When he rose from prayer he went to the disciples and found them sleeping for sheer grief. He said to them,
J Why are you asleep? Get up and pray not to be put to the test.
N He was still speaking when a number of men appeared, and at the head of them the man called Judas, one of the Twelve, who went up to Jesus to kiss him. Jesus said,
J Judas, are you betraying the Son of Man with a kiss?
N His followers, seeing what was happening, said,

C Lord, shall we use our swords?
N And one of them struck out at the high priest's servant, and cut off his right ear. But at this Jesus spoke,
J Leave off! That will do!
N And touching the man's ear he healed him.

   Then Jesus spoke to the chief priests and captains of the Temple guard and elders who had come for him. He said,
J Am I a brigand that you had to set out with swords and clubs? When I was among you in the Temple day after day you never moved to lay hands on me. But this is your hour; this is the reign of darkness.
N They seized him then and led him away, and they took him to the high priest's house. Peter followed at a distance. They had lit a fire in the middle of the courtyard and Peter sat down among them, and as he was sitting there by the blaze a servant-girl saw him, peered at him and said,
O This person was with him too.
N But he denied it, saying,
O Woman, I do not know him.
N Shortly afterwards, someone else saw him and said,
O You are another of them.
N But Peter replied,
O I am not, my friend.
N About an hour later, another man insisted, saying,
O This fellow was certainly with him. Why, he is a Galilean.
N Peter said,
O My friend, I do not know what you are talking about.
N At that instant, while he was still speaking, the cock crew, and the Lord turned and looked straight at Peter, and Peter remembered what the Lord had said to him, 'Before the cock crows today, you will have disowned me three times.' And he went outside and wept bitterly.

   Meanwhile the men who guarded Jesus were mocking and beating him. They blindfolded him and questioned him, saying,
C Play the prophet. Who hit you then?
N And they continued heaping insults on him.

   When day broke there was a meeting of the elders of the people, attended by the chief priests and scribes. He was brought before their council, and they said to him,
C If you are the Christ, tell us.
N He replied,
J If I tell you, you will not believe me, and if I question you, you will not answer. But from now on, the Son of Man will be seated at the right

N	Then they all said,
C	So you are the Son of God then?
N	He answered,
J	It is you who say I am.
N	They said,
C	What need of witnesses have we now? We have heard it for ourselves from his own lips.
N	[The whole assembly then rose, and they brought him before Pilate. They began their accusation by saying,
C	We found this man inciting our people to revolt, opposing payment of the tribute to Caesar, and claiming to be Christ, a king.
N	Pilate put to him this question,
O	Are you the king of the Jews?
N	He replied,
J	It is you who say it.
N	Pilate then said to the chief priests and the crowd,
O	I find no case against this man.
N	But they persisted,
C	He is inflaming the people with his teaching all over Judaea; it has come all the way from Galilee, where he started, down to here.
N	When Pilate heard this, he asked if the man were a Galilean; and finding that he came under Herod's jurisdiction he passed him over to Herod who was also in Jerusalem at that time.

hand of the Power of God.

Herod was delighted to see Jesus; he had heard about him and had been wanting for a long time to set eyes on him; moreover, he was hoping to see some miracle worked by him. So he questioned him at some length; but without getting any reply. Meanwhile the chief priests and the scribes were there, violently pressing their accusations. Then Herod, together with his guards, treated him with contempt and made fun of him; he put a rich cloak on him and sent him back to Pilate. And though Herod and Pilate had been enemies before, they were reconciled that same day.

Pilate then summoned the chief priests and the leading men and the people. He said,

O You brought this man before me as a political agitator. Now I have gone into the matter myself in your presence and found no case against the man in respect of all the charges you bring against him. Nor has Herod either, since he has sent him back to us. As you can see, the man has done nothing

that deserves death, so I shall have him flogged and then let him go.
N But as one man they howled,
C Away with him! Give us Barabbas!
N This man had been thrown into prison for causing a riot in the city and for murder.

    Pilate was anxious to set Jesus free and addressed them again, but they shouted back,
C Crucify him! Crucify him!
N And for the third time he spoke to them,
O Why? What harm has this man done? I have found no case against him that deserves death, so I shall have him punished and let him go.
N But they kept on shouting at the top of their voices, demanding that he should be crucified, and their shouts were growing louder.

    Pilate then gave his verdict: their demand was to be granted. He released the man they asked for, who had been imprisoned for rioting and murder, and handed Jesus over to them to deal with as they pleased.

    As they were leading him away they seized on a man, Simon from Cyrene, who was coming in from the country, and made him shoulder the cross and carry it behind Jesus. Large numbers of people followed him, and of women too who mourned and lamented for him. But Jesus turned to them and said,
J Daughters of Jerusalem, do not weep for me; weep rather for yourselves and for your children. For the days will surely come when people will say, 'Happy are those who are barren, the wombs that have never borne, the breasts that have never suckled!' Then they will begin to say to the mountains, 'Fall on us!'; to the hills, 'Cover us!' For if men use the green wood like this, what will happen when it is dry?
N Now with him they were also leading out two other criminals to be executed.

    When they reached the place called The Skull, they crucified him there and the criminals also, one on the right, the other on the left. Jesus said,
J Father, forgive them; they do not know what they are doing.
N Then they cast lots to share out his clothing. The people stayed there watching him. As for the leaders, they jeered at him, saying,
C He saved others; let him save himself if he is the Christ of God, the Chosen One.
N The soldiers mocked him too, and when they approached to offer him vinegar they said,

24 MARCH

C If you are the king of the Jews, save yourself.
N Above him there was an inscription: 'This is the King of the Jews.'
   One of the criminals hanging there abused him, saying,
O Are you not the Christ? Save yourself and us as well.
N But the other spoke up and rebuked him,
O Have you no fear of God at all? You got the same sentence as he did, but in our case we deserved it: we are paying for what we did. But this man has done nothing wrong. Jesus, remember me when you come into your kingdom.
N He replied,
J Indeed, I promise you, today you will be with me in paradise.
N It was now about the sixth hour and, with the sun eclipsed, a darkness came over the whole land until the ninth hour. The veil of the Temple was torn right down the middle; and when Jesus had cried out in a loud voice, he said,
J Father, into your hands I commit my spirit.
N With these words he breathed his last.

All kneel and pause a moment.

   When the centurion saw what had taken place, he gave praise to God and said,
O This was a great and good man.
N And when all the people who had gathered for the spectacle saw what had happened, they went home beating their breasts.
   All his friends stood at a distance; so also did the women who had accompanied him from Galilee, and they saw all this happen.]

   Then a member of the council arrived, an upright and virtuous man named Joseph. He had not consented to what the others had planned and carried out. He came from Arimathaea, a Jewish town, and he lived in the hope of seeing the kingdom of God. This man went to Pilate and asked for the body of Jesus. He then took it down, wrapped it in a shroud and put him in a tomb which was hewn in stone in which no one had yet been laid. It was Preparation Day and the sabbath was imminent.

   Meanwhile the women who had come from Galilee with Jesus were following behind. They took note of the tomb and of the position of the body.

   Then they returned and prepared spices and ointments. And on the sabbath day they rested, as the law required.

   [The Gospel of the Lord.]

Shorter Form, verses 23:1-49. Read between [ ]

After the narrative of the Passion, a brief homily should take place, if appropriate. A period of silence may also be observed.

The Creed is said, and the Universal Prayer takes place.

Prayer over the Offerings

Through the Passion of your Only
   Begotten Son, O Lord,
may our reconciliation with you
   be near at hand,
so that, though we do not merit it
   by our own deeds,
yet by this sacrifice made once
   for all,
we may feel already the effects
   of your mercy.
Through Christ our Lord.

Preface: The Passion of the Lord.

It is truly right and just,
   our duty and our salvation,
always and everywhere to give
   you thanks,
Lord, holy Father, almighty
   and eternal God,
through Christ our Lord.

For, though innocent, he suffered
   willingly for sinners
and accepted unjust condemnation
   to save the guilty.
His Death has washed away our sins,
and his Resurrection has purchased
   our justification.

And so, with all the Angels,
we praise you, as in joyful
   celebration we acclaim:

Holy, Holy, Holy Lord God of hosts...

Super oblata

Per Unigeniti tui passionem
placatio tua nobis, Domine,
   sit propinqua,
quam, etsi nostris operibus
   non meremur,
interveniente sacrificio singulari,
tua percipiamus
   miseratione præventi.
Per Christum Dominum nostrum.

Præfatio: De dominica Passione.

Vere dignum et iustum est,
   æquum et salutare,
nos tibi semper et ubique
   gratias agere:
Domine, sancte Pater, omnipotens
   æterne Deus:
per Christum Dominum nostrum.

Qui pati pro impiis dignatus
   est innocens,
et pro sceleratis
   indebite condemnari.
Cuius mors delicta nostra detersit,
et iustificationem nobis
   resurrectio comparavit.

Unde et nos cum omnibus Angelis
   te laudamus,
iucunda celebratione clamantes:

Sanctus, Sanctus, Sanctus. . .

Communion Antiphon Mt 26:42

Father, if this chalice cannot pass
   without my drinking it,
your will be done.

Prayer after Communion

Nourished with these sacred gifts,
we humbly beseech you, O Lord,
that, just as through the death
   of your Son
you have brought us to hope
   for what we believe,
so by his Resurrection
you may lead us to where you call.
Through Christ our Lord.

Prayer over the People

Look, we pray, O Lord,
   on this your family,
for whom our Lord Jesus Christ
did not hesitate to be delivered
   into the hands of the wicked
and submit to the agony
   of the Cross.
Who lives and reigns
   for ever and ever.

Ant. ad communionem

Pater, si non potest
   hic calix transire,
nisi bibam illum, fiat voluntas tua.

Post communionem

Sacro munere satiati,
supplices te, Domine, deprecamur,
ut, qui fecisti nos
morte Filii tui sperare
   quod credimus,
facias nos, eodem resurgente,
pervenire quo tendimus.
Per Christum Dominum nostrum.

Oratio super populum

Respice, quæsumus, Domine,
   super hanc familiam tuam,
pro qua Dominus noster
   Iesus Christus
non dubitavit manibus
   tradi nocentium,
et crucis subire tormentum.
Qui vivit et regnat
   in sæcula sæculorum.

THE SACRED PASCHAL TRIDUUM

In the Sacred Triduum, the Church solemnly celebrates the greatest mysteries of our redemption, keeping by means of special celebrations the memorial of her Lord, crucified, buried, and risen.

The Paschal Fast should also be kept sacred. It is to be celebrated everywhere on the Friday of the Lord's Passion and, where appropriate, prolonged also through Holy Saturday as a way of coming, with spirit uplifted, to the joys of the Lord's Resurrection.

For a fitting celebration of the Sacred Triduum, a sufficient number of lay ministers is required, who must be carefully instructed as to what they are to do.

The singing of the people, the ministers, and the Priest Celebrant has a special importance in the celebrations of these days, for when texts are sung, they have their proper impact.

Pastors should, therefore, not fail to explain to the Christian faithful, as best they can, the meaning and order of the celebrations and to prepare them for active and fruitful participation.

The celebrations of the Sacred Triduum are to be carried out in cathedral and parochial churches and only in those churches in which they can be performed with dignity, that is, with a good attendance of the faithful, an appropriate number of ministers, and the means to sing at least some of the parts.

Consequently, it is desirable that small communities, associations, and special groups of various kinds join together in these churches to carry out the sacred celebrations in a more noble manner.

28 March

THURSDAY OF THE LORD'S SUPPER
(MAUNDY THURSDAY)

If we listen attentively to the Gospel, we can discern two different dimensions in the event of the washing of the feet. The cleansing that Jesus offers his disciples is first and foremost simply his action – the gift of purity, of the "capacity for God" that is offered to them. But the gift then becomes a model, the duty to do the same for one another. The gift and example overall, which we find in the passage on the washing of the feet, is a characteristic of the nature of Christianity in general. Christianity is not a type of moralism, simply a system of ethics. It does not originate in our action, our moral capacity. Christianity is first and foremost a gift: God gives himself to us – he does not give something, but himself. And this does not only happen at the beginning, at the moment of our conversion. He constantly remains the One who gives. He continually offers us his gifts. He always precedes us. This is why the central act of Christian being is the Eucharist: gratitude for having been gratified, joy for the new life that he gives us.

(Pope Benedict XVI)

In accordance with a most ancient tradition of the Church, on this day all Masses without the people are forbidden.

At the Evening Mass

The Mass of the Lord's Supper is celebrated in the evening, at a convenient time, with the full participation of the whole local community and with all the Priests and ministers exercising their office.

All Priests may concelebrate even if they have already concelebrated the Chrism Mass on this day, or if they have to celebrate another Mass for the good of the Christian faithful.

Where a pastoral reason requires it, the local Ordinary may permit another Mass to be celebrated in churches and oratories in the evening and, in case of genuine necessity, even in the morning, but only for the faithful who are in no way able to participate in the evening Mass. Care should, nevertheless, be taken that celebrations of this sort do not take place for the advantage of private persons or special small groups, and do not prejudice the evening Mass.

Holy Communion may only be distributed to the faithful during Mass; but it may be brought to the sick at any hour of the day.

The altar may be decorated with flowers with a moderation that accords with the character of this day. The tabernacle should be entirely empty; but a sufficient amount of bread should be consecrated in this Mass for the Communion of the clergy and the people on this and the following day.

Entrance Antiphon Cf. Ga 6:14

We should glory in the Cross
of our Lord Jesus Christ,
in whom is our salvation,
  life and resurrection,
through whom we are saved
  and delivered.

Ant. ad introitum

Nos autem gloriari oportet
  in cruce Domini nostri
  Iesu Christi,
in quo est salus,
  vita et resurrectio nostra,
per quem salvati et liberati sumus.

The Gloria in excelsis (Glory to God in the highest) is said. While the hymn is being sung, bells are rung, and when it is finished, they remain silent until the Gloria in excelsis of the Easter Vigil, unless, if appropriate, the Diocesan Bishop has decided otherwise. Likewise, during this same period, the organ and other musical instruments may be used only so as to support the singing.

Collect

O God, who have called us
  to participate
in this most sacred Supper,
in which your Only Begotten Son,
when about to hand himself over
  to death,
entrusted to the Church a sacrifice
  new for all eternity,
the banquet of his love,
grant, we pray,
that we may draw from so great
  a mystery,
the fullness of charity and of life.
Through our Lord Jesus Christ,
  your Son,
who lives and reigns with you
  in the unity of the Holy Spirit,
one God, for ever and ever.

Collecta

Sacratissimam, Deus,
  frequentantibus Cenam,
in qua Unigenitus tuus,
  morti se traditurus,
novum in sæcula sacrificium
dilectionisque suæ convivium
  Ecclesiæ commendavit,
da nobis, quæsumus,
  ut ex tanto mysterio
plenitudinem caritatis hauriamus
  et vitæ.
Per Dominum nostrum Iesum
  Christum Filium tuum,
qui tecum vivit et regnat
  in unitate Spiritus Sancti,
Deus, per omnia sæcula sæculorum.

FIRST READING

A reading from the book of Exodus 12:1-8,11-14

Instructions concerning the Passover meal.

The Lord said to Moses and Aaron in the land of Egypt, 'This month is to be the first of all the others for you, the first month of your year. Speak to the whole community of Israel and say, "On the tenth day of this month each man must take an animal from the flock, one for each family: one animal for each household. If the household is too small to eat the animal, a man must join with his neighbour, the nearest to his house, as the number of persons requires. You must take into account what each can eat in deciding the number for the animal. It must be an animal without blemish, a male one year old; you may take it from either sheep or goats. You must keep it till the fourteenth day of the month when the whole assembly of the community of Israel shall slaughter it between the two evenings. Some of the blood must then be taken and put on the two doorposts and the lintel of the houses where it is eaten. That night, the flesh is to be eaten, roasted over the fire; it must be eaten with unleavened bread and bitter herbs. You shall eat it like this: with a girdle round your waist, sandals on your feet, a staff in your hand. You shall eat it hastily; it is a passover in honour of the Lord. That night, I will go through the land of Egypt and strike down all the first-born in the land of Egypt, man and beast alike, and I shall deal out punishment to all the gods of Egypt, I am the Lord. The blood shall serve to mark the houses that you live in. When I see the blood I will pass over you and you shall escape the destroying plague when I strike the land of Egypt. This day is to be a day of remembrance for you, and you must celebrate it as a feast in the Lord's honour. For all generations you are to declare it a day of festival, for ever.'"

The word of the Lord.

Responsional Psalm

Ps 115:12-13,15-18. R. Cf. 1 Co 10:16

R. **The blessing-cup that we bless
is a communion with the blood of Christ.**

How can I repay the Lord
for his goodness to me?
The cup of salvation I will raise;
I will call on the Lord's name. R.

O precious in the eyes of the Lord
is the death of his faithful.
Your servant, Lord, your servant am I;
you have loosened my bonds. R.

A thanksgiving sacrifice I make:
I will call on the Lord's name.
My vows to the Lord I will fulfil
before all his people. R.

SECOND READING

A reading from the first letter of St Paul to the Corinthians 11:23-26

Every time you eat this bread and drink this cup, you are proclaiming the death of the Lord.

This is what I received from the Lord, and in turn passed on to you: that on the same night that he was betrayed, the Lord Jesus took some bread, and thanked God for it and broke it, and he said, 'This is my body, which is for you; do this as a memorial of me.' In the same way he took the cup after supper, and said,'This cup is the new covenant in my blood. Whenever you drink it, do this as a memorial of me.' Until the Lord comes, therefore, every time you eat this bread and drink this cup, you are proclaiming his death.

The word of the Lord.

Gospel Acclamation Jn 13:34

R. **Praise and honour to you, Lord Jesus!**
I give you a new commandment:
love one another just as I have loved you, says the Lord.
R. **Praise and honour to you, Lord Jesus!**

GOSPEL

A reading from the holy Gospel according to John 13:1-15

Now he showed how perfect his love was.

It was before the festival of the Passover, and Jesus knew that the hour had come for him to pass from this world to the Father. He had always loved those who were his in the world, but now he showed how perfect his love was.

They were at supper, and the devil had already put it into the mind of Judas Iscariot son of Simon, to betray him. Jesus knew that the Father had put everything into his hands, and that he had come from God and was returning to God, and he got up from table, removed his outer garment and, taking a towel, wrapped it round his waist; he then poured water into a basin and began to wash the disciples' feet and to wipe them with the towel he was wearing.

He came to Simon Peter, who said to him, 'Lord, are you going to wash my feet?' Jesus answered, 'At the moment you do not know what I am doing, but later you will understand.' 'Never!' said Peter 'You shall never wash my feet.' Jesus replied, 'If I do not wash you, you can have nothing in common with me.' 'Then, Lord,' said Simon Peter 'not only my feet, but my hands and my head as well!' Jesus said, 'No one who has taken a bath needs washing, he is clean all over. You too are clean, though not all of you are.' He knew who was going to betray him, that was why he said, 'though not all of you are.'

When he had washed their feet and put on his clothes again he went back to the table. 'Do you understand' he said 'what I have done to you? You call me Master and Lord, and rightly; so I am. If I, then, the Lord and Master, have washed your feet, you should wash each other's feet. I have given you an example so that you may copy what I have done to you.'

The Gospel of the Lord.

After the proclamation of the Gospel, the Priest gives a homily in which light is shed on the principal mysteries that are commemorated in this Mass, namely, the institution of the Holy Eucharist and of the priestly Order, and the commandment of the Lord concerning fraternal charity.

The Washing of Feet

After the Homily, where a pastoral reason suggests it, the Washing of Feet follows.

The men who have been chosen are led by the ministers to seats prepared in a suitable place. Then the Priest (removing his chasuble if necessary) goes to each one, and, with the help of the ministers, pours water over each one's feet and then dries them.

Meanwhile some of the following antiphons or other appropriate chants are sung.

Antiphon 1   Cf. Jn 13:4,5,15

After the Lord had risen from supper,
he poured water into a basin
and began to wash the feet
   of his disciples:
he left them this example.

Antiphona 1

Postquam surrexit Dominus a cena,
misit aquam in pelvim,
et cœpit lavare
   pedes discipulorum:
hoc exemplum reliquit eis.

Antiphon 2   Cf. Jn 13:12,13,15

The Lord Jesus,
   after eating supper
   with his disciples,
washed their feet and said to them:
Do you know what I, your Lord
   and Master, have done for you?
I have given you an example,
   that you should do likewise.

Antiphona 2

Dominus Iesus, postquam cenavit
   cum discipulis suis,
lavit pedes eorum, et ait illis:
'Scitis quid fecerim vobis ego,
   Dominus et Magister?
Exemplum dedi vobis,
   ut et vos ita faciatis.'

Antiphon 3 — Jn 13:6,7,8

Lord, are you to wash my feet?
   Jesus said to him in answer:
If I do not wash your feet,
   you will have no share with me.

V. So he came to Simon Peter
   and Peter said to him:
– Lord, are you to wash my feet?...

V. What I am doing,
   you do not know for now,
   but later you will come to know.
– Lord, are you to wash my feet?...

Antiphon 4 — Cf. Jn 13:14

If I, your Lord and Master,
   have washed your feet,
how much more should you wash
   each other's feet?

Antiphon 5 — Jn 13:35

This is how all will know that you
   are my disciples:
if you have love for one another.

V. Jesus said to his disciples:
– This is how all will know...

Antiphon 6 — Jn 13:34

I give you a new commandment,
that you love one another
as I have loved you, says the Lord.

Antiphon 7 — 1 Co 13:13

Let faith, hope and charity,
   these three, remain among you,
but the greatest of these is charity.

V. Now faith, hope and charity,
   these three, remain;
but the greatest of these is charity.
– Let faith, hope and charity...

Antiphona 3

Domine, tu mihi lavas pedes?
   Respondit Iesus et dixit ei:
Se non lavero tibi pedes,
   non habebis partem mecum.

V. Venit ergo ad Simonem Petrum,
   et dixit ei Petrus:
– Domine, tu mihi lavas pedes?...

V. Quod ego facio,
   tu nescis modo:
   scies autem postea.
– Domine, tu mihi lavas pedes?...

Antiphona 4

Si ego, Dominus et Magister vester,
   lavi vobis pedes:
quanto magis debetis alter alterius
   lavare pedes?

Antiphona 5

In hoc cognoscent omnes,
   quia discipuli mei estis,
si dilectionem habueritis
   ad invicem.

V. Dixit Iesus discipulis suis.
– In hoc cognoscent omnes...

Antiphona 6

Mandatum novum do vobis,
   ut diligatis invicem,
sicut dilexi vos, dicit Dominus.

Antiphona 7

Maneant in vobis fides, spes,
   caritas, tria hæc:
maior autem horum est caritas.

V. Nunc autem manent fides, spes,
   caritas, tria hæc:
maior horum est caritas.
– Maneant in vobis fides...

After the Washing of Feet, the Priest washes and dries his hands, puts the chasuble back on, and returns to the chair, and from there he directs the Universal Prayer.

The Creed is not said.

The Liturgy of the Eucharist

At the beginning of the Liturgy of the Eucharist, there may be a procession of the faithful in which gifts for the poor may be presented with the bread and wine.

Meanwhile the following, or another appropriate chant, is sung.

Ant. Where true charity is dwelling,
God is present there.
V. By the love of Christ we have
been brought together:
V. let us find in him our gladness
and our pleasure;
V. may we love him and revere him,
God the living,
V. and in love respect each other
with sincere hearts.

Ant. Where true charity is dwelling,
God is present there.
V. So when we as one are gathered
all together,
V. let us strive to keep our minds
free of division;
V. may there be an end to malice,
strife and quarrels,
V. and let Christ our God
be dwelling here among us.

Ant. Where true charity is dwelling,
God is present there.
V. May your face thus be our vision,
bright in glory,
V. Christ our God, with all
the blessed Saints in heaven:
V. such delight is pure and faultless,
joy unbounded,
V. which endures through
countless ages
world without end. Amen.

Ant. Ubi caritas est vera,
Deus ibi est.
V. Exsultemus et in
ipso iucundemur.
V. Congregavit nos in unum
Christi amor.
V. Timeamus et amemus
Deum vivum.
V. Et ex corde diligamus nos sincero

Ant. Ubi caritas est vera,
Deus ibi est.
V. Simul ergo cum in
unum congregamur:
V. Ne nos mente dividamur,
caveamus.
V. Cessent iurgia maligna,
cessent lites.
V. Et in medio nostri sit
Christus Deus.

Ant. Ubi caritas est vera,
Deus ibi est.
V. Simul quoque cum beatis
videamus
V. Glorianter vultum tuum,
Christe Deus:
V. Gaudium, quod est immensum
atque probum,
V. Sæcula per infinita sæculorum.
Amen.

Prayer over the Offerings

Grant us, O Lord, we pray,
that we may participate worthily
 in these mysteries,
for whenever the memorial
 of this sacrifice is celebrated
the work of our redemption
 is accomplished.
Through Christ our Lord.

Preface I of the Most Holy Eucharist, pp.68-69.
If the Roman Canon is said, the following special forms are used.

Celebrating the most sacred day
on which our Lord Jesus Christ
was handed over for our sake,
and in communion with those
 whose memory we venerate,
especially the glorious
 ever-Virgin Mary,
Mother of our God and Lord,
 Jesus Christ,
and blessed Joseph, her Spouse,
your blessed Apostles and Martyrs,
Peter and Paul, Andrew,
(James, John,
Thomas, James, Philip,
Bartholomew, Matthew,
Simon and Jude;
Linus, Cletus, Clement, Sixtus,
Cornelius, Cyprian,
Lawrence, Chrysogonus,
John and Paul,
Cosmas and Damian)
and all your Saints;
we ask that through their merits
 and prayers,
in all things we may be defended
by your protecting help.
(Through Christ our Lord. Amen.)

Super oblata

Concede nobis,
 quæsumus, Domine,
hæc digne frequentare mysteria,
quia, quoties huius hostiæ
 commemoratio celebratur,
opus nostræ redemptionis exercetur.
Per Christum Dominum nostrum.

Communicantes, et diem
 sacratissimum celebrantes,
quo Dominus noster Iesus Christus
pro nobis est traditus,
sed et memoriam venerantes,
in primis gloriosæ semper
 Virginis Mariæ,
Genetricis eiusdem Dei et Domini
 nostri Iesu Christi:
sed et beati Ioseph,
 eiusdem Virginis Sponsi,
et beatorum Apostolorum ac
 Martyrum tuorum,
Petri et Pauli, Andreæ,
(Iacobi, Ioannis,
Thomæ, Iacobi, Philippi,
Bartholomæi, Matthæi,
Simonis et Thaddæi:
Lini, Cleti, Clementis, Xysti,
Cornelii, Cypriani,
Laurentii, Chrysogoni,
Ioannis et Pauli,
Cosmæ et Damiani)
et omnium Sanctorum tuorum;
quorum meritis precibusque concedas,
ut in omnibus protectionis tuæ
 muniamur auxilio.
(Per Christum Dominum nostrum.
 Amen.)

Therefore, Lord, we pray:
graciously accept this oblation of
 our service,
that of your whole family,
which we make to you
as we observe the day
on which our Lord Jesus Christ
handed on the mysteries
 of his Body and Blood
for his disciples to celebrate;
order our days in your peace,
and command that we be delivered
 from eternal damnation
and counted among the flock of
 those you have chosen.
(Through Christ our Lord. Amen.)
Be pleased, O God, we pray,
to bless, acknowledge,
and approve this offering
 in every respect;
make it spiritual and acceptable,
so that it may become for us
the Body and Blood of your most
 beloved Son,
our Lord Jesus Christ.
On the day before he was to suffer
for our salvation and the salvation
 of all,
that is today,
he took bread in his holy
 and venerable hands,
and with eyes raised to heaven
to you, O God, his almighty Father,
giving you thanks,
 he said the blessing,
broke the bread
and gave it to his disciples, saying:

Take this, all of you,
 and eat of it,
for this is my Body,
which will be given up for you.

Hanc igitur oblationem
 servitutis nostræ,
sed et cunctæ familiæ tuæ,
quam tibi offerimus ob diem,
in qua Dominus noster Iesus Christus
tradidit discipulis suis
Corporis et Sanguinis
 sui mysteria celebranda,
quæsumus, Domine,
ut placatus accipias:
diesque nostros in tua pace
 disponas,
atque ab æterna damnatione
 nos eripi
et in electorum tuorum iubeas
 grege numerari.
(Per Christum Dominum nostrum.
 Amen.)
Quam oblationem tu, Deus,
 in omnibus, quæsumus,
benedictam, adscriptam, ratam,
rationabilem, acceptabilemque
 facere digneris:
ut nobis Corpus et Sanguis fiat
 dilectissimi Filii tui,
Domini nostri Iesu Christi.

Qui, pridie quam pro nostra
omniumque salute pateretur,
hoc est hodie,
accepit panem in sanctus ac
 venerabiles manus suas,
et elevatis oculis in cælum
ad te Deum Patrem
 suum omnipotentem,
tibi gratias agens benedixit,
fregit, deditque discipulis suis, dicens:

Accipite et manducate
 ex hoc omnes:
hoc est enim Corpus meum,
quod pro vobis tradetur.

Then follows the remainder of the Roman Canon as usual (see pp.86-93) and the Communion Rite, pp.120-121.

At an appropriate moment during Communion, the Priest entrusts the Eucharist from the table of the altar to Deacons or acolytes or other extraordinary ministers, so that afterwards it may be brought to the sick who are to receive Holy Communion at home.

Communion Antiphon 1 Co 11:24-25	Ant. ad communionem
This is the Body that will be given up for you;	Hoc Corpus, quod pro vobis tradetur:
this is the Chalice of the new covenant in my Blood, says the Lord;	hic calix novi testamenti est in meo Sanguine, dicit Dominus;
do this, whenever you receive it, in memory of me.	hoc facite, quotiescumque sumitis, in meam commemorationem.

After the distribution of Communion, the ciborium with hosts for Communion on the following day is left on the altar. The Priest, standing at the chair, says the Prayer after Communion.

Prayer after Communion	Post communionem
Grant, almighty God, that, just as we are renewed by the Supper of your Son in this present age, so we may enjoy his banquet for all eternity. Who lives and reigns for ever and ever.	Concede nobis, omnipotens Deus, ut, sicut Cena Filii tui reficimur temporali, ita satiari mereamur æterna. Per Christum Dominum nostrum.

The Transfer of the Most Blessed Sacrament

After the Prayer after Communion, the Priest puts incense in the thurible while standing, blesses it and then, kneeling, incenses the Blessed Sacrament three times. Then, having put on a white humeral veil, he rises, takes the ciborium, and covers it with the ends of the veil.

A procession is formed in which the Blessed Sacrament, accompanied by torches and incense, is carried through the church to a place of repose prepared in a part of the church or in a chapel suitably decorated. A lay minister with a cross, standing between two other ministers with lighted candles leads off. Others carrying lighted candles follow. Before the Priest carrying the Blessed Sacrament comes the thurifer with a smoking thurible. Meanwhile, the hymn Pange, lingua (exclusive of the last two stanzas) or another eucharistic chant is sung.

When the procession reaches the place of repose, the Priest, with the help of the Deacon if necessary, places the ciborium in the tabernacle, the door of which remains open. Then he puts incense in the thurible and, kneeling, incenses the Blessed Sacrament, while Tantum ergo Sacramentum or another eucharistic chant is sung. Then the Deacon or the Priest himself places the Sacrament in the tabernacle and closes the door.

After a period of adoration in silence, the Priest and ministers genuflect and return to the sacristy.

At an appropriate time, the altar is stripped and, if possible, the crosses are removed from the church. It is expedient that any crosses which remain in the church be veiled.

Vespers (Evening Prayer) is not celebrated by those who have attended the Mass of the Lord's Supper.

The faithful are invited to continue adoration before the Blessed Sacrament for a suitable length of time during the night, according to local circumstances, but after midnight the adoration should take place without solemnity.

If the celebration of the Passion of the Lord on the following Friday does not take place in the same church, the Mass is concluded in the usual way and the Blessed Sacrament is placed in the tabernacle.

29 March

FRIDAY OF THE PASSION OF THE LORD
(GOOD FRIDAY)

The liturgy applies to Jesus's descent into the night of death the words of Psalm 23[24]: "Lift up your heads, O gates; be lifted up, O ancient doors!" The gates of death are closed, no one can return from there. There is no key for those iron doors. But Christ has the key. His Cross opens wide the gates of death, the stern doors. They are barred no longer. His Cross, his radical love, is the key that opens them. The love of the One who, though God, became man in order to die – this love has the power to open those doors. This love is stronger than death.

(Pope Benedict XVI)

On this and the following day, by a most ancient tradition, the Church does not celebrate the Sacraments at all, except for Penance and the Anointing of the Sick.

On this day, Holy Communion is distributed to the faithful only within the celebration of the Lord's Passion; but it may be brought at any hour of the day to the sick who cannot participate in this celebration.

The altar should be completely bare: without a cross, without candles and without cloths.

The Celebration of the Passion of the Lord

On the afternoon of this day, about three o'clock (unless a later hour is chosen for a pastoral reason), there takes place the celebration of the Lord's Passion consisting of three parts, namely, the Liturgy of the Word, the Adoration of the Cross, and Holy Communion.

The Priest and the Deacon, if a Deacon is present, wearing red vestments as for Mass, go to the altar in silence and, after making a reverence to the altar, prostrate themselves or, if appropriate, kneel and pray in silence for a while. All others kneel.

Then the Priest, with the ministers, goes to the chair where, facing the people, who are standing, he says, with hands extended, one of the following prayers, omitting the invitation Let us pray.

Prayer

Remember your mercies, O Lord,
and with your eternal protection
   sanctify your servants,
for whom Christ your Son,
by the shedding of his Blood,
established the Paschal Mystery.
Who lives and reigns
   for ever and ever.
R. Amen.

Or:

O God, who by the Passion
   of Christ your Son, our Lord,
abolished the death inherited
   from ancient sin
by every succeeding generation,
grant that just as,
   being conformed to him,
we have borne by the law of nature
the image of the man of earth,
so by the sanctification of grace
we may bear the image of the Man
   of heaven.
Through Christ our Lord.
R. Amen.

Oratio

Reminiscere miserationum
   tuarum, Domine,
et famulos tuos æterna
   protectione sanctifica,
pro quibus Christus, Filius tuus,
per suum cruorem instituit
   paschale mysterium.
Qui vivit et regnat
   in sæcula sæculorum.
R. Amen.

Vel:

Deus, qui peccati veteris
   hereditariam mortem,
in qua posteritatis genus
   omne successerat,
Christi Filii tui, Domini nostri,
   passione solvisti,
da, ut conformes eidem facti,
sicut imaginem terreni hominis
naturæ necessitate portavimus,
ita imaginem cælestis
gratiæ sanctificatione portemus.
Per Christum Dominum nostrum.
R. Amen.

FIRST PART:

The Liturgy of the Word

FIRST READING

A reading from the prophet Isaiah 52:13-53:12

He was pierced through our faults.

See, my servant will prosper,
he shall be lifted up, exalted, rise to great heights.

As the crowds were appalled on seeing him
– so disfigured did he look
that he seemed no longer human –
so will the crowds be astonished at him,
and kings stand speechless before him;
for they shall see something never told
and witness something never heard before:
'Who could believe what we have heard,
and to whom has the power of the Lord been revealed?'

Like a sapling he grew up in front of us,
like a root in arid ground.
Without beauty, without majesty (we saw him),
no looks to attract our eyes;
a thing despised and rejected by men,
a man of sorrows and familiar with suffering,
a man to make people screen their faces;
he was despised and we took no account of him.

And yet ours were the sufferings he bore,
ours the sorrows he carried.
But we, we thought of him as someone punished,
struck by God, and brought low.
Yet he was pierced through for our faults,
crushed for our sins.
On him lies a punishment that brings us peace,
and through his wounds we are healed.

We had all gone astray like sheep,
each taking his own way,
and the Lord burdened him
with the sins of all of us.

Harshly dealt with, he bore it humbly,
he never opened his mouth,
like a lamb that is led to the slaughter-house,
like a sheep that is dumb before its shearers
never opening its mouth.

By force and by law he was taken;
would anyone plead his cause?
Yes, he was torn away from the land of the living;
for our faults struck down in death.
They gave him a grave with the wicked,
a tomb with the rich,
though he had done no wrong
and there had been no perjury in his mouth.
The Lord has been pleased to crush him with suffering.
If he offers his life in atonement,
he shall see his heirs, he shall have a long life
and through him what the Lord wishes will be done.
His soul's anguish over
he shall see the light and be content.
By his sufferings shall my servant justify many,
taking their faults on himself.

Hence I will grant whole hordes for his tribute,
he shall divide the spoil with the mighty,
for surrendering himself to death
and letting himself be taken for a sinner,
while he was bearing the faults of many
and praying all the time for sinners.

   The word of the Lord.

Responsorial Psalm Ps 30:2,6,12-13,15-17,25. R. Lk 23:46

R. Father, into your hands I commend my spirit.

   In you, O Lord, I take refuge.
   Let me never be put to shame.
   In your justice, set me free.
   Into your hands I commend my spirit.
   It is you who will redeem me, Lord. **R.**

In the face of all my foes
I am a reproach,
an object of scorn to my neighbours
and of fear to my friends. R.

Those who see me in the street
run far away from me.
I am like a dead man, forgotten in men's hearts,
like a thing thrown away. R.

But as for me, I trust in you, Lord,
I say: 'You are my God.'
My life is in your hands, deliver me
from the hands of those who hate me. R.

Let your face shine on your servant.
Save me in your love.
Be strong, let your heart take courage,
all who hope in the Lord. R.

SECOND READING

A reading from the letter to the Hebrews 4:14-16; 5:7-9

He learnt to obey through suffering and became for all who obey him the source of eternal salvation.

Since in Jesus, the Son of God, we have the supreme high priest who has gone through to the highest heaven, we must never let go of the faith that we have professed. For it is not as if we had a high priest who was incapable of feeling our weaknesses with us; but we have one who has been tempted in every way that we are, though he is without sin. Let us be confident, then, in approaching the throne of grace, that we shall have mercy from him and find grace when we are in need of help.

During his life on earth, he offered up prayer and entreaty, aloud and in silent tears, to the one who had the power to save him out of death, and he submitted so humbly that his prayer was heard. Although he was Son, he learnt to obey through suffering; but having been made perfect, he became for all who obey him the source of eternal salvation.

The word of the Lord.

Gospel Acclamation
Ph 2:8-9

R. Glory and praise to you, O Christ!
Christ was humbler yet,
even accepting death, death on a cross.
But God raised him high
and gave him the name which is above all names.
R. Glory and praise to you, O Christ!

GOSPEL

The symbols in the following passion narrative represent:

N Narrator   J Jesus   O Other single speaker
C Crowd, or more than one speaker

The passion of our Lord Jesus Christ according to John   18:1-19:42

N Jesus left with his disciples and crossed the Kedron valley. There was a garden there, and he went into it with his disciples. Judas the traitor knew the place well, since Jesus had often met his disciples there, and he brought the cohort to this place together with a detachment of guards sent by the chief priests and the Pharisees, all with lanterns and torches and weapons. Knowing everything that was going to happen to him, Jesus then came forward and said,

J Who are you looking for?

N They answered,

C Jesus the Nazarene.

N He said,

J I am he.

N Now Judas the traitor was standing among them. When Jesus said, 'I am he', they moved back and fell to the ground. He asked them a second time,

J Who are you looking for?

N They said,

C Jesus the Nazarene.

N Jesus replied,

J I have told you that I am he. If I am the one you are looking for, let these others go.

N This was to fulfil the words he has spoken: 'Not one of those you gave me have I lost.'

Simon Peter, who carried a sword, drew it and wounded the high priest's servant, cutting off his right ear. The servant's name was Malchus. Jesus said to Peter,

J Put your sword back in its scabbard; am I not to drink the cup that the Father has given me?

N The cohort and its captain and the Jewish guards seized Jesus and bound him. They took him first to Annas, because Annas was the father-in-law of Caiaphas, who was high priest that year. It was Caiaphas who had suggested to the Jews, 'It is better for one man to die for the people.'

Simon Peter, with another disciple, followed Jesus. This disciple, who was known to the high priest, went with Jesus into the high priest's palace, but Peter stayed outside the door. So the other disciple, the one known to the high priest, went out, spoke to the woman who was keeping the door and brought Peter in. The maid on duty at the door said to Peter,

O Aren't you another of that man's disciples?

N He answered,

O I am not.

N Now it was cold, and the servants and guards had lit a charcoal fire and were standing there warming themselves; so Peter stood there too, warming himself with the others.

The high priest questioned Jesus about his disciples and his teaching. Jesus answered,

J I have spoken openly for all the world to hear; I have always taught in the synagogue and in the Temple where all the Jews meet together: I have said nothing in secret. But why ask me? Ask my hearers what I taught: they know what I said.

N At these words, one of the guards standing by gave Jesus a slap in the face, saying,

O Is that the way to answer the high priest?

N Jesus replied,

J If there is something wrong in what I said, point it out; but if there is no offence in it, why do you strike me?

N Then Annas sent him, still bound, to Caiaphas, the high priest. As Simon Peter stood there warming himself, someone said to him,

O Aren't you another of his disciples?

N He denied it saying,

O I am not.

N One of the high priest's servants, a relation of the man whose ear Peter had cut off, said,

O Didn't I see you in the garden with him?

N Again Peter denied it, and at once a cock crew.

	They then led Jesus from the house of Caiaphas to the Praetorium. It was now morning. They did not go into the Praetorium themselves or they would be defiled and unable to eat the passover. So Pilate came outside to them and said,
O	What charge do you bring against this man?
N	They replied,
C	If he were not a criminal, we should not be handing him over to you.
N	Pilate said,
O	Take him yourselves, and try him by your own Law.
N	The Jews answered,
C	We are not allowed to put a man to death.
N	This was to fulfil the words Jesus had spoken indicating the way he was going to die.
	So Pilate went back into the Praetorium and called Jesus to him, and asked,
O	Are you the king of Jews?
N	Jesus replied,
J	Do you ask this of your own accord, or have others spoken to you about me?
N	Pilate answered,
O	Am I a Jew? It is your own people and the chief priests who have handed you over to me: what have you done?
N	Jesus replied,
J	Mine is not a kingdom of this world; if my kingdom were of this world, my men would have fought to prevent me being surrendered to the Jews. But my kingdom is not of this kind.
N	Pilate said,
O	So you are the king then?
N	Jesus answered,
J	It is you who say it. Yes, I am a king. I was born for this; I came into the world for this; to bear witness to the truth, and all who are on the side of truth listen to my voice.
N	Pilate said,
O	Truth? What is that?
N	And with that he went out again to the Jews and said,
O	I find no case against him. But according to a custom of yours I should release one prisoner at the Passover; would you like me, then, to release the king of Jews?
N	At this they shouted:

C Not this man, but Barabbas.
N Barabbas was a brigand.
   Pilate then had Jesus taken away and scourged; and after this, the soldiers twisted some thorns into a crown and put it on his head, and dressed him in a purple robe. They kept coming up to him and saying,
C Hail, king of the Jews!
N and they slapped him in the face.
   Pilate came outside again and said to them,
O Look, I am going to bring him out to you to let you see that I find no case.
N Jesus then came out wearing the crown of thorns and the purple robe. Pilate said,
O Here is the man.
N When they saw him the chief priests and the guards shouted,
C Crucify him! Crucify him!
N Pilate said,
O Take him yourselves and crucify him: I can find no case against him
N The Jews replied,
C We have a Law, and according to the Law he ought to die, because he has claimed to be the son of God.
N When Pilate heard them say this his fears increased. Re-entering the Praetorium, he said to Jesus,
O Where do you come from?
N But Jesus made no answer. Pilate then said to him,
O Are you refusing to speak to me? Surely you know I have power to release you and I have power to crucify you?
N Jesus replied,
J You would have no power over me if it had not been given you from above; that is why the one who handed me over to you has the greater guilt.
N From that moment Pilate was anxious to set him free, but the Jews shouted,
C If you set him free you are no friend of Caesar's; anyone who makes himself king is defying Caesar.
N Hearing these words, Pilate had Jesus brought out, and seated himself on the chair of judgement at a place called the Pavement, in Hebrew Gabbatha. It was Passover Preparation Day, about the sixth hour. Pilate said to the Jews,
O Here is your king.
N They said,
C Take him away, take him away. Crucify him!

N Pilate said,
O Do you want me to crucify your king?
N The chief priests answered,
C We have no king except Caesar.
N So in the end Pilate handed him over to them to be crucified.

   They then took charge of Jesus, and carrying his own cross he went out of the city to the place of the skull, or, as it was called in Hebrew, Golgotha, where they crucified him with two others, one on either side with Jesus in the middle. Pilate wrote out a notice and had it fixed to the cross; it ran: 'Jesus the Nazarene, King of the Jews.' This notice was read by many of the Jews, because the place where Jesus was crucified was not far from the city, and the writing was in Hebrew, Latin and Greek. So the Jewish chief priests said to Pilate,

C You should not write 'King of the Jews', but 'This man said: I am King of the Jews'.
N Pilate answered,
O What I have written, I have written.
N When the soldiers had finished crucifying Jesus they took his clothing and divided it into four shares, one for each soldier. His undergarment was seamless, woven in one piece from neck to hem; so they said to one another,
C Instead of tearing it, let's throw dice to decide who is to have it.
N In this way the words of scripture were fulfilled:
   They shared out my clothing among them.
   They cast lots for my clothes.
   This is exactly what the soldiers did.

   Near the cross of Jesus stood his mother and his mother's sister, Mary the wife of Clopas, and Mary of Magdala. Seeing his mother and the disciple he loved standing near her, Jesus said to his mother,
J Woman, this is your son.
N Then to the disciple he said,
J This is your mother.
N And from that moment the disciple made a place for her in his home.

   After this, Jesus knew that everything had now been completed, and to fulfil the scripture perfectly he said:
J I am thirsty.
N A jar full of vinegar stood there, so putting a sponge soaked in vinegar on a hyssop stick they held it up to his mouth. After Jesus had taken the vinegar he said,

J It is accomplished;
N and bowing his head he gave up the spirit.

All kneel and pause a moment.

N It was Preparation Day, and to prevent the bodies remaining on the cross during the sabbath – since that sabbath was a day of special solemnity – the Jews asked Pilate to have the legs broken and the bodies taken away. Consequently the soldiers came and broke the legs of the first man who had been crucified with him and then of the other. When they came to Jesus, they found that he was already dead, and so instead of breaking his legs one of the soldiers pierced his side with a lance; and immediately there came out blood and water. This is the evidence of one who saw it – trustworthy evidence, and he knows he speaks the truth – and he gives it so that you may believe as well. Because all this happened to fulfil the words of scripture:

   Not one bone of his will be broken,
and again, in another place scripture says:

   They will look on the one whom they have pierced.

   After this, Joseph of Arimathaea, who was a disciple of Jesus – though a secret one because he was afraid of the Jews – asked Pilate to let him remove the body of Jesus. Pilate gave permission, so they came and took it away. Nicodemus came as well – the same one who had first come to Jesus at night – time – and he brought a mixture of myrrh and aloes, weighing about a hundred pounds. They took the body of Jesus and wrapped it with the spices in linen cloths, following the Jewish burial custom. At the place where he had been crucified there was a garden, and in the garden a new tomb in which no one had yet been buried. Since it was the Jewish Day of Preparation and the tomb was near at hand, they laid Jesus there.

The Gospel of the Lord.

After the reading of the Lord's Passion, the Priest gives a brief homily and, at its end, the faithful may be invited to spend a short time in prayer.

The Solemn Intercessions

The Liturgy of the Word concludes with the Solemn Intercessions, which take place in this way: the Deacon, if a Deacon is present, or if he is not, a lay minister, stands at the ambo, and sings or says the invitation in which the intention is expressed. Then all pray in silence for a while, and afterwards the Priest, standing at the chair or, if appropriate, at the altar, with hands extended, sings or says the prayer.

The faithful may remain either kneeling or standing throughout the entire period of the prayers.

Before the Priest's prayer, in accord with tradition, it is permissible to use the Deacon's invitations Let us kneel – Let us stand, (Flectamus genua – Levate), with all kneeling for silent prayer.

The Conferences of Bishops may provide other invitations to introduce the prayer of the Priest.

In a situation of grave public need, the Diocesan Bishop may permit or order the addition of a special intention.

The prayer is sung in the simple tone or, if the invitations Let us kneel – Let us stand (Flectamus genua – Levate) are used, in the solemn tone.

I. For Holy Church

Let us pray, dearly beloved,
   for the holy Church of God,
that our God and Lord be pleased
   to give her peace,
to guard her and to unite her
   throughout the whole world
and grant that, leading our life
   in tranquillity and quiet,
we may glorify God
   the Father almighty.

Prayer in silence. Then the Priest says:

Almighty ever-living God,
who in Christ revealed your glory
   to all the nations,
watch over the works of your mercy,
that your Church, spread
   throughout all the world,
may persevere with steadfast faith
   in confessing your name.
Through Christ our Lord.
R. Amen.

II. For the Pope

Let us pray also for our most
   Holy Father Pope N.,
that our God and Lord,
who chose him for the
   Order of Bishops,

I. Pro sancta Ecclesia

Oremus, dilectissimi nobis,
   pro Ecclesia sancta Dei,
ut eam Deus et Dominus noster
pacificare, adunare
   et custodire dignetur
toto orbe terrarum,
detque nobis, quietam et tranquillam
   vitam degentibus,
glorificare Deum
   Patrem omnipotentem.

Omnipotens sempiterne Deus,
qui gloriam tuam omnibus
   in Christo gentibus revelasti:
custodi opera misericordiæ tuæ,
ut Ecclesia tua, toto orbe diffusa,
stabili fide in confessione
   tui nominis perseveret.
Per Christum Dominum nostrum.
R. Amen.

II. Pro Papa

Oremus et pro beatissimo
   Papa nostro N.,
ut Deus et Dominus noster,
qui elegit eum
   in ordine episcopatus,

may keep him safe and unharmed
  for the Lord's holy Church,
to govern the holy People of God.

Prayer in silence. Then the Priest says:
Almighty ever-living God,
by whose decree all things
  are founded,
look with favour on our prayers
and in your kindness protect
  the Pope chosen for us,
that, under him,
  the Christian people,
governed by you their maker,
may grow in merit by reason
  of their faith.
Through Christ our Lord.
R. Amen.

III. For all orders and degrees of the faithful

Let us pray also for our Bishop N.,
for all Bishops, Priests,
  and Deacons of the Church
and for the whole
  of the faithful people.

Prayer in silence. Then the Priest says:
Almighty ever-living God,
by whose Spirit the whole body
  of the Church
is sanctified and governed,
hear our humble prayer
  for your ministers,
that, by the gift of your grace,
all may serve you faithfully.
Through Christ our Lord.
R. Amen.

salvum atque incolumem custodiat
  Ecclesiæ suæ sanctæ,
ad regendum populum
  sanctum Dei.

Omnipotens sempiterne Deus,
cuius iudicio universa fundantur,
respice propitius ad preces nostras,
et electum nobis Antistitem
  tua pietate conserva,
ut christiana plebs,
  quæ te gubernatur auctore,
sub ipso Pontifice,
  fidei suæ meritis augeatur.
Per Christum Dominum nostrum.
R. Amen.

III. Pro omnibus ordinibus gradibusque fidelium

Oremus et pro Episcopo nostro N.,
pro omnibus Episcopis, presbyteris,
  diaconis Ecclesiæ,
et universa plebe fidelium.

Omnipotens sempiterne Deus,
cuius Spiritu totum corpus Ecclesiæ
sanctificatur et regitur,
exaudi nos pro ministris
  tuis supplicantes,
ut, gratiæ tuæ munere, ab omnibus
  tibi fideliter serviatur.
Per Christum Dominum nostrum.
R. Amen.

IV. For catechumens

Let us pray also
    for (our) catechumens,
that our God and Lord
may open wide the ears
    of their inmost hearts
and unlock the gates of his mercy,
that, having received forgiveness
    of all their sins
through the waters of rebirth,
they, too, may be one with Christ
    Jesus our Lord.

Prayer in silence. Then the Priest says:

Almighty ever-living God,
who make your Church ever
    fruitful with new offspring,
increase the faith and understanding
    of (our) catechumens,
that, reborn in the font of Baptism,
they may be added to the number
    of your adopted children.
Through Christ our Lord.
R. Amen.

V. For the unity of Christians

Let us pray also for all our brothers
    and sisters who believe in Christ,
that our God and Lord may
    be pleased,
as they live the truth,
to gather them together and keep
    them in his one Church.

Prayer in silence. Then the Priest says:

Almighty ever-living God,
who gather what is scattered
and keep together what you
    have gathered,
look kindly on the flock of your Son,

IV. Pro catechumenis

Oremus et pro
    catechumenis (nostris),
ut Deus et Dominus noster
adaperiat aures
    præcordiorum ipsorum
ianuamque misericordiæ,
ut, per lavacrum regenerationis
accepta remissione
    omnium peccatorum,
et ipsi inveniantur in Christo Iesu
    Domino nostro.

Omnipotens sempiterne Deus,
qui Ecclesiam tuam nova semper
    prole fecundas,
auge fidem et intellectum
    catechumenis (nostris),
ut, renati fonte baptismatis,
tadoptionis tuæ filiis aggregentur.
Per Christum Dominum nostrum.
R. Amen.

V. Pro unitate Christianorum

Oremus et pro universis fratribus
    in Christum credentibus,
ut Deus et Dominus noster eos,
    veritatem facientes,
in una Ecclesia sua congregare
    et custodire dignetur.

Omnipotens sempiterne Deus,
qui dispersa congregas
    et congregata conservas,
ad gregem Filii tui placatus intende,
ut, quos unum baptisma sacravit,

that those whom one Baptism
  has consecrated
may be joined together by integrity
  of faith
and united in the bond of charity.
Through Christ our Lord.
R. Amen.

VI. For the Jewish people
Let us pray also for the Jewish people,
to whom the Lord our God
  spoke first,
that he may grant them to advance
  in love of his name
and in faithfulness to his covenant.
Prayer in silence. Then the Priest says:
Almighty ever-living God,
who bestowed your promises on
  Abraham and his descendants,
graciously hear the prayers
  of your Church,
that the people you first made
  your own
may attain the fullness
  of redemption.
Through Christ our Lord.
R. Amen.

VII. For those who do not believe in Christ
Let us pray also for those who
  do not believe in Christ,
that, enlightened by the Holy Spirit,
they, too, may enter on the way
  of salvation.
Prayer in silence. Then the Priest says:
Almighty ever-living God,
grant to those who do not
  confess Christ
that, by walking before you
  with a sincere heart,

eos et fidei iungat integritas
et vinculum societ caritatis.
Per Christum Dominum nostrum.
R. Amen.

VI. Pro Iudæis
Oremus et pro Iudæis,
ut, ad quos prius locutus est
  Dominus Deus noster,
eis tribuat in sui nominis amore
et in sui fœderis fidelitate proficere.

Omnipotens sempiterne Deus,
qui promissiones tuas Abrahæ
  eiusque semini contulisti,
Ecclesiæ tuæ preces
  clementer exaudi,
ut populus acquisitionis prioris
ad redemptionis mereatur
  plenitudinem pervenire.
Per Christum Dominum nostrum.
R. Amen.

VII. Pro iis qui Christum non credunt
Oremus et pro iis qui in Christum
  non credunt,
ut, luce Sancti Spiritus illustrati,
viam salutis et ipsi valeant introire.

Omnipotens sempiterne Deus,
fac ut qui Christum
  non confitentur,
coram te sincero corde ambulantes,
  inveniant veritatem,

they may find the truth,
and that we ourselves, being
    constant in mutual love
and striving to understand more
    fully the mystery of your life,
may be made more perfect witnesses
    to your love in the world.
Through Christ our Lord. R. Amen.

VIII. For those who do not believe in God

Let us pray also for those who
    do not acknowledge God,
that, following what is right
    in sincerity of heart,
they may find the way
    to God himself.

Prayer in silence. Then the Priest says:

Almighty ever-living God,
who created all people
to seek you always by desiring you
and, by finding you, come to rest,
grant, we pray,
that, despite every harmful obstacle,
all may recognise the signs
    of your fatherly love
and the witness of the good works
done by those who believe in you,
and so in gladness confess you,
the one true God and Father
    of our human race.
Through Christ our Lord. R. Amen.

IX. For those in public office

Let us pray also for those
    in public office,
that our God and Lord
may direct their minds and hearts
    according to his will
for the true peace and freedom of all.

nosque, mutuo proficientes
    semper amore
et ad tuæ vitæ mysterium plenius
    percipiendum sollicitos,
perfectiores effice tuæ testes
    caritatis in mundo.
Per Christum Dominum nostrum.
R. Amen.

VIII. Pro iis qui in Deum non credunt

Oremus et pro iis qui Deum
    non agnoscunt,
ut, quæ recta sunt sincero
    corde sectantes,
ad ipsum Deum
    pervenire mereantur.

Omnipotens sempiterne Deus,
qui cunctos homines condidisti,
ut te semper desiderando quærerent
et inveniendo quiescerent,
præsta, quæsumus,
ut inter noxia quæque obstacula
omnes, tuæ signa pietatis
et in te credentium testimonium
bonorum operum percipientes,
te solum verum Deum nostrique
    generis Patrem
gaudeant confiteri.
Per Christum Dominum nostrum.
R. Amen.

IX. Pro rempublicam moderantibus

Oremus et pro omnibus
    rempublicam moderantibus,
ut Deus et Dominus noster
mentes et corda eorum secundum
    voluntatem suam dirigat
ad veram omnium pacem
    et libertatem.

Prayer in silence. Then the Priest says:

Almighty ever-living God,
in whose hand lies every
　human heart
and the rights of peoples,
look with favour, we pray,
on those who govern
　with authority over us,
that throughout the whole world,
the prosperity of peoples,
the assurance of peace,
and freedom of religion
may through your gift
　be made secure.
Through Christ our Lord. R. Amen.

X. For those in tribulation

Let us pray, dearly beloved,
to God the Father almighty,
that he may cleanse the world
　of all errors,
banish disease, drive out hunger,
unlock prisons, loosen fetters,
granting to travellers safety,
　to pilgrims return,
health to the sick,
　and salvation to the dying.

Prayer in silence. Then the Priest says:

Almighty ever-living God,
comfort of mourners,
　strength of all who toil,
may the prayers of those who cry out
　in any tribulation
come before you,
that all may rejoice,
because in their hour of need
your mercy was at hand.
Through Christ our Lord.
R. Amen.

Omnipotens sempiterne Deus,
in cuius manu sunt hominum
　corda et iura populorum,
respice benignus ad eos,
　qui nos in potestate moderantur,
ut ubique terrarum populorum
　prosperitas,
pacis securitas et religionis libertas,
te largiente, consistant.
Per Christum Dominum nostrum.
R. Amen.

X. Pro tribulatis

Oremus, dilectissimi nobis,
　Deum Patrem omnipotentem,
ut cunctis mundum
　purget erroribus,
morbos auferat, famem depellat,
aperiat carceres, vincula solvat,
viatoribus securitatem,
　peregrinantibus reditum,
infirmantibus sanitatem
atque morientibus
　salutem indulgeat.

Omnipotens sempiterne Deus,
mæstorum consolatio,
　laborantium fortitudo,
perveniant ad te preces
de quacumque
　tribulatione clamantium,
ut omnes sibi in necessitatibus suis
misericordiam tuam
　gaudeant affuisse.
Per Christum Dominum nostrum.
R. Amen.

SECOND PART:

THE ADORATION OF THE HOLY CROSS

After the Solemn Intercessions, the solemn Adoration of the Holy Cross takes place. Of the two forms of the showing of the Cross presented here, the more appropriate one, according to pastoral needs, should be chosen.

The Showing of the Holy Cross

First Form

The Deacon accompanied by ministers, or another suitable minister, goes to the sacristy, from which, in procession, accompanied by two ministers with lighted candles, he carries the Cross, covered with a violet veil, through the church to the middle of the sanctuary.

The Priest, standing before the altar and facing the people, receives the Cross, uncovers a little of its upper part and elevates it while beginning the Ecce lignum Crucis (Behold the wood of the Cross). He is assisted in singing by the Deacon or, if need be, by the choir. All respond, Come, let us adore. At the end of the singing, all kneel and for a brief moment adore in silence, while the Priest stands and holds the Cross raised.

Behold the wood of the Cross, on which hung the salvation of the world. R. Come, let us adore.	Ecce lignum Crucis, in quo salus mundi pependit. R. Venite, adoremus.

Then the Priest uncovers the right arm of the Cross and again, raising up the Cross, begins, Behold the wood of the Cross and everything takes place as above.

Finally, he uncovers the Cross entirely and, raising it up, he begins the invitation Behold the wood of the Cross a third time and everything takes place like the first time.

Second Form

The Priest or the Deacon accompanied by ministers, or another suitable minister, goes to the door of the church, where he receives the unveiled Cross, and the ministers take lighted candles; then the procession sets off through the church to the sanctuary. Near the door, in the middle of the church, and before the entrance of the sanctuary, the one who carries the Cross elevates it, singing, Behold the wood of the Cross, to which all respond, Come, let us adore. After each response all kneel and for a brief moment adore in silence, as above.

The Adoration of the Holy Cross

Then, accompanied by two ministers with lighted candles, the Priest or the Deacon carries the Cross to the entrance of the sanctuary or to another suitable place and there puts it down or hands it over to the ministers to hold. Candles are placed on the right and left sides of the Cross.

For the Adoration of the Cross, first the Priest Celebrant alone approaches, with the chasuble and his shoes removed, if appropriate. Then the clergy, the lay ministers, and the faithful approach, moving as if in procession, and showing reverence to the Cross by a simple genuflection or by some other sign appropriate to the usage of the region, for example, by kissing the Cross.

Only one Cross should be offered for adoration. If, because of the large number of people, it is not possible for all to approach individually, the Priest, after some of the clergy and faithful have adored, takes the Cross and, standing in the middle before the altar, invites the people in a few words to adore the Holy Cross and afterwards holds the Cross elevated higher for a brief time, for the faithful to adore it in silence.

While the adoration of the Holy Cross is taking place, the antiphon Crucem tuam adoramus (We adore your Cross, O Lord), the Reproaches, the hymn Crux fidelis (Faithful Cross) or other suitable chants are sung, during which all who have already adored the Cross remain seated.

Chants to be Sung during the Adoration of the Holy Cross

Ant. We adore your Cross, O Lord,
we praise and glorify your
    holy Resurrection,
for behold, because of the wood
    of a tree
joy has come to the whole world.

Ant. Crucem tuam
    adoramus, Domine,
et sanctam resurrectionem tuam
    laudamus et glorificamus:
ecce enim propter lignum
venit gaudium in universo mundo.

Cf. Ps 66:2

May God have mercy on us
    and bless us;
may he let his face shed its light
    upon us
and have mercy on us.
And the antiphon is repeated:
We adore...

Deus misereatur nostri,
    et benedicat nobis:
illuminet vultum suum super nos,
et misereatur nostri.

Crucem tuam...

THE REPROACHES

Parts assigned to one of the two choirs separately are indicated by the numbers 1 (first choir) and 2 (second choir); parts sung by both choirs together are marked: 1 and 2. Some of the verses may also be sung by two cantors.

1 and 2 My people,
    what have I done to you?
Or how have I grieved you?
    Answer me!

1 et 2 Popule meus,
    quid feci tibi?
Aut in quo contristavi te?
    Responde mihi!

1 Because I led you out of the land of Egypt, you have prepared a Cross for your Saviour.	1 Quia eduxi te de terra Ægypti: parasti Crucem Salvatori tuo.

1 Hagios o Theos,
2 Holy is God,
1 Hagios Ischyros,
2 Holy and Mighty,
1 Hagios Athanatos,
   eleison himas.
2 Holy and Immortal One,
   have mercy on us.
	1 Hagios o Theos.
	2 Sanctus Deus.
	1 Hagios Ischyros.
	2 Sanctus Fortis.
	1 Hagios Athanatos,
	   eleison himas.
	2 Sanctus Immortalis,
	   miserere nobis.

1 and 2 Because I led you out
   through the desert forty years
and fed you with manna and
   brought you into a land of plenty,
you have prepared a Cross
   for your Saviour.
	1 et 2 Quia eduxi te per desertum
	   quadraginta annis,
	et manna cibavi te,
	et introduxi te in terram
	   satis bonam:
	parasti Crucem Salvatori tuo.

1 Hagios o Theos,
2 Holy is God,
1 Hagios Ischyros,
2 Holy and Mighty,
1 Hagios Athanatos, eleison himas.
2 Holy and Immortal One,
   have mercy on us.
	1 Hagios o Theos.
	2 Sanctus Deus.
	1 Hagios Ischyros.
	2 Sanctus Fortis.
	1 Hagios Athanatos, eleison himas.
	2 Sanctus Immortalis,
	   miserere nobis.

1 and 2 What more should I have
   done for you and have not done?
Indeed, I planted you as my most
   beautiful chosen vine
and you have turned very bitter
   for me,
for in my thirst you gave me
   vinegar to drink
and with a lance you pierced your
   Saviour's side.
	1 et 2 Quid ultra debui facere tibi,
	   et non feci?
	Ego quidem plantavi te
	vineam electam
	   meam speciosissimam:
	et tu facta es mihi nimis amara:
	aceto namque sitim meam potasti,
	et lancea perforasti latus
	   Salvatori tuo.

1 Hagios o Theos, 2 Holy is God,	1 Hagios o Theos. 2 Sanctus Deus.

1 Hagios Ischyros,
2 Holy and Mighty,
1 Hagios Athanatos,
   eleison himas.
2 Holy and Immortal One, have mercy on us.

Cantors:
I scourged Egypt for your sake
   with its firstborn sons,
and you scourged me and handed
   me over.

1 and 2 repeat:
My people, what have I done to you?
Or how have I grieved you?
Answer me!
Cantors:
I led you out from Egypt as Pharaoh
   lay sunk in the Red Sea,
and you handed me over
   to the chief priests.

1 and 2 repeat:
My people. . .
Cantors:
I opened up the sea before you,
and you opened my side with a lance.

1 and 2 repeat:
My people. . .

Cantors:
I went before you in a pillar of cloud,
and you led me into Pilate's palace.

1 and 2 repeat:
My people. . .

1 Hagios Ischyros.
2 Sanctus Fortis.
1 Hagios Athanatos,
   eleison himas.
2 Sanctus Immortalis,
   miserere nobis.

II

Cantores:
Ego propter te flagellavi Ægyptum
cum primogenitis suis:
et tu me flagellatum tradidisti.

1 et 2 repetunt:
Popule meus, quid feci tibi?
Aut in quo contristavi te?
Responde mihi!
Cantores:
Ego eduxi te de Ægypto,
demerso Pharaone in Mare Rubrum:
et tu me tradidisti
   principibus sacerdotum.

1 et 2 repetunt:
Popule meus. . .
Cantores:
Ego ante te aperui mare:
et tu aperuisti lancea latus meum.

1 et 2 repetunt:
Popule meus. . .

Cantores:
Ego ante te præivi in columna nubis:
et tu me duxisti ad prætorium Pilati.

1 et 2 repetunt:
Popule meus. . .

Cantors:
I fed you with manna in the desert,
and on me you rained blows
 and lashes.

1 and 2 repeat:
My people. . .

Cantors:
I gave you saving water
 from the rock to drink,
and for drink you gave me gall
 and vinegar.

1 and 2 repeat:
My people. . .

Cantors:
I struck down for you the kings
 of the Canaanites,
and you struck my head with a reed.

1 and 2 repeat:
My people. . .

Cantors:
I put in your hand a royal sceptre,
and you put on my head
 a crown of thorns.

1 and 2 repeat:
My people. . .

Cantors:
I exalted you with great power,
and you hung me on the scaffold
 of the Cross.

1 and 2 repeat:
My people. . .

Cantores:
Ego te pavi manna per desertum:
et tu me cecidisti alapis et flagellis.

1 et 2 repetunt:
Popule meus. . .

Cantores:
Ego te potavi aqua salutis de petra:
et tu me potasti felle et aceto.

1 et 2 repetunt:
Popule meus. . .

Cantores:
Ego propter te Chananæorum
 reges percussi:
et tu percussisti arundine
 caput meum.

1 et 2 repetunt:
Popule meus. . .

Cantores:
Ego dedi tibi sceptrum regale:
et tu dedisti capiti meo spineam
 coronam.

1 et 2 repetunt:
Popule meus. . .

Cantores:
Ego te exaltavi magna virtute:
et tu me suspendisti
 in patibulo Crucis.

1 et 2 repetunt:
Popule meus. . .

HYMN

All:

Faithful Cross the Saints rely on,
Noble tree beyond compare!
Never was there such a scion,
Never leaf or flower so rare.
Sweet the timber, sweet the iron,
Sweet the burden that they bear!

Cantors:

Sing, my tongue, in exultation
Of our banner and device!
Make a solemn proclamation
Of a triumph and its price:
How the Saviour of creation
Conquered by his sacrifice!

All:

Faithful Cross the Saints rely on,
Noble tree beyond compare!
Never was there such a scion,
Never leaf or flower so rare.

Cantors:

For, when Adam first offended,
Eating that forbidden fruit,
Not all hopes of glory ended
With the serpent at the root:
Broken nature would be mended
By a second tree and shoot.

All:

Sweet the timber, sweet the iron,
Sweet the burden that they bear!

Cantors:

Thus the tempter was outwitted
By a wisdom deeper still:
Remedy and ailment fitted,
Means to cure and means to kill;
That the world might be acquitted,
Christ would do his Father's will.

Omnes:

Crux fidelis, inter omnes
   arbor una nobilis,
Nulla talem silva profert,
   flore, fronde, germine!
Dulce lignum dulci clavo
   dulce pondus sustinens!

Cantores:

Pange, lingua, gloriosi
   prœlium certaminis,
Et super crucis tropæo
   dic triumphum nobilem,
Qualiter Redemptor orbis
   immolatus vicerit.

Omnes:

Crux fidelis, inter omnes
   arbor una nobilis,
Nulla talem silva profert,
   flore, fronde, germine!

Cantores:

De parentis protoplasti
   fraude factor condolens,
Quando pomi noxialis
   morte morsu corruit,
Ipse lignum tunc notavit,
   damna ligni ut solveret.

Omnes:

Dulce lignum dulci clavo
   dulce pondus sustinens!

Cantores:

Hoc opus nostræ salutis
   ordo depoposcerat,
Multiformis perditoris
   arte ut artem falleret,
Et medelam ferret inde,
   hostis unde læserat.

All:

Faithful Cross the Saints rely on,
Noble tree beyond compare!
Never was there such a scion,
Never leaf or flower so rare.

Cantors:

So the Father, out of pity
For our self-inflicted doom,
Sent him from the heavenly city
When the holy time had come:
He, the Son and the Almighty,
Took our flesh in Mary's womb.

All:

Sweet the timber, sweet the iron,
Sweet the burden that they bear!

Cantors:

Hear a tiny baby crying,
Founder of the seas and strands;
See his virgin Mother tying
Cloth around his feet and hands;
Find him in a manger lying
Tightly wrapped in swaddling-bands!

All:

Faithful Cross the Saints rely on,
Noble tree beyond compare!
Never was there such a scion,
Never leaf or flower so rare.

Cantors:

So he came, the long-expected,
Not in glory, not to reign;
Only born to be rejected,
Choosing hunger, toil and pain,
Till the scaffold was erected
And the Paschal Lamb was slain.

All:

Sweet the timber, sweet the iron,
Sweet the burden that they bear!

Cantors:

No disgrace was too abhorrent:
Nailed and mocked and

Omnes:

Crux fidelis, inter omnes
  arbor una nobilis,
Nulla talem silva profert,
  flore, fronde, germine!

Cantores:

Quando venit ergo sacri
  plenitudo temporis,
Missus est ab arce Patris
Natus, orbis conditor,
Atque ventre virginali
  carne factus prodiit.

Omnes:

Dulce lignum dulci clavo
  dulce pondus sustinens!

Cantores:

Vagit infans inter arta
  conditus præsepia,
Membra pannis involuta
  Virgo Mater alligat,
Et manus pedesque et crura
  stricta cingit fascia.

Omnes:

Crux fidelis, inter omnes
  arbor una nobilis,
Nulla talem silva profert,
  flore, fronde, germine!

Cantores:

Lustra sex qui iam peracta,
  tempus implens corporis,
se volente, natus ad hoc,
  passioni deditus,
agnus in crucis levatur
  immolandus stipite.

Omnes:

Dulce lignum dulci clavo
  dulce pondus sustinens!

Cantores:

En acetum, fel, arundo,
Mite corpus perforatur,

parched he died;
Blood and water, double warrant,
Issue from his wounded side,
Washing in a mighty torrent
Earth and stars and oceantide.

All:
Faithful Cross the Saints rely on,
Noble tree beyond compare!
Never was there such a scion,
Never leaf or flower so rare.

Cantors:
Lofty timber,
    smooth your roughness,
Flex your boughs for blossoming;
Let your fibres lose their toughness,
Gently let your tendrils cling;
Lay aside your native gruffness,
Clasp the body of your King!

All:
Sweet the timber, sweet the iron,
Sweet the burden that they bear!

Cantors:
Noblest tree of all created,
Richly jewelled and embossed:
Post by Lamb's blood consecrated;
Spar that saves the tempest-tossed;
Scaffold-beam which, elevated,
Carries what the world has cost!

All:
Faithful Cross the Saints rely on,
Noble tree beyond compare!
Never was there such a scion,
Never leaf or flower so rare.

sputa, clavi, lancea;
sanguis unde profluit;
Terra, pontus, astra, mundus
    quo lavantur flumine!

Omnes:
Crux fidelis, inter omnes
    arbor una nobilis,
Nulla talem silva profert,
    flore, fronde, germine!

Cantores:
Flecte ramos, arbor alta,
    tensa laxa viscera,
Et rigor lentescat ille,
    quem dedit nativitas,
Ut superni membra Regis
    miti tendas stipite.

Omnes:
Dulce lignum dulci clavo
    dulce pondus sustinens!

Cantores:
Sola digna tu fuisti
    ferre sæcli pretium
Atque portum præparare
    nauta mundo naufrago,
Quem sacer cruor perunxit
    fusus Agni corpore.

Omnes:
Crux fidelis, inter omnes
    arbor una nobilis,
Nulla talem silva profert,
    flore, fronde, germine!

The following conclusion is never to be omitted:

All:
Wisdom, power, and adoration
To the blessed Trinity

Omnes:
Æqua Patri Filioque,
    inclito Paraclito,

For redemption and salvation
Through the Paschal Mystery,
Now, in every generation,
And for all eternity. Amen.

Sempiterna sit beatæ
  Trinitati gloria;
cuius alma nos redemit
  atque servat gratia. Amen.

In accordance with local circumstances or popular traditions and if it is pastorally appropriate, the Stabat Mater may be sung, as found in the Graduale Romanum, or another suitable chant in memory of the compassion of the Blessed Virgin Mary.

When the adoration has been concluded, the Cross is carried by the Deacon or a minister to its place at the altar. Lighted candles are placed around or on the altar or near the Cross.

THIRD PART:

Holy Communion

A cloth is spread on the altar, and a corporal and the Missal put in place. Meanwhile the Deacon or, if there is no Deacon, the Priest himself, putting on a humeral veil, brings the Blessed Sacrament back from the place of repose to the altar by a shorter route, while all stand in silence. Two ministers with lighted candles accompany the Blessed Sacrament and place their candlesticks around or upon the altar.

When the Deacon, if a Deacon is present, has placed the Blessed Sacrament upon the altar and uncovered the ciborium, the Priest goes to the altar and genuflects.

Then the Priest, with hands joined, says aloud:

At the Saviour's command
and formed by divine teaching,
we dare to say:

Præceptis salutaribus moniti,
et divina institutione formati,
audemus dicere:

The Priest, with hands extended says, and all present continue:

Our Father, who art in heaven,
hallowed be thy name;
thy kingdom come,
thy will be done
on earth as it is in heaven.
Give us this day our daily bread,
and forgive us our trespasses,
as we forgive those who trespass
   against us;
and lead us not into temptation,
but deliver us from evil.

Pater noster, qui es in cælis:
sanctificetur nomen tuum;
adveniat regnum tuum;
fiat voluntas tua, sicut in cælo,
   et in terra.
Panem nostrum cotidianum
   da nobis hodie;
et dimitte nobis debita nostra,
sicut et nos dimittimus
   debitoribus nostris;
et ne nos inducas in tentationem;
sed libera nos a malo.

With hands extended, the Priest continues alone:

Deliver us, Lord, we pray,
   from every evil,

Libera nos, quæsumus, Domine,
   ab omnibus malis,

graciously grant peace in our days,	da propitius pacem in diebus nostris,
that, by the help of your mercy,	ut, ope misericordiæ tuæ adiuti,
and safe from all distress,	we may be always free from sin
as we await the blessed hope	et a peccato simus semper liberi
and the coming of our Saviour,	et ab omni perturbatione securi:
Jesus Christ.	exspectantes beatam spem
	et adventum Salvatoris nostri
	Iesu Christi.

He joins his hands.

The people conclude the prayer, acclaiming:

For the kingdom,	Quia tuum est regnum,
the power and the glory are yours	et potestas,
now and for ever.	et gloria in sæcula.

Then the Priest, with hands joined, says quietly:

May the receiving of your Body and Blood,	Perceptio Corporis tui, Domine Iesu Christe,
Lord Jesus Christ,	non mihi proveniat in iudicium
not bring me to judgement and condemnation,	et condemnationem:
but through your loving mercy	sed pro tua pietate prosit mihi
be for me protection in mind and body	ad tutamentum mentis et corporis,
and a healing remedy.	et ad medelam percipiendam.

The Priest then genuflects, takes a particle, and, holding it slightly raised over the ciborium, while facing the people, says aloud:

Behold the Lamb of God,	Ecce Agnus Dei, ecce qui tollit
behold him who takes away the sins of the world.	peccata mundi.
Blessed are those called	Beati qui ad cenam
to the supper of the Lamb.	Agni vocati sunt.

And together with the people he adds once:

Lord, I am not worthy	Domine, non sum dignus,
that you should enter under my roof,	ut intres sub tectum meum,
but only say the word	sed tantum dic verbo,
and my soul shall be healed.	et sanabitur anima mea.

And facing the altar, he reverently consumes the Body of Christ, saying quietly:

| May the Body of Christ keep me safe for eternal life. | Corpus Christi custodiat me in vitam æternam. |

He then proceeds to distribute Communion to the faithful. During Communion, Psalm 21 or another appropriate chant may be sung.

When the distribution of Communion has been completed, the ciborium is taken by the Deacon or another suitable minister to a place prepared outside the church or, if circumstances so require, it is placed in the tabernacle.

Then the Priest says: Let us pray, and, after a period of sacred silence, if circumstances so suggest, has been observed, he says the Prayer after Communion.

Almighty ever-living God,
who have restored us to life
by the blessed Death
    and Resurrection of your Christ,
preserve in us the work
    of your mercy,
that, by partaking of this mystery,
we may have a life unceasingly
    devoted to you.
Through Christ our Lord.
R. Amen.
	Omnipotens sempiterne Deus,
	qui nos Christi tui beata morte
	    et resurrectione reparasti,
	conserva in nobis opus
	    misericordiæ tuæ,
	ut huius mysterii participatione
	perpetua devotione vivamus.
	Per Christum Dominum nostrum.
	R. Amen.

For the Dismissal the Deacon or, if there is no Deacon, the Priest himself, may say the invitation Bow down for the blessing.

Then the Priest, standing facing the people and extending his hands over them, says this Prayer over the People:

May abundant blessing, O Lord,
    we pray,
descend upon your people,
who have honoured the Death
    of your Son
in the hope of their resurrection:
may pardon come,
comfort be given,
holy faith increase,
and everlasting redemption
    be made secure.
Through Christ our Lord.
R. Amen.
	Super populum tuum,
	    quæsumus, Domine,
	qui mortem Filii tui in spe suæ
	    resurrectionis recoluit,
	benedictio copiosa descendat,
	indulgentia veniat,
	    consolatio tribuatur,
	fides sancta succrescat,
	    redemptio sempiterna firmetur.
	Per Christum Dominum nostrum.
	R. Amen.

And all, after genuflecting to the Cross, depart in silence.

After the celebration, the altar is stripped, but the Cross remains on the altar with two or four candlesticks.

Vespers (Evening Prayer) is not celebrated by those who have been present at the solemn afternoon liturgical celebration.

EASTER SUNDAY OF THE RESURRECTION OF THE LORD

30 March

THE EASTER VIGIL IN THE HOLY NIGHT

During the Easter Vigil, the Church reads the account of creation as a prophecy. In the resurrection, we see the most sublime fulfilment of what this text describes as the beginning of all things. God says once again: "Let there be light!" The resurrection of Jesus is an eruption of light. Death is conquered, the tomb is thrown open. The Risen One himself is Light, the Light of the world. With the resurrection, the Lord's day enters the nights of history. Beginning with the resurrection, God's light spreads throughout the world and throughout history. Day dawns. This Light alone – Jesus Christ – is the true light, something more than the physical phenomenon of light. He is pure Light: God himself, who causes a new creation to be born in the midst of the old, transforming chaos into cosmos.

(Pope Benedict XVI)

By most ancient tradition, this is the night of keeping vigil for the Lord (Ex 12:42), in which, following the Gospel admonition (Lk 12:35-37), the faithful, carrying lighted lamps in their hands, should be like those looking for the Lord when he returns, so that at his coming he may find them awake and have them sit at his table.

Of this night's Vigil, which is the greatest and most noble of all solemnities, there is to be only one celebration in each church. It is arranged, moreover, in such a way that after the Lucernarium and Easter Proclamation (which constitutes the first part of this Vigil), Holy Church meditates on the wonders the Lord God has done for his people from the beginning, trusting in his word and promise (the second part, that is, the Liturgy of the Word) until, as day approaches, with new members reborn in Baptism (the third part), the Church is called to the table the Lord has prepared for his people, the memorial of his Death and Resurrection until he comes again (the fourth part).

The entire celebration of the Easter Vigil must take place during the night, so that it begins after nightfall and ends before daybreak on the Sunday.

The Mass of the Vigil, even if it is celebrated before midnight, is a paschal Mass of the Sunday of the Resurrection.

Anyone who participates in the Mass of the night may receive Communion again at Mass during the day. A Priest who celebrates or concelebrates the Mass of the night may again celebrate or concelebrate Mass during the day.

The Easter Vigil takes the place of the Office of Readings.

FIRST PART:

THE SOLEMN BEGINNING OF THE VIGIL OR LUCERNARIUM

The Blessing of the Fire and Preparation of the Candle

A blazing fire is prepared in a suitable place outside the church. When the people are gathered there, the Priest approaches with the ministers, one of whom carries the paschal candle. The processional cross and candles are not carried.

Where, however, a fire cannot be lit outside the church, the rite is carried out as below.

The Priest and faithful sign themselves while the Priest says: In the name of the Father, and of the Son, and of the Holy Spirit, and then he greets the assembled people in the usual way and briefly instructs them about the night vigil in these or similar words:

The Priest is usually assisted by a Deacon. If, however, there is no Deacon, the duties of his Order, except those indicated below, are assumed by the Priest Celebrant or by a concelebrant.

The Priest and Deacon vest as at Mass, in white vestments.

Candles should be prepared for all who participate in the Vigil. The lights of the church are extinguished.

Dear brethren (brothers and sisters), on this most sacred night, in which our Lord Jesus Christ passed over from death to life, the Church calls upon her sons and daughters, scattered throughout the world, to come together to watch and pray. If we keep the memorial of the Lord's paschal solemnity in this way, listening to his word and celebrating his mysteries, then we shall have the sure hope of sharing his triumph over death and living with him in God.	Fratres carissimi, hac sacratissima nocte, in qua Dominus noster Iesus Christus de morte transivit ad vitam, Ecclesia invitat filios dispersos per orbem terrarum, ut ad vigilandum et orandum conveniant. Si ita memoriam egerimus Paschatis Domini, audientes verbum et celebrantes mysteria eius, spem habebimus participandi triumphum eius de morte et vivendi cum ipso in Deo.

Then the Priest blesses the fire, saying with hands extended:

Let us pray.	Oremus.
O God, who through your Son bestowed upon the faithful the fire of your glory, sanctify ✠ this new fire, we pray, and grant that, by these paschal celebrations, we may be so inflamed with heavenly desires, that with minds made pure we may attain festivities of unending splendour. Through Christ our Lord. R. Amen.	Deus, qui per Filium tuum claritatis tuæ ignem fidelibus contulisti, novum hunc ignem ✠ sanctifica, et concede nobis, ita per hæc festa paschalia cælestibus desideriis inflammari, ut ad perpetuæ claritatis puris mentibus valeamus festa pertingere. Per Christum Dominum nostrum. R. Amen.

After the blessing of the new fire, one of the ministers brings the paschal candle to the Priest, who cuts a cross into the candle with a stylus. Then he makes the Greek letter Alpha above the cross, the letter Omega below, and the four numerals of the current year between the arms of the cross, saying meanwhile:

1. Christ yesterday and today	1. Christus heri et hodie
2. the Beginning and the End	2. Principium et Finis
3. the Alpha	3. Alpha
4. and the Omega	4. et Omega
5. All time belongs to him	5. Ipsius sunt tempora
6. and all the ages	6. et sæcula
7. To him be glory and power	7. Ipsi gloria et imperium
8. through every age and for ever. Amen	8. per universa æternitatis sæcula. Amen

When the cutting of the cross and of the other signs has been completed, the Priest may insert five grains of incense into the candle in the form of a cross, meanwhile saying:

1. By his holy	1. Per sua sancta vulnera
2. and glorious wounds,	2. gloriosa
3. may Christ the Lord	3. custodiat
4. guard us	4. et conservet nos
5. and protect us. Amen.	5. Christus Dominus. Amen.

Where, because of difficulties that may occur, a fire is not lit, the blessing of fire is adapted to the circumstances. When the people are gathered in the church as on other occasions, the Priest comes to the door of the church, along with the ministers carrying the paschal candle. The people, insofar as is possible, turn to face the Priest.

The greeting and address take place as above; then the fire is blessed and the candle is prepared, as above.

The Priest lights the paschal candle from the new fire, saying:

May the light of Christ rising in glory dispel the darkness of our hearts and minds.	Lumen Christi gloriose resurgentis dissipet tenebras cordis et mentis.

As regards the preceding elements, Conferences of Bishops may also establish other forms more adapted to the culture of the different peoples.

Procession

When the candle has been lit, one of the ministers takes burning coals from the fire and places them in the thurible, and the Priest puts incense into it in the usual way. The Deacon or, if there is no Deacon, another suitable minister, takes the paschal candle and a procession forms. The thurifer with the smoking thurible precedes the Deacon or other minister who carries the paschal candle. After them follows the Priest with the ministers and the people, all holding in their hands unlit candles.

At the door of the church the Deacon, standing and raising up the candle, sings:

The Light of Christ.	Lumen Christi.

And all reply:

Thanks be to God.	Deo gratias.

The Priest lights his candle from the flame of the paschal candle.

Then the Deacon moves forward to the middle of the church and, standing and raising up the candle, sings a second time:

The Light of Christ.	Lumen Christi.

And all reply:

Thanks be to God.	Deo gratias.

All light their candles from the flame of the paschal candle and continue in procession.

When the Deacon arrives before the altar, he stands facing the people, raises up the candle and sings a third time:

The Light of Christ.	Lumen Christi.

And all reply:

Thanks be to God.	Deo gratias.

Then the Deacon places the paschal candle on a large candlestand prepared next to the ambo or in the middle of the sanctuary.

The Easter Proclamation (Exsultet)

Arriving at the altar, the Priest goes to his chair, gives his candle to a minister, puts incense into the thurible and blesses the incense as at the Gospel at Mass. The Deacon goes to the Priest and saying, Your blessing, Father, asks for and receives a blessing from the Priest, who says in a low voice:

May the Lord be in your heart and on your lips, that you may proclaim his paschal praise worthily and well, in the name of the Father and of the Son, ✠ and of the Holy Spirit. The Deacon replies: **Amen.**	Dominus sit in corde tuo et in labiis tuis, ut digne et competenter annunties suum paschale præconium: in nomine Patris, et Filii, ✠ et Spiritus Sancti. Amen.

This blessing is omitted if the Proclamation is made by someone who is not a Deacon.

The Deacon, after incensing the book and the candle, proclaims the Easter Proclamation (Exsultet) at the ambo or at a lectern, with all standing and holding lighted candles in their hands.

The Easter Proclamation may be made, in the absence of a Deacon, by the Priest himself or by another concelebrating Priest. If, however, because of necessity, a lay cantor sings the Proclamation, the words Therefore, dearest friends up to the end of the invitation are omitted, along with the greeting The Lord be with you.

The Proclamation may also be sung in the shorter form p.351.

Longer Form of the Easter Proclamation

Exult, let them exult, the hosts of heaven, exult, let Angel ministers of God exult, let the trumpet of salvation sound aloud our mighty King's triumph!	Exsultet iam angelica turba cælorum: exsultent divina mysteria: et pro tanti Regis victoria tuba insonet salutaris.
Be glad, let earth be glad, as glory floods her, ablaze with light from her eternal King, let all corners of the earth be glad, knowing an end to gloom and darkness.	Gaudeat et tellus tantis irradiata fulgoribus: et, æterni Regis splendore illustrata, totius orbis se sentiat amisisse caliginem.

Rejoice, let Mother Church
  also rejoice,
arrayed with the lightning
  of his glory,
let this holy building shake with joy,
filled with the mighty voices
  of the peoples.

(Therefore, dearest friends,
standing in the awesome glory
  of this holy light,
invoke with me, I ask you,
the mercy of God almighty,
that he, who has been pleased
  to number me,
though unworthy, among the Levites,
may pour into me his light
  unshadowed,
that I may sing this candle's
  perfect praises.)

(V. The Lord be with you.
R. And with your spirit.)
V. Lift up your hearts.
R. We lift them up to the Lord.
V. Let us give thanks to the Lord
  our God.
R. It is right and just.
It is truly right and just,
with ardent love of mind and heart
and with devoted service of our voice,
to acclaim our God invisible,
  the almighty Father,
and Jesus Christ, our Lord, his Son,
  his Only Begotten.

Who for our sake paid Adam's debt
  to the eternal Father,
and, pouring out his own dear Blood,
wiped clean the record of our
  ancient sinfulness.

Lætetur et mater Ecclesia,
tanti luminis adornata fulgoribus:
et magnis populorum vocibus hæc
  aula resultet.

(Quapropter astantes vos,
  fratres carissimi,
ad tam miram huius sancti
  luminis claritatem,
una mecum, quæso,
Dei omnipotentis
  misericordiam invocate.
Ut, qui me non meis meritis
intra Levitarum numerum dignatus
  est aggregare,
luminis sui claritatem infundens,
cerei huius laudem
  implere perficiat.)

(V. Dominus vobiscum.
R. Et cum spiritu tuo.)
V. Sursum corda.
R. Habemus ad Dominum.
V. Gratias agamus Domino
  Deo nostro.
R. Dignum et iustum est.
Vere dignum et iustum est,
invisibilem Deum
  Patrem omnipotentem
Filiumque eius Unigenitum,
Dominum nostrum
  Iesum Christum,
toto cordis ac mentis affectu
  et vocis ministerio personare.

Qui pro nobis æterno Patri Adæ
  debitum solvit,
et veteris piaculi cautionem
  pio cruore detersit.

These then are the feasts of Passover,
 in which is slain the Lamb,
    the one true Lamb,
 whose Blood anoints the doorposts
    of believers.
	Hæc sunt enim festa paschalia,
	 in quibus verus ille Agnus occiditur,
	 cuius sanguine postes
	    fidelium consecrantur.

This is the night,
 when once you led our forebears,
    Israel's children,
 from slavery in Egypt
 and made them pass dry-shod
    through the Red Sea.
	Hæc nox est,
	 in qua primum patres nostros,
	 filios Israel eductos de Ægypto,
	 Mare Rubrum sicco vestigio
	    transire fecisti.

This is the night that with a pillar of fire banished the darkness of sin.	Hæc igitur nox est, quæ peccatorum tenebras columnæ illuminatione purgavit.

This is the night
 that even now, throughout the world,
 sets Christian believers apart
    from worldly vices
 and from the gloom of sin,
 leading them to grace
 and joining them to his holy ones.
	Hæc nox est,
	 quæ hodie per universum mundum
	    in Christo credentes,
	 a vitiis sæculi et caligine
	    peccatorum segregatos,
	 reddit gratiæ, sociat sanctitati.

This is the night,
 when Christ broke the prison-bars
    of death
 and rose victorious
    from the underworld.
	Hæc nox est,
	 in qua, destructis vinculis mortis,
	 Christus ab inferis victor ascendit.

Our birth would have been no gain,
 had we not been redeemed.
 O wonder of your humble care for us!
 O love, O charity beyond all telling,
 to ransom a slave you gave away
    your Son!
	Nihil enim nobis nasci profuit,
	    nisi redimi profuisset.
	 O mira circa nos tuæ pietatis
	    dignatio!
	 O inæstimablilis dilectio caritatis:
	 ut servum redimeres,
	    Filium tradidisti!

O truly necessary sin of Adam,
 destroyed completely by the Death
    of Christ!
	O certe necessarium
	    Adæ peccatum,
	 quod Christi morte deletum est!

O happy fault
that earned so great,
   so glorious a Redeemer!
	O felix culpa,
	quæ talem ac tantum meruit
	   habere Redemptorem!

O truly blessed night,
worthy alone to know the time
   and hour
when Christ rose
   from the underworld!
	O vere beata nox,
	quæ sola meruit scire tempus
	   et horam,
	in qua Christus ab inferis resurrexit!

This is the night of which it is written: The night shall be as bright as day, dazzling is the night for me, and full of gladness.	Hæc nox est, de qua scriptum est: Et nox sicut dies illuminabitur: et nox illuminatio mea in deliciis meis.

The sanctifying power of this night
dispels wickedness,
   washes faults away,
restores innocence to the fallen,
   and joy to mourners,
drives out hatred, fosters concord,
   and brings down the mighty.
	Huius igitur sanctificatio noctis
	   fugat scelera, culpas lavat:
	et reddit innocentiam lapsis
	   et mæstis lætitiam.
	Fugat odia, concordiam parat
	   et curvat imperia.

On this, your night of grace,
   O holy Father,
accept this candle, a solemn offering,
the work of bees and of your
   servants' hands,
an evening sacrifice of praise,
this gift from your most holy Church.
	In huius igitur noctis gratia,
	suscipe, sancte Pater, laudis huius
	   sacrificium vespertinum,
	quod tibi in hac cerei
	   oblatione sollemni,
	per ministrorum manus
	de operibus apum,
	   sacrosancta reddit Ecclesia.

But now we know the praises
   of this pillar,
which glowing fire ignites
   for God's honour,
a fire into many flames divided,
yet never dimmed by sharing
   of its light,
for it is fed by melting wax,
drawn out by mother bees
to build a torch so precious.
	Sed iam columnæ huius
	   præconia novimus,
	quam in honorem Dei rutilans
	   ignis accendit.
	Qui, licet sit divisus in partes,
	mutuati tamen luminis detrimenta
	   non novit.
	Alitur enim liquantibus ceris,
	quas in substantiam pretiosæ
	   huius lampadis
	apis mater eduxit.

O truly blessed night,
when things of heaven are wed
    to those of earth,
and divine to the human.
Therefore, O Lord,
we pray you that this candle,
hallowed to the honour of
    your name,
may persevere undimmed,
to overcome the darkness
    of this night.
Receive it as a pleasing fragrance,
and let it mingle with
    the lights of heaven.
May this flame be found still burning
by the Morning Star:
the one Morning Star who never sets,
Christ your Son,
who, coming back
    from death's domain,
has shed his peaceful light
    on humanity,
and lives and reigns
    for ever and ever.
R. Amen.

O vere beata nox,
in qua terrenis cælestia,
    humanis divina iunguntur!

Oramus ergo te, Domine,
ut cereus iste in honorem tui
    nominis consecratus,
ad noctis huius
    caliginem destruendam,
indeficiens perseveret.

Et in odorem suavitatis acceptus,
supernis luminaribus misceatur.
Flammas eius lucifer
    matutinus inveniat:

Ille, inquam, lucifer,
    qui nescit occasum:
Christus Filius tuus,
qui, regressus ab inferis, humano
    generi serenus illuxit,
et vivit et regnat
    in sæcula sæculorum.

R. Amen.

Shorter Form of the Easter Proclamation

Exult, let them exult,
    the hosts of heaven,
exult, let Angel ministers
    of God exult,
let the trumpet of salvation
sound aloud our mighty
    King's triumph!
Be glad, let earth be glad, as glory
    floods her,
ablaze with light from her
    eternal King,
let all corners of the earth be glad,
knowing an end to gloom
    and darkness.

Exsultet iam angelica
    turba cælorum:
exsultent divina mysteria:
et pro tanti Regis victoria tuba
    insonet salutaris.

Gaudeat et tellus tantis
    irradiata fulgoribus:
et, æterni Regis splendore illustrata,
totius orbis se sentiat
    amisisse caliginem.

Rejoice, let Mother Church
  also rejoice,
arrayed with the lightning
  of his glory,
let this holy building shake with joy,
filled with the mighty voices
  of the peoples.

(V. The Lord be with you.
R. And with your spirit.)
V. Lift up your hearts.
R. We lift them up to the Lord.
V. Let us give thanks to the Lord
  our God.
R. It is right and just.

It is truly right and just,
with ardent love of mind and heart
and with devoted service of our voice,
to acclaim our God invisible,
  the almighty Father,
and Jesus Christ, our Lord, his Son,
  his Only Begotten.

Who for our sake paid Adam's debt
  to the eternal Father,
and, pouring out his own dear Blood,
wiped clean the record
  of our ancient sinfulness.

These then are the feasts of Passover,
in which is slain the Lamb,
  the one true Lamb,
whose Blood anoints the doorposts
  of believers.

This is the night,
when once you led our forebears,
  Israel's children,
from slavery in Egypt
and made them pass dry-shod
  through the Red Sea.

Lætetur et mater Ecclesia,
tanti luminis adornata fulgoribus:
et magnis populorum vocibus hæc
  aula resultet.

(V. Dominus vobiscum.
R. Et cum spiritu tuo.)
V. Sursum corda.
R. Habemus ad Dominum.
V. Gratias agamus Domino
  Deo nostro.
R. Dignum et iustum est.

Vere dignum et iustum est,
invisibilem Deum
  Patrem omnipotentem
Filiumque eius Unigenitum,
Dominum nostrum
  Iesum Christum,
toto cordis ac mentis affectu
  et vocis ministerio personare.

Qui pro nobis æterno Patri Adæ
  debitum solvit,
et veteris piaculi cautionem pio
  cruore detersit.

Hæc sunt enim festa paschalia,
in quibus verus ille
  Agnus occiditur,
cuius sanguine postes
  fidelium consecrantur.

Hæc nox est,
in qua primum patres nostros,
  filios Israel
eductos de Ægypto,
Mare Rubrum sicco vestigio
  transire fecisti.

This is the night that with a pillar of fire banished the darkness of sin.	Hæc igitur nox est, quæ peccatorum tenebras columnæ illuminatione purgavit.

This is the night
that even now, throughout the world,
sets Christian believers apart
    from worldly vices
and from the gloom of sin,
leading them to grace
and joining them to his holy ones.
	Hæc nox est,
	quæ hodie per universum mundum
	    in Christo credentes,
	a vitiis sæculi et caligine
	    peccatorum segregatos,
	reddit gratiæ, sociat sanctitati.

This is the night,
when Christ broke the prison-bars
    of death
and rose victorious
    from the underworld.
	Hæc nox est,
	in qua, destructis vinculis mortis,
	Christus ab inferis victor ascendit.

O wonder of your humble care for us!
O love, O charity beyond all telling,
to ransom a slave you gave away
    your Son!
	O mira circa nos tuæ
	    pietatis dignatio!
	O inæstimablilis dilectio caritatis:
	ut servum redimeres,
	    Filium tradidisti!

O truly necessary sin of Adam, destroyed completely by the Death of Christ!	O certe necessarium Adæ peccatum, quod Christi morte deletum est!

O happy fault
that earned so great,
    so glorious a Redeemer!
	O felix culpa,
	quæ talem ac tantum meruit
	    habere Redemptorem!

The sanctifying power of this night
dispels wickedness,
    washes faults away,
restores innocence to the fallen,
    and joy to mourners.
	Huius igitur sanctificatio noctis
	    fugat scelera, culpas lavat:
	et reddit innocentiam lapsis
	    et mæstis lætitiam.

O truly blessed night,
when things of heaven are wed
    to those of earth,
and divine to the human.
	O vere beata nox,
	in qua terrenis cælestia,
	    humanis divina iunguntur!

On this, your night of grace,
    O holy Father,
accept this candle, a solemn offering,
the work of bees and of your
	In huius igitur noctis gratia,
	suscipe, sancte Pater, laudis huius
	    sacrificium vespertinum,
	quod tibi in hac cerei

servants' hands,
an evening sacrifice of praise,
this gift from your most
 holy Church.

Therefore, O Lord,
we pray you that this candle,
hallowed to the honour
 of your name,
may persevere undimmed,
to overcome the darkness
 of this night.
Receive it as a pleasing fragrance,
and let it mingle with the lights
 of heaven.
May this flame be found
 still burning
by the Morning Star:
the one Morning Star who never sets,
Christ your Son,
who, coming back from
 death's domain,
has shed his peaceful light
 on humanity,
and lives and reigns
 for ever and ever.
R. Amen.

oblatione sollemni,
per ministrorum manus
de operibus apum,
 sacrosancta reddit Ecclesia.

Oramus ergo te, Domine,
ut cereus iste in honorem tui
 nominis consecratus,
ad noctis huius
 caliginem destruendam,
indeficiens perseveret.
Et in odorem suavitatis acceptus,
supernis luminaribus misceatur.
Flammas eius lucifer
 matutinus inveniat:
Ille, inquam, lucifer,
 qui nescit occasum:
Christus Filius tuus,
qui, regressus ab inferis,
 humano generi serenus illuxit,
et vivit et regnat
 in sæcula sæculorum.
R. Amen.

SECOND PART:

The Liturgy of the Word

In this Vigil, the mother of all Vigils, nine readings are provided, namely seven from the Old Testament and two from the New (the Epistle and Gospel), all of which should be read whenever this can be done, so that the character of the Vigil, which demands an extended period of time, may be preserved.

Nevertheless, where more serious pastoral circumstances demand it, the number of readings from the Old Testament may be reduced, always bearing in mind that the reading of the Word of God is a fundamental part of this Easter Vigil. At least three readings should be read from the Old Testament, both from the Law and from the Prophets, and their respective Responsorial Psalms should be sung. Never, moreover, should the reading of chapter 14 of Exodus with its canticle be omitted.

After setting aside their candles, all sit. Before the readings begin, the Priest instructs the people in these or similar words:

Dear brethren (brothers and sisters),
now that we have begun
  our solemn Vigil,
let us listen with quiet hearts
  to the Word of God.
Let us meditate on how God in
  times past saved his people
and in these, the last days, has sent
  us his Son as our Redeemer.
Let us pray that our God may
  complete this paschal work
  of salvation
by the fullness of redemption.

Vigiliam sollemniter ingressi,
  fratres carissimi,
quieto corde nunc verbum
  Dei audiamus.
Meditemur, quomodo Deus
  populum suum
elapsis temporibus salvum fecerit,
et novissime nobis Filium suum
  miserit Redemptorem.
Oremus, ut Deus noster hoc
  paschale salvationis opus
ad plenam redemptionem perficiat.

Then the readings follow. A reader goes to the ambo and proclaims the reading. Afterwards a psalmist or a cantor sings or says the Psalm with the people making the response. Then all rise, the Priest says, Let us pray and, after all have prayed for a while in silence, he says the prayer corresponding to the reading. In place of the Responsorial Psalm a period of sacred silence may be observed, in which case the pause after Let us pray is omitted.

FIRST READING

A reading from the book of Genesis   1:1-2:2

God saw all he made, and indeed it was very good.

| [In the beginning God created the heavens and the earth.] Now the earth was a formless void, there was darkness over the deep, and God's spirit hovered over the water.

God said, 'Let there be light,' and there was light. God saw that light was good, and God divided light from darkness. God called light 'day', and darkness he called 'night'. Evening came and morning came: the first day.

God said, 'Let there be a vault in the waters to divide the waters in two.' And so it was. God made the vault, and it divided the waters above the vault from the waters under the vault. God called the vault 'heaven'. Evening came and morning came: the second day.

God said, 'Let the waters under heaven come together into a single mass, and let dry land appear.' And so it was. God called the dry land 'earth' and the mass of waters 'seas', and God saw that it was good.

God said, 'Let the earth produce vegetation: seed-bearing plants, and fruit trees bearing fruit with their seed inside, on the earth.' And so it was.

The earth produced vegetation: plants bearing seed in their several kinds, and trees bearing fruit with their seed inside in their several kinds. God saw that it was good. Evening came and morning came: the third day.

God said, 'Let there be lights in the vault of heaven to divide day from night, and let them indicate festivals, days and years. Let them be lights in the vault of heaven to shine on the earth.' And so it was. God made the two great lights: the greater light to govern the day, the smaller light to govern the night, and the stars. God set them in the vault of heaven to shine on the earth, to govern the day and the night and to divide light from darkness. God saw that it was good. Evening came and morning came: the fourth day.

God said, 'Let the waters teem with living creatures, and let birds fly above the earth within the vault of heaven.' And so it was. God created great sea-serpents and every kind of living creature with which the waters teem, and every kind of winged creature. God saw that it was good. God blessed them, saying, 'Be fruitful, multiply, and fill the waters of the seas, and let the birds multiply upon the earth.' Evening came and morning came: the fifth day.

God said, 'Let the earth produce every kind of living creature: cattle, reptiles, and every kind of wild beast.' And so it was. God made every kind of wild beast, every kind of cattle, and every kind of land reptile. God saw that it was good.

[God said, 'Let us make man in our own image, in the likeness of ourselves, and let them be masters of the fish of the sea, the birds of heaven, the cattle, all the wild beasts and all the reptiles that crawl upon the earth.'

God created man in the image of himself,
in the image of God he created him,
male and female he created them.

God blessed them, saying to them, 'Be fruitful, multiply, fill the earth and conquer it. Be masters of the fish of the sea, the birds of heaven and all living animals on the earth.' God said, 'See, I give you all the seed-bearing plants that are upon the whole earth, and all the trees with seed-bearing fruit; this shall be your food. To all wild beasts, all birds of heaven and all living reptiles on the earth I give all the foliage of plants for food.' And so it was. God saw all he had made, and indeed it was very good. Evening came and morning came: the sixth day.

Thus heaven and earth were completed with all their array. On the seventh day God completed the work he had been doing. He rested on the seventh day after all the work he had been doing.

The word of the Lord.]

Shorter Form, verses 1, 26-31. Read between [ ]

Responsorial Psalm

Ps 103:1-2,5-6,10,12-14,24,35. R. Cf. v.30

R. **Send forth your spirit, O Lord,**
and renew the face of the earth.

Bless the Lord, my soul!
Lord God, how great you are,
clothed in majesty and glory,
wrapped in light as in a robe! R.

You founded the earth on its base,
to stand firm from age to age.
You wrapped it with the ocean like a cloak:
the waters stood higher than the mountains. R.

You make springs gush forth in the valleys:
they flow in between the hills.
On their banks dwell the birds of heaven;
from the branches they sing their song. R.

From your dwelling you water the hills;
earth drinks its fill of your gift.
You make the grass grow for the cattle
and the plants to serve man's needs. R.

How many are your works, O Lord!
In wisdom you have made them all.
The earth is full of your riches.
Bless the Lord, my soul! R.

Alternative Psalm

Ps 32:4-7,12-13,20,22. R. v.5

R. **The Lord fills the earth with his love.**

The word of the Lord is faithful
and all his works to be trusted.
The Lord loves justice and right
and fills the earth with his love. R.

By his word the heavens were made,
by the breath of his mouth all the stars.
He collects the waves of the ocean;
he stores up the depths of the sea. R.

They are happy, whose God is the Lord,
the people he has chosen as his own.
From the heavens the Lord looks forth,
he sees all the children of men. R.

Our soul is waiting for the Lord.
The Lord is our help and our shield.
May your love be upon us, O Lord,
as we place all our hope in you. R.

R. **The Lord fills the earth with his love.**

Prayer

Let us pray.

Almighty ever-living God,
who are wonderful in the ordering
  of all your works,
may those you have
  redeemed understand
that there exists nothing
  more marvellous
than the world's creation
  in the beginning
except that, at the end of the ages,
Christ our Passover
  has been sacrificed.
Who lives and reigns
  for ever and ever.
R. Amen.

Oremus.

Omnipotens sempiterne Deus,
qui es in omnium operum tuorum
  dispensatione mirabilis,
intellegant redempti tui,
  non fuisse excellentius,
quod initio factus est mundus,
quam quod in fine sæculorum
Pascha nostrum immolatus
  est Christus.
Qui vivit et regnat
  in sæcula sæculorum.
R. Amen.

Or, On the creation of man:

O God, who wonderfully created
  human nature
and still more wonderfully
  redeemed it,
grant us, we pray,
to set our minds against
  the enticements of sin,
that we may merit to attain
  eternal joys.
Through Christ our Lord.
R. Amen.

Deus, qui mirabiliter creasti hominem
et mirabilius redemisti,
da nobis, quæsumus,
contra oblectamenta peccati mentis
  ratione persistere,
ut mereamur ad æterna
  gaudia pervenire.
Per Christum Dominum nostrum.
R. Amen.

SECOND READING

A reading from the book of Genesis   22:1-18

The sacrifice of Abraham, our father in faith.

[God put Abraham to the test. 'Abraham, Abraham,' he called. 'Here I am' he replied. 'Take your son,' God said 'your only child Isaac, whom you love, and go to the land of Moriah. There you shall offer him as a burnt offering, on a mountain I will point out to you.']

Rising early next morning Abraham saddled his ass and took with him two of his servants and his son Isaac. He chopped wood for the burnt offering and started on his journey to the place God had pointed out to him. On the third day Abraham looked up and saw the place in the distance. Then Abraham said to his servants, 'Stay here with the donkey. The boy and I will go over there; we will worship and come back to you.'

Abraham took the wood for the burnt offering, loaded it on Isaac, and carried in his own hands the fire and the knife. Then the two of them set out together. Isaac spoke to his father Abraham, 'Father' he said. 'Yes, my son' he replied. 'Look,' he said 'here are the fire and the wood, but where is the lamb for the burnt offering?' Abraham answered, 'My son, God himself will provide the lamb for the burnt offering.' Then the two of them went on together.

[When they arrived at the place God had pointed out to him, Abraham built an altar there, and arranged the wood. Then he bound his son Isaac and put him on the altar on top of the wood. Abraham stretched out his hand and seized the knife to kill his son.

But the angel of the Lord called to him from heaven. 'Abraham, Abraham' he said. 'I am here' he replied. 'Do not raise your hand against the boy' the angel said. 'Do not harm him, for now I know you fear God. You have not refused me your son, your only son.' Then looking up, Abraham saw a ram caught by its horns in a bush. Abraham took the ram and offered it as a burnt-offering in place of his son.] Abraham called this place 'The Lord provides', and hence the saying today: On the mountain the Lord provides.

[The angel of the Lord called Abraham a second time from heaven. 'I swear by my own self – it is the Lord who speaks – because you have done this, because you have not refused me your son, your only son, I will shower blessings on you, I will make your descendants as many as the stars of heaven and the grains of sand on the seashore. Your descendants shall gain possession of the gates of their enemies. All the nations of the earth shall bless themselves by your descendants, as a reward for your obedience.

The word of the Lord.]

Shorter Form, verses 1-2,9-13,15-18. Read between [ ]

Responsorial Psalm
Ps 15:5,8-11, R. v.1

R. **Preserve me, God, I take refuge in you.**

O Lord, it is you who are my portion and cup;
it is you yourself who are my prize.
I keep the Lord ever in my sight:
since he is at my right hand, I shall stand firm. R.

And so my heart rejoices, my soul is glad;
even my body shall rest in safety.
For you will not leave my soul among the dead,
nor let your beloved know decay. R.

You will show me the path of life,
the fullness of joy in your presence,
at your right hand happiness for ever. R.

Prayer

Let us pray.

O God, supreme Father
  of the faithful,
who increase the children
  of your promise
by pouring out the grace
  of adoption
throughout the whole world
and who through the Paschal Mystery
make your servant Abraham father
  of nations,
as once you swore,
grant, we pray,
that your peoples may enter worthily
into the grace to which you call them.
Through Christ our Lord.
R. Amen.

Oremus.

Deus, Pater summe fidelium,
qui promissionis tuæ filios diffusa
  adoptionis gratia
in toto terrarum orbe multiplicas,
et per paschale sacramentum
Abraham puerum tuum
universarum, sicut iurasti,
  gentium efficis patrem,
da populis tuis digne ad gratiam
  tuæ vocationis intrare.
Per Christum Dominum nostrum.
R. Amen.

The following reading must always be read.

THIRD READING

A reading from book of Exodus
14:15-15:1

The sons of Israel went on dry ground right into the sea.

The Lord said to Moses, 'Why do you cry to me so? Tell the sons of Israel to march on. For yourself, raise your staff and stretch out your hand over the sea and part it for the sons of Israel to walk through the sea on dry ground. I for my part will make the heart of the Egyptians so stubborn that they will follow them. So shall I win myself glory at the expense of Pharaoh, of all his army, his chariots, his horsemen. And when I have won glory for myself, at the expense of Pharaoh and his chariots and his army, the Egyptians will learn that I am the Lord.'

Then the angel of the Lord, who marched at the front of the army of Israel, changed station and moved to their rear. The pillar of cloud changed station from the front to the rear of them, and remained there. It came between the camp of the Egyptians and the camp of Israel. The cloud was dark, and the night passed without the armies drawing any closer the whole night long. Moses stretched out his hand over the sea. The Lord drove back the sea with a strong easterly wind all night, and he made dry land of the sea. The waters parted and the sons of Israel went on dry ground right into the sea, walls of water to right and to left of them. The Egyptians gave chase: after them they went, right into the sea, all Pharaoh's horses, his chariots, and his horsemen. In the morning watch, the Lord looked down on the army of the Egyptians from the pillar of fire and of cloud, and threw the army into confusion. He so clogged their chariot wheels that they could scarcely make headway. 'Let us flee from the Israelites,' the Egyptians cried 'the Lord is fighting for them against the Egyptians!' 'Stretch out your hand over the sea,' the Lord said to Moses 'that the waters may flow back on the Egyptians and their chariots and their horsemen.' Moses stretched out his hand over the sea and, as day broke, the sea returned to its bed. The fleeing Egyptians marched right into it, and the Lord overthrew the Egyptians in the very middle of the sea. The returning waters overwhelmed the chariots and the horsemen of Pharaoh's whole army, which had followed the Israelites into the sea; not a single one of them was left. But the sons of Israel had marched through the sea on dry ground, walls of water to right and to left of them. That day, the Lord rescued Israel from the Egyptians, and Israel saw the Egyptians lying dead on the shore. Israel witnessed the great act that the Lord had performed against the Egyptians, and the people venerated the Lord; they put their faith in the Lord and in Moses, his servant.

It was then that Moses and the sons of Israel sang this song in honour of the Lord:

The choir takes up the Responsorial Psalm immediately.

Responsorial Psalm
Ex 15:1-6,17-18. R. v.1

R. **I will sing to the Lord, glorious his triumph!**

I will sing to the Lord, glorious his triumph!
Horse and rider he has thrown into the sea!
The Lord is my strength, my song, my salvation.
This is my God and I extol him,
my father's God and I give him praise. R.

The Lord is a warrior! The Lord is his name.
The chariots of Pharaoh he hurled into the sea,
the flower of his army is drowned in the sea.
The deeps hide them; they sank like a stone. R.

Your right hand, Lord, glorious in its power,
your right hand, Lord, has shattered the enemy.
In the greatness of your glory you crushed the foe. R.

You will lead your people and plant them on your mountain,
the place, O Lord, where you have made your home,
the sanctuary, Lord, which your hands have made.

Prayer

Let us pray.
O God, whose ancient wonders
remain undimmed in splendour
   even in our day,
for what you once bestowed
   on a single people,
freeing them from
   Pharaoh's persecution
by the power of your right hand,
now you bring about as the salvation
   of the nations
through the waters of rebirth,
grant, we pray,
   that the whole world
may become children of Abraham
and inherit the dignity
   of Israel's birthright.
Through Christ our Lord.
R. Amen.

Oremus.
Deus, cuius antiqua miracula
etiam nostris temporibus
   coruscare sentimus,
dum, quod uni populo
a persecutione Pharaonis liberando
dexteræ tuæ potentia contulisti,
id in salutem gentium
per aquam regenerationis operaris,
præsta, ut in Abrahæ filios
et in Israeliticam dignitatem
totius mundi transeat plenitudo.
Per Christum Dominum nostrum.
R. Amen.

Or:

O God, who by the light
    of the New Testament
have unlocked the meaning
of wonders worked in former times,
so that the Red Sea prefigures
    the sacred font
and the nation delivered from slavery
foreshadows the Christian people,
grant, we pray, that all nations,
obtaining the privilege of Israel
    by merit of faith,
may be reborn by partaking
    of your Spirit.
Through Christ our Lord.
R. Amen.

Vel:

Deus, qui primis temporibus
impleta miracula novi testamenti
    luce reserasti,
ut et Mare Rubrum forma sacri
    fontis exsisteret,
et plebs a servitute liberata
christiani populi
    sacramenta præferret,
da, ut omnes gentes,
Israelis privilegium merito
    fidei consecutæ,
Spiritus tui participatione
    regenerentur.
Per Christum Dominum nostrum.
R. Amen.

FOURTH READING

A reading from the prophet Isaiah   54:5-14

With everlasting love the Lord your redeemer has taken pity on you.

Now your creator will be your husband,
his name, the Lord of hosts;
your redeemer will be the Holy One of Israel,
he is called the God of the whole earth.
Yes, like a forsaken wife, distressed in spirit,
the Lord calls you back.
Does a man cast off the wife of his youth?
says your God.

I did forsake you for a brief moment,
but with great love will I take you back.
In excess of anger, for a moment
I hid my face from you.
But with everlasting love I have taken pity on you,
says the Lord, your redeemer.

I am now as I was in the days of Noah
when I swore that Noah's waters
should never flood the world again.
So now I swear concerning my anger with you
and the threats I made against you;

for the mountains may depart,

the hills be shaken,
but my love for you will never leave you;
and my covenant of peace with you will never be shaken,
says the Lord who takes pity on you.

Unhappy creature, storm-tossed, disconsolate,
see, I will set your stones on carbuncles
and your foundations on sapphires.
I will make rubies your battlements,
your gates crystal,
and your entire wall precious stones.
Your sons will all be taught by the Lord.
The prosperity of your sons will be great.
You will be founded on integrity;
remote from oppression, you will have nothing to fear;
remote from terror, it will not approach you.

The word of the Lord.

Responsorial Psalm

Ps 29:2,4-6,11-13. R. v.2

R. **I will praise you, Lord, you have rescued me.**

I will praise you, Lord, you have rescued me
and have not let my enemies rejoice over me.
O Lord, you have raised my soul from the dead,
restored me to life from those who sink into the grave. R.

Sing psalms to the Lord, you who love him,
give thanks to his holy name.
His anger lasts but a moment; his favour through life.
At night there are tears, but joy comes with dawn. R.

The Lord listened and had pity.
The Lord came to my help.
For me you have changed my mourning into dancing,
O Lord my God, I will thank you for ever. R.

Prayer

Let us pray.
Almighty ever-living God,
surpass, for the honour of your name,
what you pledged to the Patriarchs
   by reason of their faith,
and through sacred adoption increase
   the children of your promise,
	Oremus.
	Omnipotens sempiterne Deus,
	multiplica in honorem nominis tui
	quod patrum fidei spopondisti,
	et promissionis filios sacra
	   adoptione dilata,
	ut, quod priores sancti non

so that what the Saints of old never
   doubted would come to pass
your Church may now see in great
   part fulfilled.
Through Christ our Lord. R. Amen.

dubitaverunt futurum,
Ecclesia tua magna ex parte iam
   cognoscat impletum.
Per Christum Dominum nostrum.
R. Amen.

Alternatively, other prayers may be used from among those which follow the readings that have been omitted.

FIFTH READING

A reading from the prophet Isaiah   55:1-11

Come to me and your soul will live, and I will make an everlasting covenant with you.

Thus says the Lord:

Oh, come to the water all you who are thirsty;
though you have no money, come!
Buy corn without money, and eat,
and, at no cost, wine and milk.
Why spend money on what is not bread,
your wages on what fails to satisfy?
Listen, listen to me, and you will have good things to eat
and rich food to enjoy.
Pay attention, come to me;
and your soul will live.

With you I will make an everlasting covenant
out of the favours promised to David.
See, I have made of you a witness to the peoples,
a leader and a master of the nations.
See, you will summon a nation you never knew,
those unknown will come hurrying to you,
for the sake of the Lord your God,
of the Holy One of Israel who will glorify you.

Seek the Lord while he is still to be found,
call to him while he is still near.
Let the wicked man abandon his way,
the evil man his thoughts.
Let him turn back to the Lord who will take pity on him,
to our God who is rich in forgiving;
for my thoughts are not your thoughts,
my ways not your ways – it is the Lord who speaks.
Yes, the heavens are as high above earth
as my ways are above your ways,
my thoughts above your thoughts.

Yes, as the rain and the snow come down from the heavens and do not return without watering the earth, making it yield and giving growth to provide seed for the sower and bread for the eating, so the word that goes from my mouth does not return to me empty, without carrying out my will and succeeding in what it was sent to do.

The word of the Lord.

Responsional Psalm   Is 12:2-6. R. v.3

R. **With joy you will draw water from the wells of salvation.**

Truly God is my salvation,
I trust, I shall not fear.
For the Lord is my strength, my song,
he became my saviour.
With joy you will draw water
from the wells of salvation. R.

Give thanks to the Lord, give praise to his name!
Make his mighty deeds known to the peoples,
declare the greatness of his name. R.

Sing a psalm to the Lord
for he has done glorious deeds,
make them known to all the earth!
People of Zion, sing and shout for joy
for great in your midst is the Holy One of Israel. R.

Prayer

Let us pray.

Almighty ever-living God,
sole hope of the world,
who by the preaching
　of your Prophets
unveiled the mysteries
　of this present age,
graciously increase the longing
　of your people,
for only at the prompting
　of your grace
do the faithful progress in any
　kind of virtue.
Through Christ our Lord.
R. Amen.

Oremus.

Omnipotens sempiterne Deus,
spes unica mundi,
qui prophetarum tuorum præconio
præsentium temporum
　declarasti mysteria,
auge populi tui vota placatus,
quia in nullo fidelium nisi ex tua
　inspiratione proveniunt
quarumlibet incrementa virtutum.
Per Christum Dominum nostrum.
R. Amen.

SIXTH READING

A reading from the prophet Baruch 3:9-15,32-4:4

In the radiance of the Lord make your way to light.

Listen, Israel, to commands that bring life;
hear, and learn what knowledge means.
Why, Israel, why are you in the country of your enemies,
growing older and older in an alien land,
sharing defilement with the dead,
reckoned with those who go to Sheol?
Because you have forsaken the fountain of wisdom.
Had you walked in the way of God,
you would have lived in peace for ever.
Learn where knowledge is, where strength,
where understanding, and so learn
where length of days is, where life,
where the light of the eyes and where peace.
But who has found out where she lives,
who has entered her treasure house?

But the One who knows all knows her,
he has grasped her with his own intellect,
he has set the earth firm for ever
and filled it with four-footed beasts,
he sends the light – and it goes,
he recalls it – and trembling it obeys;
the stars shine joyfully at their set times:
when he calls them, they answer, 'Here we are';
they gladly shine for their creator.
It is he who is our God,
no other can compare with him.
He has grasped the whole way of knowledge,
and confided it to his servant Jacob,
to Israel his well-beloved;
so causing her to appear on earth
and move among men.

This is the book of the commandments of God,
the Law that stands for ever;
those who keep her live,
those who desert her die.
Turn back, Jacob, seize her,

in her radiance make your way to light:
do not yield your glory to another,
your privilege to a people not your own.
Israel, blessed are we:
what pleases God has been revealed to us.

   The word of the Lord.

Responsorial Psalm   Ps 18:8-11. R. Jn 6:69

R. **You have the message of eternal life, O Lord.**

   The law of the Lord is perfect,
   it revives the soul.
   The rule of the Lord is to be trusted,
   it gives wisdom to the simple. R.

   The precepts of the Lord are right,
   they gladden the heart.
   The command of the Lord is clear,
   it gives light to the eyes. R.

   The fear of the Lord is holy,
   abiding for ever.
   The decrees of the Lord are truth
   and all of them just. R.

   They are more to be desired than gold,
   than the purest of gold
   and sweeter are they than honey,
   than honey from the comb. R.

Prayer

Let us pray.

O God, who constantly increase
   your Church
by your call to the nations,
graciously grant
to those you wash clean
   in the waters of Baptism
the assurance of your
   unfailing protection.
Through Christ our Lord.
R. Amen.

Oremus.

Deus, qui Ecclesiam tuam
semper gentium
   vocatione multiplicas,
concede propitius,
ut, quos aqua baptismatis abluis,
continua protectione tuearis.
Per Christum Dominum nostrum.
R. Amen.

SEVENTH READING

A reading from the prophet Ezekiel 36:16-28

I shall pour clean water over you, and I shall give you a new heart.

The word of the Lord was addressed to me as follows: 'Son of man, the members of the House of Israel used to live in their own land, but they defiled it by their conduct and actions. I then discharged my fury at them because of the blood they shed in their land and the idols with which they defiled it. I scattered them among the nations and dispersed them in foreign countries. I sentenced them as their conduct and actions deserved. And now they have profaned my holy name among the nations where they have gone, so that people say of them, "These are the people of the Lord; they have been exiled from his land." But I have been concerned about my holy name, which the House of Israel has profaned among the nations where they have gone. And so, say to the House of Israel, "The Lord says this: I am not doing this for my sake, House of Israel, but for the sake of my holy name, which you have profaned among the nations where you have gone. I mean to display the holiness of my great name, which has been profaned among the nations, which you have profaned among them. And the nations will learn that I am the Lord – it is the Lord who speaks – when I display my holiness for your sake before their eyes. Then I am going to take you from among the nations and gather you together from all the foreign countries, and bring you home to your own land. I shall pour clean water over you and you will be cleansed; I shall cleanse you of all your defilement and all your idols. I shall give you a new heart, and put a new spirit in you; I shall remove the heart of stone from your bodies and give you a heart of flesh instead. I shall put my spirit in you, and make you keep my laws and sincerely respect my observances. You will live in the land which I gave your ancestors. You shall be my people and I will be your God."'

The word of the Lord.

Responsorial Psalm
Pss 41:3,5; 42:3,4. R. Ps 41:1

R. **Like the deer that yearns for running streams,
so my soul is yearning for you, my God.**

My soul is thirsting for God.
the God of my life;
when can I enter and see
the face of God? R.

These things I will remember
as I pour out my soul:
how I would lead the rejoicing crowd
into the house of God,
amid cries of gladness and thanksgiving,
the throng wild with joy. R.

O send forth your light and your truth;
let these be my guide.
Let them bring me to your holy mountain
to the place where you dwell. R.

And I will come to the altar of God,
the God of my joy.
My redeemer, I will thank you on the harp,
O God, my God. R.

If a Baptism takes place the Responsorial Psalm which follows the Fifth Reading (see p.366), is used, or Psalm 50 as follows.

Responsorial Psalm
Ps 50:12-15,18,19. R. v.12

R. **A pure heart create for me, O God.**

A pure heart create for me, O God,
put a steadfast spirit within me.
Do not cast me away from your presence,
nor deprive me of your holy spirit. R.

Give me again the joy of your help;
with a spirit of fervour sustain me,
that I may teach transgressors your ways
and sinners may return to you. R.

For in sacrifice you take no delight,
burnt offering from me you would refuse,
my sacrifice, a contrite spirit.
A humbled, contrite heart you will not spurn. R.

Prayer

Let us pray.

O God of unchanging power
  and eternal light,
look with favour on the wondrous
  mystery of the whole Church
and serenely accomplish the work
of human salvation,
which you planned from all eternity;
may the whole world know and see
that what was cast down is raised up,
what had become old is made new,
and all things are restored
  to integrity through Christ,
just as by him they came into being.
Who lives and reigns
  for ever and ever.

R. Amen.

Or:

O God, who by the pages
  of both Testaments
instruct and prepare us to celebrate
  the Paschal Mystery,
grant that we may comprehend
  your mercy,
so that the gifts we receive
  from you this night
may confirm our hope of the gifts
  to come.
Through Christ our Lord.

R. Amen.

Oremus.

Deus, incommutabilis virtus
  et lumen æternum,
respice propitius ad totius
  Ecclesiæ mirabile sacramentum,
et opus salutis humanæ
perpetuæ dispositionis effectu
tranquillius operare;
totusque mundus experiatur
  et videat
deiecta erigi, inveterata renovari
et per ipsum Christum redire
  omnia in integrum,
a quo sumpsere principium.
Qui vivit et regnat
  in sæcula sæculorum.

R. Amen.

Vel:

Deus, qui nos ad celebrandum
  paschale sacramentum
utriusque Testamenti
  paginis instruis,
da nobis intellegere
  misericordiam tuam,
ut ex perceptione
  præsentium munerum
firma sit exspectatio futurorum.
Per Christum Dominum nostrum.

R. Amen.

After the last reading from the Old Testament with its Responsorial Psalm and its prayer, the altar candles are lit, and the Priest intones the hymn Gloria in excelsis Deo (Glory to God in the highest), which is taken up by all, while bells are rung, according to local custom.

The complete musical setting of the Latin text is found in the Graduale Romanum.

When the hymn is concluded, the Priest says the Collect in the usual way.

Collect

Let us pray.

O God, who make this most sacred night radiant
with the glory
of the Lord's Resurrection,
stir up in your Church a spirit of adoption,
so that, renewed in body and mind,
we may render you undivided service.
Through our Lord Jesus Christ, your Son,
who lives and reigns with you
in the unity of the Holy Spirit,
one God, for ever and ever.

Collecta

Oremus.

Deus, qui hanc sacratissimam noctem
gloria dominicæ resurrectionis illustras,
excita in Ecclesia tua adoptionis spiritum,
ut, corpore et mente renovati,
puram tibi exhibeamus servitutem.
Per Dominum nostrum Iesum Christum Filium tuum,
qui tecum vivit et regnat
in unitate Spiritus Sancti,
Deus, per omnia sæcula sæculorum.

FIRST READING

A reading from the letter of St Paul to the Romans 6:3-11

Christ, having been raised from the dead, will never die again.

When we were baptised in Christ Jesus we were baptised in his death; in other words, when we were baptised we went into the tomb with him and joined him in death, so that as Christ was raised from the dead by the Father's glory, we too might live a new life.

If in union with Christ we have imitated his death, we shall also imitate him in his resurrection. We must realise that our former selves have been crucified with him to destroy this sinful body and to free us from the slavery of sin. When a man dies, of course, he has finished with sin.

But we believe that having died with Christ we shall return to life with him: Christ, as we know, having been raised from the dead will never die again. Death has no power over him any more. When he died, he died, once for all, to sin, so his life now is life with God; and in that way, you too must consider yourselves to be dead to sin but alive for God in Christ Jesus.

The word of the Lord.

After the Epistle has been read, all rise, then the Priest solemnly intones the Alleluia three times, raising his voice by a step each time, with all repeating it. If necessary, the psalmist intones the Alleluia.

Responsorial Psalm   Ps 117:1-2,16-17,22-23

R. **Alleluia, alleluia, alleluia!**
Give thanks to the Lord for he is good,
for his love has no end.
Let the sons of Israel say:
'His love has no end.' R.

The Lord's right hand has triumphed;
his right hand raised me.
I shall not die, I shall live
and recount his deeds. R.

The stone which the builders rejected
has become the corner stone.
This is the work of the Lord,
a marvel in our eyes. R.

The Priest, in the usual way, puts incense in the thurible and blesses the Deacon. At the Gospel lights are not carried, but only incense.

GOSPEL

A reading from the holy Gospel according to Luke   24:1-12
Why look among the dead for someone who is alive?

On the first day of week, at the first sign of dawn, the women went to the tomb with the spices they had prepared. They found that the stone had been rolled away from the tomb, but on entering discovered that the body of the Lord Jesus was not there. As they stood there not knowing what to think, two men in brilliant clothes suddenly appeared at their side. Terrified, the women lowered their eyes. But the two men said to them, 'Why look among the dead for someone who is alive? He is not here; he has risen. Remember what he told you when he was still in Galilee: that the Son of Man had to be handed over into the power of sinful men and be crucified, and rise again on the third day?' And they remembered his words.

When the women returned from the tomb they told all this to the Eleven and to all the others. The women were Mary of Magdala, Joanna, and Mary the mother of James. The other women with them also told the apostles, but this story of theirs seemed pure nonsense, and they did not believe them.

Peter, however, went running to the tomb. He bent down and saw the binding cloths, but nothing else; he then went back home, amazed at what had happened.

The Gospel of the Lord.
After the Gospel, the Homily, even if brief, is not to be omitted.

THIRD PART:

Baptismal Liturgy

After the Homily the Baptismal Liturgy begins. The Priest goes with the ministers to the baptismal font, if this can be seen by the faithful. Otherwise a vessel with water is placed in the sanctuary.

Catechumens, if there are any, are called forward and presented by their godparents in front of the assembled Church or, if they are small children, are carried by their parents and godparents.

Then, if there is to be a procession to the baptistery or to the font, it forms immediately. A minister with the paschal candle leads off, and those to be baptised follow him with their godparents, then the ministers, the Deacon, and the Priest. During the procession, the Litany is sung. When the Litany is completed, the Priest gives the address.

If, however, the Baptismal Liturgy takes place in the sanctuary, the Priest immediately makes an introductory statement in these or similar words.

If there are candidates to be baptised:

Dearly beloved,
with one heart and one soul,
   let us by our prayers
come to the aid of these our brothers
   and sisters in their blessed hope,
so that, as they approach the font
   of rebirth,
the almighty Father may bestow
   on them
all his merciful help.
	Precibus nostris, carissimi,
	fratrum nostrorum beatam spem
	   unanimes adiuvemus,
	ut Pater omnipotens ad fontem
	   regenerationis euntes
	omni misericordiæ suæ
	   auxilio prosequatur.

If the font is to be blessed, but no one is to be baptised:

Dearly beloved,
let us humbly invoke upon
   this font
the grace of God the almighty Father,
that those who from it are born anew
may be numbered among the
   children of adoption in Christ.
	Dei Patris omnipotentis gratiam,
	   carissimi,
	super hunc fontem
	   supplices invocemus,
	ut qui ex eo renascentur
	adoptionis filiis in
	   Christo aggregentur.

The Litany

The Litany is sung by two cantors, with all standing (because it is Easter Time) and responding.

If, however, there is to be a procession of some length to the baptistery, the Litany is sung during the procession; in this case, those to be baptised are called forward before the procession begins, and the procession takes place led by the paschal candle, followed by the catechumens with their godparents, then the ministers, the Deacon, and the Priest. The address should occur before the Blessing of Water.

If no one is to be baptised and the font is not to be blessed, the Litany is omitted, and the Blessing of Water takes place at once.

In the Litany the names of some Saints may be added, especially the Titular Saint of the church and the Patron Saints of the place and of those to be baptised.

Lord, have mercy.		Kyrie, eleison.	
	Lord, have mercy.		Kyrie, eleison.
Christ, have mercy.		Christe, eleison.	
	Christ, have mercy.		Christe, eleison.
Lord, have mercy.		Kyrie, eleison.	
	Lord have mercy.		Kyrie, eleison.
Holy Mary,		Sancta Maria,	
Mother of God,	pray for us.	Mater Dei,	ora pro nobis.
Saint Michael,	pray for us.	Sancte Michael,	ora pro nobis.
Holy Angels of God,	pray for us.	Sancti Angeli Dei,	orate pro nobis.
Saint John the Baptist,	pray for us.	Sancte Ioannes Baptista,	ora pro nobis.
Saint Joseph,	pray for us.	Sancte Ioseph,	ora pro nobis.
Saint Peter and Saint Paul,	pray for us.	Sancti Petre et Paule,	orate pro nobis.
Saint Andrew,	pray for us.	Sancte Andrea,	ora pro nobis.
Saint John,	pray for us.	Sancte Ioannes,	ora pro nobis.
Saint Mary Magdalene,	pray for us.	Sancta Maria Magdalena,	ora pro nobis.
Saint Stephen,	pray for us.	Sancte Stephane,	ora pro nobis.
Saint Ignatius of Antioch,	pray for us.	Sancte Ignati Antiochene,	ora pro nobis.
Saint Lawrence,	pray for us.	Sancte Laurenti,	ora pro nobis.
Saint Perpetua and Saint Felicity,	pray for us.	Sanctæ Perpetua et Felicitas,	orate pro nobis.
Saint Agnes,	pray for us.	Sancta Agnes,	ora pro nobis.
Saint Gregory,	pray for us.	Sancte Gregori,	ora pro nobis.
Saint Augustine,	pray for us.	Sancte Augustine,	ora pro nobis.

Saint Athanasius,	pray for us.	Sancte Athanasi,	ora pro nobis.
Saint Basil,	pray for us.	Sancte Basili,	ora pro nobis.
Saint Martin,	pray for us.	Sancte Martine,	ora pro nobis.
Saint Benedict,	pray for us.	Sancte Benedicte,	ora pro nobis.

Saint Francis and
   Saint Dominic,   pray for us.
Saint Francis Xavier,   pray for us.

Saint John Vianney,   pray for us.

Saint Catherine
   of Siena,   pray for us.
Saint Teresa of Jesus,   pray for us.
All holy men and women,
   Saints of God,   pray for us.
Lord, be merciful
   Lord, deliver us, we pray.
From all evil,
   Lord, deliver us, we pray.
From every sin,
   Lord, deliver us, we pray.
From everlasting death,
   Lord, deliver us, we pray.
By your Incarnation,
   Lord, deliver us, we pray.
By your Death and Resurection,
   Lord, deliver us, we pray.

By the out-pouring of the Holy
   Spirit,   Lord, deliver us, we pray.
Be merciful to us sinners,
   Lord we ask you to hear our prayer.

If there are candidates to be baptised
Bring these chosen ones to new birth
   through the grace of Baptism,
   Lord, we ask you, hear our prayer.

If there is no one to be baptised:

Sancti Francisce
   et Dominice,   orate pro nobis.
Sancte Francisce
   (Xavier),   ora pro nobis.
Sancte Ioannes
   Maria (Vianney),   ora pro nobis.
Sancta Catharina
   (Senensis),   ora pro nobis.
Sancta Teresia a Iesu, ora pro nobis.
Omnes Sancti
   et Sanctæ Dei,   orate pro nobis.
Propitius esto,   libera nos, Domine.

Ab omni malo, libera nos, Domine.

Ab omni peccato,
   libera nos, Domine.
A morte perpetua,
   libera nos, Domine.
Per incarnationem tuam,
   libera nos, Domine.
Per mortem et
   resurrectionem tuam,
   libera nos, Domine.
Per effusionem Spiritus Sancti,
   libera nos, Domine.

Peccatores,   te rogamus, audi nos.

Ut hos electos per gratiam
   Baptismi regenerare digneris
   te rogamus, audi nos.

Make this font holy by your grace
   for the new birth of your children,
Lord, we ask you, hear our prayer.

Jesus, Son of the Living God,
   Lord, we ask you, hear our prayer.

Christ, hear us.   Christ, hear us.
Christ, graciously hear us.
   Christ graciously hear us.

Ut hunc fontem,
   regenerandis tibi filiis,
   gratia tua sanctificare digneris
             te rogamus, audi nos.
Iesu, Fili Dei vivi,
             te rogamus, audi nos.

Christe, audi nos. Christe, audi nos.
Christe, exaudi nos.
             Christe, exaudi nos.

If there are candidates to be baptised, the Priest, with hands extended, says the following prayer:

Almighty ever-living God,
be present by the mysteries of your
   great love
and send forth the spirit of adoption
to create the new peoples
brought to birth for you in the font
   of Baptism,
so that what is to be carried out
   by our humble service
may be brought to fulfilment
   by your mighty power.
Through Christ our Lord.
R. Amen.

Omnipotens sempiterne Deus,
adesto magnæ pietatis
   tuæ sacramentis,
et ad recreandos novos populos,
quos tibi fons baptismatis parturit,
spiritum adoptionis emitte,
ut, quod nostræ humilitatis
   gerendum est ministerio,
virtutis tuæ impleatur effectu.
Per Christum Dominum nostrum.
R. Amen.

Blessing of Baptismal Water

The Priest then blesses the baptismal water, saying the following prayer with hands extended:

O God, who by invisible power
accomplish a wondrous effect
through sacramental signs
and who in many ways have
   prepared water, your creation,
to show forth the grace of Baptism;

O God, whose Spirit
in the first moments
   of the world's creation
hovered over the waters,

Deus, qui invisibili potentia
per sacramentorum signa
   mirabilem operaris effectum,
et creaturam aquæ multis
   modis præparasti,
ut baptismi gratiam demonstraret;

Deus, cuius Spiritus
super aquas inter ipsa mundi
   primordia ferebatur,
ut iam tunc virtutem sanctificandi

so that the very substance of water
would even then take to itself
   the power to sanctify;

O God, who by the outpouring
   of the flood
foreshadowed regeneration,
so that from the mystery of one
   and the same element of water
would come an end to vice
   and a beginning of virtue;

O God, who caused the children
   of Abraham
to pass dry-shod through the Red Sea,
so that the chosen people,
set free from slavery to Pharaoh,
would prefigure the people
   of the baptised;

O God, whose Son,
baptised by John in the waters
   of the Jordan,
was anointed with the Holy Spirit,
and, as he hung upon the Cross,
gave forth water from his side
   along with blood,
and after his Resurrection,
   commanded his disciples:
'Go forth, teach all nations,
   baptising them
in the name of the Father and of the
   Son and of the Holy Spirit',
look now, we pray, upon the face
   of your Church
and graciously unseal for her
   the fountain of Baptism.

May this water receive
   by the Holy Spirit
the grace of your Only Begotten Son,

---

aquarum natura conciperet;

Deus, qui regenerationis speciem
in ipsa diluvii effusione signasti,
ut unius eiusdemque
   elementi mysterio
et finis esset vitiis et origo virtutum;

Deus, qui Abrahæ filios
per Mare Rubrum sicco vestigio
   transire fecisti,
ut plebs, a Pharaonis
   servitute liberata,
populum baptizatorum
   præfiguraret;

Deus, cuius Filius, in aqua Iordanis
   a Ioanne baptizatus,
Sancto Spiritu est inunctus,
et, in cruce pendens,
una cum sanguine aquam de latere
   suo produxit,
ac, post resurrectionem suam,
   discipulis iussit:

'Ite, docete omnes gentes,
   baptizantes eos
in nomine Patris et Filii
   et Spiritus Sancti':
respice in faciem Ecclesiæ tuæ,
eique dignare fontem
   baptismatis aperire.

Sumat hæc aqua Unigeniti tui
   gratiam de Spiritu Sancto,
ut homo, ad imaginem

so that human nature,
 created in your image,
and washed clean through
 the Sacrament of Baptism
from all the squalor of the life of old,
may be found worthy to rise
 to the life of newborn children
through water and the Holy Spirit.

tuam conditus,
sacramento baptismatis
a cunctis squaloribus
 vetustatis ablutus,
in novam infantiam
ex aqua et Spiritu Sancto
 resurgere mereatur.

And, if appropriate, lowering the paschal candle into the water either once or three times, he continues:

May the power of the Holy Spirit,
O Lord, we pray,
come down through your Son
into the fullness of this font,

Descendat, quæsumus, Domine,
in hanc plenitudinem fontis
per Filium tuum virtus
 Spiritus Sancti,

and, holding the candle in the water, he continues:

so that all who have been buried
 with Christ
by Baptism into death
may rise again to life with him.
Who lives and reigns with you
 in the unity of the Holy Spirit,
one God, for ever and ever.
R. **Amen.**

ut omnes, cum Christo consepulti
per baptismum in mortem,
ad vitam cum ipso resurgant.
Qui tecum vivit et regnat
 in unitate Spiritus Sancti,
Deus, per omnia sæcula sæculorum.
R. **Amen.**

Then the candle is lifted out of the water, as the people acclaim:

Springs of water, bless the Lord;
praise and exalt him above all
 for ever.

Benedicite, fontes, Domino,
laudate et superexaltate eum
 in sæcula.

After the blessing of baptismal water and the acclamation of the people, the Priest, standing, puts the prescribed questions to the adults and the parents or godparents of the children, as is set out in the respective Rites of the Roman Ritual, in order for them to make the required renunciation.

If the anointing of the adults with the Oil of Catechumens has not taken place beforehand, as part of the immediately preparatory rites, it occurs at this moment.

Then the Priest questions the adults individually about the faith and, if there are children to be baptised, he requests the triple profession of faith from all the parents and godparents together, as is indicated in the respective Rites.

Where many are to be baptised on this night, it is possible to arrange the rite so that, immediately after the response of those to be baptised and of the godparents and the parents, the Celebrant asks for and receives the renewal of baptismal promises of all present.

When the interrogation is concluded, the Priest baptises the adult elect and the children.

After the Baptism, the Priest anoints the infants with chrism. A white garment is given to each, whether adults or children. Then the Priest or Deacon receives the paschal candle from the hand of the minister, and the candles of the newly baptised are lighted. For infants the rite of Ephphetha is omitted.

Afterwards, unless the baptismal washing and the other explanatory rites have occurred in the sanctuary, a procession returns to the sanctuary, formed as before, with the newly baptised or the godparents or parents carrying lighted candles. During this procession, the baptismal canticle Vidi aquam (I saw water) or another appropriate chant is sung.

If adults have been baptised, the Bishop or, in his absence, the Priest who has conferred Baptism, should at once administer the Sacrament of Confirmation to them in the sanctuary, as is indicated in the Roman Pontifical or Roman Ritual.

The Blessing of Water

If no one present is to be baptised and the font is not to be blessed, the Priest introduces the faithful to the blessing of water, saying:

Dear brothers and sisters, let us humbly beseech the Lord our God to bless this water he has created, which will be sprinkled upon us as a memorial of our Baptism. May he graciously renew us, that we may remain faithful to the Spirit whom we have received.	Dominum Deum nostrum, fratres carissimi, suppliciter exoremus, ut hanc creaturam aquæ benedicere dignetur, super nos aspergendam in nostri memoriam baptismi. Ipse autem nos adiuvare dignetur, ut Spiritui, quem accepimus, fideles maneamus.

And after a brief pause in silence, he proclaims the following prayer, with hands extended:

Lord our God, in your mercy be present to your people who keep vigil on this most sacred night, and, for us who recall the wondrous work of our creation	Domine Deus noster, populo tuo hac nocte sacratissima vigilanti adesto propitius; et nobis, mirabile nostræ creationis opus, sed et redemptionis nostræ

and the still greater work
   of our redemption,
graciously bless this water.
For you created water to make
   the fields fruitful
and to refresh and cleanse our bodies.
You also made water the instrument
   of your mercy:
for through water you freed
   your people from slavery
and quenched their thirst
   in the desert;
through water the Prophets
   proclaimed the new covenant
you were to enter upon
   with the human race;
and last of all,
through water, which Christ made
   holy in the Jordan,
you have renewed our
   corrupted nature
in the bath of regeneration.
Therefore, may this water be for us
a memorial of the Baptism
   we have received,
and grant that we may share
in the gladness of our brothers
   and sisters,
who at Easter have received
   their Baptism.
Through Christ our Lord.
R. Amen.

   mirabilius, memorantibus,
hanc aquam benedicere tu dignare.

Ipsam enim tu fecisti,
ut et arva fecunditate donaret,
et levamen corporibus nostris
   munditiamque præberet.

Aquam etiam tuæ ministram
   misericordiæ condidisti;
nam per ipsam solvisti tui
   populi servitutem
illiusque sitim in deserto sedasti;
per ipsam novum fœdus
   nuntiaverunt prophetæ,
quod eras cum hominibus initurus;
per ipsam denique, quam Christus
   in Iordane sacravit,
corruptam naturæ
   nostræ substantiam
in regenerationis lavacro renovasti.

Sit igitur hæc aqua nobis suscepti
   baptismatis memoria,
et cum fratribus nostris,
   qui sunt in Paschate baptizati,
gaudia nos tribuas sociare.
Per Christum Dominum nostrum.
R. Amen.

The Renewal of Baptismal Promises

When the Rite of Baptism (and Confirmation) has been completed or, if this has not taken place, after the blessing of water, all stand, holding lighted candles in their hands, and renew the promise of baptismal faith, unless this has already been done together with those to be baptised.

The Priest addresses the faithful in these or similar words:

Dear brethren (brothers and sisters), through the Paschal Mystery we have been buried with Christ in Baptism, so that we may walk with him in newness of life. And so, now that our Lenten observance is concluded, let us renew the promises of Holy Baptism, by which we once renounced Satan and his works and promised to serve God in the holy Catholic Church. And so I ask you:

Priest: Do you renounce Satan?
All: I do.

Priest: And all his works?
All: I do.

Priest: And all his empty show?
All: I do.

Or:

Priest: Do you renounce sin, so as to live in the freedom of the children of God?
All: I do.

Priest: Do you renounce the lure of evil, so that sin may have no mastery over you?
All: I do.

Priest: Do you renounce Satan, the author and prince of sin?
All: I do.

Per paschale mysterium, fratres carissimi, in baptismo consepulti sumus cum Christo, ut cum eo in novitate vitæ ambulemus. Quapropter, quadragesimali observatione absoluta, sancti baptismatis promissiones renovemus, quibus olim Satanæ et operibus eius abrenuntiavimus, et Deo in sancta Ecclesia catholica servire promisimus. Quapropter:

Sacerdos: Abrenutiatis Satanæ?
Omnes: Abrenuntio.

Sacerdos: Et omnibus operibus eius?
Omnes: Abrenuntio.

Sacerdos: Et omnibus pompis eius?
Omnes: Abrenuntio.

Vel:

Sacerdos: Abrenuntiatis peccato, ut in libertate filiorum Dei vivatis?
Omnes: Abrenuntio.

Sacerdos: Abrenuntiatis seductionibus iniquitatis, ne pecccatum vobis dominetur?
Omnes: Abrenuntio.

Sacerdos: Abrenuntiatis Satanæ, qui est auctor et princeps peccati?
Omnes: Abrenuntio.

If the situation warrants, this second formula may be adapted by Conferences of Bishops according to local needs.

Then the Priest continues:

Priest: Do you believe in God, the Father almighty,
Creator of heaven and earth?
All: I do.

Priest: Do you believe in Jesus Christ, his only Son, our Lord,
who was born of the Virgin Mary,
suffered death and was buried,
rose again from the dead
and is seated at the right hand of the Father?
All: I do.

Priest: Do you believe in the Holy Spirit,
the holy Catholic Church,
the communion of saints,
the forgiveness of sins,
the resurrection of the body,
and life everlasting?
All: I do.

And the Priest concludes:

And may almighty God, the Father of our Lord Jesus Christ,
who has given us new birth by water and the Holy Spirit
and bestowed on us forgiveness of our sins,
keep us by his grace,
in Christ Jesus our Lord,
for eternal life.
All: Amen.

Sacerdos: Creditis in Deum Patrem omnipotentem,
creatorem cæli et terræ?
Omnes: Credo.

Sacerdos: Creditis in Iesum Christum, Filium eius unicum,
Dominum nostrum,
natum ex Maria Virgine,
passum et sepultum,
qui a mortuis resurrexit
et sedet ad dexteram Patris?
Omnes: Credo.

Sacerdos: Creditis in Spiritum Sanctum,
sanctam Ecclesiam catholicam,
sanctorum communionem,
remissionem peccatorum,
carnis resurrectionem et
vitam æternam?
Omnes: Credo.

Et Deus omnipotens, Pater Domini nostri Iesu Christi,
qui nos regeneravit ex aqua et Spiritu Sancto,
quique nobis dedit remissionem peccatorum,
ipse nos custodiat gratia sua,
in Christo Iesu Domino nostro,
in vitam æternam.
Omnes: Amen.

The Priest sprinkles the people with the blessed water, while all sing:

Antiphon

I saw water flowing from the Temple,
from its right-hand side, alleluia;
and all to whom this water came were saved
and shall say: Alleluia, alleluia.

Vidi aquam egredientem de templo,
a latere dextro, alleluia;
et omnes, ad quos pervenit aqua ista, salvi facti sunt
et dicent: Alleluia, alleluia.

Another chant that is baptismal in character may also be sung.

Meanwhile the newly baptised are led to their place among the faithful.

If the blessing of baptismal water has not taken place in the baptistery, the Deacon and the ministers reverently carry the vessel of water to the font.

If the blessing of the font has not occurred, the blessed water is put aside in an appropriate place.

After the sprinkling, the Priest returns to the chair where, omitting the Creed, he directs the Universal Prayer, in which the newly baptised participate for the first time.

FOURTH PART:
The Liturgy of the Eucharist

The Priest goes to the altar and begins the Liturgy of the Eucharist in the usual way.

It is desirable that the bread and wine be brought forward by the newly baptised or, if they are children, by their parents or godparents.

Prayer over the Offerings	Super oblata
Accept, we ask, O Lord, the prayers of your people with the sacrificial offerings, that what has begun in the paschal mysteries may, by the working of your power, bring us to the healing of eternity. Through Christ our Lord.	Suscipe, quæsumus, Domine, preces populi tui cum oblationibus hostiarum, ut, paschalibus initiata mysteriis, ad æternitatis nobis medelam, te operante, proficiant. Per Christum Dominum nostrum.

Preface I of Easter: The Paschal Mystery (...on this night above all...), pp.52-55.

In the Eucharistic Prayer, a commemoration is made of the baptised and their godparents in accord with the formulas which are found in the Roman Missal and Roman Ritual for each of the Eucharistic Prayers.

Before the Ecce Agnus Dei (Behold the Lamb of God), the Priest may briefly address the newly baptised about receiving their first Communion and about the excellence of this great mystery, which is the climax of Initiation and the centre of the whole of Christian life.

It is desirable that the newly baptised receive Holy Communion under both kinds, together with their godfathers, godmothers, and Catholic parents and spouses, as well as their lay catechists. It is even appropriate that, with the consent of the Diocesan Bishop, where the occasion suggests this, all the faithful be admitted to Holy Communion under both kinds.

Communion Antiphon 1 Co 5:7-8	Ant. ad communionem
Christ our Passover has been sacrificed; therefore let us keep the feast with the unleavened bread of purity and truth, alleluia.	Pascha nostrum immolatus est Christus; itaque epulemur in azymis sinceritatis et veritatis, alleluia.

Psalm 117 may appropriately be sung.

Prayer after Communion

Pour out on us, O Lord,
   the Spirit of your love,
and in your kindness make those
   you have nourished
by this paschal Sacrament
one in mind and heart.
Through Christ our Lord.

Solemn Blessing

May almighty God bless you
through today's Easter Solemnity
and, in his compassion,
defend you from every assault of sin.
R. Amen.

And may he, who restores you
   to eternal life
in the Resurrection
   of his Only Begotten,
endow you with the prize
   of immortality.
R. Amen.

Now that the days of the Lord's
   Passion have drawn to a close,
may you who celebrate
   the gladness of the Paschal Feast
come with Christ's help,
   and exulting in spirit,
to those feasts that are celebrated
   in eternal joy.
R. Amen.

And may the blessing
   of almighty God,
the Father, and the Son,
   ✠ and the Holy Spirit,
come down on you and remain
   with you for ever.
R. Amen.

Post communionem

Spiritum nobis, Domine,
   tuæ caritatis infunde,
ut, quos sacramentis
   paschalibus satiasti,
tua facias pietate concordes.
Per Christum Dominum nostrum.

Benedictio sollemnis

Benedicat vos omnipotens Deus,
hodierna interveniente
   sollemnitate paschali,
et ab omni miseratus defendat
   incursione peccati.
R. Amen.

Et qui ad æternam vitam
in Unigeniti sui resurrectione
   vos reparat,
vos præmiis
   immortalitatis adimpleat.
R. Amen.

Et qui, expletis passionis
   dominicæ diebus,
paschalis festi gaudia celebratis,
ad ea festa, quæ lætitiis
   peraguntur æternis,
ipso opitulante, exsultantibus
animis veniatis.
R. Amen.

Et benedictio Dei omnipotentis,
Patris, et Filii, ✠ et Spiritus Sancti,
descendat super vos
   et maneat semper.
R. Amen.

The final blessing formula from the Rite of Baptism of Adults or of Children may also be used, according to circumstances.

To dismiss the people the Deacon or, if there is no Deacon, the Priest himself sings or says:

Go forth, the Mass is ended, alleluia, alleluia.	Ite, missa est, alleluia, alleluia.
Or:	Vel:
Go in peace, alleluia, alleluia.	Ite in pace, alleluia, alleluia
All reply:	Omnes respondent:
Thanks be to God, alleluia, alleluia.	Deo gratias, alleluia, alleluia.

This practice is observed throughout the Octave of Easter.
The paschal candle is lit in all the more solemn liturgical celebrations of this period.

31 March

At the Mass during the Day

We know that Christ has truly risen from the dead. Yes, indeed! This is the fundamental core of our profession of faith; this is the cry of victory that unites us all today. And if Jesus is risen, and is therefore alive, who will ever be able to separate us from him? Who will ever be able to deprive us of the love of him who has conquered hatred and overcome death? The Easter proclamation spreads throughout the world with the joyful song of the Alleluia. Let us sing it with our lips, and let us sing it above all with our hearts and our lives, with a manner of life that is "unleavened", that is to say, simple, humble, and fruitful in good works. The Risen One goes before us and he accompanies us along the paths of the world. He is our hope, He is the true peace of the world.

(Pope Benedict XVI)

Entrance Antiphon Cf. Ps 138:18,5-6

I HAVE risen, and I am with you still, alleluia.
You have laid your hand upon me, alleluia.
Too wonderful for me,
  this knowledge, alleluia, alleluia.

Or: Lk 24:34; Cf. Rv 1:6
The Lord is truly risen, alleluia.
To him be glory and power
for all the ages of eternity, alleluia, alleluia.

Ant. ad introitum

RESURREXI, et adhuc tecum sum, alleluia:
posuisti super me manum tuam, alleluia:
mirabilis facta est scientia tua, alleluia, alleluia.

Vel:
Surrexit Dominus vere, alleluia.
Ipsi gloria et imperium
per universa æternitatis sæcula, alleluia, alleluia.

The Gloria in excelsis (Glory to God in the highest) is said.

Collect

O God, who on this day,
through your Only Begotten Son,
have conquered death
and unlocked for us the path
   to eternity,
grant, we pray, that we who keep
the solemnity of the
   Lord's Resurrection
may, through the renewal brought
   by your Spirit,
rise up in the light of life.
Through our Lord Jesus Christ,
   your Son,
who lives and reigns with you
   in the unity of the Holy Spirit,
one God, for ever and ever.

Collecta

Deus, qui hodierna die,
   per Unigenitum tuum,
æternitatis nobis aditum,
   devicta morte, reserasti,
da nobis, quæsumus,
ut, qui resurrectionis dominicæ
   sollemnia colimus,
per innovationem tui Spiritus
in lumine vitæ resurgamus.
Per Dominum nostrum Iesum
   Christum Filium tuum,
qui tecum vivit et regnat
   in unitate Spiritus Sancti,
Deus, per omnia sæcula sæculorum.

FIRST READING

A reading from the Acts of the Apostles   10:34,37-43

We have eaten and drunk with him after his resurrection.

Peter addressed Cornelius and his household: 'You must have heard about the recent happenings in Judaea; about Jesus of Nazareth and how he began in Galilee, after John had been preaching baptism. God had anointed him with the Holy Spirit and with power, and because God was with him, Jesus went about doing good and curing all who had fallen into the power of the devil. Now I, and those with me, can witness to everything he did throughout the countryside of Judaea and in Jerusalem itself: and also to the fact that they killed him by hanging him on a tree, yet three days afterwards God raised him to life and allowed him to be seen, not by the whole people but only by certain witnesses God had chosen beforehand. Now we are those witnesses – we have eaten and drunk with him after his resurrection from the dead – and he has ordered us to proclaim this to his people and to tell them that God has appointed him to judge everyone, alive or dead. It is to him that all the prophets bear this witness: that all who believe in Jesus will have their sins forgiven through his name.'

   The word of the Lord.

Responsional Psalm   Ps 117:1-2,16-17,22-23. R. v. 24

R. **This day was made by the Lord;
we rejoice and are glad**.
Or: **Alleluia, alleluia, alleluia!**

Give thanks to the Lord for he is good,
for his love has no end.
Let the sons of Israel say:
'His love has no end.' R.

The Lord's right hand has triumphed;
his right hand raised me.
I shall not die, I shall live
and recount his deeds. R.

The stone which the builders rejected
has become the corner stone.
This is the work of the Lord,
a marvel in our eyes. R.

SECOND READING

A reading from the letter of St Paul to the Colossians   3:1-4

You must look for the things that are in heaven, where Christ is.

Since you have been brought back to true life with Christ, you must look for the things that are in heaven, where Christ is, sitting at God's right hand. Let your thoughts be on heavenly things, not on the things that are on the earth, because you have died, and now the life you have is hidden with Christ in God. But when Christ is revealed – and he is your life – you too will be revealed in all your glory with him.

The word of the Lord.

ALTERNATIVE SECOND READING

A reading from the first letter of St Paul to the Corinthians   5:6-8

Get rid of the old yeast, and make yourselves into a completely new batch of bread.

You must know how even a small amount of yeast is enough to leaven all the dough, so get rid of all the old yeast, and make yourselves into a completely new batch of bread, unleavened as you are meant to be. Christ, our Passover, has been sacrificed; let us celebrate the feast, by getting rid of all the old yeast of evil and wickedness, having only the unleavened bread of sincerity and truth.

The word of the Lord.

The sequence is said or sung on this day. On the weekdays of the Octave of Easter, its use is optional.

SEQUENCE

Christians, to the Paschal Victim
    offer sacrifice and praise.
The sheep are ransomed
    by the Lamb;
and Christ, the undefiled,
hath sinners to his Father reconciled.

Death with life contended:
    combat strangely ended!
Life's own Champion, slain,
    yet lives to reign.

Tell us, Mary:
    say what thou didst see
    upon the way.

The tomb the Living did enclose;
I saw Christ's glory as he rose!
The angels there attesting;
shroud with grave-clothes resting.
Christ, my hope, has risen:
he goes before you into Galilee.
That Christ is truly risen
    from the dead we know.
Victorious king, thy mercy show!

Victimæ paschali laudes
    immolent Christiani.
Agnus redemit oves:
    Christus innocens Patri
    reconciliavit peccatores.

Mors et vita duello
    conflixere mirando:
    dux vitæ mortuus regnat vivus.

Dic nobis, Maria,
    quid vidisti in via?
Sepulcrum Christi viventis,
    gloriam vidi resurgentis.
Angelicos testes,
    sudarium et vestes.
Surrexit Christus spes mea:
    præcedet vos in Galilæam.
Scimus Christum surrexisse
    a mortuis vere:
tu nobis, victor Rex, miserere.

Gospel Acclamation

1 Co 5:7-8

R. **Alleluia, alleluia!**
Christ, our passover, has been sacrificed;
let us celebrate the feast then, in the Lord.
R. **Alleluia!**

GOSPEL

A reading from the holy Gospel according to John   20:1-9

He must rise from the dead.

It was very early on the first day of the week and still dark, when Mary of Magdala came to the tomb. She saw that the stone had been moved away from the tomb and came running to Simon Peter and the other disciple, the one Jesus loved. 'They have taken the Lord out of the tomb' she said 'and we don't know where they have put him.'

So Peter set out with the other disciple to go to the tomb. They ran together, but the other disciple, running faster than Peter, reached the tomb first; he bent down and saw the linen cloths lying on the ground, but did not go in. Simon Peter who was following now came up, went right into the tomb, saw the linen cloths on the ground, and also the cloth that had been over his head; this was not with the linen cloths but rolled up in a place by itself. Then the other disciple who had reached the tomb first also went in; he saw and he believed. Till this moment they had failed to understand the teaching of scripture, that he must rise from the dead.

The Gospel of the Lord.

The Creed is said. However, in Easter Sunday Masses which are celebrated with a congregation, the rite of the renewal of baptismal promises may take place after the homily, according to the text used at the Easter Vigil (pp.381-384). In that case the Creed is omitted.

Prayer over the Offerings

Exultant with paschal gladness,
    O Lord,
we offer the sacrifice
by which your Church
is wondrously reborn and nourished.
Through Christ our Lord.

Super oblata

Sacrificia, Domine,
    paschalibus gaudiis
exsultantes offerimus,
quibus Ecclesia tua
mirabiliter renascitur et nutritur.
Per Christum Dominum nostrum.

Preface I of Easter, The Paschal Mystery, pp.52-55.

When the Roman Canon is used, the proper forms of the Communicantes (In communion with those) and Hanc igitur (Therefore, Lord, we pray) are said.

Communion Antiphon 1 Co 5:7-8

Christ our Passover has been
    sacrificed, alleluia;
therefore let us keep the feast
    with the unleavened bread
of purity and truth, alleluia, alleluia.

Ant. ad communionem

Pascha nostrum immolatus
    est Christus, alleluia;
itaque epulemur
    in azymis sinceritatis
et veritatis, alleluia, alleluia.

Prayer after Communion

Look upon your Church, O God,
with unfailing love and favour,
so that, renewed by the paschal
    mysteries,
she may come to the glory
    of the resurrection.
Through Christ our Lord.

Post communionem

Perpetuo, Deus, Ecclesiam tuam
    pio favore tuere,
ut, paschalibus renovata mysteriis,
ad resurrectionis perveniat claritatem.
Per Christum Dominum nostrum.

To impart the blessing at the end of Mass, the Priest may appropriately use the formula of Solemn Blessing for the Mass of the Easter Vigil, p.385.

For the dismissal of the people, the following is sung or said:

Go forth, the Mass is ended, alleluia, alleluia.	Ite, missa est, alleluia, alleluia.
Or:	Vel:
Go in peace, alleluia, alleluia. R. Thanks be to God, alleluia, alleluia.	Ite in pace, alleluia, alleluia R. Deo gratias, alleluia, alleluia.

7 April

SECOND SUNDAY OF EASTER

(or of Divine Mercy)

"Fear not, I am the first and the last, and the living one; I died, and behold I am alive for evermore". We hear these comforting words in the Second Reading taken from the Book of Revelation. They invite us to turn our gaze to Christ, to experience his reassuring presence. To each person, whatever his condition, even if it were the most complicated and dramatic, the Risen One repeats: "Fear not!"; I died on the Cross but now "I am alive for evermore"; "I am the first and the last, and the living one".

(Blessed Pope John Paul II)

Entrance Antiphon   1 P 2:2

LIKE newborn infants,
you must long for the pure, spiritual milk,
that in him you may grow
to salvation, alleluia.

Or: 4 Esdr 2:36-37

Receive the joy of your glory,
giving thanks to God,
who has called you into the heavenly kingdom, alleluia.

Ant. ad introitum

QUASI modo geniti infantes,
rationabile, sine dolo
lac concupiscite,
ut in eo crescatis in salutem,
alleluia.

Vel:

Accipite iucunditatem gloriæ vestræ,
gratias agentes Deo,
qui vos ad cælestia regna vocavit,
alleluia.

The Gloria in excelsis (Glory to God in the highest) is said.

Collect

God of everlasting mercy,
who, in the very recurrence
   of the paschal feast
kindle the faith of the people you
   have made your own,
increase, we pray, the grace you
   have bestowed,
that all may grasp
   and rightly understand
in what font they have been washed,
by whose Spirit they have
   been reborn,
by whose Blood they have
   been redeemed.
Through our Lord Jesus Christ,
   your Son,
who lives and reigns with you
   in the unity of the Holy Spirit,
one God, for ever and ever.

Collecta

Deus misericordiæ sempiternæ,
qui in ipso paschalis festi recursu
fidem sacratæ tibi plebis accendis,
auge gratiam quam dedisti,
ut digna omnes intellegentia
   comprehendant,
quo lavacro abluti, quo
Spiritu regenerati,
quo sanguine sunt redempti.
Per Dominum nostrum Iesum
   Christum Filium tuum,
qui tecum vivit et regnat
   in unitate Spiritus Sancti,
Deus, per omnia sæcula sæculorum.

FIRST READING

A reading from the Acts of the Apostles   5:12-16

The numbers of men and women who came to believe in the Lord increased steadily.

The faithful all used to meet by common consent in the Portico of Solomon. No one else even dared to join them, but the people were loud in their praise and the numbers of men and women who came to believe in the Lord increased steadily. So many signs and wonders were worked among the people at the hands of the apostles and the sick were even taken out into the streets and laid on beds and sleeping-mats in the hope that at least the shadow of Peter might fall across some of them as he went past. People even came crowding in from the towns round about Jerusalem, bringing with them their sick and those tormented by unclean spirits, and all of them were cured.

   The word of the Lord.

Responsional Psalm

Ps 117:2-4,22-27. R. v.1

R. **Give thanks to the Lord for he is good,
for his love has no end.**
Or: **Alleluia, alleluia, alleluia!**

Let the sons of Israel say:
'His love has no end.'
Let the sons of Aaron say:
'His love has no end.'
Let those who fear the Lord say:
'His love has no end.' R.

The stone which the builders rejected
has become the corner stone.
This is the work of the Lord
a marvel in our eyes.
This day was made by the Lord;
we rejoice and are glad. R.

O Lord, grant us salvation;
O Lord, grant success.
Blessed in the name of the Lord
is he who comes.
We bless you from the house of the Lord;
the Lord God is our light. R.

SECOND READING

A reading from the book of the Apocalypse 1:9-13,17-19
I was dead and now I am to live for ever and ever.

My name is John, and through our union in Jesus I am your brother and share your sufferings, your kingdom, and all you endure. I was on the island of Patmos for having preached God's word and witnessed for Jesus; it was the Lord's day and the Spirit possessed me, and I heard a voice behind me, shouting like a trumpet, 'Write down all that you see in a book.' I turned round to see who had spoken to me, and when I turned I saw seven golden lamp-stands and, surrounded by them, a figure like a Son of man, dressed in a long robe tied at the waist with a golden girdle.

When I saw him, I fell in a dead faint at his feet, but he touched me with his right hand and said, 'Do not be afraid; it is I, the First and the Last; I am the Living One. I was dead and now I am to live for ever and ever, and I hold the keys of death and of the underworld. Now write down all that you see of present happenings and things that are still to come.'

The word of the Lord.

Easter Sequence can be sung here, see p.389.

Gospel Acclamation   Jn 20:29

R. **Alleluia, alleluia!**
Jesus said: 'You believe because you can see me.
Happy are those who have not seen and yet believe.'
R. **Alleluia!**

GOSPEL

A reading from the holy Gospel according to John   20:19-31

Eight days later, Jesus came.

In the evening of that same day, the first day of the week, the doors were closed in the room where the disciples were, for fear of the Jews. Jesus came and stood among them. He said to them, 'Peace be with you,' and showed them his hands and his side. The disciples were filled with joy when they saw the Lord, and he said to them again, 'Peace be with you.

'As the Father sent me,
so am I sending you.'
After saying this he breathed on them and said:
'Receive the Holy Spirit.
For those whose sins you forgive,
they are forgiven;
for those whose sins you retain,
they are retained.'

Thomas, called the Twin, who was one of the Twelve, was not with them when Jesus came. When the disciples said, 'We have seen the Lord,' he answered, 'Unless I see the holes that the nails made in his hands and can put my finger into the holes they made, and unless I can put my hand into his side, I refuse to believe.' Eight days later the disciples were in the house again and Thomas was with them. The doors were closed, but Jesus came in and stood among them. 'Peace be with you,' he said. Then he spoke to Thomas, 'Put your finger here; look, here are my hands. Give me your hand; put it into my side. Doubt no longer but believe.' Thomas replied, 'My Lord and my God!'

Jesus said to him:
'You believe because you can see me.
Happy are those who have not seen and yet believe.'

There were many other signs that Jesus worked and the disciples saw, but they are not recorded in this book. These are recorded so that you may believe that Jesus is the Christ, the Son of God, and that believing this you may have life through his name.

The Gospel of the Lord.

The Creed is said.

Prayer over the Offerings | Super oblata

Accept, O Lord, we pray,
the oblations of your people
(and of those you have brought
　to new birth),
that, renewed by confession of your
　name and by Baptism,
they may attain unending happiness.
Through Christ our Lord.

| Suscipe, quæsumus, Domine,
　plebis tuæ
(et tuorum renatorum) oblationes,
ut, confessione tui nominis
　et baptismate renovati,
sempiternam beatitudinem
　consequantur.
Per Christum Dominum nostrum.

Preface I of Easter (. . .on this day above all. . .), pp.52-55.

When the Roman Canon is used, the proper forms of Communicantes (In communion with those) and Hanc igitur (Therefore, Lord, we pray) are said.

Communion Antiphon Cf. Jn 20:27 | Ant. ad communionem

Bring your hand and feel the place
　of the nails,
and do not be unbelieving
　but believing, alleluia.

| Mitte manum tuam,
　et cognosce loca clavorum,
et noli esse incredulus,
　sed fidelis, alleluia.

Prayer after Communion | Post communionem

Grant, we pray, almighty God,
that our reception of this paschal
　Sacrament
may have a continuing effect
in our minds and hearts.
Through Christ our Lord.

| Concede, quæsumus,
　omnipotens Deus,
ut paschalis perceptio sacramenti
continua in nostris
　mentibus perseveret.
Per Christum Dominum nostrum.

A formula of Solemn Blessing, pp.136-139, may be used.

For the dismissal of the people, the following is sung or said: Go forth, the Mass is ended, alleluia, alleluia. Or: Go in peace, alleluia, alleluia. The people respond: Thanks be to God, alleluia, alleluia.

8 April

THE ANNUNCIATION OF THE LORD

The Annunciation, recounted at the beginning of Saint Luke's Gospel, is a humble, hidden event – no one saw it, no one except Mary knew of it –, but at the same time it was crucial to the history of humanity. When the Virgin said her "yes" to the Angel's announcement, Jesus was conceived and with him began the new era of history that was to be ratified in Easter as the "new and eternal Covenant". In fact, Mary's "yes" perfectly mirrors that of Christ himself when he entered the world, as the Letter to the Hebrews says, interpreting Psalm 40[39]: "As is written of me in the book, I have come to do your will, O God" (Heb 10:7). The Son's obedience was reflected in that of the Mother and thus, through the encounter of these two "yeses", God was able to take on a human face. This is why the Annunciation is a Christological feast as well, because it celebrates a central mystery of Christ: the Incarnation.

(Pope Benedict XVI)

Solemnity

Entrance Antiphon — Heb 10:5,7

THE Lord said,
as he entered the world:
Behold, I come to do your will,
  O God.

Ant. ad introitum

DOMINUS ingrediens
mundum dixit:
Ecce venio ut faciam,
  Deus, voluntatem tuam.

The Gloria in excelsis (Glory to God in the highest) is said.

Collect

O God, who willed that your Word
should take on the reality
  of human flesh
in the womb of the Virgin Mary,
grant, we pray,
that we, who confess our Redeemer
  to be God and man,
may merit to become partakers
  even in his divine nature.
Who lives and reigns with you
  in the unity of the Holy Spirit,
one God, for ever and ever.

Collecta

Deus, qui Verbum tuum in utero
  Virginis Mariæ
veritatem carnis humanæ
  suscipere voluisti,
concede, quæsumus,
ut, qui Redemptorem nostrum
Deum et hominem confitemur,
ipsius etiam divinæ naturæ
  mereamur esse consortes.
Per Dominum nostrum Iesum
  Christum Filium tuum,
qui tecum vivit et regnat
  in unitate Spiritus Sancti,
Deus, per omnia sæcula sæculorum.

FIRST READING

A reading from the prophet Isaiah 7:10-14; 8:10
The maiden is with child.

The Lord spoke to Ahaz and said, 'Ask the Lord your God for a sign for yourself coming either from the depths of Sheol or from the heights above.' 'No,' Ahaz answered, 'I will not put the Lord to the test.'

Then Isaiah said:

Listen now, House of David:
are you not satisfied with trying the patience of men
without trying the patience of my God, too?
The Lord himself, therefore,
will give you a sign.
It is this: the maiden is with child
and will soon give birth to a son
whom she will call Emmanuel,
a name which means 'God-with-us'.

The word of the Lord.

Responsional Psalm Ps 39:7-11. R. vv.8,9

R. **Here I am, Lord!**
I come to do your will.

You do not ask for sacrifice and offerings,
but an open ear.
You do not ask for holocaust and victim.
Instead, here am I. R.

In the scroll of the book it stands written
that I should do your will.
My God, I delight in your law
in the depth of my heart. R.

Your justice I have proclaimed
in the great assembly.
My lips I have not sealed;
you know it, O Lord. R.

I have not hidden your justice in my heart
but declared your faithful help.
I have not hidden your love and your truth
from the great assembly. R.

SECOND READING

A reading from the letter to the Hebrews 10:4-10

I was commanded in the scroll of the book, 'God, here I am! I am coming to obey your will.'

Bulls' blood and goats' blood are useless for taking away sins, and this is what Christ said, on coming into the world:

> You who wanted no sacrifice or oblation,
> prepared a body for me.
> you took no pleasure in holocausts or sacrifices for sin;
> then I said,
> just as I was commanded in the scroll of the book,
> 'God, here I am! I am coming to obey your will.'

Notice that he says first: You did not want what the Law lays down as the things to be offered, that is: the sacrifices, the oblations, the holocausts and the sacrifices for sin, and you took no pleasure in them; and then he says: Here I am! I am coming to obey your will. He is abolishing the first sort to replace it with the second. And this will was for us to be made holy by the offering of his body made once and for all by Jesus Christ.

The word of the Lord.

Gospel Acclamation
Jn 1:14,12

R. **Alleluia, alleluia!**
The Word was made flesh,
he lived among us,
and we saw his glory.
R. **Alleluia!**

GOSPEL

A reading from the Gospel according to Luke 1:26-38

Listen! You are to conceive and bear a son.

The angel Gabriel was sent by God to a town in Galilee called Nazareth, to a virgin betrothed to a man named Joseph, of the house of David; and the virgin's name was Mary. He went in and said to her, "Rejoice, so highly favoured! The Lord is with you.' She was deeply disturbed by these words and asked herself what this greeting could mean, but the angel said to her, 'Mary, do not be afraid; you have won God's favour. Listen! You are to conceive and bear a son, and you must name him Jesus. He will be great and will be called Son of the Most High. The Lord God will give him the throne of his ancestor David; he will rule over the House of Jacob for ever and his reign will have no end.' Mary said to the angel, 'But how can this come about, since I am a virgin?' 'The Holy Spirit will come upon you, the angel answered, 'and the power of the Most High will cover you with its shadow. And so the child will be holy and will be called Son of God. Know this too: your kinswoman Elizabeth also, in her old age, herself conceived a son, and she whom people called barren is now in her sixth month, for nothing is impossible to God.' 'I am the handmaid of the Lord,' said Mary, 'let what you have said be done to me.' And the angel left her.

The Gospel of the Lord.

The Creed is said. At the words and was incarnate all genuflect.

Prayer over the Offerings

Be pleased, almighty God,
to accept your Church's offering,
so that she,
    who is aware that her beginnings
lie in the Incarnation of your Only
    Begotten Son,
may rejoice to celebrate his
    mysteries on this Solemnity.
Who lives and reigns
    for ever and ever.

Super oblata

Ecclesiæ tuæ munus, omnipotens
    Deus, dignare suscipere,
ut, quæ in Unigeniti
    tui incarnatione
primordia sua constare cognoscit,
ipsius gaudeat hac sollemnitate
    celebrare mysteria.
Per Christum Dominum nostrum.

Preface: The Mystery of the Incarnation.

It is truly right and just,
    our duty and our salvation,
always and everywhere
    to give you thanks,
Lord, holy Father,
    almighty and eternal God,
through Christ our Lord.

For the Virgin Mary heard with faith
that the Christ was to be born
    among men and for men's sake
by the overshadowing power
    of the Holy Spirit.

Præfatio: De mysterio Incarnationis

Vere dignum et iustum est,
    æquum et salutare,
nos tibi semper et ubique
    gratias agere:
Domine, sancte Pater,
    omnipotens æterne Deus:
per Christum Dominum nostrum.

Quem inter homines et propter
    homines nasciturum,
Spiritus Sancti obumbrante virtute,
a cælesti nuntio Virgo
    fidenter audivit

Lovingly she bore him in her
    immaculate womb,
that the promises to the children
    of Israel might come about
and the hope of nations be
    accomplished beyond all telling.

Through him the host of Angels
    adores your majesty
and rejoices in your presence for ever.

May our voices, we pray,
    join with theirs
in one chorus of exultant praise,
    as we acclaim:

Holy, Holy, Holy Lord God of hosts...

Communion Antiphon Is 7:14

Behold, a Virgin shall conceive
    and bear a son;
and his name will be called
    Emmanuel.

Prayer after Communion

Confirm in our minds the
    mysteries of the true faith,
we pray, O Lord,
so that, confessing that he who was
    conceived of the Virgin Mary
is true God and true man,
we may, through the saving power
    of his Resurrection,
merit to attain eternal joy.
Through Christ our Lord.

et immaculatis visceribus
    amanter portavit,
ut et promissiones filiis Israel
    perficeret veritas,
et gentium exspectatio pateret
    ineffabiliter adimplenda.

Per quem maiestatem tuam adorat
    exercitus Angelorum,
ante conspectum tuum
    in æternitate lætantium.

Cum quibus et nostras voces
    ut admitti iubeas, deprecamur,
socia exsultatione dicentes:

Sanctus, Sanctus, Sanctus...

Ant. ad communionem

Ecce Virgo concipiet,
    et pariet Filium;
et vocabitur nomen
    eius Emmanuel.

Post communionem

In mentibus nostris,
    quæsumus, Domine,
veræ fidei sacramenta confirma,
ut, qui conceptum de Virgine
Deum verum et
    hominem confitemur,
per eius salutiferæ
    resurrectionis potentiam,
ad æternam mereamur
    pervenire lætitiam.
Per Christum Dominum nostrum.

14 April

THIRD SUNDAY OF EASTER

"It is the Lord!" (Jn 21:7). This exclamation of the Apostle John emphasises the intense emotion experienced by the disciples on recognizing the risen Jesus, who appeared to them for the third time on the shore of the Sea of Tiberias. After a long night of loneliness and toil, the dawn arrives and his appearance radically changes everything: the darkness is overcome by light, the fruitless work becomes an easy and abundant catch of fish, the feeling of tiredness and loneliness is transformed into joy and peace. Since then, these same sentiments enliven the Church. If at a superficial level it sometimes seems that the darkness of evil and the toil of everyday life have the upper hand, the Church knows with certainty that the light of Easter now shines eternally on those who follow Christ. The great message of the Resurrection fills the hearts of the faithful with inner joy and renewed hope.

(Blessed Pope John Paul II)

Entrance Antiphon   Cf. Ps 65:1-2

CRY out with joy to God,
   all the earth;
O sing to the glory of his name.
O render him glorious praise,
   alleluia.

Ant. ad introitum

IUBILATE Deo, omnis terra,
   psalmum dicite nomini eius,
date gloriam laudi eius, alleluia.

The Gloria in excelsis (Glory to God in the highest) is said.

Collect

May your people exult for ever,
   O God,
in renewed youthfulness of spirit,
so that, rejoicing now in the restored
   glory of our adoption,
we may look forward
   in confident hope
to the rejoicing of the day
   of resurrection.
Through our Lord Jesus Christ,
   your Son,
who lives and reigns with you
   in the unity of the Holy Spirit,
one God, for ever and ever.

Collecta

Semper exsultet populus tuus, Deus,
renovata animæ iuventute,
ut, qui nunc lætatur in adoptionis
   se gloriam restitutum,
resurrectionis diem spe certæ
   gratulationis exspectet.
Per Dominum nostrum Iesum
   Christum Filium tuum,
qui tecum vivit et regnat
   in unitate Spiritus Sancti,
Deus, per omnia sæcula sæculorum.

FIRST READING

A reading from the Acts of the Apostles   5:27-32,40-41

We are witnesses of all this, we and the Holy Spirit.

The high priest demanded an explanation of the apostles. 'We gave you a formal warning' he said 'not to preach in this name, and what have you done? You have filled Jerusalem with your teaching, and seem determined to fix the guilt of this man's death on us.' In reply Peter and the apostles said, 'Obedience to God comes before obedience to men; it was the God of our ancestors who raised up Jesus, but it was you who had him executed by hanging on a tree. By his own right hand God has now raised him up to be leader and saviour, to give repentance and forgiveness of sins through him to Israel. We are witnesses to all this, we and the Holy Spirit whom God has given to those who obey him.' They warned the apostles not to speak in the name of Jesus and released them. And so they left the presence of the Sanhedrin glad to have had the honour of suffering humiliation for the sake of the name.

The word of the Lord.

Responsorial Psalm   Ps 29:2,4-6,11-13. R. v.2

R. **I will praise you, Lord,
you have rescued me.**
Or: Alleluia!

I will praise you, Lord, you have rescued me
and have not let my enemies rejoice over me.
O Lord, you have raised my soul from the dead,
restored me to life from those who sink into the grave. R.

Sing psalms to the Lord, you who love him,
give thanks to his holy name.
His anger lasts but a moment; his favour through life.
At night there are tears, but joy comes with dawn. R.

The Lord listened and had pity.
The Lord came to my help.
For me you have changed my mourning into dancing;
O Lord my God, I will thank you for ever. R.

SECOND READING

A reading from the book of the Apocalypse 5:11-14

The Lamb that was sacrificed is worthy to be given riches and power.

In my vision, I, John, heard the sound of an immense number of angels gathered round the throne and the animals and the elders; there were ten thousand times ten thousand of them and thousands upon thousands, shouting, 'The Lamb that was sacrificed is worthy to be given power, riches, wisdom, strength, honour, glory and blessing.' Then I heard all the living things in creation – everything that lives in the air, and on the ground, and under the ground, and in the sea, crying, 'To the One who is sitting on the throne and to the Lamb, be all praise, honour, glory and power, for ever and ever.' And the four animals said, 'Amen'; and the elders prostrated themselves to worship.

The word of the Lord.

Gospel Acclamation Cf. Lk 24:32

R. **Alleluia, alleluia!**
Lord Jesus, explain the scriptures to us.
Make our hearts burn within us as you talk to us.
R. **Alleluia!**

Or:

R. **Alleluia, alleluia!**
Christ has risen: he who created all things,
and has granted his mercy to men.
R. **Alleluia!**

GOSPEL

A reading from the holy Gospel according to John 21:1-19

Jesus stepped forward, took the bread and gave it to them, and the same with the fish.

[Jesus showed himself again to the disciples. It was by the Sea of Tiberias, and it happened like this: Simon Peter, Thomas called the Twin, Nathanael from Cana in Galilee, the sons of Zebedee and two more of his disciples were together. Simon Peter said, 'I'm going fishing.' They replied, 'We'll come with you.' They went out and got into the boat but caught nothing that night.

It was light by now and there stood Jesus on the shore, though the disciples did not realise that it was Jesus. Jesus called out, 'Have you caught anything, friends?' And when they answered, 'No,' he said, 'Throw the net out to starboard and you'll find something.' So they dropped the net, and there were so many fish that they could not haul it in. The disciple Jesus loved said to Peter, 'It is the Lord.' At these words 'It is the Lord', Simon Peter, who had practically nothing on, wrapped his cloak round him and jumped into the water. The other disciples came on in the boat, towing the net and the fish; they were only about a hundred yards from land.

As soon as they came ashore they saw that there was some bread there, and a charcoal fire with fish cooking on it. Jesus said, 'Bring some of the fish you have just caught.' Simon Peter went aboard and dragged the net to the shore, full of big fish, one hundred and fifty-three of them; and in spite of there being so many the net was not broken. Jesus said to them, 'Come and have breakfast.' None of the disciples was bold enough to ask, 'Who are you?'; they knew quite well it was the Lord. Jesus then stepped forward, took the bread and gave it to them, and the same with the fish. This was the third time that Jesus showed himself to the disciples after rising from the dead.]

After the meal Jesus said to Simon Peter, 'Simon son of John, do you love me more than these others do?' He answered 'Yes Lord, you know I love you.' Jesus said to him, 'Feed my lambs.' A second time, he said to him, 'Simon son of John, do you love me?' He replied, 'Yes, Lord, you know I love you.' Jesus said to him, 'Look after my sheep.' Then he said to him a third time, 'Simon son of John, do you love me?' Peter was upset that he asked him the third time, 'Do you love me?' and said, 'Lord, you know everything; you know I love you.' Jesus said to him, 'Feed my sheep.

'I tell you most solemnly,
when you were young
you put on your own belt
and walked where you liked;
but when you grow old
you will stretch out your hands,
and somebody else will put a belt round you
and take you where you would rather not go.'

In these words he indicated the kind of death by which Peter would give glory to God. After this he said, 'Follow me.'

[The Gospel of the Lord.]

Shorter Form, verses 1-14. Read between [ ]

The Creed is said.

Prayer over the Offerings

Receive, O Lord, we pray,
these offerings of your
    exultant Church,
and, as you have given her cause
    for such great gladness,
grant also that the gifts we bring
may bear fruit in perpetual happiness.
Through Christ our Lord.

Preface of Easter, pp.52-57.

Communion Antiphon   Lk 24:35

The disciples recognised
    the Lord Jesus
in the breaking of the bread,
    alleluia.

Optional: Cf. Jn 21:12-13

Jesus said to his disciples:
    Come and eat.
And he took bread and gave it
    to them, alleluia.

Prayer after Communion

Look with kindness upon your
    people, O Lord,
and grant, we pray,
that those you were pleased
    to renew by eternal mysteries
may attain in their flesh
the incorruptible glory
    of the resurrection.
Through Christ our Lord.

Super oblata

Suscipe munera, Domine,
    quæsumus, exsultantis Ecclesiæ,
et cui causam tanti gaudii præstitisti,
perpetuæ fructum concede lætitiæ.
Per Christum Dominum nostrum.

Ant. ad communionem

Cognoverunt discipuli
    Dominum Iesum
in fractione panis, alleluia.

Ad libitum

Dixit Iesus discipulis suis:
    Venite, prandete.
Et accepit panem, et dedit eis,
    alleluia.

Post communionem

Populum tuum, quæsumus,
    Domine, intuere benignus,
et, quem æternis dignatus
    es renovare mysteriis,
ad incorruptibilem glorificandæ
    carnis resurrectionem
pervenire concede.
Per Christum Dominum nostrum.

A formula of Solemn Blessing, pp.136-139, may be used.

21 April

FOURTH SUNDAY OF EASTER

In presenting the mystery of the Church in our time, the Second Vatican Council gave priority to the category of "communion". In this perspective, the rich variety of gifts and ministries acquires great importance for the People of God. All the baptised are called to contribute to the work of salvation. In the Church, however, there are some vocations which are dedicated especially to the service of communion. The person primarily responsible for Catholic communion is the Pope, Successor of Peter and Bishop of Rome; with him, the Bishops, successors of the Apostles, are custodians and teachers of unity, assisted by the priests. But consecrated persons and all the faithful are also at the service of communion. At the heart of Church communion is the Eucharist: the different vocations draw from this supreme Sacrament the spiritual power to build constantly, in charity, the one ecclesial Body.

(Pope Benedict XVI)

Entrance Antiphon   Cf. Ps 32:5-6

THE merciful love of the Lord
fills the earth;
by the word of the Lord the
  heavens were made, alleluia.

Ant. ad introitum

MISERICORDIA Domini plena
est terra;
verbo Domini cæli firmati sunt,
alleluia

The Gloria in excelsis (Glory to God in the highest) is said.

Collect

Almighty ever-living God,
lead us to a share in the joys
  of heaven,
so that the humble flock may reach
where the brave Shepherd
  has gone before.
Who lives and reigns with you
  in the unity of the Holy Spirit,
one God, for ever and ever.

Collecta

Omnipotens sempiterne Deus,
deduc nos ad societatem
  cælestium gaudiorum,
ut eo perveniat humilitas gregis,
quo processit fortitudo pastoris.
Per Dominum nostrum Iesum
  Christum Filium tuum,
qui tecum vivit et regnat
  in unitate Spiritus Sancti,
Deus, per omnia sæcula sæculorum.

FIRST READING

A reading from the Acts of the Apostles   13:14,43-52

We must turn to the pagans.

Paul and Barnabas carried on from Perga till they reached Antioch in Pisidia. Here they went to synagogue on the Sabbath and took their seats.

When the meeting broke up, many Jews and devout converts joined Paul and Barnabas, and in their talks with them Paul and Barnabas urged them to remain faithful to the grace God had given them.

The next sabbath almost the whole town assembled to hear the word of God. When they saw the crowds, the Jews, prompted by jealousy, used blasphemies and contradicted everything Paul said. Then Paul and Barnabas spoke out boldly. 'We had to proclaim the word of God to you first, but since you have rejected it, since you do not think yourselves worthy of eternal life, we must turn to the pagans. For this is what the Lord commanded us to do when he said:

I have made you a light for the nations,
so that my salvation may reach the ends of the earth.'

It made the pagans very happy to hear this and they thanked the Lord for his message; all who were destined for eternal life became believers. Thus the word of the Lord spread through the whole countryside.

But the Jews worked upon some of the devout women of the upper classes and the leading men of the city and persuaded them to turn against Paul and Barnabas and expel them from their territory. So they shook the dust from their feet in defiance and went off to Iconium; but the disciples were filled with joy and the Holy Spirit.

The word of the Lord.

Responsional Psalm   Ps 99:1-3,5. R. v.3

R. **We are his people, the sheep of his flock.**
   Or: Alleluia!

Cry out with joy to the Lord, all the earth.
Serve the Lord with gladness.
Come before him, singing for joy. R.

Know that he, the Lord, is God.
He made us, we belong to him,
we are his people, the sheep of his flock. R.

Indeed, how good is the Lord,
eternal his merciful love.
He is faithful from age to age. R.

SECOND READING

A reading from the book of the Apocalypse   7:9,14-17

The Lamb will be their shepherd and will lead them to springs of living water.

I, John, saw a huge number, impossible to count, of people from every nation, race, tribe and language; they were standing in front of the throne and in front of the Lamb, dressed in white robes and holding palms in their hands. One of the elders said to me, 'These are the people who have been through the great persecution, and because they have washed their robes white again in the blood of the Lamb, they now stand in front of God's throne and serve him day and night in his sanctuary; and the One who sits on the throne will spread his tent over them. They will never hunger or thirst again; neither the sun nor scorching wind will ever plague them, because the Lamb who is at the throne will be their shepherd and will lead them to springs of living water; and God will wipe away all tears from their eyes.'

The word of the Lord.

Gospel Acclamation   Jn 10:14

R. **Alleluia, alleluia!**
I am the good shepherd, says the Lord;
I know my own sheep and my own know me.
R. **Alleluia!**

GOSPEL

A reading from the holy Gospel according to John   10:27-30

I give eternal life to the sheep that belong to me.

Jesus said:

'The sheep that belong to me listen to my voice;
I know them and they follow me.
I give them eternal life;
they will never be lost
and no one will ever steal them from me.
The Father who gave them to me is greater than anyone,
and no one can steal from the Father.
The Father and I are one.'

The Gospel of the Lord.

The Creed is said.

Prayer over the Offerings

Grant, we pray, O Lord,
that we may always find delight
  in these paschal mysteries,
so that the renewal constantly
  at work within us
may be the cause of our unending joy.
Through Christ our Lord.

Preface of Easter, pp.52-57.

Communion Antiphon

The Good Shepherd has risen,
who laid down his life for his sheep
and willingly died for his flock,
  alleluia.

Prayer after Communion

Look upon your flock,
  kind Shepherd,
and be pleased to settle
  in eternal pastures
the sheep you have redeemed
by the Precious Blood of your Son.
Who lives and reigns
  for ever and ever.

Super oblata

Concede, quæsumus, Domine,
semper nos per hæc mysteria
  paschalia gratulari,
ut continua nostræ
  reparationis operatio
perpetuæ nobis fiat causa lætitiæ.
Per Christum Dominum nostrum.

Ant. ad communionem

Surrexit Pastor bonus,
qui animam suam posuit pro
  ovibus suis,
et pro grege suo mori dignatus est,
  alleluia.

Post communionem

Gregem tuum, Pastor bone,
  placatus intende,
et oves, quas pretioso Filii tui
  sanguine redemisti,
in æternis pascuis collocare digneris.
Per Christum Dominum nostrum.

A formula of Solemn Blessing, pp.136-139, may be used.

In England

23 April

SAINT GEORGE, MARTYR, PATRON OF ENGLAND

The Church's action is credible and effective only to the extent to which those who belong to her are prepared to pay in person for their fidelity to Christ in every circumstance. When this readiness is lacking, the crucial argument of truth on which the Church herself depends is also absent. Dear brothers and sisters, as in early times, today too Christ needs apostles ready to sacrifice themselves. He needs witnesses and martyrs.

(Pope Benedict XVI)

SAINT GEORGE, MARTYR, PATRON OF ENGLAND
Solemnity

Entrance Antiphon
Cf. Mt 25:34

REJOICE, you Saints, in the presence of the Lamb;
a kingdom has been prepared for you
from the foundation of the world, alleluia.

Or:
Ps 90:13

On the asp and the viper you will tread,
and trample the young lion and the dragon, alleluia.

The Gloria in excelsis (Glory to God in the highest) is said.

Collect

God of hosts,
who so kindled the fire of charity
in the heart of Saint George your martyr
that he bore witness to the risen Lord
both by his life and by his death,
grant us through his intercession, we pray,
the same faith and power of love,
that we who rejoice in his triumph
may be led to share with him
in the fullness of the resurrection.
Through our Lord Jesus Christ, your Son,
who lives and reigns with you in the unity of the Holy Spirit,
one God, for ever and ever.

FIRST READING

A reading from the book of the Apocalypse
12:10-12

In the face of death they would not cling to life.

I, John, heard a voice shout from heaven, 'Victory and power and empire for ever have been won by our God, and all authority for his Christ, now that the persecutor, who accused our brothers day and night before our God, has been brought down. They have triumphed over him by the blood of the Lamb and by the witness of their martyrdom, because even in the face of death they would not cling to life. Let the heavens rejoice and all who live there.'

The word of the Lord.

Responsorial Psalm
Ps 30

R. **Those who are sowing in tears
will sing when they reap.**

When the Lord delivered Zion from bondage,
it seemed like a dream.

Then was our mouth filled with laughter,
on our lips there were songs. R.

The heathens themselves said: 'What marvels
the Lord worked for them!'
What marvels the Lord worked for us!
Indeed we were glad. R.

Deliver us, O Lord, from our bondage
as streams in dry land.
Those who are sowing in tears
will sing when they reap. R.

They go out, they go out, full of tears,
carrying seed for the sowing;
they come back, they come back, full of song,
carrying their sheaves. R.

A second reading is chosen from the Common of Martyrs.

Gospel Acclamation   Mt 23:9-10

R. **Alleluia, alleluia!**
Happy the man who stands firm,
for he has proved himself,
and will win the crown of life.
R. **Alleluia!**

GOSPEL

A reading from the holy Gospel according to John   15:18-21
If they persecuted me, they will persecute you.

Jesus said to his disciples:
  'If the world hates you,
  remember that it hated me before you.
  If you belonged to the world,
  the world would love you as its own;
  but because you do not belong to the world,
  because my choice withdrew you from the world,
  therefore the world hates you.
  Remember the words I said to you:
  A servant is not greater than his master.
  If they persecuted me,
  they will persecute you too;
  if they kept my word,
  they will keep yours as well.

But it will be on my account that they will do all this,
because they do not know the one who sent me.'

The Gospel of the Lord.

ALTERNATIVE GOSPEL

A reading from the holy Gospel according to John 15:1-8

Whoever remains in me, with me in him, bears fruit in plenty.

Jesus said to his disciples:
'I am the true vine,
and my Father is the vinedresser.
Every branch in me that bears no fruit
he cuts away,
and every branch that does bear fruit he prunes
to make it bear even more.
You are pruned already,
by means of the word that I have spoken to you.
Make your home in me, as I make mine in you.
As a branch cannot bear fruit all by itself,
but must remain part of the vine,
neither can you unless you remain in me.
I am the vine,
you are the branches.
Whoever remains in me, with me in him,
bears fruit in plenty;
for cut off from me you can do nothing.
Anyone who does not remain in me
is like a branch that has been thrown away
– he withers;
these branches are collected and thrown on the fire,
and they are burnt.
If you remain in me
and my words remain in you,
you may ask what you will
and you shall get it.
It is to the glory of my Father that you should bear much fruit,
and then you will be my disciples.'

The Gospel of the Lord.

The Creed is said.

Prayer over the Offerings

Receive, we pray, O Lord,
the sacrifice of conciliation and praise,
which we offer to your majesty
in commemoration of the blessed Martyr Saint George,
that it may lead us to forgiveness
and confirm us in constant thanksgiving.
Through Christ our Lord.

Preface I or II of Holy Martyrs, pp.72-73.

Communion Antiphon   Cf. 2 Tm 2:11-12

If we have died with Christ, we shall also live with him;
if we persevere, we shall also reign with him, alleluia.

Prayer after Communion

Rejoicing on this festival day, O Lord,
we have received your heavenly gifts;
grant, we pray,
that we who in this divine banquet
proclaim the death of your Son
may merit with Saint George to be partakers
in his resurrection and glory.
Through Christ our Lord.

---

28 April

FIFTH SUNDAY OF EASTER

"I, John, saw the holy city, new Jerusalem, coming down out of heaven from God". The splendid vision of the heavenly Jerusalem, which today's Liturgy of the Word presents to us again, closes the Book of Revelation and the whole series of sacred books which comprise the Bible. With this magnificent description of the City of God, the author of Revelation indicates the definitive defeat of evil and the achievement of perfect communion between God and men. From the beginning, the history of salvation aims at this goal. Before the community of believers, who are also called to proclaim the Gospel and to witness to their own faith in Christ amid various trials, the supreme goal shines forth: the heavenly Jerusalem! We are all advancing towards that goal, where the saints and martyrs have preceded us down the centuries. On our earthly pilgrimage, these brethren of ours, who have passed victoriously through "great tribulations", serve as an example, incentive and encouragement to us.

(Blessed Pope John Paul II)

Entrance Antiphon   Cf. Ps 97:1-2

O SING a new song to the Lord,
for he has worked wonders;
in the sight of the nations
he has shown his deliverance,
   alleluia.

Ant. ad introitum

CANTATE Domino
canticum novum,
quia mirabilia fecit Dominus;
ante conspectum gentium revelavit
   iustitiam suam, alleluia.

The Gloria in excelsis (Glory to God in the highest) is said.

Collect

Almighty ever-living God,
constantly accomplish the Paschal
   Mystery within us,
that those you were pleased
   to make new in Holy Baptism
may, under your protective care,
   bear much fruit
and come to the joys of life eternal.
Through our Lord Jesus Christ,
   your Son,
who lives and reigns with you
   in the unity of the Holy Spirit,
one God, for ever and ever.

Collecta

Omnipotens sempiterne Deus,
semper in nobis paschale
   perfice sacramentum,
ut, quos sacro baptismate dignatus
   es renovare,
sub tuæ protectionis auxilio multos
   fructus afferant,
et ad æternæ vitæ gaudia
   pervenire concedas.
Per Dominum nostrum Iesum
   Christum Filium tuum,
qui tecum vivit et regnat
   in unitate Spiritus Sancti,
Deus, per omnia sæcula sæculorum.

FIRST READING

A reading from the Acts of the Apostles   14:21-27

They gave an account to the church of all that God had done with them.

Paul and Barnabas went back through Lystra and Iconium to Antioch. They put fresh heart into the disciples, encouraging them to persevere in the faith. 'We all have to experience many hardships' they said 'before we enter the kingdom of God.' In each of these churches they appointed elders, and with prayer and fasting they commended them to the Lord in whom they had come to believe.

   They passed through Pisidia and reached Pamphylia. Then after proclaiming the word at Perga they went down to Attalia and from there sailed for Antioch, where they had originally been commended to the grace of God for the work they had now completed.

On their arrival they assembled the church and gave an account of all that God had done with them, and how he had opened the door of faith to the pagans.

The word of the Lord.

Responsorial Psalm
Ps 144:8-13. R. Cf. v.1

R. I will bless your name for ever, O God my King.
  Or: Alleluia!

The Lord is kind and full of compassion,
slow to anger, abounding in love.
How good is the Lord to all,
compassionate to all his creatures. R.

All your creatures shall thank you, O Lord,
and your friends shall repeat their blessing.
They shall speak of the glory of your reign
and declare your might, O God,
to make known to men your mighty deeds
and the glorious splendour of your reign. R.

Yours is an everlasting kingdom;
your rule lasts from age to age. R.

SECOND READING

A reading from the book of the Apocalypse
21:1-5

God will wipe away all tears from their eyes.

I, John, saw a new heaven and a new earth; the first heaven and the first earth had disappeared now, and there was no longer any sea. I saw the holy city, and the new Jerusalem, coming down from God out of heaven, as beautiful as a bride all dressed for her husband. Then I heard a loud voice call from the throne, 'You see this city? Here God lives among men. He will make his home among them; they shall be his people, and he will be their God; his name is God-with-them. He will wipe away all tears from their eyes; there will be no more death, and no more mourning or sadness. The world of the past has gone.'

Then the One sitting on the throne spoke: 'Now I am making the whole of creation new.'

The word of the Lord.

Gospel Acclamation
Jn 13:34
R. **Alleluia, alleluia!**
Jesus said: 'I give you a new commandment:
love one another, just as I have loved you.'
R. **Alleluia!**

GOSPEL
A reading from the holy Gospel according to John 13:31-35
I give you a new commandment: love one another.

When Judas had gone Jesus said:
'Now has the Son of Man been glorified,
and in him God has been glorified.
If God has been glorified in him,
God will in turn glorify him in himself,
and will glorify him very soon.
My little children,
I shall not be with you much longer.
I give you a new commandment:
love one another;
just as I have loved you,
you also must love one another.
By this love you have for one another,
everyone will know that you are my disciples.'

The Gospel of the Lord.

The Creed is said.

Prayer over the Offerings

O God, who by the
    wonderful exchange
    effected in this sacrifice
have made us partakers of the one
    supreme Godhead,
grant, we pray,
that, as we have come to know
    your truth,
we may make it ours by a worthy
    way of life.
Through Christ our Lord.
Preface of Easter, pp.52-57.

Super oblata

Deus, qui nos, per huius sacrificii
    veneranda commercia,
unius summæque divinitatis
    participes effecisti,
præsta, quæsumus,
ut, sicut tuam
    cognovimus veritatem,
sic eam dignis
    moribus assequamur.
Per Christum Dominum nostrum.

Communion Antiphon Cf. Jn 15:1,5

I am the true vine and you are the branches, says the Lord.
Whoever remains in me, and I in him, bears fruit in plenty, alleluia.

Prayer after Communion

Graciously be present to your people, we pray, O Lord,
and lead those you have imbued with heavenly mysteries
to pass from former ways to newness of life.
Through Christ our Lord.

Ant. ad communionem

Ego sum vitis vera et vos palmites, dicit Dominus;
qui manet in me et ego in eo, hic fert fructum multum, alleluia.

Post communionem

Populo tuo, quæsumus, Domine, adesto propitius,
et, quem mysteriis cælestibus imbuisti,
fac ad novitatem vitæ de vetustate transire.
Per Christum Dominum nostrum.

A formula of Solemn Blessing, pp.136-139, may be used.

5 May

SIXTH SUNDAY OF EASTER

This Sunday's Gospel, taken from Chapter Fourteen of the Gospel according to St John, gives us an implicit spiritual portrait of the Virgin Mary when Jesus says: "Whoever loves me will keep my word, and my Father will love him, and we will come to him and make our home with him". These words are addressed to the disciples but can be applied to a maximum degree precisely to the One who was the first and perfect disciple of Jesus. Mary, in fact, observed first and fully the words of her Son, showing that she loved him not only as a mother, but first of all as a humble and obedient handmaid. For this reason God the Father loved her and the Most Holy Trinity made its dwelling place in her.

(Pope Benedict XVI)

Entrance Antiphon Cf. Is 48:20

PROCLAIM a joyful sound and let it be heard;
proclaim to the ends of the earth:
The Lord has freed his people, alleluia.

Ant. ad introitum

VOCEM iucunditatis annuntiate, et audiatur,
annuntiate usque ad extremum terræ:
liberavit Dominus populum suum, alleluia.

The Gloria in excelsis (Glory to God in the highest) is said.

Collect

Grant, almighty God,
that we may celebrate with heartfelt
    devotion these days of joy,
which we keep in honour
    of the risen Lord,
and that what we relive
    in remembrance
we may always hold to in what we do.
Through our Lord Jesus Christ,
    your Son,
who lives and reigns with you
    in the unity of the Holy Spirit,
one God, for ever and ever.

Collecta

Fac nos, omnipotens Deus,
    hos lætitiæ dies,
quos in honorem Domini
    resurgentis exsequimur,
affectu sedulo celebrare,
ut quod recordatione percurrimus
semper in opere teneamus.
Per Dominum nostrum Iesum
    Christum Filium tuum,
qui tecum vivit et regnat
    in unitate Spiritus Sancti,
Deus, per omnia sæcula sæculorum.

FIRST READING

A reading from the Acts of the Apostles   15:1-2,22-29

It has been decided by the Holy Spirit and by ourselves not to saddle you with any burden beyond these essentials.

Some men came down from Judaea and taught the brothers, 'Unless you have yourselves circumcised in the tradition of Moses you cannot be saved.' This led to disagreement, and after Paul and Barnabas had had a long argument with these men it was arranged that Paul and Barnabas and others of the church should go up to Jerusalem and discuss the problem with the apostles and elders.

Then the apostles and elders decided to choose delegates to send to Antioch with Paul and Barnabas; the whole church concurred with this. They chose Judas known as Barsabbas and Silas, both leading men in the brotherhood, and gave them this letter to take with them:

'The apostles and elders, your brothers, send greetings to the brothers of pagan birth in Antioch, Syria and Cilicia. We hear that some of our members have disturbed you with their demands and have unsettled your minds. They acted without any authority from us, and so we have decided unanimously to elect delegates and to send them to you with Barnabas and Paul, men we highly respect who have dedicated their lives to the name of our Lord Jesus Christ. Accordingly we are sending you Judas and

Silas, who will confirm by word of mouth what we have written in this letter. It has been decided by the Holy Spirit and by ourselves not to saddle you with any burden beyond these essentials: you are to abstain from food sacrificed to idols, from blood, from the meat of strangled animals and from fornication. Avoid these, and you will do what is right. Farewell.'

The word of the Lord.

Responsorial Psalm

Ps 66:2-3,5-6,8. R. v.4

R. **Let the peoples praise you, O God;**
let all the peoples praise you.
Or: **Alleluia!**

O God, be gracious and bless us
and let your face shed its light upon us.
So will your ways be known upon earth
and all nations learn your saving help. R.

Let the nations be glad and exult
for you rule the world with justice.
With fairness you rule the peoples,
you guide the nations on earth. R.

Let the peoples praise you, O God;
let all the peoples praise you.
May God still give us his blessing
till the ends of the earth revere him. R.

SECOND READING

A reading from the book of the Apocalypse   21:10-14,22-23

He showed me the holy city coming down out of heaven.

In the spirit, the angel took me to the top of an enormous high mountain and showed me Jerusalem, the holy city, coming down from God out of heaven. It had all the radiant glory of God and glittered like some precious jewel of crystal-clear diamond. The walls of it were of a great height, and had twelve gates; at each of the twelve gates there was an angel, and over the gates were written the names of the twelve tribes of Israel; on the east there were three gates, on the north three gates, on the south three gates, and on the west three gates. The city walls stood on twelve foundation stones, each one of which bore the name of one of the twelve apostles of the Lamb.

I saw that there was no temple in the city since the Lord God Almighty and the Lamb were themselves the temple, and the city did not need the sun or the moon for light, since it was lit by the radiant glory of God and the Lamb was a lighted torch for it.

The word of the Lord.

Gospel Acclamation   Jn 14:23

R. **Alleluia, alleluia!**
Jesus said: 'If anyone loves me he will keep my word,
and my Father will love him, and we shall come to him.'
R. **Alleluia!**

GOSPEL

A reading from the holy Gospel according to John   14:23-29
The Holy Spirit will remind you of all I have said to you.

Jesus said to his disciples:
'If anyone loves me he will keep my word,
and my Father will love him,
and we shall come to him
and make our home with him.
Those who do not love me do not keep my words.
And my word is not my own:
it is the word of the one who sent me.
I have said these things to you
while still with you;
but the Advocate, the Holy Spirit,
whom the Father will send in my name,
will teach you everything
and remind you of all I have said to you.
Peace I bequeath to you,
my own peace I give you,
a peace the world cannot give, this is my gift to you.
Do not let your hearts be troubled or afraid.
You heard me say:
I am going away, and shall return.
If you loved me you would have been glad to know that I am going to the Father,

for the Father is greater than I.
I have told you this now before it happens,
so that when it does happen you may believe.'

The Gospel of the Lord.

The Creed is said.

Prayer over the Offerings

May our prayers rise up to you,
  O Lord,
together with the sacrificial offerings,
so that, purified by your graciousness,
we may be conformed to the
  mysteries of your mighty love.
Through Christ our Lord.

Preface of Easter, pp.52-57.

Super oblata

Ascendant ad te, Domine,
  preces nostræ
cum oblationibus hostiarum,
ut, tua dignatione mundati,
sacramentis magnæ
  pietatis aptemur.
Per Christum Dominum nostrum.

Communion Antiphon Jn 14:15-16

If you love me, keep my
  commandments, says the Lord,
and I will ask the Father and he will
  send you another Paraclete,
to abide with you for ever, alleluia.

Ant. ad communionem

Si diligitis me, mandata mea
  servate, dicit Dominus.
Et ego rogabo Patrem, et alium
  Paraclitum dabit vobis,
ut maneat vobiscum in æternum,
  alleluia.

Prayer after Communion

Almighty ever-living God,
who restore us to eternal life
  in the Resurrection of Christ,
increase in us, we pray, the fruits
  of this paschal Sacrament
and pour into our hearts
  the strength of this saving food.
Through Christ our Lord.

Post communionem

Omnipotens sempiterne Deus,
qui ad æternam vitam in Christi
  resurrectione nos reparas,
fructus in nobis paschalis
  multiplica sacramenti,
et fortitudinem cibi salutaris nostris
  infunde pectoribus.
Per Christum Dominum nostrum.

A formula of Solemn Blessing, pp.136-139, may be used.

In Scotland

12 May

SEVENTH SUNDAY OF EASTER

From Luke, and especially from John, we know that Jesus, during the Last Supper, also prayed to the Father – prayers which also contain a plea to his disciples of that time and of all times. Here I would simply like to take one of these which, as John tells us, Jesus repeated four times in his Priestly Prayer. How deeply it must have concerned him! It remains his constant prayer to the Father on our behalf: the prayer for unity. Jesus explicitly states that this prayer is not meant simply for the disciples then present, but for all who would believe in him. He prays that all may be one "as you, Father, are in me and I am in you, so that the world may believe". Christian unity can exist only if Christians are deeply united to him, to Jesus.

(Pope Benedict XVI)

Entrance Antiphon   Cf. Ps 26:7-9

O LORD, hear my voice,
for I have called to you;
of you my heart has spoken:
    Seek his face;
hide not your face from me,
    alleluia.

Ant. ad introitum

EXAUDI, Domine, vocem meam,
qua clamavi ad te.
Tibi dixit cor meum,
    quæsivi vultum tuum,
vultum tuum requiram;
ne avertas faciem tuam a me,
    alleluia.

The Gloria in excelsis (Glory to God in the highest) is said.

Collect

Graciously hear our supplications,
    O Lord,
so that we, who believe that
    the Saviour of the human race
is with you in your glory,
may experience, as he promised,
until the end of the world,
his abiding presence among us.
Who lives and reigns with you
    in the unity of the Holy Spirit,
one God, for ever and ever.

Collecta

Supplicationibus nostris, Domine,
    adesto propitius,
ut, sicut humani generis Salvatorem
tecum in tua credimus maiestate,
ita eum usque
    ad consummationem sæculi
manere nobiscum,
sicut ipse promisit, sentiamus.
Qui tecum vivit et regnat
    in unitate Spiritus Sancti,
Deus, per omnia sæcula sæculorum.

FIRST READING

A reading from the Acts of the Apostles 7:55-60

I can see the Son of Man standing at the right hand of God.

Stephen, filled with the Holy Spirit, gazed into heaven and saw the glory of God, and Jesus standing at God's right hand. 'I can see heaven thrown open' he said 'and the Son of Man standing at the right hand of God.' At this all the members of the council shouted out and stopped their ears with their hands; then they all rushed at him, sent him out of the city and stoned him. The witnesses put down their clothes at the feet of a young man called Saul. As they were stoning him, Stephen said in invocation, 'Lord Jesus, receive my spirit.' Then he knelt down and said aloud, 'Lord, do not hold this sin against them'; and with these words he fell asleep.

The word of the Lord.

Responsorial Psalm
Ps 96:1-2,6-7,9. R. vv.1-9

R. **The Lord is king, most high above all the earth.**
   Or: **Alleluia!**

The Lord is king, let earth rejoice,
the many coastlands be glad.
His throne is justice and right. R.

The skies proclaim his justice;
all peoples see his glory.
All you spirits, worship him. R.

For you indeed are the Lord
most high above all the earth
exalted far above all spirits. R.

SECOND READING

A reading from the book of the Apocalypse 22:12-14,16-17,20

Come, Lord Jesus.

I, John, heard a voice speaking to me: 'Very soon now, I shall be with you again, bringing the reward to be given to every man according to what he deserves. I am the Alpha and the Omega, the First and the Last, the Beginning and the End. Happy are those who will have washed their robes clean, so that they will have the right to feed on the tree of life and can come through the gates into the city.'

I, Jesus, have sent my angel to make these revelations to you for the sake of the churches. I am of David's line, the root of David and the bright star of the morning.

The Spirit and the Bride say, 'Come.' Let everyone who listens answer, 'Come.' Then let all who are thirsty come; all who want it may have the water of life, and have it free.

The one who guarantees these revelations repeats his promise: I shall indeed be with you soon. Amen; come, Lord Jesus.

The word of the Lord.

Gospel Acclamation
Cf. Jn 14:18

R. **Alleluia, alleluia!**
I will not leave you orphans, says the Lord;
I will come back to you, and your hearts will be full of joy.
R. **Alleluia!**

GOSPEL

A reading from the holy Gospel according to John   17:20-26

May they be completely one.

Jesus raised his eyes to heaven and said:
'Holy Father,
I pray not only for these,
but for those also
who through their words will believe in me.
May they all be one.
Father, may they be one in us
as you are in me and I am in you,
so that the world may believe it was you who sent me.
I have given them the glory you gave to me,
that they may be one as we are one.
With me in them and you in me,
may they be so completely one
that the world will realise that it was you who sent me
and that I have loved them as much as you love me.
Father,
I want those you have given me
to be with me where I am,
so that they may always see the glory
you have given me
because you loved me
before the foundation of the world.
Father, Righteous One,

the world has not known you,
but I have known you,
and these have known
that you have sent me.
I have made your name known to them
and will continue to make it known,
so that the love with which you loved me may be in them,
and so that I may be in them.'

The Gospel of the Lord.

The Creed is said.

Prayer over the Offerings

Accept, O Lord, the prayers
  of your faithful
with the sacrificial offerings,
that through these acts
  of devotedness
we may pass over to the glory
  of heaven.
Through Christ our Lord.

Super oblata

Suscipe, Domine, fidelium preces
cum oblationibus hostiarum,
ut, per hæc piæ devotionis officia,
ad cælestem gloriam transeamus.
Per Christum Dominum nostrum.

Preface of Easter, or of the Ascension, pp.52-59.

Communion Antiphon   Jn 17:22

Father, I pray that they may be one
as we also are one, alleluia.

Ant. ad communionem

Rogo, Pater, ut sint unum,
sicut et nos unum sumus, alleluia.

Prayer after Communion

Hear us, O God our Saviour,
and grant us confidence,
that through these sacred mysteries
there will be accomplished
  in the body of the whole Church
what has already come to pass
  in Christ her Head.
Who lives and reigns
  for ever and ever.

Post communionem

Exaudi nos, Deus, salutaris noster,
ut per hæc sacrosancta mysteria
in totius Ecclesiæ confidamus
  corpore faciendum,
quod eius præcessit in capite.
Per Christum Dominum nostrum.

A formula of Solemn Blessing, pp.136-139, may be used.

In England, Wales & Ireland

12 May

THE ASCENSION OF THE LORD

St Bernard of Clairvaux explains that Jesus' Ascension into Heaven is accomplished in three steps: "The first is the glory of the Resurrection; the second is the power to judge; and the third is sitting at the right hand of the Father" (Sermo de Ascensione Domini 60, 2). Such an event is preceded by the blessing of the disciples, whom he prepares to receive the gift of the Holy Spirit, in order that salvation is proclaimed everywhere. Jesus himself says to them: "You are witnesses of these things. And behold, I send the promise of my Father upon you". The Lord draws the gaze of the Apostles, our gaze toward Heaven to show how to travel the road of good during earthly life. Nevertheless, he remains within the framework of human history, he is near to each of us and guides our Christian journey: he is the companion of the those persecuted for the faith, he is in the heart of those who are marginalised, he is present in those whom the right to life is denied. We can hear, see and touch our Lord Jesus in the Church, especially through the word and the sacraments.

(Pope Benedict XVI)

Solemnity

At the Vigil Mass

This Mass is used on the evening of the day before the Solemnity, either before or after First Vespers (Evening Prayer I) of the Ascension.

Entrance Antiphon   Ps 67:33,35

YOU kingdoms of the earth,
  sing to God;
praise the Lord, who ascends above
  the highest heavens;
his majesty and might are in
  the skies, alleluia.

Ant. ad introitum

REGNA terræ cantate Deo,
  psallite Domino,
qui ascendit super cælum cæli;
magnificentia et virtus eius
  in nubibus, alleluia.

The Gloria in excelsis (Glory to God in the highest) is said.

Collect

O God, whose Son today ascended
  to the heavens
as the Apostles looked on,
grant, we pray, that, in accordance
  with his promise,

Collecta

Deus, cuius Filius hodie in cælos,
Apostolis astantibus, ascendit,
concede nobis, quæsumus,
ut secundum eius promissionem
et ille nobiscum semper in terris

we may be worthy for him to live
with us always on earth,
and we with him in heaven.
Who lives and reigns with you
in the unity of the Holy Spirit,
one God, for ever and ever.

et nos cum eo in cælo
vivere mereamur.
Qui tecum vivit et regnat
in unitate Spiritus Sancti,
Deus, per omnia sæcula sæculorum.

FIRST READING

A reading from the Acts of the Apostles 1:1-11

He was lifted up while they looked on.

In my earlier work, Theophilus, I dealt with everything Jesus had done and taught from the beginning until the day he gave his instructions to the apostles he had chosen through the Holy Spirit, and was taken up to heaven. He had shown himself alive to them after his Passion by many demonstrations: for forty days he had continued to appear to them and tell them about the kingdom of God. When he had been at table with them, he had told them not to leave Jerusalem, but to wait there for what the Father had promised. 'It is', he had said, 'what you have heard me speak about: John baptised with water but you, not many days from now, will be baptised with the Holy Spirit.'

Now having met together, they asked him, 'Lord, has the time come? Are you going to restore the kingdom to Israel?' He replied, 'It is not for you to know times or dates that the Father has decided by his own authority, but you will receive power when the Holy Spirit comes on you, and then you will be my witnesses not only in Jerusalem but throughout Judaea and Samaria, and indeed to the ends of the earth.'

As he said this he was lifted up while they looked on, and a cloud took him from their sight. They were still staring into the sky when suddenly two men in white were standing near them and they said, 'Why are you men from Galilee standing here looking into the sky? Jesus who has been taken up from you into heaven, this same Jesus will come back in the same way as you have seen him go there.'

The word of the Lord.

Responsorial Psalm

Ps 46:2-3,6-7,8-9. R. v.6

R. **God goes up with shouts of joy
the Lord goes up with trumpet blast.**
Or: **Alleluia!**

All peoples, clap your hands,
cry to God with shouts of joy!

For the Lord, the Most High, we must fear,
great king over all the earth. R.

God goes up with shouts of joy;
the Lord goes up with trumpet blast.
Sing praise for God, sing praise,
sing praise to our king, sing praise. R.

God is king of all the earth.
Sing praise with all your skill.
God is king over the nations;
God reigns on his holy throne. R.

R. **God goes up with shouts of joy**
the Lord goes up with trumpet blast.
Or: **Alleluia!**

SECOND READING

A reading from the letter to the Hebrews 9:24-28,10:19-23

Christ entered into heaven itself.

It is not as though Christ had entered a man-made sanctuary which was only modelled on the real one; but it was heaven itself, so that he could appear in the actual presence of God on our behalf. And he does not have to offer himself again and again, like the high priest going into the sanctuary year after year with the blood that is not his own, or else he would have had to suffer over and over again since the world began. Instead of that, he has made his appearance once and for all, now at the end of the last age, to do away with sin by sacrificing himself. Since men only die once, and after that comes judgement, so Christ, too, offers himself only once to take the faults of many on himself, and when he appears a second time, it will not be to deal with sin but to reward with salvation those who are waiting for him.

In other words, brothers, through the blood of Jesus we have the right to enter the sanctuary, by a new way which he had opened for us, a living opening through the curtain, that is to say, his body. And we have the supreme high priest over all the house of God. So as we go in, let us be sincere in heart and filled with faith, our minds sprinkled and free from any trace of bad conscience and our bodies washed with pure water. Let us keep firm in the hope we profess, because the one who made the promise is faithful.

The word of the Lord.

Gospel Acclamation

Mt 28:19,20

R. **Alleluia, alleluia!**
Go, make disciples of all nations;
I am with you always; yes, to the end of time.
R. **Alleluia!**

GOSPEL

A reading from the holy Gospel according to Luke 24:46-53

As he blessed them he was carried up to heaven.

Jesus said to his disciples: 'You see how it is written that the Christ would suffer and on the third day rise from the dead, and that, in his name, repentance for the forgiveness of sins would be preached to all the nations, beginning from Jerusalem. You are witnesses to this.

'And now I am sending down to you what the Father has promised. Stay in the city then, until you are clothed with the power from on high.' Then he took them out as far as the outskirts of Bethany, and lifting up his hands he blessed them. Now as he blessed them, he withdrew from them and was carried up to heaven. They worshipped him and then went back to Jerusalem full of joy; and they were continually in the Temple praising God.

The Gospel of the Lord.

The Creed is said.

Prayer over the Offerings	Super oblata
O God, whose Only Begotten Son, our High Priest, is seated ever-living at your right hand to intercede for us, grant that we may approach with confidence the throne of grace and there obtain your mercy. Through Christ our Lord.	Deus, cuius Unigenitus, Pontifex noster, semper vivens sedet ad dexteram tuam ad interpellandum pro nobis, concede nos adire cum fiducia ad thronum gratiæ, ut misericordiam tuam consequamur. Per Christum Dominum nostrum.

Preface I or II of the Ascension of the Lord, pp.58-59.
When the Roman Canon is used, the proper form of the Communicantes (In communion with those) is said.

Communion Antiphon Cf. Heb 10:12	Ant. ad communionem
Christ, offering a single sacrifice for sins, is seated for ever at God's right hand, alleluia.	Christus, unam pro peccatis offerens hostiam, in sempiternum sedet in dextera Dei, alleluia.

Prayer after Communion

May the gifts we have received
    from your altar, Lord,
kindle in our hearts a longing
    for the heavenly homeland
and cause us to press forward,
    following in
    the Saviour's footsteps,
to the place where for our sake
    he entered before us.
Who lives and reigns
    for ever and ever.

Post communionem

Quæ ex altari tuo, Domine,
    dona percepimus,
accendant in cordibus nostris
    cælestis patriæ desiderium,
et quo præcursor pro nobis
    introivit Salvator,
faciant nos, eius vestigia
    sectantes, contendere.
Qui vivit et regnat
    in sæcula sæculorum.

A formula of Solemn Blessing, pp.138-139, may be used.

At the Mass during the Day

Entrance Antiphon   Ac 1:11

MEN of Galilee, why gaze
    in wonder at the heavens?
This Jesus whom you saw
    ascending into heaven
will return as you saw him go,
    alleluia.

Ant. ad introitum

VIRI Galilæi, quid admiramini
    aspicientes in cælum?
Quemadmodum vidistis eum
    ascendentem in cælum,
    ita veniet, alleluia.

The Gloria in excelsis (Glory to God in the highest) is said.

Collect

Gladden us with holy joys,
    almighty God,
and make us rejoice with
    devout thanksgiving,
for the Ascension of Christ your Son
is our exaltation,
and, where the Head has gone
    before in glory,
the Body is called to follow in hope.
Through our Lord Jesus Christ,
    your Son,
who lives and reigns with you
in the unity of the Holy Spirit,
one God, for ever and ever.

Collecta

Fac nos, omnipotens Deus, sanctis
    exsultare gaudiis,
et pia gratiarum actione lætari,
quia Christi Filii tui ascensio est
    nostra provectio,
et quo processit gloria capitis,
    eo spes vocatur et corporis.
Per Dominum nostrum Iesum
    Christum Filium tuum,
qui tecum vivit et regnat
in unitate Spiritus Sancti,
Deus, per omnia sæcula sæculorum.

Or:

Grant, we pray, almighty God,
that we, who believe that your Only
　Begotten Son, our Redeemer,
ascended this day to the heavens,
may in spirit dwell already
　in heavenly realms.
Who lives and reigns with you
　in the unity of the Holy Spirit,
one God, for ever and ever.

Vel:

Concede, quæsumus,
　omnipotens Deus,
ut, qui hodierna die
Unigenitum tuum
　Redemptorem nostrum
ad cælos ascendisse credimus,
ipsi quoque mente
　in cælestibus habitemus.
tecum vivit et regnat
　in unitate Spiritus Sancti,
Deus, per omnia sæcula sæculorum.

FIRST READING

A reading from the Acts of the Apostles　　　　　　　　1:1-11

He was lifted up while they looked on.

In my earlier work, Theophilus, I dealt with everything Jesus had done and taught from the beginning until the day he gave his instructions to the apostles he had chosen through the Holy Spirit, and was taken up to heaven. He had shown himself alive to them after his Passion by many demonstrations: for forty days he had continued to appear to them and tell them about the kingdom of God. When he had been at table with them, he had told them not to leave Jerusalem, but to wait there for what the Father had promised. 'It is', he had said, 'what you have heard me speak about: John baptised with water but you, not many days from now, will be baptised with the Holy Spirit.'

　Now having met together, they asked him, 'Lord, has the time come? Are you going to restore the kingdom to Israel?' He replied, 'It is not for you to know times or dates that the Father has decided by his own authority, but you will receive power when the Holy Spirit comes on you, and then you will be my witnesses not only in Jerusalem but throughout Judaea and Samaria, and indeed to the ends of the earth.'

　As he said this he was lifted up while they looked on, and a cloud took him from their sight. They were still staring into the sky when suddenly two men in white were standing near them and they said, 'Why are you men from Galilee standing here looking into the sky? Jesus who has been taken up from you into heaven, this same Jesus will come back in the same way as you have seen him go there.'

　The word of the Lord.

Responsorial Psalm
Ps 46:2-3,6-7,8-9. R. v.6

R. **God goes up with shouts of joy**
the Lord goes up with trumpet blast.
Or: **Alleluia!**

All peoples, clap your hands,
cry to God with shouts of joy!
For the Lord, the Most High, we must fear,
great king over all the earth. R.

God goes up with shouts of joy;
the Lord goes up with trumpet blast.
Sing praise for God, sing praise,
sing praise to our king, sing praise. R.

God is king of all the earth.
Sing praise with all your skill.
God is king over the nations;
God reigns on his holy throne. R.

SECOND READING

A reading from the letter to the Hebrews
9:24-28,10:19-23

Christ entered into heaven itself.

It is not as though Christ had entered a man-made sanctuary which was only modelled on the real one; but it was heaven itself, so that he could appear in the actual presence of God on our behalf. And he does not have to offer himself again and again, like the high priest going into the sanctuary year after year with the blood that is not his own, or else he would have had to suffer over and over again since the world began. Instead of that, he has made his appearance once and for all, now at the end of the last age, to do away with sin by sacrificing himself. Since men only die once, and after that comes judgement, so Christ, too, offers himself only once to take the faults of many on himself, and when he appears a second time, it will not be to deal with sin but to reward with salvation those who are waiting for him.

In other words, brothers, through the blood of Jesus we have the right to enter the sanctuary, by a new way which he had opened for us, a living opening through the curtain, that is to say, his body. And we have the supreme high priest over all the house of God. So as we go in, let us be sincere in heart and filled with faith, our minds sprinkled and free from any trace of bad conscience and our bodies washed with pure water. Let us keep firm in the hope we profess, because the one who made the promise is faithful.

The word of the Lord.

Gospel Acclamation
Mt 28:19,20

R. **Alleluia, alleluia!**
Go, make disciples of all nations;
I am with you always; yes, to the end of time.
R. **Alleluia!**

GOSPEL

A reading from the holy Gospel according to Luke 24:46-53

As he blessed them he was carried up to heaven.

Jesus said to his disciples: 'You see how it is written that the Christ would suffer and on the third day rise from the dead, and that, in his name, repentance for the forgiveness of sins would be preached to all the nations, beginning from Jerusalem. You are witnesses to this.

'And now I am sending down to you what the Father has promised. Stay in the city then, until you are clothed with the power from on high.' Then he took them out as far as the outskirts of Bethany, and lifting up his hands he blessed them. Now as he blessed them, he withdrew from them and was carried up to heaven. They worshipped him and then went back to Jerusalem full of joy; and they were continually in the Temple praising God.

The Gospel of the Lord.

The Creed is said.

Prayer over the Offerings	Super oblata

We offer sacrifice now
   in supplication, O Lord,
to honour the wondrous Ascension
   of your Son:
grant, we pray,
that through this most holy exchange
we, too, may rise up to
   the heavenly realms.
Through Christ our Lord.
	Sacrificium, Domine,
	   pro Filii tui supplices
	venerabili nunc
	   ascensione deferimus:
	præsta, quæsumus,
	   ut his commerciis sacrosanctis
	ad cælestia consurgamus.
	Per Christum Dominum nostrum.

Preface I or II of the Ascension of the Lord, pp.58-59.
When the Roman Canon is used, the proper form of the Communicantes (In communion with those) is said.

Communion Antiphon Mt 28:20	Ant. ad communionem
Behold, I am with you always, even to the end of the age, alleluia.	Ecce ego vobiscum sum omnibus diebus, usque ad consummationem sæculi, alleluia.

Prayer after Communion

Almighty ever-living God,
who allow those on earth
   to celebrate divine mysteries,
grant, we pray,
that Christian hope may draw
   us onward
to where our nature is united
   with you.
Through Christ our Lord.

Post communionem

Omnipotens sempiterne Deus,
qui in terra constitutos divina
   tractare concedis,
præsta, quæsumus,
ut illuc tendat christianæ
   devotionis affectus,
quo tecum est nostra substantia.
Per Christum Dominum nostrum.

A formula of Solemn Blessing, pp.138-139, may be used.

---

19 May

PENTECOST SUNDAY

In the solemn celebration of Pentecost we are invited to profess our faith in the presence and in the action of the Holy Spirit and to invoke his outpouring upon us, upon the Church and upon the whole world. With special intensity, let us make our own the Church's invocation: Veni, Sancte Spiritus! It is such a simple and spontaneous invocation, yet also extraordinarily profound, which came first of all from the heart of Christ. The Spirit is indeed the gift that Jesus asked and continues to ask of his Father for his friends; the first and principal gift that he obtained for us through his Resurrection and Ascension into heaven.

Today's Gospel passage, which has the Last Supper as its context, speaks to us of this prayer of Christ. The Lord Jesus said to his disciples: "If you love me, you will keep my commandments. And I will pray the Father, and he will give you another Counsellor, to be with you for ever". Here the praying heart of Jesus is revealed to us, his filial and fraternal heart. This prayer reaches its apex and its fulfilment on the Cross, where Christ's invocation is one with the total gift that he makes of himself, and thus his prayer becomes, so to speak, the very seal of his self-gift out of love of the Father and humanity.

(Pope Benedict XVI)

At the Vigil Mass
EXTENDED FORM

This Vigil Mass may be celebrated on the Saturday evening, either before or after First Vespers (Evening Prayer I) of Pentecost Sunday.

In churches where the Vigil Mass is celebrated in an extended form, this may be done as follows.

a) If First Vespers (Evening Prayer I) celebrated in choir or in common immediately precede Mass, the celebration may begin either from the introductory verse and the hymn (Veni, creator Spiritus) or else from the singing of the Entrance Antiphon with the procession and greeting of the Priest; in either case the Penitential Act is omitted (Cf. General Instruction of the Liturgy of the Hours, nos. 94 and 96).

Then the Psalmody prescribed for Vespers follows, up to but not including the Short Reading.

After the Psalmody, omitting the Penitential Act, and if appropriate, the Kyrie (Lord, have mercy), the Priest says the prayer Grant, we pray, almighty God, that the splendour, as at the Vigil Mass.

b) If Mass is begun in the usual way, after the Kyrie (Lord, have mercy), the Priest says the prayer Grant, we pray, almighty God, that the splendour, as at the Vigil Mass.

Then the Priest may address the people in these or similar words:

Dear brethren (brothers and sisters), we have now begun our Pentecost Vigil, after the example of the Apostles and disciples who with Mary, the Mother of Jesus, persevered in prayer, awaiting the Spirit promised by the Lord; like them, let us, too, listen with quiet hearts to the Word of God. Let us meditate on how many great deeds God in times past did for his people and let us pray that the Holy Spirit, whom the Father sent as the first fruits for those who believe, may bring to perfection his work in the world.	Vigiliam Pentecostes ingressi, fratres carissimi, ad exemplum Apostolorum et discipulorum qui, cum Maria, Matre Iesu, instabant in oratione, exspectantes Spiritum a Domino promissum, quieto corde nunc verbum Dei audiamus. Meditemur quanta fecit Deus populo suo et oremus, ut Spiritus Sanctus quem Pater misit primitias credentibus, opus suum in mundo perficiat.

Then follow the readings proposed as options in the Lectionary. A reader goes to the ambo and proclaims the reading. Afterwards a psalmist or a cantor sings or says the Psalm with the people making the response. Then all rise, the Priest says, Let us pray and, after all have prayed for a while in silence, he says the prayer corresponding to the reading. In place of the Responsorial Psalm a period of sacred silence may be observed, in which case the pause after Let us pray is omitted.

FIRST READING

A reading from the book of Genesis 11:1-9

It was named Babel because there the language of the whole earth was confused.

Throughout the earth men spoke the same language, with the same vocabulary. Now as they moved eastwards they found a plain in the land of Shinar where they settled. They said to one another, 'Come, let us make bricks and bake them in the fire.' – For stone they used bricks, and for mortar they used bitumen. – 'Come,' they said 'let us build ourselves a town and a tower with its top reaching heaven. Let us make a name for ourselves, so that we may not be scattered about the whole earth.'

Now the Lord came down to see the town and the tower that the sons of man had built. 'So they are all a single people with a single language!' said the Lord. 'This is but the start of their undertakings! There will be nothing too hard for them to do. Come, let us go down and confuse their language on the spot so that they can no longer understand one another.' The Lord scattered them thence over the whole face of the earth, and they stopped building the town. It was named Babel therefore, because there the Lord confused the language of the whole earth. It was from there that the Lord scattered them over the whole face of the earth.

The word of the Lord.

Responsorial Psalm Ps 32:10-11,12-13,14-15 R. v.12b

R. **Happy the people the Lord has chosen as his own.**

He frustrates the designs of the nations,
he defeats the plans of the peoples.
His own designs shall stand for ever,
the plans of his heart from age to age. R.

They are happy, whose God is the Lord,
the people he has chosen as his own.
From the heavens the Lord looks forth,
he sees all the children of men. R.

From the place where he dwells he gazes
on all the dwellers on the earth,
he who shapes the hearts of them all
and considers all their deeds. R.

Prayer

Let us pray.
Grant, we pray, almighty God,
that your Church may always
   remain that holy people,
formed as one by the unity
of Father, Son and Holy Spirit,
which manifests to the world
the Sacrament of your holiness
   and unity
and leads it to the perfection
   of your charity.
Through Christ our Lord.
R. Amen.

Oremus.
Concede, qucesumus,
   omnipotens Deus,
ut Ecclesia tua semper ea plebs
   sancta permaneat
de unitate Patris et Filii
   et Spiritus Sancti adunata,
quce tuce sanctitatis
   et unitatis sacramentum
mundo manifestet
et ipsum ad perfectionem
   tuce conducat caritatis.
Per Christum Dominum nostrum.
R. Amen.

SECOND READING

A reading from the book of Exodus 19:3-8,16-20
The Lord came down on the mountain of Sinai before all the people.

Moses went up to God, and the Lord called to him from the mountain, saying, 'Say this to the House of Jacob, declare this to the sons of Israel, "You yourselves have seen what I did with the Egyptians, how I carried you on eagle's wings and brought you to myself. From this you know that now, if you obey my voice and hold fast to my covenant, you of all the nations shall be my very own, for all the earth is mine. I will count you a kingdom of priests, a consecrated nation." Those are the words you are to speak to the sons of Israel.' So Moses went and summoned the elders of the people, putting before them all that the Lord had bidden him. Then all the people answered as one, 'All that the Lord has said, we will do.'

Now at daybreak on the third day there were peals of thunder on the mountain and lightning flashes, a dense cloud, and a loud trumpet blast, and inside the camp all the people trembled. Then Moses led the people out of the camp to meet God; and they stood at the bottom of the mountain. The mountain of Sinai was entirely wrapped in smoke, because the Lord had descended on it in the form of fire. Like smoke from a furnace the smoke went up, and the whole mountain shook violently. Louder and louder grew the sound of the trumpet. Moses spoke, and God answered him with peals of thunder. The Lord came down on the mountain of Sinai, on the mountain top, and the Lord called Moses to the top of the mountain.

The word of the Lord.

Responsorial Psalm
Dn 3:52,53,54,55,56. R. v.52b

R. **To you glory and praise for evermore.**

You are blest, Lord God of our fathers. R.
Blest your glorious holy name. R.
You are blest in the temple of your glory. R.
You are blest on the throne of your kingdom. R.
You are blest who gaze into the depths. R.
You are blest in the firmament of heaven. R.

Or
Ps 18:8,9,10,11. R. Jn v.6:68c

R. **You have the message of eternal life, O Lord.**

The law of the Lord is perfect,
it revives the soul.
The rule of the Lord is to be trusted,
it gives wisdom to the simple. R.

The precepts of the Lord are right,
they gladden the heart.
The command of the Lord is clear,
it gives light to the eyes. R.

The fear of the Lord is holy,
abiding for ever.
The decrees of the Lord are truth
and all of them just. R.

They are more to be desired than gold,
than the purest of gold
and sweeter are they than honey,
than honey from the comb. R.

Prayer

Let us pray.	Oremus.
O God, who in fire and lightning gave the ancient Law to Moses on Mount Sinai and on this day manifested the new covenant in the fire of the Spirit, grant, we pray, that we may always be aflame with that same Spirit whom you wondrously poured out on your Apostles,	Deus, qui in fulgure ignis in monte Sinai legem antiquam Moysi dedisti et fœdus novum in igne Spiritus hoc die manifestasti, presta, quæsumus, ut illo iugiter Spiritu ferveamus, quem Apostolis tuis ineffabiliter infudisti,

and that the new Israel,
gathered from every people,
may receive with rejoicing
the eternal commandment
    of your love.
Through Christ our Lord.
R. Amen.

et novus Israel,
ex omni populo congregatus,
mandatum æternum tui amoris
    lætanter accipiat.
Per Christum Dominum nostrum.
R. Amen.

THIRD READING

A reading from the prophet Ezekiel 37:1-14

Dry bones, I am going to make the breath enter you, and you will live.

The hand of the Lord was laid on me, and he carried me away by the spirit of the Lord and set me down in the middle of a valley, a valley full of bones. He made me walk up and down among them. There were vast quantities of these bones on the ground the whole length of the valley; and they were quite dried up. He said to me, 'Son of man, can these bones live?' I said, 'You know, Lord.' He said, 'Prophesy over these bones. Say, "Dry bones, hear the word of the Lord. The Lord says this to these bones: I am now going to make the breath enter you, and you will live. I shall put sinews on you, I shall make flesh grow on you, I shall cover you with skin and give you breath, and you will live, and you will learn that I am the Lord."' I prophesied as I had been ordered. While I was prophesying, there was a noise, a sound of clattering; and the bones joined together. I looked, and saw that they were covered with sinews; flesh was growing on them and skin was covering them, but there was no breath in them. He said to me, 'Prophesy to the breath; prophesy, son of man. Say to the breath, "The Lord says this: Come from the four winds, breath; breathe on these dead; let them live!"' I prophesied as he had ordered me, and the breath entered them; they came to life again and stood up on their feet, a great, an immense army.

Then he said, 'Son of man, these bones are the whole House of Israel. They keep saying, "Our bones are dried up, our hope has gone; we are as good as dead." So prophesy. Say to them, "The Lord says this: I am now going to open your graves; I mean to raise you from your graves, my people, and lead you back to the soil of Israel. And you will know that I am the Lord, when I open your graves and raise you from your graves, my people. And I shall put my spirit in you, and you will live, and I shall resettle you on your own soil; and you will know that I, the Lord have said and done this – it is the Lord who speaks."'

The word of the Lord.

Responsorial Psalm
Ps 106:2-3,4-5,6–7,8–9. R. v.1

R. **O give thanks to the Lord, for he is good;
for his love has no end.**
Or: **Alleluia!**

Let them say this, the Lord's redeemed,
whom he redeemed from the hand of the foe
and gathered from far-off lands,
from east and west, north and south. R.

Some wandered in the desert, in the wilderness,
finding no way to a city they could dwell in.
Hungry they were and thirsty;
their soul was fainting within them. R.

Then they cried to the Lord in their need
and he rescued them from their distress
and he led them along the right way,
to reach a city they could dwell in. R.

Let them thank the Lord for his love,
for the wonders he does for men.
For he satisfies the thirsty soul;
he fills the hungry with good things. R.

Prayer

Let us pray.
Lord, God of power,
who restore what has fallen
and preserve what you have restored,
increase, we pray, the peoples
to be renewed by the sanctification
  of your name,
that all who are washed clean
  by holy Baptism
may always be directed
  by your prompting.
Through Christ our Lord.
R. Amen.

Or:
O God, who have brought us
  to rebirth by the word of life,
pour out upon us your Holy Spirit,
that, walking in oneness of faith,

Oremus.
Domine, Deus virtutum,
qui coliapsa reparas
  et reparata conservas,
auge populos in tui nominis
  sanctificatione renovandos,
ut omnes, qui sacro
  Baptismate diluuntur,
tua semper inspiratione dirigantur.
Per Christum Dominum nostrum.
R. Amen.

Vel:
Deus, qui nos verbo vitæ regenerasti,
effunde super nos
  Spiritum Sanctum tuum,
ut, in unitate fidei ambulantes,

we may attain in our flesh
the incorruptible glory
   of the resurrection.
Through Christ our Lord.
R. Amen.

Or:

May your people exult for ever,
   O God,
in renewed youthfulness of spirit,
so that, rejoicing now in the restored
   glory of our adoption,
we may look forward
in confident hope
to the rejoicing of the day
   of resurrection.
Through Christ our Lord.
R. Amen.

ad incorruptibilem glorificandæ
   carnis resurrectionem
pervenlre mereamur.
Per Christum Dominum nostrum.
R. Amen.

Vel:

Semper exsultet populus
   tuus, Deus,
Spiritu Sancto tuo renovata
   animce iuventute,
ut, qui nunc lætatur in adoptionis
   se gloriam restitutum,
resurrectionis diem spe certæ
   gratulationis exspectet.
Per Christum Dominum nostrum.
R. Amen.

FOURTH READING

A reading from the prophet Joel   3:1-5

I will pour out my spirit on all people.

Thus says the Lord:
   'I will pour out my spirit on all mankind.
   Your sons and daughters shall prophesy,
   your old men shall dream dreams,
   and your young men see visions.
   Even on the slaves, men and women,
   will I pour out my spirit in those days.
   I will display portents in heaven and on earth,
   blood and fire and columns of smoke.'
The sun will be turned into darkness,
and the moon into blood,
before the day of the Lord dawns,
that great and terrible day.
All who call on the name of the Lord will be saved,
for on Mount Zion there will be some who have escaped,
as the Lord has said,
and in Jerusalem some survivors whom the Lord will call.

   The word of the Lord.

Responsorial Psalm
Ps103:1-2a,24,35c,27–28,29bc-30. R. v.30

R. **Send forth your Spirit, O Lord,
and renew the face of the earth.**
Or: **Alleluia!**

Bless the Lord, my soul!
Lord God, how great you are,
clothed in majesty and glory,
wrapped in light as in a robe! R.

How many are your works, O Lord!
In wisdom you have made them all.
The earth is full of your riches.
Bless the Lord, my soul. R.

All of these look to you
to give them their food in due season.
You give it, they gather it up:
you open your hand, they have their fill. R.

You take back your spirit, they die,
returning to the dust from which they came.
You send forth your spirit, they are created;
and you renew the face of the earth. R.

Prayer

Let us pray.	Oremus.
Fulfil for us your gracious promise, O Lord, we pray, so that by his coming the Holy Spirit may make us witnesses before the world to the Gospel of our Lord Jesus Christ. Who lives and reigns for ever and ever.	Promissionem tuam, quæsumus, Domine, super nos propitiatus adimple, ut Spiritus Sanctus adveniens nos coram mundo testes efficiat Evangelii Domini nostri Iesu Christi. Qui tecum vivit et regnat in sæcula sæculorum.
R. Amen.	R. Amen.

Then the Priest intones the hymn Gloria in excelsis Deo (Glory to God in the highest).
When the hymn is concluded, the Priest says the Collect in the usual way: Almighty ever-living God, who willed, as here below (p.443).
Then the reader proclaims the reading from the Apostle (Rm 8:22-27) pp.444-445, and Mass continues in the usual way.

At the Vigil Mass
SIMPLE FORM

If Vespers (Evening Prayer) are joined to Mass, after Communion with the Communion Antiphon (On the last day), the Magnificat is sung, with its Vespers antiphon (Veni, Sancte Spiritus); then the Prayer after Communion is said and the rest follows as usual.

This Mass is used on the Saturday evening, either before or after First Vespers (Evening Prayer I) of Pentecost Sunday.

Entrance Antiphon Rm 5:5; Cf. 8:11

THE love of God has been poured into our hearts through the Spirit of God dwelling within us, alleluia.

Ant. ad introitum

CARITAS Dei diffusa est in cordibus nostris per inhabitantem Spiritum eius in nobis, alleluia.

The Gloria in excelsis (Glory to God in the highest) is said.

Collect

Almighty ever-living God,
who willed the Paschal Mystery
to be encompassed as a sign
　in fifty days,
grant that from out
　of the scattered nations
the confusion of many tongues
may be gathered by heavenly grace
into one great confession
　of your name.
Through our Lord Jesus Christ,
　your Son,
who lives and reigns with you
　in the unity of the Holy Spirit,
one God, for ever and ever.

Collecta

Omnipotens sempiterne Deus,
qui paschale sacramentum
quinquaginta dierum voluisti
　mysterio contineri,
præsta, ut, gentium
　facta dispersione,
divisiones linguarum ad unam
　confessionem tui nominis
cælesti munere congregentur.
Per Dominum nostrum Iesum
　Christum Filium tuum,
qui tecum vivit et regnat
　in unitate Spiritus Sancti,
Deus, per omnia sæcula sæculorum.

Or:

Grant, we pray, almighty God,
that the splendour of your glory
may shine forth upon us
and that, by the bright rays
　of the Holy Spirit,
the light of your light may confirm
　the hearts
of those born again by your grace.

Vel:

Præsta, quæsumus,
　omnipotens Deus,
ut claritatis tuæ super nos
　splendor effulgeat,
et lux tuæ lucis corda eorum,
qui per tuam gratiam sunt renati,
Sancti Spiritus
　illustratione confirmet.

Through our Lord Jesus Christ, your Son, who lives and reigns with you in the unity of the Holy Spirit, one God, for ever and ever.	Per Dominum nostrum Iesum Christum Filium tuum, qui tecum vivit et regnat in unitate Spiritus Sancti, Deus, per omnia sæcula sæculorum.

FIRST READING

There is a choice of four texts for the First Reading: Either Genesis 11:1-9 (On Babel), p.436; or Exodus 19:3-8,16-20 (On God's descent on Mount Sinai), p.437; or Ezekiel 37:1-14 (On the dry bones and God's spirit), p.439; or Joel 3:1-5 (On the outpouring of the Spirit), p.441.

Responsorial Psalm   Ps 103:1-2,24,27-30,35. R. Cf. v.30

R. **Send forth your spirit, O Lord,
and renew the face of the earth.**
Or: **Alleluia!**

Bless the Lord, my soul!
Lord God, how great you are,
clothed in majesty and glory,
wrapped in light as in a robe! R.

How many are your works, O Lord!
In wisdom you have made them all.
The earth is full of your riches.
Bless the Lord, my soul. R.

All of these look to you
to give them their food in due season.
You give it, they gather it up:
you open your hand, they have their fill. R.

You take back your spirit, they die,
returning to the dust from which they came.
You send forth your spirit, they are created;
and you renew the face of the earth. R.

SECOND READING

A reading from the letter of St Paul to the Romans   8:22-27

The Spirit himself expresses our plea in a way that could never be put into words.

From the beginning till now the entire creation, as we know, has been groaning in one great act of giving birth; and not only creation, but all of us who possess the first-fruits of the Spirit, we too groan inwardly as we wait for our bodies to be set free. For we must be content to hope that we shall be saved – our salvation is not in sight, we should not have to be hoping for it if it were – but, as I say, we must hope to be saved since we are not saved yet – it is something we must wait for with patience.

The Spirit too comes to help us in our weakness. For when we cannot choose words in order to pray properly, the Spirit himself expresses our plea in a way that could never be put into words, and God who knows everything in our hearts knows perfectly well what he means, and that the pleas of the saints expressed by the Spirit are according to the mind of God.

The word of the Lord.

Gospel Acclamation

R. **Alleluia, alleluia!**
Come, Holy Spirit, fill the hearts of your faithful
and kindle in them the fire of your love.
R. **Alleluia!**

GOSPEL

A reading from the holy Gospel according to John 7:37-39
From his breast shall flow fountains of living water.

On the last day and greatest day of the festival, Jesus stood there and cried out:

'If any man is thirsty, let him come to me!
Let the man come and drink who believes in me!'

As scripture says: From his breast shall flow fountains of living water.

He was speaking of the Spirit which those who believed in him were to receive; for there was no Spirit as yet because Jesus had not yet been glorified.

The Gospel of the Lord.
The Creed is said.

Prayer over the Offerings

Pour out upon these gifts
  the blessing of your Spirit,
we pray, O Lord,
so that through them your Church
  may be imbued with such love
that the truth of your saving mystery
may shine forth for the whole world.
Through Christ our Lord.

Super oblata

Præsentia munera,
  quæsumus, Domine,
Spiritus tui benedictione perfunde,
ut per ipsa Ecclesiæ tuæ
  ea dilectio tribuatur,
per quam salutaris mysterii toto
  mundo veritas enitescat.
Per Christum Dominum nostrum.

Preface: The Mystery of Pentecost.

It is truly right and just,
  our duty and our salvation,
always and everywhere
  to give you thanks,
Lord, holy Father,
  almighty and eternal God.

For, bringing your Paschal Mystery
  to completion,
you bestowed the Holy Spirit today
on those you made
  your adopted children
by uniting them to your Only
  Begotten Son.
This same Spirit,
  as the Church came to birth,
opened to all peoples
  the knowledge of God
and brought together the many
  languages of the earth
in profession of the one faith.

Therefore, overcome with paschal joy,
every land, every people exults
  in your praise
and even the heavenly Powers,
  with the angelic hosts,
sing together the unending hymn
  of your glory,
as they acclaim:

Holy, Holy, Holy Lord God of hosts...

Præfatio: De mysterio Pentecostes.

Vere dignum et iustum est,
  æquum et salutare,
nos tibi semper et ubique
  gratias agere:
Domine, sancte Pater,
  omnipotens æterne Deus.

Tu enim, sacramentum
  paschale consummans,
quibus, per Unigeniti tui consortium,
filios adoptionis esse tribuisti,
hodie Spiritum Sanctum es largitus;
qui, principio nascentis Ecclesiæ,
et cunctis gentibus scientiam
  indidit deitatis,
et linguarum diversitatem in unius
  fidei confessione sociavit.

Quapropter, profusis
  paschalibus gaudiis,
totus in orbe terrarum
  mundus exsultat.
Sed et supernæ virtutes atque
  angelicæ potestates
hymnum gloriæ tuæ concinunt,
  sine fine dicentes:

Sanctus, Sanctus, Sanctus. . .

When the Roman Canon is used, the proper form of the Communicantes (In communion with those) is said.

Communion Antiphon   Jn 7:37

On the last day of the festival,
  Jesus stood and cried out:
If anyone is thirsty, let him come
  to me and drink, alleluia.

Ant. ad communionem

Ultimo festivitatis die, stabat Iesus
  et clamabat dicens:
Si quis sitit, veniat ad me et bibat,
  alleluia.

### Prayer after Communion	### Post communionem
May these gifts we have consumed benefit us, O Lord, that we may always be aflame with the same Spirit, whom you wondrously poured out on your Apostles. Through Christ our Lord.	Hæc nobis, Domine, munera sumpta proficiant, ut illo iugiter Spiritu ferveamus, quem Apostolis tuis ineffabiliter infudisti. Per Christum Dominum nostrum.

A formula of Solemn Blessing, pp.138-141, may be used.

To dismiss the people the Deacon or, if there is no Deacon, the Priest himself sings or says:

Go forth, the Mass is ended, alleluia, alleluia.	Ite, missa est, alleluia, alleluia.
Or:	Vel:
Go in peace, alleluia, alleluia.	Ite in pace, alleluia, alleluia.
And the people reply:	Omnes respondent:
Thanks be to God, alleluia, alleluia.	R. Deo gratias, alleluia, alleluia.

At the Mass during the Day

### Entrance Antiphon Ws 1:7	### Ant. ad introitum
THE Spirit of the Lord has filled the whole world and that which contains all things understands what is said, alleluia.	SPIRITUS Domini replevit orbem terrarum, et hoc quod continet omnia scientiam habet vocis, alleluia.
Or: Rm 5:5; Cf. 8:11	Vel:
The love of God has been poured into our hearts through the Spirit of God dwelling within us, alleluia.	Caritas Dei diffusa est in cordibus nostris per inhabitantem Spiritum eius in nobis, alleluia.

The Gloria in excelsis (Glory to God in the highest) is said.

### Collect	### Collecta
O God, who by the mystery of today's great feast sanctify your whole Church in every people and nation,	Deus, qui sacramento festivitatis hodiernæ universam Ecclesiam tuam in omni gente et natione sanctificas,

pour out, we pray, the gifts
   of the Holy Spirit
across the face of the earth
and, with the divine grace that
   was at work
when the Gospel
   was first proclaimed,
fill now once more the hearts
   of believers.
Through our Lord Jesus Christ,
   your Son,
who lives and reigns with you
   in the unity of the Holy Spirit,
one God, for ever and ever.

in totam mundi latitudinem
   Spiritus Sancti dona defunde,
et, quod inter ipsa evangelicæ
   prædicationis exordia
operata est divina dignatio,
nunc quoque per credentium
   corda perfunde.
Per Dominum nostrum Iesum
   Christum Filium tuum,
qui tecum vivit et regnat
   in unitate Spiritus Sancti,
Deus, per omnia sæcula sæculorum.

FIRST READING

A reading from the Acts of the Apostles 2:1-11

They were all filled with the Holy Spirit and began to speak.

When Pentecost day came round, the apostles had all met in one room, when suddenly they heard what sounded like a powerful wind from heaven, the noise of which filled the entire house in which they were sitting; and something appeared to them that seemed like tongues of fire; these separated and came to rest on the head of each of them. They were all filled with the Holy Spirit, and began to speak foreign languages as the Spirit gave them the gift of speech.

Now there were devout men living in Jerusalem from every nation under heaven, and at this sound they all assembled, each one bewildered to hear these men speaking his own language. They were amazed and astonished. 'Surely' they said 'all these men speaking are Galileans? How does it happen that each of us hears them in his own native language? Parthians, Medes and Elamites; people from Mesopotamia, Judaea and Cappadocia, Pontus and Asia, Phrygia and Pamphylia, Egypt and the parts of Libya round Cyrene; as well as visitors from Rome – Jews and proselytes alike – Cretans and Arabs; we hear them preaching in our own language about the marvels of God.'

The word of the Lord.

Responsional Psalm
Ps 103:1,24,29-31,34. R. Cf. v.30

R. **Send forth your Spirit, O Lord,
and renew the face of the earth**.
Or: **Alleluia!**

Bless the Lord, my soul!
Lord God, how great you are.
How many are your works, O Lord!
The earth is full of your riches. R.

You take back your spirit, they die,
returning to the dust from which they came.
You send forth your spirit, they are created;
and you renew the face of the earth. R.

May the glory of the Lord last for ever!
May the Lord rejoice in his works!
May my thoughts be pleasing to him.
I find my joy in the Lord. R.

The readings for Year C are included in full below. The readings for Year A may also be used for the Second Reading and Gospel on this feast: Co 12:3-7,12-13; Jn 20:19-23.

SECOND READING

A reading from the letter of St Paul to the Romans   8:8-17

Everyone moved by the Spirit is a son of God.

People who are interested only in unspiritual things can never be pleasing to God. Your interests, however, are not in the unspiritual, but in the spiritual, since the Spirit of God has made his home in you. In fact, unless you possessed the Spirit of Christ you would not belong to him. Though your body may be dead it is because of sin, but if Christ is in you then your spirit is life itself because you have been justified; and if the Spirit of him who raised Jesus from the dead is living in you, then he who raised Jesus from the dead will give life to your own mortal bodies through his Spirit living in you.

So then, my brothers, there is no necessity for us to obey our unspiritual selves or to live unspiritual lives. If you do live in that way, you are doomed to die; but if by the Spirit you put an end to the misdeeds of the body you will live.

Everyone moved by the Spirit is a son of God. The spirit you received is not the spirit of slaves bringing fear into your lives again; it is the spirit of sons, and it makes us cry out, 'Abba, Father!' The Spirit himself and our spirit bear united witness that we are children of God. And if we are children we are heirs as well: heirs of God and coheirs with Christ, sharing his sufferings so as to share his glory.

The word of the Lord.

SEQUENCE

The sequence may be said or sung.

Holy Spirit, Lord of light,
From the clear celestial height
Thy pure beaming radiance give.

Come, thou Father of the poor,
Come with treasures which endure;
Come, thou light of all that live!

Thou, of all consolers best,
Thou, the soul's delightful guest,
Dost refreshing peace bestow.

Thou in toil art comfort sweet;
Pleasant coolness in the heat;
Solace in the midst of woe.

Light immortal, light divine,
Visit thou these hearts of thine,
And our inmost being fill:

If thou take thy grace away,
Nothing pure in man will stay;
All his good is turned to ill.

Heal our wounds,
 our strength renew;
On our dryness pour thy dew;
Wash the stains of guilt away.

Bend the stubborn heart and will;
Melt the frozen, warm the chill;
Guide the steps that go astray.

Thou, on us who evermore
Thee confess and thee adore,
thy sevenfold gifts descend:

Give us comfort when we die,
Give us life with thee on high;
Give us joys that never end.

Veni, Sancte Spiritus,
 et emitte cælitus
lucis tuæ radium.

Veni, pater pauperum,
 veni, dator munerum,
veni, lumen cordium.

Consolator optime,
 dulcis hospes animæ,
dulce refrigerium.

In labore requies,
 in æstu temperies,
in fletu solacium.

O lux beatissima,
 reple cordis intima
tuorum fidelium.

Sine tuo numine,
nihil est in homine,
nihi est innoxium.

Lava quod est sordidum,
riga quod est aridum,
sana quod est saucium.

Flecte quod est rigidum,
fove quod est frigidum,
rege quod est devium.

Da tuis fidelibus,
 in te confidentibus,
sacrum septenarium.

Da virtutis meritum
 da salutis exitum,
da perenne gaudium.

Gospel Acclamation

R. **Alleluia, alleluia!**
Come, Holy Spirit, fill the hearts of your faithful
and kindle in them the fire of your love.
R. **Alleluia!**

GOSPEL

A reading from the holy Gospel according to John 14:15-16,23-26

The Holy Spirit will teach you everything.

Jesus said to his disciples:

'If you love me you will keep my commandments.
I shall ask the Father,
and he will give you another Advocate
to be with you for ever.

'If anyone loves me he will keep my word,
and my Father will love him,
and we shall come to him
and make our home with him.
Those who do not love me do not keep my words.
And my word is not my own;
it is the word of the one who sent me.
I have said these things to you
while still with you;
but the Advocate, the Holy Spirit,
whom the Father will send in my name,
will teach you everything
and remind you of all I have said to you.'

The Gospel of the Lord.

The Creed is said.

Prayer over the Offerings

Grant, we pray, O Lord,
that, as promised by your Son,
the Holy Spirit may reveal to us
   more abundantly
the hidden mystery of this sacrifice
and graciously lead us into all truth.
Through Christ our Lord.

Preface: The Mystery of Pentecost.

It is truly right and just,
   our duty and our salvation,
always and everywhere
   to give you thanks,
Lord, holy Father,
   almighty and eternal God.

Super oblata

Præsta, quæsumus, Domine,
ut, secundum promissionem
   Filii tui,
Spiritus Sanctus huius nobis sacrificii
copiosius revelet arcanum,
et omnem propitius reseret veritatem.
Per Christum Dominum nostrum.

Præfatio: De mysterio Pentecostes.

Vere dignum et iustum est,
   æquum et salutare,
nos tibi semper et ubique
   gratias agere:
Domine, sancte Pater,
   omnipotens æterne Deus.

For, bringing your Paschal Mystery
    to completion,
you bestowed the Holy Spirit today
on those you made
    your adopted children
by uniting them to your Only
    Begotten Son.
This same Spirit,
    as the Church came to birth,
opened to all peoples
    the knowledge of God
and brought together the many
    languages of the earth
in profession of the one faith.

Therefore, overcome with paschal joy,
every land, every people exults
    in your praise
and even the heavenly Powers,
    with the angelic hosts,
sing together the unending hymn
    of your glory,
as they acclaim:

Holy, Holy, Holy Lord God of hosts...

Tu enim, sacramentum
    paschale consummans,
quibus, per Unigeniti tui consortium,
filios adoptionis esse tribuisti,
hodie Spiritum Sanctum es largitus;
qui, principio nascentis Ecclesiæ,
et cunctis gentibus scientiam
    indidit deitatis,
et linguarum diversitatem in unius
    fidei confessione sociavit.

Quapropter, profusis
    paschalibus gaudiis,
totus in orbe terrarum
    mundus exsultat.
Sed et supernæ virtutes atque
    angelicæ potestates
hymnum gloriæ tuæ concinunt,
sine fine dicentes:

Sanctus, Sanctus, Sanctus. . .

Communion Antiphon   Ac 2:4,11
They were all filled
    with the Holy Spirit
and spoke of the marvels of God,
alleluia.

Ant. ad communionem
Repleti sunt omnes Spiritu Sancto,
loquentes magnalia Dei, alleluia.

Prayer after Communion
O God, who bestow heavenly gifts
    upon your Church,
safeguard, we pray, the grace you
    have given,
that the gift of the Holy Spirit
    poured out upon her
may retain all its force
and that this spiritual food
may gain her abundance
    of eternal redemption.
Through Christ our Lord.

Post communionem
Deus, qui Ecclesiæ tuæ cælestia
    dona largiris,
custodi gratiam quam dedisti,
ut Spiritus Sancti vigeat semper
    munus infusum,
et ad æternæ
    redemptionis augmentum
spiritalis esca proficiat.
Per Christum Dominum nostrum.

A formula of Solemn Blessing, pp.138-141, may be used.
To dismiss the people the Deacon or, if there is no Deacon, the Priest himself sings or says:

Go forth, the Mass is ended, alleluia, alleluia.	Ite, missa est, alleluia, alleluia.
Or:	Vel:
Go in peace, alleluia, aleluia.	Ite in pace, alleluia, alleluia.
And the people reply:	Omnes respondent:
Thanks be to God, alleluia, alleluia.	Deo gratias, alleluia, alleluia.

With Easter Time now concluded, the paschal candle is extinguished. It is desirable to keep the paschal candle in the baptistery with due honour so that it is lit at the celebration of Baptism and the candles of those baptised are lit from it.

26 May

THE MOST HOLY TRINITY

After the Easter Season that ended last Sunday with Pentecost, the Liturgy has returned to "Ordinary Time". This does not mean, however, that Christians must be less any committed: indeed, having entered divine life through the sacraments, we are called daily to be open to the action of divine Grace, to progress in love of God and of neighbour. This Sunday of the Most Holy Trinity, in a certain sense sums up God's revelation which was brought about through the Paschal Mysteries: Christ's death and Resurrection, his Ascension to the right hand of the Father and the outpouring of the Holy Spirit. The human mind and language are inadequate to explain the relationship that exists between the Father, the Son and the Holy Spirit; yet the Fathers of the Church sought to illustrate the mystery of the Triune God by living it with deep faith in their own lives.

(Pope Benedict XVI)

Solemnity

Entrance Antiphon

BLEST be God the Father,
and the Only Begotten Son of God,
and also the Holy Spirit,
for he has shown us
his merciful love.

Ant. ad introitum

BENEDICTUS sit Deus Pater,
Unigenitusque Dei Filius,
Sanctus quoque Spiritus,
quia fecit nobiscum
misericordiam suam.

The Gloria in excelsis (Glory to God in the highest) is said.

Collect

God our Father, who by sending
  into the world
the Word of truth and the Spirit
  of sanctification
made known to the human race
  your wondrous mystery,
grant us, we pray, that in professing
  the true faith,
we may acknowledge the Trinity
  of eternal glory
and adore your Unity,
  powerful in majesty.
Through our Lord Jesus Christ,
  your Son,
who lives and reigns with you
  in the unity of the Holy Spirit,
one God, for ever and ever.

Collecta

Deus Pater, qui Verbum veritatis
et Spiritum sanctificationis
  mittens in mundum,
admirabile mysterium tuum
  hominibus declarasti,
da nobis, in confessione veræ fidei,
æternæ gloriam
  Trinitatis agnoscere,
et Unitatem adorare
  in potentia maiestatis.
Per Dominum nostrum Iesum
  Christum Filium tuum,
qui tecum vivit et regnat
  in unitate Spiritus Sancti,
Deus, per omnia sæcula sæculorum.

FIRST READING

A reading from the book of Proverbs   8:22-31

Before the earth came into being, Wisdom was born.

The Wisdom of God cries aloud:

  The Lord created me when his purpose first unfolded,
  before the oldest of his works.
  From everlasting I was firmly set,
  from the beginning, before earth came into being.
  The deep was not, when I was born,
  there were no Springs to gush with water.
  Before the mountains were settled,
  before the hills, I came to birth;
  before he made the earth, the countryside,
  or the first grains of the world's dust.
  When he fixed the heavens firm, I was there,
  when he drew ring on the surface of the deep,
  when he thickened the cloud above,
  when he fixed fast the springs of the deep,
  when he assigned the sea its boundaries

– and the waters will not invade the shore –
when he laid down the foundations of the earth,
I was by his side, a master craftsman,
delighting in him day after day,
ever at play in his presence,
at play everywhere in the world,
delighting to be with the sons of men.

The word of the Lord.

Responsional Psalm   Ps 8:4-9. R. v.2

R. **How great is your name, O Lord our God,
through all the earth!**

When I see the heavens, the work of your hands,
the moon and the stars which you arranged,
what is man that you should keep him in mind,
mortal man that you care for him? R.

Yet you have made him little less than a god;
with glory and honour you crowned him,
gave him power over the works of your hand,
put all things under his feet. R.

All of them, sheep and cattle,
yes, even the savage beasts,
birds of the air, and fish
that make their way through the waters. R.

SECOND READING

A reading from the letter of St Paul to the Romans   5:1-5

To God, through Christ, in the love poured out by the Spirit.

Through our Lord Jesus Christ, by faith we are judged righteous and at peace with God, since it is by faith and through Jesus that we have entered this state of grace in which we can boast about looking forward to God's glory. But that is not all we can boast about; we can boast about our sufferings. These sufferings bring patience, as we know, and patience brings perseverance, and perseverance brings hope, and this hope is not deceptive, because the love of God has been poured into our hearts by the Holy Spirit which has been given us.

The word of the Lord.

Gospel Acclamation
Cf. Rv 1:8

R. **Alleluia, alleluia!**
Glory be to the Father, and to the Son,
   and to the Holy Spirit,
the God who is, who was, and who is to come.
R. **Alleluia!**

GOSPEL

A reading from the holy Gospel according to John 16:12-15

Everything the Father has is mine; all the Spirit tells you will be taken from what is mine.

Jesus said to his disciples:

'I still have many things to say to you
but they would be too much for you now.
But when the Spirit of truth comes
he will lead you to the complete truth,
since he will not be speaking as from himself
but will say only what he has learnt;
and he will tell you of the things to come.
He will glorify me,
since all he tells you
will be taken from what is mine.
Everything the Father has is mine;
that is why I said:
All he tells you
will be taken from what is mine.'

The Gospel of the Lord.

The Creed is said.

Prayer over the Offerings

Sanctify by the invocation
   of your name,
we pray, O Lord our God,
this oblation of our service,
and by it make of us an eternal
   offering to you.
Through Christ our Lord.

Super oblata

Sanctifica, quæsumus,
   Domine Deus noster,
per tui nominis invocationem,
hæc munera nostræ servitutis,
et per ea nosmetipsos tibi perfice
   munus æternum.
Per Christum Dominum nostrum.

Preface: The Mystery of the Most Holy Trinity.

It is truly right and just,
  our duty and our salvation,
always and everywhere
  to give you thanks,
Lord, holy Father,
  almighty and eternal God.

For with your Only Begotten Son
  and the Holy Spirit
you are one God, one Lord:
not in the unity of a single person,
but in a Trinity of one substance.

For what you have revealed to us
  of your glory
we believe equally of your Son
and of the Holy Spirit,
so that, in the confessing of the true
  and eternal Godhead,
you might be adored in what
  is proper to each Person,
their unity in substance,
and their equality in majesty.

For this is praised by Angels
  and Archangels,
Cherubim, too, and Seraphim,
who never cease to cry out each day,
as with one voice they acclaim:

Holy, Holy, Holy Lord God of hosts...

Communion Antiphon   Ga 4:6

Since you are children of God,
God has sent into your hearts
  the Spirit of his Son,
the Spirit who cries out:
  Abba, Father.

Præfatio: De mysterio Sanctissimæ Trinitatis.

Vere dignum et iustum est,
  æquum et salutare,
nos tibi semper et ubique
  gratias agere:
Domine, sancte Pater,
  omnipotens æterne Deus:

Qui cum Unigenito Filio tuo
  et Spiritu Sancto
unus es Deus, unus es Dominus:
non in unius singularitate personæ,
sed in unius Trinitate substantiæ.

Quod enim de tua gloria,
  revelante te, credimus,
hoc de Filio tuo,
hoc de Spiritu Sancto,
sine discretione sentimus.
Ut in confessione veræ
  sempiternæque Deitatis,
et in personis proprietas,
et in essentia unitas,
et in maiestate adoretur æqualitas.

Quem laudant Angeli
  atque Archangeli,
Cherubim quoque ac Seraphim,
qui non cessant clamare cotidie,
  una voce dicentes:

Sanctus, Sanctus, Sanctus . . .

Ant. ad communionem

Quoniam autem estis filii,
misit Deus Spiritum Filii sui
  in corda vestra
clamantem: Abba, Pater.

Prayer after Communion

May receiving this Sacrament,
   O Lord our God,
bring us health of body and soul,
as we confess your eternal holy
   Trinity and undivided Unity.
Through Christ our Lord.

Post communionem

Proficiat nobis ad salutem
   corporis et animæ,
Domine Deus noster,
   huius sacramenti susceptio,
et sempiternæ sanctæ Trinitatis
eiusdemque individuæ
   Unitatis confessio.
Per Christum Dominum nostrum.

2 June

THE MOST HOLY BODY AND BLOOD OF CHRIST (CORPUS CHRISTI)

The Eucharist is the food reserved for those who in Baptism were delivered from slavery and have become sons; it is the food that sustained them on the long journey of the exodus through the desert of human existence. Like the manna for the people of Israel, for every Christian generation the Eucharist is the indispensable nourishment that sustains them as they cross the desert of this world, parched by the ideological and economic systems that do not promote life but rather humiliate it. It is a world where the logic of power and possessions prevails rather than that of service and love; a world where the culture of violence and death is frequently triumphant. Yet Jesus comes to meet us and imbues us with certainty: he himself is "the Bread of life". He repeated this to us in the words of the Gospel Acclamation: "I am the living bread from Heaven, if any one eats of this bread, he will live for ever".

(Pope Benedict XVI)

Solemnity

Where the Solemnity of the Most Holy Body and Blood of Christ is not a Holyday of Obligation, it is assigned to the Sunday after the Most Holy Trinity as its proper day.

Entrance Antiphon   Cf. Ps 80:17

HE fed them with
   the finest wheat
and satisfied them with honey
   from the rock.

Ant. ad introitum

CIBAVIT eos ex adipe frumenti,
   et de petra melle saturavit eos.

The Gloria in excelsis (Glory to God in the highest) is said.

Collect

O God, who in this
 wonderful Sacrament
have left us a memorial
 of your Passion,
grant us, we pray,
so to revere the sacred mysteries
 of your Body and Blood
that we may always experience
 in ourselves
the fruits of your redemption.
Who live and reign with God
 the Father
in the unity of the Holy Spirit,
 one God, for ever and ever.

Collecta

Deus, qui nobis sub
 sacramento mirabili
passionis tuæ memoriam reliquisti,
tribue, quæsumus,
ita nos Corporis et Sanguinis tui
 sacra mysteria venerari,
ut redemptionis tuæ fructum
 in nobis iugiter sentiamus.
Qui vivis et regnas cum Deo Patre
in unitate Spiritus Sancti,
Deus, per omnia sæcula sæculorum.

FIRST READING

A reading from the book of Genesis 14:18-20

He brought bread and wine.

Melchizedek king of Salem brought bread and wine; he was a priest of God Most High. He pronounced this blessing:

'Blessed be Abraham by God Most High, creator of heaven and earth,
 and blessed be God Most High for handing over your enemies to you.'

And Abraham gave him a tithe of everything.

The word of the Lord.

Responsorial Psalm

Ps 109:1-4. R. v.4

R. **You are a priest for ever,
a priest like Melchizedek of old.**

The Lord's revelation to my Master:
'Sit on my right:
I will put your foes beneath your feet.' R.

The Lord will send from Zion
your sceptre of power:
rule in the midst of all your foes. R.

A prince from the day of your birth
on the holy mountains;
from the womb before the dawn I begot you. R.

The Lord has sworn an oath he will not change.
'You are a priest for ever,
a priest like Melchizedek of old.' R.

R. **You are a priest for ever,
a priest like Melchizedek of old.**

SECOND READING
A reading from the first letter of St Paul to the Corinthians 11:23-26

Every time you eat this bread and drink this cup, you are proclaiming the Lord's death.

This is what I received from the Lord, and in turn passed on to you: that on the same night that he was betrayed, the Lord Jesus took some bread, and thanked God for it and broke it, and he said, 'This is my body, which is for you; do this as a memorial of me.' In the same way he took the cup after supper, and said, 'This cup is the new covenant in my blood. Whenever you drink it, do this as a memorial of me.' Until the Lord comes, therefore, every time you eat this bread and drink this cup, you are proclaiming his death.

The word of the Lord.

SEQUENCE
The Sequence may be said or sung in full, or using the shorter form indicated by the asterisked verses.

Sing forth, O Zion, sweetly sing	Lauda Sion Salvatorem
The praises of thy Shepherd-King,	Lauda ducem et pastorem
In hymns and canticles divine;	In hymnis et canticis.
Dare all thou canst, thou hast no song	Quantum potes, tantum aude:
Worthy his praises to prolong,	Quia major omni laude,
So far surpassing powers like thine.	Nec laudare sufficis.
Today no theme of common praise	Laudis thema specialis,
Forms the sweet burden of thy lays –	Panis vivus et vitalis,
The living, life-dispensing food –	Hodie proponitur.
That food which at the sacred board	Quem in sacræ mensa cenæ,
Unto the brethren twelve our Lord	Turbæ fratrum duodenæ
His parting legacy bestowed.	Datum non ambigitur.
Then be the anthem clear and strong,	Sit laus plena, sit sonora,
Thy fullest note, thy sweetest song,	Sit iucunda, sit decora
The very music of thy breast:	Mentis iubilatio.

For now shines forth the day sublime	Dies enim solemnis agitur,
That brings remembrance of the time	In qua mensæ prima recolitur
When Jesus first his table blessed.	Huius institutio.
Within our new King's banquet-hall	In hac mensa novi Regis,
They meet to keep the festival	Novum Pascha novæ legis,
That closed the ancient paschal rite:	Phase vetus terminat.
The old is by the new replaced;	Vetustatem novitas,
The substance hath the shadows chased;	Umbram fugat veritas,
And rising day dispels the night.	Noctem lux eliminat.
Christ willed what He Himself had done	Quod in cœna Christus gessit,
Should be renewed while time should run,	Faciendum hoc expressit
in memory of His parting hour:	In sui memoriam.
Thus, tutored in His school divine,	Docti sacris institutis,
We consecrate the bread and wine;	Panem, vinum, in salutis
And lo – a Host of saving power.	Consecramus hostiam.
This faith to Christian men is given –	Dogma datur Christianis,
Bread is made flesh by words from heaven:	Quod in carnem transit panis,
Into his Blood the wine is turned:	Et vinum in sanguinem.
What though it baffles nature's powers	Quod non capis, quod non vides,
Of sense and sight? This faith of ours	Animosa firmat fides,
Proves more than nature e'er discerned.	Præter rerum ordinem.
Concealed beneath the two-fold sign	Sub diversis speciebus,
Meet symbols of the gifts divine,	Signis tantum, et non rebus,
There lie the mysteries adored:	Latent res eximiæ.
The living body is our food;	Caro cibus, sanguis potus:
Our drink the ever precious blood;	Manet tamen Christus totus,
In each, one undivided Lord.	Sub utraque specie.
Not he that eateth it divides	A sumente non concisus,
The sacred food, which whole abides	Non confractus, non divisus:
Unbroken still, nor knows decay;	Integer accipitur.
Be one, or be a thousand fed,	Sumit unus, sumunt mille:

They eat alike the Living Bread
    Which, still received,
    ne'er wastes away.

The good, the guilty share therein,
With sure increase of grace or sin,
    The ghostly life, or ghostly death:
Death to the guilty; to the good
Immortal life. See how one food
    Man's joy or woe accomplisheth.

We break the Sacrament; but bold
And firm thy faith shall keep its hold;
Deem not the whole doth
    more enfold
    Than in the fractured part resides:
Deem not that Christ doth broken lie;
'Tis but the sign that meets the eye;
The hidden deep reality
    In all its fulness still abides.

*Behold the bread of angels, sent
For pilgrims in their banishment,
The bread for God's true
    children meant,
    That may not unto dogs be given:
Oft in the olden types foreshadowed;
In Isaac on the altar bowed,
And in the ancient paschal food,
    And in the manna sent
    from heaven.

*Come then, good shepherd,
    bread divine,
Still show to us Thy mercy sign;
Oh, feed us still, still keep us Thine;
So may we see Thy glories shine
    In fields of immortality;

*O Thou, the wisest, mightiest, best,
Our present food, our future rest,

Quantum isti, tantum ille:
    Nec sumptus consumitur.

Sumunt boni, sumunt mali:
Sorte tamen inæquali,
    Vitæ vel interitus.
Mors est malis, vita bonis:
Vide paris sumptionis
    Quam sit dispar exitus.

Fracto demum Sacramento,
Ne vacilles, sed memento,
Tantum esse sub fragmento,
    Quantum toto tegitur.
Nulla rei fit scissura:
Signi tantum fit fractura:
Qua nec status nec statura
    Signati minuitur.

*Ecce panis Angelorum,
Factus cibus viatorum:
Vere panis filiorum,
    Non mittendus canibus.
In figuris præsignatur,
Cum Isaac immolatur:
Agnus paschæ deputatur
    Datur manna patribus.

*Bone pastor, panis vere,
Iesu, nostri miserere:
Tu nos pasce, nos tuere:
Tu nos bona fac videre
    In terra viventium.

*Tu, qui cuncta scis et vales:
Qui nos pascis hic mortales:

Come, make us each Thy
   chosen guest,
Coheirs of Thine, and comrades blest
   With saints whose dwelling
   is with Thee.
Amen. Alleluia.

Tuos ibi commensales,
Cohæredes et sodales,
   Fac sanctorum civium.
Amen. Alleluia.

Gospel Acclamation

Jn 6:51

R. **Alleluia, alleluia!**
I am the living bread which has come down from heaven,
says the Lord;
Anyone who eats this bread will live for ever.
R. **Alleluia!**

GOSPEL

A reading from the holy Gospel according to Luke   9:11-17

They all ate as much as they wanted.

Jesus made the crowds welcome and talked to them about the kingdom of God; and he cured those who were in need of healing.

   It was late afternoon when the Twelve came to him and said, 'Send the people away, and they can go to the villages and farms round about to find lodging and food; for we are in a lonely place here.' He replied, 'Give them something to eat yourselves.' But they said, 'We have no more than five loaves and two fish, unless we are to go ourselves and buy food for all these people.' For there were about five thousand men. But he said to his disciples, 'Get them to sit down in parties of about fifty.' They did so and made them all sit down. Then he took the five loaves and the two fish, raised his eyes to heaven, and said the blessing over them; then he broke them and handed them to his disciples to distribute among the crowd. They all ate as much as they wanted, and when the scraps remaining were collected they filled twelve baskets.

   The Gospel of the Lord.

The Creed is said.

Prayer over the Offerings

Grant your Church, O Lord,
   we pray,
the gifts of unity and peace,
whose signs are to be seen in mystery
in the offerings we here present.
Through Christ our Lord.

Super oblata

Ecclesiæ tuæ, quæsumus, Domine,
unitatis et pacis propitius
   dona concede,
quæ sub oblatis muneribus
   mystice designantur.
Per Christum Dominum nostrum.

Preface of the Most Holy Eucharist I or II, pp.68-71.

Communion Antiphon — Jn 6:57

Whoever eats my flesh
   and drinks my blood
remains in me and I in him,
   says the Lord.

Prayer after Communion

Grant, O Lord, we pray,
that we may delight for all eternity
in that share in your divine life,
which is foreshadowed in the
   present age
by our reception of your precious
   Body and Blood.
Who live and reign for ever and ever.

Ant. ad communionem

Qui manducat meam carnem
   et bibit meum sanguinem,
in me manet et ego in eo,
   dicit Dominus.

Post communionem

Fac nos, quæsumus, Domine,
divinitatis tuæ sempiterna
   fruitione repleri,
quam pretiosi Corporis et
   Sanguinis tui
temporalis perceptio præfigurat.
Qui vivis et regnas in
   sæcula sæculorum.

It is desirable that a procession take place after the Mass in which the Host to be carried in the procession is consecrated. However, nothing prohibits a procession from taking place even after a public and lengthy period of adoration following the Mass. If a procession takes place after Mass, when the Communion of the faithful is over, the monstrance in which the consecrated host has been placed is set on the altar. When the Prayer after Communion has been said, the Concluding Rites are omitted and the procession forms.

7 June

THE MOST SACRED HEART OF JESUS

We are celebrating the feast of the Sacred Heart of Jesus, and in the liturgy we peer, as it were, into the heart of Jesus opened in death by the spear of the Roman soldier. Jesus's heart was indeed opened for us and before us – and thus God's own heart was opened. The liturgy interprets for us the language of Jesus's heart, which tells us above all that God is the shepherd of mankind, and so it reveals to us Jesus's priesthood, which is rooted deep within his heart; so too it shows us the perennial foundation and the effective criterion of all priestly ministry, which must always be anchored in the heart of Jesus and lived out from that starting-point.

(Pope Benedict XVI)

Entrance Antiphon Ps 32:11,19

THE designs of his Heart
are from age to age,
to rescue their souls from death,
and to keep them alive in famine.

Ant. ad introitum

COGITATIONES Cordis eius
in generatione et generationem,
ut eruat a morte animas eorum
et alat eos in fame.

The Gloria in excelsis (Glory to God in the highest) is said.

Collect

Grant, we pray, almighty God,
that we, who glory in the Heart
    of your beloved Son
and recall the wonders of his love
    for us,
may be made worthy to receive
an overflowing measure of grace
from that fount of heavenly gifts.
Through our Lord Jesus Christ,
    your Son,
who lives and reigns with you
    in the unity of the Holy Spirit,
one God, for ever and ever.

Collecta

Concede, quæsumus,
    omnipotens Deus,
ut qui, dilecti Filii tui
    Corde gloriantes,
eius præcipua in nos beneficia
    recolimus caritatis,
de illo donorum fonte cælesti
supereffluentem gratiam
    mereamur accipere.
Per Dominum nostrum Iesum
    Christum Filium tuum,
qui tecum vivit et regnat
    in unitate Spiritus Sancti,
Deus, per omnia sæcula sæculorum.

Or:

O God, who in the Heart of your Son,
wounded by our sins,
bestow on us in mercy
the boundless treasures of your love,
grant, we pray,
that, in paying him the homage
    of our devotion
we may also offer worthy reparation.
Through our Lord Jesus Christ,
    your Son,
who lives and reigns with you
    in the unity of the Holy Spirit,
one God, for ever and ever.

Vel:

Deus, qui nobis in Corde Filii tui,
nostris vulnerato peccatis,
infinitos dilectionis thesauros
misericorditer largiri dignaris,
concede, quæsumus,
ut, illi devotum pietatis nostræ
    præstantes obsequium,
dignæ quoque satisfactionis
    exhibeamus officium.
Per Dominum nostrum Iesum
    Christum Filium tuum,
qui tecum vivit et regnat
    in unitate Spiritus Sancti,
Deus, per omnia sæcula sæculorum.

FIRST READING

A reading from the prophet Ezekiel 34:11-16

I myself will pasture my sheep, I myself will show them where to rest.

The Lord God says this: I am going to look after my flock myself and keep all of it in view. As a shepherd keeps all his flock in view when he stands up in the middle of his scattered sheep, so shall I keep my sheep in view. I shall rescue them from wherever they have been scattered during the mist and darkness. I shall bring them out of the countries where they are; I shall gather them together from foreign countries and bring them back to their own land. I shall pasture them on the mountains of Israel, in the ravines and in every inhabited place in the land. I shall feed them in good pasturage; the high mountains of Israel will be their grazing ground. There they will rest in good grazing ground; they will browse in rich pastures on the mountains of Israel. I myself will pasture my sheep, I myself will show them where to rest – it is the Lord who speaks. I shall look for the lost one, bring back the stray, bandage the wounded and make the weak strong. I shall watch over the fat and healthy. I shall be a true shepherd to them.

The word of the Lord.

Responsorial Psalm Ps 22. R. v.1

R. **The Lord is my shepherd;**
there is nothing I shall want.

The Lord is my shepherd;
there is nothing I shall want.
Fresh and green are the pastures
where he gives me repose.
Near restful waters he leads me,
to revive my drooping spirit. R.

He guides me along the right path;
he is true to his name.
If I should walk in the valley of darkness
no evil would I fear.
You are there with your crook and your staff;
with these you give me comfort. R.

You have prepared a banquet for me
in the sight of my foes.
My head you have anointed with oil;
my cup is overflowing. R.

Surely goodness and kindness shall follow me
all the days of my life.
In the Lord's own house shall I dwell
for ever and ever. R.

SECOND READING

A reading from the letter of St Paul to the Romans 5:5-11
What proves that God loves us is that Christ died for us.

The love of God has been poured into our hearts by the Holy Spirit which has been given us. We were still helpless when at his appointed moment Christ died for sinful men. It is not easy to die even for a good man – though of course for someone really worthy, a man might be prepared to die – but what proves that God loves us is that Christ died for us while we were still sinners. Having died to make us righteous, is it likely that he would now fail to save us from God's anger? When we were reconciled to God by the death of his Son, we were still enemies; now that we have been reconciled, surely we may count on being saved by the life of his Son? Not merely because we have been reconciled but because we are filled with joyful trust in God, through our Lord Jesus Christ, through whom we have already gained our reconciliation.

The word of the Lord.

Gospel Acclamation
Mt 11:29

R. **Alleluia, alleluia!**
Shoulder my yoke and learn from me,
for I am gentle and humble in heart.
R. **Alleluia!**

Alternative Gospel Acclamation
Jn 10:14

R. **Alleluia, alleluia!**
I am the good shepherd, says the Lord;
I know my own sheep and my own know me.
R. **Alleluia!**

GOSPEL

A reading from the holy Gospel according to Luke 15:3-7
Rejoice with me, I have found my sheep that was lost.

Jesus spoke this parable to the scribes and Pharisees:

'What man among you with a hundred sheep, losing one, would not leave the ninety-nine in the wilderness and go after the missing one till he found it? And when he found it, would he not joyfully take it on his shoulders and then, when he got home, call together his friends and neighbours? "Rejoice with me," he would say "I have found my sheep that was lost." In the same way, I tell you, there will be more rejoicing in heaven over one repentant sinner than over ninety-nine virtuous men who have no need of repentance.'

The Gospel of the Lord.

The Creed is said.

Prayer over the Offerings

Look, O Lord, we pray,
   on the surpassing charity
in the Heart of your beloved Son,
that what we offer may be a gift
   acceptable to you
and an expiation of our offences.
Through Christ our Lord.

Super oblata

Respice, quæsumus, Domine,
ad ineffabilem Cordis dilecti Filii
   tui caritatem,
ut quod offerimus sit tibi
   munus acceptum
et nostrorum expiatio delictorum.
Per Christum Dominum nostrum.

Preface: The boundless charity of Christ

It is truly right and just,
   our duty and our salvation,
always and everywhere
   to give you thanks,
Lord, holy Father,
   almighty and eternal God,
through Christ our Lord.

For raised up high on the Cross,
he gave himself up for us
   with a wonderful love
and poured out blood and water
   from his pierced side,
the wellspring of the
   Church's Sacraments,
so that, won over to the open heart
   of the Saviour,
all might draw water joyfully
   from the springs of salvation.

And so, with all the Angels
   and Saints,
we praise you, as without end
   we acclaim:

Holy, Holy, Holy Lord God of hosts...

Præfatio: De immense caritate Christi

Vere dignum et iustum est,
   æquum et salutare,
nos tibi semper et ubique
   gratias agere,
Domine, sancte Pater,
   omnipotens æterne Deus:
per Christum Dominum nostrum:

Qui, mira caritate, exaltatus in cruce,
pro nobis tradidit semetipsum,
atque de transfixo latere sanguinem
   fudit et aquam,
ex quo manarent
   Ecclesiæ sacramenta,
ut omnes, ad Cor apertum
   Salvatoris attracti,
iugiter haurirent e fontibus salutis
   in gaudio.

Et ideo, cum Sanctis
   et Angelis universis,
te collaudamus, sine fine dicentes:

Sanctus, Sanctus, Sanctus . . .

Communion Antiphon Cf. Jn 7:37-38

Thus says the Lord:
Let whoever is thirsty
　 come to me and drink.
Streams of living water will flow
from within the one
　 who believes in me.

Or: Jn 19:34

One of the soldiers opened his side
　 with a lance,
and at once there came forth blood
　 and water.

Prayer after Communion

May this sacrament of charity,
　 O Lord,
make us fervent with the fire
　 of holy love,
so that, drawn always to your Son,
we may learn to see him
　 in our neighbour.
Through Christ our Lord.

Ant. ad communionem

Dicit Dominus:
Si quis sitit,
　 veniat ad me et bibat.
Qui credit in me,
　 flumina de ventre eius
　 fluent aquæ vivæ.

Vel:

Unus militum lancea
　 latus eius aperuit,
et continuo exivit sanguis et aqua.

Post communionem

Sacramentum caritatis, Domine,
sancta nos faciat dilectione fervere,
qua, ad Filium tuum semper attracti,
ipsum in fratribus
　 agnoscere discamus.
Qui vivit et regnat
　 in sæcula sæculorum.

9 June

TENTH SUNDAY IN ORDINARY TIME

Entrance Antiphon Cf. Ps 26:1-2

THE Lord is my light and my
　 salvation; whom shall I fear?
The Lord is the stronghold
　 of my life; whom should I dread?
When those who do evil draw near,
　 they stumble and fall.

Ant. ad introitum

DOMINUS illuminatio mea,
　 et salus mea, quem timebo?
Dominus defensor vitæ meæ,
　 a quo trepidabo?
Qui tribulant me inimici mei,
　 ipsi infirmati sunt.

Collect

O God, from whom all good
  things come,
grant that we, who call on you
  in our need,
may at your prompting discern
  what is right,
and by your guidance do it.
Through our Lord Jesus Christ,
  your Son,
who lives and reigns with you
  in the unity of the Holy Spirit,
one God, for ever and ever.

Collecta

Deus, a quo bona
  cuncta procedunt,
tuis largire supplicibus,
ut cogitemus, te inspirante,
  quæ recta sunt,
et, te gubernante, eadem faciamus.

Per Dominum nostrum Iesum
  Christum Filium tuum,
qui tecum vivit et regnat
  in unitate Spiritus Sancti,
Deus, per omnia sæcula sæculorum.

FIRST READING

A reading from the first book of the Kings   17:17-24

Look, your son is alive.

The son of the mistress of the house fell sick; his illness was so severe that in the end he had no breath left in him. And the woman said to Elijah, 'What quarrel have you with me, man of God? Have you come here to bring my sins home to me and to kill my son?' 'Give me your son,' he said, and taking him from her lap, carried him to the upper room where he was staying and laid him on his own bed. He cried out to the Lord, 'Lord my God, do you mean to bring grief to the widow who is looking after me by killing her son?' He stretched himself on the child three times and cried out to the Lord, 'Lord my God, may the soul of this child, I beg you, come into him again!' The Lord heard the prayer of Elijah and the soul of the child returned to him again and he revived. Elijah took the child, brought him down from the upper room into the house, and gave him to his mother. 'Look,' Elijah said 'your son is alive.' And the woman replied, 'Now I know you are a man of God and the word of the Lord in your mouth is truth itself.'

    The word of the Lord.

Responsorial Psalm   Ps 29:2,4-6,11-13. R. v.2

R. **I will praise you, Lord,**
  you have rescued me.

  I will praise you, Lord, you have rescued me
  and have not let my enemies rejoice over me.
  O Lord, you have raised my soul from the dead,
  restored me to life from those who sink into the grave. R.

Sing psalms to the Lord, you who love him,
give thanks to his holy name.
His anger lasts a moment; his favour through life.
At night there are tears, but joy comes with dawn. R.

The Lord listened and had pity.
The Lord came to my help.
For me you have changed my mourning into dancing;
O Lord my God, I will thank you for ever. R.

SECOND READING

A reading from the letter of St Paul to the Galatians 1:11-19

God revealed his Son to me, so that I might preach the Good News about him to the pagans.

The Good News I preached is not a human message that I was given by men, it is something I learnt only through a revelation of Jesus Christ. You must have heard of my career as a practising Jew, how merciless I was in persecuting the Church of God, how much damage I did to it, how I stood out among other Jews of my generation, and how enthusiastic I was for the traditions of my ancestors.

Then God, who had specially chosen me while I was still in my mother's womb, called me through his grace and chose to reveal his Son in me, so that I might preach the Good News about him to the pagans. I did not stop to discuss this with any human being, nor did I go up to Jerusalem to see those who were already apostles before me, but I went off to Arabia at once and later went straight back from there to Damascus. Even when after three years I went up to Jerusalem to visit Cephas and stayed with him for fifteen days, I did not see any of the other apostles; I only saw James, the brother of the Lord.

The word of the Lord.

Gospel Acclamation Cf. Ep 1:17,18

R. **Alleluia, alleluia!**
May the Father of our Lord Jesus Christ
enlighten the eyes of our mind
so that we can see what hope his call holds for us.
R. **Alleluia!**

Or: Lk 7:16

R. **Alleluia, alleluia!**
A great prophet has appeared among us;
God has visited his people.
R. **Alleluia!**

GOSPEL

A reading from the holy Gospel according to Luke 7:11-17

Young man, I tell you to get up.

Jesus went to a town called Nain, accompanied by his disciples and a great number of people. When he was near the gate of the town it happened that a dead man was being carried out for burial, the only son of his mother, and she was a widow. And a considerable number of the townspeople were with her. When the Lord saw her he felt sorry for her. 'Do not cry' he said. Then he went up and put his hand on the bier and the bearers stood still, and he said, 'Young man, I tell you to get up.' And the dead man sat up and began to talk, and Jesus gave him to his mother. Everyone was filled with awe and praised God saying, 'A great prophet has appeared among us; God has visited his people.' And this opinion of him spread throughout Judaea and all over the countryside.

The Gospel of the Lord.

Prayer over the Offerings | Super oblata

Look kindly upon our service,
  O Lord, we pray,
that what we offer
may be an acceptable oblation to you
and lead us to grow in charity.
Through Christ our Lord.

Respice, Domine, quæsumus,
  nostram propitius servitutem,
ut quod offerimus sit tibi
  munus acceptum,
et nostræ caritatis augmentum.
Per Christum Dominum nostrum.

Preface of Sundays in Ordinary Time I-VIII, pp.60-67.

Communion Antiphon   Ps 17:3 | Ant. ad communionem

The Lord is my rock, my fortress,
  and my deliverer;
my God is my saving strength.

Dominus firmamentum meum,
et refugium meum, et liberator meus.
Deus meus adiutor meus.

Or: 1 Jn 4:16 | Vel:

God is love, and whoever
  abides in love
abides in God, and God in him.

Deus caritas est,
  et qui manet in caritate
in Deo manet et Deus in eo.

Prayer after Communion | Post communionem

May your healing work, O Lord,
free us, we pray, from doing evil
and lead us to what is right.
Through Christ our Lord.

Tua nos, Domine,
  medicinalis operatio,
et a nostris perversitatibus
  clementer expediat,
et ad ea quæ sunt recta perducat.
Per Christum Dominum nostrum.

16 June

ELEVENTH SUNDAY IN ORDINARY TIME

<table>
<tr><td>

Entrance Antiphon   Cf. Ps 26:7,9

O LORD, hear my voice,
   for I have called to you;
  be my help.
Do not abandon or forsake me,
  O God, my Saviour!

</td><td>

Ant. ad introitum

EXAUDI, Domine, vocem meam,
   qua clamavi ad te.
Adiutor meus esto,
  ne derelinquas me,
neque despicias me,
   Deus salutaris meus.

</td></tr>
<tr><td>

Collect

O God, strength of those
   who hope in you,
graciously hear our pleas,
and, since without you mortal
   frailty can do nothing,
grant us always the help
   of your grace,
that in following your commands
we may please you by our resolve
   and our deeds.
Through our Lord Jesus Christ,
   your Son,
who lives and reigns with you
   in the unity of the Holy Spirit,
one God, for ever and ever.

</td><td>

Collecta

Deus, in te sperantium fortitudo,
invocationibus nostris
   adesto propitius,
et, quia sine te nihil potest
   mortalis infirmitas,
gratiæ tuæ præsta semper auxilium,
ut, in exsequendis mandatis tuis,
et voluntate tibi
   et actione placeamus.
Per Dominum nostrum Iesum
   Christum Filium tuum,
qui tecum vivit et regnat
   in unitate Spiritus Sancti,
Deus, per omnia sæcula sæculorum.

</td></tr>
</table>

FIRST READING

A reading from the second book of Samuel   12:7-10,13

The Lord forgives your sin; you are not to die.

Nathan said to David, 'The Lord the God of Israel says this, "I anointed you king over Israel; I delivered you from the hands of Saul; I gave your master's house to you, his wives into your arms; I gave you the House of Israel and of Judah; and if this were not enough, I would add as much again for you. Why have you shown contempt for the Lord, doing what displeases him? You have struck down Uriah the Hittite with the sword, taken his wife for your own, and killed him with the sword of the Ammonites. So now the sword will never be far from your House, since you have shown contempt for me and taken the wife of Uriah the Hittite to be your wife."'

David said to Nathan, 'I have sinned against the Lord.' Then Nathan said to David, 'The Lord, for his part, forgives your sin; you are not to die.'

The word of the Lord.

Responsional Psalm
Ps 31:1-2,5,7,11. R. Cf. v.5

R. **Forgive, Lord, the guilt of my sin.**

Happy the man whose offence is forgiven
whose sin is remitted.
O happy the man to whom the Lord
imputes no guilt,
in whose spirit is no guile. R.

But now I have acknowledged my sins:
my guilt I did not hide.
I said: 'I will confess
my offence to the Lord.'
And you, Lord, have forgiven
the guilt of my sin. R.

You are my hiding place, O Lord;
you save me from distress.
You surround me with cries of deliverance. R.

Rejoice, rejoice in the Lord,
exult, you just!
O come, ring out your joy,
all you upright of heart. R.

SECOND READING

A reading from the letter of St Paul to the Galatians 2:16,19-21

I live now not with my own life but with the life of Christ who lives in me.

We acknowledge that what makes a man righteous is not obedience to the Law, but faith in Jesus Christ. We had to become believers in Christ Jesus no less than you had, and now we hold that faith in Christ rather than fidelity to the Law is what justifies us, and that no one can be justified by keeping the Law. In other words, through the Law I am dead to the Law, so that now I can live for God. I have been crucified with Christ, and I live now not with my own life but with the life of Christ who lives in me. The life I now live in this body I live in faith: faith in the Son of God who loved me and who

16 JUNE

sacrificed himself for my sake. I cannot bring myself to give up God's gift: if the Law can justify us, there is no point in the death of Christ.

The word of the Lord.

Gospel Acclamation
Jn 14:6

R. **Alleluia, alleluia!**
I am the Way, the Truth and the Life, says the Lord;
no one can come to the Father except through me.
R. **Alleluia!**

Or:
1 Jn 4:10

R. **Alleluia, alleluia!**
God so loved us when he sent his Son
to be the sacrifice that takes our sins away.
R. **Alleluia!**

GOSPEL
A reading from the holy Gospel according to Luke   7:36-8:3
Her many sins have been forgiven, or she would not have shown such great love.

[One of the Pharisees invited Jesus to a meal. When he arrived at the Pharisee's house and took his place at table, a woman came in, who had a bad name in the town. She had heard he was dining with the Pharisee and had brought with her an alabaster jar of ointment. She waited behind him at his feet, weeping, and her tears fell on his feet, and she wiped them away with her hair; then she covered his feet with kisses and anointed them with the ointment.

When the Pharisee who had invited him saw this, he said to himself, 'If this man were a prophet, he would know who this woman is that is touching him and what a bad name she has.' Then Jesus took him up and said, 'Simon, I have something to say to you.' 'Speak, Master' was the reply. 'There was once a creditor who had two men in his debt; one owed him five hundred denarii, the other fifty. They were unable to pay, so he pardoned them both. Which of them will love him more?' 'The one who was pardoned more, I suppose' answered Simon. Jesus said, 'You are right.'

Then he turned to the woman. 'Simon,' he said 'you see this woman? I came into your house, and you poured no water over my feet, but she has poured out her tears over my feet and wiped them away with her hair. You gave me no kiss, but she has been covering my feet with kisses ever since I came in. You did not anoint my head with oil, but she has anointed my feet with ointment. For this reason I tell you that her sins, her many sins, must have been forgiven her, or she would not have shown such great love.

It is the man who is forgiven little who shows little love.' Then he said to her, 'Your sins are forgiven.' Those who were with him at table began to say to themselves, 'Who is this man, that he even forgives sins?' But he said to the woman, 'Your faith has saved you; go in peace.']

Now after this he made his way through towns and villages, preaching, and proclaiming the Good News of the kingdom of God. With him went the Twelve, as well as certain women who had been cured of evil spirits and ailments: Mary surnamed the Magdalene, from whom seven demons had gone out, Joanna the wife of Herod's steward Chuza, Susanna, and several others who provided for them out of their own resources.

[The Gospel of the Lord.]

Shorter Form, verses 36-50. Read between [ ]

Prayer over the Offerings

O God, who in the offerings presented here
provide for the twofold needs of human nature,
nourishing us with food and renewing us
   with your Sacrament,
grant, we pray,
that the sustenance they provide
may not fail us in body or in spirit.
Through Christ our Lord.

Super oblata

Deus, qui humani generis utramque substantiam
præsentium munerum et alimento vegetas
   et renovas sacramento,
tribue, quæsumus, ut eorum
et corporibus nostris subsidium
   non desit et mentibus.
Per Christum Dominum nostrum.

Preface of Sundays in Ordinary Time I-VIII, pp.60-67.

Communion Antiphon   Ps 26:4

There is one thing I ask of the Lord, only this do I seek:
to live in the house of the Lord all the days of my life.

Or: Jn 17:11

Holy Father, keep in your name those you have given me,
that they may be one as we are one, says the Lord.

Ant. ad communionem

Unum petii a Domino, hoc requiram,
ut inhabitem in domo Domini omnibus diebus vitæ meæ.

Vel:

Pater sancte,
   serva eos in nomine tuo,
quos dedisti mihi, ut sint unum
   sicut et nos, dicit Dominus.

Prayer after Communion

As this reception of your
   Holy Communion, O Lord,
foreshadows the union
   of the faithful in you,
so may it bring about unity
   in your Church.
Through Christ our Lord.

Post communionem

Hæc tua, Domine,
   sumpta sacra communio,
sicut fidelium in te
   unionem præsignat,
sic in Ecclesia tua unitatis
   operetur effectum.
Per Christum Dominum nostrum.

23 June

TWELFTH SUNDAY IN ORDINARY TIME

Entrance Antiphon   Cf. Ps 27:8-9

THE Lord is the strength
   of his people,
a saving refuge for the one
   he has anointed.
Save your people, Lord,
   and bless your heritage,
and govern them for ever.

Ant. ad introitum

DOMINUS fortitudo plebis suæ,
   et protector salutarium Christi
   sui est.
Salvum fac populum
   tuum, Domine,
et benedic hereditati tuæ,
et rege eos usque in sæculum.

Collect

Grant, O Lord,
that we may always revere and love
   your holy name,
for you never deprive
   of your guidance
those you set firm
   on the foundation of your love.
Through our Lord Jesus Christ,
   your Son,
who lives and reigns with you
   in the unity of the Holy Spirit,
one God, for ever and ever.

Collecta

Sancti nominis tui, Domine,
timorem pariter et amorem fac nos
   habere perpetuum,
quia numquam tua
   gubernatione destituis,
quos in soliditate tuæ
   dilectionis instituis.
Per Dominum nostrum Iesum
   Christum Filium tuum,
qui tecum vivit et regnat
   in unitate Spiritus Sancti,
Deus, per omnia sæcula sæculorum.

FIRST READING

A reading from the prophet Zechariah 12:10-11; 13:1

They will look on the one whom they have pierced.

It is the Lord who speaks: 'Over the House of David and the citizens of Jerusalem I will pour out a spirit of kindness and prayer. They will look on the one whom they have pierced; they will mourn for him as for an only son, and weep for him as people weep for a first-born child. When that day comes, there will be great mourning in Judah, like the mourning of Hadadrimmon in the plain of Megiddo. When that day comes, a fountain will be opened for the House of David and the citizens of Jerusalem, for sin and impurity.'

The word of the Lord.

Responsorial Psalm Ps 62:2-6,8-9, R. v. 2

R. **For you my soul is thirsting,
O God, my God.**

O God, you are my God, for you I long;
for you my soul is thirsting.
My body pines for you
like a dry, weary land without water. R.

So I gaze on you in the sanctuary
to see your strength and your glory.
For your love is better than life,
my lips will speak your praise. R.

So I will bless you all my life,
in your name I will lift up my hands.
My soul shall be filled as with a banquet,
my mouth shall praise you with joy. R.

For you have been my help;
in the shadow of your wings I rejoice.
My soul clings to you;
your right hand holds me fast. R.

SECOND READING

A reading from the letter of St Paul to the Galatians 3:26-29

All baptised in Christ, you have all clothed yourselves in Christ.

You are, all of you, sons of God through faith in Christ Jesus. All baptised in Christ, you have all clothed yourselves in Christ, and there are no more distinctions between Jew and Greek, slave and free, male and female, but all of you are one in Christ Jesus. Merely by belonging to Christ you are the posterity of Abraham, the heirs he was promised.

The word of the Lord.

Gospel Acclamation

Jn 8:12

R. **Alleluia, alleluia!**
I am the light of the world, says the Lord;
anyone who follows me
will have the light of life.
R. **Alleluia!**

Or:

Jn 10:27

R. **Alleluia, alleluia!**
The sheep that belong to me listen to my voice,
says the Lord,
I know them and they follow me.
R. **Alleluia!**

GOSPEL

A reading from the holy Gospel according to Luke 9:18-24

You are the Christ of God. The Son of Man is destined to suffer grievously.

One day when Jesus was praying alone in the presence of his disciples he put this question to them, 'Who do the crowds say I am?' And they answered, 'John the Baptist; others Elijah; and others say one of the ancient prophets come back to life.' 'But you,' he said 'who do you say I am?' It was Peter who spoke up. 'The Christ of God' he said. But he gave them strict orders not to tell anyone anything about this.

'The Son of Man' he said 'is destined to suffer grievously, to be rejected by the elders and chief priests and scribes and to be put to death, and to be raised up on the third day.'

Then to all he said, 'If anyone wants to be a follower of mine, let him renounce himself and take up his cross every day and follow me. For anyone who wants to save his life will lose it; but anyone who loses his life for my sake, that man will save it.'

The Gospel of the Lord.

Prayer over the Offerings

Receive, O Lord, the sacrifice
 of conciliation and praise
and grant that,
 cleansed by its action,
we may make offering of a heart
 pleasing to you.
Through Christ our Lord.

Preface of Sundays in Ordinary Time I-VIII, pp.60-67.

Communion Antiphon Ps 144:15

The eyes of all look to you, Lord,
and you give them their food
 in due season.

Or: Jn 10:11,15

I am the Good Shepherd,
and I lay down my life for my sheep,
 says the Lord.

Prayer after Communion

Renewed and nourished
by the Sacred Body and Precious
 Blood of your Son,
we ask of your mercy, O Lord,
that what we celebrate
 with constant devotion
may be our sure pledge
 of redemption.
Through Christ our Lord.

Super oblata

Suscipe, Domine,
 sacrificium placationis et laudis,
et præsta, ut,
 huius operatione mundati,
beneplacitum tibi nostræ mentis
 offeramus affectum.
Per Christum Dominum nostrum.

Ant. ad communionem

Oculi omnium in te sperant,
 Domine,
et tu das illis escam
 in tempore opportuno.

Vel:

Ego sum pastor bonus,
et animam meam pono pro ovibus
 meis, dicit Dominus.

Post communionem

Sacri Corporis et Sanguinis pretiosi
 alimonia renovati,
quæsumus, Domine,
 clementiam tuam,
ut, quod gerimus
 devotione frequenti,
certa redemptione capiamus.
Per Christum Dominum nostrum.

24 June

THE NATIVITY OF SAINT JOHN THE BAPTIST

Today, the liturgy invites us to celebrate the Solemnity of the Birth of Saint John the Baptist, whose life was totally directed to Christ, as was that of Mary, Christ's Mother. John the Baptist was the forerunner, the "voice" sent to proclaim the Incarnate Word. Thus, commemorating his birth actually means celebrating Christ, the fulfilment of the promises of all the prophets, among whom the greatest was the Baptist, called to "prepare the way" for the Messiah. All the Gospels introduce the narrative of Jesus' public life with the account of his baptism by John in the River Jordan. When Jesus, after receiving baptism, emerged from the water, John saw the Spirit descending upon him in the form of a dove. It was then that he "knew" the full reality of Jesus of Nazareth and began to make him "known to Israel", pointing him out as the Son of God and Redeemer of man: "Behold, the Lamb of God, who takes away the sin of the world!".

(Pope Benedict XVI)

Solemnity

At the Vigil Mass

This Mass is used on the evening of 23 June, either before or after First Vespers (Evening Prayer I) of the Solemnity.

Entrance Antiphon Lk 1:15-14

HE will be great in the sight of the Lord
and will be filled with the Holy Spirit,
even from his mother's womb;
and many will rejoice at his birth.

Ant. ad introitum

HIC erit magnus coram Domino,
et Spiritu Sancto replebitur adhuc
  ex utero matris suæ,
et multi in nativitate
  eius gaudebunt.

The Gloria in excelsis (Glory to God in the highest) is said.

Collect

Grant, we pray, almighty God,
that your family may walk in the
  way of salvation
and, attentive to what Saint John
  the Precursor urged,
may come safely to the One

Collecta

Præsta, quæsumus,
  omnipotens Deus,
ut familia tua per viam
  salutis incedat,
et, beati Ioannis Præcursoris
  hortamenta sectando,

| he foretold, our Lord Jesus Christ. Who lives and reigns with you in the unity of the Holy Spirit, one God, for ever and ever. | ad eum quem prædixit, secura perveniat, Dominum nostrum Iesum Christum. Qui tecum vivit et regnat in unitate Spiritus Sancti, Deus, per omnia sæcula sæculorum. |

FIRST READING

A reading from the prophet Jeremiah 1:4-10

Before I formed you in the womb, I knew you.

In the days of Josiah, the word of the Lord was addressed to me, saying,

'Before I formed you in the womb I knew you;
before you came to birth I consecrated you;
I have appointed you as prophet to the nations.'

I said, 'Ah, Lord, look, I do not know how to speak: I am a child!'

But the Lord replied,

'Do not say, "I am a child."
Go now to those to whom I send you
and say whatever I command you.
Do not be afraid of them,
for I am with you to protect you –
it is the Lord who speaks!'

Then the Lord put out his hand and touched my mouth and said to me:

'There! I am putting my words into your mouth.
Look, today I am setting you
over nations and over kingdoms,
to tear up and to knock down,
to destroy and to overthrow,
to build and to plant.'

The word of the Lord.

Responsorial Psalm

Ps 70:1-6,15,17. R. v.6

R. **From my mother's womb you have been my help.**

In you, O Lord, I take refuge;
let me never be put to shame.
In your justice rescue me, free me:
pay heed to me and save me. R.

Be a rock where I can take refuge,
a mighty stronghold to save me;
for you are my rock, my stronghold.
Free me from the hand of the wicked. R.

It is you, O Lord, who are my hope,
my trust, O Lord, since my youth.
On you I have leaned from my birth,
from my mother's womb you have been my help. R.

My lips will tell of your justice
and day by day of your help.
O God, you have taught me from my youth
and I proclaim your wonders still. R.

SECOND READING

A reading from the first letter of St Peter 1:8-12

It was this salvation that the prophets were looking and searching so hard for.

You did not see Jesus Christ, yet you love him; and still without seeing him, you are already filled with joy so glorious that it cannot be described, because you believe; and you are sure of the end to which your faith looks forward, that is, the salvation of your souls.

It was this salvation that the prophets were looking and searching so hard for; their prophecies were about the grace which was to come to you. The Spirit of Christ which was in them foretold the sufferings of Christ and the glories that would come after them, and they tried to find out at what time and in what circumstances all this was to be expected. It was revealed to them that the news they brought of all the things which have now been announced to you, by those who preached to you the Good News through the Holy Spirit sent from heaven, was for you and not for themselves. Even the angels long to catch a glimpse of these things.

The word of the Lord.

Gospel Acclamation Cf. Jn 1:7; Lk 1:17

R. **Alleluia, alleluia!**
He came as a witness,
as a witness to speak for the light,
preparing for the Lord a people fit for him.
R. **Alleluia!**

GOSPEL

A reading from the holy Gospel according to Luke 1:5-17

She is to bear you a son and you must name him John.

In the days of King Herod of Judaea there lived a priest called Zechariah who belonged to the Abijah section of the priesthood, and he had a wife, Elizabeth by name, who was a descendant of Aaron. Both were worthy in the sight of God, and scrupulously observed all the commandments and observances of the Lord. But they were childless: Elizabeth was barren and they were both getting on in years.

Now it was the turn of Zechariah's section to serve, and he was exercising his priestly office before God when it fell to him by lot, as the ritual custom was, to enter the Lord's sanctuary and burn incense there. And at the hour of incense the whole congregation was outside, praying.

Then there appeared to him the angel of the Lord, standing on the right of the altar of incense. The sight disturbed Zechariah and he was overcome with fear. But the angel said to him, 'Zechariah, do not be afraid, your prayer has been heard. Your wife Elizabeth is to bear you a son and you must name him John. He will be your joy and delight and many will rejoice at his birth, for he will be great in the sight of the Lord; he must drink no wine, no strong drink. Even from his mother's womb he will be filled with the Holy Spirit, and he will bring back many of the sons of Israel to the Lord their God. With the spirit and power of Elijah, he will go before him to turn the hearts of fathers towards their children and the disobedient back to the wisdom that the virtuous have, preparing for the Lord a people fit for him.'

The Gospel of the Lord.

The Creed is said.

Prayer over the Offerings

Look with favour, O Lord,
upon the offerings made
   by your people
on the Solemnity of
   Saint John the Baptist,
and grant that what we celebrate
   in mystery
we may follow with deeds
   of devoted service.
Through Christ our Lord.

Super oblata

Munera populi tui, Domine,
   propitius intende,
in beati Ioannis Baptistæ
   sollemnitate delata,
et præsta, ut,
   quæ mysterio gerimus,
debitæ servitutis actione sectemur.
Per Christum Dominum nostrum.

24 JUNE

Proper Preface, as in the following Mass, p.489.

Communion Antiphon — Lk 1:68

Blessed be the Lord,
   the God of Israel!
He has visited his people
   and redeemed them.

Prayer after Communion

May the marvellous prayer of Saint
   John the Baptist
accompany us who have
   eaten our fill
at this sacrificial feast, O Lord,
and, since Saint John
   proclaimed your Son
to be the Lamb who would
   take away our sins,
may he implore now for us
   your favour.
Through Christ our Lord.

Ant. ad communionem

Benedictus Dominus Deus Israel,
quia visitavit et fecit redemptionem
   plebi suæ.

Post communionem

Sacris dapibus satiatos,
beati Ioannis Baptistæ nos,
   Domine,
præclara comitetur oratio,
et, quem Agnum nostra ablaturum
   crimina nuntiavit,
ipsum Filium tuum poscat nobis
   fore placatum.
Qui vivit et regnat
   in sæcula sæculorum.

At the Mass during the Day

Entrance Antiphon — Jn 1:6-7; Lk 1:17

A MAN was sent from God,
   whose name was John.
He came to testify to the light,
to prepare a people fit for the Lord.

Ant. ad introitum

FUIT homo missus a Deo,
   cui nomen erat Ioannes.
Hic venit, ut testimonium
   perhiberet de lumine,
parare Domino plebem perfectam.

The Gloria in excelsis (Glory to God in the highest) is said.

Collect

O God, who raised up
   Saint John the Baptist
to make ready a nation fit for
   Christ the Lord,
give your people, we pray,
the grace of spiritual joys

Collecta

Deus, qui beatum Ioannem
   Baptistam suscitasti,
ut perfectam plebem
   Christo Domino præpararet,
da populis tuis spiritualium
   gratiam gaudiorum,

and direct the hearts
>of all the faithful
into the way of salvation and peace.
Through our Lord Jesus Christ,
>your Son,
who lives and reigns with you
>in the unity of the Holy Spirit,
one God, for ever and ever.

et omnium fidelium mentes
>dirige in viam salutis et pacis.
Per Dominum nostrum
>Iesum Christum Filium tuum,
qui tecum vivit et regnat
>in unitate Spiritus Sancti,
Deus, per omnia sæcula sæculorum.

FIRST READING

A reading from the prophet Isaiah 49:1-6
I will make you the light of the nations.

Islands, listen to me,
pay attention, remotest peoples.
The Lord called me before I was born,
from my mother's womb he pronounced my name.

He made my mouth a sharp sword,
and hid me in the shadow of his hand.
He made me into a sharpened arrow,
and concealed me in his quiver.

He said to me, 'You are my servant (Israel)
in whom I shall be glorified';
while I was thinking, 'I have toiled in vain,
I have exhausted myself for nothing';
and all the while my cause was with the Lord,
my reward with my God.
I was honoured in the eyes of the Lord,
my God was my strength.

And now the Lord has spoken,
he who formed me in the womb to be his servant,
to bring Jacob back to him,
to gather Israel to him:
'It is not enough for you to be my servant,
to restore the tribes of Jacob and bring back the survivors of Israel;
I will make you the light of the nations
so that my salvation may reach to the ends of the earth.'

>The word of the Lord.

Responsorial Psalm

Ps 138:1-3,13-15. R. v.14

R. **I thank you for the wonder of my being.**

O Lord, you search me and you know me,
you know my resting and my rising,
you discern my purpose from afar.
You mark when I walk or lie down,
all my ways lie open to you. R.

For it was you who created my being,
knit me together in my mother's womb.
I thank you for the wonder of my being,
for the wonders of all your creation. R.

Already you knew my soul,
my body held no secret from you
when I was being fashioned in secret
and moulded in the depths of the earth. R.

SECOND READING

A reading from the Acts of the Apostles 13:22-26

Jesus, whose coming was heralded by John.

Paul said: 'God made David the king of our ancestors, of whom he approved in these words, "I have elected David son of Jesse, a man after my own heart, who will carry out my whole purpose." To keep his promise, God has raised up for Israel one of David's descendants, Jesus, as Saviour, whose coming was heralded by John when he proclaimed a baptism of repentance for the whole people of Israel. Before John ended his career he said, "I am not the one you imagine me to be; that one is coming after me and I am not fit to undo his sandal."

'My brothers, sons of Abraham's race, and all you who fear God, this message of salvation is meant for you.'

The word of the Lord.

Gospel Acclamation

Cf. Lk 1:76

R. **Alleluia, alleluia!**
As for you, little child, you shall be called
a prophet of God, the Most High.
You shall go ahead of the Lord
to prepare his ways before him.
R. **Alleluia!**

GOSPEL

A reading from the holy Gospel according to Luke 1:57-66,80

His name is John.

The time came for Elizabeth to have her child, and she gave birth to a son; and when her neighbours and relations heard that the Lord had shown her so great a kindness, they shared her joy.

Now on the eighth day they came to circumcise the child; they were going to call him Zechariah after his father, but his mother spoke up. 'No,' she said 'he is to be called John.' They said to her, 'But no one in your family has that name', and made signs to his father to find out what he wanted him called. The father asked for a writing-tablet and wrote, 'His name is John.' And they were all astonished. At that instant his power of speech returned and he spoke and praised God. All their neighbours were filled with awe and the whole affair was talked about throughout the hill country of Judaea. All those who heard of it treasured it in their hearts. 'What will this child turn out to be?' they wondered. And indeed the hand of the Lord was with him. Meanwhile, the child grew up and his spirit matured. And he lived out in the wilderness until the day he appeared openly to Israel.

The Gospel of the Lord.

The Creed is said.

Prayer over the Offerings

We place these offerings on your altar, O Lord,
to celebrate with fitting honour the nativity of him
who both foretold the coming of the world's Saviour
and pointed him out when he came.
Who lives and reigns for ever and ever.

Super oblata

Tua, Domine, muneribus altaria cumulamus,
illius nativitatem honore debito celebrantes,
qui Salvatorem mundi et cecinit affuturum,
et adesse monstravit.
Qui vivit et regnat in sæcula sæculorum.

Preface: The mission of the Precursor

It is truly right and just,
  our duty and our salvation,
always and everywhere
  to give you thanks,
Lord, holy Father,
  almighty and eternal God,
through Christ our Lord.

In his Precursor, Saint John
  the Baptist,
we praise your great glory,
for you consecrated him
  for a singular honour
among those born of women.

His birth brought great rejoicing;
even in the womb he leapt for joy
at the coming of human salvation.
He alone of all the prophets
pointed out the Lamb of redemption.

And to make holy the flowing waters,
he baptised the very author
  of Baptism
and was privileged to bear him
  supreme witness
by the shedding of his blood.

And so, with the Powers of heaven,
we worship you constantly on earth,
and before your majesty
without end we acclaim:

Holy, Holy, Holy Lord God of hosts...

Communion Antiphon Cf. Lk 1:78

Through the tender mercy
  of our God,
the Dawn from on high will visit us.

Præfatio: De missione Præcursoris

Vere dignum et iustum est,
  æquum et salutare,
nos tibi semper et ubique
  gratias agere:
Domine, sancte Pater,
  omnipotens æterne Deus:
per Christum Dominum nostrum.

In cuius Præcursore beato Ioanne
tuam magnificentiam collaudamus,
quem inter natos mulierum honore
  præcipuo consecrasti.

Qui cum nascendo multa gaudia
  præstitisset,
et nondum editus exsultasset
  ad humanæ salutis adventum,
ipse solus omnium prophetarum
Agnum redemptionis ostendit.

Sed et sanctificandis etiam
  aquæ fluentis
ipsum baptismatis lavit auctorem,
et meruit fuso sanguine supremum
illi testimonium exhibere.

Et ideo, cum cælorum virtutibus,
in terris te iugiter prædicamus,
maiestati tuæ sine fine clamantes:

Sanctus, Sanctus, Sanctus...

Ant. ad communionem

Per viscera misericordiæ Dei nostri,
visitavit nos Oriens ex alto.

Prayer after Communion

Having feasted at the banquet
   of the heavenly Lamb,
we pray, O Lord,
that, finding joy in the nativity
   of Saint John the Baptist,
your Church may know as
   the author of her rebirth
the Christ whose coming
   John foretold.
Who lives and reigns
   for ever and ever.

Post communionem

Cælestis Agni convivio refecti,
quæsumus, Domine,
   ut Ecclesia tua,
sumens de beati Ioannis Baptistæ
   generatione lætitiam,
quem ille prænuntiavit venturum,
suæ regenerationis
   cognoscat auctorem.
Qui vivit et regnat
   in sæcula sæculorum.

In Ireland and Scotland
29 June

In England and Wales
30 June

SAINTS PETER AND PAUL, APOSTLES

In their great wealth, the biblical texts of this Eucharistic Liturgy on the Solemnity of the Holy Apostles Peter and Paul highlight a theme that could be summed up in these words: God is close to his faithful servants and delivers them from all evil and delivers the Church from negative powers. It is the theme of the Church's freedom, that presents an historical aspect and another that is more profoundly spiritual. We see that Jesus' promise "the powers of death shall not prevail against" the Church does indeed include the historical experiences of persecution that Peter and Paul and other Gospel witnesses suffered, but goes beyond them, with the intention of assuring protection, especially from threats of a spiritual kind. Therefore a guarantee exists of the freedom that God assures the Church, freedom both from material ties that seek to prevent or to coerce her mission and from spiritual and moral evils that can tarnish her authenticity and credibility.

(Pope Benedict XVI)

Solemnity

At the Vigil Mass

This Mass is used on the evening of 28 June in Ireland and Scotland, or 29 June in England and Wales, either before or after First Vespers (Evening Prayer I) of the Solemnity.

Entrance Antiphon

PETER the Apostle, and Paul the teacher of the Gentiles,
these have taught us your law, O Lord.

Ant. ad introitum

PETRUS apostolus et Paulus doctor gentium,
ipsi nos docuerunt legem tuam, Domine.

The Gloria in excelsis (Glory to God in the highest) is said.

Collect

Grant, we pray, O Lord our God,
that we may be sustained
by the intercession of the blessed Apostles Peter and Paul,
that, as through them you gave your Church
the foundations of her heavenly office,
so through them you may help her to eternal salvation.
Through our Lord Jesus Christ, your Son,
who lives and reigns with you
in the unity of the Holy Spirit,
one God, for ever and ever.

Collecta

Da nobis, quæsumus, Domine Deus noster,
beatorum apostolorum Petri et Pauli
intercessionibus sublevari,
ut, per quos Ecclesiæ tuæ superni muneris
rudimenta donasti,
per eos subsidia perpetuæ salutis impendas.
Per Dominum nostrum Iesum Christum Filium tuum,
qui tecum vivit et regnat
in unitate Spiritus Sancti,
Deus, per omnia sæcula sæculorum.

FIRST READING

A reading from the Acts of the Apostles 3:1-10

I will give you what I have: in the name of Jesus, walk!

Once, when Peter and John were going up to the Temple for the prayers at the ninth hour, it happened that there was a man being carried past. He was a cripple from birth; and they used to put him down every day near the Temple entrance called the Beautiful Gate so that he could beg from the people going in. When this man saw Peter and John on their way into the Temple he begged from them. Both Peter and John looked straight at him and said, 'Look at us.' He turned to them expectantly, hoping to get something from them, but Peter said, 'I have neither silver nor gold, but I will give you what I have: in the name of Jesus Christ the Nazarene, walk!' Peter then took him by the hand and helped him to stand up. Instantly his feet and ankles became firm, he jumped up, stood, and began to walk, and he went with them into the Temple, walking and jumping and praising God. Everyone could see him walking and praising God, and they recognised him as the man who used to sit begging at the Beautiful Gate of the Temple. They were all astonished and unable to explain what had happened to him.

The word of the Lord.

Responsorial Psalm
Ps 18:2-5. R. v.5

R. **Their word goes forth through all the earth.**

The heavens proclaim the glory of God
and the firmament shows forth the work of his hands.
Day unto day takes up the story
and night unto night makes known the message. R.

No speech, no word, no voice is heard
yet their span extends through all the earth,
their words to the utmost bounds of the world. R.

SECOND READING

A reading from the letter of St Paul to the Galatians 1:11-20

God specially chose me while I was still in my mother's womb.

The Good News I preached is not a human message that I was given by men, it is something I learnt only through a revelation of Jesus Christ. You must have heard of my career as a practising Jew, how merciless I was in persecuting the Church of God, how much damage I did to it, how I stood out among other Jews of my generation, and how enthusiastic I was for the traditions of my ancestors.

Then God, who had specially chosen me while I was still in my mother's womb, called me through his grace and chose to reveal his Son in me, so that I might preach the Good News about him to the pagans. I did not stop to discuss this with any human being, nor did I go up to Jerusalem to see those who were already apostles before me, but I went off to Arabia at once and later went straight back from there to Damascus. Even when after three years I went up to Jerusalem to visit Cephas and stayed with him for fifteen days, I did not see any of the other apostles; I only saw James, the brother of the Lord, and I swear before God that what I have just written is the literal truth.

The word of the Lord.

Gospel Acclamation
Jn 21:17

R. **Alleluia, alleluia!**
Lord, you know everything;
you know I love you.
R. **Alleluia!**

GOSPEL

A reading from the holy Gospel according to John 21:15-19

Feed my lambs, feed my sheep.

After Jesus had shown himself to his disciples and eaten with them, he said to Simon Peter, 'Simon son of John, do you love me more than these others do?' He answered, 'Yes Lord, you know I love you.' Jesus said to him, 'Feed my lambs.' A second time he said to him, 'Simon son of John, do you love me?' He replied, 'Yes, Lord, you know I love you.' Jesus said to him, 'Look after my sheep.' Then he said to him a third time, 'Simon son of John, do you love me?' Peter was upset that he asked him the third time, 'Do you love me?' and said, 'Lord, you know everything; you know I love you.' Jesus said to him, 'Feed my sheep.

> 'I tell you most solemnly,
> when you were young
> you put on your own belt
> and walked where you liked;
> but when you grow old
> you will stretch out your hands,
> and somebody else will put a belt round you
> and take you where you would rather not go.'

In these words he indicated the kind of death by which Peter would give glory to God. After this he said, 'Follow me.'

The Gospel of the Lord.

The Creed is said.

Prayer over the Offerings

We bring offerings to your altar,
   O Lord,
as we glory in the solemn feast
of the blessed Apostles Peter
   and Paul,
so that the more we doubt our
   own merits,
the more we may rejoice that we
   are to be saved
by your loving kindness.
Through Christ our Lord.

Super oblata

Munera, Domine,
   tuis altaribus adhibemus,
de beatorum apostolorum
   Petri et Pauli
sollemnitatibus gloriantes,
ut quantum sumus de nostro
   merito formidantes,
tantum de tua benignitate
   gloriemur salvandi.
Per Christum Dominum nostrum.

Proper Preface, as in the following Mass, pp.497-498.

Communion Antiphon Cf. Jn 21:15,17

Simon, Son of John, do you love
  me more than these?
Lord, you know everything;
  you know that I love you.

Prayer after Communion

By this heavenly Sacrament,
  O Lord, we pray,
strengthen your faithful,
whom you have enlightened with
  the teaching of the Apostles.
Through Christ our Lord.

Ant. ad communionem

Simon Ioannis, diligis me plus his?
Domine, tu omnia nosti;
tu scis, Domine, quia amo te.

Post communionem

Cælestibus sacramentis,
  quæsumus, Domine,
fideles tuos corrobora,
quos Apostolorum doctrina
  illuminasti.
Per Christum Dominum nostrum.

A formula of Solemn Blessing, pp.144-145, may be used.

At the Mass during the Day

Entrance Antiphon

THESE are the ones who,
  living in the flesh,
planted the Church with their blood;
they drank the chalice of the Lord
and became the friends of God.

Ant. ad introitum

ISTI sunt qui, viventes in carne,
  plantaverunt Ecclesiam
  sanguine suo:
calicem Domini biberunt,
  et amici Dei facti sunt.

The Gloria in excelsis (Glory to God in the highest) is said.

Collect

O God, who on the Solemnity
  of the Apostles Peter and Paul
give us the noble and holy joy
  of this day,
grant, we pray, that your Church
may in all things follow the teaching
of those through whom she received
the beginnings of right religion.
Through our Lord Jesus Christ,
  your Son,
who lives and reigns with you
  in the unity of the Holy Spirit,
one God, for ever and ever.

Collecta

Deus, qui huius diei venerandam
  sanctamque lætitiam
in apostolorum Petri et Pauli
  sollemnitate tribuisti,
da Ecclesiæ tuæ eorum in omnibus
  sequi præceptum,
per quos religionis sumpsit exordium.
Per Dominum nostrum Iesum
  Christum Filium tuum,
qui tecum vivit et regnat
  in unitate Spiritus Sancti,
Deus, per omnia sæcula sæculorum.

FIRST READING

A reading from the Acts of the Apostles 12:1-11

Now I know the Lord really did save me from Herod.

King Herod started persecuting certain members of the Church. He beheaded James the brother of John, and when he saw that this pleased the Jews he decided to arrest Peter as well. This was during the days of Unleavened Bread, and he put Peter in prison, assigning four squads of four soldiers each to guard him in turns. Herod meant to try Peter in public after the end of Passover week. All the time Peter was under guard the Church prayed to God for him unremittingly.

On the night before Herod was to try him, Peter was sleeping between two soldiers, fastened with double chains, while guards kept watch at the main entrance to the prison. Then suddenly the angel of the Lord stood there, and the cell was filled with light. He tapped Peter on the side and woke him. 'Get up!' he said 'Hurry!' – and the chains fell from his hands. The angel then said, 'Put on your belt and sandals.' After he had done this, the angel next said, 'Wrap your cloak round you and follow me.' Peter followed him, but had no idea that what the angel did was all happening in reality; he thought he was seeing a vision. They passed through two guard posts one after the other, and reached the iron gate leading to the city. This opened of its own accord; they went through it and had walked the whole length of one street when suddenly the angel left him. It was only then that Peter came to himself. 'Now I know it is all true,' he said. 'The Lord really did send his angel and has saved me from Herod and from all that the Jewish people were so certain would happen to me.'

The word of the Lord.

Responsorial Psalm

Ps 33:2-9. R. v.5. Alt. R. v.8

R. **From all my terrors the Lord set me free.**
Or: **The angel of the Lord rescues those who revere him.**

I will bless the Lord at all times
his praise always on my lips;
in the Lord my soul shall make its boast.
The humble shall hear and be glad. R.

Glorify the Lord with me.
Together let us praise his name.
I sought the Lord and he answered me;
from all my terrors he set me free. R.

Look towards him and be radiant;
let your faces not be abashed.
This poor man called; the Lord heard him
and rescued him from all his distress. R.

The angel of the Lord is encamped
around those who revere him, to rescue them.
Taste and see that the Lord is good.
He is happy who seeks refuge in him. R.

R. **From all my terrors the Lord set me free.**
Or: **The angel of the Lord rescues those who revere him.**

SECOND READING

A reading from the second letter of St Paul to Timothy   4:6-8,17-18
All there is to come now is the crown of righteousness reserved for me.

My life is already being poured away as a libation, and the time has come for me to be gone. I have fought the good fight to the end; I have run the race to the finish; I have kept the faith; all there is to come now is the crown of righteousness reserved for me, which the Lord, the righteous judge, will give to me on that Day; and not only to me but to all those who have longed for his Appearing.

The Lord stood by me and gave me power, so that through me the whole message might be proclaimed for all the pagans to hear; and so I was rescued from the lion's mouth. The Lord will rescue me from all evil attempts on me, and bring me safely to his heavenly kingdom. To him be glory for ever and ever. Amen.

The word of the Lord.

Gospel Acclamation   Mt 16:18

R. **Alleluia, alleluia!**
You are Peter and on this rock I will build my Church.
And the gates of the underworld can never hold out against it.
R. **Alleluia!**

GOSPEL

A reading from the holy Gospel according to Matthew   16:13-19
You are Peter, and I will give you the keys of the kingdom of heaven.

When Jesus came to the region of Caesarea Philippi he put this question to his disciples, 'Who do people say the Son of Man is?' And they said, 'Some say he is John the Baptist, some Elijah, and others Jeremiah or one of the prophets.' 'But you,' he said 'who do you say I am?' Then Simon Peter spoke up, 'You are the Christ,' he said 'the Son of the living God.' Jesus replied, 'Simon son of Jonah, you are a happy man! Because it was not flesh and blood that revealed this to you but my Father in heaven. So I now say to you: You are Peter and on this rock I will build my Church. And the gates of the underworld can never hold out against it. I will give you the keys of the kingdom of heaven: whatever you bind on earth shall be considered bound in heaven; whatever you loose on earth shall be considered loosed in heaven.'

The Gospel of the Lord.

The Creed is said.

Prayer over the Offerings

May the prayer of the Apostles,
O Lord,
accompany the sacrificial gift
that we present to your name
for consecration,
and may their intercession make us
devoted to you
in celebration of the sacrifice.
Through Christ our Lord.

Preface: The twofold mission of Peter and Paul in the Church.

It is truly right and just,
our duty and our salvation,
always and everywhere to give
you thanks,
Lord, holy Father,
almighty and eternal God.

For by your providence
the blessed Apostles Peter and Paul
bring us joy:
Peter, foremost in confessing
the faith,
Paul, its outstanding preacher,
Peter, who established the early

Super oblata

Hostiam, Domine, quam nomini
tuo exhibemus sacrandam,
apostolica prosequatur oratio,
nosque tibi reddat in sacrificio
celebrando devotos.
Per Christum Dominum nostrum.

Præfatio: De duplici missione Petri et Pauli in Ecclesia.

Vere dignum et iustum est,
æquum et salutare,
nos tibi semper et ubique
gratias agere:
Domine, sancte Pater,
omnipotens æterne Deus.

Quia nos beati apostoli
Petrus et Paulus
tua dispositione lætificant:
hic princeps fidei confitendæ,
ille intellegendæ clarus assertor;
hic reliquiis Israel instituens
Ecclesiam primitivam,

Church from the remnant of Israel,
Paul, master and teacher of the Gentiles that you call.

And so, each in a different way
gathered together the one family of Christ;
and revered together throughout the world,
they share one Martyr's crown.

And therefore, with all the Angels and Saints,
we praise you, as without end we acclaim:

Holy, Holy, Holy Lord God of hosts...

ille magister et doctor gentium vocandarum.

Sic diverso consilio unam Christi familiam congregantes,
par mundo venerabile, una corona sociavit.

Et ideo, cum Sanctis et Angelis universis
te collaudamus, sine fine dicentes:

Sanctus, Sanctus, Sanctus...

Communion Antiphon Cf. Mt 16:16,18

Peter said to Jesus:
You are the Christ,
the Son of the living God.
And Jesus replied: You are Peter,
and upon this rock I will build my Church.

Ant. ad communionem

Dixit Petrus ad Iesum:
Tu es Christus, Filius Dei vivi.
Respondit Iesus: Tu es Petrus,
et super hanc petram ædificabo Ecclesiam meam.

Prayer after Communion

Grant us, O Lord,
who have been renewed by this Sacrament,
so to live in the Church,
that, persevering in the breaking of the Bread
and in the teaching of the Apostles,
we may be one heart and one soul,
made steadfast in your love.
Through Christ our Lord.

Post communionem

Da nobis, Domine,
hoc sacramento refectis,
ita in Ecclesia conversari,
ut, perseverantes in fractione panis
Apostolorumque doctrina,
cor unum simus et anima una,
tua caritate firmati.
Per Christum Dominum nostrum.

A formula of Solemn Blessing, pp. 144-147, may be used.

In Ireland and Scotland
30 June

THIRTEENTH SUNDAY IN ORDINARY TIME

Entrance Antiphon   Ps 46:2

All peoples, clap your hands.
Cry to God with shouts of joy!

Ant. ad introitum

Omnes gentes,
plaudite manibus,
iubilate Deo in voce exsultationis.

Collect

O God, who through the grace of adoption
chose us to be children of light,
grant, we pray,
that we may not be wrapped
   in the darkness of error
but always be seen to stand
   in the bright light of truth.
Through our Lord Jesus Christ,
   your Son,
who lives and reigns with you
   in the unity of the Holy Spirit,
one God, for ever and ever.

Collecta

Deus, qui, per adoptionem gratiæ,
lucis nos esse filios voluisti,
præsta, quæsumus, ut errorum
   non involvamur tenebris,
sed in splendore veritatis semper
   maneamus conspicui.
Per Dominum nostrum Iesum
   Christum Filium tuum,
qui tecum vivit et regnat
   in unitate Spiritus Sancti,
Deus, per omnia sæcula sæculorum.

FIRST READING

A reading from the first book of the Kings   19:16,19-21

Elisha rose and followed Elijah.

The Lord said to Elijah: 'Go, you are to anoint Elisha son of Shaphat, of Abel Meholah, as prophet to succeed you.'

Leaving there, Elijah came on Elisha son of Shaphat as he was ploughing behind twelve yoke of oxen, he himself being with the twelfth. Elijah passed near to him and threw his cloak over him. Elisha left his oxen and ran after Elijah. 'Let me kiss my father and mother, then I will follow you' he said. Elijah answered, 'Go, go back, for have I done anything to you?' Elisha turned away, took the pair of oxen and slaughtered them. He used the plough for cooking the oxen, then gave to his men, who ate. He then rose, and followed Elijah and became his servant.

The word of the Lord.

Responsorial Psalm
Ps 15:1-2,5,7-11. R. Cf. v.5

R. **O Lord, it is you who are my portion.**

> Preserve me, God, I take refuge in you.
> I say to the Lord: 'You are my God.'
> O Lord, it is you who are my portion and cup;
> it is you yourself who are my prize. R.

> I will bless the Lord who gives me counsel,
> who even at night directs my heart.
> I keep the Lord ever in my sight:
> since he is at my right hand, I shall stand firm. R.

> And so my heart rejoices, my soul is glad;
> even my body shall rest in safety.
> For you will not leave my soul among the dead,
> nor let your beloved know decay. R.

> You will show me the path of life,
> the fullness of joy in your presence
> at your right hand happiness for ever. R.

SECOND READING

A reading from the letter of St Paul to the Galatians 5:1,13-18

You were called to liberty.

When Christ freed us, he meant us to remain free. Stand firm, therefore, and do not submit again to the yoke of slavery.

My brothers, you were called, as you know, to liberty; but be careful, or this liberty will provide an opening for self-indulgence. Serve one another, rather, in works of love, since the whole of the Law is summarised in a single command: Love your neighbour as yourself. If you go snapping at each other and tearing each other to pieces, you had better watch or you will destroy the whole community.

Let me put it like this: if you are guided by the Spirit you will be in no danger of yielding to self-indulgence, since self-indulgence is the opposite of the Spirit, the Spirit is totally against such a thing, and it is precisely because the two are so opposed that you do not always carry out your good intentions. If you are led by the Spirit, no law can touch you.

The word of the Lord.

Gospel Acclamation

1 S 3:9; Jn 6:68

R. **Alleluia, alleluia!**
Speak, Lord, your servant is listening:
you have the message of eternal life.
R. **Alleluia!**

GOSPEL

A reading from the holy Gospel according to Luke 9:51-62
Jesus resolutely took the road for Jerusalem. I will follow you wherever you go.

As the time drew near for him to be taken up to heaven, Jesus resolutely took the road for Jerusalem and sent messengers ahead of him. These set out, and they went into a Samaritan village to make preparations for him, but the people would not receive him because he was making for Jerusalem. Seeing this, the disciples James and John said, 'Lord, do you want us to call down fire from heaven to burn them up?' But he turned and rebuked them, and they went off to another village.

As they travelled along they met a man on the road who said to him, 'I will follow you wherever you go.' Jesus answered, 'Foxes have holes and the birds of the air have nests, but the Son of Man has nowhere to lay his head.'

Another to whom he said, 'Follow me,' replied, 'Let me go and bury my father first.' But he answered, 'Leave the dead to bury their dead; your duty is to go and spread the news of the kingdom of God.'

Another said, 'I will follow you, sir, but first let me go and say good-bye to my people at home.' Jesus said to him, 'Once the hand is laid on the plough, no one who looks back is fit for the kingdom of God.'

The Gospel of the Lord.

Prayer over the Offerings	Super oblata
O God, who graciously accomplish the effects of your mysteries, grant, we pray, that the deeds by which we serve you may be worthy of these sacred gifts. Through Christ our Lord.	Deus, qui mysteriorum tuorum dignanter operaris effectus, præsta, quæsumus, ut sacris apta muneribus fiant nostra servitia. Per Christum Dominum nostrum.

Preface of Sundays in Ordinary Time I-VIII, pp.60-67.

Communion Antiphon Cf. Ps 102:1	Ant. ad communionem
Bless the Lord, O my soul, and all within me, his holy name.	Benedic, anima mea, Domino, et ea quæ intra me sunt nomini sancto eius.

Or: Jn 17:20-21

O Father, I pray for them,
   that they may be one in us,
that the world may believe that you
   have sent me, says the Lord.

Prayer after Communion

May this divine sacrifice
   we have offered and received
fill us with life, O Lord, we pray,
so that, bound to you
   in lasting charity,
we may bear fruit that lasts for ever.
Through Christ our Lord.

Vel:

Pater, pro eis rogo,
   ut ipsi in nobis unum sint,
ut credat mundus quia tu me
   misisti, dicit Dominus.

Post communionem

Vivificet nos, quæsumus, Domine,
divina quam obtulimus
   et sumpsimus hostia,
ut, perpetua tibi caritate coniuncti,
fructum qui semper
   maneat afferamus.
Per Christum Dominum nostrum.

---

7 July

FOURTEENTH SUNDAY IN ORDINARY TIME

Entrance Antiphon Cf. Ps 47:10-11

YOUR merciful love, O God,
   we have received in the midst
   of your temple.
Your praise, O God, like your name,
reaches the ends of the earth;
your right hand is filled
   with saving justice.

Collect

O God, who in the abasement
   of your Son
have raised up a fallen world,
fill your faithful with holy joy,
for on those you have rescued
   from slavery to sin

Ant. ad introitum

SUSCEPIMUS, Deus,
misericordiam tuam
in medio templi tui.
Secundum nomen tuum, Deus,
ita et laus tua in fines terræ;
iustitia plena est dextera tua.

Collecta

Deus, qui in Filii tui humilitate
iacentem mundum erexisti,
fidelibus tuis sanctam
   concede lætitiam,
ut, quos eripuisti a
   servitute peccati,

you bestow eternal gladness.
Through our Lord Jesus Christ,
   your Son,
who lives and reigns with you
   in the unity of the Holy Spirit,
one God, for ever and ever.

gaudiis facias perfrui sempiternis.
Per Dominum nostrum
   Iesum Christum Filium tuum,
qui tecum vivit et regnat
   in unitate Spiritus Sancti,
Deus, per omnia sæcula sæculorum.

FIRST READING

A reading from the prophet Isaiah   66:10-14
Towards her I send flowing peace, like a river.

Rejoice, Jerusalem,
be glad for her, all you who love her!
Rejoice, rejoice for her,
all you who mourned her!

That you may be suckled, filled,
from her consoling breast,
that you may savour with delight
her glorious breasts.

For thus says the Lord:
Now towards her I send flowing
peace, like a river,
and like a stream in spate
the glory of the nations.

At her breast will her nurslings be carried
and fondled in her lap.
Like a son comforted by his mother
will I comfort you.
And by Jerusalem you will be comforted.

At the sight your heart will rejoice,
and your bones flourish like the grass.
To his servants the Lord will reveal his hand.

   The word of the Lord.

Responsorial Psalm   Ps 65:1-7,16,20. R. v.1

R. **Cry out with joy to God all the earth.**
   Cry out with joy to God all the earth,
   O sing to the glory of his name.
   O render him glorious praise.
   Say to God: 'How tremendous your deeds! R.

'Before you all the earth shall bow;
shall sing to you, sing to your name!'
Come and see the works of God,
tremendous his deeds among men. R.

He turned the sea into dry land,
they passed through the river dry-shod.
Let our joy then be in him;
he rules for ever by his might. R.

Come and hear, all who fear God.
I will tell what he did for my soul.
Blessed be God who did not reject my prayer
nor withhold his love from me. R.

R. **Cry out with joy to God all the earth**.

SECOND READING

A reading from the letter of St Paul to the Galatians 6:14-18
The marks on my body are those of the Lord Jesus.

The only thing I can boast about is the cross of our Lord Jesus Christ, through whom the world is crucified to me, and I to the world. It does not matter if a person is circumcised or not; what matters is for him to become an altogether new creature. Peace and mercy to all who follow this rule, who form the Israel of God. I want no more trouble from anybody after this; the marks on my body are those of Jesus. The grace of our Lord Jesus Christ be with your spirit, my brothers. Amen.

The word of the Lord.

Gospel Acclamation
Jn 15:15

R. **Alleluia, alleluia!**
I call you friends, says the Lord,
because I have made known to you
everything I have learnt from my Father.
R. **Alleluia!**

Or:
Col 3:15,16

R. **Alleluia, alleluia!**
May the peace of Christ
reign in your hearts,
because it is for this that you were called together
as part of one body.
R. **Alleluia!**

GOSPEL

A reading from the holy Gospel according to Luke 10:1-12,17-20

Your peace will rest on that man.

[The Lord appointed seventy-two others and sent them out ahead of him, in pairs, to all the towns and places he himself was to visit. He said to them, 'The harvest is rich but the labourers are few, so ask the Lord of the harvest to send labourers to his harvest. Start off now, but remember, I am sending you out like lambs among wolves. Carry no purse, no haversack, no sandals. Salute no one on the road. Whatever house you go into, let your first words be, "Peace to this house!" And if a man of peace lives there, your peace will go and rest on him; if not, it will come back to you. Stay in the same house, taking what food and drink they have to offer, for the labourer deserves his wages; do not move from house to house. Whenever you go into a town where they make you welcome, eat what is set before you. Cure those in it who are sick, and say, "The kingdom of God is very near to you."] But whenever you enter a town and they do not make you welcome, go out into its streets and say, "We wipe off the very dust of your town that clings to our feet, and leave it with you. Yet be sure of this: the kingdom of God is very near." I tell you, that on that day it will not go as hard with Sodom as with that town.'

The seventy-two came back rejoicing. 'Lord,' they said 'even the devils submit to us when we use your name.' He said to them, 'I watched Satan fall like lightning from heaven. Yes, I have given you power to tread underfoot serpents and scorpions and the whole strength of the enemy; nothing shall ever hurt you. Yet do not rejoice that the spirits submit to you; rejoice rather that your names are written in heaven.'

[The Gospel of the Lord.]

Shorter Form, verses 1-9. Read between [ ]

Prayer over the Offerings

May this oblation dedicated
   to your name
purify us, O Lord,
and day by day bring our conduct
closer to the life of heaven.
Through Christ our Lord.

Super oblata

Oblatio nos, Domine,
   tuo nomini dicata purificet,
et de die in diem ad cælestis vitæ
   transferat actionem.
Per Christum Dominum nostrum.

Preface of Sundays in Ordinary Time I-VIII, pp.60-67.

Communion Antiphon Ps 33:9

Taste and see that the Lord is good;
blessed the man who seeks refuge
   in him.

Ant. ad communionem

Gustate et videte,
   quoniam suavis est Dominus;
beatus vir, qui sperat in eo.

Or: Mt 11:28

Come to me, all who labour
   and are burdened,
and I will refresh you, says the Lord.

Vel:

Venite ad me, omnes qui laboratis
   et onerati estis,
et ego reficiam vos, dicit Dominus.

Prayer after Communion

Grant, we pray, O Lord,
that, having been replenished
   by such great gifts,
we may gain the prize of salvation
and never cease to praise you.
Through Christ our Lord.

Post communionem

Tantis, Domine, repleti muneribus,
præsta, quæsumus, ut et salutaria
   dona capiamus,
et a tua numquam laude cessemus.
Per Christum Dominum nostrum.

---

14 July

FIFTEENTH SUNDAY IN ORDINARY TIME

Entrance Antiphon Cf. Ps 16:15

AS for me, in justice I shall
   behold your face;
I shall be filled with the vision
   of your glory.

Ant. ad introitum

EGO autem cum iustitia
   apparebo in conspectu tuo;
satiabor dum manifestabitur
   gloria tua.

Collect

O God, who show the light
    of your truth
to those who go astray,
so that they may return
    to the right path,
give all who for the faith they profess
are accounted Christians
the grace to reject whatever
    is contrary to the name of Christ
and to strive after all that does
    it honour.
Through our Lord Jesus Christ,
    your Son,
who lives and reigns with you
    in the unity of the Holy Spirit,
one God, for ever and ever.

Collecta

Deus, qui errantibus,
    ut in viam possint redire,
veritatis tuæ lumen ostendis,
da cunctis qui christiana
    professione censentur,
et illa respuere, quæ huic inimica
    sunt nomini,
et ea quæ sunt apta sectari.
Per Dominum nostrum Iesum
    Christum Filium tuum,
qui tecum vivit et regnat
    in unitate Spiritus Sancti,
Deus, per omnia sæcula sæculorum.

FIRST READING

A reading from the book of Deuteronomy 30:10-14

The Word is very near to you for your observance.

Moses said to the people: 'Obey the voice of the Lord your God, keeping those commandments and laws of his that are written in the Book of this Law, and you shall return to the Lord your God with all your heart and soul.

'For this Law that I enjoin on you today is not beyond your strength or beyond your reach. It is not in heaven, so that you need to wonder, "Who will go up to heaven for us and bring it down to us, so that we may hear it and keep it?" Nor is it beyond the seas, so that you need to wonder, "Who will cross the seas for us and bring it back to us, so that we may hear it and keep it?" No, the Word is very near to you, it is in your mouth and in your heart for your observance.'

The word of the Lord.

Responsorial Psalm
Ps 68:14,17,30-31,33-34,36-37. R. Cf. v.33

R. **Seek the Lord, you who are poor,**
and your hearts will revive.

This is my prayer to you,
my prayer for your favour.
In your great love, answer me, O God,

with your help that never fails:
Lord, answer, for your love is kind;
in your compassion, turn towards me. R.

As for me in my poverty and pain
let your help, O God, lift me up.
I will praise God's name with a song;
I will glorify him with thanksgiving. R.

The poor when they see it will be glad
and God-seeking hearts will revive;
for the Lord listens to the needy
and does not spurn his servants in their chains. R.

For God will bring help to Zion
and rebuild the cities of Judah.
The sons of his servants shall inherit it;
those who love his name shall dwell there. R.

R. **Seek the Lord, you who are poor,
and your hearts will revive.**

Alternative Responsorial Psalm   Ps 18:8-11. R. v.9

R. **The precepts of the Lord
gladden the heart.**

The law of the Lord is perfect,
it revives the soul.
The rule of the Lord is to be trusted,
it gives wisdom to the simple. R.

The precepts of the Lord are right,
they gladden the heart.
The command of the Lord is clear,
it gives light to the eyes. R.

The fear of the Lord is holy,
abiding for ever.
The decrees of the Lord are truth
and all of them just. R.

They are more to be desired than gold
than the purest of gold
and sweeter are they than honey,
than honey from the comb. R.

SECOND READING

A reading from the letter of St Paul to the Colossians   1:15-20

All things were created through Christ and for him.

Christ Jesus is the image of the unseen God
and the first-born of all creation,
for in him were created
all things in heaven and on earth:
everything visible and everything invisible,
Thrones, Dominations, Sovereignties, Powers –
all things were created through him and for him.
Before anything was created, he existed,
and he holds all things in unity.
Now the Church is his body,
he is its head.
As he is the Beginning,
he was first to be born from the dead,
so that he should be first in every way;
because God wanted all perfection
to be found in him
and all things to be reconciled through him and for him,
everything in heaven and everything on earth,
when he made peace
by his death on the cross.

The word of the Lord.

Gospel Acclamation   Jn 10:27

R. **Alleluia, alleluia!**
The sheep that belong to me listen to my voice,
says the Lord,
I know them and they follow me.
R. **Alleluia!**

Or: Cf. Jn 6:63,68

R. **Alleluia, alleluia!**
Your words are spirit, Lord,
and they are life:
you have the message of eternal life.
R. **Alleluia!**

GOSPEL

A reading from the holy Gospel according to Luke 10:25-37

Who is my neighbour?

There was a lawyer who, to disconcert Jesus, stood up and said to him, 'Master, what must I do to inherit eternal life?' He said to him, 'What is written in the law? What do you read there?' He replied, 'You must love the Lord your God with all your heart, with all your soul, with all your strength, and with all your mind, and your neighbour as yourself.' 'You have answered right,' said Jesus 'do this and life is yours.'

But the man was anxious to justify himself and said to Jesus, 'And who is my neighbour?' Jesus replied, 'A man was once on his way down from Jerusalem to Jericho and fell into the hands of brigands; they took all he had, beat him and then made off, leaving him half dead. Now a priest happened to be travelling down the same road, but when he saw the man, he passed by on the other side. In the same way a Levite who came to the place saw him, and passed by on the other side. But a Samaritan traveller who came upon him was moved with compassion when he saw him. He went up and bandaged his wounds, pouring oil and wine on them. He then lifted him on to his own mount, carried him to the inn and looked after him. Next day, he took out two denarii and handed them to the innkeeper. "Look after him," he said "and on my way back I will make good any extra expense you have." Which of these three, do you think, proved himself a neighbour to the man who fell into the brigands' hands?' 'The one who took pity on him' he replied. Jesus said to him, 'Go, and do the same yourself.'

The Gospel of the Lord.

Prayer over the Offerings

Look upon the offerings
   of the Church, O Lord,
as she makes her prayer to you,
and grant that, when consumed
   by those who believe,
they may bring ever greater holiness.
Through Christ our Lord.

Super oblata

Respice, Domine, munera
   supplicantis Ecclesiæ,
et pro credentium
   sanctificationis incremento
sumenda concede.
Per Christum Dominum nostrum.

Preface of Sundays in Ordinary Time I-VIII, pp.60-67.

Communion Antiphon Cf. Ps 83:4-5

The sparrow finds a home,
and the swallow a nest for her young:
by your altars, O Lord of hosts,
  my King and my God.
Blessed are they who dwell
  in your house,
for ever singing your praise.

Or: Jn 6:57

Whoever eats my flesh
  and drinks my blood
remains in me and I in him,
  says the Lord.

Prayer after Communion

Having consumed these gifts,
  we pray, O Lord,
that, by our participation
  in this mystery,
its saving effects upon us may grow.
Through Christ our Lord.

Ant. ad communionem

Passer invenit sibi domum,
et turtur nidum,
  ubi reponat pullos suos.
Altaria tua, Domine virtutum,
  Rex meus, et Deus meus!
Beati qui habitant in domo tua,
in sæculum sæculi laudabunt te.

Vel:

Qui manducat meam carnem
  et bibit meum sanguinem,
in me manet et ego in eo,
  dicit Dominus.

Post communionem

Sumptis muneribus,
  quæsumus, Domine,
ut, cum frequentatione mysterii,
crescat nostræ salutis effectus.
Per Christum Dominum nostrum.

---

21 July

SIXTEENTH SUNDAY IN ORDINARY TIME

Entrance Antiphon Ps 53:6,8

SEE, I have God for my help.
The Lord sustains my soul.
I will sacrifice to you
  with willing heart,
and praise your name, O Lord,
  for it is good.

Ant. ad introitum

ECCE Deus adiuvat me,
et Dominus susceptor
  est animæ meæ.
Voluntarie sacrificabo tibi,
et confitebor nomini tuo, Domine,
  quoniam bonum est.

Collect

Show favour, O Lord, to your servants
and mercifully increase the gifts
  of your grace,
that, made fervent in hope,
  faith and charity,
they may be ever watchful
  in keeping your commands.
Through our Lord Jesus Christ,
  your Son,
who lives and reigns with you
  in the unity of the Holy Spirit,
one God, for ever and ever.

Collecta

Propitiare, Domine, famulis tuis,
et clementer gratiæ tuæ super eos
  dona multiplica,
ut, spe, fide et caritate ferventes,
semper in mandatis tuis vigili
  custodia perseverent.
Per Dominum nostrum Iesum
  Christum Filium tuum,
qui tecum vivit et regnat
  in unitate Spiritus Sancti,
Deus, per omnia sæcula sæculorum.

FIRST READING

A reading from the book of Genesis 18:1-10

Lord, do not pass your servant by.

The Lord appeared to Abraham at the Oak of Mamre while he was sitting by the entrance of the tent during the hottest part of the day. He looked up, and there he saw three men standing near him. As soon as he saw them he ran from the entrance of the tent to meet them, and bowed to the ground. 'My Lord,' he said 'I beg you, if I find favour with you, kindly do not pass your servant by. A little water shall be brought; you shall wash your feet and lie down under the tree. Let me fetch a little bread and you shall refresh yourselves before going further. That is why you have come in your servant's direction.' They replied, 'Do as you say.'

  Abraham hastened to the tent to find Sarah. 'Hurry,' he said 'knead three bushels of flour and make loaves.' Then running to the cattle Abraham took a fine and tender calf and gave it to the servant, who hurried to prepare it. Then taking cream, milk and the calf he had prepared, he laid all before them, and they ate while he remained standing near them under the tree.

  'Where is your wife Sarah?' they asked him. 'She is in the tent' he replied. Then his guest said, 'I shall visit you again next year without fail and your wife will then have a son.'

  The word of the Lord.

Responsional Psalm
Ps 14:2-5. R. v.1

R. **The just will live in the presence of the Lord**.

Lord, who shall dwell on your holy mountain?
He who walks without fault;
he who acts with justice
and speaks the truth from his heart;
he who does not slander with his tongue. R.

He who does no wrong to his brother,
who casts no slur on his neighbour,
who holds the godless in disdain,
but honours those who fear the Lord. R.

He who keeps his pledge, come what may;
who takes no interest on a loan
and accepts no bribes against the innocent.
Such a man will stand firm for ever. R.

SECOND READING

A reading from the letter of St Paul to the Colossians   1:24-28

A mystery hidden for centuries has now been revealed to God's saints.

It makes me happy to suffer for you, as I am suffering now, and in my own body to do what I can to make up all that has still to be undergone by Christ for the sake of his body, the Church. I became the servant of the Church when God made me responsible for delivering God's message to you, the message which was a mystery hidden for generations and centuries and has now been revealed to his saints. It was God's purpose to reveal it to them and to show all the rich glory of this mystery to pagans. The mystery is Christ among you, your hope of glory: this is the Christ we proclaim, this is the wisdom in which we thoroughly train everyone and instruct everyone, to make them all perfect in Christ.

The word of the Lord.

Gospel Acclamation
Cf. Ac 16:14

R. **Alleluia, alleluia!**
Open our heart, O Lord,
to accept the words of your Son.
R. **Alleluia!**

Or: Cf. Lk 8:15

R. **Alleluia, alleluia!**
Blessed are those who,
with a noble and generous heart,
take the word of God to themselves
and yield a harvest through their perseverance.
R. **Alleluia!**

GOSPEL

A reading from the holy Gospel according to Luke 10:38-42
Martha welcomed Jesus into her house. Mary has chosen the better part.

Jesus came to a village, and a woman named Martha welcomed him into her house. She had a sister called Mary, who sat down at the Lord's feet and listened to him speaking. Now Martha who was distracted with all the serving said, 'Lord, do you not care that my sister is leaving me to do the serving all by myself? Please tell her to help me.' But the Lord answered 'Martha, Martha,' he said 'you worry and fret about so many things, and yet few are needed, indeed only one. It is Mary who has chosen the better part; it is not to be taken from her.'

The Gospel of the Lord.

Prayer over the Offerings

O God, who in the one
   perfect sacrifice
brought to completion varied
   offerings of the law,
accept, we pray, this sacrifice
   from your faithful servants
and make it holy, as you blessed
   the gifts of Abel,
so that what each has offered
   to the honour of your majesty
may benefit the salvation of all.
Through Christ our Lord.

Super oblata

Deus, qui legalium
   differentiam hostiarum
unius sacrificii perfectione sanxisti,
accipe sacrificium a devotis
   tibi famulis,
et pari benedictione,
   sicut munera Abel, sanctifica,
ut, quod singuli obtulerunt
   ad maiestatis tuæ honorem,
cunctis proficiat ad salutem.
Per Christum Dominum nostrum.

Preface of Sundays in Ordinary Time I-VIII, pp.60-67.

Communion Antiphon Ps 110:4-5

The Lord, the gracious, the merciful,
has made a memorial of his wonders;
he gives food to those who fear him.

Or: Rv 3:20

Behold, I stand at the door
   and knock, says the Lord.
If anyone hears my voice
   and opens the door to me,
I will enter his house and dine
   with him, and he with me.

Prayer after Communion

Graciously be present to your
   people, we pray, O Lord,
and lead those you have imbued
   with heavenly mysteries
to pass from former ways
   to newness of life.
Through Christ our Lord.

Ant. ad communionem

Memoriam fecit mirabilium suorum
misericors et miserator Dominus;
escam dedit timentibus se.

Vel:

Ecce sto ad ostium et pulso,
   dicit Dominus:
si quis audierit vocem meam,
   et aperuerit mihi ianuam,
intrabo ad illum, et cenabo
   cum illo, et ipse mecum.

Post communionem

Populo tuo, quæsumus, Domine,
   adesto propitius,
et, quem mysteriis
   cælestibus imbuisti,
fac ad novitatem vitæ
   de vetustate transire.
Per Christum Dominum nostrum.

28 July

SEVENTEENTH SUNDAY IN ORDINARY TIME

Entrance Antiphon Cf. Ps 67:6-7,36

GOD is in his holy place,
   God who unites those
   who dwell in his house;
he himself gives might and strength
   to his people.

Ant. ad introitum

DEUS in loco sancto suo;
   Deus qui inhabitare facit
unanimes in domo,
ipse dabit virtutem et fortitudinem
   plebi suæ.

Collect

O God, protector of those
  who hope in you,
without whom nothing has firm
  foundation, nothing is holy,
bestow in abundance your mercy
  upon us
and grant that, with you as our ruler
  and guide,
we may use the good things that pass
in such a way as to hold fast even now
to those that ever endure.
Through our Lord Jesus Christ,
  your Son,
who lives and reigns with you
  in the unity of the Holy Spirit,
one God, for ever and ever.

Collecta

Protector in te sperantium, Deus,
sine quo nihil est validum,
  nihil sanctum,
multiplica super nos
misericordiam tuam
ut, te rectore, te duce, sic bonis
  transeuntibus nunc utamur,
ut iam possimus
  inhærere mansuris.

Per Dominum nostrum Iesum
  Christum Filium tuum,
qui tecum vivit et regnat
  in unitate Spiritus Sancti,
Deus, per omnia sæcula sæculorum.

FIRST READING

A reading from the book of Genesis   18:20-32

I trust my Lord will not be angry, but give me leave to speak.

The Lord said, 'How great an outcry there is against Sodom and Gomorrah! How grievous is their sin! I propose to go down and see whether or not they have done all that is alleged in the outcry against them that has come up to me. I am determined to know.'

The men left there and went to Sodom while Abraham remained standing before the Lord. Approaching him he said, 'Are you really going to destroy the just man with the sinner? Perhaps there are fifty just men in the town. Will you really overwhelm them, will you not spare the place for the fifty just men in it? Do not think of doing such a thing: to kill the just man with the sinner, treating just and sinner alike! Do not think of it! Will the judge of the whole earth not administer justice?' The Lord replied, 'If at Sodom I find fifty just men in the town, I will spare the whole place because of them.'

Abraham replied, 'I am bold indeed to speak like this to my Lord, I who am dust and ashes. But perhaps the fifty just men lack five: will you destroy the whole city for five?' 'No,' he replied, 'I will not destroy it if I find forty-five just men there.' Again Abraham said to him, 'Perhaps there will only be forty there.' 'I will not do it' he replied 'for the sake of the forty.'

Abraham said, 'I trust my Lord will not be angry, but give me leave to speak: perhaps there will only be thirty there.' 'I will not do it' he replied 'if I find thirty there.' He said, 'I am bold indeed to speak like this, but perhaps there will only be twenty there.' 'I will not destroy it' he replied 'for the sake of the twenty.' He said, 'I trust my Lord will not be angry if I speak once more: perhaps there will only be ten.' 'I will not destroy it' he replied 'for the sake of the ten.'

The word of the Lord.

Responsorial Psalm

Ps 137:1-3,6-8. R. v.3

R. **On the day I called,
you answered me, O Lord.**

I thank you, Lord, with all my heart,
you have heard the words of my mouth.
In the presence of the angels I will bless you.
I will adore before your holy temple. R.

I thank you for your faithfulness and love
which excel all we ever knew of you.
On the day I called, you answered;
you increased the strength of my soul. R.

The Lord is high yet he looks on the lowly
and the haughty he knows from afar.
Though I walk in the midst of affliction
you give me life and frustrate my foes. R.

You stretch out your hand and save me,
your hand will do all things for me.
Your love, O Lord, is eternal,
discard not the work of your hands. R.

SECOND READING

A reading from the letter of St Paul to the Colossians   2:12-14
He has brought you to life with him, he has forgiven us all our sins.

You have been buried with Christ, when you were baptised; and by baptism, too, you have been raised up with him through your belief in the power of God who raised him from the dead. You were dead, because you were sinners and had not been circumcised: he has brought you to life with him, he has forgiven us all our sins.

He has overridden the Law, and cancelled every record of the debt that we had to pay; he has done away with it by nailing it to the cross.

The word of the Lord.

Gospel Acclamation   Jn 1:14,12

R. **Alleluia, alleluia!**
The Word was made flesh and lived among us;
to all who did accept him
he gave power to become children of God.
R. **Alleluia!**

Or: Rm 8:15

R. **Alleluia, alleluia!**
The spirit you received is the spirit of sons,
and it makes us cry out, 'Abba Father!'
R. **Alleluia!**

GOSPEL

A reading from the holy Gospel according to Luke   11:1-13
Ask, and it will be given to you.

Once Jesus was in a certain place praying, and when he had finished, one of his disciples said, 'Lord, teach us to pray, just as John taught his disciples.' He said to them, 'Say this when you pray:

"Father, may your name be held holy,
your kingdom come;
give us each day our daily bread,
and forgive us our sins,
for we ourselves forgive each one who is in debt to us.
And do not put us to the test."'

He also said to them, 'Suppose one of you has a friend and goes to him in the middle of the night to say, "My friend, lend me three loaves, because a friend of mine on his travels has just arrived at my house and I have nothing to offer him"; and the man answers from inside the house, "Do not bother me. The door is bolted now, and my children and I are in bed; I cannot get up to give it to you." I tell you, if the man does not get up and give it him for friendship's sake, persistence will be enough to make him get up and give his friend all he wants.

'So I say to you: Ask, and it will be given to you; search, and you will find; knock, and the door will be opened to you. For the one who asks always receives; the one who searches always finds; the one who knocks will always have the door opened to him. What father among you would hand his son a stone when he asked for bread? Or hand him a snake instead of a fish? Or hand him a scorpion if he asked for an egg? If you then, who are evil, know how to give your children what is good, how much more will the heavenly Father give the Holy Spirit to those who ask him!'

The Gospel of the Lord.

Prayer over the Offerings

Accept, O Lord, we pray, the offerings which we bring from the abundance of your gifts,
that through the powerful working of your grace
these most sacred mysteries may sanctify our present way of life
and lead us to eternal gladness.
Through Christ our Lord.

Super oblata

Suscipe, quæsumus,
   Domine, munera,
quæ tibi de tua largitate deferimus,
ut hæc sacrosancta mysteria,
   gratiæ tuæ operante virtute,
et præsentis vitæ nos
   conversatione sanctificent,
et ad gaudia sempiterna perducant.
Per Christum Dominum nostrum.

Preface of Sundays in Ordinary Time I-VIII, pp.60-67.

Communion Antiphon   Ps 102:2

Bless the Lord, O my soul,
and never forget all his benefits.

Ant. ad communionem

Benedic, anima mea, Domino,
et noli oblivisci omnes
   retributiones eius.

Or: Mt 5:7-8

Blessed are the merciful,
   for they shall receive mercy.

Vel:

Beati misericordes,
quoniam ipsi

Blessed are the clean of heart,
  for they shall see God.

Prayer after Communion

We have consumed, O Lord,
  this divine Sacrament,
the perpetual memorial
  of the Passion of your Son;
grant, we pray, that this gift,
which he himself gave us with love
  beyond all telling,
may profit us for salvation.
Through Christ our Lord.

  misericordiam consequentur.
Beati mundo corde,
quoniam ipsi Deum videbunt.

Post communionem

Sumpsimus, Domine,
  divinum sacramentum,
passionis Filii tui
  memoriale perpetuum;
tribue, quæsumus,
ut ad nostram salutem hoc
  munus proficiat,
quod ineffabili nobis caritate
  ipse donavit.
Qui vivit et regnat
  in sæcula sæculorum.

4 August

EIGHTEENTH SUNDAY IN ORDINARY TIME

Entrance Antiphon   Ps 69:2,6

O GOD, come to my assistance;
  O Lord, make haste to help me!
You are my rescuer, my help;
O Lord, do not delay.

Ant. ad introitum

DEUS, in adiutorium
  meum intende;
Domine, ad adiuvandum me festina.
Adiutor meus et liberator meus es tu;
Domine, ne moreris.

Collect

Draw near to your servants, O Lord,
and answer their prayers
  with unceasing kindness,
that, for those who glory in you
  as their Creator and guide,
you may restore what you
  have created
and keep safe what you have restored.

Collecta

Adesto, Domine, famulis tuis,
et perpetuam benignitatem
  largire poscentibus,
ut his, qui te auctorem et
  gubernatorem gloriantur habere,
et creata restaures,
  et restaurata conserves.

Through our Lord Jesus Christ, your Son, who lives and reigns with you in the unity of the Holy Spirit, one God, for ever and ever.	Per Dominum nostrum Iesum Christum Filium tuum, qui tecum vivit et regnat in unitate Spiritus Sancti, Deus, per omnia sæcula sæculorum.

FIRST READING

A reading from the book of Ecclesiastes 1:2; 2:21-23

What does man gain for all his toil?

Vanity of vanities, the Preacher says. Vanity of vanities. All is vanity!

For so it is that a man who has laboured wisely, skilfully and successfully must leave what is his own to someone who has not toiled for it at all. This, too, is vanity and great injustice; for what does he gain for all the toil and strain that he has undergone under the sun? What of all his laborious days, his cares of office, his restless nights? This, too, is vanity.

The word of the Lord.

Responsorial Psalm Ps 89:3-6,12-14,17. R. v.1

R. **O Lord, you have been our refuge from one generation to the next.**

You turn men back into dust
and say: 'Go back, sons of men.'
To your eyes a thousand years
are like yesterday, come and gone,
no more than a watch in the night. R.

You sweep men away like a dream,
like grass which springs up in the morning.
In the morning it springs up and flowers:
by evening it withers and fades. R.

Make us know the shortness of our life
that we may gain wisdom of heart.
Lord, relent! Is your anger for ever?
Show pity to your servants. R.

In the morning, fill us with your love;
we shall exult and rejoice all our days.
Let the favour of the Lord be upon us:
give success to the work of our hands. R.

Alternative Responsorial Psalm

Ps 94:1-2,6-9. R. vv. 7-8

R. **O that today you would listen to his voice!
Harden not your hearts.**

Come, ring out our joy to the Lord;
hail the rock who saves us.
Let us come before him, giving thanks,
with songs let us hail the Lord. R.

Come in; let us bow and bend low;
let us kneel before the God who made us
for he is our God and we
the people who belong to his pasture,
the flock that is led by his hand. R.

O that today you would listen to his voice!
'Harden not your hearts as at Meribah,
as on that day at Massah in the desert
when your fathers put me to the test;
when they tried me, though they saw my work.'

SECOND READING

A reading from the letter of St Paul to the Colossians 3:1-5,9-11

You must look for the things that are in heaven, where Christ is.

Since you have been brought back to true life with Christ, you must look for the things that are in heaven, where Christ is, sitting at God's right hand. Let your thoughts be on heavenly things, not on the things that are on the earth, because you have died, and now the life you have is hidden with Christ in God. But when Christ is revealed – and he is your life – you too will be revealed in all your glory with him.

That is why you must kill everything in you that belongs only to earthly life: fornication, impurity, guilty passion, evil desires and especially greed, which is the same thing as worshipping a false god; and never tell each other lies. You have stripped off your old behaviour with your old self, and you have put on a new self which will progress towards true knowledge the more it is renewed in the image of its creator; and in that image there is no room for distinction between Greek and Jew, between the circumcised or the uncircumcised, or between barbarian and Scythians, slave and free man. There is only Christ: he is everything and he is in everything.

The word of the Lord.

Gospel Acclamation

Cf. Jn 17:17

R. **Alleluia, alleluia!**
Your word is truth, O Lord,
consecrate us in the truth.
R. **Alleluia!**

Or:

Mt 5:3

R. **Alleluia, alleluia!**
How happy are the poor in spirit;
theirs is the kingdom of heaven.
R. **Alleluia!**

GOSPEL

A reading from the holy Gospel according to Luke   12:13-21
This hoard of yours, whose will it be?

A man in the crowd said to Jesus, 'Master, tell my brother to give me a share of our inheritance.' 'My friend,' he replied, 'who appointed me your judge, or the arbitrator of your claims?' Then he said to them, 'Watch, and be on your guard against avarice of any kind, for a man's life is not made secure by what he owns, even when he has more than he needs.'

Then he told them a parable: 'There was once a rich man who, having had a good harvest from his land, thought to himself, "What am I to do? I have not enough room to store my crops." Then he said, "This is what I will do: I will pull down my barns and build bigger ones, and store all my grain and my goods in them, and I will say to my soul: My soul, you have plenty of good things laid by for many years to come; take things easy, eat, drink, have a good time." But God said to him, "Fool! This very night the demand will be made for your soul; and this hoard of yours, whose will it be then?" So it is when a man stores up treasure for himself in place of making himself rich in the sight of God.'

The Gospel of the Lord.

Prayer over the Offerings

Graciously sanctify these gifts,
  O Lord, we pray,
and, accepting the oblation
  of this spiritual sacrifice,
make of us an eternal offering to you.
Through Christ our Lord.

Super oblata

Propitius, Domine, quæsumus,
  hæc dona sanctifica,
et, hostiæ spiritalis
  oblatione suscepta,
nosmetipsos tibi perfice
  munus æternum.
Per Christum Dominum nostrum.

Preface of Sundays in Ordinary Time I-VIII, pp.60-67.

Communion Antiphon Ws 16:20

You have given us, O Lord,
  bread from heaven,
endowed with all delights
  and sweetness in every taste.

Ant. ad communionem

Panem de cælo dedisti
  nobis, Domine,
habentem omne delectamentum,
et omnem saporem suavitatis.

Or: Jn 6:35

I am the bread of life, says the Lord;
whoever comes to me will not hunger
and whoever believes in me
  will not thirst.

Vel:

Ego sum panis vitæ, dicit Dominus.
Qui venit ad me non esuriet,
  et qui credit in me non sitiet.

Prayer after Communion

Accompany with constant
  protection, O Lord,
those you renew with these
  heavenly gifts
and, in your never-failing care
  for them,
make them worthy
  of eternal redemption.
Through Christ our Lord.

Post communionem

Quos cælesti recreas munere,
perpetuo, Domine,
  comitare præsidio,
et, quos fovere non desinis,
dignos fieri sempiterna
  redemptione concede.
Per Christum Dominum nostrum.

11 August

NINETEENTH SUNDAY IN ORDINARY TIME

Entrance Antiphon Cf. Ps 73:20,19,22,23

Look to your covenant, O Lord,
and forget not the life
 of your poor ones for ever.
Arise, O God, and defend your cause,
and forget not the cries of those
 who seek you.

Ant. ad introitum

Respice, Domine,
 in testamentum tuum,
et animas pauperum tuorum
 ne derelinquas in finem.
Exsurge, Domine,
 et iudica causam tuam,
et ne obliviscaris
 voces quærentium te.

Collect

Almighty ever-living God,
whom, taught by the Holy Spirit,
we dare to call our Father,
bring, we pray, to perfection
 in our hearts
the spirit of adoption as your sons
 and daughters,
that we may merit to enter
 into the inheritance
which you have promised.
Through our Lord Jesus Christ,
 your Son,
who lives and reigns with you
 in the unity of the Holy Spirit,
one God, for ever and ever.

Collecta

Omnipotens sempiterne Deus,
quem, docente Spiritu Sancto,
paterno nomine invocare
 præsumimus,
perfice in cordibus nostris spiritum
 adoptionis filiorum,
ut promissam hereditatem
 ingredi mereamur.
Per Dominum nostrum Iesum
 Christum Filium tuum,
qui tecum vivit et regnat
 in unitate Spiritus Sancti,
Deus, per omnia sæcula sæculorum.

FIRST READING

A reading from the book of Wisdom   18:6-9

By the same act with which you took vengeance on ours foes you made us glorious by calling us to you.

That night had been foretold to our ancestors, so that,
once they saw what kind of oaths they had put their trust in
they would joyfully take courage.

This was the expectation of your people,
the saving of the virtuous and the ruin of their enemies;
for by the same act with which you took vengeance on our foes
you made us glorious by calling us to you.
The devout children of worthy men offered sacrifice in secret
and this divine pact they struck with one accord:
that the saints would share the same blessings and dangers alike;
and forthwith they had begun to chant the hymns of the fathers.

The word of the Lord.

Responsional Psalm

Ps 32:1,12,18-20,22. R. v.12

R. **Happy the people the Lord has chosen as his own.**

Ring out your joy to the Lord, O you just;
for praise is fitting for loyal hearts.
They are happy, whose God is the Lord,
the people he has chosen as his own. R.

The Lord looks on those who revere him,
on those who hope in his love,
to rescue their souls from death,
to keep them alive in famine. R.

Our soul is waiting for the Lord.
The Lord is our help and our shield.
May your love be upon us, O Lord,
as we place all our hope in you. R.

SECOND READING

A reading from the letter to the Hebrews 11:1-2,8-19

Abraham looked forward to a city founded, designed and built by God.

[Only faith can guarantee the blessings that we hope for, or prove the existence of the realities that at present remain unseen. It was for faith that our ancestors were commended.

It was by faith that Abraham obeyed the call to set out for a country that was the inheritance given to him and his descendants, and that he set out without knowing where he was going. By faith he arrived, as a foreigner, in the Promised Land, and lived there as if in a strange country, with Isaac and Jacob, who were heirs with him of the same promise. They lived there in tents while he looked forward to a city founded, designed and built by God.

It was equally by faith that Sarah, in spite of being past the age, was made able to conceive, because she believed that he who had made the promise would be faithful to it. Because of this, there came from one man, and one who was already as good as dead himself, more descendants than could be counted, as many as the stars of heaven or the grains of sand on the seashore.]

All these died in faith, before receiving any of the things that had been promised, but they saw them in the far distance and welcomed them, recognising that they were only strangers and nomads on earth. People who use such terms about themselves make it quite plain that they are in search of their real homeland. They can hardly have meant the country they came from, since they had the opportunity to go back to it; but in fact they were longing for a better homeland, their heavenly homeland. That is why God is not ashamed to be called their God, since he has founded the city for them.

It was by faith that Abraham, when put to the test, offered up Isaac. He offered to sacrifice his only son even though the promises had been made to him and he had been told: It is through Isaac that your name will be carried on. He was confident that God had the power even to raise the dead; and so, figuratively speaking, he was given back Isaac from the dead.

[The word of the Lord.]

Shorter Form, verses 1-2,8-12. Read between [ ]

Gospel Acclamation

Cf. Mt 11:25

R. **Alleluia, alleluia!**
Blessed are you, Father,
Lord of heaven and earth,
for revealing the mysteries of the kingdom
to mere children.
R. **Alleluia!**

Or:

Mt 24:42,44

R. **Alleluia, alleluia!**
Stay awake and stand ready,
because you do not know the hour
when the Son of Man is coming.
R. **Alleluia!**

GOSPEL

A reading from the holy Gospel according to Luke 12:32-48
You too must stand ready.

[Jesus said to his disciples:] 'There is no need to be afraid, little flock, for it has pleased your Father to give you the kingdom.

'Sell your possessions and give alms. Get yourselves purses that do not wear out, treasure that will not fail you, in heaven where no thief can reach it and no moth destroy it. For where your treasure is, there will your heart be also.

['See that you are dressed for action and have your lamps lit. Be like men waiting for their master to return from the wedding feast, ready to open the door as soon as he comes and knocks. Happy those servants whom the master finds awake when he comes. I tell you solemnly, he will put on an apron, sit them down at table and wait on them. It may be in the second watch he comes, or in the third, but happy those servants if he finds them ready. You may be quite sure of this, that if the householder had known at what hour the burglar would come, he would not have let anyone break through the wall of his house. You too must stand ready, because the Son of Man is coming at an hour you do not expect.']

Peter said, 'Lord, do you mean this parable for us, or for everyone?' The Lord replied, 'What sort of steward, then, is faithful and wise enough for the master to place him over his household to give them their allowance of food at the proper time? Happy that servant if his master's arrival finds him at this employment. I tell you truly, he will place him over everything he owns. But as for the servant who says to himself, "My master is taking his time coming", and sets about beating the menservants and the maids, and eating and drinking and getting drunk, his master will come on a day he does not expect and at an hour he does not know. The master will cut him off and send him to the same fate as the unfaithful.

'The servant who knows what his master wants, but has not even started to carry out those wishes, will receive very many strokes of the lash. The one who did not know, but deserves to be beaten for what he has done, will receive fewer strokes. When a man has had a great deal given him, a great deal will be demanded of him, when a man has had a great deal given him on trust, even more will be expected of him.'

[The Gospel of the Lord.]

Shorter Form, verses 35-40. Read between [ ]

11 AUGUST

Prayer over the Offerings
Be pleased, O Lord, to accept
> the offerings of your Church,
for in your mercy you have given
> them to be offered
and by your power you
> transform them
into the mystery of our salvation.
Through Christ our Lord.

Super oblata
Ecclesiæ tuæ, Domine,
> munera placatus assume,
quæ et misericors
> offerenda tribuisti,
et in nostræ salutis potenter efficis
> transire mysterium.
Per Christum Dominum nostrum.

Preface of Sundays in Ordinary Time I-VIII, pp.60-67.

Communion Antiphon Ps 147:12,14
O Jerusalem, glorify the Lord,
who gives you your fill
> of finest wheat.

Ant. ad communionem
Lauda, Ierusalem, Dominum,
qui adipe frumenti satiat te.

Or: Cf. Jn 6:51
The bread that I will give,
> says the Lord,
is my flesh for the life of the world.

Vel:
Panis, quem ego dedero,
caro mea est pro sæculi vita,
dicit Dominus.

Prayer after Communion
May the communion
> in your Sacrament
that we have consumed, save us,
> O Lord,
and confirm us in the light
> of your truth.
Through Christ our Lord.

Post communionem
Sacramentorum tuorum, Domine,
communio sumpta nos salvet,
et in tuæ veritatis luce confirmet.
Per Christum Dominum nostrum.

15 August

THE ASSUMPTION OF THE BLESSED VIRGIN MARY

The Assumption reminds us that Mary's life, like that of every Christian, is a journey of following, following Jesus, a journey that has a very precise destination, a future already marked out: the definitive victory over sin and death and full communion with God, because as Paul says in his Letter to the Ephesians the Father "raised us up with him, and made us sit with him in the heavenly places in Christ Jesus" (Eph 2:6). This means that with Baptism we have already fundamentally been raised and are seated in the heavenly places in Christ Jesus, but we must physically attain what was previously begun and brought about in Baptism. In us, union with Christ resurrection is incomplete, but for the Virgin Mary it is complete, despite the journey that Our Lady also had to make. She has entered into the fullness of union with God, with her Son, she draws us onwards and accompanies us on our journey.

(Pope Benedict XVI)

Solemnity

At the Vigil Mass

This Mass is used on the evening of 14 August, either before or after First Vespers (Evening Prayer I) of the Solemnity.

Entrance Antiphon

GLORIOUS things are spoken of you, O Mary,
who today were exalted above
   the choirs of Angels
into eternal triumph with Christ.

Ant. ad introitum

GLORIOSA dicta sunt de te, Maria,
quæ hodie exaltata es super
   choros Angelorum,
et in æternum cum Christo triumphas.

The Gloria in excelsis (Glory to God in the highest) is said.

Collect

O God, who, looking on the lowliness
   of the Blessed Virgin Mary,
raised her to this grace,
that your Only Begotten Son was
   born of her according to the flesh
and that she was crowned this day

Collecta

Deus, qui beatam
   Virginem Mariam,
eius humilitatem respiciens,
   ad hanc gratiam evexisti,
ut Unigenitus tuus ex ipsa
   secundum carnem nasceretur,

with surpassing glory,	et hodierna die superexcellenti
grant through her prayers,	gloria coronasti,
that, saved by the mystery of your redemption,	eius nobis precibus concede, ut, redemptionis tuæ mysterio salvati,
we may merit to be exalted by you on high.	a te exaltari mereamur.
Through our Lord Jesus Christ, your Son,	Per Dominum nostrum Iesum Christum Filium tuum,
who lives and reigns with you in the unity of the Holy Spirit,	qui tecum vivit et regnat in unitate Spiritus Sancti,
one God, for ever and ever.	Deus, per omnia sæcula sæculorum.

FIRST READING

A reading from the first book of Chronicles 15:3-4,15-16; 16:1-2

They brought in the ark of God and set it inside the tent which David had pitched for it.

David gathered all Israel together in Jerusalem to bring the ark of God up to the place he had prepared for it. David called together the sons of Aaron and the sons of Levi. And the Levites carried the ark of God with the shafts on their shoulders, as Moses had ordered in accordance with the word of the Lord.

David then told the heads of the Levites to assign duties for their kinsmen as cantors, with their various instruments of music, harps and lyres and cymbals, to play joyful tunes. They brought the ark of God in and put it inside the tent that David had pitched for it; and they offered holocausts before God, and communion sacrifices. And when David had finished offering holocausts and communion sacrifices, he blessed the people in the name of the Lord.

The word of the Lord.

Responsorial Psalm Ps 131:6-7,9-10,13-14. R. v.8

R. **Go up, Lord, to the place of your rest, you and the ark of your strength.**

At Ephrata we heard of the ark;
we found it in the plains of Yearim.
'Let us go to the place of his dwelling;
let us go to kneel at his footstool.' R.

Your priests shall be clothed with holiness:
your faithful shall ring out their joy.

For the sake of David your servant
do not reject your anointed. R.

For the Lord has chosen Zion;
he has desired it for his dwelling:
'This is my resting-place for ever,
here have I chosen to live.' R.

R. **Go up, Lord, to the place of your rest,
you and the ark of your strength.**

SECOND READING

A reading from the first letter of St Paul to the Corinthians   15:54-57
He gave us victory through our Lord Jesus Christ.

When this perishable nature has put on imperishability, and when this mortal nature has put on immortality, then the words of scripture will come true: Death is swallowed up in victory. Death, where is your victory? Death, where is your sting? Now the sting of death is sin, and sin gets its power from the Law. So let us thank God for giving us the victory through our Lord Jesus Christ.

The word of the Lord.

Gospel Acclamation   Lk 11:28

R. **Alleluia, alleluia!**
Happy are those
who hear the word of God,
and keep it.
R. **Alleluia!**

GOSPEL

A reading from the holy Gospel according to Luke   11:27-28
Happy the womb that bore you!

As Jesus was speaking, a woman in the crowd raised her voice and said, 'Happy the womb that bore you and the breasts you sucked!' But he replied, 'Still happier those who hear the word of God and keep it!'

The Gospel of the Lord.

The Creed is said.

Prayer over the Offerings

Receive, we pray, O Lord,
the sacrifice of conciliation
 and praise,
which we celebrate on
 the Assumption of the holy
 Mother of God,
that it may lead us to your pardon
and confirm us in perpetual
 thanksgiving.
Through Christ our Lord.

Proper Preface, as in the following Mass, p.537.

Super oblata

Suscipe, quæsumus, Domine,
sacrificium placationis et laudis,
quod in sanctæ Dei Genetricis
 Assumptione celebramus,
ut ad veniam nos
 obtinendam perducat,
et in perpetua gratiarum
 constituat actione.
Per Christum Dominum nostrum.

Communion Antiphon   Cf. Lk 11:27

Blessed is the womb
 of the Virgin Mary,
which bore the Son
 of the eternal Father.

Ant. ad communionem

Beata viscera Mariæ Virginis,
quæ portaverunt æterni
 Patris Filium.

Prayer after Communion

Having partaken of this
 heavenly table,
we beseech your mercy,
 Lord our God,
that we, who honour
 the Assumption of the Mother
 of God,
may be freed from every threat
 of harm.
Through Christ our Lord.

Post communionem

Mensæ cælestis participes effecti,
imploramus clementiam tuam,
 Domine Deus noster,
ut, qui Assumptionem Dei
 Genetricis colimus,
a cunctis malis
 imminentibus liberemur.
Per Christum Dominum nostrum.

A formula of Solemn Blessing, pp.144-145, may be used.

At the Mass during the Day

Entrance Antiphon   Cf. Rv 12:1

A GREAT sign appeared
in heaven:
a woman clothed with the sun,
 and the moon beneath her feet,
and on her head a crown
 of twelve stars.

Ant. ad introitum

SIGNUM magnum apparuit
in cælo:
mulier amicta sole, et luna sub
 pedibus eius,
et in capite eius corona
 stellarum duodecim.

Or:

Let us all rejoice in the Lord,
as we celebrate the feast day
   in honour of the Virgin Mary,
at whose Assumption
   the Angels rejoice
and praise the Son of God.

Vel:

Gaudeamus omnes in Domino,
diem festum celebrantes sub
   honore Mariæ Virginis,
de cuius Assumptione
   gaudent Angeli,
et collaudant Filium Dei.

The Gloria in excelsis (Glory to God in the highest) is said.

Collect

Almighty ever-living God,
who assumed the Immaculate Virgin
   Mary, the Mother of your Son,
body and soul into heavenly glory,
grant, we pray,
that, always attentive to the things
   that are above,
we may merit to be sharers
   of her glory.
Through our Lord Jesus Christ,
   your Son,
who lives and reigns with you
   in the unity of the Holy Spirit,
one God, for ever and ever.

Collecta

Omnipotens sempiterne Deus,
qui immaculatam Virginem
   Mariam, Filii tui Genetricem,
corpore et anima ad cælestem
   gloriam assumpsisti,
concede, quæsumus, ut,
   ad superna semper intenti,
ipsius gloriæ mereamur
   esse consortes.
Per Dominum nostrum Iesum
   Christum Filium tuum,
qui tecum vivit et regnat
in unitate Spiritus Sancti,
Deus, per omnia sæcula sæculorum.

FIRST READING

A reading from the book of the Apocalypse   11:19; 12:1-6,10

A woman adorned with the sun standing on the moon.

The sanctuary of God in heaven opened, and the ark of the covenant could be seen inside it.

   Now a great sign appeared in heaven: a woman, adorned with the sun, standing on the moon, and with the twelve stars on her head for a crown. She was pregnant, and in labour, crying aloud in the pangs of childbirth. Then a second sign appeared in the sky, a huge red dragon which had seven heads and ten horns, and each of the seven heads crowned with a coronet. Its tail dragged a third of the stars from the sky and dropped them to the earth, and the dragon stopped in front of the woman as she was having the child, so that he could eat it as soon as it was born from its mother. The woman brought a male child into the world, the son who was to rule all nations with an iron sceptre, and the child was taken straight up to God and to his throne, while the woman escaped into the desert, where God had made a place of safety ready. Then I heard a voice shout from heaven, 'Victory and power and empire for ever have been won by our God, and all authority for his Christ.'

The word of the Lord.

Responsional Psalm   Ps 44:10-12,16. R. v.10

R. **On your right stands the queen, in garments of gold.**

The daughters of kings are among your loved ones.
On your right stands the queen in gold of Ophir.
Listen, O daughter, give ear to my words:
forget your own people and your father's house. R.

So will the king desire your beauty:
He is your lord, pay homage to him.
They are escorted amid gladness and joy;
they pass within the palace of the king. R.

SECOND READING

A reading from the first letter of St Paul to the Corinthians   15:20-26
Christ as the first-fruits and then, those who belong to him.

Christ has been raised from the dead, the first-fruits of all who have fallen asleep. Death came through one man and in the same way the resurrection of the dead has come through one man. Just as all men die in Adam, so all men will be brought to life in Christ; but all of them in their proper order: Christ as the first-fruits and then, after the coming of Christ, those who belong to him. After that will come the end, when he hands over the kingdom to God the Father, having done away with every sovereignty, authority and power. For he must be king until he has put all his enemies under his feet and the last of the enemies to be destroyed is death, for everything is to be put under his feet.

The word of the Lord.

Gospel Acclamation

R. **Alleluia, alleluia!**
Mary has been taken up into heaven;
all the choirs of angels are rejoicing.
R. **Alleluia!**

GOSPEL

A reading from the holy Gospel according to Luke 1:39-56
The Almighty has done great things for me, he has exalted up the lowly.

Mary set out and went as quickly as she could to a town in the hill country of Judah. She went into Zechariah's house and greeted Elizabeth. Now as soon as Elizabeth heard Mary's greeting, the child leapt in her womb and Elizabeth was filled with the Holy Spirit. She gave a loud cry and said, 'Of all women you are the most blessed, and blessed is the fruit of your womb. Why should I be honoured with a visit from the mother of my Lord? For the moment your greeting reached my ears, the child in my womb leapt for joy. Yes, blessed is she who believed that the promise made her by the Lord would be fulfilled.'

And Mary said:

> 'My soul proclaims the greatness of the Lord
> and my spirit exults in God my saviour;
> because he has looked upon his lowly handmaid.
> Yes, from this day forward all generations will call me blessed,
> for the Almighty has done great things for me.
> Holy is his name,
> and his mercy reaches from age to age for those who fear him.
> He has shown the power of his arm,
> he has routed the proud of heart.
> He has pulled down princes from their thrones and exalted the lowly.
> The hungry he has filled with good things, the rich sent empty away.
> He has come to the help of Israel his servant, mindful of his mercy
> – according to the promise he made to our ancestors –
> of his mercy to Abraham and to his descendants for ever.'

Mary stayed with Elizabeth about three months and then went back home.

The Gospel of the Lord.

The Creed is said.

Prayer over the Offerings

May this oblation, our tribute
  of homage,
rise up to you, O Lord,
and, through the intercession
  of the most Blessed Virgin Mary,
whom you assumed into heaven,
may our hearts,
  aflame with the fire of love,
constantly long for you.
Through Christ our Lord.

Preface: The Glory of Mary assumed into heaven.

It is truly right and just, our duty
  and our salvation,
always and everywhere to give
  you thanks,
Lord, holy Father, almighty
  and eternal God,
through Christ our Lord.

For today the Virgin Mother of God
was assumed into heaven
as the beginning and image
of your Church's coming
  to perfection
and a sign of sure hope and comfort
  to your pilgrim people;
rightly you would not allow her
to see the corruption of the tomb,
since from her own body she
  marvellously brought forth
your incarnate Son,
  the Author of all life.

And so, in company with the choirs
  of Angels,
we praise you, and with joy
  we proclaim:

Holy, Holy, Holy Lord God of hosts...

Super oblata

Ascendat ad te, Domine, nostræ
  devotionis oblatio,
et, beatissima Virgine Maria
in cælum assumpta intercedente,
corda nostra, caritatis igne succensa,
ad te iugiter aspirent.
Per Christum Dominum nostrum.

Præfatio: De Gloria Mariæ Assumptæ.

Vere dignum et iustum est,
  æquum et salutare,
nos tibi semper et ubique
  gratias agere:
Domine, sancte Pater,
  omnipotens æterne Deus:
per Christum Dominum nostrum.

Quoniam hodie Virgo Deipara
  in cælos assumpta est,
Ecclesiæ tuæ consummandæ
  initium et imago,
ac populo peregrinanti certæ spei
  et solacii documentum;
corruptionem enim sepulcri
eam videre merito noluisti,
quæ Filium tuum,
  vitæ omnis auctorem,
ineffabiliter de se
  genuit incarnatum.

Et ideo, choris angelicis sociati,
te laudamus, in gaudio confitentes:
Sanctus, Sanctus, Sanctus...

Communion Antiphon Lk 1:48-49

All generations will call me blessed,
for he who is mighty has done
  great things for me.

Ant. ad communionem

Beatam me dicent
  omnes generationes,
quia fecit mihi magna
  qui potens est.

Prayer after Communion

Having received the Sacrament
  of salvation,
we ask you to grant, O Lord,
that, through the intercession
  of the Blessed Virgin Mary,
whom you assumed into heaven,
we may be brought to the glory
  of the resurrection.
Through Christ our Lord.

Post communionem

Sumptis, Domine,
  salutaribus sacramentis,
da, quæsumus,
ut, intercessione beatæ Mariæ
  Virginis in cælum assumptæ,
ad resurrectionis
  gloriam perducamur.
Per Christum Dominum nostrum.

A formula of Solemn Blessing, p.144-145, may be used.

18 August

TWENTIETH SUNDAY IN ORDINARY TIME

Entrance Antiphon Ps 83:10-11

TURN your eyes, O God,
  our shield;
and look on the face
  of your anointed one;
one day within your courts
is better than a thousand elsewhere.

Ant. ad introitum

PROTECTOR noster,
  aspice, Deus,
et respice in faciem Christi tui,
quia melior est dies una in atriis
  tuis super millia.

Collect

O God, who have prepared
  for those who love you
good things which no eye can see,
fill our hearts, we pray,
  with the warmth of your love,
so that, loving you in all things
  and above all things,

Collecta

Deus, qui diligentibus te bona
  invisibilia præparasti,
infunde cordibus nostris
  tui amoris affectum,
ut, te in omnibus et super
  omnia diligentes,

we may attain your promises,
which surpass every human desire.
Through our Lord Jesus Christ,
　　your Son,
who lives and reigns with you
　　in the unity of the Holy Spirit,
one God, for ever and ever.

promissiones tuas, quæ omne
　　desiderium superant,
consequamur.
Per Dominum nostrum Iesum
　　Christum Filium tuum,
qui tecum vivit et regnat
　　in unitate Spiritus Sancti,
Deus, per omnia sæcula sæculorum.

FIRST READING

A reading from the prophet Jeremiah　　　　　　　　　　38:4-6,8-10

You have borne me to be a man of dissension for all the land.

The king's leading men spoke to the king. 'Let Jeremiah be put to death: he is unquestionably disheartening the remaining soldiers in the city, and all the people too, by talking like this. The fellow does not have the welfare of this people at heart so much as its ruin.' 'He is in your hands, as you know,' King Zedekiah answered 'for the king is powerless against you.' So they took Jeremiah and threw him into the well of Prince Malchiah in the Court of the Guard, letting him down with ropes. There was no water in the well, only mud, and into the mud Jeremiah sank.

　　Ebed-melech came out from the palace and spoke to the king. 'My lord king,' he said 'these men have done a wicked thing by treating the prophet Jeremiah like this: they have thrown him into the well where he will die.' At this the king gave Ebed-melech the Cushite the following order: 'Take three men with you from here and pull the prophet Jeremiah out of the well before he dies.'

　　The word of the Lord.

Responsorial Psalm　　　　　　　　　　　　　　　　Ps 39:2-4,18. R. v.14

R. **Lord, come to my aid!**

I waited, I waited for the Lord
and he stooped down to me;
he heard my cry. R.

He drew me from the deadly pit,
from the miry clay.
He set my feet upon a rock
and made my footsteps firm. R.

He put a new song into my mouth,
praise of our God.

Many shall see and fear
and shall trust in the Lord. R.

As for me, wretched and poor,
the Lord thinks of me.
You are my rescuer, my help,
O God, do not delay. R.

R. **Lord, come to my aid!**

SECOND READING

A reading from the letter to the Hebrews 12:1-4

We shall keep running steadily in the race we have started.

With so many witnesses in a great cloud on every side of us, we too, then, should throw off everything that hinders us, especially the sin that clings so easily, and keep running steadily in the race we have started. Let us not lose sight of Jesus, who leads us in our faith and brings it to perfection: for the sake of the joy which was still in the future, he endured the cross, disregarding the shamefulness of it, and from now on has taken his place at the right of God's throne. Think of the way he stood such opposition from sinners and then you will not give up for want of courage. In the fight against sin, you have not yet had to keep fighting to the point of death.

The word of the Lord.

Gospel Acclamation Cf. Ac 16:14

R. **Alleluia, alleluia!**
Open our heart, O Lord,
to accept the words of your Son.
R. **Alleluia!**

Or: Jn 10:27

R. **Alleluia, alleluia!**
The sheep that belong to me listen to my voice,
says the Lord,
I know them and they follow me.
R. **Alleluia!**

GOSPEL

A reading from the holy Gospel according to Luke 12:49-53

I am not here to bring peace, but rather division.

Jesus said to his disciples: 'I have come to bring fire to the earth, and how I wish it were blazing already! There is a baptism I must still receive, and how great is my distress till it is over!

'Do you suppose that I am here to bring peace on earth? No, I tell you, but rather division. For from now on a household of five will be divided: three against two and two against three; the father divided against the son, son against father, mother against daughter, daughter against mother, mother-in-law against daughter-in-law, daughter-in-law against mother-in-law.'

The Gospel of the Lord.

Prayer over the Offerings

Receive our oblation, O Lord,
by which is brought about
 a glorious exchange,
that, by offering what you have given,
we may merit to receive
 your very self.
Through Christ our Lord.

Preface of Sundays in Ordinary Time I-VIII, pp.60-67.

Super oblata

Suscipe, Domine, munera nostra,
quibus exercentur
 commercia gloriosa,
ut, offerentes quæ dedisti,
teipsum mereamur accipere.
Per Christum Dominum nostrum.

Communion Antiphon   Ps 129:7

With the Lord there is mercy;
in him is plentiful redemption.

Or: Jn 6:51-52

I am the living bread that came
 down from heaven, says the Lord.
Whoever eats of this bread
 will live for ever.

Ant. ad communionem

Apud Dominum misericordia,
et copiosa apud eum redemptio.

Vel:

Ego sum panis vivus, qui de cælo
 descendi, dicit Dominus:
si quis manducaverit ex hoc pane,
 vivet in æternum.

Prayer after Communion

Made partakers of Christ through
 these Sacraments,
we humbly implore your
 mercy, Lord,
that, conformed to his image
 on earth,
we may merit also to be his coheirs
 in heaven.
Who lives and reigns
 for ever and ever.

Post communionem

Per hæc sacramenta, Domine,
 Christi participes effecti,
clementiam tuam
 humiliter imploramus,
ut, eius imaginis conformes
 in terris,
et eius consortes in cælis
 fieri mereamur.
Qui vivit et regnat
 in sæcula sæculorum.

25 August

TWENTY-FIRST SUNDAY IN ORDINARY TIME

Entrance Antiphon   Cf. Ps 85:1-3

Turn your ear, O Lord,
and answer me;
save the servant who trusts in you,
my God.
Have mercy on me, O Lord,
for I cry to you all the day long.

Ant. ad introitum

Inclina, Domine, aurem tuam
ad me, et exaudi me.
Salvum fac servum tuum,
Deus meus, sperantem in te.
Miserere mihi, Domine,
quoniam ad te clamavi tota die.

Collect

O God, who cause the minds
of the faithful
to unite in a single purpose,
grant your people to love
what you command
and to desire what you promise,
that, amid the uncertainties
of this world,
our hearts may be fixed on that place
where true gladness is found.
Through our Lord Jesus Christ,
your Son,
who lives and reigns with you
in the unity of the Holy Spirit,
one God, for ever and ever.

Collecta

Deus, qui fidelium mentes unius
efficis voluntatis,
da populis tuis id amare
quod præcipis,
id desiderare quod promittis,
ut, inter mundanas varietates,
ibi nostra fixa sint corda,
ubi vera sunt gaudia.
Per Dominum nostrum Iesum
Christum Filium tuum,
qui tecum vivit et regnat
in unitate Spiritus Sancti,
Deus, per omnia sæcula sæculorum.

FIRST READING

A reading from the prophet Isaiah   66:18-21

They will bring all your brothers from all the nations.

The Lord says this: I am coming to gather the nations of every language. They shall come to witness my glory. I will give them a sign and send some of their survivors to the nations: to Tarshish, Put, Lud, Moshech, Rosh, Tubal, and Javan, to the distant islands that have never heard of me or seen my glory. They will proclaim my glory to the nations. As an offering to the Lord they will bring all your brothers, in horses, in chariots, in litters, on mules, on dromedaries, from all the nations to my holy mountain in Jerusalem, says the Lord, like Israelites bringing oblations in clean vessels to the Temple of the Lord. And of some of them I will make priests and Levites, says the Lord.

The word of the Lord.

Responsorial Psalm   Ps 116. R. Mk 16:15

R. **Go out to the whole world;
proclaim the Good News.**
   Or: **Alleluia!**

O praise the Lord, all you nations,
acclaim him all you peoples! R.

Strong is his love for us;
he is faithful for ever. R.

SECOND READING

A reading from the letter to the Hebrews   12:5-7,11-13

The Lord trains the one that he loves.

Have you forgotten that encouraging text in which you are addressed as sons? My son, when the Lord corrects you, do not treat it lightly; but do not get discouraged when he reprimands you. For the Lord trains the ones that he loves and he punishes all those that he acknowledges as his sons. Suffering is part of your training; God is treating you as his sons. Has there ever been any son whose father did not train him? Of course, any punishment is most painful at the time, and far from pleasant; but later, in those on whom it has been used, it bears fruit in peace and goodness. So hold up your limp arms and steady your trembling knees and smooth out the path you tread; there the injured limb will not be wrenched, it will grow strong again.

The word of the Lord.

Gospel Acclamation   Jn 14:23

R. **Alleluia, alleluia!**
If anyone loves me he will keep my word,
and my Father will love him,
and we shall come to him.
R. **Alleluia!**

Or: Jn 14:6

R. **Alleluia, alleluia!**
I am the Way, the Truth and the Life, says the Lord;
no one can come to the Father except through me.
R. **Alleluia!**

GOSPEL

A reading from the holy Gospel according to Luke 13:22-30

Men from east and west will come to take their places at the feast in the kingdom of God.

Through towns and villages Jesus went teaching, making his way to Jerusalem. Someone said to him, 'Sir, will there be only a few saved?' He said to them, 'Try your best to enter by the narrow door, because, I tell you, many will try to enter and will not succeed.

'Once the master of the house has got up and locked the door, you may find yourself knocking on the door, saying, "Lord, open to us" but he will answer, "I do not know where you come from." Then you will find yourself saying, "We once ate and drank in your company; you taught in our streets" but he will reply, "I do not know where you come from. Away from me, all you wicked men!"

'Then there will be weeping and grinding of teeth, when you see Abraham and Isaac and Jacob and all the prophets in the kingdom of God, and yourselves turned outside. And men from east and west, from north and south, will come to take their places at the feast in the kingdom of God.

'Yes, there are those now last who will be first, and those now first who will be last.'

The Gospel of the Lord.

Prayer over the Offerings

O Lord, who gained for yourself
   a people by adoption
through the one sacrifice offered
   once for all,
bestow graciously on us, we pray,
the gifts of unity and peace
   in your Church.
Through Christ our Lord.

Super oblata

Qui una semel hostia, Domine,
adoptionis tibi populum acquisisti,
unitatis et pacis in Ecclesia tua
propitius nobis dona concedas.
Per Christum Dominum nostrum.

Preface of Sundays in Ordinary Time I-VIII, pp.60-67.

Communion Antiphon Cf. Ps 103:13-15

The earth is replete with the fruits
of your work, O Lord;
you bring forth bread from the earth
and wine to cheer the heart.

Or: Cf. Jn 6:54

Whoever eats my flesh
and drinks my blood
has eternal life, says the Lord,
and I will raise him up on the
last day.

Prayer after Communion

Complete within us, O Lord,
we pray,
the healing work of your mercy
and graciously perfect
and sustain us,
so that in all things we may
please you.
Through Christ our Lord.

Ant. ad communionem

De fructu operum tuorum,
Domine, satiabitur terra,
ut educas panem de terra,
et vinum lætificet cor hominis.

Vel:

Qui manducat meam carnem
et bibit meum sanguinem,
habet vitam æternam,
dicit Dominus;
et ego resuscitabo eum
in novissimo die.

Post communionem

Plenum, quæsumus, Domine,
in nobis remedium tuæ
miserationis operare
ac tales nos esse perfice propitius
et sic foveri,
ut tibi in omnibus
placere valeamus.
Per Christum Dominum nostrum.

---

1 September

TWENTY-SECOND SUNDAY IN ORDINARY TIME

Entrance Antiphon Cf. Ps 85:3,5

HAVE mercy on me, O Lord,
for I cry to you all the day long.
O Lord, you are good and forgiving,
full of mercy to all who call to you.

Ant. ad introitum

MISERERE mihi, Domine,
quoniam ad te clamavi
tota die:
quia tu, Domine, suavis ac mitis es,
et copiosus in misericordia
omnibus invocantibus te.

Collect

God of might, giver of every
  good gift,
put into our hearts the love
  of your name,
so that, by deepening our sense
  of reverence,
you may nurture in us what is good
and, by your watchful care,
keep safe what you have nurtured.
Through our Lord Jesus Christ,
  your Son,
who lives and reigns with you
  in the unity of the Holy Spirit,
one God, for ever and ever.

Collecta

Deus virtutum, cuius est totum
  quod est optimum,
insere pectoribus nostris tui
  nominis amorem,
et præsta, ut in nobis,
religionis augmento,
  quæ sunt bona nutrias,
ac, vigilanti studio,
  quæ sunt nutrita custodias.
Per Dominum nostrum Iesum
  Christum Filium tuum,
qui tecum vivit et regnat
  in unitate Spiritus Sancti,
Deus, per omnia sæcula sæculorum.

FIRST READING

A reading from the book of Ecclesiasticus   3:19-21,30-31

Behave humbly, and then you will find favour with the Lord.

My son, be gentle in carrying out your business,
and you will be better loved than a lavish giver.
The greater you are, the more you should behave humbly,
and then you will find favour with the Lord;
for great though the power of the Lord is,
he accepts the homage of the humble.
There is no cure for the proud man's malady,
since an evil growth has taken root in him.
The heart of a sensible man will reflect on parables,
an attentive ear is the sage's dream.

   The word of the Lord.

Responsorial Psalm   Ps 67:4-7,10-11. R. Cf. v.11

R. **In your goodness, O God, you prepared a home for the poor.**

   The just shall rejoice at the presence of God,
   they shall exult and dance for joy.
   O sing to the Lord, make music to his name;
   rejoice in the Lord, exult at his presence. R.

Father of the orphan, defender of the widow,
such is God in his holy place.
God gives the lonely a home to live in;
he leads the prisoners forth into freedom. R.

You poured down, O God, a generous rain:
when your people were starved you gave them new life.
It was there that your people found a home,
prepared in your goodness, O God, for the poor. R.

SECOND READING

A reading from the letter to the Hebrews   12:18-19,22-24

You have to come to Mount Zion and to the city of the living God.

What you have come to is nothing known to the senses: not a blazing fire, or a gloom turning to total darkness, or a storm; or trumpeting thunder or the great voice speaking which made everyone that heard it beg that no more should be said to them. But what you have come to is Mount Zion and the city of the living God, the heavenly Jerusalem where the millions of angels have gathered for the festival, with the whole Church in which everyone is a 'first-born son' and a citizen of heaven. You have come to God himself, the supreme Judge, and been placed with spirits of the saints who have been made perfect; and to Jesus, the mediator who brings a new covenant.

The word of the Lord.

Gospel Acclamation   Jn 14:23

R. **Alleluia, alleluia!**
If anyone loves me he will keep my word,
and my Father will love him,
and we shall come to him.
R. **Alleluia!**

Or: Mt 11:29

R. **Alleluia, alleluia!**
Shoulder my yoke and learn from me,
for I am gentle and humble in heart.
R. **Alleluia!**

GOSPEL

A reading from the holy Gospel according to Luke 14:1,7-14

Everyone who exalts himself will be humbled, and the man who humbles himself will be exalted.

On a sabbath day Jesus had gone for a meal to the house of one of the leading Pharisees; and they watched him closely. He then told the guests a parable, because he had noticed how they picked the places of honour. He said this, 'When someone invites you to a wedding feast, do not take your seat in the place of honour. A more distinguished person than you may have been invited, and the person who invited you both may come and say, "Give up your place to this man." And then, to your embarrassment, you would have to go and take the lowest place. No; when you are a guest, make your way to the lowest place and sit there, so that, when your host comes, he may say, "My friend, move up higher." In that way, everyone with you at the table will see you honoured. For everyone who exalts himself will be humbled, and the man who humbles himself will be exalted.'

Then he said to his host, 'When you give a lunch or a dinner, do not ask your friends, brothers, relations or rich neighbours, for fear they repay your courtesy by inviting you in return. No; when you have a party, invite the poor, the crippled, the lame, the blind; that they cannot pay you back means that you are fortunate, because repayment will be made to you when the virtuous rise again.'

The Gospel of the Lord.

Prayer over the Offerings

May this sacred offering, O Lord,
confer on us always the blessing
   of salvation,
that what it celebrates in mystery
it may accomplish in power.
Through Christ our Lord.

Super oblata

Benedictionem nobis, Domine,
   conferat salutarem
sacra semper oblatio,
ut, quod agit mysterio,
   virtute perficiat.
Per Christum Dominum nostrum.

Preface of Sundays in Ordinary Time I-VIII, pp.60-67.

Communion Antiphon   Ps 30:20

How great is the goodness, Lord,
that you keep for those who fear you.

Or: Mt 5:9-10

Blessed are the peacemakers,
for they shall be called
    children of God.
Blessed are they who are persecuted
    for the sake of righteousness,
for theirs is the Kingdom of Heaven.

Prayer after Communion

Renewed by this bread
    from the heavenly table,
we beseech you, Lord,
that, being the food of charity,
it may confirm our hearts
and stir us to serve you
    in our neighbour.
Through Christ our Lord.

Ant. ad communionem

Quam magna multitudo dulcedinis
    tuæ, Domine,
quam abscondisti timentibus te.

Vel:

Beati pacifici,
    quoniam filii Dei vocabuntur.
Beati qui persecutionem patiuntur
    propter iustitiam,
quoniam ipsorum
    est regnum cælorum.

Post communionem

Pane mensæ cælestis refecti, te,
    Domine, deprecamur,
ut hoc nutrimentum caritatis corda
    nostra confirmet,
quatenus ad tibi ministrandum
    in fratribus excitemur.
Per Christum Dominum nostrum.

8 September

TWENTY-THIRD SUNDAY IN ORDINARY TIME

Entrance Antiphon Ps 118:137,124

YOU are just, O Lord,
    and your judgement is right;
treat your servant in accord
    with your merciful love.

Collect

O God, by whom we are redeemed
    and receive adoption,
look graciously upon your beloved
    sons and daughters,

Ant. ad introitum

IUSTUS es, Domine,
    et rectum iudicium tuum;
fac cum servo tuo secundum
    misericordiam tuam.

Collecta

Deus, per quem nobis
et redemptio venit
    et præstatur adoptio,
filios dilectionis tuæ

that those who believe in Christ
may receive true freedom
and an everlasting inheritance.
Through our Lord Jesus Christ,
    your Son,
who lives and reigns with you
    in the unity of the Holy Spirit,
one God, for ever and ever.

benignus intende,
ut in Christo credentibus
et vera tribuatur libertas,
    et hereditas æterna.
Per Dominum nostrum Iesum
    Christum Filium tuum,
qui tecum vivit et regnat
    in unitate Spiritus Sancti,
Deus, per omnia sæcula sæculorum.

FIRST READING

A reading from the book of Wisdom   9:13-18

Who can divine the will of God?

What man can know the intentions of God?
Who can divine the will of the Lord?
The reasonings of mortals are unsure
and our intentions unstable;
for a perishable body presses down the soul,
and this tent of clay weighs down the teeming mind.
It is hard enough for us to work out what is on earth,
laborious to know what lies within our reach;
who, then, can discover what is in the heavens?

As for your intention, who could have learnt it, had you not granted Wisdom
and sent your holy spirit from above?
Thus have the paths of those on earth been straightened
and men been taught what pleases you,
and saved, by Wisdom.

   The word of the Lord.

Responsorial Psalm   Ps 89:3-6,12-14,17. R. v.1

R. **O Lord, you have been our refuge
    from one generation to the next.**

   You turn men back into dust
   and say 'Go back, sons of men.'
   To your eyes a thousand years
   are like yesterday, come and gone,
   no more than a watch in the night. R.

You sweep men away like a dream,
like grass which springs up in the morning.
In the morning it springs up and flowers:
by evening it withers and fades. R.

Make us know the shortness of our life
that we may gain wisdom of heart.
Lord, relent! Is your anger for ever?
Show pity to your servants. R.

In the morning, fill us with your love;
we shall exult and rejoice all our days.
Let the favour of the Lord be upon us:
give success to the work of our hands. R.

SECOND READING

A reading from the letter of St Paul to Philemon   9-10,12-17
Have him back, not as a slave any more, but as a dear brother.

This is Paul writing, an old man now and, what is more, still a prisoner of Christ Jesus. I am appealing to you for a child of mine, whose father I became while wearing these chains: I mean Onesimus. I am sending him back to you, and with him – I could say – a part of my own self. I should have liked to keep him with me; he could have been a substitute for you, to help me while I am in the chains that the Good News has brought me. However, I did not want to do anything without your consent; it would have been forcing your act of kindness, which should be spontaneous. I know you have been deprived of Onesimus for a time, but it was only so that you could have him back for ever, not as a slave any more, but something much better than a slave, a dear brother; especially dear to me, but how much more to you, as a blood-brother as well as a brother in the Lord. So if all that we have in common means anything to you, welcome him as you would me.

The word of the Lord.

Gospel Acclamation   Jn 15:15

R. **Alleluia, alleluia!**
I call you friends, says the Lord,
because I have made known to you
everything I have learnt from my Father.
R. **Alleluia!**

Or: Ps 118:135

R. Alleluia, alleluia!
Let your face shine on your servant,
and teach me your decrees.
R. Alleluia!

GOSPEL

A reading from the holy Gospel according to Luke   14:25-33

None of you can be my disciple unless he gives up all his possessions.

Great crowds accompanied Jesus on his way and he turned and spoke to them. 'If any man comes to me without hating his father, mother, wife, children, brothers, sisters, yes and his own life too, he cannot be my disciple. Anyone who does not carry his cross and come after me cannot be my disciple.

'And indeed, which of you here, intending to build a tower, would not first sit down and work out the cost to see if he had enough to complete it? Otherwise, if he laid the foundation and then found himself unable to finish the work, the onlookers would all start making fun of him and saying, "Here is a man who started to build and was unable to finish." Or again, what king marching to war against another king would not first sit down and consider whether with ten thousand men he could stand up to the other who advanced against him with twenty thousand? If not, then while the other king was still a long way off, he would send envoys to sue for peace. So in the same way, none of you can be my disciple unless he gives up all his possessions.'

The Gospel of the Lord.

Prayer over the Offerings	Super oblata

O God, who give us the gift
   of true prayer and of peace,
graciously grant that,
   through this offering,
we may do fitting homage to your
   divine majesty
and, by partaking
   of the sacred mystery,
	Deus, auctor sinceræ
	   devotionis et pacis,
	da, quæsumus,
	   ut et maiestatem tuam
	convenienter hoc
	   munere veneremur,
	et sacri participatione mysterii

we may be faithfully united
   in mind and heart.
Through Christ our Lord.

fideliter sensibus uniamur.
Per Christum Dominum nostrum.

Preface of Sundays in Ordinary Time I-VIII, pp.60-67.

Communion Antiphon Cf. Ps 41:2-3 | Ant. ad communionem

Like the deer that yearns
   for running streams,
so my soul is yearning for you,
   my God;
my soul is thirsting for God,
   the living God.

Quemadmodum desiderat cervus
   ad fontes aquarum,
ita desiderat anima mea
   ad te, Deus:
sitivit anima mea ad Deum
   fortem vivum.

Or: Jn 8:12 | Vel:

I am the light of the world,
   says the Lord;
whoever follows me will not walk
   in darkness,
but will have the light of life.

Ego sum lux mundi,
   dicit Dominus:
qui sequitur me non ambulat
   in tenebris,
sed habebit lumen vitæ.

Prayer after Communion | Post communionem

Grant that your faithful, O Lord,
whom you nourish and endow
   with life
through the food of your Word
   and heavenly Sacrament,
may so benefit from your beloved
   Son's great gifts
that we may merit an eternal share
   in his life.
Who lives and reigns
   for ever and ever.

Da fidelibus tuis, Domine,
quos et verbi tui et cælestis
   sacramenti pabulo
nutris et vivificas,
ita dilecti Filii tui tantis
   muneribus proficere,
ut eius vitæ semper consortes
   effici mereamur.
Qui vivit et regnat
   in sæcula sæculorum.

15 September

TWENTY-FOURTH SUNDAY IN ORDINARY TIME

Entrance Antiphon   Cf. Si 36:18

GIVE peace, O Lord,
to those who wait for you,
that your prophets be found true.
Hear the prayers of your servant,
and of your people Israel.

Collect

Look upon us, O God,
Creator and ruler of all things,
and, that we may feel the working
   of your mercy,
grant that we may serve you
with all our heart.
Through our Lord Jesus Christ,
   your Son,
who lives and reigns with you
in the unity of the Holy Spirit,
one God, for ever and ever.

Ant. ad introitum

DA pacem, Domine,
sustinentibus te,
ut prophetæ tui fideles inveniantur;
exaudi preces servi tui,
   et plebis tuæ Israel.

Collecta

Respice nos, rerum omnium Deus
   creator et rector,
et, ut tuæ propitiationis
   sentiamus effectum,
toto nos tribue tibi corde servire.
Per Dominum nostrum Iesum
   Christum Filium tuum,
qui tecum vivit et regnat
in unitate Spiritus Sancti,
Deus, per omnia sæcula sæculorum.

FIRST READING

A reading from the book of Exodus   32:7-11,13-14

The Lord relented and did not bring on his people the disaster he had threatened.

The Lord spoke to Moses, 'Go down now, because your people whom you brought out of Egypt have apostasised. They have been quick to leave the way I marked out for them; they have made themselves a calf of molten metal and have worshipped it and offered it sacrifice. "Here is your God, Israel," they have cried "who brought you up from the land of Egypt!"' The Lord then said to Moses, 'I can see how headstrong these people are! Leave me, now, my wrath shall blaze out against them and devour them; of you, however, I will make a great nation.'

   But Moses pleaded with the Lord his God. 'Lord,' he said, 'why should your wrath blaze out against this people of yours whom you brought out of the land of Egypt with arm outstretched and mighty hand? Remember

Abraham, Isaac and Jacob, your servants to whom by your own self you swore and made this promise: I will make your offspring as many as the stars of heaven, and all this land which I promised I will give to your descendants, and it shall be their heritage for ever.' So the Lord relented and did not bring on his people the disaster he had threatened.

The word of the Lord.

Responsional Psalm
Ps 50:3-4,12-13,17,19. R. Lk 15:18

R. **I will leave this place and go to my father.**

Have mercy on me, God, in your kindness.
In your compassion blot out my offence.
O wash me more and more from my guilt
and cleanse me from my sin. R.

A pure heart create for me, O God,
put a steadfast spirit within me.
Do not cast me away from your presence,
nor deprive me of your holy spirit. R.

O Lord, open my lips
and my mouth shall declare your praise.
My sacrifice is a contrite spirit;
a humbled, contrite heart you will not spurn. R.

SECOND READING

A reading from the first letter of St Paul to Timothy 1:12-17
Christ Jesus came into the world to save sinners.

I thank Christ Jesus our Lord, who has given me strength, and who judged me faithful enough to call me into his service even though I used to be a blasphemer and did all I could to injure and discredit the faith. Mercy, however, was shown me, because until I became a believer I had been acting in ignorance; and the grace of our Lord filled me with faith and with the love that is in Christ Jesus. Here is a saying that you can rely on and nobody should doubt: that Christ Jesus came into the world to save sinners. I myself am the greatest of them; and if mercy has been shown to me, it is because Jesus Christ meant to make me the greatest evidence of his inexhaustible patience for all the other people who would later have to trust in him to come to eternal life. To the eternal King, the undying, invisible and only God, be honour and glory for ever and ever. Amen.

The word of the Lord.

Gospel Acclamation

Cf. Ep 1:17,18

R. **Alleluia, alleluia!**
May the Father of our Lord Jesus Christ
enlighten the eyes of our mind,
so that we can see what hope his call holds for us.
R. **Alleluia!**

Or:

2 Co 5:19

R. **Alleluia, alleluia!**
God in Christ was reconciling the world to himself,
and he has entrusted to us the news that they are reconciled.
R. **Alleluia!**

GOSPEL

A reading from the holy Gospel according to Luke

15:1-32

There will be rejoicing in heaven over one repentant sinner.

[The tax collectors and the sinners were all seeking the company of Jesus to hear what he had to say, and the Pharisees and the scribes complained. 'This man' they said 'welcomes sinners and eats with them.' So he spoke this parable to them:

'What man among you with a hundred sheep, losing one, would not leave the ninety-nine in the wilderness and go after the missing one till he found it? And when he found it, would he not joyfully take it on his shoulders and then, when he got home, call together his friends, and neighbours? "Rejoice with me," he would say "I have found my sheep that was lost." In the same way, I tell you, there will be more rejoicing in heaven over one repentant sinner than over ninety-nine virtuous men who have no need of repentance.

'Or again, what woman with ten drachmas would not, if she lost one, light a lamp and sweep out the house and search thoroughly till she found it? And then, when she had found it, call together her friends and neighbours? "Rejoice with me," she would say "I have found the drachma I lost." In the same way, I tell you, there is rejoicing among the angels of God over one repentant sinner.']

He also said, 'A man had two sons. The younger said to his father, "Father, let me have the share of the estate that would come to me." So the father divided the property between them. A few days later, the younger son got together everything he had and left for a distant country where he squandered his money on a life of debauchery.

'When he had spent it all, that country experienced a severe famine, and now he began to feel the pinch, so he hired himself out to one of the local inhabitants who put him on his farm to feed the pigs. And he would willingly have filled his belly with the husks the pigs were eating but no one offered him anything. Then he came to his senses and said, "How many of my father's paid servants have more food than they want, and here am I dying of hunger! I will leave this place and go to my father and say: Father, I have sinned against heaven and against you; I no longer deserve to be called your son; treat me as one of your paid servants." So he left the place and went back to his father.

'While he was still a long way off, his father saw him and was moved with pity. He ran to the boy, clasped him in his arms and kissed him tenderly. Then his son said, "Father, I have sinned against heaven and against you. I no longer deserve to be called your son." But the father said to his servants, "Quick! Bring out the best robe and put it on him; put a ring on his finger and sandals on his feet. Bring the calf we have been fattening, and kill it; we are going to have a feast, a celebration, because this son of mine was dead and has come back to life; he was lost and is found." And they began to celebrate.

'Now the elder son was out in the fields, and on his way back, as he drew near the house, he could hear music and dancing. Calling one of the servants he asked what it was all about. "Your brother has come" replied the servant "and your father has killed the calf we had fattened because he has got him back safe and sound." He was angry then and refused to go in, and his father came out to plead with him; but he answered his father, "Look, all these years I have slaved for you and never once disobeyed your orders, yet you never offered me so much as a kid for me to celebrate with my friends. But, for this son of yours, when he comes back after swallowing up your property – he and his women – you kill the calf we had been fattening."

'The father said, "My son, you are with me always and all I have is yours. But it was only right we should celebrate and rejoice, because your brother here was dead and has come to life; he was lost and is found."'

[The Gospel of the Lord.]

Shorter Form, verses 1-10. Read between [ ]

Prayer over the Offerings

Look with favour on our
　supplications, O Lord,
and in your kindness accept these,
　your servants' offerings,
that what each has offered
　to the honour of your name
may serve the salvation of all.
Through Christ our Lord.

Super oblata

Propitiare, Domine,
　supplicationibus nostris,
et has oblationes famulorum
　tuorum benignus assume,
ut, quod singuli ad honorem tui
　nominis obtulerunt,
cunctis proficiat ad salutem.
Per Christum Dominum nostrum.

Preface of Sundays in Ordinary Time I-VIII, pp.60-67.

Communion Antiphon Cf. Ps 35:8

How precious is your mercy, O God!
The children of men seek shelter
　in the shadow of your wings.

Ant. ad communionem

Quam pretiosa est misericordia tua,
　Deus!
Filii hominum sub umbra alarum
　tuarum confugient.

Or: Cf. 1 Co 10:16

The chalice of blessing that we bless
is a communion in the Blood
　of Christ;
and the bread that we break
is a sharing in the Body of the Lord.

Vel:

Calix benedictionis, cui benedicimus,
communicatio Sanguinis
　Christi est;
et panis, quem frangimus,
participatio Corporis Domini est.

Prayer after Communion

May the working of this heavenly
　gift, O Lord, we pray,
take possession of our minds
　and bodies,
so that its effects,
　and not our own desires,
may always prevail in us.
Through Christ our Lord.

Post communionem

Mentes nostras et corpora possideat,
quæsumus, Domine,
　doni cælestis operatio,
ut non noster sensus in nobis,
sed eius præveniat semper effectus.
Per Christum Dominum nostrum.

22 September

TWENTY-FIFTH SUNDAY IN ORDINARY TIME

Entrance Antiphon

I AM the salvation of the people,
  says the Lord.
Should they cry to me
  in any distress,
I will hear them, and I will be their
  Lord for ever.

Ant. ad introitum

SALUS populi ego sum,
  dicit Dominus.
De quacumque tribulatione
  clamaverint ad me,
exaudiam eos, et ero illorum
  Dominus in perpetuum.

Collect

O God, who founded all the
  commands of your sacred Law
upon love of you
  and of our neighbour,
grant that, by keeping your precepts,
we may merit to attain eternal life.
Through our Lord Jesus Christ,
  your Son,
who lives and reigns with you
  in the unity of the Holy Spirit,
one God, for ever and ever.

Collecta

Deus, qui sacræ legis
  omnia constituta
in tua et proximi dilectione posuisti,
da nobis, ut, tua præcepta servantes,
ad vitam mereamur
  pervenire perpetuam.
Per Dominum nostrum Iesum
  Christum Filium tuum,
qui tecum vivit et regnat
  in unitate Spiritus Sancti,
Deus, per omnia sæcula sæculorum.

FIRST READING

A reading from the prophet Amos 8:4-7

Against those who 'buy up the poor for money'.

Listen to this, you who trample on the needy
and try to suppress the poor people of the country,
you who say, 'When will the New Moon be over
so that we can sell our corn,
and sabbath, so that we can market our wheat?
Then by lowering the bushel, raising the shekel,
by swindling and tampering with the scales,
we can buy up the poor for money,
and the needy for a pair of sandals,
and get a price even for the sweepings of the wheat.'
The Lord swears it by the pride of Jacob,
'Never will I forget a single thing you have done.'

  The word of the Lord.

Responsorial Psalm

Ps 112:1-2,4-8. R. Cf. vv. 1,7

R. **Praise the Lord, who raises the poor.**
Or: **Alleluia!**

Praise, O servants of the Lord,
praise the name of the Lord!
May the name of the Lord be blessed
both now and for evermore! R.

High above all nations is the Lord,
above the heavens his glory.
Who is like the Lord, our God,
who has risen on high to his throne
yet stoops from the heights to look down,
to look down upon heaven and earth? R.

From the dust he lifts up the lowly,
from the dungheap he raises the poor
to set him in the company of princes,
yes, with the princes of his people. R.

SECOND READING

A reading from the first letter of St Paul to Timothy 2:1-8

There should be prayers offered for everyone to God, who wants everyone to be saved.

My advice is that, first of all, there should be prayers offered for everyone – petitions, intercessions and thanksgiving – and especially for kings and others in authority, so that we may be able to live religious and reverent lives in peace and quiet. To do this is right, and will please God our saviour: he wants everyone to be saved and reach full knowledge of the truth. For there is only one God, and there is only one mediator between God and mankind, himself a man, Christ Jesus, who sacrificed himself as a ransom for them all. He is the evidence of this, sent at the appointed time, and I have been named a herald and apostle of it and – I am telling the truth and no lie – a teacher of the faith and the truth to the pagans.

In every place, then, I want the men to lift their hands up reverently in prayer, with no anger or argument.

The word of the Lord.

Gospel Acclamation

Cf. Ac 16:14

R. **Alleluia, alleluia!**
Open our heart, O Lord,
to accept the words of your Son.
R. **Alleluia!**

Or: 2 Co 8:9
R. **Alleluia, alleluia!**
Jesus Christ was rich,
but he became poor for your sake,
to make you rich out of his poverty.
R. **Alleluia!**

GOSPEL

A reading from the holy Gospel according to Luke 16:1-13
You cannot be the slave of both God and money.

[Jesus said to his disciples:] 'There was a rich man and he had a steward who was denounced to him for being wasteful with his property. He called for the man and said, "What is this I hear about you? Draw me up an account of your stewardship because you are not to be my steward any longer." Then the steward said to himself, "Now that my master is taking the stewardship from me, what am I to do? Dig? I am not strong enough. Go begging? I should be too ashamed. Ah, I know what I will do to make sure that when I am dismissed from office there will be some to welcome me into their homes."

'Then he called his master's debtors one by one. To the first he said, "How much do you owe my master?" "One hundred measures of oil" was the reply. The steward said, "Here, take your bond; sit down straight away and write fifty." To another he said, "And you, sir, how much do you owe?" "One hundred measures of wheat" was the reply. The steward said, "Here, take your bond and write eighty."

'The master praised the dishonest steward for his astuteness. For the children of this world are more astute in dealing with their own kind than are the children of light.

'And so I tell you this: use money, tainted as it is, to win you friends, and thus make sure that when it fails you, they will welcome you into the tents of eternity. [The man who can be trusted in little things can be trusted in great; the man who is dishonest in little things will be dishonest in great. If then you cannot be trusted with money, that tainted thing, who will trust you with genuine riches? And if you cannot be trusted with what is not yours, who will give you what is your very own?

'No servant can be the slave of two masters: he will either hate the first and love the second, or treat the first with respect and the second with scorn. You cannot be the slave both of God and of money.'

The Gospel of the Lord.]

Shorter Form, verses 10-13. Read between [ ]

Prayer over the Offerings

Receive with favour, O Lord, we pray,
the offerings of your people,
that what they profess
　with devotion and faith
may be theirs through
　these heavenly mysteries.
Through Christ our Lord.

Super oblata

Munera, quæsumus, Domine,
　tuæ plebis propitiatus assume,
ut, quæ fidei pietate profitentur,
sacramentis cælestibus
　apprehendant.
Per Christum Dominum nostrum.

Preface of Sundays in Ordinary Time I-VIII, pp.60-67.

Communion Antiphon Ps 118:4-5

You have laid down your precepts
　to be carefully kept;
may my ways be firm in keeping
　your statutes.

Ant. ad communionem

Tu mandasti mandata tua
　custodiri nimis;
utinam dirigantur viæ meæ
ad custodiendas iustificationes tuas.

Or: Jn 10:14

I am the Good Shepherd,
　says the Lord;
I know my sheep,
　and mine know me.

Vel:

Ego sum pastor bonus,
　dicit Dominus;
et cognosco oves meas,
　et cognoscunt me meæ.

Prayer after Communion

Graciously raise up, O Lord,
those you renew
　with this Sacrament,
that we may come to possess
　your redemption
both in mystery and in the manner
　of our life.
Through Christ our Lord.

Post communionem

Quos tuis, Domine,
　reficis sacramentis,
continuis attolle benignus auxiliis,
ut redemptionis effectum
et mysteriis capiamus et moribus.
Per Christum Dominum nostrum.

29 September

TWENTY-SIXTH SUNDAY IN ORDINARY TIME

Entrance Antiphon Dn 3:31,29,30,43,42

ALL that you have done to us, O Lord,
 you have done with true judgement,
for we have sinned against you
and not obeyed
 your commandments.
But give glory to your name
and deal with us according
 to the bounty of your mercy.

Collect

O God, who manifest
 your almighty power
above all by pardoning
 and showing mercy,
bestow, we pray, your grace
 abundantly upon us
and make those hastening to attain
 your promises
heirs to the treasures of heaven.
Through our Lord Jesus Christ,
 your Son,
who lives and reigns with you
 in the unity of the Holy Spirit,
one God, for ever and ever.

Ant. ad introitum

OMNIA, quæ fecisti nobis, Domine,
in vero iudicio fecisti,
 quia peccavimus tibi,
et mandatis tuis non obœdivimus;
sed da gloriam nomini tuo,
et fac nobiscum secundum
 multitudinem misericordiæ tuæ.

Collecta

Deus, qui omnipotentiam tuam parcendo maxime
 et miserando manifestas,
multiplica super nos gratiam tuam,
ut, ad tua promissa currentes,
cælestium bonorum facias
 esse consortes.
Per Dominum nostrum Iesum
 Christum Filium tuum,
qui tecum vivit et regnat
 in unitate Spiritus Sancti,
Deus, per omnia sæcula sæculorum.

FIRST READING

A reading from the prophet Amos 6:1,4-7

Those who sprawl and those who bawl will be exiled.

The almighty Lord says this:
 Woe to those ensconced so snugly in Zion
 and to those who feel so safe on the mountain of Samaria.
 Lying on ivory beds
 and sprawling on their divans,

they dine on lambs from the flock,
and stall-fattened veal;
they bawl to the sound of the harp,
they invent new instruments of music like David,
they drink wine by the bowlful,
and use the finest oil for anointing themselves,
but about the ruin of Joseph they do not care at all.
That is why they will be the first to be exiled;
the sprawlers' revelry is over.

The word of the Lord.

Responsorial Psalm
Ps 145:6-10. R. v.2

**R. My soul, give praise to the Lord.
Or: Alleluia!**

It is the Lord who keeps faith for ever,
who is just to those who are oppressed.
It is he who gives bread to the hungry,
the Lord, who sets prisoners free. R.

It is the Lord who gives sight to the blind,
who raises up those who are bowed down.
It is the Lord who loves the just,
the Lord, who protects the stranger. R.

He upholds the widow and orphan
but thwarts the path of the wicked.
The Lord will reign for ever,
Zion's God, from age to age. R.

SECOND READING

A reading from the first letter of St Paul to Timothy 6:11-16

Do all that you have been told until the Appearing of the Lord.

As a man dedicated to God, you must aim to be saintly and religious, filled with faith and love, patient and gentle. Fight the good fight of the faith and win for yourself the eternal life to which you were called when you made your profession and spoke up for the truth in front of many witnesses. Now, before God the source of all life and before Jesus Christ, who spoke up as a witness for the truth in front of Pontius Pilate, I put to you the duty of doing all that you have been told, with no faults or failures, until the Appearing of our Lord Jesus Christ,

who at the due time will be revealed
by God, the blessed and only Ruler of all,
the King of kings and the Lord of lords,
who alone is immortal,
whose home is in inaccessible light,
whom no man has seen and no man is able to see:
to him be honour and everlasting power. Amen.

The word of the Lord.

Gospel Acclamation
Jn 10:27

R. **Alleluia, alleluia!**
The sheep that belong to me listen to my voice,
says the Lord,
I know them and they follow me.
R. **Alleluia!**

Or:
2 Co 8:9

R. **Alleluia, alleluia!**
Jesus Christ was rich,
but he became poor for your sake,
to make you rich out of his poverty.
R. **Alleluia!**

GOSPEL

A reading from the holy Gospel according to Luke
16:19-31

Good things came your way, just as bad things came the way of Lazarus. Now he is being comforted here while you are in agony.

Jesus said to the Pharisees: 'There was a rich man who used to dress in purple and fine linen and feast magnificently everyday. And at his gate there lay a poor man called Lazarus, covered with sores, who longed to fill himself with the scraps that fell from the rich man's table. Dogs even came and licked his sores. Now the poor man died and was carried away by the angels to the bosom of Abraham. The rich man also died and was buried.

'In his torment in Hades he looked up and saw Abraham a long way off with Lazarus in his bosom. So he cried out, "Father Abraham, pity me and send Lazarus to dip the tip of his finger in water and cool my tongue, for I am in agony in these flames." "My son," Abraham replied "remember that during your life good things came your way, just as bad things came the way of Lazarus. Now he is being comforted here while you are in agony.

But that is not all: between us and you a great gulf has been fixed, to stop anyone, if he wanted to, crossing from our side to yours, and to stop any crossing from your side to ours."

'The rich man replied, "Father, I beg you then to send Lazarus to my father's house, since I have five brothers, to give them warning so that they do not come to this place of torment too." "They have Moses and the prophets," said Abraham "let them listen to them." "Ah no, father Abraham," said the rich man "but if someone comes to them from the dead, they will repent." Then Abraham said to him, "If they will not listen either to Moses or to the prophets, they will not be convinced even if someone should rise from the dead."'

The Gospel of the Lord.

Prayer over the Offerings

Grant us, O merciful God,
that this our offering may find
   acceptance with you
and that through it the wellspring
   of all blessing
may be laid open before us.
Through Christ our Lord.

Super oblata

Concede nobis, misericors Deus,
ut hæc nostra oblatio tibi
   sit accepta,
et per eam nobis fons omnis
   benedictionis aperiatur.
Per Christum Dominum nostrum.

Preface of Sundays in Ordinary Time I-VIII, pp.60-67.

Communion Antiphon Cf. Ps 118:49-50

Remember your word to your servant,
   O Lord,
by which you have given me hope.
This is my comfort when I am
   brought low.

Ant. ad communionem

Memento verbi tui
   servo tuo, Domine,
in quo mihi spem dedisti;
hæc me consolata
   est in humilitate mea.

Or: 1 Jn 3:16

By this we came to know
   the love of God:
that Christ laid down his life for us;
so we ought to lay down our lives
   for one another.

Vel:

In hoc cognovimus caritatem Dei:
quoniam ille animam suam
   pro nobis posuit;
et nos debemus pro fratribus
   animas ponere.

Prayer after Communion

May this heavenly mystery, O Lord,
restore us in mind and body,
that we may be coheirs in glory
   with Christ,
to whose suffering we are united
whenever we proclaim his Death.
Who lives and reigns
   for ever and ever.

Post communionem

Sit nobis, Domine,
   reparatio mentis et corporis
cæleste mysterium, ut simus eius
   in gloria coheredes,
cui, mortem ipsius
   annuntiando, compatimur.
Qui vivit et regnat
   in sæcula sæculorum.

6 October

TWENTY-SEVENTH SUNDAY IN ORDINARY TIME

Entrance Antiphon   Cf. Est 4:17

WITHIN your will, O Lord,
   all things are established,
and there is none that can resist
   your will.
For you have made all things,
   the heaven and the earth,
and all that is held within the circle
   of heaven;
you are the Lord of all.

Ant. ad introitum

IN voluntate tua, Domine,
   universa sunt posita,
et non est qui possit resistere
   voluntati tuæ.
Tu enim fecisti omnia,
   cælum et terram,
et universa quæ cæli
   ambitu continentur;
Dominus universorum tu es.

Collect

Almighty ever-living God,
who in the abundance
   of your kindness
surpass the merits and the desires
   of those who entreat you,
pour out your mercy upon us
to pardon what conscience dreads
and to give what prayer does
   not dare to ask.
Through our Lord Jesus Christ,
   your Son,
who lives and reigns with you
   in the unity of the Holy Spirit,
one God, for ever and ever.

Collecta

Omnipotens sempiterne Deus,
   qui abundantia pietatis tuæ
et merita supplicum excedis et vota,
effunde super nos
   misericordiam tuam,
ut dimittas quæ conscientia metuit,
et adicias quod oratio non præsumit.
Per Dominum nostrum Iesum
   Christum Filium tuum,
qui tecum vivit et regnat
   in unitate Spiritus Sancti,
Deus, per omnia sæcula sæculorum.

FIRST READING

A reading from the prophet Habakkuk   1:2-3; 2:2-4

The upright man will live by his faithfulness.

How long, Lord, am I to cry for help
while you will not listen;
to cry 'Oppression!' in your ear
and you will not save?
Why do you set injustice before me,
why do you look on where there is tyranny?
Outrage and violence, this is all I see,
all is contention, and discord flourishes.
Then the Lord answered and said,

> 'Write the vision down,
> inscribe it on tablets
> to be easily read,
> since this vision is for its own time only:
> eager for its own fulfillment, it does not deceive;
> if it comes slowly, wait,
> for come it will, without fail.
> See how he flags, he whose soul is not at rights,
> but the upright man will live by his faithfulness.'

The word of the Lord.

Responsorial Psalm   Ps 94:1-2,6-9. R. v.8

**R. O that today you would listen to his voice!
Harden not your hearts.**

> Come, ring out our joy to the Lord;
> hail the rock who saves us.
> Let us come before him, giving thanks,
> with songs let us hail the Lord. R.

> Come in; let us bow and bend low;
> let us kneel before the God who made us
> for he is our God and we
> the people who belong to his pasture,
> the flock that is led by his hand. R.

> O that today you would listen to his voice!
> 'Harden not your hearts as at Meribah,

as on that day at Massah in the desert
when your fathers put me to the test;.
when they tried me, though they saw my work.' R.

SECOND READING

A reading from the second letter of St Paul to Timothy   1:6-8,13-14

Never be ashamed of witnessing to our Lord.

I am reminding you to fan into a flame the gift that God gave you when I laid my hands on you. God's gift was not a spirit of timidity, but the Spirit of power, and love, and self-control. So you are never to be ashamed of witnessing to the Lord, or ashamed of me for being his prisoner; but with me, bear the hardships for the sake of the Good News, relying on the power of God.

Keep as your pattern the sound teaching you have heard from me, in the faith and love that are in Christ Jesus. You have been trusted to look after something precious; guard it with the help of the Holy Spirit who lives in us.

The word of the Lord.

Gospel Acclamation   1 S 3:9; Jn 6:68

R. **Alleluia, alleluia!**
Speak, Lord, your servant is listening:
you have the message of eternal life.
R. **Alleluia!**

Or: 1 P 1:25

R. **Alleluia, alleluia!**
The word of the Lord remains for ever:
What is this word?
It is the Good News that has been brought to you.
R. **Alleluia!**

GOSPEL

A reading from the holy Gospel according to Luke   17:5-10

If only you had faith!

The apostles said to the Lord, 'Increase our faith.' The Lord replied, 'Were your faith the size of a mustard seed you could say to this mulberry tree, "Be uprooted and planted in the sea," and it would obey you.

'Which of you, with a servant ploughing or minding sheep, would say to him when he returned from the fields, "Come and have your meal immediately"? Would he not be more likely to say, "Get my supper laid;

make yourself tidy and wait on me while I eat and drink. You can eat and drink yourself afterwards"? Must he be grateful to the servant for doing what he was told? So with you: when you have done all you have been told to do, say, "We are merely servants: we have done no more than our duty."'

The Gospel of the Lord.

Prayer over the Offerings

Accept, O Lord, we pray,
the sacrifices instituted
   by your commands
and, through the sacred mysteries,
which we celebrate
   with dutiful service,
graciously complete
   the sanctifying work
by which you are pleased
   to redeem us.
Through Christ our Lord.

Super oblata

Suscipe, quæsumus, Domine,
sacrificia tuis instituta præceptis,
et sacris mysteriis,
quæ debitæ servitutis
   celebramus officio,
sanctificationem tuæ nobis
   redemptionis dignanter adimple.
Per Christum Dominum nostrum.

Preface of Sundays in Ordinary Time I-VIII, pp.60-67.

Communion Antiphon   Lm 3:25

The Lord is good to those
   who hope in him,
to the soul that seeks him.

Ant. ad communionem

Bonus est Dominus
   sperantibus in eum,
animæ quærenti illum.

Or: Cf. 1 Co 10:17

Though many, we are one bread,
   one body,
for we all partake of the one Bread
   and one Chalice.

Vel:

Unus panis et unum corpus
   multi sumus,
omnes qui de uno pane et de uno
   calice participamus.

Prayer after Communion

Grant us, almighty God,
that we may be refreshed
   and nourished
by the Sacrament which
   we have received,
so as to be transformed
   into what we consume.
Through Christ our Lord.

Post communionem

Concede nobis, omnipotens Deus,
ut de perceptis sacramentis
   inebriemur atque pascamur,
quatenus in id quod
   sumimus transeamus.
Per Christum Dominum nostrum.

13 October

TWENTY-EIGHTH SUNDAY IN ORDINARY TIME

<table>
<tr><td>

Entrance Antiphon   Ps 129:3-4

If you, O Lord,
should mark iniquities,
Lord, who could stand?
But with you is found forgiveness,
   O God of Israel.

</td><td>

Ant. ad introitum

Si iniquitates observaveris,
Domine,
Domine, quis sustinebit?
Quia apud te propitiatio est,
   Deus Israel.

</td></tr>
<tr><td>

Collect

May your grace, O Lord, we pray,
at all times go before us
   and follow after
and make us always determined
to carry out good works.
Through our Lord Jesus Christ,
   your Son,
who lives and reigns with you
   in the unity of the Holy Spirit,
one God, for ever and ever.

</td><td>

Collecta

Tua nos, quæsumus,
   Domine, gratia
semper et præveniat et sequatur,
ac bonis operibus iugiter præstet
   esse intentos.
Per Dominum nostrum Iesum
   Christum Filium tuum,
qui tecum vivit et regnat
   in unitate Spiritus Sancti,
Deus, per omnia sæcula sæculorum.

</td></tr>
</table>

FIRST READING

A reading from the second book of the Kings   5:14-17

Naaman returned to Elisha and acknowledged the Lord.

Naaman the leper went down and immersed himself seven times in the Jordan, as Elisha had told him to do. And his flesh became clean once more like the flesh of a little child.

   Returning to Elisha with his whole escort, he went in and stood before him. 'Now I know' he said 'that there is no God in all the earth except in Israel. Now, please, accept a present from your servant.' But Elisha replied, 'As the Lord lives, whom I serve, I will accept nothing.' Naaman pressed him to accept, but he refused. Then Naaman said, 'Since your answer is "No," allow your servant to be given as much earth as two mules may carry, because your servant will no longer offer holocaust or sacrifice to any god except the Lord.'

   The word of the Lord.

Responsional Psalm
Ps 97:1-4. R. Cf. v.2

R. The Lord has shown his salvation to the nations.

Sing a new song to the Lord
for he has worked wonders.
His right hand and his holy arm
have brought salvation. R.

The Lord has made known his salvation;
has shown his justice to the nations.
He has remembered his truth and love
for the house of Israel. R.

All the ends of the earth have seen
the salvation of our God.
Shout to the Lord all the earth,
ring out your joy. R.

SECOND READING

A reading from the second letter of St Paul to Timothy 2:8-13

If we hold firm, then we shall reign with Christ.

Remember the Good News that I carry, 'Jesus Christ risen from the dead, sprung from the race of David'; it is on account of this that I have my own hardships to bear, even to being chained like a criminal – but they cannot chain up God's news. So I bear it all for the sake of those who are chosen, so that in the end they may have the salvation that is in Christ Jesus and the eternal glory that comes with it.

Here is a saying that you can rely on:

If we have died with him, then we shall live with him.
If we hold firm, then we shall reign with him.
If we disown him, then he will disown us.
We may be unfaithful, but he is always faithful,
for he cannot disown his own self.

The word of the Lord.

Gospel Acclamation
Cf. Jn 6:63,68

R. Alleluia, alleluia!
Your words are spirit, Lord,
and they are life:
you have the message of eternal life.
R. Alleluia!

Or: 1 Th 5:18
R. **Alleluia, alleluia!**
For all things give thanks,
because this is what God expects you to do in Jesus Christ.
R. **Alleluia!**

GOSPEL

A reading from the holy Gospel according to Luke 17:11-19
No one can come back to give praise to God, except this foreigner.

On the way to Jerusalem Jesus travelled along the border between Samaria and Galilee. As he entered one of the villages, ten lepers came to meet him. They stood some way off and called to him, 'Jesus! Master! Take pity on us.' When he saw them he said, 'Go and show yourselves to the priests.' Now as they were going away they were cleansed. Finding himself cured, one of them turned back praising God at the top of his voice and threw himself at the feet of Jesus and thanked him. The man was a Samaritan. This made Jesus say, 'Were not all ten made clean? The other nine, where are they? It seems that no one has come back to give praise to God, except this foreigner.' And he said to the man, 'Stand up and go on your way. Your faith has saved you.'

The Gospel of the Lord.

Prayer over the Offerings

Accept, O Lord, the prayers
  of your faithful
with the sacrificial offerings,
that, through these acts
  of devotedness,
we may pass over to the glory
  of heaven.
Through Christ our Lord.

Super oblata

Suscipe, Domine,
fidelium preces cum
  oblationibus hostiarum,
ut, per hæc piæ devotionis officia,
ad cælestem gloriam transeamus.
Per Christum Dominum nostrum.

Preface of Sundays in Ordinary Time I-VIII, pp.60-67.

Communion Antiphon Cf. Ps 33:11

The rich suffer want and go hungry,
but those who seek the Lord
  lack no blessing.

Ant. ad communionem

Divites eguerunt et esurierunt;
quærentes autem Dominum
  non minuentur omni bono.

Or: 1 Jn 3:2

When the Lord appears,
  we shall be like him,
for we shall see him as he is.

Prayer after Communion

We entreat your majesty most
    humbly, O Lord,
that, as you feed us
    with the nourishment
which comes from the most holy
    Body and Blood of your Son,
so you may make us sharers
    of his divine nature.
Who lives and reigns
    for ever and ever.

Vel:

Cum apparuerit Dominus,
  similes ei erimus,
quoniam videbimus eum sicuti est.

Post communionem

Maiestatem tuam, Domine,
    suppliciter deprecamur,
ut, sicut nos Corporis
    et Sanguinis sacrosancti
pascis alimento,
ita divinæ naturæ facias
    esse consortes.
Per Christum Dominum nostrum.

20 October

TWENTY-NINTH SUNDAY IN ORDINARY TIME

Entrance Antiphon   Cf. Ps 16:6,8

To you I call; for you will surely
    heed me, O God;
turn your ear to me; hear my words.
Guard me as the apple of your eye;
in the shadow of your wings
    protect me.

Ant. ad introitum

Ego clamavi,
  quoniam exaudisti
  me, Deus;
inclina aurem tuam,
  et exaudi verba mea.
Custodi me, Domine,
  ut pupillam oculi;
sub umbra alarum tuarum
  protege me.

Collect

Almighty ever-living God,
grant that we may always conform
    our will to yours
and serve your majesty in sincerity
    of heart.

Collecta

Omnipotens sempiterne Deus,
fac nos tibi semper et devotam
    gerere voluntatem,
et maiestati tuæ sincero
    corde servire.

| Through our Lord Jesus Christ, your Son, who lives and reigns with you in the unity of the Holy Spirit, one God, for ever and ever. | Per Dominum nostrum Iesum Christum Filium tuum, qui tecum vivit et regnat in unitate Spiritus Sancti, Deus, per omnia sæcula sæculorum. |

FIRST READING

A reading from the book of Exodus 17:8-13

As long as Moses kept his arms raised, Israel had the advantage.

The Amalekites came and attacked Israel at Rephidim. Moses said to Joshua, 'Pick out men for yourself, and tomorrow morning march out to engage Amalek. I, meanwhile, will stand on the hilltop, the staff of God in my hand.' Joshua did as Moses told him and marched out to engage Amalek, while Moses and Aaron and Hur went up to the top of the hill. As long as Moses kept his arms raised, Israel had the advantage; when he let his arms fall, the advantage went to Amalek. But Moses's arms grew heavy, so they took a stone and put it under him and on this he sat, Aaron and Hur supporting his arms, one on one side, one on the other; and his arms remained firm till sunset. With the edge of the sword Joshua cut down Amalek and his people.

The word of the Lord.

Responsional Psalm

Ps 120. R. Cf. v.2

R. **Our help is in the name of the Lord who made heaven and earth.**

I lift up my eyes to the mountains:
from where shall come my help?
My help shall come from the Lord
who made heaven and earth. R.

May he never allow you to stumble!
Let him sleep not, your guard.
No, he sleeps not nor slumbers,
Israel's guard. R.

The Lord is your guard and your shade;
at your right side he stands.
By day the sun shall not smite you
nor the moon in the night. R.

The Lord will guard you from evil,
he will guard your soul.
The Lord will guard your going and coming
both now and for ever. R.

R. **Our help is in the name of the Lord
who made heaven and earth.**

SECOND READING

A reading from the second letter of St Paul to Timothy   3:14-4:2

The man who is dedicated to God becomes fully equipped and ready for any good work.

You must keep to what you have been taught and know to be true; remember who your teachers were, and how, ever since you were a child, you have known the holy scriptures – from these you can learn the wisdom that leads to salvation through faith in Christ Jesus. All scripture is inspired by God and can profitably be used for teaching, for refuting error, for guiding people's lives and teaching them to be holy. This is how the man who is dedicated to God becomes fully equipped and ready for any good work.

Before God and before Christ Jesus who is to be judge of the living and dead, I put this duty to you, in the name of his Appearing and of his kingdom: proclaim the message and, welcome or unwelcome, insist on it. Refute falsehood, correct error, call to obedience – but do all with patience and with the intention of teaching.

The word of the Lord.

Gospel Acclamation   Cf. Ep 1:17,18

R. **Alleluia, alleluia!**
May the Father of our Lord Jesus Christ
enlighten the eyes of our mind,
so that we can see what hope his call holds for us.
R. **Alleluia!**

Or: Heb 4:12

R. **Alleluia, alleluia!**
The word of God is something alive and active;
it can judge secret emotions and thoughts.
R. **Alleluia!**

GOSPEL

A reading from the holy Gospel according to Luke 18:1-8

God will see justice done to his chosen who cry to him.

Jesus told his disciples a parable about the need to pray continually and never lose heart. 'There was a judge in a certain town' he said 'who had neither fear of God nor respect for man. In the same town there was a widow who kept on coming to him and saying, "I want justice from you against my enemy!" For a long time he refused, but at last he said to himself, "Maybe I have neither fear of God nor respect for man, but since she keeps pestering me I must give this widow her just rights, or she will persist in coming and worry me to death."'

And the Lord said, 'You notice what the unjust judge has to say? Now will not God see justice done to his chosen who cry to him day and night even when he delays to help them? I promise you, he will see justice done to them, and done speedily. But when the Son of Man comes, will he find any faith on earth?'

The Gospel of the Lord.

Prayer over the Offerings | Super oblata

Grant us, Lord, we pray, a sincere respect for your gifts, that, through the purifying action of your grace, we may be cleansed by the very mysteries we serve. Through Christ our Lord.	Tribue nos, Domine, quæsumus, donis tuis libera mente servire, ut, tua purificante nos gratia, iisdem quibus famulamur mysteriis emundemur. Per Christum Dominum nostrum.

Preface of Sundays in Ordinary Time I-VIII, pp.60-67.

Communion Antiphon Cf.Ps 32:18-19 | Ant. ad communionem

Behold, the eyes of the Lord are on those who fear him, who hope in his merciful love, to rescue their souls from death, to keep them alive in famine.	Ecce oculi Domini super timentes eum, et in eis qui sperant super misericordia eius; ut eruat a morte animas eorum, et alat eos in fame.

Or: Mk 10:45

The Son of Man has come
to give his life as a ransom for many.

Prayer after Communion

Grant, O Lord, we pray,
that, benefiting from participation
   in heavenly things,
we may be helped by what you give
   in this present age
and prepared for the gifts
   that are eternal.
Through Christ our Lord.

Vel:

Filius hominis venit,
ut daret animam suam
   redemptionem pro multis.

Post communionem

Fac nos, quæsumus, Domine,
cælestium rerum
   frequentatione proficere,
ut et temporalibus
   beneficiis adiuvemur,
et erudiamur æternis.
Per Christum Dominum nostrum.

27 October

THIRTIETH SUNDAY IN ORDINARY TIME

Entrance Antiphon   Cf. Ps 104:3-4

LET the hearts that seek
the Lord rejoice;
turn to the Lord and his strength;
constantly seek his face.

Collect

Almighty ever-living God,
increase our faith, hope and charity,
and make us love
   what you command,
so that we may merit
   what you promise.
Through our Lord Jesus Christ,
   your Son,
who lives and reigns with you
   in the unity of the Holy Spirit,
one God, for ever and ever.

Ant. ad introitum

LÆTETUR cor
quærentium Dominum.
Quærite Dominum et confirmamini,
quærite faciem eius semper.

Collecta

Omnipotens sempiterne Deus,
da nobis fidei,
   spei et caritatis augmentum,
et, ut mereamur assequi
   quod promittis,
fac nos amare quod præcipis.
Per Dominum nostrum Iesum
   Christum Filium tuum,
qui tecum vivit et regnat
   in unitate Spiritus Sancti,
Deus, per omnia sæcula sæculorum.

FIRST READING

A reading from the book of Ecclesiasticus 35:12-14,16-19

The humble man's prayer pierces the clouds.

The Lord is a judge
who is no respecter of personages.
He shows no respect of personages to the detriment of a poor man,
he listens to the plea of the injured party.
He does not ignore the orphan's supplication,
nor the widow's as she pours out her story.

The man who with his whole heart serves God will be accepted,
his petitions will carry to the clouds.
The humble man's prayer pierces the clouds,
until it arrives he is inconsolable,
nor will he desist until the Most High takes notice of him,
acquits the virtuous and delivers judgement.
And the Lord will not be slow,
nor will he be dilatory on their behalf.

The word of the Lord.

Responsorial Psalm
Ps 32:2-3,17-19,23. R. v.7

R. **This poor man called; the Lord heard him.**

I will bless the Lord at all times,
his praise always on my lips;
in the Lord my soul shall make its boast.
The humble shall hear and be glad. R.

The Lord turns his face against the wicked
to destroy their remembrance from the earth.
The just call and the Lord hears
and rescues them in all their distress. R.

The Lord is close to the broken-hearted;
those whose spirit is crushed he will save.
The Lord ransoms the souls of his servants.
Those who hide in him shall not be condemned. R.

SECOND READING

A reading from the second letter of St Paul to Timothy 4:6-8,16-18

All there is to come now is the crown of righteousness reserved for me.

My life is already being poured away as a libation, and the time has come for me to be gone. I have fought the good fight to the end; I have run the race to the finish; I have kept the faith; all there is to come now is the crown of righteousness reserved for me, which the Lord, the righteous judge, will give to me on that Day; and not only to me but to all those who have longed for his Appearing.

The first time I had to present my defence, there was not a single witness to support me. Every one of them deserted me – may they not be held accountable for it. But the Lord stood by me and gave me power, so that through me the whole message might be proclaimed for all the pagans to hear; and so I was rescued from the lion's mouth. The Lord will rescue me from all evil attempts on me, and bring me safely to his heavenly kingdom. To him be glory for ever and ever. Amen.

The word of the Lord.

Gospel Acclamation Cf. Mt 11:25

R. **Alleluia, alleluia!**
Blessed are you, Father,
Lord of heaven and earth,
for revealing the mysteries of the kingdom
to mere children.
R. **Alleluia!**

Or: 2 Co 5:19

R. **Alleluia, alleluia!**
God was in Christ was reconciling the world to himself,
and he has entrusted to us the news that they are reconciled.
R. **Alleluia!**

GOSPEL

A reading from the holy Gospel according to Luke 18:9-14

The publican went home at rights with God; the Pharisee did not.

Jesus spoke the following parable to some people who prided themselves on being virtuous and despised everyone else: 'Two men went up to the Temple to pray, one a Pharisee, the other a tax collector. The Pharisee stood there and said this prayer to himself, "I thank you, God, that I am not grasping, unjust, adulterous like the rest of mankind, and particularly that I am not like this tax collector here. I fast twice a week; I pay tithes on all I get." The tax collector stood some distance away, not daring even to raise his eyes to heaven; but he beat his breast and said, "God, be merciful to me, a sinner." This man, I tell you, went home again at rights with God; the other did not. For everyone who exalts himself will be humbled, but the man who humbles himself will be exalted.'

The Gospel of the Lord.

Prayer over the Offerings

Look, we pray, O Lord,
on the offerings we make
   to your majesty,
that whatever is done by us
   in your service
may be directed above all
   to your glory.
Through Christ our Lord.

Super oblata

Respice, quæsumus, Domine,
munera quæ tuæ
   offerimus maiestati,
ut, quod nostro servitio geritur,
ad tuam gloriam potius dirigatur.
Per Christum Dominum nostrum.

Preface of Sundays in Ordinary Time I-VIII, pp.60-67.

Communion Antiphon Cf. Ps 19:6

We will ring out our joy at your
   saving help
and exult in the name of our God.

Ant. ad communionem

Lætabimur in salutari tuo,
et in nomine Dei
   nostri magnificabimur.

Or: Ep 5:2

Christ loved us and gave himself up
   for us,
as a fragrant offering to God.

Vel:

Christus dilexit nos, et tradidit
   semetipsum pro nobis,
oblationem Deo
   in odorem suavitatis.

Prayer after Communion

May your Sacraments, O Lord,
   we pray,
perfect in us what lies within them,
that what we now celebrate in signs
we may one day possess in truth.
Through Christ our Lord.

Post communionem

Perficiant in nobis,
   Domine, quæsumus,
tua sacramenta quod continent,
ut, quæ nunc specie gerimus,
rerum veritate capiamus.
Per Christum Dominum nostrum.

1 November

ALL SAINTS

The Solemnity of All Saints, which we celebrate today, invites us to raise our gaze to Heaven and to meditate on the fullness of the divine life which awaits us. "We are God's children now; it does not yet appear what we shall be" (1 Jn 3:2): with these words the Apostle John assures us of the reality of our profound relation to God, as too, of the certainty of our destiny. Like beloved children, therefore, we also receive the grace to support the trials of this earthly existence – the hunger and the thirst for justice, the misunderstandings, the persecutions (Cf. Mt 5:3-11) – and, at the same time, we inherit what is promised in the Gospel Beatitudes. The holiness, imprinted in us by Christ himself, is the goal of Christian life. And we have a foretaste of the gift and the beauty of sanctity every time that we participate in the Eucharistic Liturgy, the communion with the "great multitude" of holy souls, which in Heaven eternally acclaim the salvation of God and of the Lamb (Cf. Rv 7:9-10).

(Pope Benedict XVI)

Solemnity

Entrance Antiphon

LET us all rejoice in the Lord,
as we celebrate the feast day
in honour of all the Saints,
at whose festival the Angels rejoice
and praise the Son of God.

Ant. ad introitum

GAUDEAMUS omnes in Domino,
diem festum celebrantes
sub honore Sanctorum omnium,
de quorum sollemnitate
    gaudent Angeli,
et collaudant Filium Dei.

The Gloria in excelsis (Glory to God in the highest) is said.

Collect

Almighty ever-living God,
by whose gift we venerate
    in one celebration
the merits of all the Saints,
bestow on us, we pray,
through the prayers of so
    many intercessors,
an abundance of the reconciliation
    with you
for which we earnestly long.

Collecta

Omnipotens sempiterne Deus,
qui nos omnium Sanctorum
    tuorum merita
sub una tribuisti celebritate
    venerari, quæsumus,
ut desideratam nobis tuæ
    propitiationis abundantiam,
multiplicatis intercessoribus,
    largiaris.

Through our Lord Jesus Christ, your Son, who lives and reigns with you in the unity of the Holy Spirit, one God, for ever and ever.	Per Dominum nostrum Iesum Christum Filium tuum, qui tecum vivit et regnat in unitate Spiritus Sancti, Deus, per omnia sæcula sæculorum.

FIRST READING

A reading from the book of the Apocalypse 7:2-4,9-14

I saw a huge number, impossible to count, of people from every nation, race, tribe and language.

I, John, saw another angel rising where the sun rises, carrying the seal of the living God; he called in a powerful voice to the four angels whose duty was to devastate land and sea, 'Wait before you do any damage on land or at sea or to the trees, until we have put the seal on the foreheads of the servants of our God.' Then I heard how many were sealed: a hundred and forty-four thousand, out of all the tribes of Israel.

After that I saw a huge number, impossible to count, of people from every nation, race, tribe and language; they were standing in front of the throne and in front of the Lamb, dressed in white robes and holding palms in their hands. They shouted aloud, 'Victory to our God, who sits on the throne, and to the Lamb!' And all the angels who were standing in a circle round the throne, surrounding the elders and the four animals, prostrated themselves before the throne, and touched the ground with their foreheads, worshipping God with these words: 'Amen. Praise and glory and wisdom and thanksgiving and honour and power and strength to our God for ever and ever. Amen.'

One of the elders then spoke, and asked me, 'Do you know who these people are, dressed in white robes, and where they have come from?' I answered him, 'You can tell me, my Lord.' Then he said, 'These are the people who have been through the great persecution, and they have washed their robes white again in the blood of the Lamb.'

The word of the Lord.

Responsional Psalm Ps 23:1-6. R. Cf. v.6

R. Such are the men who seek your face, O Lord.

The Lord's is the earth and its fullness,
the world and all its peoples.
It is he who set it on the seas;
on the waters he made it firm. R.

Who shall climb the mountain of the Lord?
Who shall stand in his holy place?
The man with clean hands and pure heart,
who desires not worthless things. R.

He shall receive blessings from the Lord
and reward from the God who saves him.
Such are the men who seek him,
seek the face of the God of Jacob. R.

R. Such are the men who seek your face, O Lord.

SECOND READING

A reading from the first letter of St John 3:1-3

We shall see God as he really is.

Think of the love that the Father has lavished on us,
by letting us be called God's children;
and that is what we are.
Because the world refused to acknowledge him,
therefore it does not acknowledge us.
My dear people, we are already the children of God
but what we are to be in the future has not yet been revealed,
all we know is, that when it is revealed
we shall be like him
because we shall see him as he really is.
Surely everyone who entertains this hope
must purify himself, must try to be as pure as Christ.

The word of the Lord.

Gospel Acclamation Mt 11:28

R. Alleluia, alleluia!
Come to me, all of you who labour
  and are overburdened,
and I will give you rest, says the Lord.
R. Alleluia!

GOSPEL

A reading from the holy Gospel according to Matthew 5:1-12

Rejoice and be glad, for your reward will be great in heaven.

Seeing the crowds, Jesus went up the hill. There he sat down and was joined by his disciples. Then he began to speak. This is what he taught them:

'How happy are the poor in spirit;
theirs is the kingdom of heaven.
Happy the gentle:

they shall have the earth for their heritage.
Happy those who mourn:
they shall be comforted.
Happy those who hunger and thirst for what is right:
they shall be satisfied.
Happy the merciful:
they shall have mercy shown them.
Happy the pure in heart:
they shall see God.
Happy the peacemakers:
they shall be called sons of God.
Happy those who are persecuted in the cause of right:
theirs is the kingdom of heaven.

'Happy are you when people abuse you and persecute you and speak all kinds of calumny against you on my account. Rejoice and be glad, for your reward will be great in heaven.'

The Gospel of the Lord.

The Creed is said.

Prayer over the Offerings

May these offerings we bring
   in honour of all the Saints
be pleasing to you, O Lord,
and grant that, just as we believe
   the Saints
to be already assured of immortality,
so we may experience their
   concern for our salvation.
Through Christ our Lord.

Preface: The glory of Jerusalem, our mother.

It is truly right and just,
   our duty and our salvation,
always and everywhere
   to give you thanks,
Lord, holy Father,
   almighty and eternal God.

For today by your gift we celebrate
   our mother,

Super oblata

Grata tibi sint, Domine, munera,
quæ pro cunctorum offerimus
   honore Sanctorum,
et concede,
ut, quos iam credimus de sua
   immortalitate securos,
sentiamus de nostra salute sollicitos.
Per Christum Dominum nostrum.

Præfatio: De gloria matris nostræ Ierusalem

Vere dignum et iustum est,
   æquum et salutare,
nos tibi semper et ubique
   gratias agere:
Domine, sancte Pater,
   omnipotens æterne Deus:

Nobis enim hodie civitatem tuam
   quæ mater nostra est,

the festival of your city,
the heavenly Jerusalem,
  where the great array
  of our brothers and sisters
already gives you eternal praise.

Towards her, we eagerly hasten
  as pilgrims advancing by faith,
rejoicing in the glory bestowed
  upon those exalted members
  of the Church
through whom you give us,
  in our frailty, both strength
  and good example.

And so, we glorify you with the
  multitude of Saints and Angels,
as with one voice of praise
  we acclaim:

Holy, Holy, Holy Lord God of hosts...

Communion Antiphon Mt 5:8-10
Blessed are the clean of heart,
  for they shall see God.
Blessed are the peacemakers,
  for they shall be called
  children of God.
Blessed are they who are persecuted
  for the sake of righteousness,
for theirs is the Kingdom of Heaven.

Prayer after Communion
As we adore you, O God, who alone
  are holy
and wonderful in all your Saints,
we implore your grace,
so that, coming to perfect holiness
  in the fullness of your love,
we may pass from this pilgrim table
to the banquet
  of our heavenly homeland.
Through Christ our Lord.

tribuis celebrare,
cælestique Ierusalem,
ubi iam te in æternum fratrum
  nostrorum corona collaudat.

Ad quam peregrini,
  per fidem accedentes,
alacriter festinamus,
  congaudentes de Ecclesiæ
sublimium glorificatione
  membrorum,
qua simul fragilitati nostræ
  adiumenta et exempla concedis.

Et ideo, cum ipsorum
  Angelorumque frequentia,
una te magnificamus,
  laudis voce clamantes:

Sanctus, Sanctus, Sanctus...

Ant. ad communionem
Beati mundo corde, quoniam ipsi
  Deum videbunt;
beati pacifici, quoniam filii
  Dei vocabuntur;
beati qui persecutionem patiuntur
  propter iustitiam,
quoniam ipsorum
  est regnum cælorum.

Post communionem
Mirabilem te, Deus,
et unum Sanctum in omnibus
  Sanctis tuis adorantes,
tuam gratiam imploramus,
qua, sanctificationem
in tui amoris plenitudine
  consummantes,
ex hac mensa peregrinantium
ad cælestis patriæ
  convivium transeamus.
Per Christum Dominum nostrum.

A formula of Solemn Blessing, pp.146-149, may be used.

2 November

THE COMMEMORATION OF ALL THE FAITHFUL DEPARTED
(ALL SOULS' DAY)

Today we renew the hope in eternal life, truly founded on Christ's death and Resurrection. "I am risen and I am with you always", the Lord tells us, and my hand supports you. Wherever you may fall, you will fall into my hands and I will be there even to the gates of death. Where no one can accompany you any longer and where you can take nothing with you, there I will wait for you to transform for you the darkness into light. Christian hope, however, is not solely individual, it is also always a hope for others. Our lives are profoundly linked, one to the other, and the good and the bad that each of us does always effects others too. Hence, the prayer of a pilgrim soul in the world can help another soul that is being purified after death. This is why the Church invites us today to pray for our beloved deceased and to pause at their tombs in the cemeteries.

(Pope Benedict XVI)

The Masses that follow may be used at the discretion of the celebrant.

1

Entrance Antiphon Cf. 1 Th 4:14; 1 Co 15:22

Just as Jesus died and has risen again,
so through Jesus God will bring with him
those who have fallen asleep;
and as in Adam all die,
so also in Christ will all be brought to life.

Ant. ad introitum

Sicut Iesus mortuus est et resurrexit,
ita et Deus eos qui dormierunt
    per Iesum adducet cum eo.
Et sicut in Adam omnes moriuntur,
ita et in Christo
    omnes vivificabuntur.

Collect

Listen kindly to our prayers, O Lord,
and, as our faith in your Son,
raised from the dead, is deepened,

Collecta

Preces nostras, quæsumus,
    Domine, benignus exaudi,
ut, dum attollitur nostra fides

so may our hope of resurrection
   for your departed servants
also find new strength.
Through our Lord Jesus Christ,
   your Son,
who lives and reigns with you
   in the unity of the Holy Spirit,
one God, for ever and ever.

in Filio tuo a mortuis suscitato,
in famulorum tuorum
   præstolanda resurrectione
spes quoque nostra firmetur.
Per Dominum nostrum Iesum
   Christum Filium tuum,
qui tecum vivit et regnat
   in unitate Spiritus Sancti,
Deus, per omnia sæcula sæculorum.

Prayer over the Offerings

Look favourably on our offerings,
   O Lord,
so that your departed servants
may be taken up into glory
   with your Son,
in whose great mystery of love
   we are all united.
Who lives and reigns
   for ever and ever.

Preface for the Dead, pp.74-79.

Super oblata

Nostris, Domine,
   propitiare muneribus,
ut famuli tui defuncti assumantur
   in gloriam cum Filio tuo,
cuius magno pietatis
   iungimur sacramento.
Qui vivit et regnat
   in sæcula sæculorum.

Communion Antiphon Cf. Jn 11:25-26

I am the Resurrection and the Life,
   says the Lord.
Whoever believes in me, even
   though he dies, will live,
and everyone who lives and believes
   in me will not die for ever.

Ant. ad communionem

Ego sum resurrectio et vita,
   dicit Dominus.
Qui credit in me, etiam si mortuus
   fuerit, vivet;
et omnis, qui vivit et credit in me,
non morietur in æternum.

Prayer after Communion

Grant we pray, O Lord, that your
   departed servants,
for whom we have celebrated this
   paschal Sacrament,
may pass over to a dwelling place of
   light and peace.
Through Christ our Lord.

Post communionem

Præsta, quæsumus, Domine,
ut famuli tui defuncti
in mansionem lucis transeant
   et pacis,
pro quibus paschale
   celebravimus sacramentum.
Per Christum Dominum nostrum.

A formula of Solemn Blessing, pp.148-151, may be used.

2

Entrance Antiphon Cf. 4 Esdr 2:34-35

Eternal rest grant unto them, O Lord,
and let perpetual light shine
  upon them.

Collect

O God, glory of the faithful and
  life of the just,
by the Death and Resurrection
  of whose Son
we have been redeemed,
look mercifully on your
  departed servants,
that, just as they professed
  the mystery of our resurrection,
so they may merit to receive
  the joys of eternal happiness.
Through our Lord Jesus Christ,
  your Son,
who lives and reigns with you
  in the unity of the Holy Spirit,
one God, for ever and ever.

Prayer over the Offerings

Almighty and merciful God,
by means of these
  sacrificial offerings
wash away, we pray,
  in the Blood of Christ,
the sins of your departed servants,
for you purify unceasingly by your
  merciful forgiveness
those you once cleansed in the
  waters of Baptism.
Through Christ our Lord.

Preface for the Dead, pp.74-79.

Ant. ad introitum

Requiem æternam dona eis, Domine,
et lux perpetua luceat eis.

Collecta

Deus, gloria fidelium
  et vita iustorum,
cuius Filii morte et resurrectione
  redempti sumus,
propitiare famulis tuis defunctis,
ut, qui resurrectionis nostræ
  mysterium agnoverunt,
æternæ beatitudinis gaudia
  percipere mereantur.
Per Dominum nostrum Iesum
  Christum Filium tuum,
qui tecum vivit et regnat
  in unitate Spiritus Sancti,
Deus, per omnia sæcula sæculorum.

Super oblata

Omnipotens et misericors Deus,
his sacrificiis ablue, quæsumus,
  famulos tuos defunctos
a peccatis eorum
  in sanguine Christi,
ut, quos mundasti
  aqua baptismatis,
indesinenter purifices
  indulgentia pietatis.
Per Christum Dominum nostrum.

Communion Antiphon Cf. 4 Esdr 2:35,34

Let perpetual light shine upon
   them, O Lord,
with your Saints for ever,
   for you are merciful.

Prayer after Communion

Having received the Sacrament of
   your Only Begotten Son,
who was sacrificed for us
   and rose in glory,
we humbly implore you, O Lord,
for your departed servants,
that, cleansed by
   the paschal mysteries,
they may glory in the gift of the
   resurrection to come.
Through Christ our Lord.

A formula of Solemn Blessing, pp.148-151, may be used.

Ant. ad communionem

Lux æterna luceat eis, Domine,
cum Sanctis tuis in æternum,
   quia pius es.

Post communionem

Sumpto sacramento Unigeniti tui,
qui pro nobis immolatus
   resurrexit in gloria,
te, Domine, suppliciter exoramus
   pro famulis tuis defunctis,
ut, paschalibus mysteriis mundati,
futuræ resurrectionis
   munere glorientur.
Per Christum Dominum nostrum.

3

Entrance Antiphon Cf. Rm 8:11

God, who raised Jesus from the dead,
will give life also to your
   mortal bodies,
through his Spirit that dwells in you.

Collect

O God, who willed that your Only
   Begotten Son,
having conquered death,
should pass over into the realm
   of heaven,
grant, we pray,
   to your departed servants
that, with the mortality
   of this life overcome,
they may gaze eternally on you,
their Creator and Redeemer.

Ant. ad introitum

Deus, qui suscitavit Iesum a mortuis,
vivificabit et mortalia
   corpora nostra,
propter inhabitantem Spiritum
   eius in nobis.

Collecta

Deus, qui Unigenitum tuum,
   devicta morte,
ad cælestia transire fecisti,
concede famulis tuis defunctis,
ut, huius vitæ mortalitate devicta,
te conditorem et redemptorem
possint perpetuo contemplari.

Through our Lord Jesus Christ,
    your Son,
who lives and reigns with you in
    the unity of the Holy Spirit,
one God, for ever and ever.

Prayer over the Offerings

Receive, Lord, in your kindness,
the sacrificial offering we make
for all your servants who sleep
    in Christ,
that, set free from the bonds
    of death
by this singular sacrifice,
they may merit eternal life.
Through Christ our Lord.

Preface for the Dead, pp.74-79.

Communion Antiphon Cf. Ph 3:20-21

We await a saviour,
    the Lord Jesus Christ,
who will change our mortal bodies,
to conform with his glorified body.

Prayer after Communion

Through these sacrificial gifts
which we have received, O Lord,
bestow on your departed servants
    your great mercy
and, to those you have endowed
    with the grace of Baptism,
grant also the fullness of
    eternal joy.
Through Christ our Lord.

Per Dominum nostrum Iesum
    Christum Filium tuum,
qui tecum vivit et regnat
    in unitate Spiritus Sancti,
Deus, per omnia sæcula sæculorum.

Super oblata

Pro omnibus famulis tuis in Christo
    dormientibus
hostiam, Domine, suscipe
    benignus oblatam,
ut, per hoc sacrificium singulare
    vinculis mortis exuti,
vitam mereantur æternam.
Per Christum Dominum nostrum.

Ant. ad communionem

Salvatorem exspectamus
    Dominum Iesum Christum,
qui reformabit corpus
    humilitatis nostræ,
configuratum corpori claritatis suæ.

Post communionem

Multiplica, Domine,
    his sacrificiis susceptis,
super famulos tuos defunctos
    misericordiam tuam,
et, quibus donasti
    baptismi gratiam,
da eis æternorum
    plenitudinem gaudiorum.
Per Christum Dominum nostrum.

A formula of Solemn Blessing, pp.148-151, may be used.

FIRST READING

A reading from the prophet Isaiah 25:6-9
The Lord will destroy Death for ever.

On this mountain,
the Lord of hosts will prepare for all peoples
a banquet of rich food.
On this mountain he will remove
the mourning veil covering all peoples,
and the shroud enwrapping all nations,
he will destroy Death for ever.
The Lord will wipe away
the tears from every cheek;
he will take away his people's shame
everywhere on earth,
for the Lord has said so.
That day, it will be said: See, this is our God
in whom we hoped for salvation;
the Lord is the one in whom we hoped.
We exult and we rejoice
that he has saved us.

The word of the Lord.

Responsial Psalm   Ps 26:1,4,7-9,13-14. R. v.1. Alt. R. v.13

R. **The Lord is my light and my help.**

> Or: **I am sure I shall see the Lord's goodness
> in the land of the living.**

The Lord is my light and my help;
whom shall I fear?
The Lord is the stronghold of my life;
before whom shall I shrink? R.

There is one thing I ask of the Lord,
for this I long,
to live in the house of the Lord,
all the days of my life,
to savour the sweetness of the Lord,
to behold his temple. R.

O Lord, hear my voice when I call;
have mercy and answer.
It is your face, O Lord, that I seek;
hide not your face. R.

I am sure I shall see the Lord's goodness
in the land of the living.
Hope in him, hold firm and take heart.
Hope in the Lord! R.

SECOND READING

A reading from the letter of St Paul to the Romans   5:5-11

Having died to make us righteous, is it likely that he would now fail to save us from God's anger?

Hope is not deceptive, because the love of God has been poured into our hearts by the Holy Spirit which has been given us. We were still helpless when at his appointed moment Christ died for sinful men. It is not easy to die even for a good man – though of course for someone really worthy, a man might be prepared to die – but what proves that God loves us is that Christ died for us while we were still sinners. Having died to make us righteous, is it likely that he would now fail to save us from God's anger? When we were reconciled to God by the death of his Son, we were still enemies; now that we have been reconciled, surely we may count on being saved by the life of his Son? Not merely because we have been reconciled but because we are filled with joyful trust in God, through our Lord Jesus Christ, through whom we have already gained our reconciliation.

The word of the Lord.

Gospel Acclamation   Jn 6:39

R. **Alleluia, alleluia!**
It is my Father's will, says the Lord,
that I should lose nothing
of all that he has given to me,
and that I should raise it up on the last day.
R. **Alleluia!**

GOSPEL

A reading from the holy Gospel according to Luke   7:11-17

Young man, I tell you to get up.

Jesus went to a town called Nain, accompanied by his disciples and a great number of people. When he was near the gate of the town it happened that a dead man was being carried out for burial, the only son of his mother, and she was a widow. And a considerable number of the townspeople were with her. When the Lord saw her he felt sorry for her. 'Do not cry,' he said.

Then he went up and put his hand on the bier and the bearers stood still, and he said, 'Young man, I tell you to get up'. And the dead man sat up and began to talk, and Jesus gave him to his mother. Everyone was filled with awe and praised God saying, 'A great prophet has appeared among us; God has visited his people'. And this opinion of him spread throughout Judaea and all over the countryside.

    The Gospel of the Lord.

3 November

THIRTY-FIRST SUNDAY IN ORDINARY TIME

Entrance Antiphon Cf. Ps 37:22-23

FORSAKE me not, O Lord,
   my God;
be not far from me!
Make haste and come to my help,
O Lord, my strong salvation!

Ant. ad introitum

NE derelinquas me,
   Domine Deus meus,
ne discedas a me;
intende in adiutorium meum,
Domine, virtus salutis meæ.

Collect

Almighty and merciful God,
by whose gift your faithful offer you
right and praiseworthy service,
grant, we pray,
that we may hasten
   without stumbling
to receive the things you
   have promised.
Through our Lord Jesus Christ,
   your Son,
who lives and reigns with you
   in the unity of the Holy Spirit,
one God, for ever and ever.

Collecta

Omnipotens et misericors Deus,
   de cuius munere venit,
ut tibi a fidelibus tuis digne
   et laudabiliter serviatur,
tribue, quæsumus, nobis,
ut ad promissiones tuas sine
   offensione curramus.
Per Dominum nostrum Iesum
   Christum Filium tuum,
qui tecum vivit et regnat
   in unitate Spiritus Sancti,
Deus, per omnia sæcula sæculorum.

FIRST READING

A reading from the book of Wisdom 11:22-12:2

You are merciful to all because you love all that exists.

In your sight, Lord the whole world is like a grain of dust that tips the scales,
like a drop of morning dew falling on the ground.
Yet you are merciful to all, because you can do all things
and overlook men's sins so that they can repent.
Yes, you love all that exists, you hold nothing of what you have made
   in abhorrence,
for had you hated anything, you would not have formed it.
And how, had you not willed it, could a thing persist,
how be conserved if not called forth by you?
You spare all things because all things are yours, Lord, lover of life,
you whose imperishable spirit is in all.
Little by little, therefore, you correct those who offend,
you admonish and remind them of how they have sinned,
so that they may abstain from evil and trust in you, Lord.

The word of the Lord.

Responsional Psalm
Ps 144:1-2,8-11,13-14. R. Cf. v.1

R. **I will bless your name for ever,
O God my King**.

I will give you glory, O God my King,
I will bless your name for ever.
I will bless you day after day
and praise your name for ever. R.

The Lord is kind and full of compassion,
slow to anger, abounding in love.
How good is the Lord to all,
compassionate to all his creatures. R.

All your creatures shall thank you, O Lord,
and your friends shall repeat their blessing.
They shall speak of the glory of your reign
and declare your might, O God. R.

The Lord is faithful in all his words
and loving in all his deeds.
The Lord supports all who fall
and raises all who are bowed down. R.

SECOND READING

A reading from the second letter of St Paul to the Thessalonians   1:11-2:2
The name of Christ will be glorified in you and you in him.

We pray continually that our God will make you worthy of his call, and by his power fulfil all your desires for goodness and complete all that you have been doing through faith; because in this way the name of our Lord Jesus Christ will be glorified in you and you in him, by the grace of our God and the Lord Jesus Christ.

To turn now, brothers, to the coming of our Lord Jesus Christ and how we shall all be gathered round him: please do not get excited too soon or alarmed by any prediction or rumour or any letter claiming to come from us, implying that the Day of the Lord has already arrived.

The word of the Lord.

Gospel Acclamation   Lk 19:38; 2:14

R. **Alleluia, alleluia!**
Blessings on the King who comes,
in the name of the Lord!
Peace in heaven
and glory in the highest heavens!
R. **Alleluia!**

Or: Jn 3:16

R. **Alleluia, alleluia!**
God loved the world so much
that he gave his only Son,
so that everyone who believes in him
may have eternal life.
R. **Alleluia!**

GOSPEL

A reading from holy Gospel according to Luke   19:1-10
The Son of Man has come to seek out and save what was lost.

Jesus entered Jericho and was going through the town when a man whose name was Zacchaeus made his appearance; he was one of the senior tax collectors and a wealthy man. He was anxious to see what kind of man Jesus was, but he was too short and could not see him for the crowd; so he ran ahead and climbed a sycamore tree to catch a glimpse of Jesus who was to pass that way. When Jesus reached the spot he looked up and spoke to him: 'Zacchaeus, come down. Hurry, because I must stay at your house today.'

And he hurried down and welcomed him joyfully. They all complained when they saw what was happening. 'He has gone to stay at a sinner's house' they said. But Zacchaeus stood his ground and said to the Lord, 'Look, sir, I am going to give half my property to the poor, and if I have cheated anybody I will pay him back four times the amount.' And Jesus said to him, 'Today salvation has come to this house, because this man too is a son of Abraham; for the Son of Man has come to seek out and save what was lost.'

The Gospel of the Lord.

Prayer over the Offerings

May these sacrificial offerings,
   O Lord,
become for you a pure oblation,
and for us a holy outpouring
   of your mercy.
Through Christ our Lord.

Super oblata

Fiat hoc sacrificium, Domine,
   oblatio tibi munda,
et nobis misericordiæ tuæ
   sancta largitio.
Per Christum Dominum nostrum.

Preface of Sundays in Ordinary Time I-VIII, pp.60-67.

Communion Antiphon Cf. Ps 15:11

You will show me the path of life,
the fullness of joy in your presence,
   O Lord.

Ant. ad communionem

Notas mihi fecisti vias vitæ,
adimplebis me lætitia
   cum vultu tuo, Domine.

Or: Jn 6:58

Just as the living Father sent me
and I have life because of the Father,
so whoever feeds on me
shall have life because of me,
   says the Lord.

Vel:

Sicut misit me vivens Pater,
   et ego vivo propter Patrem,
et qui manducat me,
   et ipse vivet propter me,
dicit Dominus.

Prayer after Communion

May the working of your power,
   O Lord,
increase in us, we pray,
so that, renewed by these
   heavenly Sacraments,
we may be prepared by your gift
for receiving what they promise.
Through Christ our Lord.

Post communionem

Augeatur in nobis,
   quæsumus, Domine,
tuæ virtutis operatio,
ut, refecti cælestibus sacramentis,
ad eorum promissa capienda tuo
   munere præparemur.
Per Christum Dominum nostrum.

10 November

THIRTY-SECOND SUNDAY IN ORDINARY TIME

Entrance Antiphon   Ps 87:3

LET my prayer come into your presence.
Incline your ear
   to my cry for help, O Lord.

Ant. ad introitum

INTRET oratio mea in conspectu tuo;
inclina aurem tuam
   ad precem meam, Domine.

Collect

Almighty and merciful God,
graciously keep from us all adversity,
so that, unhindered in mind
   and body alike,
we may pursue in freedom of heart
the things that are yours.
Through our Lord Jesus Christ,
   your Son,
who lives and reigns with you
   in the unity of the Holy Spirit,
one God, for ever and ever.

Collecta

Omnipotens et misericors Deus,
universa nobis adversantia
   propitiatus exclude,
ut, mente et corpore pariter expediti,
quæ tua sunt liberis
   mentibus exsequamur.
Per Dominum nostrum Iesum
   Christum Filium tuum,
qui tecum vivit et regnat
   in unitate Spiritus Sancti,
Deus, per omnia sæcula sæculorum.

FIRST READING

A reading from the second book of Maccabees   7:1-2,9-14

The King of the world will raise us up to live for ever.

There were seven brothers who were arrested with their mother. The king tried to force them to taste pig's flesh, which the Law forbids, by torturing them with whips and scourges. One of them, acting as spokesman for the others, said, 'What are you trying to find out from us? We are prepared to die rather then break the Law of our ancestors.'

   With his last breath the second brother exclaimed, 'Inhuman fiend, you may discharge us from this present life, but the King of the world will raise us up, since it is for his laws that we die, to live again for ever.'

   After him, they amused themselves with the third, who on being asked for his tongue promptly thrust it out and boldly held out his hands, with these honourable words, 'It was heaven that gave me these limbs; for the sake of his laws I disdain them; from him I hope to receive them again.'

The king and his attendants were astounded at the young man's courage and his utter indifference to suffering.

When this one was dead they subjected the fourth to the same savage torture. When he neared his end he cried, 'Ours is the better choice, to meet death at men's hands, yet relying on God's promise that we shall be raised up by him; whereas for you there can be no resurrection, no new life.'

The word of the Lord.

Responsional Psalm
Ps 16:1,5-6,8,15. R. v.15

R. **I shall be filled, when I awake,
with the sight of your glory, O Lord.**

Lord, hear a cause that is just,
pay heed to my cry
Turn your ear to my prayer:
no deceit is on my lips. R.

I kept my feet firmly in your paths;
there was no faltering in my steps.
I am here and I call, you will hear me, O God.
Turn your ear to me; hear my words. R.

Guard me as the apple of your eye.
Hide me in the shadow of your wings.
As for me, in my justice I shall see your face
and be filled, when I awake, with the sight of your glory. R.

SECOND READING

A reading from the second letter of St Paul to the Thessalonians 2:16-3:5

May the Lord strengthen you in everything good that you do or say.

May our Lord Jesus Christ himself, and God our Father who has given us his love and, through his grace, such inexhaustible comfort and such sure hope, comfort you and strengthen you in everything good that you do or say.

Finally, brothers, pray for us; pray that the Lord's message may spread quickly, and be received with honour as it was among you; and pray that we may be preserved from the interference of bigoted and evil people, for faith is not given to everyone. But the Lord is faithful, and he will give you strength and guard you from the evil one, and we, in the Lord, have every confidence that you are doing and will go on doing all that we tell you. May the Lord turn your hearts towards the love of God and the fortitude of Christ.

The word of the Lord.

Gospel Acclamation   Lk 21:36

R. **Alleluia, alleluia!**
Stay awake praying at all times
for the strength to stand with confidence
before the Son of Man.
R. **Alleluia!**

Or: Rv 1:5,6

R. **Alleluia, alleluia!**
Jesus Christ is the First-born from the dead;
to him be glory and power for ever and ever.
R. **Alleluia!**

GOSPEL

A reading from the holy Gospel according to Luke   20:27-38
He is of God, not of the dead, but of the living.

[Some Sadducees – those who say that there is no resurrection – approached Jesus and they put this question to him,] 'Master, we have it from Moses in writing, that if a man's married brother dies childless, the man must marry the widow to raise up children for his brother. Well, then, there were seven brothers. The first, having married a wife, died childless. The second and then the third married the widow. And the same with all seven, they died leaving no children. Finally the woman herself died. Now, at the resurrection, to which of them will she be wife since she had been married to all seven?'

[Jesus replied, 'The children of this world take wives and husbands, but those who are judged worthy of a place in the other world and in the resurrection from the dead do not marry because they can no longer die, for they are the same as the angels, and being children of the resurrection they are sons of God. And Moses himself implies that the dead rise again, in the passage about the bush where he calls the Lord the God of Abraham, the God of Isaac and the God of Jacob. Now he is God, not of the dead, but of the living; for to him all men are in fact alive.'

The Gospel of the Lord.]

Shorter Form, verses 27,34-38. Read between [ ]

Prayer over the Offerings

Look with favour, we pray, O Lord,
upon the sacrificial gifts offered here,
that, celebrating in mystery
  the Passion of your Son,
we may honour it
  with loving devotion.
Through Christ our Lord.

Preface of Sundays in Ordinary Time I-VIII, pp.60-67.

Super oblata

Sacrificiis præsentibus, Domine,
quæsumus, intende placatus,
ut, quod passionis Filii tui
  mysterio gerimus,
pio consequamur affectu.
Per Christum Dominum nostrum.

Communion Antiphon Ps 22:1-2

The Lord is my shepherd;
  there is nothing I shall want.
Fresh and green are the pastures
  where he gives me repose,
near restful waters he leads me.

Or: Lk 24:35

The disciples recognised the Lord
  Jesus in the breaking of bread.

Ant. ad communionem

Dominus regit me,
  et nihil mihi deerit;
in loco pascuæ ibi me collocavit,
super aquam refectionis
  educavit me.

Vel:

Cognoverunt discipuli Dominum
  Iesum in fractione panis.

Prayer after Communion

Nourished by this sacred gift,
  O Lord,
we give you thanks and beseech
  your mercy,
that, by the pouring forth
  of your Spirit,
the grace of integrity may endure
in those your heavenly power
  has entered.
Through Christ our Lord.

Post communionem

Gratias tibi, Domine, referimus
  sacro munere vegetati,
tuam clementiam implorantes,
ut, per infusionem Spiritus tui,
in quibus cælestis virtus introivit,
sinceritatis gratia perseveret.
Per Christum Dominum nostrum.

17 November

THIRTY-THIRD SUNDAY IN ORDINARY TIME

Entrance Antiphon   Jr 29:11,12,14

THE Lord said: I think thoughts of peace and not of affliction.
You will call upon me,
  and I will answer you,
and I will lead back your captives
  from every place.

Collect

Grant us, we pray, O Lord our God,
the constant gladness of being
  devoted to you,
for it is full and lasting happiness
to serve with constancy
the author of all that is good.
Through our Lord Jesus Christ,
  your Son,
who lives and reigns with you
  in the unity of the Holy Spirit,
one God, for ever and ever.

Ant. ad introitum

DICIT Dominus:
  Ego cogito cogitationes pacis
  et non afflictionis;
invocabitis me, et ego exaudiam vos,
et reducam captivitatem vestram
  de cunctis locis.

Collecta

Da nobis, quæsumus,
  Domine Deus noster,
in tua semper devotione gaudere,
quia perpetua est et plena felicitas,
si bonorum omnium iugiter
  serviamus auctori.
Per Dominum nostrum Iesum
  Christum Filium tuum,
qui tecum vivit et regnat
  in unitate Spiritus Sancti,
Deus, per omnia sæcula sæculorum.

FIRST READING

A reading from the prophet Malachi   3:19-20

For you the sun of righteousness will shine out.

The day is coming now, burning like a furnace, and all the arrogant and the evil-doers will be like stubble. The day that is coming is going to burn them up, says the Lord of hosts, leaving them neither root nor stalk. But for you who fear my name, the sun of righteousness will shine out with healing in its rays.

The word of the Lord.

Responsorial Psalm

Ps 97:5-9. R. Cf. v.9

R. **The Lord comes to rule the peoples with fairness.**

Sing psalms to the Lord with the harp,
with the sound of music.
With trumpets and the sound of the horn
acclaim the King, the Lord. R.

Let the sea and all within it, thunder
the world, and all its peoples.
Let the rivers clap their hands
and the hills ring out their joy
at the presence of the Lord. R.

For the Lord comes,
he comes to rule the earth.
He will rule the world with justice
and the peoples with fairness. R.

SECOND READING

A reading from the second letter of St Paul to the Thessalonians   3:7-12

Do not let anyone have food if he refuses to work.

You know how you are supposed to imitate us: now we were not idle when we were with you, nor did we ever have our meals at anyone's table without paying for them; no, we worked night and day, slaving and straining, so as not to be a burden on any of you. This was not because we had no right to be, but in order make ourselves an example for you to follow.

We gave you a rule when we were with you: not to let anyone have any food if he refused to do any work. Now we hear that there are some of you who are living in idleness, doing no work themselves but interfering with everyone else's. In the Lord Jesus Christ, we order and call on people of this kind to go on quietly working and earning the food that they eat.

The word of the Lord.

Gospel Acclamation

Lk 21:36

R. **Alleluia, alleluia!**
Stay awake, praying at all times
for the strength to stand with confidence
before the Son of Man.
R. **Alleluia!**

Or: Lk 21:28

R. **Alleluia, alleluia!**
Stand erect, hold your heads high,
because your liberation is near at hand.
R. **Alleluia!**

GOSPEL

A reading from the holy Gospel according to Luke 21:5-19
Your endurance will win you your lives.

When some were talking about the Temple, remarking how it was adorned with fine stonework and votive offerings, Jesus said, 'All these things you are staring at now – the time will come when not a single stone will be left on another: everything will be destroyed.' And they put to him this question: 'Master,' they said 'when will this happen, then, and what sign will there be that this is about to take place?'

'Take care not to be deceived,' he said 'because many will come using my name and saying, "I am he" and, "The time is near at hand." Refuse to join them. And when you hear of wars and revolutions, do not be frightened, for this is something that must happen but the end is not so soon.' Then he said to them, 'Nation will fight against nation, and kingdom against kingdom. There will be great earthquakes and plagues and famines here and there; there will be fearful sights and great signs from heaven.

'But before all this happens, men will seize you and persecute you; they will hand you over to the synagogues and to imprisonment, and bring you before kings and governors because of my name – and that will be your opportunity to bear witness. Keep this carefully in mind: you are not to prepare your defence, because I myself shall give you an eloquence and a wisdom that none of your opponents will be able to resist or contradict. You will be betrayed even by parents and brothers, relations and friends; and some of you will be put to death. You will be hated by all men on account of my name, but not a hair of your head will be lost. Your endurance will win you your lives.'

The Gospel of the Lord.

Prayer over the Offerings

Grant, O Lord, we pray,
that what we offer in the sight
  of your majesty
may obtain for us the grace
  of being devoted to you
and gain us the prize
  of everlasting happiness.
Through Christ our Lord.

Super oblata

Concede, quæsumus, Domine,
ut oculis tuæ maiestatis
  munus oblatum
et gratiam nobis
  devotionis obtineat,
et effectum beatæ
  perennitatis acquirat.
Per Christum Dominum nostrum.

Preface of Sundays in Ordinary Time I-VIII, pp.60-67.

Communion Antiphon   Ps 72:28

To be near God is my happiness,
to place my hope in God the Lord.

Ant. ad communionem

Mihi autem adhærere Deo
  bonum est,
ponere in Domino Deo spem meam.

Or: Mk 11:23-24

Amen, I say to you:
  Whatever you ask in prayer,
believe that you will receive,
and it shall be given to you,
  says the Lord.

Vel:

Amen dico vobis,
  quidquid orantes petitis,
credite quia accipietis, et fiet vobis,
  dicit Dominus.

Prayer after Communion

We have partaken of the gifts
  of this sacred mystery,
humbly imploring, O Lord,
that what your Son commanded
  us to do
in memory of him
may bring us growth in charity.
Through Christ our Lord.

Post communionem

Sumpsimus, Domine,
  sacri dona mysterii,
humiliter deprecantes,
ut, quæ in sui commemorationem
nos Filius tuus facere præcepit,
in nostræ proficiant
  caritatis augmentum.
Per Christum Dominum nostrum.

24 November

OUR LORD JESUS CHRIST, KING OF THE UNIVERSE

Solemnity

Entrance Antiphon — Rv 5:12; 1:6

How worthy is the Lamb
who was slain,
to receive power and divinity,
and wisdom and strength
   and honour.
To him belong glory and power
   for ever and ever.

Ant. ad introitum

Dignus est Agnus,
qui occisus est,
accipere virtutem et divinitatem
et sapientiam et fortitudinem
   et honorem.
Ipsi gloria et imperium
   in sæcula sæculorum.

The Gloria in excelsis (Glory to God in the highest) is said.

Collect

Almighty ever-living God,
whose will is to restore all things
in your beloved Son,
   the King of the universe,
grant, we pray,
that the whole creation,
   set free from slavery,
may render your majesty service
and ceaselessly proclaim your praise.
Through our Lord Jesus Christ,
   your Son,
who lives and reigns with you
   in the unity of the Holy Spirit,
one God, for ever and ever.

Collecta

Omnipotens sempiterne Deus,
qui in dilecto Filio tuo,
   universorum Rege,
omnia instaurare voluisti,
concede propitius,
ut tota creatura, a servitute liberata,
tuæ maiestati deserviat ac te sine
   fine collaudet.
Per Dominum nostrum
   Iesum Christum Filium tuum,
qui tecum vivit et regnat
   in unitate Spiritus Sancti,
Deus, per omnia sæcula sæculorum.

FIRST READING

A reading from the second book of Samuel   5:1-3

They anointed David king of Israel.

All the tribes of Israel came to David at Hebron. 'Look' they said 'we are your own flesh and blood. In days past when Saul was our king, it was you who led Israel in all their exploits; and the Lord said to you, "You are the man who shall be shepherd of my people Israel, you shall be the leader of Israel.'" So all the elders of Israel came to the king at Hebron, and King David made a pact with them at Hebron in the presence of the Lord, and they anointed David king of Israel.

The word of the Lord.

Responsorial Psalm

Ps 121:1-5. R. Cf. v.2

R. **I rejoiced when I heard them say:
'Let us go to God's house.'**

I rejoiced when I heard them say:
'Let us go to God's house.'
And now our feet are standing
within your gates, O Jerusalem. R.

Jerusalem is built as a city
strongly compact.
It is there that the tribes go up,
the tribes of the Lord. R.

For Israel's law it is,
there to praise the Lord's name.
There were set the thrones of judgement
of the house of David. R.

SECOND READING

A reading from the letter of St Paul to the Colossians 1:12-20
He has created a place for us in the kingdom of the Son that he loves.

We give thanks to the Father who has made it possible for you to join the saints and with them to inherit the light.

Because that is what he has done: he has taken us out of the power of darkness and created a place for us in the kingdom of the Son that he loves, and in him, we gain our freedom, the forgiveness of our sins.

He is the image of the unseen God
and the first-born of all creation,
for in him were created
all things in heaven and on earth:
everything visible and everything invisible,
Thrones, Dominations, Sovereignties, Powers –
all things were created through him and for him.

Before anything was created, he existed,
and he holds all things in unity.
Now the Church is his body,
he is its head.
As he is the Beginning,
he was first to be born from the dead,
so that he should be first in every way;
because God wanted all perfection
to be found in him
and all things to be reconciled through him and for him,
everything in heaven and everything on earth,
when he made peace
by his death on the cross.

The word of the Lord.

Gospel Acclamation

Mk 11:9.10

R. **Alleluia, alleluia!**
Blessings on him who comes in the name of the Lord!
Blessings on the coming kingdom of our father David!
R. **Alleluia!**

GOSPEL

A reading from the holy Gospel according to Luke 23:35-43

Lord, remember me when you come into your kingdom.

The people stayed there before the cross watching Jesus. As for the leaders, they jeered at him. 'He saved others,' they said 'let him save himself if he is the Christ of God, the Chosen One.' The soldiers mocked him too, and when they approached to offer him vinegar they said, 'If you are the king of the Jews, save yourself.' Above him there was an inscription: 'This is the King of the Jews.'

One of the criminals hanging there abused him. 'Are you not the Christ?' he said. 'Save yourself and us as well.' But the other spoke up and rebuked him. 'Have you no fear of God at all?' he said. 'You got the same sentence as he did, but in our case we deserved it: we are paying for what we did. But this man has done nothing wrong. Jesus,' he said 'remember me when you come into your kingdom.' 'Indeed, I promise you,' he replied 'today you will be with me in paradise.'

The Gospel of the Lord.

The Creed is said.

Prayer over the Offerings

As we offer you, O Lord,
   the sacrifice
by which the human race
   is reconciled to you,
we humbly pray
that your Son himself may bestow
   on all nations
the gifts of unity and peace.
Through Christ our Lord.

Preface: Christ, King of the Universe.

It is truly right and just,
   our duty and our salvation,
always and everywhere
   to give you thanks,
Lord, holy Father,
   almighty and eternal God.

For you anointed your Only
   Begotten Son,
our Lord Jesus Christ,
   with the oil of gladness
as eternal Priest and King
   of all creation,
so that, by offering himself
   on the altar of the Cross
as a spotless sacrifice
   to bring us peace,
he might accomplish the mysteries
   of human redemption
and, making all created things
   subject to his rule,
he might present to the immensity
   of your majesty
an eternal and universal kingdom,
a kingdom of truth and life,
a kingdom of holiness and grace,
a kingdom of justice, love and peace.

Super oblata

Hostiam tibi, Domine,
humanæ reconciliationis
   offerentes,
suppliciter deprecamur,
ut ipse Filius tuus cunctis gentibus
unitatis et pacis dona concedat.
Qui vivit et regnat
   in sæcula sæculorum.

Præfatio: De Christo universorum Rege.

Vere dignum et iustum est,
   æquum et salutare,
nos tibi semper
   et ubique gratias agere:
Domine, sancte Pater,
   omnipotens æterne Deus:

Qui Unigenitum Filium tuum,
Dominum nostrum
   Iesum Christum,
Sacerdotem æternum
   et universorum Regem,
oleo exsultationis unxisti:
ut, seipsum in ara crucis
hostiam immaculatam
   et pacificam offerens,
redemptionis humanæ
   sacramenta perageret:
et, suo subiectis imperio
   omnibus creaturis,
æternum et universale regnum
immensæ tuæ traderet maiestati:
regnum veritatis et vitæ;
regnum sanctitatis et gratiæ;
regnum iustitiæ,
   amoris et pacis.

And so, with Angels and Archangels,
with Thrones and Dominions,
and with all the hosts and Powers
   of heaven,
we sing the hymn of your glory,
as without end we acclaim:

Holy, Holy, Holy Lord God of hosts...

Et ideo cum Angelis et Archangelis,
cum Thronis et Dominationibus,
cumque omni
   militia cælestis exercitus,
hymnum gloriæ tuæ canimus,
sine fine dicentes:

Sanctus, Sanctus, Sanctus . . .

Communion Antiphon Ps 28:10-11

The Lord sits as King for ever.
The Lord will bless his people
   with peace.

Ant. ad communionem

Sedebit Dominus Rex in æternum;
Dominus benedicet populo suo
   in pace.

Prayer after Communion

Having received the food
   of immortality,
we ask, O Lord,
that, glorying in obedience
to the commands of Christ,
   the King of the universe,
we may live with him eternally
   in his heavenly Kingdom.
Who lives and reigns
   for ever and ever.

Post communionem

Immortalitatis alimoniam consecuti,
quæsumus, Domine,
ut, qui Christi Regis universorum
gloriamur obœdire mandatis,
cum ipso in cælesti regno sine fine
   vivere valeamus.
Qui vivit et regnat
   in sæcula sæculorum.

---

30 November

In Scotland

SAINT ANDREW, APOSTLE AND MARTYR, PATRON OF SCOTLAND

The lesson of the grain of wheat that dies in order to bear fruit also has a parallel in the life of Saint Andrew. Tradition tells us that he followed the fate of his Lord and Master, ending his days in Patras, Greece. Like Peter, he endured martyrdom on a cross, the diagonal cross that we venerate today as the cross of Saint Andrew. From his example we learn that the path of each single Christian, like that of the Church as a whole, leads to new life, to eternal life, through the imitation of Christ and the experience of his cross.

(Pope Benedict XVI)

Solemnity

Entrance Antiphon Cf. Mt 4:18-19

BESIDE the Sea of Galilee,
the Lord saw two brothers,
Peter and Andrew,
and he said to them:
Come after me and I will make you
fishers of men.

Ant. ad introitum

DOMINUS secus mare Galilææ
vidit duos fratres,
Petrum et Andream,
et vocavit eos:
Venite post me, faciam vos fieri
piscatores hominum.

The Gloria in excelsis (Glory to God in the highest) is said.

Collect

We humbly implore your majesty,
O Lord,
that, just as the blessed
Apostle Andrew
was for your Church a preacher
and pastor,
so he may be for us a constant
intercessor before you.
Through our Lord Jesus Christ,
your Son,
who lives and reigns with you
in the unity of the Holy Spirit,
one God, for ever and ever.

Collecta

Maiestatem tuam, Domine,
suppliciter exoramus,
ut, sicut Ecclesiæ tuæ beatus
Andreas apostolus
exstitit prædicator et rector,
ita apud te sit pro nobis
perpetuus intercessor.
Per Dominum nostrum Iesum
Christum Filium tuum,
qui tecum vivit et regnat
in unitate Spiritus Sancti,
Deus, per omnia sæcula sæculorum.

FIRST READING

A reading from the book of Wisdom   3:1-9

He accepted them as a holocaust.

The souls of the virtuous are in the hands of God,
no torment shall ever touch them.
In the eyes of the unwise, they did appear to die,
their going looked like a disaster,
their leaving us, like annihilation;
but they are in peace.
If they experienced punishment as men see it,
their hope was rich with immortality;
slight was their affliction, great will their blessings be.
God has put them to the test

and proved them worthy to be with him;
he has tested them like gold in a furnace,
and accepted them as a holocaust.
When the time comes for his visitation they will shine out;
as sparks run through the stubble, so will they.
They shall judge nations, rule over peoples,
and the Lord will be their king for ever.
They who trust in him will understand the truth,
those who are faithful will live with him in love;
for grace and mercy await those he has chosen.

The word of the Lord.

Responsorial Psalm   Ps 30:3-4,6,8,17,21. R. v.6

R. **Into your hands, O Lord,
I commend my spirit.**

Be a rock of refuge for me,
a mighty stronghold to save me,
for you are my rock, my stronghold.
For your name's sake, lead me and guide me. R.

Into your hands I commend my spirit.
It is you who will redeem me, Lord.
As for me, I trust in the Lord:
let me be glad and rejoice in your love. R.

Let your face shine on your servant.
Save me in your love.
You hide them in the shelter of your presence
from the plotting of men. R.

SECOND READING

A reading from the letter of St Paul to the Romans   10:9-18

Faith comes from what is preached, and what is preached comes from the word of Christ.

If your lips confess that Jesus is Lord and if you believe in your heart that God raised him from the dead, then you will be saved. By believing from the heart you are made righteous; by confessing with your lips you are saved. When scripture says: those who believe in him will have no cause for shame, it makes no distinction between Jew and Greek: all belong to the same Lord who is rich enough, however many ask his help, for everyone who calls on the name of the Lord will be saved.

But they will not ask his help unless they believe in him, and they will not believe in him unless they have heard him, and they will not hear him unless they get a preacher, and they will never have a preacher unless one is sent, but as scripture says: The footsteps of those who bring good news are a welcome sound. Not everyone, of course, listens to the Good News. As Isaiah says: Lord, how many believe what we proclaimed? So faith comes from what is preached, and what is preached comes from the word of Christ.

Let me put the question: is it possible that they did not hear? Indeed they did; in the words of the psalm, their voice has gone out through all the earth, and their message to the ends of the world.

The word of the Lord.

Gospel Acclamation   2 Ch 7:16

R. **Alleluia, alleluia!**
Follow me, says the Lord,
and I will make you fishers of men.
R. **Alleluia!**

GOSPEL

A reading from the holy Gospel according to Matthew   4:18-22

And they left their nets at once and followed him.

As Jesus was walking by the Sea of Galilee he saw two brothers, Simon, who was called Peter, and his brother Andrew; they were making a cast in the lake with their net, for they were fishermen. And he said to them, 'Follow me and I will make you fishers of men.' And they left their nets at once and followed him.

Going on from there he saw another pair of brothers, James son of Zebedee and his brother John; they were in their boat with their father Zebedee, mending their nets, and he called them. At once, leaving the boat and their father, they followed him.

The Gospel of the Lord.

The Creed is said.

Prayer over the Offerings

Grant us, almighty God,
  that through these offerings,
which we bring on the feast day
  of Saint Andrew,
we may please you by what
  we have brought
and be given life by what
  you have accepted.
Through Christ our Lord.

Preface of the Apostles, pp.70-71.

Communion Antiphon Cf. Jn 1:41-42

Andrew told his brother Simon:
We have found the Messiah,
  the Christ,
and he brought him to Jesus.

Prayer after Communion

May communion in your Sacrament
  strengthen us, O Lord,
so that by the example of the
  blessed Apostle Andrew
we, who carry in our body
  the Death of Christ,
may merit to live with him in glory.
Who lives and reigns
  for ever and ever.

Super oblata

Concede nobis, omnipotens Deus,
ut his muneribus,
quæ in beati Andreæ festivitate
  deferimus,
et tibi placeamus exhibitis,
  et vivificemur acceptis.
Per Christum Dominum nostrum.

Ant. ad communionem

Dixit Andreas Simoni fratri suo:
Invenimus Messiam,
  qui dicitur Christus.
Et adduxit eum ad Iesum.

Post communionem

Roboret nos, Domine,
  sacramenti tui communio,
ut, exemplo beati Andreæ apostoli,
Christi mortificationem ferentes,
cum ipso vivere mereamur
  in gloria.
Qui vivit et regnat
  in sæcula sæculorum.

A formula of Solemn Blessing, pp.146-147, may be used.

RITE OF EUCHARISTIC EXPOSITION AND BENEDICTION

The service of Benediction developed during the Middle Ages during the Corpus Christi processions in which the Blessed Sacrament was held up for veneration. The service was subsequently used at other times throughout the year as an opportunity to give thanks for the Mass and adore Christ present under the form of bread.

Today, the Church encourages this rite to be celebrated in the context of a longer period of reading, prayer and reflection.

Exposition

First of all, the minister exposes the Blessed Sacrament while a hymn is sung, during which he incenses the Sacrament. The following or another hymn may be chosen.

O saving Victim, opening wide, The gate of heav'n to man below Our foes press on from every side; Thine aid supply, thy strength bestow. To thy great name be endless praise, Immortal Godhead, One in Three; O grant us endless length of days In our true native land with thee. Amen.	O salutaris hostia, Quæ cæli pandis ostium; Bella premunt hostilia, Da robur, fer auxilium. Uni Trinoque Domino Sit sempiterna gloria, Qui vitam sine termino Nobis donet in patria. Amen.

Adoration

A time for silent prayer, readings from Scripture, litanies or other prayers and hymns may be used. On some occasions, the Prayer of the Church might be said or sung.

Of the Glorious Body Telling | Pange Lingua

Of the glorious Body telling,
O my tongue, its mysteries sing,
And the Blood, all price excelling,
Which the world's eternal King,
In a noble womb once dwelling
Shed for the world's ransoming.

Pange lingua gloriosi
Corporis mysterium,
Sanguinisque pretiosi,
Quem in mundi pretium
Fructus ventris generosi,
Rex effudit gentium.

Given for us, for us descending,
Of a Virgin to proceed,
Man with man in
   converse blending,
Scattered he the Gospel seed,
Till his sojourn drew to ending,
Which he closed in wondrous deed.

At the last great Supper lying
Circled by his brethren's band,
Meekly with the law complying,
First he finished its command
Then, immortal Food supplying,
Gave himself with his own hand.

Word made Flesh,
   by word he maketh
Very bread his Flesh to be;
Man in wine Christ's Blood
   partaketh,
And if senses fail to see,
Faith alone the true heart waketh
To behold the mystery.

Nobis datus, nobis natus
Ex intacta Virgine,
Et in mundo conversatus,
Sparso verbi semine,
Sui moras incolatus
Miro clausit ordine.

In supremae nocte coenæ
Recumbens cum fratribus,
Observata lege plene
Cibis in legalibus,
Cibum turbæ duodenæ
Se dat suis manibus

Verbum caro, panem verum
Verbo carnem efficit,
Fitque sanguis Christi merum,
Et, si sensus deficit,
Ad firmandum cor sincerum
Sola fides sufficit.

Sweet Sacrament Divine

Sweet Sacrament divine,
Hid in thine earthly home;
Lo! round thy lowly shrine,
With suppliant hearts we come;
Jesus, to thee our voice we raise
In songs of love and heartfelt praise
Sweet Sacrament divine. (repeat)

Sweet Sacrament of peace,
Dear home of every heart,
Where restless yearnings cease,
And sorrows all depart.
There in thine ear, all trustfully,
We tell our tale of misery,
Sweet Sacrament of peace. (repeat)

Sweet Sacrament of rest,
Ark from the ocean's roar,
Within thy shelter blest
Soon may we reach the shore;
Save us, for still the tempest raves,
Save, lest we sink beneath the waves:
Sweet Sacrament of rest. (repeat)

Sweet Sacrament divine,
Earth's light and jubilee,
In thy far depths doth shine
The Godhead's majesty;
Sweet light, so shine on us, we pray
That earthly joys may fade away:
Sweet Sacrament divine. (repeat)
(Francis Stanfield)

Benediction

Towards the end of the exposition, the priest or deacon goes to the altar, genuflects and kneels. Then this hymn or a suitable alternative is sung, during which the minister incenses the sacrament.

Therefore we, before him bending This great Sacrament revere Types and shadows have their ending for the newer rite is here Faith, our outward sense befriending Makes the inward vision clear.	Tantum ergo Sacramentum Veneremur cernui, Et antiquum documentum Novo cedat ritui; Præstet fides supplementum Sensuum defectui.
Glory let us give, and blessing To the Father and the Son Honour, might, and praise addressing While eternal ages run Ever too his love confessing Who, from both, with both is one. Amen.	Genitori, Genitoque Laus et iubilatio. Salus, honor, virtus quoque Sit et benedictio; Procedenti ab utroque Compar sit laudatio. Amen.

The minister then says the following prayer (or a suitable alternative)

Let us pray. Lord Jesus Christ, you gave us the eucharist as the memorial of your suffering and death. May our worship of this sacrament of your body and blood Help us to experience the salvation you won for us and the peace of the kingdom where you live with the Father and the Holy Spirit, one God, for ever and ever. R. Amen.	Oremus. Deus, qui nobis sub sacramento mirabili passionis tuæ memoriam reliquisti: tribue, quæsumus, ita nos Corporis et Sanguinis tui sacra mysteria venerari, ut redemptionis tuæ fructum in nobis iugiter sentiamus. Qui vivis et regnas in sæcula sæculorum. R. Amen.

The Priest or Deacon now puts on the humeral veil and blesses the congregation with the Blessed Sacrament.

The Divine Praises formerly said at this point may more properly be included within the period of adoration.

The Divine Praises

Blessed be God.
Blessed be his holy Name.
Blessed be Jesus Christ, true God and true Man.
Blessed be the name of Jesus.
Blessed be his most Sacred Heart.
Blessed be his most Precious Blood.
Blessed be Jesus in the most holy Sacrament of the Altar.
Blessed be the Holy Spirit, the Paraclete.
Blessed be the great Mother of God, Mary, most holy.
Blessed be her holy and Immaculate Conception.
Blessed be her glorious Assumption.
Blessed be the name of Mary, Virgin and Mother.
Blessed be St Joseph, her spouse most chaste.
Blessed be God in his Angels and in his Saints.

Reposition

Immediately after the Blessed Sacrament is reposed in the tabernacle, the following may be sung:

Ant. Let us adore for ever
  the most holy Sacrament.

Ps. O praise the Lord,
  all you nations
Acclaim him, all you peoples
For his mercy is confirmed upon us
and the truth of the Lord
  remains for ever.

Glory be to the Father,
  and to the Son
and to the Holy Spirit
As it was in the beginning, is now
and ever shall be,
  world without end. Amen.

Ant. Let us adore for ever the most
  holy Sacrament.

Ant. Adoremus in æternum
  sanctissimum Sacramentum.

Ps. Laudate Dominum,
  omnes gentes;
laudate eum omnes populi.
Quoniam confirmata est super
  nos misericordia eius;
et veritas Domini manet
  in æternum.

Gloria Patri, et Filio,
  et Spiritui Sancto.
Sicut erat in principio,
  et nunc, et semper,
et in sæcula sæculorum. Amen.

Ant. Adoremus in æternum
  sanctissimum Sacramentum.

An alternative acclamation:
O Sacrament most holy,
  O Sacrament divine!
All praise, and all thanksgiving,
Be every moment thine!